**FROM THE COMMAND POST** boxes are used to demonstrate how some companies are implementing the latest sales concepts and practices. Each of these boxes is directed toward students gaining enhanced knowledge of the practice of personal selling.

W9-DFK-776

**KEEPING UP ONLINE** boxes provide students with a web address to log on to for special insights. Each box will include questions related to the web site noted in the box.

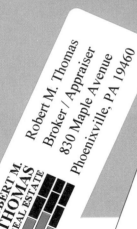

# PERSONAL SELLING

## ACHIEVING CUSTOMER SATISFACTION AND LOYALTY

### ROLPH E. ANDERSON
*Drexel University*

### ALAN J. DUBINSKY
*Purdue University*

**Houghton Mifflin Company**
*Boston   New York*

*For their unwavering love and support, this book is dedicated to*
*Sallie, Rachel, Stuart, Carrie, Elliott, and David—all of them "super salespeople"*
*in their own way—and to the memories of a wonderful brother, Joseph B. Anderson,*
*and our dear colleague, mentor, and friend, Marvin A. Jolson.*

Editor-in-Chief: George T. Hoffman

Technology Manager/Development Editor: Damaris R. Curran

Associate Project Editor: Kate Hartke

Editorial Assistant: May Jawdat

Senior Production/Design Coordinator: Sarah Ambrose

Senior Manufacturing Coordinator: Jane Spelman

Senior Marketing Manager: Steven W. Mikels

Cover image: © Susan LeVan

Part opener photo credits: p. 1, Roger Ressmeyer/Corbis; p. 65, Jose Luis Palaez/Corbis;

p. 269, JFPI Studios/Corbis; p. 401, Robert Lewine/Corbis.

Library of Congress Control Number: 2002109348

ISBN: 0-618-26045-5

123456789—QV—07 06 05 04 03

# BRIEF CONTENTS

# CONTENTS

## CHAPTER 6
## Negotiating Sales Resistance and Objections for "Win-Win" Agreements    170

INSIDE PERSONAL SELLING: *Meet Leslie Vaughan of SAS Institute*    170

## PART THREE
# Understanding and Communicating with Customers 269

## CHAPTER 9
# Understanding Organizational Markets 270

# PREFACE

apid growth in telecommunication technologies and dynamic global markets have propelled personal selling into one of the most exciting, fast-changing, and rewarding of all the business professions. Evolutionary and revolutionary technological, behavioral, and managerial forces are relentlessly and irrevocably changing the way that salespeople understand, prepare for, and accomplish their jobs. Thanks to the Internet and sophisticated computer hardware and software, salespeople have become empowered as never before and increasingly independent from their sales managers. With their notebook or handheld computers, salespeople can tap into their company intranets and instantly obtain information that their sales managers used to provide. Many salespeople feel so empowered today that they see themselves as their company's mobile field headquarters. In their expanded roles, salespeople are moving away from "selling" toward "serving" customers as consultants and business partners. These professional salespeople not only understand their customers' needs but those of their customers' customers as well. They are freer and more powerful than ever before in their ability to work creatively with customers toward profitable "win-win" relationships based on mutual trust and professionalism.

You are about to begin a journey into the wonderful world of personal selling, where you will serve largely as your own boss with few limitations on your potential success. If you have any stereotypes about salespeople, throw them away because they're probably no longer true. The field of personal selling has been changing so rapidly in recent years that only well-educated, highly trained individuals with strong customer orientations can succeed in this new competitive environment.

Those of you interested in personal selling careers need to be thoroughly prepared to assume demanding professional sales positions after graduation. But your hard work in preparation and training will pay off quickly. For example, did you know that there are more people making over $100,000 annually in personal selling than in any other career field? What's more, a sizeable number of salespeople make over a million dollars a year, and they largely manage themselves. Much of your preparation for sales will occur in college courses, particularly those involving personal selling—the intended course for this book. As such, you must be forearmed with the critical knowledge, attitudes, and skills necessary to succeed. Business recruiters, as well as those for nonprofit organizations, are interested in interviewing and hiring students who exhibit stellar professional selling qualities and strong interest in starting their careers in sales. This textbook, *Personal Selling: Achieving Customer Satisfaction and Loyalty*, is designed to assist you in becoming the kind of sales professional that all types of organizations will want to employ.

# Features of the Book

*Personal Selling: Achieving Customer Satisfaction and Loyalty* uses a pragmatic, up-to-date, realistic, upbeat, and professional approach to the study of personal selling. Our writing style is conversational, talking one-to-one with students, without pedantries. Although considerable theoretical material is presented, we use non-technical language in our analyses and always try to show the practical application of the theory. To support and complement the comprehension of crucial concepts and issues, we cite and report current research findings. Moreover, we give many "real world" company examples to allow students to further enhance their understanding of the concepts.

In reading this text, there are five basic goals that we want our readers to achieve. Specifically, we want you to (1) understand and appreciate the multi-faceted roles that salespeople play in their organizations, (2) obtain a solid conceptual background and understanding of the dynamic environment in which today's professional salespeople function, (3) develop a comprehensive and in-depth knowledge of how to apply the steps involved in the *personal selling process (PSP)* skillfully, (4) utilize an array of proven, effective tools and techniques for assessing and enhancing your abilities for personal selling, and (5) feel fully confident to assume a position in business-to-business sales. To accomplish these objectives, we first provide an overview of personal selling. Then, we discuss, illustrate, and analyze the *personal selling process (PSP)*. In each of the chapters on the PSP, we depict the process as a revolving wheel of seven interacting, overlapping steps, and highlight the step or steps covered in that particular chapter. Next, we direct our attention to topics related to enhancing students' understanding of customers and persuasively communicating with them. Finally, we offer advice and suggestions on how to achieve success in the sales field by developing long-term, mutually satisfying relationships with customers that lead to repeat purchasing loyalty and higher profits.

As a complement to this text, we provide a frequently updated web site, **http://college.hmco.com/business/students/**, that presents additional material on personal selling that we were unable to include in the text. By periodically clicking onto this web site, you will be able to enhance and update your knowledge of the textbook material.

## Text Content and Organization

Every textbook needs an organizational format to help readers. *Personal Selling: Achieving Customer Satisfaction and Loyalty* is subdivided into four sections covering fourteen chapters.

**Part I. Overview of Personal Selling** The first section, "Overview of Personal Selling," introduces the career field of personal selling to students and describes the dynamic selling environment in which modern salespeople operate. Chapter 1, "Introduction to Personal Selling: It's a Great Life!" discusses such topics as the differences between yesterday's and today's salesperson, customer-oriented selling vis-à-vis the marketing concept, sales job opportunities and advantages, telecommunication advances in selling, and salespeople's career paths. In chapter 2, "The Ever-Changing Personal Selling Environment," we analyze the key evolutionary and revolutionary factors influencing personal selling. These include *behavioral* forces (e.g., more expert and demanding buyers, rising customer expectations, internationalization of markets), *technological* forces (e.g., sales force automation, virtual sales offices, electronic commerce), and *managerial* forces (e.g., selling cost reduction efforts, shift to direct marketing alternatives, sales force certification). All three of these megatrends are relentlessly and irrevocably changing the way that salespeople understand, prepare for, and accomplish their jobs.

**Part II. The Personal Selling Process** We believe that the heart of personal selling, as well as its most exciting part, is the *personal selling process (PSP)*. This process entails seven basic steps that salespeople carry out to ultimately make a sale and engender long-run customer satisfaction and loyalty. Therefore, the second section of *Personal Selling: Achieving Customer Satisfaction and Loyalty* contains six chapters that address the PSP in detail. Chapter 3, "Prospecting for and Qualifying Prospects: Filling the Salesperson's 'Pot of Gold,'" describes the importance of prospecting, how to qualify sales leads, various kinds of prospecting sources, and basic steps in a prospecting plan. In chapter 4, "Planning the Sales Call: Steps to a Successful Approach," we focus on key issues in the preapproach and approach steps of the personal selling process. In particular, attention is paid to several useful techniques and methods for effectively executing these two steps, as well as how to deal with sales call reluctance—a bane of many salespeople.

We then move on to a discussion about preparing for and making a sales presentation and demonstration in chapter 5, "Sales Presentation and Demonstration: The Pivotal Exchange." Extensive attention is given to alternate kinds of demonstrations, preparation of written presentations (sales proposals), adaptive versus canned presentations, and making sales presentations to buyer groups. In chapter 6, "Negotiating Sales Resistance and Objections for 'Win-Win' Agreements," students learn how to attend to prospect or customer resistance or objections to buying. Major issues covered include how to plan for objections, how to deal with objections, how to overcome price resistance, and how to ensure a "win-win" outcome for both buyer and seller.

The last two chapters of this section of the text—chapter 7, "Confirming and Closing the Sale: Start of the Long-Term Relationship," and chapter 8, "Following Up: Keeping Customers Satisfied and Loyal"—pertain to consummating the sale and attending to post-sale activities. Chapter 7 deals with why some salespeople fail to close, important closing signals, when to close, effective techniques for closing, and handling rejection. Chapter 8 addresses, among other issues, the importance of customer satisfaction and loyalty, customer service expectations, assessing customer satisfaction, critical post-sale activities, and the 8Cs of customer loyalty.

**Part III. Understanding and Communicating with Customers** The third section of *Personal Selling: Achieving Customer Satisfaction and Loyalty,* "Understanding and Communicating with Customers," contains four chapters, the topics of which will enhance students' abilities to carry out effectively the steps in the personal selling process. Chapter 9, "Understanding Organizational Markets," describes the various kinds of organizational customers that business-to-business salespeople must understand, the different negotiation styles of buyers, decision-making styles of buyers, and selling in international markets. In "Strategic Understanding of Your Company, Products, Competition, and Markets" (chapter 10), we discuss the various kinds of knowledge salespeople require to do their job effectively. Chapter 11, "Communicating Effectively with Diverse Customers," describes the different dimensions of effective listening, alternative formats and types of questions to ask prospects, the use of body language and space, the four communication styles of buyers, and building trust in relationships. The final chapter of this section, "Managing Your Time and Your Territory," addresses the importance of salesperson effectiveness and efficiency, methods for using time wisely, how to avoid time traps, efficient routing alternatives, and how to prioritize accounts.

**Part IV. Achieving Success in Personal Selling** In the fourth and final section of *Personal Selling: Achieving Customer Satisfaction and Loyalty,* we focus on "Achieving Success in Personal Selling." "Ethical and Legal Considerations in Personal Selling" are covered in chapter 13 and "Starting Your Personal Selling Career" in chapter 14. Ethical issues confronting salespeople include their interactions with prospects and customers, competitors, peers, and employers. Various local, national, and international laws that affect the performance of salespeople are described, then an approach to ethical decision-making is offered. Finally, chapter 14 shows students how to use the personal selling process to obtain their initial job following graduation.

## Chapter Pedagogy

*Personal Selling: Achieving Customer Satisfaction and Loyalty* offers several special features to facilitate student learning, including the following:

- The text focuses exclusively on professional *business-to-business* selling, not on retail or door-to-door selling to consumers. Why? Because most college students today begin their sales careers after college graduation and view a job in retail sales or selling direct to consumers as unsuitable for a college-trained professional. Focusing on business-to-business selling helps students understand that personal selling is a respected, well-paid professional career replete with abundant opportunities and rewards for those who are qualified and motivated.

- Each chapter begins with a set of chapter goals. These goals address those areas most important in the respective chapter. After studying the chapter, students can review the chapter goals to assess whether or not they have indeed achieved them.

- Following each chapter's goals is a profile of a successful salesperson. These profiles present salespeople from diverse backgrounds who sell various products for different types of organizations. By reading these profiles, students will discover that there is no stereotypical profile of a successful salesperson. Individuals from all "walks of life"—with various demographic and psychographic characteristics—can be highly successful in sales.

- Near the beginning of most chapters is a wheel depicting the personal selling process (PSP) as a revolving cycle of seven interacting, overlapping stages centered on prospects and customers. The stage dealt with in that particular chapter is highlighted on the wheel. Presenting this PSP wheel in each of the chapters of Part II reinforces the interconnectedness and relationships among the seven stages—illustrating that the wheel keeps revolving so that there is really no precise beginning or end to the personal selling process.

- Sales positions are becoming more and more high-tech. This requires students to become intimately familiar with the high-tech tools and services that facilitate salespeople's jobs. Our text describes the pragmatic use of high-tech tools and the advantages (and a few disadvantages from excessive use) in skillfully using such tools to sell more efficiently and effectively.

- Today's salespeople need to be able to discern their strengths and weaknesses themselves without depending solely on feedback from their sales managers. Our text (in several chapters) includes *personal assessment tools* that students will be able to use for purposes of self-appraisal and skill building.

- Findings from the most recent academic literature in selling are incorporated into the book in useful, understandable, and interesting ways that provide students with insights for their sales careers. When research is cited, we explain and illustrate how students can use the findings to increase their own sales performance.

- Timeliness and keeping up-to-date with "real world" best practices in personal selling are critical. To enhance students' understanding of how salespeople in today's most progressive companies do their jobs, we use the most current examples (from both the online and offline business press) taken from the best business practices.

- Long-term customer loyalty, not merely customer satisfaction, leads to the highest profitability for both salespeople and their organizations. Our mantra throughout the book is the significance of attracting, cultivating, and retaining satisfied and loyal customers who are the most profitable.

- *On the Frontlines* boxes are utilized to demonstrate the activities of "real world" salespeople working with prospects and customers before, during, and after the sale.

- *It's Up to You* boxes are employed to stimulate student thinking. These boxes pose a problem to students, asking them how they would handle a particular "live" selling situation.
- *From the Command Post* boxes are used to demonstrate how some companies are implementing the latest sales concepts and practices. Each of these boxes is directed toward students' gaining enhanced knowledge of the practice of personal selling.
- *Keeping Up Online* boxes provide students with a web address to log on to for special insights. Each box will include questions related to the web site noted in the box.
- All chapters conclude with a set of key terms, chapter review questions, topics for thought and class discussion, projects for personal growth, and two cases. In the *Instructor's Resource Manual,* there are at least two role-playing cases for each chapter. All of these pedagogical tools are designed to ensure that students understand and can apply the chapter material effectively.

# A Fully Integrated Package

The *Personal Selling: Achieving Customer Satisfaction and Loyalty* text offers a comprehensive package of ancillary materials created to assist instructors and learners. An instructor web site as well as an Instructor's Resource Manual with Test Bank and a video series contain a variety of tools tied to the text and designed to facilitate instructor-led classes as well as online learning environments. The student web site is integrated with the text structure and content, thereby creating an expanded and richer learning environment for students to explore.

## Instructor's Resource Manual with Test Bank

The Instructor's Resource Manual with Test Bank is designed to be the basic source of information to support text material in each chapter of *Personal Selling: Achieving Customer Satisfaction and Loyalty*. The Instructor's Resource Manual includes suggested class schedules and detailed teaching notes for each chapter of the text; suggested responses to end-of-chapter questions, exercises, and cases; and in-class role-playing exercises. The comprehensive Test Bank includes almost 1,200 multiple-choice, true-false, and essay questions, each identified with the corresponding learning objective and page numbers for reference.

## Instructor Web Site

This rich resource offers valuable information for instructors including PowerPoint® slides, lecture outlines, and instructor resources for end-of-chapter material. The variety of information included on the site is designed to enhance the learning and teaching experience.

## HMClassPrep® CD-ROM with HMTesting and PPT

The HMClassPrep® Instructor CD includes a wide variety of instructor resources such as HMTesting and PowerPoint slides. With HMTesting, the computerized testing program, an instructor can select questions and produce test masters for easy duplication. Instructors can select their own questions or have the program select them. They can also customize tests by creating new questions, editing existing ones, and generating multiple versions of the tests. A call-in service is also available.

## PowerPoint Slides

Included on the HmClassPrep CD and the instructor web site, an extensive set of PowerPoint slides provides instructors with lecture presentations, including key figures from the text. Instructors can use the slides as is for display on computer-based projection systems, edit them to suit personal course objectives, or print them out for use in making transparency acetates or handouts for student note taking.

## Videos

A video program accompanies *Personal Selling: Achieving Customer Satisfaction and Loyalty* to illustrate important concepts from the text. Each video is designed to illustrate personal selling concepts in the text by real-world case examples presented in the video. The video segments run from 12 to 23 minutes to allow time for classroom discussion.

## Student Web Site

This site provides additional information, guidance, and activities that will help enhance the concepts presented in this text. The site offers students ACE Self-Testing, Ready Notes, Flash Cards, Web Resources, Learning Objectives, Outlines, and Company Links. In addition, the site will feature links to important job and career sites.

## Real Deal UpGrade CD-ROM

Free with a new textbook, this CD contains tools to help students succeed: chapter objectives and summaries, a glossary of key terms, tips on improving study habits, and a link to the text web site that includes both chapter-related material and general resources.

# Acknowledgments

*Personal Selling: Achieving Customer Satisfaction and Loyalty* was written with support and encouragement from many people. First, and foremost, we owe a tremendous amount of gratitude to our friend and mentor, Marvin A. Jolson, who passed away suddenly in July 2001. Marv was the quintessential personal selling teacher, researcher, practitioner, consultant, and unparalleled ambassador of personal selling. His outstanding contributions to the field are incalculable and have had a tremendous impact on us (and thus this book), as well as on the selling arena. His presence is sorely missed.

Several other colleagues and friends have had a marked influence on our professional lives. Their friendship and collegiality have been an unending source of support throughout the years and have also helped enhance our roles as teachers and authors. These meritorious individuals include Professors Paul Christ, Jim Strong, Mary Shoemaker, William Rudelius, Lucette Comer, Lawrence Chonko, Chae Un Lim, Steven Skinner, Francis Yammarino, Bert Rosenbloom, Srini Srinivasan, Burt Brodo, Stan Kligman, Larry Colfer, Brent Smith, Joe Rocereto, and the late James Comer.

We are deeply grateful for the valuable comments and suggestions that the reviewers provided during the gestation of this text. They are Bobby Cutler, Cleveland State University; C. David Shepherd, Kennessaw State University; Vicki West, Southwest Texas State University; Rajiv Mehta, New Jersey Institute of Technology; Richard Bethel, Ferris State University; Philip Gonsher, Johnson County Community College; A.E. Beatty, Northern Arizona University; Gary Walk, Lima Technical College; Susan Meyer, Colorado State University; Jeff Totten, Bemidji State University; Thomas F. Cannon, University of Texas at San Antonio; Henry Noel, College of the Southwest; and Jack Forrest, Cumberland University.

Without the assistance from our respective schools, writing *Personal Selling: Achieving Customer Satisfaction and Loyalty* would have been even more difficult than it was. Therefore, we thank Dean George P. Tsetsekos and Marketing Department Chair Trina Larsen Andras at Drexel University for their unwavering support. At Purdue University, we express our appreciation to Dean Dennis Savaiano, Interim Department Chair Richard Feinberg, and Department Chair Richard Widdows.

Most important to initiating and completing *Personal Selling: Achieving Customer Satisfaction and Loyalty* was the professional team at Houghton Mifflin. In particular, we are grateful to George Hoffman, Editor-in-Chief, for giving us the opportunity to write this book for Houghton Mifflin and for facilitating our efforts. Also, Damaris Curran, Technology Manager and Development Editor, was extremely helpful and encouraging in her diligent work on every chapter that we wrote. Her attention to detail and sound suggestions were awesome. Kate Hartke, Associate Project Editor, was also truly thorough and painstaking in her work. Shirley Webster was trenchant and good humored throughout the photograph selection process. All of the aforementioned people and many unnamed others have made significant contributions to *Personal Selling: Achieving Customer Satisfaction and Loyalty*, and it is our fervent hope that our combined efforts will give you an enjoyable and rewarding reading experience that prepares you for a career in personal selling.

Rolph E. Anderson
Alan J. Dubinsky

## ROLPH E. ANDERSON, PH.D.

Rolph Anderson is the Royal H. Gibson Sr. Professor of Business Administration and former Head of the Department of Marketing at Drexel University. Dr. Anderson earned his Ph.D. from the University of Florida, and his MBA and BA degrees from Michigan State University. He is author or co-author of 18 textbooks, including *Multivariate Data Analysis*, 5th Edition, the most frequently cited text in academic marketing.

Professor Anderson's research has been widely published in the major refereed academic journals in his field, including articles in the *Journal of Marketing Research, Journal of Marketing, Journal of Retailing, Journal of the Academy of Marketing Science, Journal of Experimental Education, Business Horizons, Journal of Global Marketing, Journal of Marketing Education, European Journal of Marketing, Journal of Business-to-Business Marketing, Industrial Marketing Management, Journal of Business and Industrial Marketing, Journal of Personal Selling & Sales Management*, and numerous others. His classic *Journal of Marketing Research* article titled "Consumer Dissatisfaction: The Effect of Disconfirmed Expectations on Perceived Product Performance" was one of the pioneering articles in the study of customer satisfaction. Co-winner of the national Mu Kappa Tau award for the best article published in the *Journal of Personal Selling and Sales Management*, he also received the journal's national "Excellence in Reviewing Award." Drexel's LeBow College of Business students have twice chosen him for their "Faculty Appreciation Award" for teaching and student service. In 1998, Dr. Anderson received the American Marketing Association Sales SIG inaugural "Excellence in Sales Scholarship Award." In 2001, Drexel's LeBow College of Business named him recipient of its "Excellence in Faculty Research" award.

He has served several professional organizations as an officer, including President, Southeast Institute for Decision Sciences (IDS); Secretary and Board of Directors, Academy of Marketing Science; Board of Directors and Vice President for Programming, American Marketing Association (Philadelphia Chapter); National Council, Institute for Decision Sciences; Board of Directors, Northeast IDS; and Co-Chair, 61st International American Marketing Association Conference. Dr. Anderson is a member of the Editorial Boards of five academic journals. In addition, he serves on the Faculty Advisory Board of the Fisher Institute for Professional Selling and as a member of the National Sales Committee of *Financial Services Advisor* magazine.

Prior to entering academia, Dr. Anderson worked in sales and managerial positions for three *Fortune 500* companies. Active as a business and government consultant, he is also a retired U.S. Navy Supply Corps Captain. Married and the father of two teenagers, Professor Anderson's biographical sketch appears in *Who's Who in America*.

## ALAN J. DUBINSKY, PH.D.

Alan Dubinsky is a Professor in the School of Family and Consumer Sciences and the Krannert School of Business at Purdue University. He earned his Ph.D. from the University of Minnesota, as well as his MBA and BS degrees. He is a former editor of the *Journal of Personal Selling and Sales Management*, the leading academic journal that focuses on selling and sales management. He has authored *Sales Training: An Analysis of Field Sales Techniques* and co-authored *Managing the Successful Sales Force*. Additionally, he has given selling skills sales training seminars to industrial salespeople, as well as marketing seminars to executives.

Dr. Dubinsky has published over 150 research articles in personal selling and sales management. They have appeared in the major journals in his field, including the *Journal of Marketing Research, Journal of Marketing, Journal of Retailing, Journal of the Academy of Marketing Science, European Journal of Marketing, Journal of Business Research, Journal of Business-to-Business Marketing, Industrial Marketing Management, Journal of Business and Industrial Marketing, Journal of Personal Selling & Sales Management, Academy of Management Journal, Journal of Applied Psychology, Personnel Psychology, Leadership Quarterly, Sloan Management Review, Business Horizons, Journal of Marketing Education*, and in numerous others.

He was co-recipient of the national Mu Kappa Tau award for the best article of the year published in the *Journal of Personal Selling and Sales Management*. His co-authored article titled "A Path-Analytic Study of a Model of Salesperson Performance" was designated as the best article of the year in the *Journal of Academy of Marketing Science*. His article "Salesperson Failure: Sales Management is the Key" that appeared in *Industrial Marketing Management* was selected for the Annual Excellence in Research Award by the American Marketing Association Selling and Sales Management Special Interest Group. In addition, his article "Transformational and Contingent Reward Leadership: Individual, Dyad, and Group Levels of Analysis" won the outstanding article of the year award in *Leadership Quarterly*. His article "Sales Force Socialization" that appeared in the *Journal of Marketing* was voted by the AMA Sales SIG as one of the top ten most influential articles in the selling and sales management literature in the 20th century. Furthermore, he has received the "Excellence in Reviewing Award" from the *Journal of Personal Selling and Sales Management*. He is a member of the Editorial Boards of three academic journals.

Dr. Dubinsky has served on the faculty of seven universities. Prior to entering academia, he was a territory manager for Burroughs Corporation (now Unisys). He also spent a year in Volunteers in Service to America (VISTA), the U.S.'s domestic Peace Corps, as a full-time volunteer, where he coordinated volunteer reading programs in public elementary schools to assist at-risk students in enhancing their literacy skills. He has a college-aged daughter.

# PART ONE

# Overview of Personal Selling

## CHAPTER 1

# Introduction to Personal Selling: It's a Great Life!

*"All glory comes from daring to begin."*
*Anonymous*

## After Reading This Chapter, You Should Understand

- How yesterday's salesperson and today's professional salesperson differ.

- What roles professional salespeople play in providing customer satisfaction within the framework of the marketing concept and customer-oriented selling.

- Many of the opportunities and advantages offered by a professional sales career.

- How telecommunications advances can help salespeople.

- The multiple career paths branching out from an initial job in personal selling.

INSIDE PERSONAL SELLING:

## Meet David Wenz of American Greetings

The first thing David Wenz noticed about selling was that every day is different. According to Wenz, a senior national account executive calling on retail chains for Cleveland-based American Greetings, "there is a routine, but no day is exactly like another."

Wenz sells greeting cards, gift wrap, accessories, and stationery for a living—which has caused some misunderstanding: "Some people expect me to have a briefcase full of cards and say, 'Look at this one.'" Instead, Wenz collaborates with his retail accounts to understand their needs and see how American Greetings can add value through appropriate products, programs, and promotions.

After college, Wenz considered a sales career because his father was in sales and the profession was familiar. "Sales seemed

to present a certain amount of freedom and independence," he remembers. "Now the autonomy is probably the most satisfying aspect of my job." Wenz sets his own schedule and plans his sales calls based on customer and company needs; his performance is measured, in large part, by his sales accomplishments.

Wenz employs technology to stay organized and productive. He uses a hand-held computer to log phone calls, check appointments, and prioritize to-do lists. He also analyzes sales data to ensure that "the right stores are getting the right products in the right quantities."

Like all American Greetings sales trainees, Wenz started in a two-week training program. He visited stores to see that company products were properly stocked and displayed; he also learned by shadowing an expert sales mentor. "A lot of my training was observing my district manager on a sales call to see how he conducted himself," Wenz says. After training, Wenz continued to chart his progress and apply what he learned to analyzing and satisfying customer needs in everyday selling situations.

With experience, sales professionals at American Greetings can move from sales representative or area supervisor to field manager or assistant district manager. The next step may be district manager—managing other salespeople—then account executive, Wenz's current position. The sales career path may continue upward to executive sales manager, sales director, and regional vice president.

Although he observes that product knowledge, confidence, and a customer orientation are all important for sales success, Wenz's biggest challenge starting out was simply learning to listen. "People may think they listen, but they don't," he says. "If you really listen to what customers say, often you will be able to answer their questions—or objections—and make the sale."

P erhaps you are wondering "Am I cut out to be a salesperson?" "Aren't top-notch salespeople just born that way?" "Do I really need a degree just to become a salesperson?" "Will I have to coerce customers to buy, and sell them products in which I don't believe?" This book and the class in which you are enrolled will take you on a journey into the exciting world of personal selling—a world that can hold great personal development and financial opportunities for professional salespeople. By the time you have completed both, you will have many new insights into your questions and into the selling profession. Those of you who take this journey with optimism will find your already favorable view of personal selling reinforced and enhanced. If you are uncertain about whether or not the selling profession is appropriate for you keep your mind open. You may be surprised and delighted by the possibilities you encounter. Read what one early advocate of personal selling had to say about the importance of personal selling:

> What the sun is to the earth, salesmanship is to business. Without the creative power of the sun . . . the earth would become a desolate wilderness . . . Salesmanship is the force that keeps business moving. . . . Salesmanship is the creator of happiness, the bulwark of continued efficient service to humanity. Without the creative force of salesmanship, the greatest inventions would have rusted away without ever reaching the user. . . . Salesmanship is the driving wheel of commerce. The individual salesperson is a cog in the wheel that keeps business moving.[1]

Like the author of the words above, we strongly believe that professional personal selling is one of the most exciting, dynamic, rewarding, and beneficial of all possible careers. At the same time, it is also one of the most misunderstood, overlooked, and underrated career fields because most people never encounter professional business-to-business salespeople, who are the focus of this book. Instead, they are often irritated by telemarketers and door-to-door salespeople who call at inconvenient hours to aggressively pitch unwanted products or services. Consumers also interact almost daily with retail store clerks, who tend to be merely order takers. The aforementioned sales jobs are considered low-level by most college students, as they do not offer the career opportunities they want, so we will seldom mention salespeople who sell primarily to households. Our goal throughout this book is to prepare students to assume a professional career in business-to-business sales, which offers unlimited earning potential and excellent career opportunities.

If you have less than favorable images of salespeople, you are in for a real awakening as you learn about the many career opportunities and stimulating challenges in professional selling today. By frequently placing the word "professional" in front of "personal selling" or "selling" in our discussions, we are emphasizing that today's successful salespeople are well-educated, well-trained, customer-relationship–oriented people who use the latest techniques and technologies to create customer satisfaction and loyalty. These professionals understand the "lifetime value" of loyal customers and focus on long-run relationships rather than mere single-transaction profitability. They understand that keeping current customers loyal is even more important than attracting new customers because over two-thirds of sales for most companies come from the repeat purchases of loyal customers. What's more, loyal customers are the most profitable because they buy the most dollar volume, cost less to serve since they have moved up on the relationship learning curve, generate positive word-of-mouth promotion for your products and services, readily purchase new products introduced by your company, are receptive to *upselling* (buying higher priced product versions) and *cross-selling* (buying other types of products), and are usually the most forgiving when problems occur. For these reasons, we consistently stress in our discussions that professional salespeople must not only satisfy customers in each and every transaction, but go that extra mile by providing pre- and post-sale customer service that provides added value and helps achieve customer loyalty. Later in this chapter and in the chapters ahead, we'll discuss more about what it means to be a professional salesperson. Now, let's begin your journey into the world of professional selling.

## WHO SELLS?

Selling, whether one considers it an art or a discipline, involves the use of persuasive communication to negotiate mutually beneficial agreements. Selling is at the heart of nearly all our relationships with other people. Although we concentrate on commercial selling situations in this book, the concepts and techniques we discuss apply to negotiating agreements in business, school, social, family, and other relationships. As a youngster, you may have sold your lawn mowing services to neighbors, or you may have sold candy to raise money for a school activity. Today you may be working part-time as a shoe salesperson or a real estate representative. Or you may be trying to cajole your parents into letting you go to Florida during spring break. Perhaps you're attempting to convince one of your friends to loan you fifty dollars for the upcoming weekend. Maybe you're trying to sell your boss on giving you a raise or a few days off. You may be struggling to induce a special person to go out with you. You may be endeavoring to convince your teacher to let you take the final exam early. Possibly you're talking your friends into voting for your favorite political candidate. In all of these situations, you're using your knowledge of people and their needs to negotiate an agreement or commitment through persuasive communication. In other words, you're selling!

Learning the principles of selling will improve anyone's chances for success in virtually any field.[2] It's been said that all professionals must be good salespeople, and all good salespeople must be professional. More than twelve million Americans sell to businesses, organizations, and consumers. Even this huge number is understated because virtually every occupational group involves an element of personal selling. Professional selling ranges from selling major appliances to consumers shopping in a department store to selling desktop computers to purchasing agents for manufacturers to selling stocks and bonds to individual investors. Our focus, however, will be on those salespeople who sell their companies' products and services to other organizations—businesses, not-for-profit organizations, or government agencies. These salespeople are professionals who consider personal selling either a lifelong career or a vital experience leading to higher-level management.

## PROFESSIONAL PERSONAL SELLING: A NEW LOOK

An *INC*. magazine article on the art of selling stated: "If you're still selling the old-fashioned way, mark our words, you won't be for long."[3] Customers of all kinds—whether consumers, businesses, not-for-profit organizations, or government agencies—are expecting and demanding more from sellers. More and more customers today perceive many products—from computers to hand drills—to be almost identical across manufacturers, or like commodities. Sellers are recognizing that they cannot continue to make profits on products seen as commodities, so firms are switching to value-added selling, which requires a whole new understanding of customers, their needs, and their ever-rising expectations. Progressive companies tell their salespeople to focus on how individual customers see the product benefits in solving their specific problems. Instead of short-run sales, companies are insisting that their salespeople concentrate on developing long-term relationships and partnerships based on professionalism and mutual trust with customers.

### New Professionalism Required

Contemporary salespeople must develop a new level of professionalism and sensitivity to customer concerns as they face increasingly diverse, multicultural, and sophisticated customers whose expectations continue to rise. The old "door-to-door" salesperson has essentially been replaced by various forms of direct marketing aided by advanced communication methods and technology. Revolutionary developments in telecommunications and computer technologies have led customers to expect better and faster service, greater values at lower prices, and much more. Today's salespeople must be more educated and better trained than ever. They must develop innovative selling strategies and tactics to negotiate "win-win" agreements with expert buyers who are generally equipped with computerized systems that can continuously monitor and analyze purchasing alternatives, product turnover, and supplier performance. These professional buyers often know as much or more than the salesperson about the products and services offered by various suppliers, so today's salespeople must be well-prepared professionals themselves in order to succeed in increasingly demanding and competitive markets. While domestic buyers are becoming more expert and demanding, foreign competition for domestic and global markets continues to intensify. Only those companies that provide truly world-class product quality, professional personal selling, and customer service will thrive in the future.[4]

Whew! We have a lot to discuss, so let's get started. In this first chapter, we begin by refuting some stereotypes and myths about salespeople. Then, we'll look at how personal selling has evolved and what it's like to be a professional salesperson today.

## Myth of the Born Salesperson

Many have long accepted the notion that "salespeople are born, not made." In other words, you can't achieve sales success without an extroverted "selling personality." In reality, though, people can develop into successful salespeople. Research suggests that personal characteristics (those with which one is born) do have some influence on sales performance, but not as much as a determined individual has in developing his or her own skills or as management has in training recruits.[5] No longer is the bubbly personality armed with a quick wit and a few clever sales techniques enough for a successful career in sales. Pushiness, brashness, and puffery have given way to polished, well-trained professionalism. Today's customer wants to deal with salespeople who are knowledgeable, honest, trustworthy, competent, and service oriented. Many of today's sales practitioners and scholars view personal selling either as an art or discipline to be learned. Most realistically, personal selling is a mixture of art *and* discipline. Some observers, however, express strong opinions one way or another about the nature of personal selling. For instance:

> Some people have more natural ability than others, but selling is not an art. It's a discipline. There's a specific selling process you have to go through, and anyone can learn it. It involves taking all the different steps, reducing them to a checklist, and then executing them one by one. There's no magic to it, and you don't need a lot of natural talent. What you need is a disciplined, organized approach to selling. If you have that, you'll outperform the great salesperson who doesn't understand the process every time. Selling can definitely be learned.[6]

## Salesperson Commitment

Salespeople's commitment to job and company can vary dramatically and affect performance. Some are almost apathetic about their daily work and are unlikely to exert much effort in improving their sales productivity or satisfying their customers. Others are intensely involved with their jobs but feel no bond with their organization. These "lone wolves" put forth high effort and show concern for their customers but are ever vigilant about seeking alternative employment where the "grass looks greener." Still other salespeople care little for their sales job but feel a high degree of commitment to their employer. They often seek close attachments to the firm but fail to conduct their selling job either efficiently or effectively.

Successful professional salespeople, unlike the foregoing three types of underachievers, display a high degree of commitment to their jobs, their customers, and their companies. They are determined to satisfy customers while achieving both their personal and organizational selling objectives. Moreover,

*The salesperson who practices customer-oriented selling identifies customer needs accurately, and engages in selling and servicing behaviors that build and maintain customer satisfaction.*

Jose Luis Palaez/Corbis

they feel a bonding with the firm—its management, staff, values, philosophies, and practices—and see themselves as team players. Such "super salespeople" are the bulwark of the most successful organizations. They seek to generate sales revenue in win-win sales agreements that benefit *both* the buyer and the seller over the short and long runs.[7]

## Marketing and Customer-Oriented Selling Concepts

Professional salespeople today tend to adopt two interrelated business philosophies. One is known as the *marketing concept.* According to Kotler and Armstrong: "The marketing concept holds that achieving organizational goals depends on determining the needs and wants of target markets and delivering the desired satisfactions more effectively and efficiently than competitors."[8] Organizations that adhere to this philosophy know that successful implementation requires that not only its sales force but also its entire administrative and sales support staff be focused on customer satisfaction. In fact, a company-wide customer orientation is needed, as described by Frank "Buck" Rodgers, former marketing vice president for IBM and author of *The IBM Way*:

> At IBM, everybody sells! . . . Every employee has been trained to think that the customer comes first—everybody from the CEO, to the people in finance, to the receptionists, to those who work in manufacturing. . . . 'IBM doesn't sell products. It sells solutions.' . . . An IBM marketing rep's success depends totally on his ability to understand a prospect's business so well that he can identify and analyze its problems and then come up with a solution that makes sense to the customer.[9]

**Customer-Oriented Selling** Focus on identifying customers' needs and engaging in selling and servicing behaviors that help build and maintain a high level of customer satisfaction and loyalty in the long run.

Closely related to the marketing concept is **customer-oriented selling.** Salespeople who practice customer-oriented selling focus on identifying their customers' needs accurately and engaging in selling and servicing behaviors that help build and maintain a high level of customer satisfaction. The focus is on building profitable, long-lasting customer relationships.[10] Customer-oriented salespeople put heavy emphasis on uncovering and addressing their customers' needs. They know their customers and they understand their customers' customers as well. Thus, they can help customers develop strategies for "selling through" to their own customers. Such efforts enhance the buyer-seller relationship and augment customer satisfaction and loyalty.[11] These top-performing salespeople make satisfying customers their major focus. Consequently, their customers respect and trust them . . . and expect to continue interacting with them in the future.[12] Even if you have no sales experience, assume that you are

# HOW CUSTOMER ORIENTED ARE YOU?

*Determine how customer oriented you are by responding to the statements below, using the following scale:*

**5–Strongly Agree  4–Agree  3–Neither Agree nor Disagree  2–Disagree  1–Strongly Disagree**

1. I want to help customers achieve their goals. ____

2. I want to serve my customers so well that they will come back to buy more from me. ____

3. It's more important to satisfy a customer than to make a big sales commission on a product that won't satisfy the customer. ____

4. I use a canned sales pitch for most sales. ____

5. I try to influence customers by providing information rather than by applying pressure. ____

6. I try to sell the product best suited to the customer's problem even if my commission is lower on that product. ____

7. I listen to customers more than I talk to them so I can understand their needs. ____

8. I try to answer a customer's questions about products as honestly as I can. ____

9. I try to help customers solve their problems even if I have to occasionally recommend a competitor's product. ____

10. I am willing to politely disagree with a customer in order to help him or her make a better decision. ____

11. I try to give customers accurate expectations about what the product will do for them. ____

12. I try to resolve customer complaints so that they want to remain my customer. ____

13. I want customers to be fully satisfied, so they will become repeat buyers from me. ____

14. I try to sell customers all I can convince them to buy, even if it's more than they really need. ____

15. I keep alert to spot weaknesses in a customer's personality so I can use them to apply buying pressure at the right time. ____

16. If I'm not sure if a product is right for a customer, I still pressure him or her to buy because it's not my job to figure out whether or not the product's right for the customer. ____

17. I usually try to persuade customers to buy the product on which I make the most commission. ____

18. I sometimes paint too rosy a picture of my products to make them sound as good as possible to customers. ____

19. If a customer doesn't ask about a particular product weakness, I don't think it's my job to mention it. ____

20. It's sometimes necessary to stretch the truth a little in describing a product to a customer. ____

21. Even when I know they're wrong, I generally pretend to agree with customers in order to please them. ____

22. I sometimes imply to a customer that something is beyond my control when it's not. ____

23. When customers come back to complain about a product I sold them, I often try to avoid them. ____

24. In negotiating with customers, my main focus is on winning the sale. ____

25. I never let customers assume something that's incorrect because over the long run my integrity and honesty are among my best sales tools. ____

The higher your score for items 1 through 3, 5 through 13, and 25, the more customer oriented you are. Total scores of 52 or higher on these items indicate a strong customer orientation; a score of less than 39 indicates a weak customer orientation.

The lower your score for items 4 and 14 through 24, the more customer oriented you are. Total scores of 24 or less indicate a strong customer orientation; a score of over 36 indicates a weak customer orientation.

***Source:*** *Robert Saxe and Barton A. Weitz, "The SOCO Scale: A Measure of the Customer Orientation of Salespeople," Journal of Marketing Research 19 (August 1982): 343–351. Reprinted with permission of the American Marketing Association.*

| | TABLE 1.1 |
|---|---|
| **CONTRASTING YESTERDAY'S AND TODAY'S SALESPEOPLE** | |

| Yesterday's Salesperson | Today's Professional Salesperson |
|---|---|
| Product oriented | Customer oriented |
| Thinks mainly about *selling* customers | Thinks mainly about *serving* customers |
| Does little sales call planning | Develops sales call strategy to achieve specific objectives |
| Makes sales pitches without listening much to customers | Listens to and communicates meaningfully with customers |
| Sales presentation focuses on product features and price | Sales presentation focuses on customer benefits |
| Thinks in terms of manipulative selling techniques | Thinks in terms of helping customers solve problems |
| Goal is to make immediate sales | Goal is to develop long-term, mutually beneficial relationships |
| Disappears once a sale is made | Follows up with customers to provide service and ensure satisfaction leading to customer loyalty |
| Works alone and has little interest in understanding customer problems | Works as a member of a team of specialists to serve customers |

**Professional Salesperson** Salesperson who sees a sales career as a true profession for which he or she must be well educated, well prepared, and thoroughly professional in order to negotiate successfully with professional buyers.

about to start a sales career and honestly answer the questions in the exercise on p. 9 to see how customer oriented you are. Then, evaluate yourself to see how you might become more customer oriented.

How well did you do on the self-assessment of your customer orientation? Do you need to change some attitudes or behaviors? Development of marketing and customer-oriented selling concepts have changed the focus of professional personal selling from a short-run emphasis on sellers' needs to a long-run emphasis on customers' needs. Contrasts between yesterday's salesperson and today's **professional salesperson** are summarized in Table 1.1.

## WHAT IS A CUSTOMER?

A customer may have many names: client, account, patron, patient, parishioner, member, fan, or voter. Whatever the name, every organization thrives, survives, or dies on the basis of how well it satisfies its customers. After all, customers are the lifeblood of both salespeople and the organizations for which they work because they provide the sales revenues on which the entire organization depends. The two basic categories of customers or markets are *consumers* and *organizations*. In order to sell successfully to consumers or organizations, sales representatives must understand how these markets buy.

*Consumer markets* consist of individuals who purchase goods and services for their own personal consumption. All customers other than ultimate consumers are organizational customers. *Organizational markets* include three types: producers, resellers, and governments.

The *producer market* consists of both manufacturing firms and nonprofit organizations that purchase goods and services for the production of additional goods and services to sell, rent, or supply. For example, General Motors may purchase sheet steel from USX and automobile tires from Goodyear to manufacture its automobiles for sale to its dealer customers. An example of a *nonprofit* producer market is a church that buys a Hammond organ to "produce" music at Sunday services.

The *reseller market* includes individuals and organizations that purchase goods to resell, rent, or conduct their own business operations. Resellers are "middlemen" (also called intermediaries) who facilitate the flow of goods from producers to ultimate users and consumers. Three common types of resellers are industrial distributors, wholesalers, and retailers. Each has its own category of customers. *Industrial distributors* sell primarily to manufacturers or producers of goods and services. *Wholesalers* sell chiefly to retailers. And *retailers* sell to consumers. For example, an industrial distributor might sell drill bits to a garage door manufacturer. A large wholesaler may buy Godiva chocolates from the Campbell Soup Company (a producer) to sell to Bloomingdale's (a retailer) for sale to its department store shoppers. A public library may become a nonprofit reseller by purchasing a Xerox copier for its patrons to use, thus providing better services to its patrons.

Finally, the *government market* includes all local, state, and federal governmental units that purchase or rent products and services to carry out the functions of government. At the national level, the Defense Supply Agency (DSA) buys for all the armed services, while the General Services Administration (GSA) buys for the civilian branches and agencies of the federal government. State and local governments also have buying functions conducted by various governmental units.

## WHAT IS A PRODUCT?

A *product* may be defined as anything offered to a market to satisfy customer needs and wants. It can be a *tangible product*, such as a forklift, or an *intangible service*, such as professional advice from an estate planner. Note, though, that this distinction between tangible products and intangible services lacks precision because nearly all products have intangible aspects and all services have tangible aspects. A computer usually comes with a warranty and may include a service contract (intangibles). And the professional advice may include a detailed written financial analysis and investment plan (tangibles).

Customers buy products for *benefits or solutions to their problems*. They do not seek laser printers as such, but want "attractive financial reports." Salespeople can never assume that the most obvious or functional benefit is the one the customer wants. And salespeople should always be thinking past their immediate customers to their customers' customers. For example, an alert salesperson noticed that many women owned several wristwatches because they sought the watch's benefit as an ornament or accessory to match their clothes rather than as a timepiece. With this information, the maker of Swatches, whose customers are wholesalers and retailers, developed and profitably sold stylish, multicolored plastic watches for their customers to sell through to consumers.

The actual problem-solving benefit a customer seeks is called the *core product*. For example, a company may want a corporate airplane for its executives' convenience in attending meetings across the country and internationally. Product characteristics such as safety features, interior styling, comfort level, range, cruising speed, fuel capacity, and a respected brand name turn this core product into something tangible such as a Cessna Citation Jet. We call the combination of a core product and product characteristics the *tangible product*. Many customers want additional tangible and intangible benefits such as credit, product use training, repair service, replacement guarantees, and warranties. The **augmented product** is the complete bundle of benefits offered by a product including its core function, various enhancing characteristics, and supplemental benefits and services.[13] We can see that tangible and intangible benefits and services blend together to form every product. We will therefore use the term *product* to refer to both products *and* services.

**Augmented Product**
Complete bundle of benefits offered by a product, including its core function, various enhancing characteristics, and supplemental benefits and services.

# DIVERSE ROLES OF THE PROFESSIONAL SALESPERSON

As products and services have become more technical, competition more intense, buyers more sophisticated, and purchase decisions more shared (by several levels of management and technical experts in organizations), personal selling has grown in complexity. Behind the basic job of the professional salesperson today lie a great many different types of selling roles, tasks, and responsibilities.

## Selling Roles Vary Across Organizations

Retailers, wholesalers, industrial distributors, manufacturers, service firms, and nonprofit organizations are some examples of employers who need salespeople. Each of these organizations employs different types of salespeople for different selling roles. For example, an IBM marketing representative who calls on large manufacturers to sell complex mainframe computers has a role different from that of the Procter & Gamble salesperson who sells laundry soap to wholesalers. Similarly, the Merrill-Lynch stockbroker who sells common stock to small investors has tasks and responsibilities different from those of the salesperson who sells construction materials to small contractors. If a customer's organization has a large and intricate structure, several salespeople from the same firm may be required to sell to various levels within that buyer organization. Out of necessity, smaller firms often train their salespeople to handle a broad range of customers and customer needs. Factors that influence the numbers and kinds of salespeople a firm will hire include the following:

- Size and characteristics of potential buyers
- Price, complexity, and type of products
- Types and number of distribution channels
- Geographic location and relative dispersion of customers
- Level of marketing and technical support required

## Selling Positions and Jobs

Selling entails an array of different activities and tasks. One researcher identified ten key categories of salesperson activities: basic selling activities, order-related tasks, product service, information/communication management, account service, conferences/meetings, training/recruitment for the firm, entertainment, out-of-town travel, and middlemen tasks.[14] Furthermore, selling can be divided into three basic roles, or jobs: (1) order taking, (2) order supporting, and (3) order creating. We see these in a continuum of sales-job complexity from mere response selling to the highly creative selling necessary to obtain new business, as follows:

**Order Taking**
- Response selling
  - Inside order taker
  - Outside order taker

**Order Supporting**
- Missionary selling

**Order Creating**
- Trade selling
- Technical selling
- Creative selling

**Order Taking.** **Order taking** entails processing routine orders or reorders for products that have already been sold to the buying firm. The major goal is to maintain the ongoing relationship with existing customers and maintain sales revenue. *Response selling* requires the salesperson simply to respond to customer requests. Response salespersons are either *inside order takers*—such as retail clerks in department stores or telephone salespersons in wholesaler organizations—or *outside order takers* who work outside of the firm's offices. These include truck driver-salespeople who travel a regular route to replenish inventories, (e.g., Frito-Lay snacks or Coca-Cola soft drinks), for customers such as retail grocery stores.

**Order Supporting.** **Order-supporting** salespeople do minimal sales generation but instead serve as an assistance-provider to customers.

**Order Taking**
Processing routine orders or reorders for products that have been sold previously to the buying firm.

**Order Supporting** The process of having minimal involvement in sales generation but instead serving as an assistance-provider to customers.

**Missionary Selling**
Educating, building good-
will, and providing serv-
ices to customers (for
example, doctors and den-
tists) by giving them samples and information
about products and serv-
ices (such as new pharma-
ceuticals and medicines to
prescribe or recommend
for their patients).

**Order Creating**  The
process of identifying
prospective buyers, providing them information,
motivating them to buy,
confirming the sale, and
following up after the sale
has been made to ensure
customer satisfaction.
Trade, technical, and creative salespeople all do
order creating in varying
degrees.

**Trade Selling**  Consists
largely of creative field
service to wholesale and
distributor customers, such
as expediting orders, taking reorders, restocking
shelves, setting up dis-
plays, providing in-store
demonstrations, and dis-
tributing samples to store
customers.

**Missionary selling** requires the salesperson to educate customers, build goodwill, and provide services. The missionary salesperson seldom takes orders from customers directly, but furnishes information about products to middlemen, who in turn recommend or sell the products to their own customers. For example, the pharmaceuticals "detail person"—a missionary sales-person—introduces physicians to new pharmaceutical drugs and related products in hopes that the physicians will prescribe these products for their patients. Distilleries, pharmaceutical houses, food manufacturers, and transportation firms commonly employ missionary salespeople to help wholesale and retail customers sell to their own customers.

Merck & Co., a major pharmaceutical firm, boosted its total sales staff by 36 percent because of its increasing number of new product introductions. In many instances physicians needed Merck detail reps to help them understand the benefits and possible side effects in prescribing the new drugs for their patients. As the number of new drugs on the market continues to explode, more and more pharmaceutical companies have increased their missionary sales calls on doctors.

**Order Creating. Order-creating** sales personnel identify prospective buyers, offer them information, stimulate them to buy, close the sale, and follow-up after completing the sale. Trade, technical, and creative salespeople engage in order creating in varying degrees. **Trade selling** generally occurs when a manufacturer sells to a distributor wholesaler—a business that resells the product rather than using it in its own business operations. Similar to response selling, the salesperson responds to customer requests. Field service, however, is more important in trade selling. The trade-selling representative expedites orders, takes reorders, restocks shelves, sets up displays, provides in-store demonstrations, and distributes samples to store customers. Trade sellers are usually discouraged from hard selling to customers.

*Technical selling* requires a specifically trained salesperson, often called a "sales engineer," to help customers solve technical problems. Technical selling resembles professional consulting and is common in such industries as steel, chemicals, heavy machinery, and computers, where product offerings tend to be complex. A sales engineer typically helps customers understand proper use of complex products, system design, and product installation and maintenance procedures.

*Creative selling* calls upon the salesperson to stimulate product demand among present and potential customers. Creative selling includes sales development and sales maintenance. *Sales development* attempts to generate new customers. *Sales maintenance* tries to ensure a continuous flow of sales from present customers. Salespeople required to do both tasks tend to spend more time on maintenance work because developing new prospects takes more time and may be less rewarding in the short run.

Although we have talked about selling positions as if each job had a definite set of tasks, it is important to realize that every selling job may include all three essential characteristics of order taking, order supporting, and order creating. An outside order taker dealing with a demanding and indecisive customer might give a convincing product explanation and create an order. And

# Using "Insiders" to Get the Sale

Simon Perez is a successful missionary salesperson for a large pharmaceutical company whose territory covers the Miami area. Simon thought that it was strange to be called a missionary salesperson when his job was not to directly sell his company's new medicines and drugs to doctors, but to educate them about their benefits and side effects. "Oh, well," he thought, "the term *missionary salesperson* probably sounds better than missionary educator." In educating doctors about his company's products, Simon tries to convince them to prescribe the products for their patients. Although Simon receives a good base salary, he also receives a quarterly bonus depending on the total dollar amount of his company's products sold in his territory. Simon heard that some of the top missionary salespeople in his company earned bonuses that were larger than their base salaries. During his first few weeks as a missionary salesperson, Simon was frustrated that the doctors in his territory were often unavailable to talk to him and even when they became available for a few minutes, there was seldom enough time to tell the doctors all that he wanted them to know.

Feeling frustrated by this inability to secure much time with the doctors, Simon began to worry if there might be something wrong with his approach. After one late Friday evening sales meeting at his company's regional headquarters, Simon asked Susan Hankens, one of his fellow missionary salespeople, how she managed to speak to doctors about the company's products. Susan laughed and told Simon that all missionary salespeople have the same problem. Doctors are very busy people who seldom have much time to sit down with salespeople of any kind. "What I do," Susan said, "is work with the office staff—the nurses, receptionists, or medical assistants—who interact with the doctor daily. They do most of my job for me. First, I make sure that they're glad to see me

because I bring in special snacks, pastries, cookies, sandwiches, or soft drinks, every time I call on them. I learn the birthdays of everybody in the office and make sure that I remember to give them a little something on that special occasion, usually a birthday cake and small gift. Sometimes I'll hang around the medical office for an hour or more talking to them about their families and telling them a little more about our products each time they get a break from their work with patients. Of course, I stay out of their way but I continue to engage them in conversation about a myriad of things of interest to them. But I always try to tell them everything they need to know about our company's new products and answer all their questions. Then, before leaving, I make sure that I've left lots of product samples for everyone along with our product brochures. I also leave my telephone number and email address in case a doctor or anyone has any more questions. My experience is that the office staff probably does a better job of educating the doctors about our products than I could do, especially since they work together and trust one another. It's great having all these busy, talented people help me do my job."

After talking with Susan, Simon tried her approach by working closely with the office staff, nurses, and medical assistants in his territory's medical offices. Although he still was unable to meet with the doctors as often as he liked, Simon felt that he had done his job when he had managed to educate the doctor's support team about his company's products. As a missionary salesperson, he realized that you don't really know how well you've done in educating prospects and customers about your company's products until quarterly sales figures come out. But Simon feels he must be doing something right because last quarter, for the first time, his bonus was larger than his base salary.

some kinds of missionary salespeople might actually "take" an order (a publisher's book representative, for example, may write out and deliver a professor's textbook order to the bookstore manager). No matter what the selling role, however, the bottom-line goal of all selling is to obtain the order. And *that* usually involves a certain amount of creativity. Read *On the Frontlines* on p. 15 to see how one salesperson had to alter his selling approach to create sales.

## WHAT DOES A PROFESSIONAL SALESPERSON DO?

**Personal Selling Process (PSP)** The seven interacting, overlapping stages that every salesperson, no matter what the product or service being sold, must carry out.

The many different types of sales situations and jobs all tend to involve seven basic stages that form the **Personal Selling Process (PSP).** In order of completion, they are (1) prospecting and qualifying, (2) planning the sales call (the preapproach), (3) approaching the prospect, (4) making the sales presentation and demonstration, (5) negotiating sales resistance or objections, (6) confirming and closing the sale, (7) following up and servicing the account. Salespeople must work through all seven interrelated stages while trying to negotiate sales agreements with prospects or customers. Although not all activities in the PSP stages require direct interaction with the prospect or customer, *both* noncustomer interaction and customer interaction activities have a dramatic impact on success with a given buyer.[15]

### Continuous Cycle or Wheel

**Wheel of Personal Selling** Depiction of the seven stages of the PSP as a continuous cycle or wheel carried out by professionals in the field of sales.

The seven stages of the PSP are best depicted as a continuous cycle or wheel of overlapping stages, as shown in Figure 1.1. Notice that once the **wheel of personal selling** is set in motion, it continues to revolve from one stage to the next. Using this depiction, it is easy to see that stage seven is not the end of the cycle but rather a new beginning, for the salesperson's follow-up and service activities generate repeat sales and purchases of new products as customer needs change over time. The wheel is not a rigid, unchangeable, continuously evolving mechanism that can't be stopped, changed, or reversed if necessary. Sometimes, the salesperson must return to, skip over, or redesign a stage in the PSP when an initial approach or turn of the wheel fails to work and requires a modified response to new information about the customer's wants or needs. Flexibility in response to customer feedback is critical in making the most effective and efficient use of the PSP concept.

### The PSP Wheel Revolves Around Prospects and Customers

As you examine Figure 1.1, keep in mind that the *center* or focus of the wheel—prospects and customers—is its most important part. Without prospects and customers, the wheel would have nothing around which to revolve! In addition, present customers are good sources of new leads—or potentially qualified prospects. Below is a brief overview; we will discuss each of the seven stages in depth later, beginning in chapter 3.

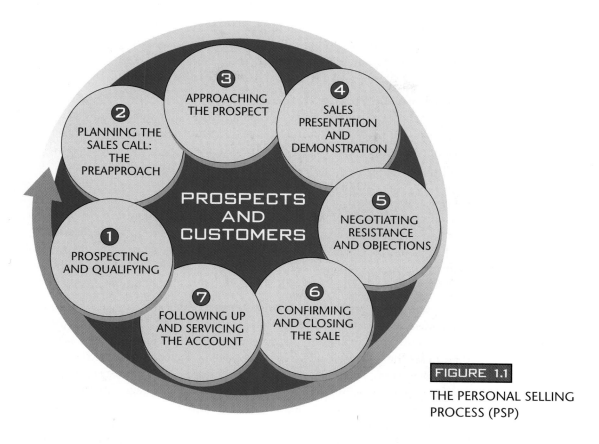

FIGURE 1.1

THE PERSONAL SELLING
PROCESS (PSP)

**Prospecting and Qualifying.**  Current-customer rosters continuously shrink
through death, bankruptcy, relocation, or switches to other suppliers. In order to
increase or even maintain sales volume, salespeople must unceasingly search for
new customers. Potential new customers are called *prospects*. Most salespeople
spend more time on prospecting than on any other selling activity. **Prospecting**
requires salespeople to obtain *leads*. A lead is basically the name and address or telephone number of a person or organization that may have a need for the company's product or service. Before a *lead* may be considered a genuine prospect, it
must be qualified in terms of *need or want*, *authority to buy*, *money to buy*, and *eligibility to buy*. An easy way to remember these four qualifiers is the acronym "NAME":
need, authority, money, and eligibility. When companies or individuals pass all
four of these screens, they become "prospects" on which to make a sales call.

**Planning the Sales Call (The Preapproach).**  In the preapproach or planning stage, the salesperson obtains detailed information about the prospective
buyer and the buying situation and then develops a strategy for ensuring a
favorable reception. Information sources include trade associations, chambers
of commerce, credit bureaus, mailing list companies, government and public
libraries, investment firms, and the Internet (using search engines such as
www.google.com or www.yahoo.com). Perhaps, the most direct source of
information is a low profile preliminary call at the prospect's business site.
While at the prospect's company site, salespeople can talk subtly to receptionists or other employees, gather company brochures and materials, and simply

**Prospecting**  First step in
the PSP where salespeople
find leads and qualify
them on four criteria:
name, authority, money,
and eligibility to buy.

observe the way the business operates. Such efforts must be undertaken diplomatically and graciously though, to avoid being viewed as a "spy" or "snoop." One means of doing this is to inform a prospect's personnel of your intentions for the visit and then ask for permission to gather information.

**Approaching the Prospect.**  The salesperson makes his or her vital first impression in the approach stage. Salespeople must quickly gain and hold a prospect's attention and interest. Depending on the situation, numerous methods for approaching the prospect can succeed, ranging widely from mutual-acquaintance or reference approaches to the customer-benefit approach. Probably the approach salespeople most often use is a *sales letter* to introduce themselves, their company, and products, and a follow-up telephone call to obtain more information and arrange a sales call appointment. In chapter 4, we'll discuss variations of the classic sales letter approach, including "seeding" (becoming a kind of "pen pal" with a company manager) and "prenotification" (obtaining permission to send sales materials). For now, keep in mind that successful salespeople learn to tailor their approach to suit each new prospect.

**Making the Sales Presentation and Demonstration.**  The sales presentation is the persuasive communication at the heart of the selling process. After asking the customer qualifying questions to uncover specific needs, the salesperson proposes the products and services that will best satisfy those needs, highlights their features, advantages, and benefits, and stimulates prospect desire for the offerings with a skillful demonstration. Success in this stage demands carefully planned strategies and tactics, followed by anticipation and rehearsal of likely interactions between buyer and seller. Like the approach stage, each sales presentation must be tailored to the prospect and the selling situation. A practical sales presentation combined with a convincing product demonstration can help secure a favorable outcome. Mere "dog and pony shows," no matter how elaborate, will seldom succeed. A salesperson who employs skillful questioning and reactive listening as prospects describe their needs stands a far better chance of thoroughly understanding the exact nature of the customer's problem, so that the sales presentation and demonstration "speak" directly to providing a solution. An effective sales presentation and demonstration must convey clearly to prospects that you are not merely selling products but are solving their problems.

**Negotiating Sales Resistance or Objections.**  Seldom do prospects or customers automatically accept the salesperson's sales proposal and sign a purchase agreement. Instead, salespeople are likely to confront customer resistance. However, do not be discouraged by prospect resistance or objections. These are usually positive signs of interest and involvement. In fact, experienced salespeople often say, "The sale doesn't begin until the prospect says 'No.'" View such objections, then, as positive requests for more information so that the prospect can justify a purchase decision. If you anticipate the customer's possible objections and prepare responses before making the sales call you will be better able to counter buyer objections with information that will confirm the sale.

**Confirming and Closing the Sale.**  In order to increase their *closing ratio* (number of orders/number of sales calls), salespeople must become skillful closers. The close is the crowning moment of the sales process, the moment for which the salesperson has worked so hard, when the customer agrees to order the product. Typically, new salespeople are shy about asking for the order. Although no closing question is more decisive than "Will you give me the order?", it need not be that blatant. Often, you can accomplish the same result with an indirect closing question such as "When do you need the product delivered?" In chapter 7 we'll describe effective ways to close a sale.

"When do I close the sale?" is another question new salespeople often ask. There is no perfect time to close the sale. An old adage says that salespeople need to know their ABCs (that is, "Always be closing"). This means you should attempt "trial closes" throughout your interaction with the prospect. Trial closes are simply attempts to make prospects show their *readiness to buy*. Examples of "trial closes" include questions such as: "Is this the kind of product you're looking for?"; "Do you think this product will solve your problem?"; "How do you like it so far?"; or "So, what do you think?"

Involving prospects directly in demonstrating the product or "trying it out" can help prospects gain confidence in the product and move them toward the close. Nonverbal trial closes can also be effective. Even a small physical act like moving the order form and pen in front of prospects may generate a reflex action to pick up the pen and sign the order. Savvy salespeople also learn to read and closely observe body language to determine the time for a close. The close can happen at any time during the sales process—in the first few minutes of the first sales call, or in the last few seconds of the sixth sales call. Skillful salespeople learn a variety of closing techniques, discussed in chapter 7, to help prospects make decisions in the buying process.

**Following Up and Servicing the Account.** Generally, it is far easier—and less costly—to keep present customers satisfied than to search out and acquire new customers. That is why, after making the sale, top-performing salespeople maintain close contact with the customer to handle any complaints and to provide customer service such as installation, repair, or credit approvals. Satisfied customers are more likely to become loyal repeat buyers. Loyal customers are the most profitable: they buy the most, cost less to serve, refer others, and are usually the most forgiving when problems occur. About 70 percent of the typical company's sales come from its current, satisfied customers.[16] And these loyal customers over their lifetimes can be worth up to ten times as much as the average customer. Companies as diverse as Pizza Hut, Home Depot, and General Motors are working to not only satisfy customers but to keep their loyalty. Pizza Hut estimates that the lifetime value of its regular customers

*The Personal Selling Process can involve selling to individual buyers or a team of buyers.*
Jeff Zarud/Corbis

## IT'S UP TO YOU

You are a salesperson for Herculon, Inc., a manufacturer of industrial equipment. You have received extensive sales training for three months, especially addressing product knowledge, competition, and selling skills. Today is your first day in your new territory. You know little about the territory or who are the most likely prospects. You have, however, the names, addresses, telephone numbers, and email addresses of key people at companies that have inquired about Herculon products or purchased from the company in the past. How will you begin working in your newly assigned territory?

is over $8,000, Home Depot figures $23,000, and Cadillac—a division of General Motors—calculates $332,000 as the lifetime value of its most loyal customers.[17] The message seems clear: Loyal customers provide "big-time" profits!

Follow-up calls can also produce sales of ancillary items or new products, and referrals to new prospects. Frequent and comprehensive follow-up is a primary means of securing long-run, satisfied, and loyal customers . . . and of keeping the *personal selling process wheel* revolving. Using what you've learned so far in this chapter, consider the situation described in *It's Up to You* above.

## USING TECHNOLOGY TO SELL BETTER

**Extranets**  Corporate networks that allow communication between a company and selected customers, suppliers, and business partners.

**Intranets**  Internal corporate networks that allow salespeople and other employees within a company to obtain information and communicate with each other.

Today's professional salespeople can enhance their productivity and customer satisfaction levels by making skillful use of the latest technologies in carrying out each of the seven steps of personal selling. For example, some salespeople use the Internet and email to prospect for customers, to notify their customers about upcoming price changes or product shortages, to introduce new products, and to ask for referrals to new prospects. **Extranets**—corporate networks that allow communication between a company and selected customers, suppliers, and business partners—often yield prospects, too. Most companies also have **intranets**—internal corporate networks that allow salespeople and other employees within a company to obtain information and communicate with each other. For instance, salespeople use their company intranets to gain quick access to the latest product prices, inventories, or delivery dates.

En route to customers' offices, salespeople often use cellular phones or car phones to let customers know about any traffic problems that might delay their arrival for a sales call appointment. Portable fax machines, pagers, cell phones with Internet capabilities, and handheld computers all help the salesperson communicate with and serve customers more efficiently and effectively.

Some companies and salespeople include impressive full-color video sales presentations and product demonstrations on their web sites. During long-term negotiations, salespeople can respond to customers' questions either by email or at a web site that provides answers to the most frequently asked questions (FAQs). Customer service (for example, installation, maintenance, and warranty information) also can be furnished on a web site. Starting in chapter 3 with our in-depth discussion of each stage in the PSP, we will further describe and provide examples of salespeople making effective and efficient use of the latest technologies. Who knows what future innovations will help salespeople do their jobs better? Read this chapter's *From the Command Post* to learn how a cement marketer has employed technology to enhance customer service.

## FROM THE COMMAND POST: CEMEX—HIGH-TECH CEMENT MARKETER

Cemex is a highly successful international marketer of cement based in Monterrey, Mexico. It established an information technology department in the mid-1980s and its first email system in 1991. It has provided a wealth of internal and external information to its employees in efforts to enhance corporate efficiency and effectiveness. In fact, the company places computers with Internet access in its employees' homes.

Concrete must be poured within ninety minutes of mixing. Ensuring that trucks travel from plants to building sites on schedule has always been a problem. Cemex now installs computers and global positioning receivers in all of its ready-mix concrete trucks. The current system calculates which truck should go where and also enables dispatchers to redirect trucks en route to a given construction site. As a result, delivery time has dropped on average from three hours to less than twenty minutes in crowded Mexico City! The system has also allowed trucks to deliver many more orders per day.

Cemex is also planning to use Construmix (the construction industry portal) to provide other services for customers who already purchase Cemex concrete online. For instance, the company is considering creating an online meeting place for all parties involved in a construction project. Blueprints would be placed on the Internet and be updated online, allowing contractors and suppliers to consult a current version of the blueprints at all times.

Cemex management believes its high-tech approach frees up employees' imagination and fosters a healthy degree of competition among company units. The company's financial success is a tribute to its efforts: Cemex has an operating margin twice that of its two largest rivals and a 5 percent greater return on assets.

*Source: From "The Cemex Way," The Economist (June 16, 2001): 75–76. Copyright © 2001 The Economist Newspaper Ltd. All rights reserved. Reprinted with permission. Further reproduction prohibited. www.economist.com.*

## BENEFITS OF PROFESSIONAL PERSONAL SELLING AS A CAREER

Selling is one of the entry-level positions most accessible to college graduates. About 15 to 20 percent of all college graduates, regardless of major, start out in selling jobs. Some companies require sales experience as a prerequisite for advancement into managerial ranks. Many chief executive officers of Fortune 500 corporations began their careers as sales representatives. Billionaire H. Ross Perot, a former top salesman for IBM who became CEO of Electronic Data Systems, says: "I sold Christmas cards and garden seeds in Texarkana, Texas. At the age of 12, I peddled newspapers in a poor section of town filled with flophouses. I never thought of doing anything besides selling."[18]

A sales career offers many benefits, particularly its initial availability to just about anyone interested in a career with unlimited opportunities where there are nearly always job openings. In the United States, more than one million new or experienced salespeople are needed annually by new and expanding businesses, so there is frequently a shortage of qualified salespeople. Sales is a great place to start for almost any managerial career. Newly promoted executives often say that the entry field they would choose if they had to start over would be sales because that's where you work directly with customers and learn the business from the bottom up. Let's take a look at some of the other benefits a salesperson can expect to share in once he or she has started a career in professional selling.

### Financial Rewards

Salespeople are among the best-paid employees in business. Almost nothing limits earnings in sales, other than the salesperson's drive and ability, especially in business-to-business selling. Earning more than one hundred thousand dollars yearly is not unusual, and some salespeople earn more than one million dollars annually. Unlike most jobs that offer small annual raises based on a boss's subjective performance evaluation or cost of living increases, the sales profession offers commissions, bonuses, and sales contest money and prizes in addition to a regular salary. Commissions are typically paid promptly on order size or profitability; individual and group bonuses are often awarded when salespeople exceed their annual sales quotas; and winners of sales contests may receive all kinds of booty (sailboats, exotic vacations, and entertainment packages), as well as prize money. People accustomed to being paid a regular salary may not like the idea of being paid partially in commissions, but they shouldn't worry. Salespeople paid solely on commissions usually earn the most money.

### Perks

In addition to potentially high earnings, sales positions include various perquisites, or "perks." Expense account benefits, for example, permit salespeople to enjoy the "good life" while doing business with customers. Dinners at top restaurants, tickets to ball games and concerts, and health and golf club memberships are some examples of legitimate business entertainment. Other perks may include use of a company credit card, company car, cell phone, or a computer for home use, and low-interest loans. Some benefits play the dual roles of recognizing and rewarding successful salespeople while allowing them to entertain and better serve their prospects and customers.

## Visibility

Beyond tangible rewards, most sales careers offer a high degree of recognition. Top-performing salespeople can become in-house celebrities known to high-level management and virtually everyone else in the company. Senior managers often give personal recognition to their highest achieving salespeople by interacting with them during special celebrations, vacation trips, or leadership seminars. For instance, at a payroll-processing company with sales of more than $100 million a year, the top ten salespeople are invited to spend a day discussing organizational issues with the CEO. At one meeting, the top ten salespeople drafted a new compensation plan for the entire sales force.

## High Demand

Despite the many opportunities and high compensation in selling, shortages of qualified salespeople often arise. For example, when IBM announced that it would have to lay off twelve thousand employees, it simultaneously reassigned three thousand people to its sales force. Mobility tends to be higher for salespeople than for most professionals because selling skills are highly transferable to other products, and virtually every organization needs quality salespeople. As key generators of sales revenue—the lifeblood of any organization—salespeople are among the first to be hired and the last to be fired.

The Internet carries many sources for sales jobs. *Sales and Marketing Management* magazine offers a special careers section at its web site: www.salesandmarketing.com/smmnew/resources/careers.asp. At several popular employment sites (for example, www.monster.com) job seekers post their resumes and look for sales opportunities by geographic areas. Opportunities for people entering sales careers are nearly always good because sales force turnover across all industries exceeds 20 percent a year. Turnover is so high partially because sales managers must often hire marginal people just to cover their territories. Many talented people never consider a sales career because they have negative ideas about selling, often including the following:

- Most salespeople are dishonest and unethical.
- All sales jobs require overnight traveling.
- Most sales jobs involve door-to-door selling.
- Most customers treat salespeople with contempt.
- Few salespeople hold college degrees.
- Salespeople must push unneeded products on people.
- Most salespeople suffer humiliating personal rejection.

Although these exaggerated negative perceptions stem from outmoded tales about traveling and door-to-door salespeople, they are so widely held that many potentially good salespeople fail to even consider sales as a career.

Admittedly, some sales jobs *do* require regular travel away from home, long working hours, continual pressure to achieve, interaction with difficult customers, frequent rejection, and constant self-management. These same conditions, however, apply to many other jobs as well.

## Job Freedom and Independence

Salespeople are like entrepreneurs or independent businesspeople in that they largely manage themselves. They set their own working hours and develop unique personal selling styles, yet still enjoy the security of working for an organization that provides medical coverage, vacation pay, and retirement benefits. Compared to the cost of starting one's own business, a sales career offers tremendous leverage for a small monetary investment. For example, a franchise may require an initial investment of two hundred thousand dollars or more and provide an annual return of less than fifty thousand dollars, even after working several years of daily long hours. A new salesperson, however, may spend less than fifteen hundred dollars on clothing and a nice briefcase and earn more than fifty thousand dollars in commissions and bonuses alone in one year of selling.

Outside salespeople seldom have a supervisor looking over their shoulders or timing their coffee breaks. In fact, if they do an outstanding job, salespeople can become somewhat like talented professional baseball or basketball players whose worth to the organization is often greater than that of their coaches. Top salespeople, like top athletes, are less likely to suffer from unfair or capricious actions on the part of a sales manager who doesn't like them. Still, salespeople cannot afford to slack off. While job freedom and control attract many people to sales, the pressure is always on, even if only self-imposed, to make a sales quota and earn higher commissions, bonuses, and other incentives. Competitive salespeople who expend great amounts of effort, however, are likely to be better producers.[19] They are also the ones who receive the rewards. Being your own boss means working for the most demanding person of all—yourself.

## Adventure and Satisfaction

Selling is adventurous because it challenges you to grow personally and professionally. It can be an invigorating experience to deal every day with people from diverse backgrounds and frames of reference. Many nonselling jobs are so routine and narrowly defined that they seldom present the employee with a challenge and may actually limit his or her personal and professional growth. Any limits on creativity and growth in selling tend to be self-imposed ones.

Selling can also give you more personal satisfaction than most jobs because the essence of your job is helping others solve their problems and achieve their goals. The better salesperson you are, the more benefits you will provide to others—your customers, company, and family, and the nation's economy. And for this you are well paid.

## KEEPING UP ONLINE: SALESAUTOPSY.COM

Salespeople the world over make numerous errors—some traumatic and some only mildly upsetting. Regardless of the seriousness of the mistake, though, salespeople can learn from their errors. Now salespeople can visit a web site designed to help professional salespeople avoid certain kinds of mistakes, or at least stop making them. Sales Autopsy (http://www.salesautopsy.com) provides numerous examples of mistakes made by real salespeople and offers an analysis of why each mistake occurred. How might you currently make use of this web site? What do you see as this web site's strengths? What are its weaknesses?

### Objective Performance Evaluation

A salesperson who shows ability will be spotted quickly. In many fields, the seniority system or office politics seem to determine how much pay an employee receives. This is not the case in sales. Sales performance is highly visible and quantifiable. The salesperson is generally rewarded in relation to his or her sales productivity (for example, sales revenue, percent of quota achieved, profitability). In fact, if the salesperson works strictly on commissions, earnings are directly proportionate to sales. Few jobs offer such objective performance appraisals.

### Contribution to Society

Salespeople make many valuable contributions to society. They improve the quality of people's lives by identifying their needs and wants, helping solve their problems, adding value to products and services, and introducing new products. By generating income for their companies, salespeople provide jobs for many other people. With intensifying worldwide competition, the success of America's professional salespeople in domestic and world markets will become increasingly important to the health of our economy.

## CAREERS FOR DIFFERENT TYPES OF INDIVIDUALS

No single background, cultural heritage, ethnic group, gender, age, or personality type assures success in selling to diverse customer types. On the contrary, some research has found that salespeople are most successful when selling to buyers who are the same gender, age, and personality type as they are;[20] that if they have more positive thoughts about the buyer and enhanced confidence, they are more likely to make the sale;[21] and that the sales effectiveness of a salesperson is related to the degree of similarity between the customer and salesperson[22]—especially with respect to their thinking alike.[23] As a result, recommendations have been made to sales managers that they try to match their salespeople with similar customer types.[24] For instance, women and minorities may be especially appropriate sales reps to call on customers who are women and minorities, particularly when they are similar in other characteristics relevant to the buying situation.

### Which Career Paths Begin with Personal Selling?

Many companies offer multiple career paths to newly hired salespeople: (1) professional selling, (2) sales management, or (3) marketing management. Figure 1.2 shows how the sales track branches out into multiple career path alternatives. Regardless of which path you take, your work challenges, desires, attitudes, and concerns will evolve as you pass through the various stages of your career.[25] And the longer you stay on your chosen path, the more prepared you will become to assume greater job responsibilities and advancement.[26]

### Choosing the Right Career Path

Following completion of an initial training program, the trainee is promoted to sales representative and, depending on the industry and company, given a title similar to one of these: marketing representative, account representative, account executive, account manager, sales representative, sales engineer, sales associate, sales coordinator, sales consultant, market specialist, territory manager, or salesperson. Typically, newly designated salespeople spend a year or

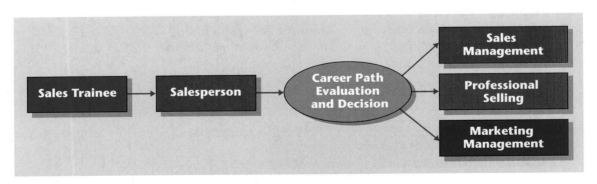

**FIGURE 1.2**

MULTIPLE CAREER PATHS IN PERSONAL SELLING

two in the field gaining essential experience before a decision is made regarding their long-term career with the company. The length of this field selling experience varies depending on the industry, company, product, market complexities, and, of course, the individual. After the salesperson has achieved success in field-selling assignments, he or she meets with the sales manager, and perhaps a human resources manager, to examine the salesperson's skills and performance record. This in-depth evaluation provides the basis for deciding the individual's best career path.

Many experienced salespeople move on to sales management or marketing management, but not everyone possesses the ability and desire to become a manager. Yet, most salespeople want to advance in their sales career. The good news is that excellent opportunities exist for advancement into higher levels of personal selling.

**Professional Selling.** If you choose the professional selling career path, you may spend three to five years as a *sales representative* before promotion to *senior sales representative*. After five to seven years in this capacity, a senior salesperson will be promoted to *master sales representative*. Top-performing master sales reps may be named *national or key account sales representatives* with responsibility for selling to a few major customers (for example, national retail chains such as Target or Home Depot).

**Sales Management**. If you choose the sales management career path, you would probably be promoted from salesperson to sales supervisor or field sales manager, with responsibility for day-to-day guidance of a few salespeople in a given sales branch. Next comes promotion to *branch sales manager*, then *district manager*, with successively larger territorial responsibilities as a manager. From district sales manager, the successive promotion steps would be *zone, division,* and *regional sales manager* although these hierarchical titles may vary from one company to another. Then comes promotion to *national sales manager* and, in some companies, *vice president of sales*. Finally comes the opportunity for a few talented people who started in sales to become *CEO*.

A close alternative to the sales management career path is the *sales management staff* route. Here, you might serve as a *sales analyst, sales training manager*, or *assistant to the sales manager*. Staff people work at every organizational level and may hold positions in sales planning, sales promotion, sales recruiting, sales analysis, or sales training. Although people in sales management staff positions have no line authority over the sales force, they frequently hold impressive titles, such as *assistant national sales manager*, and often switch over to top positions in line management after demonstrating success in their staff positions.

**Marketing Management.** Following success in field sales, you might be selected for the marketing management career path. This path often starts with promotion to a position as a *product* or *brand manager* for a product category (for example, Pillsbury's Hungry Jack biscuits). Success in product management leads to promotion to *director of product management*, then *vice president of marketing*, and maybe eventually company *president and CEO*. In sum, sales is a great place to start no matter what direction your future career takes.

## SUMMARY

*Selling* is a universal activity. At one time or another, everyone uses persuasive communication to "sell" products, services, ideas, opinions, or points of views. The marketing concept and customer-oriented selling concept have changed the basis of professional personal selling from a short-run focus on the needs of sellers to a long-run focus on the needs of customers.

*Consumers* and *organizations* form the two basic categories of customers or markets. Organizational markets, which can be either profit or nonprofit oriented, include *producers, resellers,* and *governments.* A *product* is anything offered to a market to satisfy customer needs and wants. Every product is an amalgam of a *core product,* a *tangible product,* and an *augmented product.*

Selling roles include order taking, order supporting, and order creating. Regardless of the sales posi-

tion, professional salespeople carry out seven basic stages in the personal selling process, from prospecting and qualifying to following up and servicing the account. Each of these steps benefits from applying technological resources, including handheld computers, the Internet, extranets, intranets, cell phones, beepers, and portable fax machines.

Sales careers offer opportunities for nearly anyone who is motivated to learn and earn by helping others solve their problems. Benefits include financial rewards, perquisites, a fast route to the top of an organization, job freedom and independence, personal satisfaction, objective performance evaluation, and contribution to society. Career paths that begin in personal selling tend to offer three routes: *professional personal selling, sales management,* and *marketing management.* The latter two routes can lead to senior executive positions in the company.

## KEY TERMS

| | | | |
|---|---|---|---|
| Customer-Oriented Selling | Order Supporting | Trade Selling | Prospecting |
| Professional Salesperson | Missionary Selling | Personal Selling Process (PSP) | Extranets |
| Augmented Product | Order Creating | Wheel of Personal Selling | Intranets |
| Order Taking | | | |

## CHAPTER REVIEW QUESTIONS

1. Discuss the myth of the "born" salesperson.

2. Explain the relationship between personal selling, the "marketing concept," and the "customer-oriented selling concept."

3. List and briefly describe the three kinds of profit and nonprofit organizational markets.

4. What is a product? What are the differences between the core, tangible, and augmented product?

5. Describe the seven stages in the professional personal selling process. Why do we depict them as a wheel?

6. Name the three basic selling roles and describe the continuum of sales jobs ranging from simple response selling to complex creative selling.

7. What types of creative salespeople are discussed in this chapter?

8. Give some examples of how salespeople can use different technologies to improve their efficiency and better serve prospects and customers.

9. Discuss the benefits and drawbacks of a career in personal selling.

## TOPICS FOR THOUGHT AND CLASS DISCUSSION

1. Have you ever known or met a person who appeared to be a "natural born" salesperson? What made you think he or she was a good salesperson? Based on what you now know about professional personal selling, do you think you could call this person a truly professional salesperson? Why or why not?

2. What kind of selling might you like to do? With what products and what customers would you prefer to work? What do you think would be some advantages and disadvantages of each kind of selling for you personally?

3. Think about why you would want a career in professional personal selling. What would motivate you best? Money? Job independence? Opportunity to help people? Discuss your thoughts and feelings with classmates.

## PROJECTS FOR PERSONAL GROWTH

1. You have just inherited a pencil manufacturing business. Pencils are hardly a glamorous product, but they enjoy a large and competitive market. See if you can develop a description of your product that would help your sales staff sell the core, tangible, and augmented product.

2. Use what you have learned about what professional salespeople do to "sell" one of your classmates something in your classroom—a pen, chair, book, pair of shoes, or such. Once you've successfully sold to the classmate, try selling to your instructor.

CASE 1.1

# YOU WANT TO BE A SALESPERSON?

Paula Majors is graduating from Ohio University with a degree in marketing this June. Throughout her college studies, Paula has maintained a B grade average and been active in several campus organizations while working twenty hours a week in a local retail store. Paula comes from an achievement-oriented family. Her father is a certified public accountant who specializes in taxes, and her mother is a divorce lawyer in private practice. Everybody says that Paula has inherited her father's analytical approach to problem solving and her mother's drive and determination to do well in whatever she undertakes.

On her resume, Paula decided to keep her job objective fairly general: *Beginning-level job in sales or marketing that offers an opportunity for creative use of my abilities and career development.* After interviewing with several companies who visited campus during the fall and winter months, Paula has received three job offers—all in sales. Two of the jobs were sales trainee positions with large Fortune 500 companies where she would first complete an intensive training program before being assigned to a sales territory. The third job was as a salesperson with a small manufacturer of art supplies covering about two-thirds of the Ohio market.

With the two large companies, Paula would have a straight salary the first year while completing her training program, then go on 80 percent salary, 20 percent commission. At the small company, the training program is only three weeks long and her compensation would be 70 percent salary, 30 percent commission. Salaries for all three jobs were about the same, and each provided a car.

Paula asked three of her college professors for advice about which of the jobs she should take. Each of them gave Paula perspectives on the three jobs, but each said that the final decision was up to Paula.

Finally, Paula decided to call her parents to ask their views. She had been reluctant to do this because she knew both her mother and father were negative about a sales career. In calling home, Paula learned that her father was working late at his office, and her mother had to leave in a few minutes to meet an important client for dinner. Paula did manage to have a brief conversation with her mother. After quickly telling her mother about the three job offers, her mother replied, "Paula, you know that your father and I want you to make up your own mind about a career, but I think you ought to consider some alternatives besides sales. We'd like to see you use your education. It doesn't take any special abilities to be a salesperson—except the willingness to push products on people even when they don't need them. And where does a sales job lead? You can't be a salesperson all your life. With the constant travel and living out of a suitcase, I'd be concerned about your safety. A woman doesn't belong in sales, especially if she plans to have children. When you raise a family, you've got to settle down and be home at night with your children. Why don't you try for a large company's management training program so that you have a chance for promotion and a good salary? Maybe I'm idealistic, but I'd also like to see you choose a career where you can make a positive contribution to society. You know, make a real difference. Honey, I have to run now or I'll be late for my dinner meeting, but let's try to find some time to talk about it this weekend. Why don't you give us a call around 4 P.M. on Sunday after your father and I return from the CPA luncheon. Love you, Paula! Bye bye, for now."

Feeling a little depressed after hearing her mother's comments, Paula lay down on her sofa and began to think about what she would say to her father and mother when she called them on Sunday.

## Questions

1. Why do you think Paula's parents resist her going into a sales career? What misconceptions about personal selling do they have?
2. To convince them that sales is the right place to begin her business career, what points should Paula make when she calls her parents?
3. If Paula cannot persuade her parents to see personal selling in a positive way, what would you advise her to do?

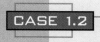

## DECISIONS! DECISIONS! WHICH CAREER PATH SHOULD I CHOOSE?

**N**earing completion of his third year as a sales representative for Admiralty Food Company in Chicago, John Drain had just received notice that his sales manager had scheduled John's annual performance evaluation for this coming Monday at 9 A.M. John felt confident about meeting with his boss for his evaluation because he was having an outstanding year and had a good chance at winning the company's salesperson of the year award. Only two other salespeople out of forty-three in the midwest region were selling at John's pace this year.

Admiralty Food sold most of its products through wholesalers or direct to large supermarket buying centers. John had more than one hundred customers, most of whom he called on about every two weeks. He believed that his track record with Admiralty was impressive by anybody's standards. He sold 105 percent of his assigned quota the first year, 115 percent the second year, nearly 135 percent the third year, and he was on track this year to reach 140 percent of quota. During each of the past three years, John had made the "CEO's Sales Club" and, along with other top performing Admiralty salespeople from around the country, won an exciting vacation. John was proud to work for Admiralty because the company had an excellent reputation for quality products and superior service.

Beginning with the fourth year in field selling for Admiralty, the annual performance evaluation for all salespeople included a discussion of their desired career path. Although salespeople were not required to declare a career path in their fourth year, the sales manager had to indicate the salesperson's seeming preference at that time. John didn't feel quite ready to make a career path decision, but he had given serious thought to the different options.

With a degree in marketing from Central Michigan University and halfway through an evening M.B.A. program at Roosevelt University, John believed all three sales/marketing career paths at Admiralty were open to him. He could continue on the *personal selling track*—progressing from field sales representative to senior sales rep to master sales rep. Or he could switch into the *sales management track,* which leads from field sales rep to key account manager, to district sales manager, to regional sales manager, to national sales manager, and perhaps senior vice president for sales. Finally, he could move into *marketing management* by becoming a brand manager for one of the company's product lines, then seek promotion to director of product management, next vice president of marketing, and eventually maybe a chance to become CEO. John recognized that each of the career paths had their pluses and minuses depending on personal needs, lifestyle, and goals.

John was engaged to be married that summer to Sylvia Maplewood, a public relations manager for Admiralty. He considered how this might affect his career strategy. Although the company had no nepotism rule, he decided it would be awkward to work in headquarters marketing and interact on a daily business basis with his wife.

John's thoughts about each of the possible career tracks are summarized below.

### Professional Personal Selling Track

John loved the freedom and independence of personal selling. He wasn't sure that he could stand being cooped up in an office all day long. By remaining in personal selling, John felt sure that he would maximize his income over the next five to seven years. He knew his commissions from his continuing top performance put his earnings ahead of nearly everyone in the sales organization except for regional sales managers and above. However, John didn't think he could maintain his torrid selling pace for more than about five years.

(continued)

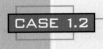

## DECISIONS! DECISIONS! WHICH CAREER PATH SHOULD I CHOOSE? (CONTINUED)

He figured his earnings would likely peak after that, and he would probably be shifted to a large national account or two where sales maintenance was most important. At that point, it might be nice to become a sales manager to guide the career development of younger salespeople, or to take on new challenges in marketing management. If he waited another five years or so to choose a career path, however, his chances of success in it would be diminished.

### Sales Management Track

John feared that the pressure of traveling and meeting sales quotas might eventually become nerve racking instead of challenging and exciting as it was now. He and Sylvia planned to have a couple of children, and John wanted to watch them grow up. He wanted time to take them to dance classes or soccer games and be home in the morning when they got up as well as at night to tuck them in bed. Sales managers were really like field marketing managers in that they spent most of their time in the office forecasting sales; preparing sales plans and budgets; setting sales goals and sales quotas; recruiting, selecting, and training new salespeople; designing sales territories; developing compensation plans; motivating and leading the salespeople; analyzing sales volume, costs, and profits by territory, product, customer, and salesperson; evaluating sales performance; and monitoring the ethical conduct of the sales force.

### Marketing Management Track

If he became a brand manager, John recognized that he might be moving into a more risky field; a brand manager's career success or failure seemed to depend on successful new products. At the annual sales meeting last year, he remembered the comments of one of the company's brand managers at dinner:

"Brand managers have a lot of responsibility but little authority. Our job is to develop marketing strategies, improve present products, develop new products, and manage the marketing mixes for all of them within a fiercely competitive and changing marketing environment. If a new product is successful, you can just hang onto its coat tails and let it pull you to success. But if you get identified with a product failure, you'd better get your resume up to date. When you're a salesperson, you can always blame unsuccessful products on headquarters marketing, but brand managers can't blame product failures on the sales force."

In moving from the sales force to brand management, John feared that he might be trading in the day-to-day pressures of selling for career-threatening pressures. In addition, John had heard from his fiancée that politics could be subtle at headquarters, and he would probably have to tone down his natural tendency toward candor. Moreover, he noticed that the top marketing positions seemed to be filled disproportionately by people with Ivy League M.B.A.s. All in all, though, John decided that moving into marketing management was the best way to go if you wanted to become one of the top officers in the company.

Reviewing his own strengths and weaknesses, John listed the following strengths: *communication skills, analytical ability, product knowledge, drive, ambition, extroverted personality, well organized, results oriented, competitive.* Under weaknesses, he wrote: *impatient, nonpolitical, distaste for tedious paperwork,* and *too honest for own good.*

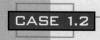

## DECISIONS! DECISIONS! WHICH CAREER PATH SHOULD I CHOOSE? (CONTINUED)

**Questions**

1. Do you think John should declare a career path now? If not, why not?
2. Taking into account John's attitudes, strengths, and weaknesses, what advice would you give John about each of the three career paths for him? If forced to choose, which career path would be best for John? Explain your answer.

## CHAPTER 2

# The Ever-Changing Personal Selling Environment

*"If today's salespeople don't innovate and automate, they'll evaporate."*

*Anonymous*

## After Reading This Chapter, You Should Understand:

- What megatrends are affecting personal selling now and what megatrends will affect personal selling in the foreseeable future.

- How developments in telecommunications technology are dramatically changing personal selling.

- Why rising personal selling costs are encouraging salespeople and their companies to make increasing use of alternative direct-marketing techniques.

- What current trends in information management will affect how salespeople do their jobs.

- Why today's professional salespeople need to be much like micromarketing managers in their expanding roles.

INSIDE PERSONAL SELLING:

## Meet Julie Wroblewski of eFunds

Julie Wroblewski obtains most of her sales leads from a technology that barely existed ten years ago—and some of the services she sells are even newer. Wroblewski is an account executive for eFunds, which provides electronic payment software and processing solutions as well as both the data and the analysis tools to help companies make decisions about financial risk (fraud, for example). Customers include banks, financial services firms, retailers, electronic funds networks, government agencies, and e-commerce firms.

Technology is a vital part of the personal selling environment for eFunds. "I get most of my leads through our web site," Wroblewski says. Prospects visit the site (www.efunds.com), then call or email the company for more information. A group at eFunds headquarters screens these

requests and sends them on to reps for personal contact.

Because they've browsed the web site, prospects usually have a general idea of what eFunds can do for them. Still, Wroblewski carefully investigates each prospect's unique needs and situation. To save time and money, she schedules as many as ten conference calls per week so various eFunds technical specialists can discuss solutions to prospects' problems. For a typical conference call, she says, "I learn about the prospect's needs and expectations ahead of time, gather a pool of eFunds experts, and we work through the agenda with the prospect's business people." A growing number of prospects do business globally, which means people in other countries sometimes participate in these conference calls.

To spot sales opportunities, Wroblewski reads the *Wall Street Journal, Fast Company,* and several technology magazines. "But what is really new for sales folks in today's environment are Internet sources like *Wall Street Journal Online* and online newsletters," she observes. "I can have news

about particular firms forwarded to my email inbox. This keeps me up-to-date about prospects and companies where I'm trying to make an appointment."

Technology also affects what Wroblewski sells. One of eFunds' newest offerings is a service that allows online shoppers to pay with electronic checks that look much like ordinary bank checks. Consumers without credit cards like the convenience, and merchants pay lower fees than they would for processing credit-card payments.

Not long ago, Wroblewski began talking with an education company that wanted to start accepting Internet checks. After an initial phone call to discuss the prospect's situation, "We set up a time for eFunds experts to meet face-to-face with their management," she says, "and we presented our proposal using a PowerPoint electronic presentation." She followed up with periodic conference calls to address technical issues, supplemented by emails to provide additional details. After nine months, she closed the deal—and now eFunds powers the electronic checks on this customer's web site.

**W**hat an exciting and challenging time it is to be—or plan on being—a salesperson! Salespeople today face an incredibly dynamic selling environment that offers them enormous opportunities but also some major challenges. Marketplace changes are occurring at such a breakneck pace that some salespeople feel as though they are trapped on a high-tech treadmill going faster and faster. Evolutionary and revolutionary forces are relentlessly altering how salespeople understand, prepare for, and accomplish their jobs. Change is inevitable in every field, of course, but several dramatic changes make personal selling one of today's most volatile—yet exciting—careers.

Thanks largely to continuous innovations in telecommunications technology, salespeople are becoming increasingly empowered and independent of their sales managers. They are continuing to move away from "selling" toward "serving" the customer by becoming more like customer consultants and business partners. Creative ways to provide greater value-added service and to develop mutually profitable, ongoing customer–seller partnerships are constantly emerging. The challenges of this changing personal selling environment need not make you uneasy, because this dynamism also brings many exciting benefits that we will learn more about in this chapter.

## MEGATRENDS AFFECTING PERSONAL SELLING

**Sales Megatrends** Major behavioral, technological, and managerial trends that influence how salespeople perform their jobs.

Salespeople, to become successful or maintain their success, must recognize and adapt to several *megatrends* in order to enhance their effectiveness and efficiency. Three major forces—*behavioral, technological*, and *managerial*—are influencing buyer-seller relationships and how salespeople do their jobs.[1] Outlined in Table 2.1 are the key elements of each of these three forces. In this chapter, we will discuss the nature of these inexorable forces—or **sales megatrends**—and their probable effects on salespeople and their work.

### Behavioral Forces

Buyers' attitudes, preferences, and behaviors, as well as competitors' efforts, are changing frequently, so salespeople must stay alert and flexible to quickly modify their selling strategies and approaches. Let's briefly discuss some of these factors.

**More Expert and Demanding Buyers.** Organizational buyers are becoming increasingly skillful at obtaining value for their expenditures. Companies are developing more efficient purchasing processes and using professional buying committees composed of purchasing, engineering, finance, marketing, legal, and operations management. Sales presentations to these diverse expert buying committees and to all other customers who treat purchases like long-term investments require a talented new type of professional salesperson. Most sales organizations are providing intensified training to help salespeople deal effectively in these complex selling situations.

| TABLE 2.1 |
| --- |

## MAJOR FORCES AFFECTING PERSONAL SELLING

### Behavioral Forces

| | |
| --- | --- |
| • More Expert and Demanding Buyers | • Expanding Power of Giant Retailers |
| • Rising Customer Expectations | • Globalization of Markets |
| • Micro-Segmentation of Domestic Markets | |

### Technological Forces

| | |
| --- | --- |
| • Sales Force Automation<br>  • Portable Computers<br>  • Electronic Data Interchange<br>  • Videoconferencing<br>  • Cellular Phones and Satellite Pagers<br>  • Voice Mail<br>  • Electronic Mail | • Virtual Sales Offices<br><br>• Electronic Commerce<br>  • Internet<br>  • Extranets<br>  • Intranets |

### Managerial Forces

| | |
| --- | --- |
| • Selling Cost Reduction Efforts | • Certification of Salespeople |
| • Shift to Direct Marketing Alternatives<br>  • Direct Mail<br>  • Telemarketing<br>  • Teleselling<br>  • Computer Salespeople<br>  • Facsimile<br>  • Electronic Mail | |

**Rising Customer Expectations.**  Salespeople must reconcile themselves to the fact that human expectations are probably infinitely elastic (that is, they will continually rise). Organizational buyers are less and less tolerant of inferior products. Japanese automobile manufacturers, for example, are pushing quality and service to such high levels that one American car part manufacturer found that it could not compete successfully in the international market:

> After marketing automobile gaskets for years in the United States, the company assumed it could also become a major player in the world market. It set its initial sights on Japan. Unfortunately, it found limited success because, even though its gaskets exceeded all U.S. auto manufacturers' requirements, they weren't good enough for the Japanese producers. Why? Although U.S. car owners are used to seeing an occasional drop of oil on the garage floor—especially from a car with over 50,000 miles—a single drop of oil in Japan is ample justification for a complaint to the manufacturer.

Today's and tomorrow's customers will expect ever-higher quality products and services. Successful sales representatives must not become defensive about the limitations of their company's products or services. Instead, they must be willing and able to look at their offerings from the perspectives of their most critical customers. And, as the company's "eyes and ears in the field," salespeople should promptly report customer complaints to their sales managers. Their companies can use this critical information to improve their products and services for higher levels of customer satisfaction.

**Micro-Segmentation of Domestic Markets.** The United States has become increasingly multicultural and multilingual. Selling in major parts of Miami, New York City, Los Angeles, Chicago, Philadelphia, Detroit, and San Antonio—in fact, in most large cities—will increasingly require the salesperson to understand different cultures, languages, tastes, and preferences for everything from food and clothing to cosmetics. Sales forces that fail to understand and adapt to this rich mix of wants and needs will miss reaching several large, fast-growing markets.

Some companies have responded to this multicultural mosaic by dividing the United States into distinct markets based on unique cultural and ethnic tastes and preferences. These companies then allocate a percentage of their advertising budget to regional promotion, and in some instances the regional ad budget may be elevated as regional success grows. Many organizational sellers are also developing and marketing specialized products that exemplify their regional sales approach; for example, product variations—for everything from food to clothing to music—sold in the Southwest differ from those sold in the Northwest. Goya Foods, which employs a Spanish-speaking sales force that serves both large retailers and the *bodegas* (Hispanic mom-and-pop stores), has already won a major share of the diverse Hispanic market by catering to the special tastes and preferences of consumers who have immigrated to the United States from Mexico, Puerto Rico, Venezuela, and Cuba.

**Expanding Power of Giant Retailers.** Only a few retailers today account for more than half of total retail sales. Large retail organizations—such as Wal-Mart, Target, Home Depot, and Best Buy—have gained and continue to gain an increasing share of the consumer's dollar. As these giant retailers grow bigger and exceed the size and power of the manufacturers that supply them, they dictate the buyer-seller relationship. For instance, several dominant retailers are bypassing wholesalers and distributors to buy directly from manufacturers who give them "key account" (large account) status and special attention. Also, large retailers such as Wal-Mart are leveraging electronic data interchange (EDI) technology to force out middlemen and to require manufacturers' direct sales organizations to assume the functions and administrative costs of "just-in-time" inventory control, order billing, and sales promotion. Changing demands of giant retailers and methods of serving them have contributed to the evolutionary change in the supplier–giant retailer relationship.

To meet the demands of giant retailers, large manufacturers such as Procter & Gamble have set up sales offices near or sometimes even within the retailer's headquarters. The growing dominance of these giant retailers has led

## IT'S UP TO YOU

**Y**ou have just been assigned to your territory, which has many potential organizational customers. Competition is keen, however, and customers tend to buy chiefly on price—they want the best value for their money. Concomitantly, prospects and customers in your territory have increasing expectations of their suppliers and the service they should provide. Knowing that price is the major driver of prospects and customers and that your firm is not the lowest-priced seller, you are stumped about how you can succeed in this territory. How will you begin to build your sales program? What resources will you call on within your organization and outside it? What technologies and tools might come to your aid?

to establishing single-sourcing, multiyear contracts with manufacturers. In such instances, an agreement between the buyer and the seller allows one manufacturer to be the single supplier for a given product (or array of products); in return, though, the manufacturer must provide an extremely high level of service and support to the large retailer. Giant supermarkets have gained so much leverage over producers that they often charge "slotting fees" to allow manufacturers to place their products on the retail shelves. For example, if a cereal manufacturer wants a large grocery chain to stock a newly launched cereal, the retailer may demand that the seller pay *up front* a fee for filling precious shelf space with the new product. Doing so reduces the grocery retailer's financial risk associated with taking on a new product. As giant retailers have gained power, many small manufacturers and suppliers have simply stopped calling on them, unable or unwilling to meet their costly demands. In view of this retailing megatrend, salespeople must remain alert to skillfully and nimbly respond to the growing needs and demands of their large retail customers. Keeping in mind the megatrends discussed to this point, consider the personal selling situation presented in *It's Up To You* above.

**Globalization of Markets.**  With its large population, high discretionary income levels, and political stability, the United States currently is the world's most attractive market. Companies based in Asia (particularly those in Japan, South Korea, Hong Kong, and Taiwan), as well as many from the European Union (especially those in Germany, France, and Great Britain), have captured huge market shares of the most basic U.S. industries: automobiles, steel, electronic components, televisions, home appliances, industrial chemicals, textiles, and machine tools. Many foreign manufacturers and service companies are also establishing operations in the United States, particularly in the automobile and electronic appliances markets.

Thus, the U.S. domestic market has given way to a world market invaded by companies from around the globe.[2] This situation has led more and more U.S. firms seeking sales growth to become major exporters of their products. In fact, numerous U.S.-based firms such as Colgate-Palmolive, Apple

## *Even "IT" Managers Want to Have Fun*

Security on the web is a major headache for Information Technology (IT) managers and customers alike. Hackers bent on creating mischief or actual theft of data or money keep many IT managers awake at night. After all, if a web site is not secure, the potential for rampant harm to the site's organization and its customers looms large. Consequently, numerous firms have sprung up to sell safeguards against hacker invaders. A major problem for security service companies, however, is how to get their names and service offerings in front of target markets.

Web advertising is frequently used by network security service providers to reach target markets who are usually "heavy users" of the Web. These promotional efforts, though, are often obscured by the plethora of competing advertisements. One creative solution has been to develop and install an intriguing game (similar to popular video games) on a security provider's web site aimed directly at IT managers. When IT managers and their subordinates click on the banner ad for the game, they are whisked to the security provider's web site, where they download and play the game. Although the game revolves around computer security issues, it is fun to play and specifically designed to capture the attention and interest of IT professionals.

While enjoying the game, IT players also learn how the security protection provider's products can protect a web site. Given the complexity of security products, several levels in a buying firm (including IT) tend to be involved in their purchase. Clever and challenging games can garner a large following of potential security service buyers, especially when augmented by promotional activities such as game contests, publicity, and referrals. Bottom Line: Even when you're selling a serious product to business professionals, it can be done successfully in a fun way.

Computer, Coca-Cola, and IBM already generate more than half their annual sales revenue from exports. This requires many U.S. salespeople to learn how to sell in foreign countries. Language, customs, culture, politics, ethics, laws, economies, market information, and distribution channels are just a few of the areas where differences can make international selling much more challenging but potentially more rewarding for salespeople willing to make the extra effort. The future economic health of the United States depends partially on how well salespeople and sales managers do their jobs as competition from foreign products and services intensifies. Fortunately, many organizational sellers are preparing their sales personnel to sell in foreign cultures.[3] (In subsequent chapters in this book, we will discuss selling in foreign markets.)

### Technological Forces

Probably the most obvious and dramatic influences on personal selling today are technological innovations, especially in telecommunications. Today's successful salespeople are those who make skillful and efficient use of technology to increase their efficiency and productivity in serving customers. Sales force automation, virtual sales offices, and electronic commerce using the Internet, extranets, and intranets are some dominant technological forces requiring changes in the way personal selling is conducted. Before we examine these topics, first read *On the Frontlines* and see how technology is being used in creative and fun ways to capture the attention of business prospects.

**Sales Force Automation.** Sales force automation (SFA) refers to the use of high-tech tools that help the salesperson work effectively and efficiently. Salespeople rely on a host of SFA innovations, including portable (laptop, notebook, or handheld) computers, electronic data interchange, videoconferencing, cellular phones, satellite pagers, voice mail, and electronic mail. SFA tools provide a cornucopia of benefits for organizational sales personnel. In fact, one study found that the more strategic, administrative, and operating issues management considered in justifying the purchase of SFA technology, the greater the benefits realized from SFA.[4] Let's briefly discuss the more prevalent SFA technologies.

***Portable Computers.*** Some of the most exciting changes in the buyer-seller relationship are coming via sophisticated portable computers that range in size from laptop to notebook to handheld. Combined with creative software, these tools have empowered salespeople and helped reduce or eliminate much of their tedious paperwork (for example, filling out sales call reports, order forms, and expense reports). Other software is assisting sales personnel to manage their customer accounts (organizing accounts, targeting e-promotions, timing sales calls), thus enhancing their productivity. Salespeople use email with attachments to send pamphlets, brochures, or preformatted sales letters tailored to the needs of prospects and customers. Most importantly, salespeople use computers and other handheld devices to tap in directly to huge data banks of information about credit, production, and shipping instead of requesting data from their sales manager or other home office sources.

Salespeople also use their computers to develop and improve customer relationships. For example, some salespeople keep their prospects and customers informed by emailing them a monthly newsletter that provides important information about new products, upcoming price changes, or early alerts about possible product shortages. Instead of relying on traditional hardcopy sales materials, CD-ROM technology allows salespeople to customize sales presentations on their portable computers, then promptly email them (with attachments) to customers. Resourceful salespeople are finding many ways to use technology to better serve their customers and their companies—and those ways are only limited by a salesperson's creativity and resourcefulness.

***Electronic Data Interchange (EDI).*** EDI refers to the linking together of channel member computer systems to allow real-time exchanges of information between manufacturers and resellers (that is, retailers, wholesalers, or distributors). For instance, a retailer's computers can be linked to the manufacturer's computers so that real time retail sales automatically update the retailer's product mix and the manufacturer's production schedules. The EDI linkage automatically transmits purchase orders, invoices, price quotations, shipping dates, reports, and promotional information to the manufacturer. Similarly, EDI provides retailers with product sales data, consumer purchasing patterns, customer-tailored promotions and merchandising, product profitability analyses, and demand forecasts based on sales trends. To illustrate, independent retailers who sell Hallmark greeting cards at locations throughout the United States use EDI to transmit orders and receive acknowledgment and delivery dates within seconds from Hallmark's Kansas City, Missouri, headquarters. Orders are not only filled faster, thereby reducing store "out-of-stocks," they also are no longer lost in the mail.

As more business buying is handled by EDI systems, the role of the salesperson is changing:

> No longer is catalog, price, and technical information transported to the buyer through the salesperson. . . . No longer is the salesperson required to be a physical conduit for order information . . . the salesperson . . . [will have] fewer functions to perform in the traditional sales role. . . . Because of the reduction in routine, labor intensive, uncreative order processing, the salesperson can devote more time in a creative, consulting role.[5]

Salespeople who excel at this consultative role will build higher levels of trust with customers and thereby enhance development of mutually profitable buying and selling relationships. Ideally, all salespeople should strive to serve their prospects and customers as knowledgeable consultants to help them sell through to their own customers. Helping customers improve their profitability over the long run helps the salesperson and his or her company. Savvy salespeople ought to keep in mind a paraphrase of an old slogan: "If our customers don't do well, we won't do well." EDI is a key technological tool that can facilitate salespeople practicing the preceding maxim.

***Videoconferencing.*** This tool is usually a corporate (internal) satellite television system that allows simulated face-to-face interaction among geographically separated individuals. Individuals can videoconference using desktop or laptop computers, or large rooms of people at different locations can communicate via huge monitors. Many companies have cut the cost of travel and employee "downtime" by substituting videoconferencing or teleconferencing, as it's sometimes called, for national and regional conferences. In fact, a recent study found that technology has decreased the amount of travel for 63 percent of executives, as teleconferencing has become one of their major alternatives.[6] Much like face-to-face interaction, widely dispersed salespeople (and their managers) can use desktop videoconferences for sales meetings, training, and customer interaction without leaving their individual virtual offices. General Electric managers stay in touch with their different sales forces and markets by an internal communication system. Once a week, field salespeople conduct a videoconference with personnel in various corporate divisions around the world to talk about market opportunities and challenges and to decide on prompt action.

Salespeople generally are able to spend less than a third of their time in face-to-face selling. If videoconferencing can convert part of the time salespeople spend traveling, waiting to see customers, and attending internal sales meetings to time spent with customers, sales and customer satisfaction might experience significant boosts.

### Cellular Phones and Satellite Pagers.

Mobile communications innovations, especially cellular phones and satellite pagers (beepers), are helping salespeople keep in touch with customers, their managers, and the home office even when hundreds or thousands of miles away. Indeed, many companies supply their sales forces with cell phones and pagers to enhance their salespeople's customer orientation and improve productivity.[7] Cell phones enable salespeople to obtain the latest customer information or relevant home office information en route to a customer's place of business; to alert customers about unavoidable delays, such as a car breakdown or traffic jam; and to speak with drivers in company delivery trucks who can check on customer orders. Furthermore, beepers can provide sales personnel with timely information, as well as inform them that prospects, customers, management, or other company personnel are trying to reach them.

*Cell phones are only one of many technological tools salespeople use to improve their productivity.*

Photo Disc

### Voice Mail.

Voice mail—various electronic methods of sending and receiving voice messages—is dramatically improving the efficiency of sales force communications. AT&T has determined that 75 percent of all business communications are not completed on the first try. The reasons for this failure are shown in Figure 2.1. Staying in touch with office support people, answering customer inquiries, keeping distributors informed about product availability and delivery dates, and carrying out numerous other telephone communications consume a lot of a salesperson's time. Voice mail ensures that the salesperson connects every time to leave a message.

Many salespeople use voice mail to keep in touch with their sales managers while on the road calling on wholesalers, distributors, or independent retailers. Before they used voice mail, most of these salespeople were on the phone every night updating their managers on their daily activities and discussing problems. Now their evenings are freer because they can dial into the system whenever they like to leave messages and retrieve information left by their sales managers.

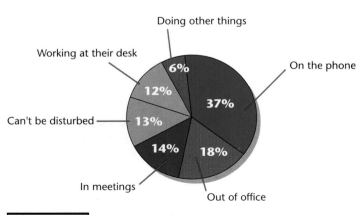

**FIGURE 2.1**

WHERE ARE PEOPLE WHEN YOU CALL THEM?
*Source:* Sam Lobue, "Tired of Telephone Tag? Voice (Message) Your Opinion," *Marketing News* (November 7, 1988): 20.

***Electronic Mail.*** Electronic mail (email) is the transmission of electronic messages between two or more computers. Electronic messages can be sent to a single receiver's email address or written on an electronic "bulletin board" for hundreds or even thousands of computer users to see at the same time. Instead of enduring the frustration of playing telephone tag with a customer, sales peer, or sales manager, salespeople can always leave electronic mail for the addressee, who can read the message when convenient. Email is as fast as a phone call and usually less subject to misunderstandings because the message is in text format for the receiver to read several times if necessary. A company can cut its information handling costs by 60 percent or more by replacing regular mail and filing cabinets with electronic mail and storage. One popular handheld device for managing email is Research in Motion's "Blackberry," which includes a tiny keyboard that enables salespeople to read, write, forward, reply, delete, or file their messages while keeping only one email address and mailbox.[8]

**Virtual Sales Offices.** More than ten million U.S. employees conduct business from virtual offices (for example, one's home or car). As one salesperson says: "I'll drive about forty thousand miles this year. My [car] is my office. Or should I say it's [my company's] mobile world headquarters."[9]

Salespeople are more empowered today than ever before. Powerful portable computers, telecommunications software, handheld fax machines, pagers, cell phones, and voice mail enable salespeople to have mobile virtual offices that allow them to keep in contact with customers, sales managers, and coworkers anywhere without concern for geographic distance. Companies are also assigning more decision-making authority to field salespeople, making it unnecessary for them to report to a sales manager for authorization. Electronic automation is enabling field salespeople to become increasingly self-sufficient, thereby eliminating the need for many branch sales offices. To illustrate, IBM has a telecommuting program in two of its divisions. The company asked sales personnel not to come into the office except to deliver sales presentations, to pick up their mail, or to take a break from working at home. IBM saved millions of dollars in overhead costs from this initiative, and most of those participating prefer it to working at the office. Virtual sales offices also afford salespeople the opportunity to teach customers how to access their suppliers' communications technologies, such as EDI or extranets, to help them answer their questions or obtain the latest information on products and prices. As such, the actual products today's salespeople offer customers increasingly have become consulting and professional advice.

**Electronic Commerce.** Electronic commerce includes all the activities of companies and other organizations that use the Internet. Mostly these activities consist of using the Internet and proprietary networks such as intranets and extranets—to sell products and services and expedite communication.

***Internet.*** Considered the backbone of the information superhighway, the Internet is one of the most important technological tools today. It enables virtually instantaneous interactions among manufacturers, intermediaries or middlemen, and households. More than 97 percent of large businesses have established web sites,[10] and business-to-business (B2B) Internet purchases exceed $1.4 trillion.[11] Salespeople frequently use this electronic channel for prospecting. Some sales personnel view the Internet as a worldwide electronic yellow pages. For instance, a salesperson planning cold calls on companies in a suburb of a major city can utilize an online database service to develop a list of the suburb's businesses along with their sales volume and names of key executives. Many salespeople also develop networks or centers of influence through special online forums where prospects for their products are likely to log on.

**Intranets.** An intranet is an *internal* company network that looks and feels like the Internet because it uses the same tools, such as *Netscape Navigator* or *Microsoft Explorer* web browsers. But intranets are proprietary company networks that link salespeople, other employees, and business affiliates through personal computers and other devices. Organizations use intranets for diverse functions, including email, team projects, and desktop publishing. Intranets are an ideal solution for a mobile sales force or a diverse sales force that needs instant access to a lot of rapidly changing information. For instance, a California software-solutions provider uses an intranet system as the primary information supplier for its two-hundred-person sales force. Instead of using dated manuals and countless photocopies and memos, the firm simply posts its sales-related data—everything from information about sales processes to news about competitors and product specifications—on its internal intranet server.

**Extranets.** Another important business use of electronic channels is a corporate maintained extranet to provide customer support and service. Transferring customer support information to a web site is a labor-efficient and cost-effective way of distributing information to thousands of current and potential customers. Extranets can provide prospects and customers an array of product and technical information, design guides, videos, and graphics. Beyond prospecting and customer support, some companies use their extranets as direct sales channels. For example, Ernst & Young provides online consulting services for small companies, and Vanguard Group, one of the world's largest mutual fund sellers, uses an extranet to provide education on financial topics for its different tiers of customers who log on with their passwords.

For B2B sales, the Internet and its related electronic variations offer powerful, low-cost ways to locate high-quality prospects, provide customer service, conduct research on prospects and customers, sell to organizational buyers, support sales channels, and facilitate communications. Research has found that the amount a firm spends on the Internet (budget allocation) and the extent to which the firm uses the Internet (usage) affect sales management activities and can positively influence sales performance and sales efficiency.[12] Thus, salespeople need to know how to use the Internet, intranets, and extranets to their advantage and for the benefit of their prospects and customers. Read *From the Command Post*, on p. 46, to see how one firm has used e-commerce beneficially.

## Managerial Forces

In response to the dynamic behavioral and technological megatrends, sales organizations are trying various strategies to achieve profitable sales growth and closer customer relationships. Among these strategies are (1) cost reduction efforts, (2) a shift from field selling to direct marketing alternatives, and (3) certification of salespeople.

## FROM THE COMMAND POST: CARRIER CORPORATION—KEEPING THINGS COOL

Carrier Corporation is the largest producer of air conditioning, heating, and refrigeration equipment in the world. Its products are used primarily in commercial and residential buildings, as well as in trucks. In an effort to boost sales, Carrier turned to the Web, and its success has been phenomenal.

Carrier has been able to identify and target web site visitors with the products they are most likely to purchase by offering visitors a discount on shipping if they provide their zip code. With zip code information, Carrier can determine the characteristics of a particular visitor's zip code area and match those characteristics with the kinds of products most likely needed by individuals in that zip code. For instance, web site ads offer visitors with zip codes in wealthy areas air conditioning systems with remote controls. Visitors living in zip code areas with many multiple family dwellings are offered window unit air conditioners. Carrier's technology allows it to offer the right product to the right site visitor in twenty milliseconds!

Returns from this system have been overwhelming. Revenues per visitor have increased from $1.47 to $37.42. And the number of individuals who have visited the site *and* made a purchase has increased 2,673 percent! How's that for a cool number?

**Source:** *From SellingPower.com, CRM Newsletter (October 8, 2001). Reprinted with permission.*

---

**Selling Cost Reduction Efforts.** Median cost of a business-to-business sales call—although it varies widely by industry and company—is now more than $250. For some large industrial companies, unusual complexity of both the selling process and the product itself can lead to sales call costs of four hundred to one thousand dollars or more.

To reduce selling costs, many manufacturers and service providers are aggressively seeking alternatives to large national sales forces. Some large manufacturers are cutting costs by reaching customers through distributors and other kinds of middlemen (for example, independent brokers, manufacturers' agents). Other companies are turning to part-time salespeople to help call on buying organizations such as wholesalers and retailers. Still others are using **direct marketing** techniques, such as direct mail, inbound and outbound **telemarketing,** and **teleselling** (conducting the entire sales process on "fast-forward" via telephone). Rather than fight or fear these additional sales methods, field salespeople should jump on the bandwagon and cooperate with these hybrid approaches to better serve customers and improve their companies' efficiency and effectiveness. The end result should be an increasing sales pie for all sales force members no matter what the selling channel used to reach prospects and customers.

**Shift to Direct-Marketing Alternatives.** Several direct marketing alternatives for selling to organizational buyers either support or bypass field salespeople. These include *direct mail, telemarketing, teleselling, computer salespeople, facsimile,* and *electronic mail.* The speed with which some direct marketing methods, such as facsimile and email, reach the customer has produced the nickname "salespeople on wings."

**Direct Marketing**
Selling alternatives that bypass or partially substitute for field salespeople, including *direct mail, telemarketing, teleselling, computer salespeople, facsimile,* and *electronic mail.*

**Telemarketing** Use of telephone by support staff to help salespeople identify prospects, gather information, and answer inquiries.

**Teleselling** Conducting the entire personal selling process via telephone.

**Direct Mail.** "Snail mail" (or postal mail) remains an effective direct sales channel for many organizational buyers. The fastest growing segment of direct mail is catalog sales. Applying database marketing techniques, mailing list companies use computers to generate the names and addresses of prospects based on company demographics (for example, annual sales volume, type of products sold, number of employees, geographical location). For instance, a large office products manufacturer restructured its sales force to reach approximately three million small businesses it believed needed its products. Instead of making field sales calls on each prospect, though, it employed advertising and direct mail for many of the smallest businesses.

**Telemarketing.** A marketing strategy conducted entirely by telephone to support or sometimes substitute for personal, face-to-face customer interactions is called *telemarketing*. Most often sellers use telemarketing to generate leads and qualify prospects. More than 250,000 U.S. businesses use either outbound or inbound telemarketing. *Outbound telemarketing* places telephone calls to customers at their businesses instead of making costly sales calls in person. While a sales representative can average five face-to-face calls a day, a telemarketer can make up to fifteen phone contacts per hour. Although the final sale may not be closed over the telephone, telemarketers can qualify prospects for the field sales force to call upon. *Inbound telemarketing* uses an organization's inside sales personnel to respond to customers who call a toll-free number to obtain information or place orders. Such call-in leads from promotional campaigns can be targeted and prioritized for timely follow-up by the field sales force. Larger firms are using telemarketing to work with marginally profitable accounts. Smaller firms that cannot afford large field sales forces are using telemarketing to expand geographical markets. As shown in Figure 2.2, telemarketing has many applications, but it also has its strengths and weaknesses.

| APPLICATIONS | ADVANTAGES | DISADVANTAGES |
| --- | --- | --- |
| • prospecting<br>• setting sales appointments<br>• taking customer orders<br>• maintaining goodwill<br>• informing customers about new products and services<br>• notifying customers about special offers<br>• handling customer complaints<br>• reactivating past customers<br>• keeping contact with marginal accounts<br>• providing service<br>• answering customer inquiries | • saves time<br>• low cost<br>• flexible<br>• convenient<br>• can reach almost anyone<br>• yields higher profits<br> | • lacks multisensory appeal (sight, touch, smell)<br>• obscures observable demographic information (age, sex, race)<br>• makes refusals easier<br>• incurs cost of telephone calls<br>• requires brief persuasive messages |

**FIGURE 2.2**

TELEMARKETING APPLICATIONS, ADVANTAGES, AND DISADVANTAGES

***Teleselling.*** Teleselling is a fundamental shift in buyer-seller relationships. Whereas telemarketing generates *warm leads* to pass on to the field sales force, teleselling handles the *entire* selling process from beginning to end via telephone. Although its process resembles the traditional field selling steps, the entire teleselling process proceeds on "fast forward" during one or more telephone calls. Instead of being tightly scripted like typical telemarketing, teleselling uses a flexible but systematic approach much like a salesperson making a face-to-face sales call. Sophisticated database marketing allows telesellers to efficiently contact targeted customers. Telesellers typically have high repeat sales ratios because they provide customers with buying convenience and prompt service. Customers can reach product knowledgeable telesellers by phone whenever they want, and they can complete transactions promptly at their own initiative. Teleselling is a cost-effective supplement or alternative to field sales. IBM has moved many of its former field salespeople into teleselling cubicles where some of the salespeople have sharply increased their annual sales and incomes. In organizational markets where large, complex sales and long negotiations require personal contact, numerous companies are using hybrid selling by combining telesales reps with field reps and telemarketers to achieve better market penetration and customer support.

***Computer Salespeople.*** In a growing number of organizations, computer "salespeople" are replacing their human counterparts. These firms use interactive computers and kiosks to perform some, if not all, of the sales work. Such sales tools can, for instance, provide customers with requested product information, calculate product operating costs, compare product price and features with alternative models and with competitors' products, write up an order, and transmit the order to the factory. *From the Command Post* discusses a company that has had great success in using a "talking" computer salesperson.

***Facsimile.*** Faxing is an increasingly popular and inexpensive way to deliver sales promotions and various information to prospects and customers while avoiding wasteful unopened junk mail. A page of text or a chart can be faxed in about twenty seconds at the cost of a short long-distance phone call. Faxes overcome problems of delayed transportation, unreliable couriers, and frustrating games of telephone tag. A fax can be sent virtually anywhere in the world at anytime, whether the receiving office is open or not, and the information will await the addressee's arrival.

***Email.*** The prevalence of personal computers in U.S. businesses makes email an inexpensive way to contact prospects and customers at their offices or homes with minimal interruption. Salespeople who use emails to reach large numbers of customers simultaneously must be careful that their emails target receptive people. Few people are receptive to unwanted emails, or "spam" as it's often called. Spamming is flooding the Internet with copies of the same message, in an attempt to reach people who would not otherwise choose to receive it. Most spam is commercial advertising, often for dubious products or get-rich-quick schemes. Therefore, when sending large volume emails, you will want to take precautions to ensure that your ISP doesn't erroneously mis-

## FROM THE COMMAND POST: IS THE SALESPERSON LIVE . . . OR NOT?

A floor-covering distributor in the southeastern United States uses a talking computer—an order processing system that responds to floor-covering retailers' or installers' telephone calls in a natural-sounding human voice. The firm's microcomputer can handle up to eight orders at a time, twenty-four hours a day, over an ordinary touch-tone telephone. Customers can place orders even on Saturdays, when the company is closed. Callers simply press the appropriate buttons on the touch-tone phone to enter their orders. The computer also checks and automatically updates inventories and handles various contingencies. For example, if an item is out of stock, the computer can suggest an alternative to the customer. If that substitute is unacceptable, the computer will ask if the caller would like to speak with a salesperson. As the system expands and becomes more sophisticated, the distributor hopes to free up current order takers so that they can make more outgoing sales calls. Such efforts clearly are designed to foster the distributor's customer service orientation.

take your mailings for spam. Since the mid-1990s, AOL and EarthLink have won millions of dollars in judgments and settlements against purveyors of spam under trespass, computer fraud, and specific anti-spam laws passed by nineteen states.

Of course, many companies find emailing a powerful tool for simultaneously reaching many prospects and customers. By clicking on an embedded address in an email, prospects and customers can be sent to a desired web site to learn more about a product or service. Emails have encouraged millions of people to go to web sites selling a vast array of both industrial and consumer products and services. Creative direct marketers will keep coming up with innovative approaches to contact prospects and customers electronically.

**Certification of Salespeople.**   To many people, salespeople continue to have a negative image. This is largely because relatively few people encounter the professional business-to-business salespeople who are the primary focus of this book. Instead, they often must respond to pushy consumer salespeople who telephone them at home at inconvenient times or sometimes use sales gimmicks or a canned sales pitch to maneuver them into buying a product or service that they might not really need. This negativism has spurred efforts to certify sales personnel.

A salesperson who applies for certification usually must gain a certain amount of practical experience, enroll in educational seminars and courses, pass a sales competency exam, provide some professional references, and agree to comply with a code of conduct.[13] Two professional sales organizations—Sales and Marketing Executives International and the National Association of Sales Professionals—have been in the vanguard of promoting

# KEEPING UP ONLINE: SALES AND MARKETING EXECUTIVES INTERNATIONAL

Sales and Marketing Executives International (SME-I) is dedicated to enhancing the profession of sales and marketing. Many of the salespeople throughout the world who belong to this organization network, learn, and socialize regularly in their respective geographical locations. SME-I is especially focused on offering educational opportunities for its members. Even members who have already graduated from college find that learning need never formally end.

Investigate the SME-I web site at www.smei.org to see how you might use SME-I right now. What benefits might SME-I provide you in your selling career? What other professional sales organizations may benefit you as you advance in your selling career?

salesperson certification. Sales certification is a positive response to customer demands for increased quality, trust, and professionalism in sales. Certification can identify someone as a respected sales professional who has met high standards of knowledge, skills, and ethics—thus enhancing the salesperson's professionalism and credibility. You may wish to consider becoming a certified salesperson to enhance your position in your territory and for long-run selling success. Ask your sales manager about doing so or contact one of the aforementioned two professional sales organizations for more information. Read *Keeping Up Online* to obtain further insights about how you might benefit from becoming a member of Sales & Marketing Executives International.

## ADAPTING TO MEGATRENDS

Flexible and resourceful salespeople need not fear the proliferation of new selling alternatives to sales reps. All these methods still require human selling skills and flexible sensitivity to design and carry out major parts of the sales and customer service process. Some telecommunications and computer innovations will partially substitute for salespeople in fulfilling certain sales activities, such as prospecting or routine order taking. Their more dominant role, however, will be to help professional salespeople do their jobs more effectively and efficiently, especially in selling to organizations.

Many progressive sales organizations are spending millions of dollars each year preparing their sales personnel through education, training, and the latest telecommunication equipment to deal effectively and efficiently with this dynamism. Moreover, top-performing salespeople today are ever vigilant to identify trends that affect them and to become early adopters of new technologies and selling tools to better serve their customers, their companies, and themselves. These savvy salespeople know that the phenomena confronting them can confer many benefits as well as challenges. The selling world is indeed a'changin'—and sales professionals who are flexible and adaptable can become a productive part of it.

## Trends in Information Management

Behind the megatrends that influence salespeople and how they operate are key trends in information management. Four of these trends are database marketing, data warehousing, data mining, and push technology. Each of these factors influences the manner in which sales personnel choose to perform their jobs. Let's briefly discuss each.

**Database Marketing.** A sales information database is a large computerized file of customers' and potential customers' profiles and purchase patterns. **Database marketing** allows salespeople to use the information stored in the database to identify a specific group of customers most likely to respond to a particular offer. Customers are generally contacted by direct mail or email. Specifically, database marketing can do the following:

- Identify the most profitable and least profitable customers.
- Select the most profitable market segments and individuals, then target sales efforts with greater efficiency and effectiveness.
- Direct marketing efforts to those goods, services, and market segments that require the most support.
- Increase revenue by repackaging and repricing products for various market segments.
- Evaluate opportunities for developing and offering new products and services.
- Identify the best-selling and most profitable products and services.

In its basic form, database marketing relies on processing systems that collect the details of individual or company transactions. For example, when you make a purchase using a credit or customer loyalty card, a database simultaneously records the store name, the store location, the date of the purchase, the purchase price, and oftentimes the product, among other facts. Similar data can be gathered and analyzed that pertain to companies. Over time, a transaction history and profile is created for every customer. This basic transactional system provides critical information about purchasing patterns and preferences that are valuable in creating new products and services to sell through the distribution channels.

**Database Marketing**
Use of computers to analyze prospect and customer profiles and purchase patterns to better identify and serve target markets.

*Using a company's database, telemarketing representatives can help field salespeople in the areas of sales support, order taking, customer service, and account management.*
Corbis

More resellers and manufacturers are creating databases, and their size is astounding: Ford Motor Company, 50 million names; Kraft General Foods, 2.5 million; Citicorp, 30 million; Kimberly Clark, 10 million. General Motors has a database of twelve million GM credit card holders, giving the company access to detailed data on their buying habits.

Database marketing also provides tremendous opportunities for cross-selling related products. For instance, Canon Computer Systems maintains a database of its 1.3 million customers. The company obtained a 50 percent response rate in a direct-mail solicitation asking printer owners if they wanted information on a new color scanner. As an incentive, buyers of scanners received free four ink cartridges for their printers. Such efforts easily translate to organizational selling contexts.

**Data Warehouse**
Corporate-wide database built from information systems already in place in the company.

**Data Warehousing.** A **data warehouse** is essentially an immense corporate-wide database, built with data from diverse information systems already in place in the company.

It may not be optimized for sales management purposes, but it contains information that can be. Smaller *data marts* group information from the data warehouse in formats pertaining to specific areas. A company, for instance, may have one data mart for market segmentation, another for ad campaign management, and a third for forecasting product sales. Each data mart is optimized for the particular task.

A data warehouse can be enhanced with information obtained from third-party suppliers. For example, lifestyle classifications or demographic information such as estimated household income and educational level added to customer files can aid decision making. Similarly, demographic data, such as company size, annual sales, geographic locations, growth rates, typical purchase order size, and the like can be collected and analyzed for business customers.

**Data Mining** Using statistical analyses, such as decision trees, cluster analysis, and regression analysis, to detect relevant patterns between and among variables in a database.

**Data Mining.** Insights about markets and customers obtained through sophisticated analytical techniques are collectively known as data mining. Data mining is the process of using statistical analysis to detect relevant hidden patterns in a database. Data mining software accesses the data warehouse and uses tools such as decision trees, cluster analysis, neural networks, and regression analysis to detect underlying relationships between and among variables. For example, researchers found through data mining that fathers often buy beer as an impulse purchase when buying diapers. Displaying beer close to the diapers increased sales of both products. Wal-Mart uses data mining to identify customer purchasing patterns, such as what products are typically bought together (for example, bananas and cereals or tissues and nonprescription cold medicines). Through data mining, Wal-Mart controls inventory costs, boosts sales, and improves shoppers' satisfaction.

Many other companies are using data mining techniques to create customer profiles; analyze the potential return for different pricing, promotion, and direct mail strategies; forecast sales; and generally improve customer satisfaction and loyalty.[14] Salespeople can further their long-term customer relationships by sharing data mining insights that help their customers profitably sell through to their own customers.

**Push Technology**
Combination of data warehousing and email to retrieve and send relevant information and services to prospects and customers.

**Push Technology.** The combination of email's latest iteration with data warehousing is called **push technology.** The key to a successful push strategy is knowing exactly what your customers need and exactly when they need it. The first major application of push technology is news retrieval services that deliver via email news articles containing user-specified key words. For example, if Dell, a business customer, depends on Microsoft for key software products such as Windows, lawsuits filed against Microsoft might force changes in its software products, thereby changing what Dell could promote as prepackaged software with its computers. By submitting the following keywords: "Microsoft, law suits, Windows," Dell would receive via email any news articles containing these three words, in any order. Companies can use this same technology to keep track of how they're being written about and perceived in news articles.

A more sophisticated application of push technology is in the sale, distribution, and upgrade of software applications. When the software vendor completes the latest upgrade, it can electronically upgrade its customer's computers, with minimal or no customer involvement. Whether a breaking news article concerning a customer, an alert about an unexpected increase in the price of a product, or notification that your computer software has been updated while you were at a meeting, push technology provides the precise type of information you specified for receipt and delivery. Once push technology is set in motion, the desired information is automatically delivered to you and your designated customers. Without any additional efforts after the initial setup, push technology enables salespeople to continually provide their customers with timely information and services.

Success in personal selling depends on close relationships with customers and "selling through" by understanding the changing wants and needs of your customers' customers. Push technology, skillfully employed, can enhance those relationships by making sure the customer has more relevant and less irrelevant information to work with. Moreover, when the right information is delivered at the right time, the customer spends less time searching for what's needed. Just as telesales has made significant inroads in the sales process in recent years, so will push technology in the near future.

## Information Management and Relationship Selling

As we have seen, information management includes various forms of database technology, all of which is readily available to salespeople for assessing, analyzing, anticipating, and serving customer needs. Resourceful salespeople will make use of these systematically designed and implemented database technologies to develop long-term, personalized, and profitable relationships with each of their customers. Information management and relationship selling go hand-in-hand as part of the evolutionary development of a marketing strategy called one-to-one marketing.

**One-to-One Marketing.** **One-to-one marketing** represents a sharp philosophical change from the traditional approach of viewing customers as mass markets to seeing them as individuals. Instead of trying to increase market share by selling more goods to more customers, one-to-one marketing concentrates on selling more goods, more profitably to fewer selected customers. It seeks a larger share of individual customer's wallets or expenditures rather than a larger share of some mass market. Rather than finding customers for products, one-to-one

**One-to-One Marketing**
A philosophical change from the traditional approach of looking at customers as mass markets to viewing customers as individuals. One-to-one marketing seeks to sell more products to fewer (selected) customers rather than more products to more customers.

marketing focuses on developing ongoing relationships with individual customers by providing them with exactly the products and services they want.

One-to-one marketing is not new by any means. General store owners back in the 1800s were one-to-one marketers because they knew and served the exact tastes and preferences of their relatively few customers. In this era of giant sellers with thousands of customers, it was nearly impossible to meet the tastes and preferences of individual customers until database technologies emerged. Today, marketing strategists and salespeople use database technologies to identify the specific customers they want to cultivate and to tailor products, services, and communications to meet the customer's precise expectations. One of the nation's largest financial services companies, KeyCorp, achieved a more than 350 percent return on investment by implementing one-to-one marketing. By collecting customer profiles, interests, activities, and goals on its web site and integrating the profiles into its database, KeyCorp dramatically increased its ability to serve the financial expectations of its customers and cross-sell them other products via direct mail, service tellers, and the Internet.[15]

**Salespeople: One-to-One Relationship Builders.**  Ultimately, the quality of individual relationships that salespeople develop with customers will determine the success of one-to-one marketing strategies, especially in business-to-business markets. Salespeople are the companies' real one-to-one customer relationship builders and sustainers. Tampering with these long-term customer relationships can be disastrous. To illustrate, Xerox management almost bankrupted the company when they too hastily reorganized their various sales forces and, in the process, severed many long-term customer-salesperson relationships and lost countless sales.

By taking full advantage of the customized information that database technologies provide, resourceful salespeople can better learn and even better anticipate their individual customer's exact needs and expectations—then provide them with the products and services and positive relationship experiences that contribute to cumulative customer satisfaction and loyalty. Today's professional salespeople are empowered like no previous generation of salespeople to effectively and efficiently do their sales jobs for themselves and their companies. As database technologies and applications increase in sophistication, they will no doubt continue to enhance salespeople's abilities to further long-run, trustful, satisfying, and profitable one-to-one relationships with customers.

## PROFESSIONAL SALESPEOPLE AS MICRO-MARKETING MANAGERS

As the aforementioned megatrends and information trends continue to evolve and influence personal selling and buyer-seller relationships, the role of salespeople will continue to expand and change. Instead of merely selling products, today's sales representatives are expected to serve as sales *consultants* who can offer customers expert advice on helping make their business operations more profitable. Professional salespeople must operate much like *micro-*

*marketing managers* in the field, with profit objectives for their designated territories and markets. Their expanding marketing responsibilities require them to perform diverse, expanding roles, including the following:[16]

- *Customer Partners:* Today's salespeople cannot merely know their own company's business; they must also thoroughly understand their customers' businesses—as well as the businesses of their customers' customers. They must develop partnerships with customers in order to help them achieve competitive advantages and increased profitability.
- *Market Analysts and Planners:* Salespeople must monitor changes in the marketing environment, especially competitive actions, and help devise strategies and tactics to adjust to these changes and satisfy customers.
- *Buyer-Seller Team Coordinators:* Modern salespeople must know how to use backup organizational specialists from both seller and buyer teams in marketing research, traffic management, engineering, finance, operations, and customer services to solve customer problems.
- *Customer Service Providers:* Today's prospects and customers generally expect a high level of service. They want problem-solving advice, technical assistance, financing information, and expedited deliveries. If you don't supply these services, they'll likely buy from someone else. After making a sale, salespeople must continually check back with customers to see how the product is performing. Keeping customers satisfied is largely a matter of providing good service, and top salespeople are as skillful at that as they are at persuading prospects to buy.
- *Buyer Behavior Experts:* Salespeople must study customer purchase decision processes and buyer motivations in order to better communicate with and serve customers.
- *Opportunity Spotters:* Salespeople who remain alert to unsatisfied or unrecognized customer needs and potential problems are able to recommend new products, new markets, or innovative marketing mixes.
- *Intelligence Gatherers:* Providing informational feedback from the field to headquarters marketing for strategic and tactical planning purposes is an important part of the salesperson's job. Salespeople are still the frontline "eyes and ears" of their companies.
- *Sales Forecasters:* Sales managers need salespeople's help in estimating future sales and setting sales quotas for territorial assignments and markets.
- *Marketing Cost Analysts:* Professional salespeople should concentrate on profitable sales rather than merely on sales volume or quotas. Of course, companies first need to share profit information with their salespeople, and many now do so because it can lead to more profitable sales. Recognizing the higher-level responsibilities of salespeople today, companies such as Gillette have exempted their salespeople from some routine duties and employed part-time people to set up retail displays and replenish store stock. Salespeople devote more of their efforts to creative selling and profitability analyses by customers and products.
- *Allocators of Scarce Products:* When the company's products are in short supply and demanded by competing customers, as periodically occurs with oil and gas products, you might think that the salesperson's

job is a "piece of cake." Customer relationships, however, can become especially difficult during these times. Many customers will become resentful and even switch supplier if they believe salespeople have treated them unfairly in allocating scarce products.

- *Field Public Relations People:* Because they deal with customers on a daily basis, salespeople must handle many customer problems and concerns that require sensitivity and public relations skills. Astute salespeople recognize that long-term relationships with customers matter more than profit on any one transaction.
- *Adopters of Advanced Sales Technology:* Rising sales costs are requiring sales reps to quickly adopt new technologies to improve their efficiency and effectiveness in serving customers. In the fierce competition of today and tomorrow, salespeople must creatively innovate and automate to succeed for themselves and their companies.

Today's salespeople must perform these multiple roles while serving customers in dynamic world markets that are continuously changing in response to the inexorable behavioral, technological, and managerial forces we have discussed in this chapter. In order to keep their professional edge, salespeople must remain alert to rapidly emerging market opportunities and challenges that significantly affect how they must serve their customers and represent their companies. Professional salespeople are truly their companies' "eyes and ears" in continually evolving markets. Their daily interactions with customers place salespeople in the best position to provide early alerts to their companies' management about recent competitors' actions, changing customers' needs, and the latest market developments. Analogous to professional athletes who never stop trying their hardest, whether far behind or far ahead in a game, professional salespeople strive to do their best every day for their customers, their companies, their families, and themselves.

## SUMMARY

Several megatrends are changing the way salespeople engage in their job tasks and responsibilities. These can be categorized under behavioral, technological, and managerial forces. First, there are several market factors that are having a marked impact on how field salespeople conduct their business. Second, there are revolutionary developments in telecommunications technology that are helping salespeople do their jobs better but, in some cases, partially replacing salespeople. Third, sales organizations' efforts at cost reduction, their increasing use of direct marketing alternatives, and salesperson certification are affecting buyer-seller interactions and relationships. Given these major forces, today's salespeople work in dramatically changing selling environments and must increasingly operate like micro-marketing managers in their territories.

## KEY TERMS

| | | | |
|---|---|---|---|
| Sales Megatrends | Teleselling | Data Warehouse | Push Technology |
| Direct Marketing | Database Marketing | Data Mining | One-to-One Marketing |
| Telemarketing | | | |

## CHAPTER REVIEW QUESTIONS

1. Describe the three broad megatrends affecting personal selling.

2. What specific market and competitive forces are changing the personal selling and buyer-seller relationships? What are their effects?

3. Name some major advances in telecommunications and computer technology affecting personal selling. Describe briefly how salespeople can use each to improve their effectiveness and efficiency.

4. What are some companies doing to reduce selling costs?

5. In your own words, define the term "direct marketing." Describe some tools and techniques used in direct marketing.

6. Why do some companies see selling in the United States as increasingly like selling internationally?

7. Describe the type of assistance that salespeople may receive from the company's telemarketing staff. What can field salespeople do to increase the benefits they derive from telemarketers?

8. What is teleselling? How have many former field salespeople who were transferred to teleselling increased their incomes?

9. How are information management trends affecting salespeople?

10. Why must today's professional salesperson learn to function more like a micro-marketing manager in the field?

## TOPICS FOR THOUGHT AND CLASS DISCUSSION

1. Which of the advances in telecommunications and computer technology do you think will provide the most help to salespeople over the next decade?

2. Discuss how you think salespeople can take advantage of each of the phenomena taking place under the managerial megatrend.

3. How do you think the rising cost of personal selling and the growth of direct marketing techniques will affect salespeople?

## PROJECTS FOR PERSONAL GROWTH

1. Assume that a firm has divided the United States into ten regional markets based on needs for its products—industrial lawn mowers, lawn sweepers, watering equipment, and garden tools. Also, assume that the company's CEO has asked you to prepare a map of the United States showing these regional markets. Clearly label each region according to how you identify it. For example, perhaps part of the southwestern United States may have different needs owing to the terrain and desert-like environment of the area, whereas part of Florida may be identified with abundant moisture, humidity, and tropical plants. Do any library research necessary to complete your map.

2. Ask two business-to-business salespeople about telecommunications use in their sales work. What SFA equipment has been most helpful to them? Why? How have their companies assisted them in selling and in serving prospects and customers? What other equipment would they like? What other support would they like from their companies in helping them work with prospects and customers?

## WE'RE TRYING TO CUT COSTS . . . WE CAN'T AFFORD LAPTOPS NOW!

Russ Lauver has been a field salesperson for Smith & Betz, a medium-sized manufacturer of men's clothing accessories (belts, wallets, tie clasps, cuff links, and suspenders) for the past two years. He began with S&B right after graduating from the University of Florida with a B.A. degree in marketing. Wanting to stay near home because his father was ill, Russ accepted a sales job at S&B. He figured he'd work in sales for a year until his dad's health improved and then move on. However, Russ has been surprised to find that he loves the freedom and independence of his job and the opportunity to regularly travel in three southern states. As he tells his old college friends, many of whom have moved to New York, Philadelphia, Chicago, Los Angeles, and other big cities, "I'm not getting rich, but I've got a steady job where I'm pretty much my own boss. I have a great lifestyle that allows me to golf most weekends, and until something a whole lot better comes along, I'm content where I am."

Russ drives a car as he calls on small, independent retail clothing stores located mainly in small towns in South Carolina, North Carolina, and Virginia. He earns a comfortable income, based on 70 percent salary and 30 percent commission. Most of his customers have been buying from S&B for decades, and many are about the same age as Sam Gibson, Russ's predecessor in the territory, who retired five years ago at age sixty-five. Mr. Gibson was well liked and respected by his customers. Russ was fortunate in being able to spend a month calling on customers with Mr. Gibson before he retired. Mr. Gibson always followed a routine when making sales calls and had an easy-going manner that endeared him to customers. Russ describes Mr. Gibson as "folksy, dependable, honest, and steady." He gave all his customers his home number, as well as the S&B office number; several customers would telephone him on weekends just to chat about the latest news or family events. At the end of each sales call, Mr. Gibson always told customers, "Now don't you hesitate to call me at the office or my home if you have problems with any of our products or need any special orders." Mr. Gibson always carried an impressive-sized notebook in which he recorded what took place on each of his sales calls and any tasks he needed to do for his customers.

Except for his annual vacation during the first two weeks of August, Mr. Gibson always returned customer calls within a day or two at most, and Russ has tried to do the same. When traveling in his territory, it was Mr. Gibson's habit, and now Russ's, to call the S&B office each weekday around 4 P.M. to retrieve phone messages from the regional sales manager's secretary. In this way Russ can provide excellent service to customers who leave messages at headquarters if they needed anything. Mr. Gibson's customers almost never complained about being unable to quickly obtain needed service, such as a rush order or correction of an erroneous billing. Russ is determined to keep that good relationship with his customers intact.

Homer Peabody, the Smith & Betz regional sales manager—a dear friend of Mr. Gibson—has worked for S&B for more than thirty-five years. Always supportive and complimentary to Russ, he has become a father-like mentor for Russ. Russ likes him a lot, but he isn't sure how much longer Homer will continue to work. His children are all grown and on their own, and Homer's wife, Betty, is experiencing poor health. Russ feels awkward about bringing up anything about retirement in conversations with Homer, as he doesn't want to risk offending him.

Russ is also concerned about S&B's lack of sales force or headquarters technology. Although many of Russ's retail customers still prefer to use the telephone, a growing number have told Russ that they would rather email him regarding special orders and requests. Russ has a desktop computer at

(continued)

## WE'RE TRYING TO CUT COSTS . . . WE CAN'T AFFORD LAPTOPS NOW! (CONTINUED)

home, but he travels in his territory each week, so he isn't home until the weekend. Russ doesn't want to spend his personal money to buy a laptop computer because he is trying to save for a new car. Just before Russ was hired, salespeople stopped receiving company cars. Instead, the salespeople are now reimbursed only so many cents per mile for their travel expenses. Thus, Russ believes it's critical to replace his ten-year old Ford Taurus— with 150,000 miles on it—with a new car before he has a major breakdown on the road and misses several days of sales calls.

Because Russ's boss, Homer, doesn't communicate by email and the company has neither a web site nor intranet, Russ doesn't feel any pressure to buy the laptop out of his personal funds. Instead, he believes the company ought to buy laptop computers for its ten full-time salespeople but not for the fifteen manufacturers' representatives who sell on commission for S&B as well as several other companies. Now, however, might not be a good time to suggest to Homer an investment in sales laptop computers. S&B sales have plateaued over the past few years, and the company has been desperately trying to find ways to cut costs.

Russ is twenty to thirty years younger than the nine other full-time salespeople, who all have worked for S&B for more than ten years, some as many as thirty years. He is probably the only salesperson pushing for a laptop. Of course, most of the other salespeople are more financially stable than he currently is and probably could readily buy one if they needed it.

Early this Saturday morning, Homer called Russ at his apartment and told him that he would like to travel with him during the coming week to see how things were going in his territory. Russ knew that his sales were down a little, but so were overall company sales, so it wasn't Russ's fault. Besides, he had just lost one big order last week when Sam Katz, owner of a medium-sized retail store in Charlestown, needed a rush order of two

hundred wallets because a big manufacturing company planned to give them as employee presents at their annual holiday party. Because Katz couldn't reach Russ fast enough, he bought the wallets from a competitive sales rep. If Russ had had the laptop computer, he could have received the order promptly by email and had the wallets shipped that same day by express mail to Mr. Katz. "Oh well," thought Russ, "you can't win them all, and it certainly wasn't my fault that Mr. Katz couldn't reach me because I was traveling most of that day."

Russ considered the upcoming week with Homer. What customers should he call on—the ones who suggested Russ use a laptop computer and email or the ones who didn't mind using the telephone? What arguments could he give Homer for purchasing the laptops if the company was trying to cut costs, if Homer didn't own one, and if most of Russ's customers seemed satisfied with telephoning or even postal mailing special purchase orders? Russ worried, too, that Homer might take his suggestions and comments as personal criticism—the last thing Russ wanted. Homer Peabody was like a second father to him, especially since Russ's own dad had been so ill. Maybe it would be best to say nothing to Homer, because he would probably retire soon. Russ concluded that in any case he might be looking for another job himself in a few months if sales kept falling off at S&B. Although he loved the company and the lifestyle, S&B just wasn't a progressive company, and the future seemed none too bright even though S&B products were very high quality. In fact, Russ had seen lower quality wallets selling for higher prices at a Wal-Mart store and on the retailer's web site.

Of course, Homer had told Russ that he had a great future with S&B because he was the youngest of the salespeople. On the other hand, salesperson turnover at S&B was rare because the company, largely Homer's doing, had treated them so well.

(continued)

## CASE 2.1

# WE'RE TRYING TO CUT COSTS . . . WE CAN'T AFFORD LAPTOPS NOW! (CONTINUED)

Well, it was getting late, so Russ decided to sleep on all his concerns; maybe he could sort everything out tomorrow.

### Questions

1. Which customers would you advise Russ to call on with Homer?
2. What should Russ say to Homer about purchasing laptop computers for the full-time sales force? Do you think S&B should buy laptop computers for the fifteen manufacturers' reps, too? Would any other equipment aid personal selling at S&B? If so, should S&B be asked to purchase it for the salespeople?
3. How might Russ recommend buying laptop computers without Homer seeing it as running counter to S&B's current cost-reduction push? Will the laptops pay off for S&B? Could the company expand its markets through the use of computers and email?
4. Do you think Russ should consider looking for another job now? Why or why not?
5. If Homer were to retire and recommend Russ as his successor, what actions would you advise for Russ if he became S&B's regional sales manager? How else, besides making field sales calls, might S&B reach prospects and customers? How well would the current salespeople accept your suggestions? How would you address their concerns?
6. What other situations and possible questions should Russ prepare for during his five days traveling with Homer?

# SAVORING SUCCESS AND CONTEMPLATING THE FUTURE

Gloria Pattengale was eating dinner with two of her United Business Technologies (UBT) colleagues, Vickie Brodo and Deborah Coyle, at one of the best restaurants in Los Angeles. The three had just finished three weeks of training as new sales representatives, and the dinner was part of their reward from UBT for finishing at the top of their training class. Out of twenty new sales trainees participating in the program—eight women and twelve men—Vickie had finished third, Deborah second, and Gloria first in overall scores on the six training categories: (1) role plays, (2) product demonstrations, (3) case analyses, (4) written exams, (5) use of sales force automation (SFA) equipment, and (6) peer ratings. Now, for the first time in weeks, they could relax and reflect on their experiences and what might be ahead for them at UBT. They all knew UBT quickly assigns newly trained sales representatives to individual sales territories.

While sipping their drinks and waiting for dinner, the three friends talked about the rigorous training they had just completed. They had had almost no time for relaxation, not even on weekends, because each Friday night instructors assigned time-consuming projects, such as preparing PowerPoint sales proposals or sales presentations for hypothetical customers, for completion by Monday morning. None of the three could remember ever undergoing such sustained pressure. Let's listen in on their conversation.

**GLORIA PATTENGALE:** I'm sure glad I took that selling and sales management course in college. I'd done a lot of this stuff before—like role playing and preparing sales presentations and case analyses using PowerPoint—but the UBT sales training was still the most intense pressure I've ever been under. I worked a lot harder here than I did in college. Bet some of the guys are mad because none of them ranked in the top three. They're probably having pizza tonight while we dine in the style I'd like to become accustomed to.

**VICKIE BRODO:** Earning 98 percent on that last exam made the difference for me. I just barely beat out Tom Bajier, who came up strong on the final exam, too.

**DEBORAH COYLE:** Well, we all made it. Let's drink a toast to UBT's next three superstar salespeople.

**VICKIE BRODO:** It feels great to be a winner!

**GLORIA PATTENGALE:** It sure does. But to be honest, I get a little nervous just thinking about going out into my own territory within a few days. We didn't have any training about what it's like for a woman traveling a sales territory. I wish we'd had some women trainers. I'm not sure men really understand some of the problems we can run into.

**DEBORAH COYLE:** I agree. What are we going to do when we stay overnight at a hotel? I don't want to go down to the hotel lounge alone, and I know I'm going to get bored sitting around in the room. Guess, I'll just watch a movie on television or read some good books.

**VICKIE BRODO:** You know what really worries me? Trying to do everything they expect of us besides selling. Did you see that list of salesperson duties the national sales manager put up during his lecture? Wow! All that talk about "selling through" to our customers' customers, and serving as business partners and consultants to our customers was too much. I just want to sell products to my customers and keep them satisfied. I'm not going to know enough about my customers' customers or their businesses to offer them consulting advice. They'd probably resent it anyway . . . coming from a twenty-three-year old woman on her first full-time job.

*(continued)*

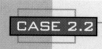

## CASE 2.2

# SAVORING SUCCESS AND CONTEMPLATING THE FUTURE (CONTINUED)

**GLORIA PATTENGALE:**  Yeah, I agree. And that wasn't all. Do you remember he said that we had to be the company's "eyes and ears" in the field by gathering intelligence about competitors' actions and changing customer needs? Won't the customers tell us their needs? I'm sure not going to spend valuable selling time trying to gather "intelligence"—whatever that means. Isn't that supposed to be the job of marketing research?

**DEBORAH COYLE:**  What worried me is when he said we need to ensure that we allocate our time to those customers and products that are most profitable. We didn't really cover that in our training. We don't even have access to total sales and profit information for our customers. Boy, if we do all the stuff they're talking about, what's left for the sales managers to do? All I'm interested in is making my sales quota and winning one of those exotic overseas trips.

**VICKIE BRODO:**  It's great being assigned a company car with a phone plus a nice laptop computer. One of the guys said the car and computer could be picked up as early as Monday if we go into the office. With my new laptop, I plan to stay in touch with my customers weekly by sending them emails. Maybe I'll even prepare a monthly newsletter to let my customers know about stuff like upcoming price changes, inventory shortages, and new product introductions. I think I'll call it *Vickie's News and Views.* I could send it as an email attachment.

**DEBORAH COYLE:**  Hey, I like that idea, Vickie! Maybe, we won't have to make so many sales calls if we handle more stuff by email. Nobody said we had to make all our sales calls in person, did they?

**GLORIA PATTENGALE:**  Say, maybe we could do a lot of the personal selling process on the Internet. I might set up a web site for my prospects and customers that will show them our product line and give them all kinds of information that they would usually ask me about. In fact, I bet somebody in the Information Technology (IT) department would put a video on my web site demonstrating how each of our products works. I know we've got a videotape like that because the CEO shows it to the financial community to promote our company and keep its stock price up. You know if we used our heads and the Internet, we could spend a lot less time doing all the paperwork involved in working with customers.

**VICKIE BRODO:**  Sorry, gals, but I've got to go. Let's plan on meeting next week around this time to discuss some more of our brilliant ideas about how to make our jobs easier. Let's each bring at least five ideas to discuss next time, Okay? Well, gotta run. See ya!

## Questions

1. In their conversation, do the women seem unnecessarily concerned about taking on their new territorial assignments? Do you think any special issues arise for saleswomen as compared to salesmen? Why or why not?

2. Do the women have an accurate understanding of what many salespeople are expected to do today? Why or why not? What can the company do to help its salespeople handle the expanded roles?

3. Are the women's ideas about making their sales jobs easier realistic? Which ones make the most sense? Which ones make the least sense? Could the company provide a lot of this information for customers on an extranet or the Internet?

4. Assume you are a friend of one of the women. What five ideas would you give her about using the Internet and other telecommunications tools to make her more effective and efficient in her sales assignments?

5. Do you think the use of high-tech equipment—laptop computers, cell phones, pagers, and the like—will help the young saleswomen appear more professional?

# PART TWO
# The Personal Selling Process

# Prospecting for and Qualifying Prospects: Filling the Salesperson's "Pot of Gold"

*"It is one of the most beautiful compensations of life, that no man can sincerely try to help another without helping himself."*

Ralph Waldo Emerson

## After Reading This Chapter, You Should Understand:

- The steps in the personal selling process.
- The importance of prospecting.
- How to qualify leads as prospects.
- Several prospecting methods.
- The steps in developing a prospecting plan.

**INSIDE PERSONAL SELLING:**
## Meet Noah Huggins of Transworld Services

What do you do when nearly every business is a potential customer? That's the situation facing Noah Huggins, a district manager for Transworld Services who sells cost recovery services. The company collects, on behalf of corporate clients, from customers who pay their bills slowly or not at all. Clients include Fortune 500 corporations, hospitals, contractors, doctors, dentists, even city and county governments. With such a broad market, Huggins has had to find efficient ways of identifying good prospects. "Prospecting and qualifying are the hardest parts of the sales job," he notes.

Transworld has no sales territories and provides no leads, so Huggins and his sales team make fifty prospecting phone calls—cold calls—and twenty in-person prospecting calls—warm calls—every day. "We

want to schedule two appointments and go on two presentations every single day," he says. "If I have to make a hundred calls to get two appointments, I make them. If I get two appointments in my first ten calls, I'm still going to make my fifty calls because I have a good chance of getting ten to fifteen appointments over the next week." When Huggins finishes one appointment, he will canvass nearby offices to try to set up more appointments.

He also gets leads from other sources, including telephone directories, web sites, publications, conventions, and trade groups. When addressing business groups, Huggins avoids a hard-sell pitch and instead emphasizes bottom-line benefits. Not long ago, he explained to a group of home inspectors and appraisers how cost-recovery services can reduce their accounts receivable, and came away with contact information for a number of prospects.

"I usually qualify prospects when I first talk to them," Huggins says, by dealing only with decision-makers to set up appointments. For example, he recently phoned a local gym, and the manager answered. Huggins asked for the owner, but the manager said the owner was rarely at the gym. The Transworld executive wondered whether the manager had the authority to buy, so he asked, "Can you make buying decisions about services?" When she said yes, he was on his way to qualifying the company, and arranged an appointment.

During the sales call, Huggins learned that the gym, under new ownership, had just fired the person who collected past-due accounts, and was struggling with collections. Now he knew that the gym had a genuine need. The manager mentioned that she had turned the gym's eleven thousand dollars in monthly losses into a sixteen thousand dollar monthly gain, an indication that the business could afford Transworld's services. Having qualified the gym as a good prospect, Huggins reviewed the manager's listing of overdue accounts and made his presentation. He closed the sale and left with a significant contract in less than an hour.

You now have some understanding of what it means to be a professional salesperson and how dynamic the selling environment is. But we've only begun to scratch the surface of professional selling. In chapters 3 through 8, we will explore the many activities that professional salespeople carry out to generate prospects, confirm sales, nurture relationships, and maintain customer satisfaction and loyalty. Put on your seat belts, sit back, and prepare to enter the heart of personal selling.

First, our discussion will center on the focal point of this book—the **Personal Selling Process (PSP).** The PSP, covered in the next six chapters, represents a set of interrelated sales stages through which salespeople must progress—from identifying legitimate prospects to closing sales and following up with customers to ensure post-sales customer satisfaction and subsequent business. Although the seven PSP stages are closely intertwined, we will describe each step separately to help you become conversant with the tasks and activities in each stage and to enhance your comprehension of how the PSP can foster selling success.

Salespeople for years have used the PSP to achieve great success for themselves, for their companies, and for their customers. In a sense, salesperson

FIGURE 3.1

THE PERSONAL SELLING PROCESS (PSP)

efforts to facilitate customer purchases and satisfaction resemble ways effective managers (or leaders) deal with their employees (or followers):

> Leadership and selling are both forms of influence. . . . Like leadership, the sales influence may be a matter of persuasion or it can derive from a participative or consensual decision. . . . In the sales-customer and the leader-follower situations, the salesperson and the leader make the attempt to change and influence the perceptions, cognitions, decisions, and behaviors of the customer and the follower. If the customer and the follower are influenced, both the selling and the leadership are *successful*. . . . If the customer and the follower are influenced *and* their needs and expectations are fulfilled, then the selling and the leadership are successful and *effective*. The selling and the leadership are successful and effective when the needs of the customers are met by a sale as a consequence of the efforts of the salesperson and when the goals of followers are achieved as a consequence of the efforts of the leader.[1]

## STAGES IN THE PERSONAL SELLING PROCESS

Professional salespeople need to master basic selling strategies and tactics, then develop their own styles to adapt to specific customer types and selling situations. As mentioned in chapter 1, countless small tasks in the PSP may be divided into seven major stages:

1. Prospecting for and Qualifying Prospects
2. Planning the Sales Call (Preapproach)
3. Approaching the Prospect
4. Making the Sales Presentation and Demonstration
5. Negotiating Prospect Resistance and Objections
6. Confirming and Closing the Sale
7. Following up and Servicing Customers

Although we have sequentially numbered the PSP stages above, it is more accurate to think of them as interacting, overlapping, and continuous stages, depicted as a cycle or wheel, in Figure 3.1. Successful selling relies on retaining *good* customers through post-sale service and relationship development, which leads to repeat sales and referrals to new prospects whom you hope to turn into customers—and so the wheel keeps turning. We will present this wheel at the beginning of chapters 3 through 8 to trace our discussion of the PSP. "Prospecting and Qualifying," the first stage of the PSP and the subject of this chapter, is highlighted on this chapter's wheel.

We strongly suggest that you read each of the six selling process chapters (we cover two stages in chapter 4) multiple times and that you look for opportunities to put to use as soon as possible the information you learn here. You might do this through membership in a student marketing or sales organization, a part-time job, role-playing with friends or fellow students, or in class discussion. Using the PSP early on will have three important and near-term benefits for you. It will (1) acquaint you with principles and methods of *real-world selling*; (2) help you decide if professional selling is the right career choice for you; and (3) give you more confidence in interviewing for professional selling jobs.

# PROSPECTING FOR AND QUALIFYING PROSPECTS

As depicted by the *Wheel of Personal Selling*, the selling process can be viewed as a continuous cycle, each stage of which connects with and indeed overlaps adjoining stages. The entire wheel turns around its *most important* part: its "axis" of *prospects* and *customers*. Although every stage of the PSP is as important as the next, the extreme importance of prospects and customers tends to make the first and seventh stages of the process seem especially significant. After all, the promise of potential customers and the security of satisfied current customers give the wheel its initial forward movement and its continuous momentum, respectively. The Prospecting and Qualifying stage of the PSP gives the wheel its initial push.

## The Importance of Prospecting

Prospecting is the process of searching for leads—people and organizations that might need your product—identifying them, then qualifying them as prospects or potential customers. It is an essential, future-oriented task. It is not done, however, without certain costs (for example, salesperson time, out-of-pocket costs, opportunity costs of failing to further develop another satisfied account). Nonetheless, prospecting should be a continuous part of the selling job. Many salespeople think of prospects as their "pot of gold" from which they can draw whenever sales are slow. To increase or even maintain sales volume, sales reps must *continually* seek out and prospect for new customers for several reasons:

- Customers switch to other suppliers.
- Customers move out of your territory.
- Customers go out of business.
- Customers die.
- Customers' businesses are taken over by another company.
- Customers have only a one-time need for the product.
- Relationships with some customers deteriorate, and they stop buying from you.
- Your buying contacts are promoted, demoted, transferred, or fired, or they retire or resign.
- You need to increase total sales.

Prospecting can produce significant benefits. Salespeople who continually prospect can generate a steady flow of sales (future sources of sales revenue come from prospects) and offset customer attrition. Also, prospecting can help create a more productive selling environment because the likelihood of your making a sale increases when you are dealing with a legitimate, or "qualified," prospect. In addition, prospecting provides a more enjoyable selling situation; your qualified prospects need the product so you avoid high-pressure selling.

## Qualifying: How a Lead Becomes a Prospect

Generally, prospecting requires more salesperson time than any other selling activity. In prospecting, you must first obtain leads to people whose firms seemingly could benefit from your company's product or service. Essentially, a **lead** is a possible buyer, sometimes called a suspect. The most basic lead information usually consists of a name, phone number, and address. You *qualify* the lead or suspect in order to create a *prospect*. Salespeople contact and call on four groups of people: (1) suspects qualified as prospects and called on; (2) suspects improperly judged as qualified and called on in error; (3) qualified nonsuspects contacted by a cold call; and (4) unqualified nonsuspects contacted by a cold call (those who reject the sales overture).[2] Clearly, your goal is to reduce dealing with individuals who fall into the second and fourth categories. Therefore, you must qualify the lead in terms of the following criteria:

> **Lead** Anything—a name, address, or telephone number—that points to a potential buyer.

- Need or want
- Authority to buy
- Money to buy
- Eligibility to buy

The lead becomes a **prospect** when the potential buyer meets all four of the qualifying criteria. As noted in chapter 1, you can easily remember this qualifying process: think of adding another **name.** Before you add this name to your list of prospects, first qualify the lead's **N**eed, then **A**uthority, **M**oney, and **E**ligibility to buy. Let's discuss each of these criteria now.

> **Prospect** A lead that has been qualified as a definite potential buyer.
>
> **NAME** An abbreviation for the process of qualifying a lead in terms of *need* for the product, *authority* to buy, *money* to be able to buy, and overall *eligibility* to buy.

**Need or Want.**  Savvy salespeople avoid wasting time and effort trying to sell products and services to people who neither need nor want them. Not only are such efforts usually nonproductive, many people consider it unethical. It's better to sell products to customers in such a way that the customers come back, not the products. Most often, in your initial contact you can quickly determine which leads have a *genuine* need or want for your products and services. Sometimes, however, you may see that the customer has an unrecognized need or is unaware of a product that can satisfy a latent need. That unrecognized need is your opportunity to explain and demonstrate your product's benefits. For example, an office manager may not appreciate the cost and timesaving advantages of having the latest model fax machine to communicate with his customers and suppliers until you point out the benefits.

**Authority to Buy.**  One of the biggest mistakes that novice salespeople make is spending too much time with people who lack sufficient purchase decision-making authority. The industrial sales rep who tries to sell the drill press to the purchasing agent in the office but doesn't bother to see the machine operator and his supervisor in the factory has failed to grasp the concept of authority to buy. Whether presenting to an individual or a group of people, the alert salesperson finds out who will influence the purchase and whose approval is necessary. Sometimes you can qualify the prospect's authority to buy by merely asking, "Whose approval is needed for this purchase?" and "What individuals in your firm have an influence on this decision?"

**Money to Buy.** Prospects must have the money or credit to buy before they can be qualified. Selling products and services to someone who has little or no chance of paying wastes your time and company resources, especially if the products must be repossessed later or written off as bad debts.

Ensuring that a prospect has sufficient capital with which to make the purchase should be a "no-brainer" for salespeople. That isn't always the case, however. For example, a salesperson at a Fortune 500 computer manufacturer spent months closing a computer sale, only to have the buyer declare bankruptcy shortly after the installation. This unfortunate selling situation could have been avoided had the salesperson done his homework to discover that his prospect was not financially sound. Sales to buyers who cannot pay are especially detrimental to a service organization because services performed cannot be repossessed. Services are intangible and perishable in that they are simultaneously produced and consumed, so service organizations often demand payment prior to performing services.

National credit rating services such as Dun & Bradstreet provide financial information about organizational buyers. For smaller companies, Better Business Bureaus, commercial banks, or local credit rating services can provide information about the lead's ability to buy. Of course, if it's just a matter of temporary cash flow, a resourceful sales rep may be able to arrange an installment or time payment plan that allows the lead to be qualified as a prospect. Lee Iacocca, a former Ford executive and CEO of Chrysler, became, in his words, "an overnight success" when he came up with an innovative idea to help people and organizations buy automobiles, as explained in his book, *Iacocca: An Autobiography:*

> While sales of 1956 Fords were poor everywhere, our district was the weakest in the entire country. I decided that any customer who bought a new 1956 Ford should be able to do so for a modest down payment of 20 percent, followed by three years of monthly payments of $56. This was a payment schedule that almost anyone could afford, and I hoped that it would stimulate sales in our district. I called my idea "56 for '56." At that time, financing for new cars was just coming into its own. "56 for '56" took off like a rocket. Within a period of only three months, the Philadelphia district moved from last place in the country all the way to first. In Dearborn, Robert S. McNamara, vice president in charge of the Ford Division—later he would become secretary of defense in the Kennedy administration—admired the plan so much that he made it part of the company's national marketing strategy. He later esti-

mated it was responsible for selling 75,000 cars. And so, after ten years of preparation, I became an overnight success. Suddenly I was known and even talked about in national headquarters. I had toiled in the pits for a good decade, but now I had a big break. My future suddenly looked a lot brighter. As a reward, I was promoted to district manager of Washington, D.C.[3]

**Eligibility to Buy.** Many organizations seek to buy products and services when they are ineligible to do so. It would be a mistake, for instance, for some manufacturers to bypass their wholesalers to sell to retailers. Essentially, these manufacturers would alienate their wholesaler customers if they sold directly to the retailer. Feeling threatened by the manufacturer, the bypassed wholesalers might retaliate and refuse to carry the manufacturers' line for distribution to other retailers.

Some small electronics retailers bypass their electronics wholesalers and purchase some of their stock from large electronics retailers who buy directly from electronics manufacturers in large quantities (thus receiving substantial trade discounts). The small retailers receive a better price from the large retailer than they would from their wholesalers. Technically, though, the small retailer is supposed to buy from the electronics wholesaler. This "gray market" kind of buying and selling can undermine the effectiveness and efficiency of the channel of distribution as well as lead to conflict among the manufacturers, wholesalers, and large and small retailers. Screening out these ineligible people in the qualifying process will provide your sales manager with solid evidence of your judgment, thoroughness, and perhaps your ethics.

*Even if your sales territory and customer base appear to be stable now, you would be wise to do some prospecting and qualifying activities every workday.*
Chuck Savage/Corbis

You must also be certain that your prospect is in *your* territory and not in that of one of your sales peers. If the account is outside your territory, the prospect is ineligible to make the purchase from you. "Stealing" an account or accidentally crossing into a sales associate's territory can create tremendous ill will and poor morale among sales force members. Therefore, when in doubt, always confirm that a prospect is indeed within your territory; if not, turn it over to the appropriate salesperson.

**Other Qualifying Criteria.** Salespeople should consider two other criteria when qualifying prospects. One is the individual's *accessibility* and the other is the prospect's long-run potential *profitability*. Accessibility refers to whether the salesperson can reach the buying organization's key decision-maker. Warren Buffet and Bill Gates may seem like ideal prospects because they have so much money, but how likely are you to reach these individuals? Similarly, a prospect who keeps

## *Is He Really Inaccessible?*

Scott, an office products salesperson, made a cold call on a small business located in his territory. In a courteous manner, Scott asked the receptionist if he could see the firm's owner, as he had a line of products that he felt certain would be of interest. The receptionist rose from her chair and walked a few steps to enter a glass-enclosed office, through which Scott could clearly see the receptionist and owner interacting. The owner was reading the newspaper and had his feet up on the desk. A moment later the receptionist returned to her desk and informed Scott that the owner was in a meeting and, therefore, was unavailable (inaccessible). Scott, tempted to leave a negative message for the boss, wisely didn't. Instead, he politely thanked the secretary and left. He didn't give up, however, because he knew this firm was growing fast and could benefit from using his company's products. Scott called three more times over two months, but the owner remained inaccessible. On Scott's fifth call, the owner finally became available . . . and this time, thanks to his congenial perseverance, Scott won a substantial sale from a formerly inaccessible account. Of course, not even the most persistent salesperson can make all accounts accessible. Each salesperson must estimate the probability that an inaccessible account will eventually become accessible and that account's long-run sales potential.

canceling appointments with you is probably trying to avoid you. But, the anecdote in *On the Frontlines* shows how even some inaccessible accounts can be reached with gracious perseverance.

The *On the Frontlines* story reminds us of the little refrain that many of us learned as children:

> 'Tis a lesson you should heed,
> Try, Try again;
> If at first you don't succeed,
> Try, Try again;
> Then your courage should appear,
> For, if you will persevere,
> You will conquer, never fear;
> Try, Try again.[4]

One other criterion when qualifying prospects is whether the prospect's business is likely to be of long-run financial benefit to the seller. A customer who requires extensive and frequent service, has extraordinary and complicated special purchasing requirements, or is a hard negotiator (especially on price) may prove unprofitable for the salesperson at almost any sales volume. A high-volume and low- or no-profit account can be a nightmare. Such prospects are better left for competitors.

**Lead Sources.**[5] The two basic ways to search for leads are either random searching or selective searching. **Random-lead searching,** sometimes called blind searching, means to generate leads by randomly calling on organizations (door-to-door canvassing) or by mass promotional appeals (advertising) to which organizations respond and thereby identify themselves as leads. Because randomly searching for leads can be inefficient, most salespeople prefer to employ more planned strategies. The application of systematic strategies to generate leads from predetermined target markets is called **selective-lead searching.**

Table 3.1 shows several random searching methods and selective searching methods that we can further divide into direct and indirect sources. Leads can also be categorized as effort and noneffort. *Noneffort leads* are supplied by the company or from an individual's voluntary inquiry or response to advertising. An *effort lead* is generated solely by the salesperson. Most leads come

**Random-Lead Searching** Generation of leads by randomly calling on organizations. Sometimes called "blind" searching.

**Selective-Lead Searching** Application of systematic strategies to generate leads from predetermined target markets.

| TABLE 3.1 |
| :-- |
| **LOOKING FOR ORGANIZATIONAL PROSPECTS** |

| **Random-Lead Searching Methods** | |
| :-- | :-- |
| Door-to-door canvassing of organizations | Advertising |
| Territory blitz of organizations | Print media |
| Cold calls on organizations | Broadcast media |
| Emails to organizations | Web sites |

| **Selective-Lead Searching Methods** | |
| :-- | :-- |
| **Direct Sources** | **Indirect Sources** |
| Friends, neighbors, acquaintances | Direct mail |
| Personal observation | Trade shows, fairs, exhibits |
| Spotters or "bird dogs" | Professional seminars and conferences |
| Endless chain | Contests |
| Centers of influence | Free gifts |
| Internet (emails) | Unsolicited inquiries |
| Prospects and former customers | Telemarketing |
| Junior salespeople and sales associates | |
| Professional sales organizations | |
| Company records | |
| Directories and lists | |
| Newsletters | |
| Surveys | |

from diligent efforts, and noneffort leads considered serendipitous.[6] *Direct sources* allow leads to be identified by name or approached directly by salespeople, whereas *indirect sources* require leads to identify themselves by responding to a general call. Each of the random and selective searching methods can be useful to professional salespeople, depending on the product and the customer mix in a given situation. Let's discuss several methods for obtaining prospects.

### Random-Lead Searching

**Door-to-Door Canvassing**
Knocking on doors in a commercial area without an appointment to locate prospects.

**Cold Calling**
Approaching or calling a business without an appointment for the purpose of prospecting or selling.

**Door-to-Door Canvassing and Cold Calls.** **Door-to-door canvassing** requires knocking on many doors in a given area, without an appointment, and introducing yourself in search of prospects. This approach can supplement other methods for obtaining leads. For instance, if you are in between scheduled sales calls, **cold calling** can be a valuable use of your time. Ideally, though, you should turn to door-to-door canvassing, which can be time consuming and ineffective, only when other lead-generating approaches are unavailable or don't seem to be working. To cut down on the frustration of cold calls that produce no shows of interest, precede your visit with some research on the company (for example, nature of the business, size, contact individual) to maximize the effectiveness of the call.

A great deal of face-to-face canvassing has been replaced by telephoning, faxing, or emailing initial sales messages to potential customers, then following up with face-to-face calls if the prospect responds or shows any interest. The best salespeople develop excellent telephone skills and can fearlessly call prospective new accounts. A slow afternoon's paperwork can be enlivened with such cold calls, and they often yield at least a few appointments, if not an actual sale.

**Territory Blitz**
An intensified version of door-to-door canvassing in which several salespeople join efforts to call on every organization in a given territory or area.

**Territory Blitz of Organizations.** A version of door-to-door canvassing is the **territory blitz** (or area blitz) where several salespeople join efforts to call on every organization within a given territory. Any leads developed during this blitz are turned over to the *regular* territory salesperson for follow-up. This often inefficient approach is seldom used today as it can be a "turn-off" if people detect this mass assault on their home turf.

**Advertising.** Various forms of *print media* (newspapers, magazines, telephone book directories, billboards, and posters) exposure can stimulate people to inquire about the product or service and thus identify themselves as good leads. *Broadcast media* (television, radio, the Internet) exposure can generate leads among audiences less likely to view print media. Some companies prepare prospects for the salesperson's call by mailing videocassettes or sending emails that demonstrate the product or service to make more efficient use of the salesperson's selling time during the actual sales call.

**Electronic Mail and Web Sites.** Some salespeople and their companies send unsolicited emails over the Internet to large numbers of people. But mass emailing requires special care and consideration for the privacy of organizations and their people. Such emails may turn off more customers than they attract. Emails should target only those companies and people most likely to need the promoted products and services. Some legitimate online marketing research firms will sell you the email addresses of companies and people who have given permission to be solicited for certain categories of products and services. Another safer approach is to establish a company web site that requires or encourages those who visit the site to provide basic qualifying information, then asks them to check a box indicating whether they would grant permission to be contacted by email about products of interest.

Sending out unsolicited, mass commercial emails may be considered "spamming" and may cause Internet providers such as AOL to cut off the emailer's access. Internet providers will cut off even highly desirable emails if they appear to be spam. Harvard University tried to send several hundred emails at the same time to high school students notifying them that they had been accepted. But AOL blocked all these emails because they looked like a spamming operation. It's always a good idea to let your Internet provider know in advance before you undertake any mass mailings.

Many recipients of frequent commercial emails quickly delete them or set up "filters" to block emails from that source in the future. The American Marketing Association has developed a code of ethics, presented in Chapter 13 of this text, which outlines a set of principles for using the Internet for online selling activities. All salespeople should be familiar with these principles before attempting to prospect online. *TRUSTe* is another nonprofit organization that has developed a "trust-mark" which it awards only to web sites that strictly adhere to its privacy principles. Email can be an effective tool for prospecting and qualifying but is best used only with permission to send such messages, and only if not sent so frequently and repetitively as to irritate recipients.

## Selective Searching: Direct Sources

**Friends, Neighbors, and Acquaintances.** Probably the easiest sources of leads for a new salesperson are people you've already met. It's hard to say no to friends, neighbors, and acquaintances, and these sources usually try to help you start up your career if they can. Many life insurance companies and other direct sellers tell new salespeople to write down the names and addresses of all their neighbors, friends, and acquaintances who might buy the product, then make telephone or personal sales calls to each.

Technical sales personnel and other business-to-business salespeople can find this approach valuable. Perhaps you are selling printing services to small businesses, and your best friend's husband just opened his own flower shop. Or maybe while chatting with people at church or temple services, you learn that one of them is planning to open up a new business location. A low-key style approach usually works best in approaching friends, neighbors, and acquaintances, though. If you come on too strong as a salesperson, even friends will start to avoid you.

**Personal Observation.** This approach is also called the "railroad crossing technique." At a rail crossing you stop, look, and listen. You do the same with personal observation. All successful salespeople pick up leads from personal observations while carrying out their daily routines. While pleasurably reading newspapers and magazines, listening to their car radio, taking a ride in the car, overhearing a conversation while dining at a restaurant, or watching television in their easy chairs, they spot leads. For instance, announcements of a company relocating to your city, expanding its operations, or replacing its vice president of purchasing provide leads for products and services ranging from construction to communications and computer equipment. Or while driving through a given geographic area you may see numerous awnings and signs with the names of companies (potential prospects) on them.

**Spotters.**  People who work in ordinary people-contact jobs for other companies are often excellent **spotters** (sometimes called "bird dogs") who can often help you obtain good leads. Bartenders, doormen, taxi drivers, and service people such as hair stylists hear the intimate conversations of many people. They learn who's looking for financial advice, larger office space, a new fleet of company cars, landscaping, office furniture, or personal computers. Within organizations, secretaries, receiving dock workers, maintenance people, and even mailroom personnel can be valuable "bird dogs" for leads.

**Endless Chain.**  A classic way to obtain leads is to ask your most recent satisfied customers to refer you to other people who might be interested in the benefits of your product or service. This is called the **endless chain** approach. This referral strategy provides you with leads already qualified, at least partially, by your current customers. Some salespeople make a point of giving inexpensive, but nice gifts to customers who refer others to them. By showing their appreciation in this tangible and memorable way, they continue to motivate customers to provide additional referrals.

**Centers of Influence.**  Salespeople from many kinds of organizational settings, as well as other professionals, such as dentists, accountants, and lawyers, subtly cultivate potential customers by joining professional, social, and civic organizations whose members are potential customers and *opinion leaders*. From such organizations, whether formal or informal, salespeople can develop **centers of influence**—individuals or groups of people whose opinions, professional activities, and lifestyles are respected among people in the salespeople's target market. Health clubs, country clubs, university alumni associations, hobby groups, professional associations, or civic organizations offer the salesperson opportunities to develop contacts and centers of influence that can lead to many potential customers. For example, a pharmaceutical salesperson may meet a well-known doctor at a club who agrees to prescribe his company's latest drug. Because the doctor is so respected, other physicians will likely decide to prescribe the same drug for their patients. Or you may sell your firm's services to a large, well-respected company and then inform other prospects in the center of influence about this firm's use of your product. Their reaction may be: "Gee, if your service is good enough for them, then it clearly is good enough for us."

**Internet.**  Salespeople frequently use the Internet for prospecting. Some sales personnel view the Internet as a worldwide electronic directory. For instance, a salesperson planning to cold call in a large office building in another city could use an online database service to develop a list of the

**Spotters**  People who work in jobs where they meet other people and who can help salespeople obtain business leads. Also called "bird dogs."

**Endless Chain**  A classic method of prospecting in which the salesperson simply asks recently satisfied customers for prospect referrals.

**Centers of Influence**  Individuals or groups of people whose opinions, professional activities, and lifestyles are respected among people in the salesperson's target markets.

building's corporate tenants along with their sales volume and names of key executives. Salespeople also prospect by developing networks or centers of influence through online forums where prospects for their products are likely to log on.

**Prospects and Former Customers.** Current prospects are nearly always excellent sources for referrals to new leads. Research has indicated that one referral can be as valuable as up to twelve cold calls.[7] However, although 80 percent of clients would be willing to give referrals, only about 20 percent are asked.[8] One study of four hundred marketing managers whose companies advertise in trade publications to generate leads found that almost 40 percent of the leads produced went completely unanswered.[9]

Even when prospects decide not to buy or quit buying from you, they may still give you leads to other potential customers. All you have to do is ask! Former prospects often appreciate your honest efforts to sell to them and generally feel a little guilty in not buying from you. So, like many nice people, they may want to "make it up to you" by supplying names of other potential customers. It is essential, however, that you retain each prospect's trust and respect if you expect referrals to other potential customers. Former customers often feel the same way—provided your relationship with them ended on good terms. But never try to "guilt" former prospects or customers into giving you referrals. When you approach former prospects or customers for referrals, first politely remind them who you are, and then simply ask if they know of any other people or organizations that might be interested in your product. In *On the Frontlines,* on p. 80, you'll discover how one super salesman succeeds with this approach.

**Junior Salespeople and Sales Associates.** When junior salespeople or "sales associates" take on much of the responsibility for developing leads and qualifying them, senior salespeople can spend their time more profitably in developing sales presentation strategies and actually selling to prospects. For instance, one salesperson for a vegetable processor made profitable use of a "quasi-sales associate." He hired and paid a high school student to place a brochure and product samples in the hands of all grocery store produce managers in a southeastern state and to ask them if they wanted the sales representative to call on them. Out of 500 produce managers contacted, 180 managers wanted to meet with the sales rep and 140 out of those 180 prospects bought!

You might ask other salespeople in your company who sell products different from yours which of their customers might be likely prospects for you. Or you might set up a "buddy system" whereby each company salesperson helps out the others with names of leads. A variation of this approach is to ask *noncompeting* salespeople in other companies for leads—and the emphasis is on noncompeting. For example, sitting in a customer's office with another sales rep gives you the opportunity to ask him or her for the name of a lead, and you can reciprocate in kind. Also, you can identify what products are used with your offerings (for example, corrugated boxes and wines bottles), and contact the salespeople selling those particular products for leads.

ON THE FRONTLINES

# Prospecting by Doing Good Deeds

Bob Tasca is a master at prospecting for new customers—individuals and companies—by doing good deeds and satisfying customers. He owns one of the most successful Ford and Mercury dealerships in the United States. Founded in 1953, his company mission is to "satisfy customers" no matter what it takes. As a result, his dealership in the tiny state of Rhode Island sells more than five thousand new and used cars annually, generating more than $130 million in business!

His organization's selling practices focus on always satisfying the customer, even when the customer is not his. In fact, some people who have bought different brand cars from other dealerships have called him when their cars have broken down by the side of the road. Tasca, unlike many other car dealers, never says, "You're not one of my customers . . . call the dealership where you bought your car." Instead, he invariably says, "One of my associates will come out promptly to pick you up and bring your car back for repair." By doing so, Tasca continually brings in new prospects without spending a dime on advertising or sales promotion. Once back at the dealership, Tasca treats these new prospects with as much care as he does his long-time customers . . . and many become new Tasca customers who recommend his dealership to others.

Rather than focusing on short-run profitability, Tasca focuses on generating long-term revenues by building customer relationships. He believes that saying "yes" to drivers with car problems can yield customers for life. Tasca also sets one price for a vehicle, rather than negotiating with customers (which can lead to price gouging). His salespeople earn commissions on how well they satisfy their customers, not on how many cars they sell.

Tasca gives his customers added value by innovative programs. For example, he has established a *Pre-Trade-in Plan*, which allows customers—whether companies or individuals—to buy new cars every two years at a mutually satisfactory price. In addition, he anticipates customer wants and needs by requesting Ford to put new features on his stable of cars before the features have even become popular (that is, he "bets" on the future). He was adding antilock brakes and air bags as standard options on his cars well ahead of his competitors. Why? Because he was confident that his customers would want them!

Tasca's efforts add up to a bevy of customers who return to his showroom again and again (oftentimes with their friends, neighbors, and business associates) to buy from the man who has made customer satisfaction his life's business mission. As a testament to Tasca's work, a phenomenal 97 percent of his customers return to the dealership when looking for a new car, and 65 percent of those actually buy.

***Source:*** *Adapted from Bob Tasca with Peter Caldwell, You Will Be Satisfied (New York: Harper Collins, 1996); Ken Liebskind, "Satisfaction is Job One," Selling Power web site archives, 1999–2001.*

**Professional Sales Organizations.** Today's professional salespeople may join the Sales & Marketing Executives International (SME-I), or less formal *tip clubs* that meet regularly over breakfast, lunch, or dinner for a short program and to share information, ideas, and perspectives on selling. Both the SME-I and tip clubs provide opportunities to gather information on leads, exchange referrals, cross-sell, and learn new selling techniques.

**Company Records.**  As a salesperson, always remember to look for—and use—possibilities right in front of you. Information available on internal company records, such as warranty cards, repair service logs, and even complaint letters, often indicate who can use a related product or service, who hasn't bought anything for a long time, or whose dissatisfaction with a current product might be solved with a new product. Timely follow-ups on these leads can be profitable.

**Mailing Lists and Directories.**  Any person or organization that has ever ordered anything by mail or telephone, requested product or service information, obtained a credit card, or applied for a mortgage or loan is probably on one or more lists. Compilation of mailing lists is big business because *targeting*—reaching the highest-potential customers—is the name of the prospecting game. Professional salespeople frequently use targeted lists purchased from mailing list providers. In addition, online or offline directories (for example, phone books, trade association directories, users' lists, manufacturing directories, service industry guides, organization directories, membership lists) provide a wealth of information. A medical products supply sales rep, for example, can make a quick sweep through a metropolitan area telephone directory and compile the office telephone numbers of oral surgeons and their locations.

**Newsletters.**  In this age of personal computers and desktop publishing programs, a few enterprising salespeople prepare periodic newsletters to mail or email to their prospects. Newsletters can keep prospects up to date on new products, upcoming price changes, seasonal discounts, special services, and newsworthy information about the industry. A page or two will do, but give your newsletter a first-class look and provide quality first-class information that reflects well on your integrity and professionalism. Be sure to clearly identify yourself as the sender by including your name, business address, email address, and telephone number on the newsletter.

If a newsletter doesn't seem right for you, simply cut out articles from magazines and newspaper and mail them to prospects with a note attached: "Mary, Thought you'd be interested in seeing the attached article. Best regards, Sally." In this way, you can develop a kind of pen-pal relationship with your prospects and customers.

**Surveys.**  Although legitimate pollsters and marketing researchers do not like it, many companies generate leads by conducting so-called surveys by mail, telephone, email, or personal interview. Some pretend to want to know a respondent's opinion on some issue when, in reality, the questions are trying to qualify the individual. An Internet variation is to send out thousands of emails seeking responses to a "survey." Respondents are considered prospects and receive follow-up emails and perhaps a telephone call or two. Salespeople who use the survey method dishonestly should be prepared for angry reactions from people who feel manipulated.

To screen out nonprospects, surveys often use opening questions such as "Do you use oil to heat your business offices?" or "Does your company maintain a jet aircraft for executive use?" or "Does your factory have central air conditioning?" Mechanically conducted surveys rely on computers that randomly dial offices and play preprogrammed messages (sometimes from celebrities). Virtually anyone who has a telephone number, unlisted or listed, can be reached this way. Those people who complete the survey have usually qualified themselves as prospects for a salesperson to call later.

### Selective Searching: Indirect Sources

**Direct Mail.** Direct mail offers many subtle ways to prospect for new customers, such as sales letters, catalogs, invitations, samples, new product mailings, advertising reprints, and emails. Salespeople or their companies can use a lead directory to do one-time mailings (via the Internet or post office) to obtain quick responses from some prospects, or they can conduct strategic mail campaigns to steadily convince more people to become prospects (see the *Direct Mail Example* on p. 83 as an example). In preparing a direct mail piece, consider the following guidelines:

- Address your letter to an individual by name and position.
- Where appropriate, use an attention-grabbing opening statement or headline.
- Make the format attractive but not too flamboyant.
- Keep the promotion straightforward and simple to understand.
- Stress customer benefits, not product features.
- Provide customer testimonials or independent research as proof for the quality of your product and the benefits stressed.
- Ask for action after the recipient has read the material (for example, call a toll-free number, mail in a coupon, or click a box on the email).
- Personalize the direct mail piece by adding a written postscript (use a special writing font if a mass mailing).
- Follow your mailing with a prompt response to recipients (for example, "May I come by to show you how our product can save you hundreds of dollars a year?").
- Keep records of the mailing results (for example, calculate the return on your mailing by comparing mailing cost to sales generated from the mailing). After all, not all mailings are equal.

**Trade Shows, Fairs, and Exhibits.** Trade shows have proven especially effective for prospecting as well as for determining prospect needs.[10] Special shows of appealing new products in diverse categories attract many people and companies. Some are just looking, but most are interested in the products or they wouldn't pay the admission and spend their time at the show. In essence, they self-select themselves as potential prospects. Names and addresses of attendees can be obtained in various ways—from requests to mail product literature to registrations for prizes or business card drawings. While at the show or exhibit, videotape presentations and product demonstrations can move attendees through part of the selling process. One caveat about trade shows: Prompt follow-up after the show is mandatory, before your prospect goes "cold." Try your hand at working a trade show exhibit in *It's Up to You,* on p. 84.

# DIRECT MAIL EXAMPLE

*Johnson & Williams Investment Planning, Inc.*
*916 W. Touhy Avenue, Suite 34*
*Chicago, IL 34790*

September 8, 2003

Ms. Susan Brophy
1407 S. Washington Street
Arlington Heights, IL 47401

Dear Ms. Brophy:

Congratulations on the recent establishment of Brophy Manufacturing. Your company no doubt is on the road to an exciting and rewarding future in Chicago's business world. As your firm travels that road, we would like to offer our services as investment portfolio managers.

In business since 1974, Johnson & Williams has earned a reputation for sound, shrewd investments and friendly, attentive client service among many leaders in the Chicagoland business community. We offer a wide variety of services and specialize in tailoring investment plans to meet the needs of each of our clients.

Perhaps you are thinking, "But I've just started out and am not really ready to begin thinking about investment/pension options for my employees." We sincerely believe that it is never too soon to begin assisting your employees in planning their financial future.

To this end, we would be pleased if you would accept our invitation for a corporate investment consultation. This consultation is absolutely free of any charge or obligation and is intended to help you assess (1) your firm's financial readiness for employee investment/pension options and (2) the kinds of investments they would like to make. In order to schedule a consultation, or if you would simply like more information about Johnson & Williams, please use the enclosed reply card and postage-paid envelope to indicate where and when you prefer to be reached by telephone, or please call us at 1-800-368-PLAN. One of our investment managers will be happy to talk with you.

With thanks for your attention, I am,

Very truly yours,


Cynthia Johnson, President

## IT'S UP TO YOU

As a salesperson for Megadisc Software Corporation, you have been assigned to work two days at one of the biggest trade shows of the year. Your company has invested a small fortune in display and demonstration equipment for the show. The Megadisc exhibit features a bank of five computers set up so that interested prospects can run demo versions of Megadisc's newest product offerings. In addition, two large laser disc-driven video monitors allow passersby to play their choice of thirty specialized file segments that describe different aspects of the Megadisc programs, which help businesses streamline computer and telecommunications hookups. Your company has sent along plenty of brochures and a sign-up sheet for exhibit visitors who would like more information. During your first day at the exhibit, dozens of people stopped by to look at your video segments and to try out the demo programs, but only two put their names on the sign-up sheet. It is now 9 A.M. on your second and last day of handling the exhibit. You are worried that Megadisc management will think you did a poor job of generating prospects. How will you generate more sign-ups today?

**Professional Seminars, Workshops, and Conferences.** Seminars, workshops, and conferences or conventions that many potential customers are likely to attend can be lead-generating "supermarkets." For example, a computer manufacturer may advertise in a local newspaper a seminar at which area businesspeople will see a demonstration of the firm's latest computer innovations. At the conclusion of the seminar, the presenter would state, "This seminar was sponsored by XYZ Computer Manufacturing. We have more information available, so if you'd like to talk with us now or want a representative to call on you, we'll be happy to do so. Several of our company's people (with big red badges) will remain in the room for the next hour to answer your questions. If you must leave now, please drop your business card into the box near the door or complete one of the information sheets. Thanks, again, for coming."

Attend as many workshops, seminars, luncheons, special sessions, and coffee breaks as you can to circulate with the members and chat with them about themselves (that is, where they work, what they do, their special interests, and so on). Exchange business cards with them and take some notes on the cards following your conversations. Obtain a list of attendees and collect all the litera-

*Seminars give salespeople the opportunity to present simultaneously their products and services to several interested parties from different organizations.*
Corbis

ture, programs, brochures, and handouts that seem relevant. After the conference, call or write to the most promising leads and prospects, remind them about how you met, recall a few pleasantries, and try to set up an appointment.

**Contests.**  Who among us hasn't excitedly opened a letter from Publishers' Clearing House or Readers' Digest that says: "You may have won ten million dollars!" Many of us do the tearing, scraping, and pasting tasks necessary to enter these contests even though our chances of winning anything are slim. Few people can resist entering a contest, especially if entering requires little effort. Contests are nearly always going on at trade shows and exhibits, and in newspapers and magazines. All you need to do to enter is submit your name and address on the handy form, and sometimes answer a few demographic or psychographic questions about yourself or your company. People who enter the contest are presumed to be interested in the prize offered, so they may be good prospects to buy it if they don't win. Even the lucky winners may not win all they need to use the prize, so they can turn out to be paying customers, too. For example, a CEO may win a free personal digital assistant (PDA). Next, she may realize that several employees in her firm might increase their effectiveness and efficiency if her company bought them PDAs as well.

**Free Gifts.**  Many companies offer inexpensive free gifts, such as a dozen golf balls or small tool sets, to people who respond to an advertisement. Although few people who see the ad respond to it, many of those who do eventually buy the product being advertised for themselves or their companies. Another method of attracting potential customers is to offer them a special prize to visit your company facility for a product demonstration. An animal breeding service used an innovative adaptation of the free gift approach to obtain the names of prospects interested in its unique service, as described in *From the Command Post*.

## FROM THE COMMAND POST: GETTING A GRIP ON THE MARKET

A large animal-breeding service in the Midwest mailed a single leather glove to each of 3,700 farmers and cattle breeders who might be interested in an artificial insemination service. The glove was imprinted with the company logo and came with a brochure entitled *Get a Better Grip on Beef A.I.* To receive the matching glove, prospects only had to mail in the reply card. A sales rep, bearing the other glove, called on each respondent. A follow-up mailing to those who didn't respond advised prospects: "You still have time to get a better grip on Beef A.I." The company reported a 47 percent total response to the two mailings and more than $110,000 in additional sales.

**Unsolicited Inquiries.** Such inquiries usually come from individuals who see a telephone directory advertisement, receive an email, browse a web site, read an article about the firm, return a magazine tear-out postcard, or respond to some other promotional campaign. Unsolicited telephone calls and letters from people asking for information are usually excellent leads because the inquirers often have qualified themselves or their companies in terms of need, authority, money, and eligibility to buy the product or service. In essence, such noneffort leads are "freebies"—they cost you nothing, yet you can benefit from them handsomely. Inside telemarketing salespeople should respond to these calls and letters, then turn the names of prospects over to the territorial salesperson. Surprisingly, some salespeople and their companies have no system for tracking such call-ins nor do they follow up on telephone and letter inquiries.

Another kind of unsolicited inquiry is generated via Internet prospecting. Many sales professionals secure valuable leads from their firm's web site or extranets for current customers. Customers who visit a company's extranet can earn monetary or product incentives by referring other potential customers. Web surfers visiting a firm's site frequently request more product or service information, which opens an opportunity for a salesperson to follow up with a phone call. By knowing what other sites potential customers visit, a company can gather more leads by setting up a hot link or ad in those areas, linking Internet surfers directly to the firm's site.[11]

**Telemarketing for Prospects.** Companies can amass numerous leads via inbound toll-free telephone responses to advertisements in magazines and newspapers, or on billboards, radio, or television or from outbound calls made by a firm's telemarketers. For example, one large data processing firm uses telemarketing to call leads and ask if and when they expect to be ready to make a purchase decision. If the prospect says in three months, the lead receives a higher priority than if the prospect answers six months. Sometimes, telemarketing generates more leads than the company's salespeople can handle. The same company ran a special lead-generating program that obtained thirteen thousand computer sales leads for seventy salespeople over a ten-month period!

A Fortune 500 manufacturer generates more than thirty thousand leads a year by providing a toll-free number at which prospective customers can obtain product literature, repair service, or a sales contract. Useful information yielded in those incoming calls goes to the company's inquiry center, which mails a questionnaire to each inquirer. Those who return their questionnaires become prospects to be called on by salespeople. *Keeping Up Online* describes a well-known company that few people would associate with the use of telemarketing.

**Marketing Information System (MIS)** Any systematized, continuous process of gathering, sorting, analyzing, evaluating, and distributing market information. Can be helpful to salespeople in obtaining leads and prospects.

## Marketing Information Systems

Many industrial companies find that they need a continuous computerized **marketing information system (MIS)** to develop leads. An MIS, a systematized, continuous process of gathering, sorting, analyzing, evaluating,

## KEEPING UP ONLINE: DUPONT COMPANY

DuPont, the chemical giant, employs former field salespeople as telemarketing reps to identify "hot prospects" for their field sales force, answer customers' technical questions, help resolve distribution problems, and even sell some products. Over 50 percent of the leads passed on to the field sales force by the telemarketers become DuPont customers. Explore DuPont's web site and think of innovative ways that the company might use it to generate more leads for their field sales force.

www.DuPont.com

and distributing market information, can be useful in prospecting. For instance, an MIS has provided great prospecting assistance at a large and successful mechanical contractor that designs, manufactures, and installs plumbing, instrumentation, heating, ventilation, air-conditioning, and fire protection equipment. The company's major sales opportunities come from construction projects, such as high-rise office buildings, commercial complexes, manufacturing and processing plants, wastewater treatment plants, and nuclear generating plants. The usual approach is to wait until specific job bid lists are published and then submit a bid along with numerous other competitors. Under such conditions, bidding amounts to a price war. In addition, successful bids wind up having to conform to job specifications determined without the contractor's input. To overcome these disadvantages of straight-bid work, the firm began promoting its engineering and construction management capabilities to customers via mail, email, and a web site. By proactively generating advance information about construction projects, the company has became involved early in project development, which generally assures them of sales.

### Sales and Marketing Executives Marketing Library

For prospecting or any other stage in the PSP, *Sales and Marketing Executives Marketing Library* at www.sell.org is an outstanding source of information and help for salespeople. The library offers (1) more than 200,000 searchable articles on sales and marketing, (2) discussions by top marketing/sales leaders about their latest strategies and ideas, (3) access to the world's first knowledge-base in sales and marketing, (4) company and industry profiles, and (5) the latest compensation data for salespeople, sales managers, and marketing managers, plus much more. This SME-I site even offers online sales training at www.TrackSelling.com.

## THE PROSPECTING PLAN

As you can now see, professional salespeople consider prospecting a critical function, not a hit-and-miss one. Therefore, to maximize prospecting activities, you must develop and execute a comprehensive prospect plan. A sound prospecting plan should have six stages.

1. *Set objectives for prospecting.* What do you hope to achieve when you prospect? To answer this question, establish specific, reasonable, quantitative goals, rather than vague ones that provide no direction. Rather than "I want to significantly increase the prospects I gain through prospecting," make your goal specific: "Through prospecting I will make sales calls for two hours per day and add five new accounts by June 1."

2. *Allocate time for prospecting.* Prospecting is too important an activity to leave until you have left over time, perhaps at the end of the day. Prospecting requires hard work, initiative, time, and creativity. Its end results should be your lifeblood as a salesperson. Just as you must make time in life to, say, rest, shop for clothes, and go to school, you must make time for prospecting. To do otherwise may leave you bereft of future sales.

3. *Become familiar with prospecting techniques.* You will want to become conversant with the various prospecting methods that we have introduced. Evaluate when to use which methods and which ones seem best suited to your industry and customer types.

4. *Choose one or more prospecting techniques.* Study these prospecting approaches over and over again and test them out. Determine which ones you feel comfortable with and which ones really work for you. As time goes by, you may opt to use some new prospecting techniques, omit ones you've been employing, and modify others.

5. *Systematize the prospecting plan.* Successful professional salespeople classify prospects and keep good prospect records. You will want to maintain accurate and detailed information about each prospect (for example, company name, contact person(s), address, phone number, type of business, products needed by the prospect, company size). You could classify prospects by product, by customer type, by geographical area, by size, or by potential. You could even categorize them by call priority: on whom you should call first, second, third, and so forth.

6. *Evaluate the results.* Carefully analyze your prospecting performance versus the prospecting objectives that you set in step 1 above. In other words, compare your outcomes with your objectives. Where your results are below goal, seek to determine the barriers to success. Where your results are above goal, determine why you exceeded your expectations. These two analyses will help you set your prospecting goals for the next period as well as your prospecting strategies and tactics. In addition, you will want to determine which prospecting techniques worked the best for you. Figure 3.2 illustrates how you may assess the effectiveness of the various prospecting methods you have employed. In this example, the salesper-

| | PROSPECTING METHODS | | | | | | | |
| Prospect | Cold calls | Centers of influence | Direct mail | Email | Internet web site | Spotters | Newsletter | Results: Qualified prospect? |
|---|---|---|---|---|---|---|---|---|
| Jones Co. | X | | | | | | | No |
| Pearson | | | | X | | | | No |
| Fox, Inc. | | | X | | | | | Yes |
| Simpson | | | | | | X | | Yes |
| Ace Mfg. | | | | | X | | | Yes |
| G&G Ltd. | | X | | | | | | No |
| Apex Inc. | | | | | | | X | Yes |
| Genus | X | | | | | | | No |
| Hyperon | | | X | | | | | Yes |
| Excelco | | | | | | | X | Yes |

**FIGURE 3.2**

PROSPECTING METHODS EVALUATION FORM

son approached ten firms (under the "Prospect" column) using seven different prospecting methods (cold calls, influence centers, direct mail, email, Internet web site, spotters, and newsletters). The salesperson determined each method's effectiveness by whether it led to a qualified prospect (under the "Results: Qualified prospect?" column). The method was deemed *effective* if it resulted in a bona fide prospect (a "yes") and *ineffective* if it did not. Of course, you may want to personalize this basic format by adding more columns (for example, actual dollar results, reasons for success or failure, and suggestions for the next call).

# PROSPECTS: THE SALESPERSON'S POT OF GOLD

Without prospects, the selling process never reaches first base. Prospects are essential to the continuous health of any sales organization. Consciously or unconsciously, whether making sales calls on present customers, listening to the car radio while driving to their next sales appointment, relaxing at home while reading the evening newspaper, or attending a party with friends and acquaintances, professional salespeople are *always* prospecting. In fact, an old maxim for salespeople is: "Apply your ABP's" (that is, Always Be Prospecting).

Prospects not only provide every selling organization with the promise of future business, but also furnish special solace for individual salespeople who must deal with the rejection and frustration that accompany every selling job. When a salesperson hasn't made a sale in some time, a long list of prospects is that "pot of gold" at the end of the faint rainbow peeking through an otherwise cloudy day that will help keep alive the hope and motivation to make the next sales call.

Although we have discussed many different approaches to generating leads and prospecting, most professional salespeople have their favorite methods and adapt each to their own individual styles. For example, some of the best make more use of centers of influence, existing records, and seminars and trade shows than do their lower-performing counterparts.[12] You may discover that some methods work best with certain products in certain markets at certain times. So, like professional golfers who choose the precise club for each situation near the green or in the rough or sand trap, choose the best approach for your selling situation. Finally, even when you think that you've done "enough" prospecting for the day or week or year, remember: Skillful prospecting efforts and professional selling success usually go hand in hand. Always try for that next prospect. After all, that next prospect could become your best customer ever.

## SUMMARY

The seven basic stages in the personal selling process should not be viewed as separate, mutually exclusive steps toward a sale, but rather as a process in which stages overlap and integrate in a continuous cycle. This cycle may be depicted as a rotating wheel with no definite end or beginning.

Whether a prospect buys or not, the salesperson should always ask for referrals, as these start the PSP wheel rotating again. Leads qualified on the basis of *need, authority, money,* and *eligibility* to buy are called prospects. Several prospecting methods are available, and they can be categorized as either *random searching* or *selective searching* approaches. Prospecting is a never ending process for professional salespeople because new prospects must continuously replace current customers who stop buying for various reasons. To be effective in prospecting, salespeople should employ a six-step

prospecting plan that starts with establishing prospecting objectives and concludes with evaluating prospecting results.

Skillful and ethical use of web sites, extranets, and emails can generate prospects who often qualify themselves in answers to log-on requests. Because of the volume of leads they generate, large industrial firms often handle leads with computerized marketing information systems (MIS). In general, the most successful salespeople are those who are the most resourceful, energetic, and skillful in finding new sources of prospects and more efficient ways to qualify them. With continuous innovations in telecommunications technology, creative and alert salespeople will identify many new opportunities for prospecting and qualifying . . . and filling up their "pots of gold."

## KEY TERMS

Personal Selling Process (PSP)

Lead

Prospect

NAME

Random-Lead Searching

Selective-Lead Searching

Door-to-Door Canvassing

Cold Calling

Territory Blitz

Spotters

Endless Chain

Centers of Influence

Marketing Information System (MIS)

## CHAPTER REVIEW QUESTIONS

1. Name and describe the seven basic stages in the selling process.

2. What four criteria determine whether a lead becomes a prospect?

3. Give several reasons why a salesperson's present customers stop buying.

4. Distinguish between random searching and selective searching for leads. Give some examples of each.

5. What is the centers-of-influence approach to finding potential customers? Why is this the preferred method for many professionals such as doctors, lawyers, insurance agents, and accountants?

6. Provide some basic guidelines for preparing a direct-mail piece to obtain leads on potential customers.

7. How can internal company records, such as warranty cards, be of value in developing lists of prospects?

8. Describe the survey approach to generating leads.

9. What is a marketing information system (MIS) and how can it help manage leads?

10. Describe the different elements of a prospecting plan.

## TOPICS FOR THOUGHT AND CLASS DISCUSSION

1. Why is prospecting and qualifying prospects such a crucial stage in the selling process? Do you think innovations in telecommunications will require salespeople to do more or less prospecting and qualifying of prospects? Why?

2. If you were hired by Fidelity Investments to contact businesses and nonprofit organizations to sell them retirement plans, which prospecting methods do you think you would use? Why?

3. In making a cold call on a medium-sized manufacturing company to sell a contract building maintenance service, how would you go about qualifying the company?

4. It's October 1 and your first day on the job as a salesperson for a central air conditioning firm in a town of about sixty-five thousand people. Your boss, the owner of Stibb's Commercial Air Conditioning, has said, "Go out and get some business customers." Until now, Mr. Stibb has relied on a small advertisement in the local telephone directory to generate sales, but because sales are particularly slow during the fall and winter months, he has hired you as his first salesperson.

Your earnings will come solely from commissions. How will you prospect for potential customers?

5. Your sister and two of her female colleagues have recently graduated from business school, pooled their limited resources, and opened up an accounting firm in three rooms on the sixteenth floor of an office building in Los Angeles. The three partners want to audit the financial statements and annual reports of small- to medium-sized companies in the metropolitan area. They all attended the same East Coast high school and college, and none of them has any long-time friends or acquaintances in Los Angeles. Although you know little about selling accounting services, you promise to come up with a strategy. What prospecting methods do you think might best help the three accountants generate potential business clients?

6. What student prospecting strategies would you recommend to a market research firm that specializes in carrying out research projects and developing marketing plans for colleges and universities?

## PROJECTS FOR PERSONAL GROWTH

1. Prepare a list of ten organizations in your area that you think would be good prospects for the products listed below. Describe your sources and criteria for selecting the organizations and explain how you would go about qualifying them.

   - Automobile leasing
   - Overnight package or freight delivery
   - Professional nursing uniform supplies
   - Bottled water for offices

2. In newspapers or trade magazines, find five examples of companies using (a) telemarketing, (b) mail-in response cards, (c) toll-free telephone numbers, (d) web sites, or (e) a combination of one or more of these to generate leads. Explain the reasoning behind the lead-generating strategy of each approach.

3. Research and prepare a report on the trade show or exhibit marketing industry. In your report, cover the following points:

   - What is a trade show or exhibit?
   - Who attends trade shows?
   - How can a company generate leads or prospects by participating in a trade show?
   - What industries hold the largest shows?
   - What cities hold the most?
   - Is the number of trade shows increasing or decreasing each year? Why?

4. While reading your local newspaper or browsing the Internet over the next few days, find two industrial firms, two nonprofit organizations (such as a church, university, or museum), and two professional service firms (such as consulting or landscaping) who are prospecting through advertising, either online or offline. Critique the effectiveness of the six advertisements in accomplishing their objectives. How would you change each?

## CASE 3.1   PROSPECTING BY DRIVING AROUND

When the phone rings, Charlie Preston knows exactly who is on the other end. It is eight o'clock Wednesday evening, and his sales manager, Melinda White, punctual as always, is making her weekly checkup call to see how Charlie did last week. Charlie and Melinda work for RealVoice Corporation, a distributor of electronic communications equipment. One of the company's exciting new products, a portable email/cell phone device called the In-Touch 200, is about the size of a pack of cards, weighs only five ounces, and can be carried in a suitcoat pocket. RealVoice is a small player in this growing but highly competitive market, and they are trying to carve out a niche by marketing their products mainly to small- and medium-sized companies. Customers and prospects for RealVoice products include companies that have many salespeople and other employees (for example, delivery, installation, and maintenance people) who spend little time at the central headquarters office.

Charlie, who has been with RealVoice for less than four months, is not looking forward to this conversation with Melinda because he had a rather lackluster week. He completed only one sale to a small account with limited long-term profit potential for RealVoice. Although the three-day company training program for new salespeople covered many different prospecting methods, Charlie prefers to drive his company car out into his territory near Portland, Oregon, and become familiar with the companies and people in it. Business growth is exploding in the area, so the telephone directories are always out of date. Only by driving around his territory can Charlie be one of the first salespeople to locate and make calls on the new companies that have recently opened for business.

During his first three months on the job, Charlie had considerable success by merely driving around until he spotted an industrial park or a company whose parking lot contained a lot of look-alike, middle-range cars—the kind usually assigned to salespeople. Even during his daily routine of putting gas in his car, eating meals, and doing personal errands, Charlie makes a point to subtly prospect for business by starting conversations with people. Charlie used this technique to find four prospects during his first four months with RealVoice, and two of them he turned into customers after only a few sales calls. But this past month his sales have really slowed, probably because many area companies are cutting costs during a current economic slow-down. Charlie picks up the phone and tries to put himself into a positive, upbeat frame of mind before he speaks.

**CHARLIE:**   Hello.

**MELINDA:**   Hi Charlie, this is Melinda. How are you doing? Just calling to see how your week went.

**CHARLIE:**   Well, it was not one of my best weeks, but I've got a lot of pots heating up on the old stove.

[Charlie has a few accounts that he is working on that hold promise, but he knows Melinda is really interested in how many sales he made this week.]

**MELINDA:**   That's good, Charlie, but first, tell me about your week. How many sales did you make?

**CHARLIE:**   Unfortunately, I sold only one account last week, but I'm only about one sales call away on two others.

[Charlie fears Melinda's notorious wrath. Another rep in the company has told him about how upset Melinda becomes when a salesperson has poor weekly numbers. Instead, Charlie is surprised to hear her reply in a mild, comforting tone.]

(continued)

# PROSPECTING BY DRIVING AROUND (CONTINUED)

**MELINDA:**   Well, why don't you give me an idea of what happened on each call, and maybe we can figure out a way to change your luck.

[Feeling relieved by Melinda's approach, Charlie proceeds to describe the past week on the road.]

**CHARLIE:**   Let me start on a positive note. I did find three prospects this week that should turn into customers eventually. Last Thursday, while I was having coffee in a doughnut shop down in Salem, I met a guy named Carl Avery, who turned out to be the sales manager of Lixon Wholesale Foods. He's a high-energy guy who has ten sales reps located throughout the state. He said that one of his frustrations is that he has a hard time reaching his sales reps during the day and has been thinking about equipping each with a portable email or cell phone device. I told him that our new *In-Touch 200* did both jobs, and he was interested. So I followed him back to his office and showed him some of our latest product brochures and let him play with my own *In-Touch 200* for a few minutes. He seemed impressed. He even called to ask Joe Lixon, the company president, to come down for a look, but Mr. Lixon had gone for the day. Anyway, I tried to close Carl and get him to buy a few for his sales force on a trial basis, but he said he wasn't quite sure he was ready. He asked me to call him back in about three weeks, after he's had a chance to educate himself more about competitive products.

On Monday I had an appointment to see the president of Waller Rubber Company. I found out about this company through a friend of mine who buys tires from them for his bicycle repair business. The president told me that they sell products throughout the United States and Canada and that they have a twenty-five–member direct sales force. I told him that his company sounded just right for our RealVoice *In-Touch 200*. He told me that he didn't have the budget this year, but he was pretty sure that he would be interested about a year from now. Just then his secretary buzzed to remind him of a meeting. So he quickly thanked me for my time and walked me to the door. As he was leaving, he yelled back to me, "Why don't you see Pete over in MR? He might be interested." I didn't know what he meant by MR, and he was gone before I could ask. I waited for a few minutes by the secretary's desk to see if she knew what MR meant, but she was so engrossed in her phone conversation, I don't think she even noticed I was standing nearby. She's kind of an airhead, so she probably wouldn't have known anyway. So I headed on out for my next appointment.

**MELINDA:**   Have you checked out Lixon Wholesale Foods and Waller Rubber Company with our credit department for advanced approval for sales to them?

**CHARLIE:**   I haven't had a chance yet, but I'll do that as soon as I'm close to a sale. They're good-sized companies with nice facilities, so I'm sure there won't be any problems with either of them.

**MELINDA:**   You're probably right, but it's a good idea to check them out credit-wise before you spend any more time with them.

**CHARLIE:**   You're right. I'll call my friend, Bob Cammarota, in the credit department tomorrow to check both companies out. Before I forget, Melinda, I want to tell you what happened today while I was having a flat tire fixed at a service station. I struck up a conversation with a guy named Walt Stauffer who turns out to be the sales manager for a company that sells auto parts to service stations. He told me that they currently sell in twenty states and have thirty-five sales

*(continued)*

## CASE 3.1

# PROSPECTING BY DRIVING AROUND (CONTINUED)

reps, but are planning to cut back in the near future. He wasn't sure how many reps they are going to keep, but he liked the idea of a combination email and cell phone in one device. He looked over my *In-Touch 200* and our brochures for several minutes; so I know he's interested. He especially liked the size and design of our product, although he thought the price was a little high. He asked whether the payments could be spread out over a longer period of time, and I told him I would get back to him on that. I got his business card, and I'll call him on Monday to set up an appointment. I think this account offers good potential.

Overall, I averaged about six in-person calls a day last week, but most of my contacts were pretty much up-front flat rejections due to budget cut-backs. I didn't even see about a third of my prospects because they were in meetings. Guess I should have used my *In-Touch 200* to call or email ahead of time to reconfirm. Times are tough in my territory now, but I'll keep charging until things turn up again.

*Reprinted with permission of Paul Christ, West Chester University of Pennsylvania.*

## Questions

1. After hearing Charlie describe his week, what do you think his sales manager, Melinda, will say to him?
2. Do Charlie's prospecting strategies sound effective and efficient for his territory? Why? Can you offer Charlie any suggestions to improve his prospecting strategies and tactics?
3. Do you think RealVoice should help Charlie develop leads? What prospecting methods could RealVoice use in order to help Charlie and other company salespeople?
4. With its new product, the *In-Touch 200*, what can Charlie and/or RealVoice management do to generate leads and stimulate sales?
5. How do you think Charlie is performing in qualifying the leads he finds? What could he do better?

## CASE 3.2

# WHEN COLD CALLING TURNS COLD

Securevest Publishing Company has been in business for fifteen years producing reference books that provide financial and market information on major corporations located in the United States. These publications sell primarily to public and college libraries. Securevest reference books, which compete with similar publications sold by companies such as Standard and Poor and Moody, are typically published once a year in a comprehensive hardcover format. Unlike many of their rivals, Securevest does not provide monthly or quarterly updates to their reference books. Instead, the company has chosen to update their product on a biannual basis, thereby saving subscribers as much as 50 percent over competitors' prices.

Price is an important selling point for many small college, city, and county libraries, whose funds for reference materials are constrained by limited budgets. In order to keep prices below those of competitive products, Securevest also provides fewer company profiles in their publications. For example, its main publication, *The Securevest Industry Report* (a two-volume set) provides users with extensive financial and market data on the top three thousand publicly held companies in the United States, whereas competitors provide information on more than ten thousand companies. Securevest management believes that including less than a third of the company profiles of competitive products is a wise choice because studies indicate that about 75 percent of all users of reference materials are primarily interested in information on the top three thousand companies. Besides *Industry Report*, Securevest's product line includes financial summaries on the top one thousand privately held U.S. firms and specific industries such as health care, financial services, and manufacturing. Most competitive products profile about five thousand privately held U.S. firms.

Securevest salespeople usually open new accounts by selling the *Securevest Industry Report*. Within two weeks of the account's establishment, the sales rep makes a follow-up call to attempt to sell other Securevest publications. Principal duties of the field sales reps are to (1) locate and sell to new accounts and (2) maintain sales to existing accounts by providing superior customer service. Securevest salespeople have been known to deliver, within hours, a new volume to a library that loses or damages a Securevest publication.

As described in the sales training manual, written thirteen years ago by the company's founder, Jeffrey Breslin, the chief method of prospecting for new subscribers is cold calling. In bold type on the second page of the *Securevest Sales Training Manual* are these words of Mr. Breslin:

> In the introductory and growth periods of the product life cycle for Securevest reference publications, cold calling is the most effective method of locating and selling new accounts. Cold calling provides the best opportunity for maximizing sales because we compete with several well-known companies. Unless we arrive on the doorstep of prospects with our quality products in hand, it is too easy for prospects who don't recognize our name to refuse us that initial sales appointment. Once prospects see the quality of our reference volumes and hear our low prices, they will realize that their dollars go further with Securevest. Your job, as a resourceful Securevest salesperson, is to reach the buyer and make the sale on that initial in-person call. Remember that we are all family here at Securevest, and headquarters is always ready to help whenever you need us.

For many years, Securevest's sales force has used the cold call approach successfully. However, within the past few years, sales reps have begun to

(continued)

## WHEN COLD CALLING TURNS COLD (CONTINUED)

experience increasing difficulty in selling to new accounts. In fact, sales to new accounts actually declined last year for the first time in the firm's history. Securevest management is quite concerned with this development. At the annual sales meeting last month, the company president and several managers conducted an open forum in which the sales reps discussed problems they were encountering, including the following:

- Many sales reps believe that the public and college libraries in their territories are mostly saturated with reference books. One salesperson wondered whether other markets existed for Securevest products besides public and college libraries.
- Recent cuts in library budgets have forced many library staffs to reduce personnel and increase workloads. Consequently, librarians in charge of purchasing reference materials are under more time pressure and will not talk to cold call sales reps. Securevest sales reps often end up talking to someone who is neither a decision-maker nor even a key influencer.
- Several sales reps expressed the opinion that budget cuts, space limitations, and

rising prices for library books and materials of all kinds are constricting new reference purchases. Librarians in this predicament stick with established, well-known products that patrons know and will use.
- Increasing Internet use by library patrons has led many libraries to purchase online access to some of the most popular reference materials for their patrons. However, budget cuts have prevented many libraries from purchasing online access to the more expensive reference books.

*Reprinted with permission of Paul Christ, West Chester University of Pennsylvania.*

### Questions

1. What are some underlying reasons why Securevest salespeople are having increasing difficulty selling to new accounts?
2. What does the situation facing Securevest salespeople seem to tell you about cold-call prospecting?
3. What alternate prospecting techniques should Securevest salespeople consider? Why?
4. If you were a Securevest salesperson, what action would you now take in your territory?

## CHAPTER 4

# Planning the Sales Call:
# Steps to a Successful Approach

*"A man surprised is half beaten."*
Thomas Fuller

## After Reading This Chapter, You Should Understand:

- Why it's important to plan and prepare for the sales call.

- How to plan the sales call.

- How to prepare prospects for the initial sales call.

- What causes sales call reluctance.

- Which strategies to use in approaching the prospect.

- Necessary steps in greeting the prospect.

- How to interact with the prospect's receptionist.

**INSIDE PERSONAL SELLING:**
## Meet Glenda Blake of Houghton Mifflin

Selling a college textbook requires homework. Before meeting with a professor, Glenda Blake, a senior sales representative for Houghton Mifflin Company, finds out what courses he or she teaches, checks course enrollment, and learns what texts are currently assigned. She also researches copyright dates because professors using a new text are unlikely to switch to another text right away.

Much of the information Blake needs to plan a sales call—the courses, the number of sections, and the instructor's name, in many cases—comes from the class schedule and college catalog. "I do as much research as I can before I knock on the door of the people making the buying decision," she says. She often asks the department secretary for information and always visits the college bookstore to see what texts are being used.

Blake keeps detailed files on every account and reviews her notes before every sales meeting. If, for example, an instructor is interested in technology, she comes prepared to talk about the technology available for a particular book. Armed with all this information, she is ready to meet the professor.

Because she may visit dozens of instructors on one campus, Blake does not make individual appointments. She investigates office hours and, if a professor is not immediately available, she sets a time to meet or returns after class. Blake always begins by reintroducing herself and her company, "because instructors don't see me every day." Then, based on her homework, she will ask about the instructor's textbook needs.

Although she is measured on sales, Blake says customers "really see me more as a consultant, someone who lets them know what is going on in the textbook business. They have so much to do: teaching, research, seeing students, grading papers, preparing for class. If I can give them information to help make a decision, they see me as an asset rather than a nuisance."

Blake had to overcome some nervousness when she first began in sales. However, because she was a reporter for her college newspaper, she knew how to get in to see and talk with all kinds of people. She also learned from her colleagues. "Early on, I was able to observe my manager and follow an experienced rep," she says. "Even now, if I see a colleague do something that works really well, I have no problem borrowing it."

Rather than rehearse a sales pitch—"I don't think it would come across as natural," Blake explains—she concentrates on understanding the customer. "I believe that if you are prepared and go in with a professional attitude and a polite personality," she says, "people will talk to you. They will help you do your job. I listen carefully and tailor what I say based on customer needs."

**Preapproach** The approach planning stage of the selling process.

**Approach** The first face-to-face contact with the prospect.

**W**ell, now you have your list of potential prospects on whom to call. You're probably anxious to go out and start calling on them. After all, "time is money." Staying in the office certainly won't help you generate any sales—or will it? Making sales calls on customers, especially first-time calls, takes preparation. Just as a baseball player takes batting practice to prepare for the game, professional salespeople "practice"—prepare themselves—for their sales calls. Failure to do so produces less than spectacular results. And you do want to be spectacular, don't you?

"Failing to plan is planning to fail" is an old saying in sales that remains true today. Unless each sales call is carefully planned and prepared before approaching the prospect, chances for success are slim. Planning is essential for salespeople to consistently achieve desired results. It enables salespeople to identify their goals and decide on the steps necessary to accomplish them. The approach planning stage of the selling process is often called the **preapproach.** Many sales managers view the preapproach as even more important than the next stage, which is the **approach** itself. Planning provides salespeople with an overall framework for decision making, not only *before* the sales call but *during* and *after* the sales call. We will consider both the preapproach and the approach stages of the selling process in this chapter.

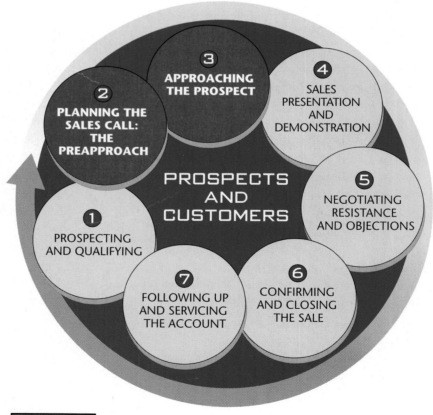

**FIGURE 4.1**

THE PERSONAL SELLING PROCESS (PSP)

## IMPORTANCE OF PLANNING THE SALES CALL

Top-performing salespeople have many reasons for taking so much care in thinking about and planning their approaches to prospects and customers. Thorough planning helps ensure their success. Let's discuss some of the major reasons for planning sales calls.

### Establishing Sales Call Focus

Each sales call should have realistic, meaningful, and measurable objectives. These objectives provide direction and focus for the sales call. Without direction, sales reps will be unfocused in their interaction with the prospect, thus squander precious time and risk incurring the prospect's displeasure for wasting his or her time, too. Clear-cut objectives enable salespeople to determine after the sales call whether they were effective (met their goals) or not, then analyze why they obtained the results they did. When establishing call objectives, some sales personnel set a *primary objective* (dominant or major result), a minimum objective (lowest acceptable result), and an optimal objective (best possible result).

One large telephone company's salespeople are taught to plan all of their sales calls to achieve one or more of three objectives:

1. *Generate sales*—sell particular products to target customers on designated sales calls.

2. *Develop the market*—lay the groundwork for generating new business by educating customers and gaining visibility with prospective buyers.

3. *Protect the market*—learn competitors' strategies and tactics and protect relationships with current customers.

### Improving Effectiveness and Efficiency

Salespeople must consider not only how quickly and directly they accomplish their sales call goals—*effectiveness*—but how many resources they use in the process—*efficiency*. Inefficient use of such resources as a salesperson's time, expense account, and promotional materials can make sales unprofitable. In planning the sales call, the salesperson must determine the desired specific goal and the exact steps necessary to reach that goal at minimal cost.

### Preparing for Customer Reaction

Top salespeople prepare for sales calls by anticipating prospects' possible responses to each step and statement in the selling process. Prospects will soon lose confidence and respect for a salesperson who is poorly prepared to respond to their questions. After all, having the necessary information *before* you see the prospect will increase your credibility, and having to respond to the prospect's question with "I don't know" won't. Establishing credibility can augment salesperson persuasiveness[1] and is a key means of enhancing customer trust in your professionalism, which strengthens the buyer-seller relationship.[2] It's a good idea for the salesperson to go through every step of the planned sales presentation from the perspective of an inquisitive and demanding potential *customer*. Putting yourself in the customer's shoes in a sales call rehearsal will enhance the success of subsequent buyer-seller interactions and ultimately selling effectiveness.[3]

### Enhancing Self-Confidence and Professionalism

*Planning is preparing for the future,* and the best-prepared salesperson is usually the most confident, professional, and successful. The very process of planning—establishing sales call objectives, determining the most effective and efficient methods with which to accomplish the objectives, anticipating and preparing for prospect reactions, and rehearsing the sales call—helps build the salesperson's confidence and professionalism. Such planning provides direction that allows the salesperson to feel comfortable about the activities in which he or she soon will engage.

### Determining Which Selling Strategies to Use

Sometimes the sales call objective is simply to introduce yourself or gather more information about the prospect's needs or to develop a closer relationship. At other times the objective may be to win a large order. Each objective, depending on the stage in the selling process and on the prospect's needs and personality, requires a different sales presentation strategy.

### Avoiding Errors

Gathering prospect information ahead of the sales call helps salespeople reduce their chances of making serious errors in front of the prospect. The information obtained can be woven into the approach, the sales presentation, and each of the other remaining steps in the PSP. A sales rep who possesses the requisite knowledge is unlikely to say something or do something that will rankle the prospect. For example, if you discover that the prospect is reluctant to use the latest technology in his firm owing to his lack of technical knowledge, you would not want to exacerbate those feelings during the call. Or, if you know that the prospect has had a good relationship with her current vendor for years, you won't want to disparage the competitor. Of course, it's never a good idea to put down any competitor.

## PLANNING FOR THE SALES CALL: SIX STEPS TO PREAPPROACH SUCCESS

The type of sales situation, customer, and products can cause preapproach planning and strategy to vary widely. Some salespeople call on hundreds of small accounts; others call on only a few big ones. Some salespeople are sales team coordinators; others operate largely on their own. Some salespeople spend weeks or months in gathering preapproach information about large potential customers. Others must size up a prospect quickly in the showroom or at an industrial trade show, rapidly plan and make an approach, qualify the prospect by asking questions and interpreting verbal and nonverbal responses, and then tailor an impromptu sales presentation to meet the prospect's dominant needs.

Although sales call planning is always essential, it *increases* in importance when

- the customer's decision is complex, high involvement, and high risk;
- future interactions and negotiations with the customer are expected;
- the customer's needs are unique;
- the customer has access to a range of alternatives; and
- the sale is critical to the salesperson.

Although the planning and preparation steps differ for initial sales calls as compared to subsequent sales calls, six basic steps lead to preapproach success, as outlined in Table 4.1. Assume a selling scenario in which you are the salesperson and think about ways you would prepare your preapproach. Start by picking a product you like. Now, how would you prepare yourself to approach a prospect with a sales proposal for this product using the six steps to preapproach success?

## Prepare the Prospect for the Initial Sales Call

A salesperson who fails to warm up a prospect before making that first *cold call*, may receive an icy reception. One approach for favorably preparing a prospect for the sales call is **seeding.**

**Seeding.** Sowing seeds for a potential future sales harvest requires prospect-focused activities carried out well in advance of a sales call. First, the salesperson identifies industries or customer categories that offer high sales potential and makes a file folder for each. Second, the salesperson quickly learns as much as possible about the most important concerns of these industries, such as new product development, product quality, return on investment, or employee turnover. Third, the salesperson keeps these needs in mind while

**Seeding** Prospect-focused activities, such as mailing pertinent news articles, carried out several weeks or months before a sales call.

---

| TABLE 4.1 |
|---|
| **SIX STEPS IN PREAPPROACH PLANNING** |
| 1. Prepare the prospect for the initial sales call. |
| 2. Sell the sales call appointment. |
| 3. Gather and analyze information about the prospect. |
| 4. Identify the prospect's problems and needs. |
| 5. Choose the best sales presentation strategy. |
| 6. Rehearse your approach. |

browsing through newspapers, trade journals, or general business magazines and cuts out any pertinent articles. Fourth, the salesperson selects specific companies with high sales potential from each of the industries and finds out the names of the key people in the buying center at each company. Fifth, the salesperson begins the campaign to develop a positive *preapproach* image for himself or herself. Several times prior to the initial sales call, the salesperson picks a relevant article from the appropriate file folder and mails it to the prospect along with a business card (but no sales literature) and a handwritten note saying something like "Hope you'll find the attached interesting." Many salespeople also use push technology (discussed in chapter 2) to deliver news articles to prospects via email. Using key words pertinent to a given prospect, a salesperson can quickly identify relevant articles. After mailing four to six articles to a prospect over a period of several weeks (the "seeding"), the salesperson has created a relationship that will probably ensure a positive reception for the initial call. An often overlooked but important point is to enclose the articles in a *distinctive* envelope to ensure the prospect remembers receiving your mailings.

### Sell the Sales Call Appointment

No one wants his or her time wasted, so the salesperson must develop a persuasive strategy to sell the prospect on the initial sales appointment. This effort is directed at piquing the prospect's attention and interest prior to making a face-to-face sales call. In essence, you must sell the prospect on why his or her time will be well spent talking with you about your product or service. One way of doing this is to *prenotify* prospects of your intention to call on them.

**Prenotification** A technique using an in-person cold call, a letter, a fax, an email, or a telephone call to send a strong signal to the prospect that the salesperson would like to schedule a sales call appointment.

**Prenotification.**  One step beyond seeding and sales promotion is the technique of **prenotification.** Whereas the aforementioned techniques simply make a prospect aware of you and your company, prenotification sends a strong signal to the prospect that you would like to make the initial sales call soon. The salesperson uses the *telephone*, a *letter*, a *fax*, an *email*, or an *in-person cold call* to prenotify the prospect of his or her intention to make the first sales call and persuades the prospect to set a specific date, time, and place for the appointment. Successful sales personnel have found prenotification to be an effective approach for achieving a set date.

**Cold Call** Initial face-to-face contact with a prospect who is not expecting the salesperson to call.

***Prenotification by Cold Call.***  Sales personnel sometimes attempt first-time face-to-face contact with a prospect without an appointment (hence the term **cold call**). Such efforts may lead to an actual meeting with the prospect or arrangement of a subsequent appointment (the "prenotification" part of the cold call). For instance, one resourceful salesperson for a large office equipment supplier often sets up appointments by making an in-person cold call on the prospect's business. If the prospect is willing to see her on the cold call, great. However, if the prospect is unavailable, this salesperson writes a date and time on her business card, hands it to the prospect's secretary, and says, "I've written a day and time on my business card to meet with Mr. Barley. Would you please ask him to call me if that time is inconvenient so we can schedule another time?" This technique might not work for everyone, but this saleswoman has such a friendly personality that she readily wins over secretaries, who then help sell the appointments to their bosses.

***Prenotification by Letter, Fax, or Email.*** Salespeople for one marketer of industrial sealing devices use written prenotifications to obtain their first sales appointment with a prospect. A week before they call on a prospect, they mail (or sometimes fax) a postcard with a list of product categories the company sells and a message saying that they look forward to visiting the prospect next week at a certain time. This way, when they arrive at the prospect's office, they can honestly tell the secretary that the prospect has been informed about the sales call. Customers generally feel obligated to accept a sales call that has been announced in advance. This technique makes the salespeople seem much more professional than salespeople who show up unexpectedly at the prospect's office. Many sales reps use a similar procedure with email. Prospect email addresses are readily available from various search engines (for example, Yahoo! at www.yahoo.com) or simply by calling the firms and asking for them.

***Prenotification by Telephone.*** One marketing researcher has found an effective three-stage approach to telephone prenotification.[4] First, you introduce yourself, your company, and your product to the prospect and obtain the prospect's permission to send product literature. Second, you mail the product literature and any product samples. Third, after allowing the prospect a short time to "digest" your mailing, you make a follow-up phone call and request a personal appointment. An illustration of this process appears in Table 4.2.

Like most telephone prenotification strategies, this three-stage approach works because it requires *commitment* from the prospect on three different occasions. At the first stage, the prospect is obliged to provide feedback expressing at least some interest in you, your company, and/or your product by granting you permission to mail product information. At the second stage, the prospect receives and, you hope, reviews the material you mailed. At the third stage, during the follow-up phone call, you attempt to (1) discover whether or not the prospect read the product literature, (2) determine the prospect's reactions to the literature, (3) encourage questions because they are the best indicators of interest in the product, and (4) arrange a day and time for a personal visit.

## Gather and Analyze Information about the Prospect

Today and tomorrow's successful salespeople will be those who have the best information about their targeted customers. Although some basic information about prospects is gathered in the prospecting stage, the salesperson usually must acquire more in-depth information for the actual sales call. The more information a salesperson has about a prospect, the better prepared he or she is to handle any situation during a sales call. Almost any relevant information can be useful. Essentials include the prospect's name and its pronunciation, nickname if preferred, job title, duties, education, work experience, level of technical expertise, purchasing authority, buying behavior, personality, after work activities and interests, and maybe even the names of family members.

TABLE 4.2

## PRENOTIFICATION BY TELEPHONE TO OBTAIN A SALES CALL APPOINTMENT

After learning the name of the purchasing agent or key decision-maker, the salesperson using the prenotification phone call approach to obtain an appointment might continue along the following lines.

When the prospect's receptionist answers the call, the salesperson can say: *Hello! My name is _____, and I'm trying to reach Mr. _____ to tell him some exciting news. Is he in?*

When the prospect answers the phone, the salesperson can say:

*Hello, Mr. _____, my name is _____, and I'm a marketing representative for _____ Company. We've developed some outstanding new materials-handling equipment and customer service concepts that can save your company many thousands of dollars yearly. Several of our current customers have already increased their profits by 10 to 20 percent using our products. Because yours is a progressive company, you might be interested in seeing our latest literature on these products. I didn't want to clutter up your mailbox with something you might discard as junk mail, so I thought it best to call first and get your permission to mail the literature. May I send you this information?*

*Good! I'll mail it today. I'll put it in a large blue folder with our company name and red horse trademark on the outside, so you'll be able to readily identify it. Is there any special department code I should type on the folder to make sure that it is routed to you as fast as possible? I'll give you a call in a few days, after you've had a chance to review the literature, to see what questions you have. Will that be okay? Good! I'll put the information in the mail today. I think you'll be pleased to see what we can offer you. I look forward to talking with you again soon, Mr. _____. Thank you for your time!*

### Possible Prospect Resistance

"Our company is not interested in any materials-handling equipment at this time."

"We're perfectly happy with the equipment we've got now."

"We don't do business over the phone."

Responses:

*Mr. _____, I'm calling purely in the spirit of "there's no harm in asking." You've got absolutely nothing to lose—and possibly a lot to gain—by looking over the literature I'll send you. I'm confident that you'll find our new equipment offers you substantial potential savings while providing better service to your customers. We're getting very positive testimonials from other customers. Two companies in your area, _____ and _____, are using the equipment and are very pleased. I'd be delighted to visit your office to answer any questions you may have about the specific benefits you can expect. And I'll also give you a videotaped demonstration in your office or a live demonstration at our local plant, whichever you prefer. So, you can't lose Mr. _____. May I mail you the literature today?*

### Tactical Hints

Don't try to hard-sell prospects. Talk to them like a friend or neighbor. Make reassuring statements like "Some of our satisfied customers were initially skeptical about the materials-handling equipment until they observed it in action and saw how it improved their company profits."

Using a basic format like the one shown in Table 4.3, salespeople can keep up-to-date records on each of their industrial prospects and customers. As relevant information emerges, it can be added to the *insights and comments* section of this form. Ideally, all of this information can be maintained on the salesperson's laptop computer so that it can be called up for review just prior to seeing the prospect.

One caveat is in order when collecting preapproach information. You must assess the information with caution. There is always a chance that the information you collect will be inaccurate or misinterpreted. Misinterpreting the information can be costly, leading to the loss of a sale or even a customer. One study found that salespeople tend to have relatively inaccurate perceptions of their customers. Specifically, sales reps inaccurately estimated the performance, price, and service levels that their customers wanted.[5] Such incorrect beliefs will lead you to perform in ways that do not satisfy the buyer.

*The more information a salesperson has regarding a prospect, the better prepared he or she will be to handle any situation during a sales call.*
Steve Prezant/Corbis

Numerous sources of information can help salespeople strategically plan their approach to organizational (business, not-for-profit, and government) prospects. Major sources (similar to those employed when prospecting) include (1) information available in various departments in the salesperson's company—marketing, accounting, credit, purchasing, and data processing; (2) federal, state, and local government reports; (3) trade association newsletters, brochures, and literature from trade shows and exhibits; (4) trade journals; (5) online and offline directories, indexes, and bibliographies; (6) mailing lists bought from commercial companies; (7) the prospect and the prospect's business (through observation); and (8) current customers of the seller. Let's discuss two sources that can be especially helpful: in-house purchasing agents and electronic directories and databases.

**In-House Purchasing Agents.** Buyers in the *seller's* purchasing department are a good source of information on business prospects because they may be procuring products and services from these companies. Because *reciprocity* (you buy from me and I'll buy from you) is a widespread business practice, it's always a good idea to see if your company is a buyer as well as a seller to the company you're calling on. This can be especially valuable if your company is large and has many different departments or groups that individually buy and sell.

**Electronic Directories and Databases.** Business data can also be purchased for computer analysis. The *Electronic Yellow Pages,* containing listings from nearly all the nation's 4,800 phone books, is the largest directory of American companies available. *ABI/Inform* presents background data on industries, companies, products, and current business topics from 550 publications.

TABLE 4.3

## ORGANIZATIONAL PROFILE

**Company Name** _____

**Address** _____

**Telephone Number** _____ **Fax Number** _____

**E-mail address** _____ **Company Web Site** _____

**Type of Business**: _____ Manufacturer _____ Wholesaler _____ Retailer _____

Service _____ Government _____ Petroleum _____ Not-for-Profit _____

Utility _____ Mine/Quarry _____ Other Organization Type _____

**Buying Pattern**: _____ Weekly _____ Monthly _____ Semiannually _____

Yearly _____ Seasonal _____ As needed _____ Other _____

### PURCHASING PATTERN

| Products Purchased | Annual $ Amount | Company Share | Brand Preferred | Competitive Suppliers |
|---|---|---|---|---|
| 1. | | | | |
| 2. | | | | |
| 3. | | | | |
| 4. | | | | |
| 5. | | | | |
| 6. | | | | |
| 7. | | | | |
| 8. | | | | |

**Totals** _____

### CUSTOMER CONTACTS

*INITIATORS:*

| | Names/Responsibilities | Department | Calling Hours |
|---|---|---|---|
| 1. | _____ | | |
| 2. | _____ | | |

| | Contacts | Dates | Results |
|---|---|---|---|
| | | | |

*GATEKEEPERS:*

| | Names/Responsibilities | Department | Calling Hours |
|---|---|---|---|
| 1. | _____ | | |
| 2. | _____ | | |

| | Contacts | Dates | Results |
|---|---|---|---|
| | | | |

**TABLE 4.3**

## ORGANIZATIONAL PROFILE (CONTINUED)

**INFLUENCERS:**

| Names/Responsibilities | Department | Calling Hours |
|---|---|---|
| 1. | | |
| 2. | | |

| Contacts | Dates | Results |
|---|---|---|
| | | |

**DECIDERS:**

| Names/Responsibilities | Department | Calling Hours |
|---|---|---|
| 1. | | |
| 2. | | |

| Contacts | Dates | Results |
|---|---|---|
| | | |

**BUYERS:**

| Names/Responsibilities | Department | Calling Hours |
|---|---|---|
| 1. | | |
| 2. | | |

| Contacts | Dates | Results |
|---|---|---|
| | | |

**USERS:**

| Names/Responsibilities | Department | Calling Hours |
|---|---|---|
| 1. | | |
| 2. | | |

| Contacts | Dates | Results |
|---|---|---|
| | | |

**Insights and Comments:** _____
_____
_____
_____
_____
_____
_____
_____

Standard & Poor's *Compustat* provides detailed balance sheet and income statement information for more than five thousand companies. *Industry Data Sources* compiles information from trade association reports, government publications, and industry studies by brokerage firms on sixty-five major industries. *Economic Information Systems (EIS)* maintains data on about four hundred thousand establishments. *TRINET* Data Base of U.S. Business Information gives sales and market share information for five hundred thousand businesses, including addresses, numbers of employees, decision-makers, sales, and market information. *Dun's Market Identifiers* reports information on more than two million U.S. businesses with ten or more employees, including address, product, financial, and marketing information.

Hundreds of online database vendors, including Compuserve, Inc., Bibliographic Retrieval Service (BRS), Dow Jones News Retrieval, and Dialog Information Services, Inc., provide access to more than two hundred databases in a variety of business and scientific fields. Some provide electronic access to hundreds of business databases, newsletters, company annual reports, and investment firm reports. As computer databanks continue to proliferate and computer software increases in versatility, salespeople will be able to obtain instant access to prospect data organized in any way desired. Only a few minutes before meeting the prospect, perhaps while waiting in the car or reception area, the salesperson will be able to electronically call up and review relevant information about the prospect, including the objectives and strategy for this particular sales call. Some companies have made rapid progress toward this scenario, as described in the *From the Command Post* below.

## FROM THE COMMAND POST: ONLINE INFORMATION SYSTEM FOR SALESPEOPLE

At one chemical producer, sales representatives obtain needed information from an online automated information system. The system updates the salespeople daily on their accounts, products, and performance. Once a field salesperson signs on at a terminal, menus appear on the screen that present different options, depending on the type of information sought. Before making a sales call, the salesperson can obtain an order status report summarizing shipments along with an explanation of the reasons for unfilled orders. Data can also be secured on specific products the customer bought this month, the previous month, and for the year to date. After obtaining data on buying activity, the salesperson can switch to another menu that shows sales forecasts for each product and the progress toward those objectives. The system was designed to make the terminals as user-friendly as possible. After less than four hours training, 95 percent of the time salespeople can locate the information they want with just two keystrokes. Salespeople are assured of the latest data because the system is hooked into the company's automated order billing system. The database is updated constantly as new orders come in and shipments go out. Thus, salespeople can obtain data on everything that occurred up to 6 P.M. the previous day.

## KEEPING UP ONLINE: PROCTER & GAMBLE COMPANY

**P**rocter & Gamble maintains a wealth of sales information on its database. How might a salesperson who sells packaging materials use this web site to learn more about P&G's packaging needs?

www.pg.com

### Identify the Prospect's Problems and Needs

Prior to the initial sales call, it is difficult to know the prospect's *specific* needs. However, by carefully analyzing the preapproach information gathered, you can often identify basic problems the prospect is facing and establish the general area of that prospect's needs. An obvious place to learn more about a prospect company's problems and needs is their web site. Consider the situation in *Keeping Up Online*, then go to Procter & Gamble's web site to gather appropriate preapproach information.

Uncovering the specific organizational problems and needs of a business prospect usually requires an initial sales call. During the call, some salespeople use a technique referred to as **SPIN** to quickly zero in on the prospect's needs and achieve commitment. Here's what SPIN stands for and how it can be used:

**SPIN** A selling technique that allows the salesperson to identify a prospect's major needs quickly. The acronym refers to *Situation, Problem, Implications,* and *Needs payoff.*

- *Situation:* First, the salesperson tries to learn about the prospect's situation. For example, a photocopier salesperson might ask, "How many copies do you make a month in your office?" "What kinds of documents do you most often copy?" "Who usually makes the decision to buy copier equipment?" Notice that the sales rep is keying in on the prospect's environment in which the product (copier) is used.
- *Problem:* Second, the salesperson identifies a problem that the prospect regularly encounters with the present products. For example, the copier sales rep might ask, "Do you have problems copying blue ink, like on blueprints?" "Do you find that your present copier is so complex that only a few people use it?" "Do you find that your present copier breaks down frequently?" All three inquiries focus on potential difficulties the prospect is currently having with her present product (copier).
- *Implication:* Third, the salesperson learns the implications, or results, of the problem. For example, the copier salesperson could ask, "Do you have to go to the trouble of changing the copier setting or have to do the messy job of changing the copier's ink supply in order to copy blue ink?" "Do you have to do other people's photocopying because they don't know how to use your present complex copier?" "Do you have to go to another department to try to get your copying done

when your copier breaks down?" Here, the salesperson examines the consequences of the prospect's using the current competitive product.

- *Needs Payoff:* Finally, the salesperson proposes a solution to the problem and asks for some kind of commitment from the prospect. For example, the sales rep might inquire, "If I could provide you with a machine that would copy blue ink, would you be interested?" "If I could supply you with a copier so simple to operate that even the CEO can use it, would you be interested?" "If I had a copier for you that seldom breaks down, would you be interested?" In this final step, the sales rep is set on arriving at a sound solution to the prospect's problem and then obtaining the prospect's commitment to making the purchase or, at least, agreement to try the product.

Note that in all of these sample questions the first commitment asked for is simply one of "interest." In most organizational selling situations, the initial sales call mainly allows the salesperson and prospect to meet and learn about each other. Pushing too hard for a close at this time might alienate the prospect. Once the prospect has indicated that he or she is interested, however, it's usually easy to convince the prospect to commit to another sales call—and a full sales presentation.

## Choose the Best Sales Presentation Strategy

After discovering the prospect's unique problems and needs, the next step to preapproach success is to choose an appropriate sales presentation strategy. Although we will discuss various sales presentation strategies in detail in the next chapter, this is a good time to mention two concepts. Together, they provide an excellent guide for choosing the most appropriate sales presentation strategy for each prospect. First, the truly customer-oriented salesperson (recall chapter 1) strives at all times to identify and solve customer problems by skillfully observing, listening, and asking probing questions. Second, the most successful salespeople learn how to "flex" (adapt) their communication styles with their prospects' communication styles (which we'll discuss in chapter 11). For now, keep these key concepts in mind as you prepare your sales presentation.

## Rehearse Your Approach

As top athletes, public speakers, and professional entertainers know, the more they practice their skills, the more successful they become. So rehearse, rehearse, rehearse until you have mastered your total sales presentation and feel comfortable and confident about it. Do not memorize a canned spiel, but keep in mind the key points you want to make in each part of the sales presentation and other stages of the selling process. Carefully planning, preparing, and rehearsing each sales call will lead you to sales success, especially when approaching a new customer or a former customer that no longer buys from your company. This latter situation is described in *It's Up To You.*

## IT'S UP TO YOU

Y ou notice in your company's records that a customer in your new territory, Excelsior Parts, bought one of your firm's heavy duty photocopiers for small businesses about five years ago. You hope that Excelsior might be ready to replace that old copier with one of the new much faster, higher print quality models. Unfortunately, the last salesperson for your territory is long gone, and she left behind no information about the account. In fact, internal records show only the address and telephone number for Excelsior Parts—nothing about what the firm does, who are its principals, how large it is, or the last time one of your firm's salespeople called there.

Surprisingly, there is no record of any service calls for Excelsior either. Your company's photocopiers are high quality, but not good enough to not need servicing for five years. It's very likely that Excelsior has already replaced the old copier with a competitor's brand. However, the old copier was a top of the line portable model costing about $4,000, so Excelsior may still have it but is obtaining service elsewhere. How do you prepare for and rehearse a sales call on a former customer that hasn't been contacted by your company in nearly five years? If your company is going to re-establish a relationship with Excelsior, it seems clear that it's up to you.

## INITIAL CALL RELUCTANCE—SALES STAGE FRIGHT

Once you have marched up all six steps to preapproach success, you may have still another barrier to overcome, especially if you are a new sales rep. One of the biggest problems new salespeople face is picking up the phone and initiating contact with prospects. Many salespeople, both experienced and novice, suffer from *sales call reluctance*. It is a kind of sales stage fright that can persist regardless of what they sell, how well they have been trained, or how much they believe in the product and the company.

Sales call reluctance can be attributed to *sales call anxiety* (SCA)—the fear of being negatively evaluated and rejected by customers. SCA has four components. One dimension is *negative evaluation of the self*. The salesperson is insecure about his or her ability to perform well and exhibit a favorable impression in front of the customer. The second element of SCA is *imagined negative evaluations from customers*. Salespeople with SCA wish to convey a strong and positive impression of themselves, yet they perceive that customers think ill of them. A third factor of SCA is *physiological symptoms*. That is, salespeople with SCA have adverse physical reactions to making sales calls (for example, sweating, shaky hands, dizziness, and an unsteady voice). The fourth component of SCA entails urges to engage in *protective actions*. Salespeople with SCA tend to employ self-protective responses during a sales call (for example, avoiding eye contact with the prospect, speaking quickly, fiddling with the hands). All of these have a detrimental impact on salespeople's performance unless they can effectively be overcome.[6]

---

TABLE 4.4

## KINDS OF SALES CALL RELUCTANCE

- **Social or Self-Image Threat**—belief that sales calls are sure to go wrong, resulting in personal humiliation.
- **Intrusion Sensitivity**—fear of upsetting prospects by interrupting and intruding on them.
- **Analysis Paralysis**—overanalyzing and over-preparing for the sales call, then becoming too petrified to take action.
- **Group Fright**—fear of making presentations before groups of people; this fear is akin to the widespread dread of public speaking.
- **Social Class or Celebrity Intimidation**—fear of contacting affluent or prominent prospects.
- **Role Ambivalence**—embarrassment about the perceived negative role of selling as a career choice.
- **Exploitation Guilt**—apprehension that family, relatives, and friends will consider sales approaches as exploitative, so such "close" prospects are ignored.

---

Sales call reluctance can take many forms. Most new salespeople suffer some of these at one time or another. One salesperson who earns in the high six figures was so worried about making sales calls that she almost dropped out of a sales career after her first year selling Samuel Adams beer to nightclubs and restaurants. She was especially reluctant to make cold calls. In her words, "My mother always taught me to be polite, and I felt that making sales calls on prospects was like showing up for dinner without being invited." Not until this young woman began to use some of the sales techniques that she had learned in school to turn cold calls into warm calls—prenotification and obtaining referrals—did her fears begin to go away. After awhile, she learned that most of her prospects and customers were pleased to see her and to talk about their business needs. So, don't worry that you might have some of the fears shown in Table 4.4. If you persist in using the techniques and skills you'll learn from this text and in your classroom exercises, your fears will desist.

Many of the above barriers to making sales calls can be gradually and even readily overcome through the following efforts:

- Listen carefully to the excuses other salespeople use to justify call reluctance and learn to objectively analyze your own excuses.
- Use supportive role-playing and discussions with sales colleagues to overcome fear.
- Make some initial prospect contacts with a partner for support; then make calls without partner support.
- Review and reenact recent sales calls with sales colleagues to constructively critique performance for signs of progress.
- Shift the focus from individual prospect personalities to sales objectives by setting them down in writing prior to making a sales call.

• Rehearse sales calls with sales colleagues to reinforce positive behaviors.
• Observe and model the behavior of successful salespeople.

Keep in mind that even the top professionals become nervous before important initial sales calls. And as famous scientist Marie Curie once said, "Nothing in life is to be feared. It is only to be understood." Think of your discomfort this way: Your nervousness shows that you really care about your prospect and your selling performance. In fact, perhaps you should worry if you are *never* nervous before an important initial sales call!

## APPROACHING THE PROSPECT

Although a letter, a telephone call, an email, or a brief cold call is often perfectly acceptable for arranging an initial sales call, most professional selling situations absolutely require that the actual approach be a well-planned, face-to-face meeting with the prospect. Despite all that we have said about the usefulness of computer and telecommunications technologies, most prospects remain most impressed—and best persuaded—by an *in-person* visit from a salesperson. And the old saying that "you never get a second chance to make a first impression," suggests how important that first contact with the prospect can be.

When we meet new people, we tend to size them up or categorize them in some way. In essence, people start to make up their minds about others within seconds after meeting them. We tend to think, "Boy, this guy is pushy" or "She really seems bright and nice." Clothes and accessories (for example, glasses, briefcase, umbrella, jewelry, pen), general grooming, facial expressions, body postures, voice tones and inflections, and choice of words all send messages.

The first few minutes of interaction between the salesperson and prospect are crucial in creating an impression that may be slow to change. In fact, a prospect may decide whether or not to buy from the salesperson within minutes of the initial interaction. Thus, we need to do all we can to make sure that the prospect's first impression of us is a positive one.[7]

The approach must build and hold the prospect's attention and interest. Business prospects are busy people, and you must convince them that meeting with you is not a waste, but in fact offers a potential benefit. Therefore, an important part of the approach is to set yourself apart from other sales reps. Just as companies try to differentiate their products to gain a competitive advantage, you want to positively differentiate yourself from all of the other salespeople a prospect may encounter.

*During the first few minutes, interactions between the salesperson and prospect create an impression that may be difficult to change.*
Corbis

| TABLE 4.5 |
|---|

## STRATEGIES FOR APPROACHING PROSPECTS

| **Non-Product-Related Approaches** | |
|---|---|
| **Self-Introduction** | Smoothly and professionally greet prospect. |
| **Mutual Acquaintance or Reference** | Mention the names of satisfied customers whom the prospect respects. |
| **Free Gift or Sample** | Offer a free gift, sample, or luncheon invitation. |
| **Dramatic Act** | Do something dramatic to capture the prospect's attention. |
| **Piquing Interest Approaches** | |
| **Customer-Benefit** | Offer the customer a benefit immediately. |
| **Curiosity** | Offer the prospect a benefit that appeals to the prospect's curiosity. |
| **Consumer-Directed Approaches** | |
| **Compliment or Praise** | Subtly but sincerely compliment the prospect. |
| **Survey** | Ask permission to obtain information about whether the prospect might need your product. |
| **Question** | Involve the prospect in two-way communication early on by asking a question. |
| **Product-Related Approaches** | |
| **Product or Ingredient** | Show the customer the product or a model of the product. |
| **Product Demonstration** | Begin demonstrating the product upon first meeting the prospect. |

Depending upon the selling situation, you can choose from several effective methods for approaching the prospect, as outlined in Table 4.5. These methods can be categorized into non-product-related approaches, piquing interest approaches, consumer-directed approaches, and product-related approaches.[8]

### Non-Product-Related Approaches

**Self-Introduction Approach.** A warm smile and firm handshake are important beginnings and endings of sales calls. In the self-introduction approach, sales reps greet prospects by name and give their own name and company. For example: "Good morning, Mr. Stevens. I'm Marie Potts from IBM, here for our ten o'clock appointment." Stating the prospect's name is a means of acknowledging the uniqueness of the prospect and potentially reducing invisible barriers between the salesperson and the prospect. Most salespeople present their business card at this point, but some prefer to wait until the close of the interview for emphasis.

**Mutual Acquaintance or Reference Approach.** Mentioning the names of satisfied customers respected by the prospect (even if they are competitors) can be a compelling approach. For example, "Your colleague, George Ferguson at Monsanto, has just switched to our process, and so have four of the top five chemical companies in the area." This kind of statement can impel prospects to think, "Gee, if they bought it, maybe I should, too." Testimonial letters from satisfied customers can be especially valuable when selling high-investment or high-risk products or services (for example, major capital expenditures on an office building or a company jet aircraft). Salespeople must avoid mere name dropping, however, because prospects will often contact the referenced person before buying. Therefore, be sure that the individual will verify your testimonial.

**Free Gift or Sample Approach.** Door-to-door salespeople long ago discovered that a cosmetic sample, key chain, or free toothbrush can help establish good will and gain entry to a prospect's home. Similarly, professional salespeople can offer prospects a luncheon invitation, a free seminar, trial use of a product, or a limited sample of services (for example, a basic estate planning analysis for a firm's managers). When a buyer who relished lemon drops kept stonewalling, one enterprising salesperson sent the buyer ten pounds of lemon drops. After receiving the candy, the buyer was so touched by such thoughtfulness that he immediately called the salesperson, arranged an appointment for the next day, and became the salesperson's best account.[9] A chemical products firm uses free gifts as an especially effective approach with its prospects. Its sales reps, who sell industrial strength cleaning solvents for use in factories, offer prospects (typically purchasing personnel or heads of custodial services) small gifts (for example, fishing lures, screwdriver kits) in return for a sales presentation. Although the gifts are not expensive, they have a favorable impact on the targeted prospects. Salespeople need to be sure not to violate legal and ethical guidelines in using this approach.

**Dramatic Approach.** Infrequently, the salesperson might attempt dramatic or attention-getting efforts if he or she seems to be running up against a brick wall. Some salespeople, for instance, have placed twenty dollars on the prospect's desk and announced, "If I can't show you in the next twenty minutes how our product does everything I claim it will, you can keep the twenty dollars." Often, they let the prospect keep the money anyway, since it's a relatively inexpensive way of ensuring attention. Even more dramatic approaches include "accidentally" dropping the product on the floor to show its durability, or holding a cigarette lighter flame under a piece of packaging material to demonstrate its fire resistance. Any dramatic approach, though, should be used with caution. Why? Because the danger in using a dramatic approach is that the prospect, if offended by such blatant showmanship, may become defensive. Nevertheless, dramatics are sometimes beneficial in capturing a prospect's full attention.

### Piquing Interest Approaches

**Customer-Benefit Approach.** Prospects seek to solve problems or obtain benefits from their purchases. Why else would they buy? The **customer-benefit approach** is designed to demonstrate vividly how the sales rep's product can provide that benefit for the prospect. Some examples of the customer-benefit approach include the following:

> **Customer-Benefit Approach** An approach whereby the salesperson offers the prospect a specific benefit that can be realized from using the salesperson's product.

- "Would you like to learn how to save 20 percent or more on your fleet automobile expenses by using our leasing plan?"
- "Our new, high-speed mainframe computer can cut your MIS costs by up to 30 percent."
- "Independent research companies have judged our compact Baby Bull bulldozer to be the best value on the market for construction firms with annual sales volume below fifty million dollars."
- "By converting your key 'person' insurance policy to our new all-business plan, you will have a million dollars more coverage at the same price you're paying now."

Notice that in each of the above illustrations, the salesperson emphasizes the product's *benefits* (the motive for buying), not its features or characteristics (qualities that can be seen, touched, smelled, and so on). Why? Because individuals buy a product for the benefits it offers, not the characteristics or features that it possesses. Features are only important if they directly translate into benefits for the buyer, as illustrated in the following example: "All of our new computers come with flat panel monitors (feature) that take up 50 percent less space on office desks (benefit), giving each employee more working space (benefit), which studies show will improve efficiency (benefit). In addition, employees will experience less eye strain (benefit), which should increase productivity and reduce absenteeism from eye-related health problems (benefits)."

**Curiosity Approach.** As we noted above, your goal in this approach is to set yourself apart in a favorable way from other salespeople. By using creativity in an offbeat but still business-like way, the prospect may become interested in seeing you because you have stimulated his or her curiosity. For example, a computer salesperson has asked prospects the following question with positive results: "May I please have three hundred seconds of your time?" Many prospects have smiled after hearing the question and have granted the salesperson an interview simply because the approach is unusual and stimulated their interest. A salesperson whose prospect wouldn't return his phone calls sent a telephone equipped with large numbers to the prospect, along with directions about how to call him and the benefits of doing so. Such an unusual approach resulted in the prospect finally agreeing to see the salesperson after several previous failed attempts.[10]

### Consumer-Directed Approaches

**Compliment or Praise Approach.** A subtly and sincerely delivered compliment can be a positive approach to a prospect that sets a pleasant atmosphere for the interview. In fact, research has found that use of praise can enhance one's persuasive ability.[11] Most prospects (or, for that matter, people in general) want positive feedback or praise. An indirect compliment is often more effective than a direct one, which may be dismissed as flattery. Some examples of the compliment approach include the following:

- "I can't help but ask you about that beautiful antique clock you have on your wall. Would you tell me something about it?"
- "Your secretary is really efficient and thoughtful. She called me at eight o'clock this morning to let me know that you would have to change our appointment to 3 P.M."
- "Congratulations on your company's recent award as one of Pittsburgh's top ten corporate 'good citizens.' That's an honor that any company would like to win."

**Survey Approach.**   Whether over the telephone or in person, the **survey approach** is widely used by salespeople selling business insurance, security systems, computerized information services, or any product where a potential need cannot be established without obtaining basic information about the prospect. Simply asking the prospect's permission to ask a few survey questions is usually an inoffensive and nonthreatening way to begin a sales call. For example, "Mr. Peters, may I ask you a few questions about your information needs? Your answers will help us determine whether you can substantially benefit by subscribing to one of our electronic information services." After receiving a yes answer, the salesperson can probe further to learn the exact nature and intensity of the prospect's needs.

**Survey Approach** An approach whereby the salesperson asks the prospect to answer a few survey questions, the responses to which establish quickly whether or not the prospect has a need for the salesperson's product.

**Question Approach.**   Asking questions is a good way to involve prospects in two-way communication. Prospects often disclose other useful information (such as the level of prospect interest) when they respond to salespeople's questions. One type of question that helps qualify prospects, for example, is, "If I could show you how your organization can increase your profits by 10 percent or more by using our new desktop publishing software, would you be willing to give me a half hour of your time?" Such a question necessitates the prospect's thoughtful consideration and quickly separates the "lookers" from the "buyers." Thus the salesperson moves along the path to an early sales close if the subsequent sales presentation meets prospect expectations. Most salespeople avoid asking questions that prospects are likely to answer negatively. The classic example of this poor approach is the retail store clerk's old standby: "May I help you?" which nearly always earns the response, "No thanks, I'm just looking." The salesperson essentially has nowhere to go from there . . . but away.

## Product-Related Approaches

**Product or Ingredient Approach.**   Most sales reps on calls like to carry a sample, model, or picture of the product. This approach allows prospects to see exactly what you are selling and permits a smooth transition into the sales presentation and demonstration. Producing a cutaway cross section of a new type of heavy-duty truck battery or hydraulic pump or a customized computer printout for a prospect can significantly enhance the impact of your first contact.

**Product Demonstration Approach.**  Demonstrating the product upon first approaching the prospect can be an excellent way to show the benefits offered and immediately involve the prospect. For example, a company that sells coffeemaker systems has outfitted a van as a traveling salesroom to introduce its coffeemaker system in supermarkets. The firm's salespeople drive the van to wholesale and retail chain headquarters and invite everyone from purchasing agents to top management to come out to the van for a cup of fresh coffee and pastry. This approach enables the sales reps to talk to the buyers in a relaxed atmosphere, free from telephone interruptions, with all the facilities needed for a demonstration. As this organization's sales manager said, "Frequently, six or seven top company executives visit the van, rather than the one or two we would have been able to see during ordinary office calls. They stay longer too—and they buy."

## GREETING THE PROSPECT

As the old maxim goes, "A picture is worth a thousand words," and that is indeed true in your initial sales encounter with the prospect. What the prospect observes in you will have a lasting impact. Thus, your first face-to-face contact can set the tone for the entire interview and also affect the long-term relationship. Even an element as fleeting as the handshake requires practice because it is the physical greeting that accompanies the salesperson's verbal greeting. Several aspects of your approach, as discussed below, will have a discernible effect on your success with the prospect.

### Mood

Your mood, or psychological state, when you call on a prospect will have a marked impact on the end result of that sales call. In fact, your mood is likely to affect how customer oriented you are and how helpful you will be with the prospect.[12] We all have bad days, but if you carry that negativity into the sales call, the end result will be less than satisfactory. Negative thinking begets more negative thinking, which leads to negative behavior and adverse results. Conversely, positive thoughts lead to positive behavior that further reinforces the positive thoughts and positive behavior, thus producing favorable outcomes. Successful sales personnel learn to bounce back from a setback and go on to the next call with positive energy and optimism.

You *can* learn to be optimistic—to overcome adversity and develop a positive mood state.[13] The technique involves three steps:

1. *Identify self-defeating beliefs and the events that trigger those beliefs.* For example, perhaps you are reluctant to make cold calls. Such activities (or events) can create self-defeating beliefs within you (for example, "I always do poorly when making cold calls.").

2. *Gather evidence to assess the accuracy of your self-defeating beliefs.* For example, what evidence supports your belief that you cannot make effective cold calls?

3. *Replace the negativity (self-defeating beliefs) with constructive and accurate beliefs.* For example, you might say to yourself, "So what if I'm not the best salesperson in the world? That doesn't mean I can't make effective cold calls. Why, even the best salespeople make bad cold calls at times. With enough practice, I will learn how to make effective cold calls and fine-tune my own methods."

## Facial Expression

Nearly all of us like to see a pleasant, smiling face, even when we're a bit down ourselves. Salespeople should practice the art of warmly smiling with their eyes as well as their mouths, while simultaneously greeting prospects. As simple as this sounds, we all know people who smile only with their mouths while their eyes remain cold or dull. Although nothing is said, many people notice this lack of harmony between the mouth and eyes. Stir up genuinely positive feelings for the prospect, and your smile and eyes will project enthusiasm and a warm, gracious disposition. And by looking the prospect in the eye, you will show respectful attention to what he or she is saying.

## Body Posture

Salespeople are usually advised to maintain a comfortable, erect posture in greeting prospects in order to project a positive attitude. In general, this is sound advice. In some cases, however, it might be better for the salesperson to bend slightly at the waist or gently bow or nod the head when greeting and shaking hands with the prospect because a "stiff" posture might imply feelings of superiority. Certainly, this is true when greeting prospects and customers from other cultures such as Japan or China. Also, when a salesperson is much taller than a prospect, it is impolite to maintain an erect posture that forces the prospect to look and reach too far upward for the greeting! Courtesy, politeness, and consideration for others will aid your common sense in determining the appropriate body posture for greeting a prospect.

## Shaking Hands

We often unconsciously judge others, and are judged by them, by the way we shake hands. Some top salespeople will tell you that it's best to let the prospect decide whether or not to shake hands. A friendly extended hand can be a positive way to begin a sales call, but it can also turn off some prospects, especially on cold calls. Of course, you must use your common sense and size up the situation. If a prospect is seated behind her desk when you put out your hand, you're forcing her to stand up, and this may not be a good way to begin. In social settings, good etiquette calls for the person in the superior position to decide whether or not to shake hands, and men have generally been taught to let women initiate handshakes. But most communication takes place between people who lack definite superior-inferior relationships; so salespeople should not force a handshake on a prospect but be ready to extend a hand whenever the situation warrants. A handshake sends a silent message about the salesperson, as illustrated in Table 4.6. Most all of us have

TABLE 4.6

## APPROPRIATE AND INAPPROPRIATE HANDSHAKES

- **Seal-the-Deal**—A firm and warm handshake with smiling eye contact communicates "trust me," particularly in U.S. culture. It says that you are confident and have nothing to hide.

- **The Fish**—Extending a limp hand to someone is like handing him or her a fish. Failure to firmly grasp the prospect's hand shows a lack of warmth and sends a negative message about your self-confidence.

- **Three-Fingered Claw**—Closing too quickly on the handshake will often result in your shaking only two or three fingers of the other person. It's an awkward feeling that both of you want to exit from as quickly as possible and certainly doesn't help create a good start with a prospect.

- **Bone Crusher**—Some salespeople, thinking that a powerful handshake sends a positive, confident message, literally crush the prospect's hand. This handshake will probably turn off most prospects because it makes them think you're trying to dominate.

- **The Pumper**—A few salespeople pump the prospect's hand like they're drawing water up from a well. If you are so boorish up front, the prospect likely will wonder about your long-run sensitivity to his or her needs.

- **The Death Grip**—Some salespeople keep shaking hands for an interminable length of time and seem unwilling to let go. A handshake is a greeting, not an embrace! Any salesperson who hangs on too long to either a man's or woman's hand may inadvertently send an unwanted sexual message.

- **The Dish Rag**—Salespeople who are nervous about meeting a prospect or customer may present a wet hand for shaking and reveal their nervousness. Even when you don't feel nervous, it's a smart practice to take a few seconds to dry your hands on your handkerchief before going in to see the prospect.

experienced each of these kinds of handshakes at one time or another. How did you feel at the time? How about your own handshake? Is it ever one of these inappropriate kinds?

### Presenting Your Business Card

Usually, presenting your business card shortly after shaking hands with a prospect will help keep your name and company in front of him or her as you talk. It's a good idea to present your business card each time you call on a prospect until you're sure that he or she knows your name and your company. Because prospects see many salespeople only once or twice a year, it is a little presumptuous to take for granted that prospects will remember you from one sales call to the next. When a sales supervisor or manager travels in your territory with you, presenting your business card to each prospect will help prevent you from being embarrassed in front of your boss should the prospect forget your name. In some cultures, such as Japan, exchanging business cards and carefully examining them is a fundamental rule of business etiquette and mutual respect.

## INTERACTION WITH THE RECEPTIONIST

As you enter the prospect's outer office, you will meet the receptionist. Receptionists are also called "buffers" or "gatekeepers" because part of their role is to keep you (and other salespeople) away from their bosses. After all, bosses are busy, and their time is important. Thus, receptionists can help or hinder your selling efforts.

What determines whether you receive the receptionist's assistance or his or her wrath? Usually, it is the behavior you exhibit with that person. Are you soft spoken, well mannered, and polite? Or are you boisterous, insincerely flattering or flirtatious, and ill mannered? The former encourages the receptionist to smooth your way with the prospect. The latter style will likely lead to stumbling blocks being placed between you and the prospect.

Buyers often complain that salespeople are rude, particularly to receptionists. As one company executive says, "What really bothers me is when they treat my receptionist like trash."[14] Any salesperson who would be this inconsiderate and let's face it, stupid, probably won't succeed in sales. To gain a receptionist's help, you should be sure to do the following:

- Give the receptionist your business card.
- Speak clearly and audibly to help the receptionist pronounce and spell your name correctly.
- Be friendly but not fresh.
- Don't try to wheedle confidential information about the prospect or the firm out of the receptionist.
- Act like a guest, because that's what you are.
- Be patient. Many delays are unavoidable, so don't fume about them.
- Be courteous and respectful.
- Don't ignore the receptionist on your way out. Always thank the receptionist for his or her cooperation prior to leaving the prospect's business.

An example of a salesperson's using a unique approach to deal successfully with a receptionist is provided in the *On the Frontlines* on p. 124.

## IMPROVING ONE'S SELF-IMAGE

Although all of the foregoing discussion is sound, positive advice for salespeople in their daily approaches and interactions with prospects and customers, some salespeople have found that they need to go much further to solve the long-run problem of *self-image*. They feel that they must change their self-image before they can really live out a daily mood of optimism. Dr. Maxwell Maltz, the plastic surgeon who wrote *Psycho-Cybernetics*, found that although he could improve people's physical appearances dramatically, many of his patients retained their old, negative self-images.[15] He realized that unless a patient's mental self-image was changed, plastic surgery was of little avail in improving the patient's overall attitude.

## *Silence is Golden*

A former professional mime who had become a business forms distributor was trying to get his foot in the door with a company in his territory. The firm's stern receptionist repeatedly rebuffed him. She would neither provide him with names of buyers nor accept his business card. The sales rep was stymied. He knew that he sold products that the receptionist's firm would use, if only he could see the decision-makers.

After being turned away again and again, he decided to take a chance and hark back to his skills as a mime. As he approached the receptionist, he told her that he thought there was some kind of obstacle between them. Then, using his mime talents, he began "building" an imaginary wall around the receptionist's desk and proceeded to go around her desk several times. Eventually, he "found" a doorknob with which he opened a make-believe door. He then walked through the door and handed the receptionist his card.

After reading the card, she began laughing uproariously. In fact, she was so amused that she "ordered" the buyer to witness the performance. The buyer, impressed and entertained, made an appointment with the mime-turned-salesperson and ultimately became a devoted customer.

***Source:*** *From Micah Bertin, "How to Break Through an Invisible Wall," SellingPower.com,* Most Memorable Sale, *October 5, 2001. Reprinted with permission.*

Viewed as a magnificent computer, the human mind is "programmed" daily by whatever thoughts are allowed to enter. As you go through life, you accumulate many "files" containing life experiences. How you interpret those files of experiences continually writes new programs for your mental computer. Over time, you develop a subconscious pattern of loading the stored file automatically whenever you encounter a new situation that resembles a previous one. Thus, to break out of the pattern of running the same old programs over and over again, we need to rewrite some of the files that go into our mind-computers. Even though much of our self-image was formed in childhood, it is never too late to repair or change a damaged self-image. In fact, any successful person has undoubtedly rewritten some mental files. Many top performers in sales and other competitive fields work diligently at programming themselves to view every failure as a kind of success. Every failure is, after all, at least a learning experience. To reprogram your self-image, Maltz suggests counting all the positive experiences in your life each night before you fall asleep. Start at the earliest age you can remember, and recall every positive event you can: the time you won the school playground race, the praise your teacher gave you for the picture you drew, the compliment you received from your coach about the game you played, a grade you earned, praise you received on a school project, the promotion you earned on your part-time job, or the time a classmate called you "smart," "cute," or "nice."

These recollections, no matter how small they seem, are worth storing in your mind as you rewrite your old negative files with fresh, positive ones. You may not accomplish a self-transformation overnight, or even in a few weeks, but each day you will make some progress . . . and before you know it, you will have a more positive self-image and greater success will surely follow.

One of the best pieces of advice for new or discouraged salespeople is to first accept yourself as you are now and then slowly move from there toward self-improvement. After all, as a famous poster says, "God Don't Make No Junk." You are a worthy human being who has something valuable to contribute to others. Dr. Maxwell Maltz sums up the case for self-acceptance in this way:

> Accept yourself as you are—and start from there. Learn to emotionally tolerate imperfection in yourself. It is necessary to intellectually recognize our shortcomings, but disastrous to hate ourselves because of them. Differentiate between your "self" and your behavior. . . . Don't hate yourself because you're not perfect. You have lots of company.[16]

## SUMMARY

In the preapproach stage of the PSP, the salesperson must carefully plan the sales call and establish specific goals for achievement. Depending on the particular selling situation, the level of planning varies, but it must always be done for each sales call. Seeding and prenotification are effective and efficient ways to prepare a prospect for the sales call. Demographic and psychographic information about organizational (business, not-for-profit, and government) prospects can be obtained from either internal or external sources. Selling the prospect on the appointment is a preliminary step that can help ensure a favorable reception for the sales call. Sales call reluctance, which is common among new salespeople, can prove an impediment to sales success until it's overcome by putting into practice good sales techniques and philosophy.

Approach strategies must be matched with the type of prospect and the selling situation. Even the salesperson's initial greeting during the approach can be critical in establishing rapport with a prospect. Always treat receptionists with the utmost courtesy and respect as they can have a key influence on the salesperson's success in the approach stage. Finally, a salesperson has several ways to improve his or her daily mood—and even long-run self-image—which will reflect a more favorable personality to prospects and customers.

## KEY TERMS

| | | | |
|---|---|---|---|
| Preapproach | Seeding | Cold Call | Customer-Benefit Approach |
| Approach | Prenotification | SPIN | Survey Approach |

## CHAPTER REVIEW QUESTIONS

1. Give some basic reasons for planning sales calls.

2. What are the six steps to preapproach success?

3. Define *seeding* and briefly explain how this technique can be used.

4. What do each of the letters in *SPIN* stand for? Give an example of the SPIN approach.

5. Describe the prenotification phone call approach to obtaining the initial sales appointment.

6. List several kinds of sales stage fright. What would you do to overcome these fears?

7. Name as many different approach strategies as you can and briefly give a sales example of each.

8. How might a salesperson overcome a poor self-image?

## TOPICS FOR THOUGHT AND CLASS DISCUSSION

1. What strategy would you use to arrange a sales appointment for each of the following situations:

   - Selling a corporate jet to a CEO
   - Selling lighting fixtures to the chief administrator of a large city hospital
   - Selling the arrangements committee of the American Marketing Association on choosing your resort hotel for the AMA's annual summer educators' conference three years from now

2. You have a salesperson friend who fears calling prospects on the phone to arrange sales appointments. You'd like to help him or her overcome this fear. What's your advice?

3. You've tried many different approaches with an organizational prospect who seems nice enough but just isn't impressed with you. Finally, you decide to risk a dramatic approach. Describe some dramatic approaches you might use. What risks accompany this approach?

## PROJECTS FOR PERSONAL GROWTH

1. Choose two companies in your hometown, one large and one small, and plan an approach (preapproach) strategy for each of them.

2. Using the mutual acquaintance or reference approach and the customer-benefit approach strategies, role play how you would execute each one in these two situations: (a) you are a textbook salesperson for a large publisher calling on the chair of the marketing department at a state university; and (b) you are a salesperson for a security guard company calling on a large retail store manager.

3. With a classmate, demonstrate each of the types of handshakes listed below. Describe your feelings as you perform each handshake.

   *Seal-the-Deal, Fish, Three-Fingered Claw, Bone Crusher, Pumper, Death Grip, and the Dish Rag.*

4. Develop an organizational prospect profile on your favorite company. You might start by going online using a basic search engine such as Google, then request an annual report or other descriptive materials from the company or obtain it at your school library. Use sources at your library such as Standard and Poor's, Dun & Bradstreet, or Value Line to learn more about the company and its financial situation. Note: You might want to practice cold calling by contacting representatives within the company itself, but be sure to indicate that you are a student working on a project before requesting pamphlets and other materials or information; otherwise, you may hear a quick "hang-up."

# THE REALLY COLD INITIAL SALES CALL

John Gibbons smiles as he drives past the college library. He remembers the many long nights he spent there cramming for tests and finishing reports. But all that is finally over, and now he has his first job. It feels good. Since his graduation eight months ago, he has been a salesperson for Electronic Business Communications Company (EBCC), and his old college town is part of his territory. John is driving by the campus on his way to the east side of town, where industrial parks and business campuses have sprouted over the past five years. He believes this area of town holds great sales potential, and he tells his passenger, Matt Block, that he is eager to "press the flesh and sell some EBCC machines."

Matt Block has been a sales manager for ten years and is respected and liked by his sales reps. One of the reasons his people like him is his low-key management style. He rarely tells his reps how to run their territories unless they are in trouble or ask for his advice. Matt hired John and likes his enthusiasm, but over the past few months he has become concerned with John's performance. His sales are not rising as quickly as those of other new EBCC salespeople. Matt understands that new reps often have problems, but experience has taught him that new reps should begin to show substantial signs of improvement by their sixth month in a sales territory. Because John is still finding it difficult to make sales in his eighth month, Matt is going along on his calls today to try to find out why.

**MATT:** Where are we headed?

**JOHN:** We're going over to the east side of town. That's where the growth seems to be happening. Several new businesses have moved in, and a few big companies have started branch offices there.

**MATT:** What kind of businesses?

**JOHN:** I'm not really sure. I just remember when I was in college here, my business professors kept talking about this section of town being a booming area, so I thought we should make sure that EBCC is in on the ground floor.

*[They enter the east side of town and quickly come upon an industrial park.]*

**JOHN:** Look over there, Matt. There's Marshall Company. I think I've heard of that company before. Don't they sell insurance or some type of financial service?

**MATT:** I really don't know. Can't say that I've heard of them.

**JOHN:** Well, if they are an insurance or financial services company, they sure can use some EBCC machines.

*[John pulls the car into the parking lot, and both men get out. John carries a briefcase containing his selling aids. They enter the building and approach the receptionist.]*

**RECEPTIONIST:** Good morning. May I help you?

**JOHN:** Yes, we're here to see the person who handles the ordering of electronic office equipment.

**RECEPTIONIST:** I'm not sure who that is. Do you know the name?

**JOHN:** No, I don't. Do you think you could call someone to find out who it is?

**RECEPTIONIST:** *[Looking a little annoyed.]* Let me see.

*[The receptionist picks up the phone and dials a number. After explaining to the person on the other end of the line what John wants, she waits a moment, thanks the person, and hangs up.]*

(continued)

## THE REALLY COLD INITIAL SALES CALL (CONTINUED)

**RECEPTIONIST:**  You want to go to Personnel. Go down the hallway and make the first right. Then it's the first office on the right.

**JOHN:**  Okay, thanks. *[When John and Matt reach the Personnel office, they come to the desk of Margaret Page, the front desk secretary.]*

**MARGARET:**  Yes, sir. What can I do for you?

**JOHN:**  *[Handing his business card to her.]* I would like to see the person who orders your office equipment, please.

**MARGARET:**  Do you have an appointment?

**JOHN:**  No, I didn't know that one was required.

**MARGARET:**  Mr. Ford sees sales representatives only by appointment.

**JOHN:**  Well, could you just tell him that two representatives from EBCC are here?

**MARGARET:**  *[Sounding impatient.]* I'm sorry, but he is busy now. In fact, his schedule is booked tight all day.

**JOHN:**  All right, would you tell him that we dropped by, and that I'll try another time. Thank you.

*[John and Matt leave the building and head to the car. As they get in the car, John turns to Matt.]*

**JOHN:**  Well, no luck on the first one. You know, that has happened to me a lot lately. I've been having bad luck getting in to see buyers. Do you have any advice that might help me?

**MATT:**  *[Thinking to himself, "This guy needs some serious help."]* Maybe I do. Let's drive over to that coffee place we passed on the way here and talk.

### Questions

1. What do you think are John's major problems as a salesperson?
2. Outline a strategy for John in making initial sales call appointments so that he isn't turned away so often.
3. What first-meeting approach might John use to win over "gatekeepers" such as receptionists and administrative secretaries?
4. What kind of training program do you think EBCC has for new salespeople? What would you suggest that the program include?

## APPROACHING PROSPECTS TO SELL A "GOTTA HAVE IT" PRODUCT

Jodi Miller recently took a sales position with Midwest Carpet Distributors selling a new line of area rugs. Midwest Carpet is excited about the Nedecon line of area rugs because it will allow retailers of furniture and floor coverings to enter the area rug business with virtually no inventory. Midwest considers this an important selling point because high inventory costs often keep both types of retailers out of the market. This is especially true for furniture stores, many of which also shun the rug business because of the slow turnover. Although profit margins are excellent on rugs, furniture stores need to keep most of their inventory dollars in furniture and related stock.

The Nedecon line has several innovations. For example, the patented computer injection dying system produces intricate patterns using tufted carpet production technology at moderate costs compared to the competition's machine-woven rugs. A Nedecon six-by-nine-foot rug retails for $699, half the cost of a machine-woven rug. Nedecon has decided to sell the rugs through independent carpet distributors such as Midwest Carpet, who stock the rugs and provide second-day delivery to retailers. To become a Nedecon rug dealer, a retailer simply buys three rugs (one of each size) and pays fifty dollars for a truly eye-catching display that exhibits two-by-two-foot swatches of all the patterns in the line. Each swatch represents one-quarter of a rug's pattern. The top of the display is a flat two-by-two-foot square with perpendicular eight-foot mirrors on two sides. By fitting the swatch against the mirrors on the top of the display and looking into the mirrors, one can see the full repeat of the pattern. Consumers can also view the rugs in a professional-looking pattern book attached to the display. Armed with this stunning display and the promise of second-day delivery, retailers can enter the rug business without making a significant inventory commitment.

Jodi is excited about the new line, and she has already started to telephone accounts in the Toledo area that she considers good prospects. One of the first accounts she calls is a moderately high-end furniture store, Thrush's Interiors. The conversation goes like this:

"Hello, this is Jodi Miller from Midwest Carpets. May I talk to someone about the possibility of Thrush's taking on an area rug line?"

"We don't sell area rugs," answers a nasal voice.

"I see. Well, I have a beautiful line of area rugs that requires no inventory on your part and guarantees second-day delivery and substantial profit for you." A twenty-second dead silence ensues. Jodi stammers, "Uh, would you be interested in such a line?"

"We don't handle area rugs; please hold," replies the voice. After about two minutes, the hold button clicks off and the same voice says "Thrush Interiors."

"Hello. Yes, well, if your firm did consider buying rugs, which of your buyers would have responsibility for the purchase?"

"I have no idea," says the voice. "We don't handle rugs."

"Yes, you've made that clear. Would you be so kind as to ask one of your buyers who would have responsibility for rugs?" asks an increasingly frustrated Jodi.

"Hold, please," the voice hisses. After what seems like ten minutes, the voice returns. "Mr. Hestvik said that we don't handle rugs and have no plans to take on a rug line. He said no buyer is assigned to area rugs."

"I see. Thank you," replies Jodi softly.

Jodi is really disappointed by the outcome of her phone call. Thrush's would be a perfect account for the Nedecon rug line. If only she could talk to the right person.

(continued)

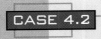

# APPROACHING PROSPECTS TO SELL A "GOTTA HAVE IT" PRODUCT (CONTINUED)

Jodi spends the remaining part of the week trying to set up appointments to show the rug line and mostly failing. When telephoning, the receptionist or secretary frequently refuses to let her speak with a buyer. This is especially frustrating because Jodi prides herself on being a superior salesperson and believes that scheduling appointments with buyers is time efficient and demonstrates the salesperson's professionalism.

A week later, Jodi is in the neighborhood of the Thrush store. She decides to drop in to see if she was right about Thrush Interiors being an ideal account for the area rugs. She walks in and begins browsing around the store. As she envisions how a Nedecon area rug would look in each display, she feels certain that this account would be a natural for the Nedecon rug line. One of Thrush's salespeople walks over, introduces herself, and asks what rooms Jodi is decorating. "Oh, I'm not decorating any rooms. My name is Jodi Miller. I'm with Midwest Carpet Distributors, and we've got a great new line of area rugs that I was thinking would be a natural for Thrush's. What's really neat about them is that dealers don't need to stock the line because we guarantee second-day delivery. Here, take a look at these patterns." Jodi hands the pattern book to the salesman.

The salesman looks at the pattern book and after a minute asks, "What's the retail price for these rugs?"

"Four hundred and ninety-nine dollars for the four-by-sixes, and eight hundred and ninety-nine for the nine-by-twelves. The rugs are made from tufted carpet using a computerized injection dying technology that creates a product almost as good as a machine-woven rug at half the price," Jodi explains quickly.

"Hey, that's not bad! Maria, look at these rugs. We could sell these. I've tried to tell our head buyer, Sam Hestvik, to stock area rugs, but he always says he doesn't have any available inventory dollars, and doesn't need another slow-moving line."

"Well, the pictures look nice, Marty, but I wonder what the goods look like," replies Maria, another Thrush salesperson.

"Wait here two minutes, and I'll bring you some samples," says Jodi, as she hustles out to her station wagon. Jodi knows that these two can't buy the line, but after such a long, relatively unsuccessful week, she needs some positive feedback. Anyway, she is interested in whether they think the line is worthwhile. "Here's a four-by-six and a six-by-nine," says Jodi, as she spreads two rugs out on the floor and begins brushing the pile.

The two Thrush salespeople start to examine the rugs carefully. At one point, Jodi thinks they are going to rip the rugs up in their intense inspection. They ask numerous questions and seem satisfied with Jodi's answers. They also seem to listen as she describes the Nedecon area rug program.

"This would be perfect for us Maria—no inventory, fifty-six patterns, second-day delivery, reasonable prices, an attractive product. What a great add-on item!" exclaims Marty.

"You're right. Now, how can we convince Hestvik to take it on?" asks Maria.

"He's always interested in add-on sales. He'll go for this. What's he doing now?" asked Marty.

"I think he's working on the inventory."

"Jodi, let me take your samples in to show him. I'll be right back." Marty hurries into the back offices. Jodi can't believe her good fortune. One of the store salespeople is actually going to sell the line for her! She can't help feeling that she should have gone along to explain the program, but Marty was so impulsive that he disappeared before Jodi could even suggest it. After five minutes, Marty comes back looking upset.

"That stupid clown. He told me that I should stick to selling, and he'll do the buying. I think

(continued)

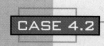

## APPROACHING PROSPECTS TO SELL A "GOTTA HAVE IT" PRODUCT (CONTINUED)

he's jealous of my interior design degree, so he hates to accept any of my suggestions. I'd be a much better buyer than that no-taste accountant. As usual, he brought up those vases I suggested he buy two years ago that didn't sell well. He never even looked at the rugs. Sorry, I guess I didn't help you any."

"Marty, you never should have gone in there while he was working on his precious inventory figures," scolds Maria, "You know how grouchy he gets when he learns how much we have in stock."

"That's the irony of it. This program doesn't require any inventory, but Hestvik thinks 'new line' means more inventory. The guy's got a closed mind and won't listen to new ideas."

Jodi thanks her two new friends, gives them the pattern books that Marty requested, and leaves the store with the strong feeling that sell-

ing this line is going to be tougher than she thought.

*Reprinted with permission of James T. Strong, University of Akron.*

### Questions

1. What do you think of Jodi Miller's general approach to selling the new line of area rugs? What could she do differently to obtain appointments with buyers?
2. Critique Jodi's performance in trying to sell the area rugs to Thrush's. What positive moves did she make? What mistakes did she make? How would you have handled this account?
3. What might Jodi do now to sell the area rugs to Thrush's?
4. What strategies would you advise Jodi to use in (a) scheduling appointments with retail buyers, (b) preparing for the sales call, and (c) approaching prospects for the first time?

## CHAPTER 5

# Sales Presentation and Demonstration: The Pivotal Exchange

*"One of the best ways to persuade others is with your ears."*
*Dean Rusk*

## After Reading This Chapter, You Should Understand:

- Alternative sales presentation strategies.
- Guidelines for effective sales presentations and demonstrations to organizational prospects.
- Preparation of written sales presentations.
- Sales presentation strategies for different prospect categories.
- Use of adaptive and canned sales presentations.
- Sales presentations to prospect groups.
- How to make a sales presentation memorable.

## INSIDE PERSONAL SELLING:
### Meet Greg Genova of Kennametal

As a senior metal working systems engineer for Kennametal, Inc., Greg Genova has to speak two languages. He has to know the language of management—to talk about cash flow and return on investment—as well as the language of machine operators on the shop floor—to discuss set-up ease and cutting rates. Kennametal is the largest marketer of metal cutting tools in America, with annual sales of approximately $1.8 billion. Its customers are companies in aerospace, automotive, construction and farm machinery, power generation and transmission equipment, and home appliances.

Early in the sales process, Genova learns as much as he can about a prospect's business so he can demonstrate how Kennametal products will enhance productivity. "I look for opportunities where our products can have a significant impact in a

short time," he says. "If you can improve the bottom line immediately, that wins the customer over. In some cases, I had a product in my car that made a productivity increase while I was still in the customer's plant."

Showing prospects what Kennametal's products will do is essential, stresses Genova. Although he can talk about a product's features and benefits, companies are sometimes skeptical until they see results. Moreover, Genova must convince both management and machine operators of his products' value. Otherwise, the operators might sabotage the demonstration and tell management that the new product does not work. Because Genova has operated factory equipment—"and I have the scars on my hands to prove it"—he has the credibility to enlist the operators' trust and cooperation during a demonstration.

On occasion, Genova has the opportunity to unseat an entrenched competitor by demonstrating the superior advantages and benefits of Kennametal products. He recently heard from an aerospace company that had a contract to manufacture jet engine mounts. The company had previously made the part from a different steel alloy but had not allowed for the use of a new government-mandated alloy that was more difficult to cut. As a result, the company was spending thousands of dollars more than expected to fulfill the contract.

Despite an existing relationship with a Kennametal competitor, the company put out a call to anybody who could help solve the problem. Genova visited the plant and analyzed the situation. He found that the company's machines were removing one to three cubic inches of metal per minute in cutting the alloy. "I was able to go in and show that Kennametal's tools could remove 33 cubic inches of metal per minute," Genova recalls. This dramatic demonstration of product speed and superiority won the account for Kennametal. "We ended up saving the company over a million dollars on the contract," he says. "They actually made me supplier of the year."

**133**

**Y**our prospect's attention and interest have been piqued, and he's eager to learn more about your product and how it can benefit his company. "Will it make us more productive?" "Will it save us money?" "Will our manufacturing operations run more smoothly?" "Will it increase our sales?" "Will it improve customer satisfaction with our products and services?" These are just some of the questions the prospect hopes you can answer. To answer such queries in an understandable, compelling, and convincing fashion, you must give an energetic, high-quality sales presentation. As you make your presentation, you may want to keep in mind the objectives of many professional entertainers. Talk show hosts, actors and actresses, and comedians try to keep their audiences on the edge of their seats, that is, attentive, interested, and excited. You should aspire to capture and retain your prospect's enthusiasm for your product or service. Anxious about your ability to do this? Don't worry! By the end of this chapter, you will see how to give sales presentations that can have lasting and favorable effects on prospects.

A *sales presentation* can be defined as those activities involved in presenting the product to the prospect, demonstrating its strengths, and explaining

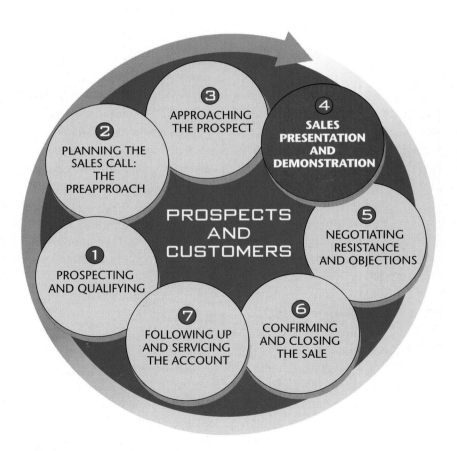

FIGURE 5.1

THE PERSONAL SELLING PROCESS

what it will do for the prospect. This stage is the heart of the PSP for two reasons. First, the sales presentation is halfway through the PSP. So far, a qualified prospect has been identified, preliminary information about the prospect has been collected, and the salesperson has approached the prospect to pique his or her interest. Second, it is at this point that the salesperson attempts to arouse the prospect's desire for and conviction to buy the product, ultimately making a transition toward closing the sale.

Many people think of a presentation as a situation in which something is being shown or displayed to a passive person or group of people. However, successful salespeople think of the sale presentation and demonstration as the *pivotal exchange* between seller and buyer in the sequence of exchanges that make up the selling process. When planning their sales presentations and demonstration strategies, the best salespeople make room for *buyers'* descriptions of problems, needs, ideas, and questions and expect to actively solicit their participation at every phase of the presentation. This approach to personal selling is best exemplified in the consultative *problem-solving strategy*, the major perspective of our discussion in this chapter. We will also discuss several other sales presentation strategies.

## THE FIRST SALES CALL AND THE SALES PRESENTATION

In chapter 4 we discussed planning and preparing for your first sales call with a new prospect. Once you have established initial contact with a prospect, however, when does the sales presentation begin? The answer to this question depends on the industry in which you're selling and the selling situation itself. If you're a paper company sales representative trying to dislodge a competitor, and the buyer—who may have seen ten other salespeople that day—gives you exactly five minutes of her time, you would be wise to minimize the usual ice-breaking conversation and begin your presentation, or offer to come back another day. But if you represent a large computer technology company and are trying to convince a prospect corporation that it needs a multimillion-dollar mainframe computer installation, you will no doubt make several sales calls just to gather information from various people within the organization before you feel ready to make a sales presentation to a key decision-maker or decision-making committee.

Remember this, however: In a sense, whenever you interact with the prospect or his or her company colleagues, you are *always* making a presentation. Although you may not actually be presenting and demonstrating your product, you are representing your company and yourself. Therefore, your behavior—both verbal and nonverbal—*is* a presentation of sorts. The information that you gathered in the preapproach stage can prove especially valuable now as a guide to your "presentation" conduct.

# PLANNING THE SALES PRESENTATION

An active, participatory exchange during a sales presentation may become routine once you have established a good relationship with your buyer. But how do you plan that first big presentation with a new prospect so that you're not the only one doing the talking? Before planning the sales presentation tactics, the professional salesperson first develops an overall strategy for handling the chain of interactions with the prospect. In planning the sales presentation and demonstration strategy for organizational prospects, salespeople often find it helpful to think in terms of five basic stages, as denoted in Table 5.1: *gathering information, identifying prospect needs, preparing and presenting the sales proposal, confirming the sale and/or the relationship,* and *ensuring customer satisfaction.*

## Gathering Information

Even a well-prepared sales presentation may contain some tentative data and information based on assumptions or opinions. You can use small talk to verify some of this information while simultaneously sizing up the prospect: *What type of person is this? What kind of mood is he or she in? What communication style should I use? Which persuasive appeals might work best?* Too much small talk, however, can be detrimental to the sales process. A chronic complaint of organizational buyers is that salespeople talk too much, fail to ask the right questions, and do not really listen to the buyer. Such salespeople dominate the conversation and ignore the specific and unique concerns of their prospects. If you're not listening, you can't ever really identify prospect problems and needs and arrive at a sound solution.

Top-performing salespeople understand that the first step in the sales presentation is to gather all the relevant information they can about prospects and their perceived problems. First, they make sure they're talking to decision-makers (those with authority to buy) or key influencers, so neither party's time is wasted. Next, they ask probing questions to encourage prospects to

| TABLE 5.1 |
|---|
| **PLANNING THE SALES PRESENTATION AND DEMONSTRATION** |
| • Gathering information |
| • Identifying prospect needs |
| • Preparing and presenting the sales proposal |
| • Confirming the sale and/or the relationship |
| • Ensuring customer satisfaction |

provide information on perceived problems, objectives, financial status, needs, and personal feelings. Like a doctor's patient, sometimes prospects know only that they have a problem, but not what it is; so they'll describe the symptoms. In such cases, even after talking with the prospect, salespeople may need to play the role of a doctor or even Sherlock Holmes, whose observations, probing questions, and insightful analyses always enabled him to discover the underlying facts that led to the correct solution.

### Identifying the Prospect's Problems and Needs

Using a consultative, problem-solving approach, the professional salesperson can efficiently uncover the prospect's perceived problems and needs by skillful questioning and careful listening. "What led you to switch suppliers in the past?" "How do you currently deal with this situation?" "How long has this problem been occurring?" Note that the emphasis is *always* on the prospect's perceptions of his or her needs, *not* the salesperson's. Each of the foregoing questions deals solely with the prospect's needs. It matters little what the salesperson thinks he or she is selling; what really matters is what the prospect thinks he or she is buying. People and companies buy for their own unique reasons, and until the salesperson uncovers those unique reasons in a given situation, a sale will seldom take place. Today's professional salespeople spend more time defining client needs than on any other part of the sales presentation process. Only after clearly understanding the prospect's perceived needs can a salesperson discover what product benefits to focus on in the sales presentation.

### Preparing and Presenting the Sales Proposal

Before you "go on stage" (make a sales presentation), you will want to prepare yourself to give a superb performance.

**Professional Approach to Sales Presentations.** A traditional salesperson makes a standard product-oriented presentation and sales proposal to all prospects, regardless of their individual needs. In contrast, the professional approach custom tailors the sales presentation and proposal to the client's specific business situation, needs, and individual communication style. Each presentation should match a particular buyer's unique combination of these variables.[1] Furthermore, the salesperson must adapt the terminology to the buyer. For instance, technical language is appropriate for technically well-versed buyers but inappropriate for prospects with sketchy technical sophistication. Salespeople often must adjust their sales presentation to some particularly challenging prospects, as shown in Table 5.2.

**FAB Leads to SELLS.** Salespeople must first uncover each customer's needs and wants, then present their product's features, advantages, and benefits **(FAB)**—that will appeal *most* to that customer. Let's describe the three parts of the FAB selling approach.

**FAB** A memory-aid acronym standing for a product's *f*eatures, *a*dvantages, and *b*enefits that will appeal most to a salesperson's customer.

1. *Features* are a product or service's relatively obvious characteristics: what the customer can see, touch, hear, taste, or smell. In the case of a laptop computer for office use, some of its features may be a rich-looking

TABLE 5.2

## PROSPECT CATEGORIES AND STRATEGY

**Skeptical Sid and Sally.** Be conservative in the sales presentation. Avoid puffery; stay with the facts. Understate a little, especially in areas where the prospect is knowledgeable.

**Silent Sam and Sue.** To encourage Silent Sam or Sue to talk, ask questions and be more personal than usual. Encourage them to tell you about some of their interests, problems, and successes.

**Paula and Pete Procrastinator.** Summarize benefits that will be lost if they don't act quickly. Reassure them that they have the authority and the ability to make decisions. Use a little showmanship to overcome their indecision.

**Gussy and Garfield Grouch.** Ask questions to uncover any underlying problems. Encourage them to tell their story.

**Edith Ego and Ollie Opinionated.** Listen attentively to whatever they say, agree with their views, cater to their wishes, and subtly flatter their egos.

**Irma and Irwin Impulsive.** Speed up the sales presentation, omit unneeded details, and hit the high points. Try to close early if the situation seems right.

**Mary and Melvin Methodical.** Slow down the sales presentation to adjust your tempo to theirs. Provide additional explanations for each key point and include many details.

**Teresa and Tim Timid or Carol and Corey Cautious.** Talk at a gentle, comfortable, deliberate pace. Use a simple, straightforward, logical presentation. Reassure them on each key point.

**Tom and Thelma Talkative.** Don't allow their continuous "small talk" to take your sales presentation off on a tangent. Listen politely, but move back on track as quickly as possible. Say something like, "By the way, that reminds me that our product has . . ." Then wrap up the sales presentation as quickly as you can.

**Cathy and Charlie Chip-on-the-Shoulder.** Don't argue or become defensive with them. Remain calm, sincere, and friendly. Agree with them as much as you can. Show respect for them.

*Source:* Rolph E. Anderson, Joseph F. Hair, Alan J. Bush, *Professional Sales Management,* 1988. Copyright © 1998 The McGraw-Hill Companies. Reproduced with permission of The McGraw-Hill Companies.

carrying case; its light weight; large memory size; internal modem; noiseless keys; multicolored screen projection; and built-in alarm clock. As noted in chapter 4, it's important to keep in mind that features matter little to prospects unless they can be translated into customer benefits.

2. *Advantages* are product performance characteristics that show how it can help the customer better solve a problem than do present products. A salesperson may inform the customer that this laptop is the most reliable on the market and that it is completely shock resistant. Claims like this, however, must be provable. The salesperson could roughly drop the laptop on a table, then show that the computer is still at the same point in the word-processing program as it was prior to the shock. This might adequately demonstrate the laptop's advantages to the prospect.

3. *Benefits* are what the customer wants from the product, and they must be demonstrated with the prospect involved as much as possible. The salesperson who discovers that a prospect wants laptop computers for company managers to pose "what if" questions for the marketing database system might invite the prospect to run a simulation on the laptop. Likewise, if the prospect's sales force wants a laptop that is easy to carry and lightweight, the salesperson can invite them to lift the laptop by just one finger. These invitations to experience the product sharply increase demonstration impact.

Although the three aspects of the FAB selling approach need not be covered in any particular order, it's usually best to present the customer benefit early because that's the customer's "hot button" and reason for buying. Consider the following illustrations of the FAB selling formula:

- "You'll be able to produce dazzling professional full-color reports and memos *(benefit)* with this new portable *(advantage)* Hewlett-Packard inkjet printer with its interface kit for Apple computers *(feature)*."
- "Your team's win-loss record should quickly improve *(benefit)* with this new lightweight but incredibly strong titanium baseball bat *(features)* because it enables the batter to swing faster and hit the ball up to 50 percent harder *(advantage)*, thus changing many former soft line outs into smashing line drives *(benefit)*."

These two illustrations point to the broad range of use for the FAB selling approach. Low-tech or high-tech, all products have features, advantages, and benefits. But remember that it's the benefits that make prospects and customers want to buy.

It's always important to include *trial closes* or subtle attempts to move toward the close whenever appropriate in the sales presentation. The acronym "SELLS" will help you remember to cover FAB and include trial closes:

- *S*how your product's key features.
- *E*xplain its major advantages.
- *L*ead into specific benefits for the prospect.
- *L*et the prospect do most of the talking.
- *S*tart a trial close and use more throughout the presentation.

When you make a sales presentation, concentrate on the benefits customers want and how best they can use the product to achieve those benefits. When you make sales presentations to business resellers such as distributors, wholesalers, or retailers, always include financial information and a marketing strategy that show how to profitably *resell* the product to the customers of these middlemen. Finally, you must sell the prospect on the higher *value* of the product's benefits relative to its cost, and the *added value* of buying this brand from your company

Organizational buyers want to maximize the value received for their dollars, so they compare the bundle of product benefits offered by competitive products. **Value added** refers to the extra benefits, from the prospect's perspective, that a seller's product offerings have over those of competitors. Added value can come from the brand's reputation for quality or the seller's guarantees or special customer service. For example, one imaging technologies firm adds value to its diagnostic ultrasound equipment by providing a free,

**Value Added**  Extra benefits, from the prospect's perspective, that one salesperson and his or her products and services have over those of competitors.

automatic one-year warranty extension from the date of any breakdown. This firm's competitors offer only the standard one-year warranty.

### Confirming the Relationship and the Sale

In traditional sales negotiations, the salesperson spends the most time working to overcome buyer resistance and to close the sale by prevailing over the "stubborn" customer. Such salespeople see prospects as adversaries or challengers to be hustled into early purchase commitments. Professional salespeople, on the other hand, see their prospects as *business partners*. They uncover the problems and needs of their prospect partners through attentive listening and by serving as a trusted adviser and friend. Only when they fully understand a prospect's needs and believe that they have the best product to satisfy those needs, should sales reps start their trial closes: "Are these benefits the ones you're seeking?" "How do you feel about this product's ability to solve the problems you've outlined?"

### Ensuring Customer Satisfaction

Some underperforming salespeople tend to neglect customer service. Immediately after the sale, their interest, contact, and relationship with the customer fall off rapidly. This shortsighted approach usually causes these salespeople extra work trying to rebuild rapport with the customer. A truly professional salesperson never lets the relationship with the customer wither in the first place. He or she makes a commitment to provide full service and assistance to the buyer before, during, and after the sale and to ensure post-purchase customer satisfaction. Professional salespeople understand that fully satisfying current customers generates repeat sales, referrals to other prospects, and increased sales as customer needs grow.[2]

Top performing salespeople are always seeking new ways to better serve their customers. They join sales organizations such as *Sales and Marketing Executives International*, attend sales and marketing seminars, compare notes with other salespeople, and make a habit of reading sales books, journals, and magazines such as *Sales and Marketing Management*. A quarterly academic publication, with a sizable salesperson and sales manager readership, is the *Journal of Personal Selling & Sales Management (JPSSM)*, described in *Keeping Up Online* below.

## KEEPING UP ONLINE: JOURNAL OF PERSONAL SELLING & SALES MANAGEMENT (JPSSM)

**JPSSM,** a research-based journal in the fields of personal selling and sales management, serves a diverse readership that includes sales professionals, professors, researchers, trainers, and students. Readers of *JPSSM* do so chiefly to (1) gain a broader perspective of selling and sales management beyond the boundaries of personal experi-ence and (2) stay abreast of the knowledge explosion in selling and sales management, including the latest research findings and evolving concepts. You can visit their web site and view some of their offerings at http://mkt.cba.cmich.edu/jpssm/. How might salespeople make use of *JPSSM* to assist them in their selling positions?

# GENERAL GUIDELINES FOR EFFECTIVE SALES PRESENTATIONS

As you now know, making a sales presentation is not a haphazard activity. Much thought and care must go into your presentation if you are to be successful in your selling efforts. To achieve effective personal communication with prospects during sales presentations and demonstrations, salespeople should observe four basic principles.

1. *Participation:* Prospects who actively participate in the sales presentation and demonstration retain more information and tend to develop more favorable attitudes toward the product.

2. *Association:* Prospects remember new information better if they can connect it to their personal knowledge, past experiences, and frames of reference.

3. *Transfer:* Prospects who see the product being used in situations similar to their own can better visualize the benefits they will derive from the product.

4. *Insight:* Product demonstrations should weave the facts and figures from the sales presentation into the prospect's own experience because this often leads to special insights that favorably impress the prospect.[3]

Some salespeople have found success by being somewhat flamboyant in their sales presentations and demonstrations. Never be reluctant to develop your own style, because this uniqueness can be an effective sales tool that sets you apart from the competition, as illustrated in *From the Command Post,* on p. 142.

## Effective Sales Demonstrations

"One picture is worth a thousand words, and one demonstration is worth a thousand pictures" is a well-known axiom among professional salespeople. To bring their sales presentations to life, most successful salespeople try to make realistic, often dramatic, product *demonstrations.* Prospects want to understand a product with all their senses. They want to see, hear, feel, smell, and taste a product where appropriate before making a purchase decision. So the best salespeople work to involve as many prospect senses as possible in their demonstrations. One sales rep for a shatterproof glass producer led his company's sales force year after year in sales. He did this using a creative demonstration: aggressively hitting the shatterproof glass with a hammer in front of prospects. But he became an even bigger success when rather than striking the glass himself, he handed the hammer to prospects and asked them to hit the glass. Few other tactics could so effectively increase their direct involvement and understanding of the product.

The demonstration can be a powerful selling tool, but it calls for careful planning and practice. Strategic planning of the demonstration enables the salesperson to follow procedures and prepare in advance for all of the

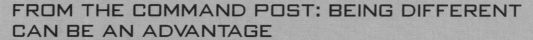

# FROM THE COMMAND POST: BEING DIFFERENT CAN BE AN ADVANTAGE

Did you ever wonder how companies and their salespeople fight through all the promotional "clutter" so that their messages are seen or heard by their target markets? With great difficulty, that's how! Competition tends to be keen in most industries, so promotional messages are numerous and frequent. In fact, these competitive promotions often seem to have little impact other than to cancel or offset each other. Consequently, many marketing communication programs and salespeople's selling efforts are ineffective. Thus, the onus often falls on field salespeople to develop communication and sales programs that truly "awaken" awareness and interest in the target audience.

Getting in the door with prospects and extant customers requires creativity and a willingness to try something unusual that will clearly differentiate the firm from its competitors. Some firms have discovered that custom-designing of invitations (a type of sales presentation) for fundraisers, marketing events, and other gatherings can have a salutary effect on their recipients. Using arresting mailers can generate significantly higher response rates.

Several factors contribute to high response rates. For instance, a vendor's style is as significant as a person's style. Designing a mailer with a new twist that grabs the reader's attention can project a stimulating style for the company. Also, crafting eye-catching pieces that strike readers' senses by being unusual (e.g., in size or personalization) rather than having a mass-produced tenor is advantageous. Third, designing elaborate mailers incorporating unusual materials (e.g., three-dimensional cut-outs or pieces of cloth or plastic) can set the supplier apart from competition. Finally, mailers should reflect clearly the event that is being promoted. Doing so sets the tone and starts people talking about the activity.

So, what characterizes a successful communication program that supports the sales force's efforts? One that offers uniqueness, not "me-tooism."

eventualities. The following are seven basic planning steps in preparing for the demonstration:

1. Select benefits to demonstrate that fit the prospect's needs.
2. Decide what to say about the benefits from the prospect's perspective.
3. Select sales aids that involve most human senses and have the most positive impact.
4. Precheck all sales aids to make sure everything is working smoothly.
5. Decide when and where to make the demonstration. Usually a controlled environment is best.
6. Figure out how to involve the prospect. Remember the motto: "If they try it, they'll buy it."
7. Prepare a written demonstration outline. Include three columns: (1) Benefit to demonstrate, (2) what to say, and (3) what to do.
8. Rehearse the demonstration many times until you have the right wording and timing of actions—but don't try to memorize the *entire* demonstration, otherwise it will likely appear canned and perfunctory.

## Dressing for Selling Success

An important part of any sales presentation is the salesperson's personal appearance. Many companies hire consultants to conduct seminars for their salespeople on personal grooming, selecting clothing and accessories, and using body language. A few salespeople have been successful despite dressing in bizarre ways, but most professional salespeople make sure that their appearance helps them makes sales. What's the best way to dress? As with many other facets of professional selling, the answer depends on the prospects, selling situations, and products, but we offer some general advice in Table 5.3.

## Effective Behavior and Listening Principles

How salespeople behave during sales presentations and demonstrations is critical. Inappropriate behavior—as seen through the eyes of the *prospect*—can ruin even a solid presentation or demonstration. Similarly, a salesperson who shows poor listening attentiveness or frequently interrupts when the prospect

---

**TABLE 5.3**

### DRESSING FOR SALES PRESENTATION SUCCESS

- **Goal:** Your goal is to convey trustworthiness, reliability, confidence, and professionalism to prospects.

- **Clothes:** Wear conservatively cut clothes in muted or neutral colors that make little obvious impression but subliminally speak of power, confidence, and success. Avoid bright hues, intricate patterns, or anything that's trendy or showy. Dark blue is nearly always safe.

- **Makeup:** Saleswomen should wear only moderate makeup unless they represent a cosmetics company and are showing off a new line. If your makeup says, "I'd rather be partying than doing business," securing your prospect's serious attention will be an uphill battle.

- **Jewelry:** Neither salesmen nor saleswomen should wear ostentatious or noisy jewelry that can suggest a preoccupation with appearance. Salesmen are safest wearing no jewelry at all, and saleswomen should wear only conservative jewelry.

- **Briefcase:** Choose a conservative, unobtrusive briefcase in dark brown or cordovan. A flat zipper case is a good choice because it helps you look organized and like someone who deals only with important matters. Replace your case when it starts to show wear.

- **Business Cards:** Choose simple, dignified business cards without gaudy logos or emblems. Always carry them in a special metal or leather business card case to keep them from becoming dirty or dog-eared.

- **Writing Pen:** Never ask a customer to sign a twenty-thousand-dollar order with a thirty-five-cent ballpoint pen. Carry a fine pen and always keep it handy so you don't have to fumble to find it.

*Source:* David Severson, "When a Sales Pitch Won't Do," *Training & Development Journal* (June 1985), 18–19. Copyright June 1985, *Training & Development Journal*, American Society for Training & Development. Reprinted with permission. All rights reserved.

---

| TABLE 5.4 |
| :-- |
| **BEHAVIORAL GUIDELINES FOR EFFECTIVE SALES PRESENTATIONS AND DEMONSTRATIONS** |

- Establish rapport early.
- Include in your introductory remarks questions that will grab the prospect's attention and involvement.
- Look for and use responsive behaviors.
- Connect prospect needs and product benefits with respected reference groups.
- Combine factual and emotional appeals.
- Assume an initial relatively firm negotiating position.
- Help prospects draw the right conclusions.
- Use humor with discretion and only where appropriate.
- Never disparage another individual or company.
- Avoid making puns, which can come off as childish.
- Never tell ethnic jokes or offensive jokes of any kind.
- Readily admit minor weaknesses in the product, as this increases your credibility with prospects and customers.

---

is talking gives the impression that the salesperson considers the prospect's problems and needs unimportant. Always keep your deportment consistent with your prospects' business setting and personal values and beliefs. Most important, listen carefully and respectfully to your prospect.[4] Table 5.4 is a list of professional behaviors salespeople employ when making successful presentations and demonstrations. In Table 5.5 we offer important guidelines for effective listening during presentations and demonstrations. Although you may consider some of these suggestions obvious, many buyers can recount horror stories of salespeople who failed to behave in accordance with these basic guidelines and thus failed to garner sales from the buyers.

## SALES PRESENTATIONS TO GROUPS

Sales presentations to organizational prospects and customers must include a business strategy (also called a business plan) that explains how the product can profitably be resold or used to make other products. Organizational customers must be convinced that the overall business strategy is sound before they will buy the product. Because the purchasing decision is so important to their success, large organizational customers will often ask salespeople to make presentations to a group of company employees, including people from purchasing, accounting, marketing, production, engineering, and finance.[5] To

| TABLE 5.5 |
| --- |
| **KEYS TO GOOD LISTENING** |

- Stop, look, and listen! You cannot listen when you're talking, and you won't grasp the subtle meaning of words unless you're closely watching the prospect's body language. Never interrupt prospects while they're talking. Wait until prospects have finished talking before you respond.

- Make prospects feel comfortable and uninhibited about talking freely with you by listening in a nonjudgmental way. Avoid either positively or negatively critiquing their statements; just understand what they're saying.

- Ask nonthreatening, probing questions to clarify the prospect's comments. Doing so shows that you're listening, encourages the prospect to talk more, and helps you both to understand the communication that has taken place.

- Empathize with prospects and their problems, and if applicable, tell them specifically how you relate to their problems. Make the prospect's needs more important than your own.

- Give prospects your full attention, both mentally and physically. Do not yawn, allow your eyes to glaze over, doodle, tap fingers, shuffle papers, or allow your mind to wander while the prospect is talking. Continue to look and be interested.

- Keep your emotions under control. No matter what happens, keep cool. An emotional person is unlikely to hear or see clearly. Avoid arguments. Even if you win, you'll probably lose the sale.

- Make notes of major points in your discussion with the prospect at the first opportunity, probably in the car before driving to your next appointment.

- Some top salespeople send the prospect a memorandum summarizing each meeting. Before doing so, however, ask the prospect if he or she would welcome this. Unless he or she agrees, keep your notes to yourself. Of course, a thank-you note for the prospect's time is always appropriate.

assist you in making a presentation, you may want to make a *presentation planning checklist*. The checklist (which can be adapted for different types of presentations) will provide you with direction for your presentation, improve your preparation, and enhance your comfort level prior to and during the presentation. On pp. 146 and 147, you will find one kind of presentation-planning checklist.

### Sales Presentation Format

Salespeople succeed using many different kinds of group presentations. One popular group presentation format follows this sequence: *problem, product, benefits, evidence, summary,* and *action.* An abbreviated version of a salesperson's presentation, using this standard format, is shown on p. 148.

*Because purchasing decisions are important to their success, large organizational customers often ask salespeople to make presentations to a group.*
Corbis

# PRESENTATION PLANNING CHECKLIST

1. Who is the prospect?

   Company name _____

   People to see _____

   Address _____

   Phone number _____

   Fax number _____

   Email address _____

2. Date, time, and place of appointment:

   Date _____ Time _____ Place _____

3. Statements of customer problem and/or opportunity as related to our product/service offerings:

   _____

   _____

4. Major buying motives of the prospect (if known):

   _____

5. Objectives of the presentation:

   Major objectives _____

   _____

   Minor objectives _____

   _____

6. Preferred Communication Style:

   a. Amiable _____     b. Analytical _____

   c. Expressive _____     d. Driver _____

7. Important customer benefits to be stressed:

   _____

   _____

8. Evidence needed to support my claims (competitive comparisons, test results, testimonials, etc.):

   _____

   _____

9. Other information needed (terms, delivery schedules, etc.):

   _____

   _____

(continued)

# PRESENTATION PLANNING CHECKLIST (CONTINUED)

10. Sales tools needed (e.g., brochures, audio-visual equipment, samples):

    _____

    _____

11. To start the presentation, I will: _____

    _____

    • state objectives and approach: _____

    _____

    • establish rapport by: _____

    _____

    • attract attention, obtain interest, and transition by: _____

    _____

12. I anticipate the following objections and will respond to them as follows:

    a. objection #1: _____

       response: _____

    b. objection #2: _____

       response: _____

13. To close the sale, I will ask for the order by:

    _____

    _____

14. To ensure customer satisfaction, I will follow up with these actions:

    _____

    _____

15. I have rehearsed the presentation to emphasize the following key customer benefits:

    _____

    _____

16. If other people from my company are involved in the presentation, we all understand our roles, as well as the roles of the others.

                                                        Name of Person

    Individual Role 1. _____       _____

    Individual Role 2. _____       _____

17. I have planned to be flexible during the presentation and will be able to adapt my presentation if the situation warrants it. Possible adaptive strategies include:

    _____

# GROUP PRESENTATION EXAMPLE

1. **Problem:** "Good morning. I'm delighted to be at Santa's Workshop Company this morning and to have this chance to talk with you and to bring you some good news. First, based on my discussions with many of you, it is my understanding that the poor adhesive quality of the glue you're currently using has been a major source of customer complaints and merchandise returns to retailers. Two of your newest toys are being recalled at a cost of several hundred thousand dollars because the glue is simply not holding. Is that essentially correct? *[Additional discussion of the problem may take place here as members of the prospect group clarify the specific nature of their collective and individual needs. Information gathered here can help the salesperson to make some adjustments in the focus of the sales presentation.]*

2. **Product:** Well, I'm delighted to report that our new product, *Fantastic Glue*, is the answer to your problem. *Fantastic Glue* is a revolutionary new adhesive recently developed and tested at our research laboratories that will be available next month. I've got a sample of it right here, in the bright blue tube on the table. After four years of intense effort, our research scientists developed this unbelievable product that more than doubles the holding properties of any other industrial strength glue on the market, and what's more, it sets up twice as fast.

3. **Benefits:** *Fantastic Glue* will completely solve your product adhesion problems, raise customer satisfaction, and increase your company's reputation for quality products. Your customer complaint department people may become as lonely as the Maytag repairman. At the same time, your company's annual profits will jump by several thousand dollars, not only from increased sales, but because *Fantastic Glue's* fast-setting properties will make your gluing operations nearly twice as efficient, saving you hundreds of hours of employee time and labor. Equally important, you'll see a noticeable improvement in employee morale on the production line.

4. **Evidence:** Our packaging and shipping department has been using *Fantastic Glue* for the past three months now, and everybody gives it rave reviews. I know from my personal experience that *Fantastic Glue* is terrific. I've taken samples home to repair some broken toys and appliances in my own home. My wife and kids think I'm brilliant now that I can repair just about anything that gets broken. Let me prove it to you. Here's one of the broken toys returned by one of your unhappy customers. I'll just brush on a little *Fantastic Glue*, and one minute later, I'll challenge anyone to pull the two pieces apart. [*Salesperson performs the demonstration with help of prospects.*] Now, isn't that truly fantastic!

5. **Summary:** Well, there you have it. You've seen the incredible qualities and benefits yourself. *Fantastic Glue* will immediately solve your adhesive problems, stop the customer complaints about broken toys, enhance your company's reputation for quality thereby increasing sales, improve production line morale, and dramatically improve your company's profits by making your gluing operations more time and cost efficient.

6. **Action:** I've got some more good news for you. As a special incentive for new buyers to try *Fantastic Glue*, we're offering a 20 percent discount with a double-your-money-back guarantee. In fact, if you order today, I'll even personally guarantee that *Fantastic Glue* will be delivered to you by this Thursday so you can start solving those gluing problems as soon as possible. How many gallons do you think you'll need? [*Salesperson takes out the order pad and pen.*]

Depending on the situation and the prospect audience, a standardized sales presentation format can often work well. However, the professional salesperson first answers three basic questions to ensure that the presentation is both appropriately tailored (aligned) for the audience and consistent with several guidelines. Table 5.6 outlines these questions and guidelines, and we discuss them below.

## Alignment of the Sales Presentation

Generally, the more precisely a sales presentation's content and communication style are aligned or matched with the audience's characteristics, desired benefits, and communication style, the more effective the presentation will be. Creating an alignment requires you to ask three crucial questions.

1. *Who Is the Prospect Audience?* Top salespeople always identify and confirm their audience before delivering their sales presentations. Some salespeople have been known to make sales presentations focused on highly technical aspects of a product, only to learn later that the audience included no engineers or technicians, only marketing and finance people. Find out what information the prospect organization requires before it will make the purchase. Until they know their prospects' characteristics and interests, even the best sales presenters can't communicate persuasively. This should be researched before the sales presentation is prepared and confirmed at the start of the presentation. Probably the most straightforward way to confirm the audience before you start the presentation is to ask, "It's my understanding that everyone in the room is an engineer. Is that correct?"

2. *What Benefits Are the Prospects Seeking?* Depending on their type of business or nonprofit activities and the macroenvironment, organizations

---

TABLE 5.6

## SALES PRESENTATION ALIGNMENT AND GUIDELINES FOR PROSPECT GROUPS

**Questions Regarding Alignment of the Sales Presentation**

1. Who is the audience?_____
2. What benefits are they seeking?_____
3. How do they prefer to communicate?_____

**Guidelines for Sales Presentations**

- Begin with an audience-focused statement of purpose.
- Translate the product into customer benefits.
- Energize the sales presentation and demonstration.
- Encourage interaction and participation.
- Show your commitment to customer service.
- Ask for specific action.
- Critique the sales presentation.

may have unique problems and needs at different stages in their life cycle. In general, however, the sales presentation's perspective should be carrying out the organization's primary functions. For example, a sales presentation to retailers and wholesalers needs to explain how they can profitably resell the product, and a sales presentation to industrial firms needs to focus on how the product will improve profitability in producing and marketing the buying firm's products.

3. *How Do the Prospects Prefer to Communicate?* Find out ahead of the sales presentation how the prospect group communicates with each other, so you can prepare and rehearse appropriately. Several questions need to be answered: What special jargon and gestures do they use? How do they normally dress—business suits, sports coats, or blue collars? What beliefs and attitudes underlie their business relationships and decisions? What do they recognize as achievements and why? How do they regard time? Do they prefer a formal style or a more relaxed style? How is space handled? Do they sit or stand close together? Do they make frequent eye contact? How do they prefer to receive information: color transparencies, slides, flipcharts, videotapes, printed material, PowerPoint, or verbal communication? Do they prefer open, give-and-take discussions?

## Group Sales Presentation Guidelines

After aligning the sales presentation content and communication style with the audience, professional salespeople generally follow seven basic guidelines.

1. *Begin with an Audience-Focused Statement of Purpose.* Many salespeople outline their sales presentations according to the points *they want to make* to prospects. However, the most effective presentations focus on what the *audience wants* to hear. The opening purpose statement should clarify the presentation goals and approach, as noted in the following example:

> Our purpose today is to show you how ABC Company can help you solve your product quality problems. Our approach will be to show you how we solve similar problems in various industries and companies by presenting four different scenarios. Finally, we have these four goals for this presentation: (1) to illustrate our understanding of your problem, (2) to demonstrate the benefits provided by our new punch press, (3) to show how it will pay for itself within the first year of use, and (4) to explain how we will maintain and service the equipment to ensure that it remains in top working order.

2. *Translate the Product into Prospect Benefits.* Prospects are interested in benefits or solutions to *their* problems, not necessarily the benefits the salesperson thinks he or she is selling. All the snazzy features and advantages of the product or service will have little impact unless you can hit the prospects' "hot buttons"—their desired benefits.

The best salespeople realize that they are selling *expected outcomes*—the results the prospect expects from the product, *not* the results the salesperson assumes the prospect expects. If the salesperson has not yet been able to pinpoint major benefits sought by the prospect, sometimes the product demonstration will reveal which benefits prospects value most.

When emphasizing the product's benefits, you should use *specific, positive* statements, rather than general, vague statements. For example, DON'T say, "Our competitors can't do this." Instead, DO say, "Our product is unmatched by competition, as we have over 97 percent up time." DON'T say, "This motor has outstanding performance." Rather, DO say, "This motor can turn 4500 rpms with minimum maintenance."

3. *Energize the Sales Presentation to Make It Memorable.* A sad tie can spoil the appearance of a suit, but **SAD TIE** is an acronym memory aid to salespeople in planning ways to spice up a sales presentation, as explained on p. 152. Such efforts enhance the clarity of the presentation and credibility of the seller.

> **SAD TIE** A memory-aid acronym standing for *s*tatistics, *a*nalogies, *d*emonstrations, *t*estimonials, *i*ncidents, and *e*xhibits, one or all of which the salesperson may use to spice up a sales presentation.

4. *Encourage Interaction and Participation.* In developing a relationship, nothing works better than personal give-and-take discussions. Salespeople can learn more about prospect needs and perceptions through direct discussions than from any market research technique. Essentially, such efforts are implicitly directed at taking the "pulse" of the sales presentation through prospect feedback. Learning to subtly facilitate and manage a group discussion while directing it along the sales presentation track is a talent that develops only after much role-playing or actual experience. Some salespeople try to involve prospects at various points during and after the sales presentation by asking, "Are there any questions?" Unfortunately, this approach seldom stimulates much response from the audience and does little to strengthen buyer-seller communication. A better way to obtain prospect involvement after completing part of the sales presentation is for the salesperson to ask a specific question such as, "Could you tell me how the system I've laid out might help you in your work?" or "Now, would you want one large central workstation or would a group of smaller ones best meet your needs?" If no one volunteers to answer even specific questions like these, the salesperson can direct the question in a nonthreatening way to a particular member of the buying group. For example, you might ask, "Mary, how do you think this system will fit in with your company's data processing needs?" or "Bill, how might your manufacturing plant benefit from this hydraulic pumping system?" In addition, when demonstrating the product, ask prospects to operate the product (if feasible and safe) to help familiarize them with the functioning of the product. Doing so should enhance their ability to see the benefits that they can realize from the product. Just as car salespeople ask prospects to take a test drive to "get the feel" of an automobile, prospects' participation in a demonstration can give them increased awareness of the strengths of the product under consideration as well as how it will help their business operations.

## SAD TIE

**S—*Statistics:*** Business audiences are particularly receptive to a few statistics, because they use them to make their own sales pitches to their bosses. Too many numbers, however, can be confusing; so show just enough to make key points. It's best to also show the numbers in a graphic form such as a pie or bar chart.

**A—*Analogies, Similes, and Metaphors:*** Innovative use of *analogies, similes,* and *metaphors* can bring special life to sales presentations. Most salespeople will tell you that analogies are an effective way to win people over to your way of thinking. *Analogies* enable prospects to better visualize and comprehend something complex by relating it to something different but familiar and easier to understand. For instance, talking about a billion dollars is rather vague until you tell people how many miles that many dollars would stretch if laid end to end, or how many hundred-thousand-dollar homes you could buy with it. *Similes* are direct comparisons usually preceded by the prepositions *like* or *as.* For example: "An Apple computer greets you like an old friend every time you turn it on" or "Our cellular car phone makes you feel as if you never left home." *Metaphors* are implied comparisons that use a seemingly inappropriate word or phrase to create a dramatic visual image. For example: "Our new razor *skates* smoothly over your face." "The *eye* and *ear* of this lightweight camcorder will *see* and *hear* everything you do."

**D—*Demonstrations:*** Use actual product demonstrations or simulations to bring benefits to life for the prospect and create a memorable impression. Nothing is more impressive to prospects than seeing, feeling, touching, tasting, or smelling the product benefits. Some salespeople are so confident in their products that they believe: "If they try it, they'll buy it."

**T—*Testimonials:*** Support your position with expert testimony. People will be more easily persuaded if you provide testimonial support from an objective source that the prospect respects. The product testimonial doesn't have to be a direct one, but can be implied: "Did you notice that the *Today Show* uses our cordless microphones?" "Do you know that the president wears the same brand of suit?"

**I—*Incidents:*** Describing an unusual but relevant incident brings a point home and usually makes a lasting impression. For example, if you're selling a new heating plant system, you could relate a specific experience of a well-known and respected company that saved money using the same system.

**E—*Exhibits:*** An exhibit is a selling prop and can take many forms. It can be a display at a trade show, the flipchart you're using as you talk, or a model of the product. The purpose of an exhibit is to help bring the sales presentation to life and enhance the sales presentation performance. For example, if you're making a presentation to a company interested in buying laptop computers for their executives, you could show a display of different laptops used by businesspeople over the years, ranging from the early "luggable" fifty-pound model to today's miniaturized versions that you want them to buy.

5. *Show Your Commitment to Customer Service.* It's important to show prospects and customers that you care about fully satisfying their business needs and that your service will continue after the sale. Explain your professional selling philosophy to them. Let them know that you want a *permanent* business relationship or partnership with them and that your success depends on their success. Telling them that you want them to be

lifetime customers, not merely one-time customers, shows that you are committed to customer satisfaction and service. Make such pronouncements, however, only if you really mean them and plan to back them up with exceptional service. Giving lip service to such ideals without following through will come back to haunt you and your company. Raising customer expectations without meeting those expectations only serves to foster customer dissatisfaction and loss of future sales.

6. *Ask for Specific Action.* Just as with sales presentations to individual buyers, it is important and necessary for salespeople to seek some kind of commitment from a group of buyers. Although salespeople should try to close a sale whenever possible, they must be prepared to seek other specific actions by prospects. Every sales call should include several possible secondary objectives in case a purchase commitment cannot be obtained. Maybe the prospects can be persuaded to try a small amount of the product on a trial basis or schedule an appointment for another sales presentation to a larger buying committee. By accomplishing one or more of their secondary objectives, salespeople learn to view nearly every sales call as at least a partial success that furthers the prospect-seller relationship and moves closer to future mutually satisfying sales agreements. This perspective clearly is preferable to that of a salesperson who believes that every sales presentation must lead to a close. A sales attitude that a sale must be made on every call can lead salespeople to become too pushy and even rude, two nemeses of buyers.[6]

7. *Critique the Sales Presentation.* Professional football teams review game films weekly to identify strengths and weaknesses in their previous game and prepare for the next one. Similarly, salespeople can critique every group (or single person) sales presentation and prepare for the next. If other members of the seller organization attended the sales presentation, they too can help the salesperson by offering their perspectives. Here are several questions to ask.

- Was the sales presentation executed from the prospects' viewpoint?
- Which benefits seemed most important to prospects? Why?
- What product features and advantages did prospects seem most interested in?
- What did you learn about the prospects that you want to include in the next sales presentation?
- Did you attempt enough *trial closes?* How did the prospect react to each? Which ones worked best?
- Which of your sales presentation goals were achieved? Which were not achieved?
- Which presentation format did you use? How well did it work?
- Overall, what parts of the sales presentation could you have done better?

For maximum benefit, conduct your debriefings both orally and in writing while encouraging a positive climate for candor and learning. Feedback and corrective action stimulate learning and lead to improved performance in subsequent sales presentations.

# SALES PRESENTATION STRATEGIES

Several alternative presentation strategies ought to be considered in preparing effective sales presentations to achieve specific objectives. As summarized in Table 5.7, these include the stimulus response, formula, need satisfaction, consultative problem solving, depth selling, and team selling approaches. Let's briefly discuss each of these six basic sales presentation strategies.

### Stimulus-Response

Stimulus-response strategies call for stimuli (selling points) to be presented in such a way as to elicit favorable responses from prospects while leading them toward the sales close. In order to obtain a series of "yes" responses from the prospect while demonstrating the product, the sales rep may ask leading questions such as the following: "Aren't you surprised to see how smoothly and efficiently this new computerized lathe works compared to your current ones?" This sales presentation technique is widely used for training new salespeople, but it may come across as robot-like and disingenuous if rigidly followed. This approach can sometimes work for novice salespeople talking to relatively naive prospects, but salespeople who deal with sophisticated buyers should seldom employ the stimulus-response approach except perhaps briefly in the product demonstration to help clarify benefits for the prospects.

### Formula

Formula sales presentation strategies tend to focus on the products offered rather than on the prospect's needs, but they do have the advantage of encouraging prospect involvement. *AIDA* is the name of one commonly employed formula. It tries to move prospects toward a purchase decision by sequentially progressing through four mental states: *attention, interest, desire,* and *action.* Sales reps must capture their prospects' undivided attention, then arouse their interest by describing benefits and pointing out advantages to them, stimulate their desire for the benefits by offering proof, and finally motivate them to take prompt purchase action.

An industrial strength vacuum cleaner salesperson calling on a large factory might make effective use of a formula sales presentation, even using the most stereotypical salesperson demonstration. First, the salesperson sprinkles sawdust or metal scrapings around the prospect's factory floor to dramatically draw the prospect's *attention.* As the dismayed plant manager's anxiety grows, the salesperson gains *interest* by saying: "Now wouldn't you like to see this mess cleaned up quickly and quietly?" Of course, the prospect's *desire* is to do

*Formula sales presentations encourage prospect involvement by sequentially obtaining the prospect's awareness, interest, desire, and action.*

Roger Ball/Corbis

## TABLE 5.7

## SALES PRESENTATION STRATEGIES

| Strategy | Approach | Advantage or Disadvantage |
|----------|----------|---------------------------|
| **Stimulus-Response** | Salesperson asks a series of positive leading questions. | Customer develops habit of answering "yes," which may lead to a positive response to the closing question. Can appear manipulative to more sophisticated prospects. |
| **Formula** | Salesperson leads the prospect through the mental states of buying (AIDA: attention, interest, desire, and action). | Prospect is led toward purchase action one step at a time, as the prospect participates in the interview. May come across as too mechanical and rehearsed to win prospect's trust and confidence. |
| **Need-Satisfaction** | Salesperson tries to find the prospect's dominant but often latent buying needs; skillful listening, questioning, and use of certain image-producing words will help the salesperson uncover the critical need or needs to be satisfied if the sale is to be won. | Salesperson listens and responds to the prospect while "leading" the prospect to buy; the salesperson learns dominant buyer needs and motivations. Salesperson must not overlook latent needs of prospect not articulated. |
| **Consultative Problem-Solving** | Salesperson carefully listens and asks probing questions to more fully understand the prospect's problems and specific needs, then recommends the best alternative solutions. | By working together to understand and solve customer problems, a trustful, consultative relationship with the prospect is created. Salesperson and buyer negotiations focus on "win-win" outcome. |
| **Depth Selling** | Salesperson employs a skillful mix of several sales presentation methods. | A customized mix of the best features of all of the strategies that helps realize most of their advantages. Depth selling requires exceptional salesperson skill and experience. |

(continued)

| | | TABLE 5.7 |
|---|---|---|
| **SALES PRESENTATION STRATEGIES (CONTINUED)** | | |
| **Strategy** | **Approach** | **Advantage or Disadvantage** |
| **Team Selling** | Salesperson, in concert with other company personnel, sells the product/service benefits and avoids intragroup conflicts by promoting harmony. Salesperson must identify and cater to the needs of each interest group. | Team selling involves counterparts from both the buyer and seller organizations interacting and cooperating to find solutions to problems. Salesperson serves as coordinator of the buyer-seller team interactions. |

exactly that and immediately, so the salesperson plugs the cord into the outlet, and the vacuum neatly cleans up all the particles. Demonstrating the benefits of the industrial vacuum usually can relieve and delight the prospect so much that the plant manager may be motivated to purchase (action) on the spot. Of course, using a little understated humor before and during such a classic salesperson's demonstration would probably go a long way in making it successful. For example, you might say: "Before I start this demonstration, your electricity is working, isn't it?" After a "yes" answer, the salesperson continues: "Good, now you've probably never seen nor heard of the demonstration I'm about to give, but it will show you just how well our industrial strength vacuum will work in your plant."

## Need-Satisfaction

Need-satisfaction strategies avoid talking about the product or service until the salesperson has discovered the prospects' dominant needs or wants. Through skillful questioning, the salesperson encourages prospects to reveal their psychographic make-up (attitudes, interests, opinions, personality, and life style) and needs. Need-satisfaction strategy requires the salesperson to be a patient, perceptive listener and observer of body language in order to fully understand what the prospect is saying and feeling. This approach is most appropriate when the potential purchase involves a significant economic and psychological commitment on the part of the prospect. Misreading the prospect's dominant buying motives will lose the sale, so the need-satisfaction strategy requires considerable selling practice and experience to be effective. Some dominant needs are latent and may not be articulated because of embarrassment, guilt, or unawareness; so, the salesperson must "read between the lines" as the prospect describes his or her needs. A prospect may express the *manifest needs* for transportation, safety, and comfort in buying a carpooling van for the firm, but an alert salesperson may also detect a strong *latent need* for status as the prospect talks. Unless the van satisfies this unspoken but perhaps dominant status need, the sale may fall through.

## Consultative Problem-Solving

The most frequently recommended and generally most successful sales presentation strategy for today's professional salespeople is *consultative problem-solving*. Consultative problem-solving sales presentations focus on the prospect's problems, *not* the seller's products. It emphasizes the partnership of buyer and seller and stresses "win-win" outcomes in negotiations, which is why most salespeople and customers see it as the *best* sales presentation method. This approach is most often used by sellers of complex technical products who seek to establish long-term relationships built on mutual trust, confidence, and respect. For example, an electronics company considering the purchase of some robots for an assembly line versus the alternative of upgrading its current manual equipment would probably prefer a problem-solving sales presentation strategy that would analyze the pros and cons of each possible solution from the buyer's perspective.

In applying problem-solving strategies salespeople must make full use of their listening and questioning skills to understand the prospect's problem and discover precise needs. Several face-to-face meetings, telephone calls, emails, in-depth research, and the help of backup technical specialists may be required to prepare a final written proposal that accurately analyzes the prospect's problems and recommends alternative solutions along with their advantages and disadvantages. Contrasted with traditional canned formula presentations, dramatic product demonstrations, or splashy multimedia shows, the consultative problem-solving approach to sales presentations is rather uncomplicated, as described by a salesperson in *On the Frontlines* on p. 158.

## Depth Selling

Depth selling is a strategic mix of several sales presentation strategies. For example, a sales representative might start with an overall formula strategy, such as AIDA (attention, interest, desire, action), while using probing need-satisfaction questions to discover buying motives; then turn to stimulus-response questions to encourage the prospect to think positively about the product; and finally move to the consultative problem-solving strategy to suggest alternative solutions and win the prospect's confidence. Effectively employing the depth-selling presentation strategy requires a skillful, perceptive, and flexible mastery of sales presentation strategies, so it's most often used by veteran salespeople.

## Team Selling

As organizational buying functions become more centralized and buying committees more expert, team-selling strategies are becoming increasingly important. Team selling is a response to the growing buyer insistence that sellers spend less time pitching products to them and more time helping them solve their problems. A team selling approach significantly increases the chances for reaching most members of the buying center.

There are two types of selling teams—core selling teams and selling centers.[7] A **core selling team** is comprised of assigned members of the selling

**Core Selling Team**
Members of the selling firm assigned to particular prospects or customers to develop and maintain ongoing buyer-seller relationships with them.

# A Consultative Problem-Solving Sales Presentation

I used to think that lacking a dazzling sales presentation style worked against me, but no more. Recently, I earned my biggest commission ever, and it was the easiest sales presentation I ever made. Four competitive salespeople and I were scheduled to make a sales presentation to a local manufacturer. I'd been up against these four sales reps before, and I knew each of them would make a multimedia, show-biz type sales presentation to try for the business. Recognizing that I didn't have a high-tech sales presentation or the kind of flare to beat them at their game, I decided not to play their game at all. Instead, I spent my time trying to learn as much as I could about the prospect's problems. First, I went to the library and read about the prospect in various sources that the reference librarian helped me find. Then, I talked to several noncompeting salespeople who have done business with the company. Next, I took a personal plant tour arranged by one of the plant supervisors to see how the prospect's assembly line operates. During the tour, I asked my supervisor friend and other employees I met a bunch of questions. Any question that didn't get answered to my satisfaction I wrote down in my little notebook.

On the day of the sales presentation, I didn't bring any audiovisual aids at all, just my notebook of questions and a couple of pens. After saying hello and shaking hands with the four people (from purchasing, engineering, production, and finance) who were going to hear my presentation, I opened up by asking a question. "I understand you have some problems at your Chicago assembly plant. Do you mind giving me your perspectives on the problems?"

They each took turns talking. As soon as they all had said everything they wanted in response to that question, I asked another question. And it kept going like that. I'd ask a question, and they're answer it, oftentimes providing a lot of interesting information that I wouldn't have thought to ask for. After a while, we were talking back and forth like members of the same team, working for the same company and come to think of it, we were!

They probably talked 90 percent of the time, which was fine with me because I was taking notes and gathering all the information I needed: when and why they believed the problems had started, what it would take to solve the problems, how they would go about selecting a supplier, and how the purchasing process would be set up. At the end of three hours, I summarized what I thought had been said, and they helped me clarify a few points. Then, I said: "I'm confident that we can provide the right products and service to solve your problems, and I'll send you a written proposal within a week." Two weeks after receiving the proposal, one of them called to say that my company had won the contract. They didn't even quibble over price; they just told me to move ahead on the contract as fast as possible.

Later, as I got to know the four quite well, one of them told me that my sales presentation was the only one that asked for their perspectives on their company's problems. All the other sales presentations took up the entire time doing an elaborate "dog-and-pony" show that centered on the products they had to sell. As the customer put it, "They were trying to sell products; you were trying to help us solve our problems."

firm who work together to develop and maintain particular prospects or customer relationships. The team tends to stay together for the duration of the buyer-seller relationship. A **selling center** consists of selling organization members assigned to a certain prospect to close a particular sales transaction. After the sale is consummated, the selling center is likely to disband. Both kinds of selling teams consist of individuals from different parts of the company brought together to marshal the resources necessary to work effectively with the customer or prospect. The strength of team selling is highlighted below:

> . . . selling firms often have a great opportunity to deliver high levels of value, in both real and perceived terms, to their customers by effectively marshaling resources and expertise from across their entire enterprise. A real competitive advantage can be gained if salespeople . . . can effectively locate and deploy the expertise that may reside outside the selling organization [sales department].[8]

Depending on the organization, the customer, and the sales situation, the exact nature of team selling can vary widely. Team selling usually takes place at one of three distinct levels.[9] At the first level, team selling simply means that the field salesperson is supported closely by the branch sales manager, the district sales manager, and perhaps the national sales manager. At a second level, team selling implies that the salesperson's field efforts are closely integrated with customer-oriented efforts in other in-house departments, such as engineering, manufacturing, accounting, customer service, market research, advertising, and sales promotion. In this stage the salesperson serves as a coordinator of all company activities that impinge on the customer and constantly asks the question, "Where can I find the best resources to help solve a specific customer need or problem?"

At the third and highest level, all of the seller team members, whether technical, administrative staff, or managerial, work directly with their counterparts in the buyer organization. From the presidents of the two companies on down there are open lines of communication, interaction, and cooperation between counterparts in both seller and buyer organizations. The salesperson acts as the coordinator and contact person for the buyer and sales teams, which may consist of specialists from marketing, finance, engineering, production, or research and development. Specialists from the seller team work closely with their counterparts from the buyer team to make sure that the selling team understands and responds to all facets of customer needs and problems. For instance, the traffic manager of the seller organization will coordinate product delivery with the receiving manager at the customer organization, and the seller's advertising manager may work with the buyer's advertising manager on cooperative advertising campaigns aimed at the product's ultimate consumer or user. Customer-supplier relationships are so integrated in some high-tech companies that the customer is allowed to choose preferred after-sale support team members from the supplier's organization. Being selected to provide customer service as a member of a support team is an honor that generates considerable competition among support personnel. *It's Up to You,* on p. 160, gives you a chance to consider an impromptu decision often necessary during sales presentations.

**Selling Center** Selling organization members assigned to a certain prospect to close a particular sales transaction. After the sale is consummated, the selling center is likely to disband.

## IT'S UP TO YOU

You are thirty minutes into a planned sixty-minute sales presentation to a buying group in a conference room of a pesticide manufacturer. During your presentation on a new specialty chemical, you have paused several times to ask if there are any questions, and each time all buying group members have shaken their heads "no." The room is warm, and you are concerned that you are talking too much and losing your small audience's attention. To revive them, you are thinking about pausing to tell a funny and relevant, although risqué, joke, but you are not sure how the conservative-looking prospects will react.

Another option is to mention that it's very warm in the room, so perhaps it is a good time to take a five-minute break for everyone to refresh, but you're afraid that you'll lose some of your audience if you take a break. Still another way to perk up the audience might be to ask two or three people specific questions about how they plan to use the product in their respective areas of responsibility. You don't have much time to decide what to do as you can see that some members of the buying group are already glancing at their watches and beginning to stir restlessly. What are you going to do? Think fast!

## ADAPTIVE VERSUS CANNED SALES PRESENTATIONS

**Adaptive Selling**
Modifying each sales presentation and demonstration to accommodate each individual prospect.

The opportunity to customize or adapt each presentation to individual prospects differentiates personal selling from any other promotional tool. **Adaptive selling** stresses the unique advantage skilled salespeople have in adjusting their selling behavior to the particular prospect and selling situation.[10] Traditional salespeople usually make a relatively standard or habitual sales presentation that doesn't vary too much with different prospects or customers. But salespeople who modify their presentations to adapt to specific prospect or customer needs and behaviors have proven to be more effective than those who do not.[11] It may seem obvious but only salespeople who are predisposed to engage in adaptive selling are likely to do so during the sales call.[12] Successful professional salespeople not only mentally prepare themselves to adapt their sales presentation to the prospect or customer, but they remain alert to opportunities to do so throughout the sales presentation and demonstration. For instance, if a buyer for Hertz's fleet of automobiles shows more interest in safety than gas mileage, then an observant salesperson for General Motors quickly adapts the sales presentation and demonstration to emphasize the safety benefits of GM cars. Remaining adaptable, however, does not mean that the salesperson should not have a sound, basic structure for his or her sales presentation and demonstration. Some sales managers, in their efforts to improve efficiency while controlling the accuracy and ethics of the sales message, have found structured or **canned (or programmed) selling** to be best for some types of prospects, selling situations, and salespeople. Salespeople, however, tend to think of canned and adaptive sales presentations as polar extremes. Many believe that increasing structure decreases the professional salesperson's role in the sales presentation. Some salespeople protest, "Anybody can read a script or play a video."

**Canned (or Programmed) Selling** Any highly structured or patterned selling approach.

Although most salespeople prefer wide latitude and flexibility in deciding what to say and show prospects, the best sales presentations may often blend the canned and adaptive approaches.[13] In his book *Superselling*, comedian Johnny Carson's long-time sidekick Ed McMahon, who has sold everything from vegetable slicers on Atlantic City's boardwalk to countless products on television, says

> I believe that perfecting your presentation is probably the most important work you can do now to advance your sales career. . . . I rehearsed my entire sales interview down to each lifted eyebrow and dropped tone. . . . There is only one way you can free your mind to give a professional, order-winning performance: You have to know your lines. . . . Without even thinking, you have to be able to adapt your presentations to the buyer and the circumstances under which you're selling. Questions such as the following should be running through your mind constantly as you work to fit what you say to suit the person you're trying to persuade:
>
> How is this prospect reacting?
>
> Should I speed up or slow down?
>
> Should I get more technical or should I skip the heavy data?
>
> What will get this buyer excited about my product?
>
> What's my best close?
>
> Why isn't this guy smiling?[14]

While the debate between canned and adaptive approaches continues, salespeople are making increasing use of multi-media aides and computer-developed sales presentation materials. Many salespeople find that these tools enliven their sales presentations and help keep prospects interested. Moreover, they enable salespeople to present prospect-focused information efficiently and effectively, while they closely observe the prospect's reaction and appropriately adapt later parts of the sales presentation.

Occasionally, the risk of coming across too slick to prospects arises. A highly programmed, multimedia presentation to decision-makers in a consumer products company may position a salesperson as a skilled professional. This same presentation to a group of conservative engineering managers at a public utility may come off as orchestrated hucksterism. It is essential for the salesperson to know the prospect's normal communication methods and styles before making a sales presentation and demonstration, and to adapt aptly to the prospects' responses. Do you think you are or will be an adaptive salesperson? Take the following test to see how adaptive you are now.

# HOW ADAPTIVE ARE YOU?

*Assume that you are a salesperson, and respond to each of the following statements to determine how adaptive you would be in dealing with a prospect or a customer. Use the following scale when responding to each statement:*

**5-Strongly Agree    4-Agree    3-Neither Agree nor Disagree    2-Disagree    1-Strongly Disagree**

____ 1. Each customer requires a unique approach.

____ 2. When I feel that my sales approach is not working, I can easily change to another approach.

____ 3. I like to experiment with different sales approaches.

____ 4. I am very flexible in the selling approach I use.

____ 5. I feel that most buyers can be dealt with in different manners.

____ 6. I change my approach from one customer to another.

____ 7. I can easily use a wide variety of selling approaches.

____ 8. I use varied sales approaches.

____ 9. It is easy for me to modify my sales presentation if the situation calls for it.

____ 10. Basically, I use a different approach with most customers.

____ 11. I am very sensitive to the needs of my customers.

____ 12. I find it easy to adapt my presentation style to most buyers.

____ 13. I vary my sales style from situation to situation.

____ 14. I try to understand how one customer differs from another.

____ 15. I feel confident that I can effectively change my planned presentation when necessary.

____ 16. I treat each of my buyers differently.

Add up your scores for the sixteen questions. A score of 64 or higher indicates that your adaptability is strong; a score of 32 or less indicates that your adaptability is weak and needs work.

***Source:*** *Adapted from Rosann L. Spiro and Barton A. Weitz, "Adaptive Selling: Conceptualization, Measurement, and Nomological Validity,"* Journal of Marketing Research *27 (February 1990): 60–61. Reprinted with permission of the American Marketing Association.*

## WRITTEN PRESENTATIONS

**Written Presentation**
In sales presentations to organizational prospects, the salesperson's explanation of how the prospect can profitably use the product. Also called a sales proposal or business plan.

Whether used at the time of the verbal sales presentation or mailed as a follow-up after the sales call, a **written presentation** (also called a sales proposal or business plan) can be effective in winning sales. Written presentations force salespeople to be specific about prospect needs and ensure that the salespeople do their homework. Putting the sales presentation in writing also enables the prospect to share information with other key decision-makers in the company. Written presentations, usually from ten to twenty pages long, allow the salesperson to reinforce the material presented orally and to bring in more material, such as detailed financial analyses that cannot be adequately covered in a verbal presentation. Each written sales presentation should contain the following:

- statement of the prospect's problem (or opportunity)
- problem solution (that is, the seller's product offering that will address the prospect's problem)
- detailed listing of the product's specifications
- cost-benefit analysis (information regarding what the prospect will receive for the money spent over the life of the product)
- financial analysis of the sale (for example, leasing arrangements, terms, interest rate)
- timetable (an enumeration of the key events that will occur after the prospect has agreed to make the purchase)
- written contract (order form)

Salespeople who think they cannot afford time out from selling to write sales presentations must learn that they *are* selling when they're writing sales proposals. Persuasive proposals win sales. Carefully study the tips for writing effective sales presentations noted in Table 5.8.

---

TABLE 5.8

## TIPS FOR A WRITTEN SALES PRESENTATION

- Make sure you spell all prospect company names and titles correctly. Nothing turns off prospects more than a salesperson who doesn't take time to ensure correct spelling of names and titles.

- Make the opening paragraph exciting and interesting so prospects will look forward to reading your sales proposal. (For example, *We're delighted to tell you that our sales proposal will show how we can save your company several thousand dollars during the coming year.*)

- Be positive and upbeat in a natural, conversational writing style.

- Tailor each written sales presentation to a specific prospect or customer.

- Use a logical format along with a creative but professional look.

- Sequence benefits in the most effective order, usually in term of importance to the prospect.

- Use powerful action-oriented words while minimizing tentative words such as *maybe, promising, per chance, tentatively, hopeful, perhaps, likely, apt,* or *possible.*

- Never disparage competitors or their products and services.

- Use paragraph headings, occasional bold or italicized type, graphs, tables, charts, figures, and pictures to clarify material, add interest, and guide prospects through the narrative.

- Provide an incentive (for example, a limited-time discount, free gift, special services) to purchase or take other desired action (such as requesting more information) promptly.

- Personalize the proposal with a handwritten note in a postscript (PS).

- Double check and proofread everything before mailing, faxing, or e-mailing.

## SELLING THE LONG-TERM RELATIONSHIP

The most successful strategy for selling to organizations has proven to be developing a long-term relationship of mutual trust and professionalism. Organizations across the board—whether manufacturers, resellers, or governments—are continually seeking to improve quality and reduce costs. Closer supplier relationships, longer-term contracts, and fewer suppliers are elements of an ever-growing trend toward achieving these goals. As one director of purchasing at an automotive manufactuer puts it: "We're no longer just asking who should supply this part number for this product program. Instead, we're asking ourselves who should be our supplier for this product line for multiple product programs." Selling the long-term relationship is not just another strategy. It is fast becoming the *only* viable strategy for salespeople.

## SUMMARY

The sales presentation and demonstration form the pivotal exchange between buyers and sellers and as such should be based on a carefully developed strategy. Although several sales presentation strategies are available, most professional salespeople use the consultative problem-solving strategy, which requires full use of their listening and questioning skills to understand the prospect's problems and needs. Consultative problem solving emphasizes the partnership of the buyer and seller. When making sales presentations and demonstrations to an individual or group (either orally or in writing), salespeople need to understand and follow some basic guidelines. In addition, they need to practice adaptive selling to enhance their effectiveness with increasingly demanding and sophisticated prospects and customers.

## KEY TERMS

| | | | |
|---|---|---|---|
| FAB | SAD TIE | Selling Center | Canned (or Programmed) Selling |
| Value Added | Core Selling Team | Adaptive Selling | Written Presentation |

## CHAPTER REVIEW QUESTIONS

1. Why are the sales presentation and demonstration so important in the personal selling process?

2. What are the basic steps in planning the sales presentation?

3. Explain the difference between adaptive and canned sales presentations.

4. List and briefly describe the basic sales presentation strategies. Which one is generally considered best for professional salespeople? Why?

5. What is the consultative problem-solving sales presentation strategy? Give an example of a selling situation where this strategy would be especially appropriate.

6. Why are clothing and accessories important considerations in making an effective sales presentation?

7. In making presentations to groups, what does the acronym *SAD TIE* stand for?

8. Define and give an example of each of the following aids for sales presentations: (a) analogies, (b) similes, and (c) metaphors.

9. Give some basic guidelines for written sales presentations.

## TOPICS FOR THOUGHT AND CLASS DISCUSSION

1. Why do you think the consultative problem-solving sales presentation is the most successful strategy for professional salespeople? What are the benefits of this strategy to the prospect or customer?

2. Name at least five special prospect categories and describe an appropriate strategy for a sales presentation to each.

3. Which do you think is more effective for most business-to-business selling, an *oral* or a *written* sales presentation? Why?

4. Do you think sales presentations and demonstrations are more important for tangible products or for intangible services? Why?

## PROJECTS FOR PERSONAL GROWTH

1. Contact two business-to-business salespeople and ask them about their sales presentation preparation methods, dress style during the presentation, and demonstration techniques.

2. Research the following two industries and report on the methods and approaches each uses to sell its products: (1) airplane manufacturers, and (2) household products manufacturers.

3. Contact three salespeople (one who sells to manufacturers, one who sells to resellers, and one who sells to the national government) and ask them how they prepare for their sales presentations and demonstrations. Are there major differences? Compare and contrast the preparation done by each of the three salespeople.

4. With a classmate, take turns playing the role of a publishing company sales rep trying to sell a new textbook to a college professor who might be nicknamed "Skeptical Sid." Then prepare a *written* sales presentation to sell a textbook to the instructor of your personal selling class. Depending on how creative or cooperative your instructor is, you may want to ask him or her to play one of the prospect stereotypes described in Table 5.2.

5. Assume that you are a sales representative for a manufacturer of automatic fire sprinkler systems for commercial buildings. Outline sales presentations using each of the seven basic strategies. For each strategy, create and then describe the individual or group of prospects to whom you're presenting.

## CASE 5.1

# SELF-ANALYSIS OF A SALES PRESENTATION

Peter Kimball, a sales representative for United Container Company, is sitting in front of the desk of Mark Spearman, the head purchasing agent for Modern Office Equipment Company. Just after Peter finished his twenty-minute sales presentation, Mr. Spearman's secretary buzzed him for an important phone call. Picking up the phone, Mr. Spearman spun his chair around so that his back was to Peter, and he is now deeply engaged in conversation with the person on the other end. While Mr. Spearman is talking on the phone, Peter reflects on his sales presentation and wonders what else he can do to convince Mr. Spearman to purchase his line of shipping containers. Modern Office Equipment Company would be a big account to land. Prior to making the sales call, Peter had carefully developed and rehearsed a sales presentation strategy. His presentation incorporated results of his research on Modern online and at his local library plus some perspectives he elicited from noncompeting salespeople about Mr. Spearman, an analytical person who's mainly interested in buying at the lowest price. Peter continues to think about whether or not he adequately covered the five basic objectives of his sales presentation and what he should do when Mr. Spearman hangs up the phone. Here are Peter's thoughts on each of his five sales call objectives:

1. *Build rapport.* Initially, Mr. Spearman acted low key and analytical, just as I was told he would. But I caught his interest by asking him several nonthreatening questions about his son, who I know is a football player at the University of Missouri. I think my gently probing questions put him in the right frame of mind to respond to my questions and even prompted him to ask a few of his own.

2. *Uncover problems and perceived needs.* At first, when I asked him to describe some of his major packaging problems, he claimed Modern didn't have any special packaging problems. I told him how amazing that was and that most of my other customers have a lot of packaging problems; otherwise I'd be standing in a bread line somewhere. Hearing that, he laughed, loosened up a little, and admitted that his company occasionally experienced some "minor" problems when Modern equipment was damaged in customers' warehouses. Mr. Spearman elaborated: "Usually the damage is caused by forklift trucks cutting through our heavy-duty cardboard boxes and puncturing our equipment. Although we're really not responsible for damage in the customer's warehouse, our company philosophy is that 'the customer is always right,' so we allow them to return any damaged equipment still in the packing box. Guess it would help if our packing boxes were made of tougher material, but we get a great price on the heavy-duty cardboard boxes."

3. *Learn how satisfied Modern is with its current supplier.* When I asked how satisfied Modern is with its current supplier, Mr. Spearman said everybody in the company seemed "satisfied," except perhaps the quality control manager who handles customer complaints about equipment. Although he didn't say so, I think Modern's major supplier is Megastar Container because I saw some Megastar cardboard box flats outside the warehouse near where I parked my car. Mr. Spearman didn't seem interested in even talking about buying our metal containers, even though I told him they would eliminate any problems of equipment damage in shipping or storage, and the price was only about 15 percent higher than for heavy-duty cardboard containers. Anyway, I've already put our product brochure for the metal containers on his desk. When I asked him if he would consider changing suppliers if we could offer him a lower price for the same quality of product he was buying now, he replied that he would have to see the total sales proposal, not just the price. I'll have to prepare him a written sales proposal. Maybe I should prepare four different sales proposals, one for each quality of

(continued)

## SELF-ANALYSIS OF A SALES PRESENTATION
(CONTINUED)

container we sell. That's a lot of work. Maybe Bob or Jennifer in Marketing will help me out in preparing the proposals, because I'm going to need some information from them.

4. *Demonstrate that United Container has the right products to solve Modern's problems and satisfy its needs.* I gave him several brochures about our products and carefully pointed out the features and benefits of our four major packaging products. I also stressed that United takes great pride in its reputation for customer service and keeping customers satisfied. But, darn it, I couldn't quickly find our latest price listing sheet. I must have left it on the prospect's desk at my first sales call. I probably shouldn't have left my laptop computer in the trunk of my car either, because I know that I could go to our intranet to find prices. But he would probably want the prices in writing anyway. Oh well, I'll send Mr. Spearman our new price sheet when I mail him the written sales proposals next week.

5. *Convince Mr. Spearman that he can trust me and that United Container Company can deliver quality products at fair prices backed up by excellent service.* I showed him a list of other companies we sell to, and he seemed impressed. I told him that I will personally service his account once a month and that I always carry a beeper that will allow him to reach me in case of an emergency. When I mentioned that our company was spending a lot of money on research to develop new environmentally safe packaging products, I must have hit his "hot button" because his eyes really lit up and he asked several questions

about what we were doing. He said that he was chairing a committee on environmental issues for the Purchasing Agent Association and that the PAA was holding a regional conference in three months on the topic of environmental packaging. Mr. Spearman is going to present a paper at the conference, and Modern's vice president of marketing will be a major speaker.

I asked if our company could help him at this meeting, and he gave me some suggestions that I'll follow up on with some of our R&D people. Maybe I should ask him whether he knows about the union strike that began at Megastar yesterday. They might not even be able to deliver containers unless they have a lot more inventory than we have. Of course, I don't want to sound like I'm knocking a competitor.

Just as Peter is mulling over his last thought, Mr. Spearman finishes his phone call, spins his chair around to face him, and says: "Now, where were we?"

### Questions

1. What should Peter say and do now? How do you think Mr. Spearman will react? Why?
2. What do you think about Peter's sales presentation? What could he have done better?
3. What advice would you give Peter for capitalizing on the interest Mr. Spearman showed in environmental packaging?
4. Should Peter mention the union strike at Megastar?

## CASE 5.2   WHAT MAKES HIM SO SUCCESSFUL?

Wanda Soules is a new salesperson for Corbet Corporation, a small pharmaceutical company. After graduating near the top of her class with a degree in biology from an Ivy League university, Wanda had interviewed with several companies for a job in research and development. She took a couple of interviews in technical sales—mainly as a lark because her college roommate had challenged her to do it. Surprisingly, the two sales interviews convinced Wanda to switch directions and start her business career in sales with Corbet. After completing an intensive one-month training program, which concentrated mainly on product knowledge and role plays of sales calls, Wanda was assigned to a territory that mostly consisted of small, private medical practices, retail store pharmacies, and hospitals.

Wanda did well in training and felt she learned a great deal about the company's products and the proper "steps" in selling. But her first month was disappointingly slow, even though she faithfully followed the same selling steps she had learned in the training program. After Wanda's second slow month, her sales manager suggested that she spend a day traveling with one of the company's rising star sales reps, Dan Clover. Wanda was a little perturbed to be asked to tag along behind another salesperson who had only about a year more selling experience than she had. And Dan was only twenty-two years old—her own age! She felt she could learn more from a real veteran rep. Wanda also knew that Dan didn't even have a technical degree. Nevertheless, she had to comply with her sales manager's request. On Monday, this is how her day goes:

The two young missionary reps meet for breakfast at 7 A.M. Dan suggests that Wanda just observe everything during the calls but hold her comments until the end of the day, when they can sit down together to critique the entire day. Wanda says nothing but thinks to herself, "He's condescending to me . . . and I know more than he does." The first call is at 8 A.M. at a center-city drugstore pharmacy run by a father-and-son team. As they leave the car, Wanda is surprised to see Dan remove his suitcoat

and roll up his shirtsleeves. She is about to remark that she really doesn't think it's appropriate to be so casual (after all, they're representing a respected company with an image to uphold), but, remembering Dan's request to watch the day's progression with an open mind, Wanda resists the temptation to say anything. As they enter the store and head back to the pharmacy department, Wanda notices that neither pharmacist has a white lab coat on and their sleeves are rolled up. Dan and the senior pharmacist head back to his office with Wanda tagging behind. They chat casually about fishing while Wanda stands by, silently but impatiently waiting for them to get down to business. "What a waste of time," Wanda thinks to herself, as the two men talk on and on about fishing. "Dan probably hasn't memorized the sales presentation that we were taught, so he's trying to sidetrack the conversation to keep from being embarrassed in front of me." While they talk, Wanda glances around the office at all the nature scenes on the walls. Many show the father and son pharmacists, each with a rod and reel, wading in mountain streams up to their hips. Wanda considers them tranquil scenes, but somewhat monotonous. Even the magazines on the coffee table look alike: *Field and Stream, Wildlife, Hunting and Fishing,* and *Backpacking.* "Boy, I'd hate to be stuck a long time in this room," she says to herself. Finally, the two stop chatting and Dan mentions the new drug they should have been discussing the entire time. Dan speaks briefly about the benefits of the new drug and leaves some information. Wanda is dumbfounded. They've been here for twenty-five minutes, and Dan has only talked about their company's products for five minutes. And even more amazing, as they are leaving, the senior pharmacist says, "I'll give the new drug a try, Dan, to see how it works. I'll call you with my order by the end of next week."

Their next call is with Dr. Stanley Hafer at a suburban hospital outside of the city. Wanda notices that Dan rolls down his sleeves and replaces his jacket before entering the hospital. After signing in at the security desk, they are escorted to the

(continued)

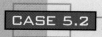

## WHAT MAKES HIM SO SUCCESSFUL? (CONTINUED)

doctor's office by the doctor's nurse, Ruth Blair. Wanda is surprised to hear Dan's conversation with the nurse. He speaks to her about Corbet's new product, asks her opinion on some of the company's other products, and even leaves a sample and some product brochures with her. Wanda can't believe that Dan is wasting all this time and energy on the nurse when everyone knows that it's the doctors who make all the decisions. After Dan has spent about fifteen minutes with the nurse (while Wanda tries not to act upset), they go in to see Dr. Hafer. They have only a few minutes with the doctor, who is expected in surgery shortly. Wanda is surprised that the doctor asks only a couple of questions about the drug before excusing himself and heading out the door. As he leaves, Dr. Hafer calls back: "Leave your product brochures and a sample with my nurse, Mrs. Blair." On the way out of the medical office, Dan stops to say goodbye to Mrs. Blair, and Wanda is interested to hear her say, "I'm sure the doctor will give your new drug a try. Why don't you call me next week to check on how we like it?"

The third call of the day is at a small medical practice about four blocks away from the hospital. As they enter the room, Dan greets the nurse by her first name, Sandra. Wanda can't believe how informal Dan is acting with Sandra—telling her jokes and asking about her son's Little League games. Wanda thinks, "How could this guy be one of the company's rising young stars? He wastes time on every call, and he doesn't stick to the sales steps that we were taught in the training program. Matter of fact, he seems to change his style and approach on each call. He isn't the least bit consistent or professional!"

The last call of the morning is at Dr. Beverly Pruett's office at another private medical clinic. After announcing themselves at the receptionist's desk, Dan and Wanda wait quietly in the reception room for about fifteen minutes before the nurse asks them to come in. Dan's behavior finally seems appropriate. He doesn't say anything other than a polite hello to the nurse. As they enter the doctor's office, Wanda notices that Dan's whole attitude has changed from that exhibited in the previous sales calls. He waits for the doctor to sit before seating himself. He goes through the entire presentation (just the way they were trained to in class). The doctor stops Dan and asks him several different questions. Wanda is impressed with Dan's direct, no-nonsense answers. She is also surprised that Dan doesn't take the opportunity to expand on certain points and bring up other products. Wanda knows that the appointment is supposed to last only twenty minutes, but what harm would it do to take a little extra time? Wanda is startled to realize that Dan has neatly condensed into twenty minutes a presentation that normally takes her forty-five minutes. When all points have been covered, Dan concludes the presentation by graciously but directly asking for the order. It is interesting to observe the doctor glance at her watch, think over the information for a few long seconds, and then agree to place an order for the new product.

By the end of the day, Wanda is really confused. Dan doesn't use the same sales technique twice. Sometimes he calls the prospect by a first name, sometimes not. Sometimes he goes through the entire presentation, sometimes only parts. In certain offices he seems to spend more time talking about other subjects than the company's products. On certain calls he comes right out and asks for the order, but on others he simply thanks the doctor for his or her time. He doesn't seem to be following a prepared script, yet each call seems to produce a sale. Wanda is really unsure what, if anything, she has learned from watching Dan. Perhaps it will be sorted out when they critique the day together as they head for a nearby coffee shop.

### Questions

1. What do you think Dan will tell Wanda about his selling philosophy and use of different sales presentation strategies?
2. Describe in a few sentences the most important lesson you think Wanda should have learned on her day in the field with Dan.
3. What advice would you offer Wanda to help her sell more successfully in her sales territory?

## CHAPTER 6

# Negotiating Sales Resistance and Objections for "Win-Win" Agreements

*"Everything is worth what its purchaser will pay for it."*
*Publilius Syrus*

## After Reading This Chapter, You Should Understand:

- Why objections and sales resistance are important to personal selling.

- The various kinds of buyer resistance and objections.

- How to deal with prospect resistance.

- The importance of win-win negotiation outcomes.

- How to plan for objections.

- How to overcome objections to price.

- Techniques for negotiating resistance and objections.

## INSIDE PERSONAL SELLING:
## *Meet Leslie Vaughan of SAS Institute*

Leslie Vaughan has found the most difficult sales resistance is simply prospect "niceness." Vaughan is a senior account executive for SAS Institute, selling information delivery software to insurance companies in North Carolina and Virginia. SAS, the world's largest privately held software firm, helps companies develop more profitable relationships with customers and suppliers and helps management analyze business data to make informed decisions about issues such as customer profitability and possible fraud.

During her ten years in sales, Vaughan has identified two kinds of sales resistance. "Either they hesitate," she says, "or they are very nice yet evasive—they never intend to do anything." With hesitant prospects, she digs deeper to uncover and answer objections; with nice but evasive prospects, however, she has had to change

her approach. "For years I didn't ask questions I didn't want answered," she notes. "But if people are genuinely nice, that approach doesn't get you anywhere. So I changed my style and now ask very direct questions about their concerns."

Starting with the first sales visit, Vaughan probes directly but tactfully to learn about prospects' problems, their knowledge of SAS, and any reservations they may have. This sets the stage for open conversations throughout the sales cycle, as she continues to flush out hidden issues through questions such as "Have you heard anything you're concerned about? Are you hesitant about anything? Is anything holding you back from making a decision?"

Vaughan has also found that some objections are symptoms of other concerns. For example, a customer may object to SAS's price, but the real issue is licensing rather than buying the software. Since SAS only licenses its software for yearly renewal and does not discount price, she must explain how customers benefit because SAS constantly improves its software by adding valuable new functionality. This is clearly a persuasive argument because 98 percent of customers renew every year—and 67 percent decide to spend even more with SAS.

Actually inviting objections helped clinch a major sale to a large insurance company where management was excited about SAS's software. Looking ahead, however, Vaughan realized that successful implementation would be nearly impossible without the expertise of the prospect's information technology personnel. As a result, she says, "Very early in the sales cycle, I insisted that management get the information technology people involved, even knowing they would have tons of objections."

This move, which carried some risk, lengthened the sales cycle by four months as Vaughan and SAS technical experts worked to overcome a variety of real and invalid objections, many of which boiled down to "We've always done things our own way." As discussions continued month after month, higher-level decision-makers became involved and the project grew bigger than anyone imagined—but ultimately the sale "became a huge win for everybody," she summarizes.

**171**

**Y**ogi Berra, a great former catcher for the New York Yankees, once said, "It ain't over 'til it's over." His statement couldn't be more apt than in selling. You may have generated tremendous enthusiasm from the prospect during your sales presentation. You may have given a skillful and impressive presentation and demonstration—and even had your prospect try your product during the demonstration. In fact, you may believe that you did everything right. So, you ask yourself silently, "Why wouldn't the prospect give me a sales order after such a stellar presentation?" Why? Because prospects rarely embrace any sales proposition wholeheartedly. They usually have anxieties about the purchase, and their objections and sales resistance is merely part of the buying-selling process.

"Without sales resistance, I wouldn't have a job," is a comment often heard from successful salespeople. They understand that if prospects put up no resistance to buying, then the first seller to reach them would make the sale, and trained salespeople wouldn't be needed at all. Most professional salespeople appreciate that a certain amount of prospect resistance indicates interest, which is a healthy way to start negotiations between buyers and sellers. Some salespeople even call objections "their best friends" or "rungs on the ladder of selling success" because serious negotiations seldom begin until the prospect's objections surface.

## WHAT ARE BUYER OBJECTIONS AND RESISTANCE?

**Objection** Anything that the prospect or customer says or does that impedes the sales negotiations.

**Objections** can be defined as statements, questions, or actions by the prospect that indicate resistance or an unwillingness to buy . . . at least yet. Buyer objections and resistance can be both a challenge and an opportunity. Some novice salespeople let initial prospect objections so discourage them that they all but lose the sale at that point. In reality, however, chances for a sale increase when prospects raise objections. Why? Because when prospects raise objections, it usually means they are tuned into and interested in your selling proposition. Therefore, don't be discouraged when you encounter sales resistance—and don't take it personally. The *objections or sales resistance* stage of the PSP entails activities that will enable you to identify and deal successfully with prospect objections.

### Reasons for Objections

Prospects and customers raise objections for myriad reasons. Some rationales seem logical, and others do not, as you can see below:

- People will almost always raise objections, even if they are totally sold on the product. This action is a function of human nature. Essentially, prospects try to rationalize the decision and want information to help them do this . . . and besides, they don't want the salesperson to think that they are a pushover.

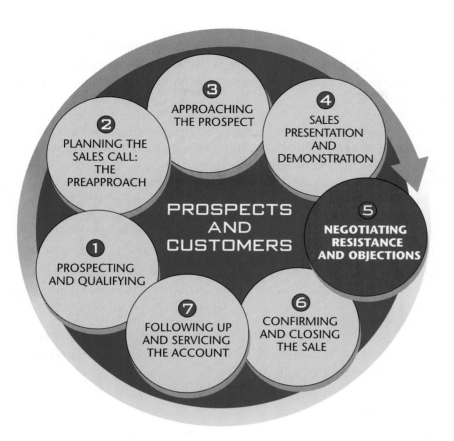

**FIGURE 6.1**

THE PERSONAL SELLING PROCESS

- The prospect may seek reassurance that the product will perform as promised. Perhaps the prospect tends to believe what you have said about the product but wants you to reaffirm your selling proposition (for example, "A major benefit of our system is that it has only 1/2 percent downtime, which will minimize production line disruption.").
- The prospect may have been trained to raise objections as a matter of buying technique or negotiation strategy. Just as professional buyers are trained to sell effectively, purchasing personnel are trained in buying strategies and techniques that will afford their firm the "best" buy.
- The prospect may lack the authority to buy but covers up this fact by raising several smokescreen objections. Through effective prospect qualifying, though, the salesperson should encounter this situation less frequently over time.
- A few prospects will raise objections merely to be an irritant to salespeople or have fun seeing them work for the order. In other words, these prospects seem to delight in the perceived game of negotiating with salespeople.

- An objection may actually be the prospect's appeal for assistance in justifying a decision to buy. For example, the prospect may say, "Gee, your price is very high." But the prospect may be thinking, "Tell me how my company can afford or justify spending the money to buy your clearly superior product."
- Some prospects raise objections so that they can bargain for a better deal. Irrespective of how low your price might be compared to competition, some prospects are obsessed with gaining an even lower price so that they can feel "victorious."
- Prospects may raise an objection because they have a bias against the salesperson's company or product type or, in rare cases, simply dislike the salesperson. For instance, the prospect may have done business with your firm years ago, had a bad experience, and is determined to never buy from your firm again.

Regardless of the reason for an objection, don't view sales resistance as a sign of impending failure. Although you may have your work cut out for you to overcome the prospect's sales resistance and close the sale, think of objections as a request for more information and an overall positive sign in the selling process. If you've done your homework in the first four steps of the PSP, chances are you will be able to effectively address the prospect's objections and consummate the deal.

### Signs of Interest

Prospect objections usually are *positive* signs of interest and involvement in the sales presentation. As noted above, objections are often indirect ways for prospects to say that they want to know more. Prospects may be saying, "Persuade me or give me more evidence so that I can convince my boss that I've made the right decision." Professional buyers sometimes purposely make negative statements about some aspect of a product in order to elicit more information from the salesperson that they can use in defending the purchase decision up the line. For instance, a purchasing agent for a large manufacturer may say, "I like your product, but we require just-in-time (JIT) delivery to keep our costs low, and I'm afraid that your company won't be able to provide the quick response we need." Maybe the sales rep can honestly answer, "I'm glad you raised that point because we're already working with IBM and General Electric on a JIT basis. We know that to compete in most industries today, you need fast response to customer requests, shorter lead times, lower stockouts, and less waste and scrap. That's why we exchange information with customers via computer linkups. I'm confident that you'll find our JIT system as good as any available." This sort of response should reassure the purchasing agent and dispel that potential barrier to buying. Each time a salesperson can answer a specific prospect or customer objection, another obstacle in the path to the sale is removed.

### Nonverbal Resistance

Prospect or customer resistance is part of nearly every negotiation. It might not even be active resistance. Sometimes prospects show resistance through

## KEEPING UP ONLINE: SALES AND MARKETING MANAGEMENT (S&MM)

**S**&MM is one of the more popular trade publications read by salespeople and their managers. Each issue is replete with suggestions about how to improve one's personal selling efforts or managerial skills. Today's dynamic selling arena calls for salespeople to continually update their knowledge, capabilities, and tools in their selling repertoire. Take a look at the *S&MM* web site at www.salesandmarketing.com. Why do you think many salespeople find it so useful? How might *S&MM* assist you now?

silence or through body language such as shaking their head, frowning, glancing at the time frequently, playing with their watch or some desk accessory, reading their mail while the salesperson talks, yawning or exhaling a big breath, or just looking bored, puzzled, or expressionless. When salespeople spot this passive kind of resistance, they must find some way to perk up the presentation and involve the prospect.

You can often find up-to-date, sound advice on improving the overall selling process, including negotiating sales objections and subtle kinds of resistance, in the monthly issues of *Sales and Marketing Management* magazine, described in *Keeping Up Online* above.

## KINDS OF OBJECTIONS

Sales resistance tends to be of two kinds: invalid or valid. Salespeople need to recognize each in negotiating with a prospect or customer.

### Invalid Objections

**Invalid objections** are typically (1) irrelevant, harassing objections, (2) untruthful objections, or (3) delaying actions or hidden reasons for not buying. Irrelevant objections are difficult to overcome because rather than deal with the salesperson in a straightforward, honest manner, prospects play a cat-and-mouse game unconnected to the actual sales offering.

Prospects who regularly use invalid or untruthful objections are revealing their basic insincerity—and questionable business conduct. Some salespeople may prefer to not waste precious selling time calling on such disingenuous buyers.

Obviously delaying or stalling objections usually produce prospect statements such as, "I've got to prepare for a meeting in ten minutes, so I don't have time to talk now," or "Around here, all decisions are shared, so just leave your product literature for us to look over and we'll get back to you if we're interested." Salespeople might deal with these obvious put-offs by replying as follows:

**Invalid Objections**
Delaying or stalling actions or hidden reasons for not buying.

"How about our getting together after your meeting, say around three o'clock or tomorrow morning if that's more convenient?"

"Okay, why don't you share the product literature with the rest of the team. I'll come back Friday morning around ten o'clock to tell you more about the benefits we can provide."

Hidden objections are sometimes too personal or embarrassing for the prospect to reveal, so they remain *unspoken*. Examples include the following:

- "I'm not going to buy from you because I always buy from my old friend, Charlie."
- "Your company is too small and unknown for me to justify buying from you to my boss."
- "I don't like your style. You act and sound arrogant and patronizing to me."

Uncovering hidden objections like those above is difficult because the prospect is unlikely to ever reveal them to the salesperson. Sometimes the salesperson can learn about the prospect's hidden objections by cultivating a relationship with a receptionist, secretary, or other employee in the firm who knows why the prospect isn't receptive. However, this can be a long-term process and may not be worth the effort because even if the hidden reasons are identified, they will still be major obstacles to the sale.

### Valid Objections

**Valid Objections**
Sincere concerns that the prospect needs answered before he or she will be willing to buy.

**Valid objections** (the main focus of this chapter) are sincere concerns that the prospect needs answered before he or she is willing to make the commitment to buy. They are relevant to the current buying situation and are truthful as far as the prospect knows. Once these valid objections are identified, they can be dealt with in a variety of ways that we'll describe later in this chapter. You are likely to be more successful if you treat most objections as valid and, therefore, address them as being truthful and real. Table 6.1 enumerates common objections that you are likely to encounter in your selling efforts. How might you respond to each one? By the end of the chapter, you'll know!

## IDENTIFYING AND DEALING WITH THE PROSPECT'S KEY OBJECTION

Determining the customer's dominant or key objection is one of the most difficult and intriguing tasks of salespeople. Why? Because prospects often give several reasons for not buying, but maybe none is the *dominant* reason. Generally, however, one objection acts like a keystone in the buyer's "arch of resistance," as depicted in Figure 6.2. Here the key objection is the product's styling, though the buyer also objects to the price, delivery terms, service contract terms, and lack of accessories. If the sales rep confronting this particular arch of resistance can show the buyer an acceptable product style and thus knock out the dominant or **keystone objection,** the other objections that make up the arch of resistance may well fall quickly thereafter.

**Keystone Objection**
The customer's most important objection.

How can you uncover the keystone objection? One subtle way to start is by engaging the prospect in informal conversation before the sales presentation.

## TABLE 6.1

## COMMON OBJECTIONS

### Price Objections

Product isn't worth the price.

Price isn't competitive.

Discounts are insufficient.

Terms are out of line.

### Product Objections

Product characteristics are less than ideal for the prospect.

Product characteristics are not superior to the product currently in use.

Product characteristics are not competitive.

### Distribution Objections

Lead time is too long.

Minimum order requirements are unacceptable.

Delivery arrangements are inadequate.

Questions regarding who pays transportation costs.

The salesperson's company is unwilling to provide consignment sales.

Inadequate damage and return goods policy.

### Promotion Objections

Cooperative advertising is minimal.

No free samples or display merchandise are available.

No "push money" for reseller salespeople is offered.

No advertising support is provided.

### Miscellaneous Objections

Company reputation is poor.

Buyer prefers a local supplier.

Buyer wishes to do business with a national company.

Lingering concerns over past problems doing business with the company.

Buyer prefers to keep the status quo.

Encourage the prospect to reveal his or her personal concerns by asking probing questions, such as the following:

- "I guess you've been involved in a lot of planning and decision making for this new installation?"

KEYSTONE

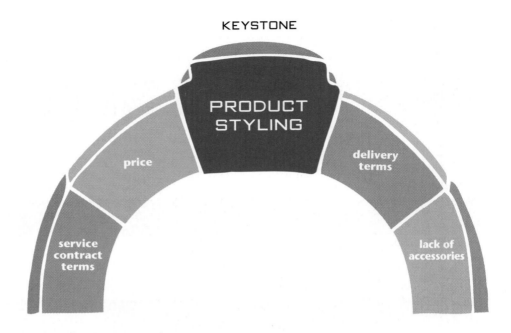

**FIGURE 6.2**

KEYSTONE IN THE ARCH OF RESISTANCE

- "Have you decided exactly what you're going to need?"
- "What special features or benefits are you looking for?"
- "What are your major concerns in purchasing and installing the new equipment?"
- "Are you leaning toward any special kind of equipment or particular features?"
- "What led you to change suppliers in the past?"

When you successfully identify and resolve the buyer's key objection, you will have a powerful opportunity to resolve many or all of the other objections in short order. This is especially true if the key objection is taken care of quickly. In this case, your next statement to the buyer should be, "I'm glad we resolved that issue. Now I'm confident that we can iron out these other sticking points without much difficulty." A word to the wise, however: Don't be overconfident. It takes a skilled salesperson to identify, "nail down," and resolve the key objection without allowing another, lesser objection to become the new key objection. If the negotiations threaten to take this turn, you might try reminding the buyer that you thought that the problem just resolved was the biggest one and that this or that other objection was relatively minor. Otherwise, resign yourself quickly (and as happily as possible) to starting back at square one in the negotiations. Table 6.2 outlines a process for uncovering and overcoming objections.

As with most areas of personal selling, it's helpful to have an overall sequential process to think about and follow. Of course, seldom can the process be followed by rote, as one or more steps may have to be skipped,

| TABLE 6.2 |
| --- |

# PROCESS FOR UNCOVERING
# AND OVERCOMING OBJECTIONS

1. **Start with the Proper Attitude.** An antagonistic "seller versus buyer" attitude is inappropriate. Don't view the buyer as a rival or as antagonistic when he or she raises objections. Successful salespeople welcome objections. They view objections as an indication that a purchase decision may be close at hand. After all, objections are typically raised prior to making the sale.

2. **Uncover the Objection.** If the objection is not stated, you must probe for the objection. You will need to determine what's going on in the buyer's mind when the selling process is being impeded, but no specific objection has been raised. Start the prospect talking about reasons for not buying.

3. **Clarify the Objection.** You need to identify the real objection. What's really leading the prospect to be reluctant to make the purchase? For example, the prospect may say, "The price is too high." In relation to what is it too high? Competitive products? Budget constraints? You may want to paraphrase or repeat the objection if it's unclear to you and ask whether you understand the objection correctly. Doing so will give you more time to think about how to deal with the objection.

4. **Acknowledge the Objection.** In most cases valid objections should be acknowledged (for example, "Bill, you have raised an important point"). In doing so, you are merely telling the prospect that he or she has brought up a reasonable objection. People like to be praised; you are offering positive input to the prospect when you acknowledge the objection.

5. **Handle the Objection.** In most cases, your prior preparation will enable you to anticipate and promptly handle most objections. However, you should generally delay handling an objection if you encounter the following situations:
   (a) *An early price objection arises.* Generally, you want to address the price issue after you have presented the product's features, advantages, and benefits so that you will then be in a better position to justify the price.
   (b) *Frequent, harassing objections emerge.* The prospect may just be in a mad mood that day or feel antagonistic toward your company. In such situations, it's usually best to just listen and avoid responding to unreasonable objections, as your response may lead to confrontations with a prospect. In such situations, perhaps you can graciously excuse yourself by saying something like, "I apologize, but can we make another appointment? I'm running late today, and we'll need more time to thoroughly discuss the issues you're bringing up." With a gracious exit, maybe the prospect will be in a better mood next time so that serious negotiations can be conducted.
   (c) *A logical reason for discussing the objection later in the presentation exists,* for example, the prospect raises an objection about delivery dates and installation service before you have even started talking about the specific product desired or learned about its availability. In such cases, you might say, "I'm confident that we'll be able to meet your requirements in those areas, but first we'll need to determine exactly which of our products will best fit your needs."

altered, or returned to in response to prospect and customer reactions. Sometimes, you'll have to take two steps forward and one or more steps backward in the process. On a few rare occasions, you may not have to follow the process at all and can move directly to close the sale, as the customer is already presold by product literature and earlier sales calls that you've made at the company. When such a situation arises, jump over all the other intermediate steps of the process and go right to the sales close. Remember you're not in the business of making sales presentations. Your overall objective is to sell your company's products and services and develop long-term mutually profitable relationships with customers. The steps in the sales process and each part of it are merely guidelines to help you move toward your ultimate objectives. If a shorter route to your objectives opens up, feel flexible and confident enough to take it. A sequential flow-chart approach to follow in dealing with objections in shown in Figure 6.3.

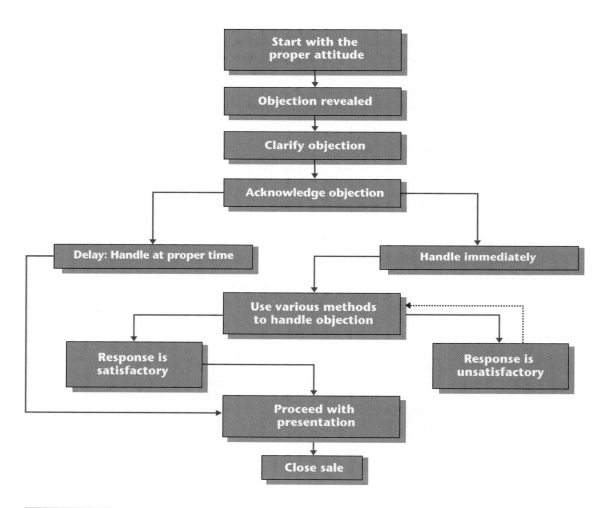

**FIGURE 6.3**

FLOW-CHART APPROACH FOR HANDLING OBJECTIONS

## NEGOTIATING WITH PROSPECTS AND CUSTOMERS

In dealing with prospect or customer objections, the operative word is "negotiation." Several dictionaries define *negotiation* as "mutual discussion and arrangement of the terms of a transaction or agreement." This definition implies mutual understanding, respect, and satisfaction between the negotiating parties. Negotiation does not mean manipulating or outfoxing an opponent in a contest. Instead, negotiation in professional selling means that buyers and sellers work together to reach mutually satisfying agreements and solve problems of shared interest. Thus, both the buyer and the seller come out of the negotiation as winners . . . and that's the only outcome that will further a long-term relationship.

### Negotiation Strategies

Buyers use negotiations to obtain various objectives, including lower price, higher quality, special services, concessions on delivery or payment, and increased cooperative efforts. The best way to negotiate with prospects is to draw them into creative partnerships.[1] The following are several basic strategies and tactics for moving a customer away from resistance to a problem-solving mentality.

- Take a relatively firm negotiating position initially so that when you compromise, the prospect will feel that he or she negotiated a bargain. This approach also helps you find the lowest possible combination of price and terms acceptable to the buyer.
- Avoid making the first concession except on a minor point. Studies show that those who make the first concession tend to give away too much in each concession and usually get the worse end of the agreement.
- Keep track of the issues resolved during the discussions. Frequent recaps help confirm the steady progress being made.
- Concentrate on problem-solving approaches that satisfy the needs of both the buyer and the seller. Neither party in the negotiations should use unequal leverage or power to force an unfair solution, because that will hurt the long-term business relationship. Salespeople should always think of the lifetime value of the customer, not just the profit that can be made on any single transaction.
- Focus on issues where you and the prospect agree most. Leave the areas of widest disagreement until last. Reaching amicable agreements on several easier issues sets up a pattern for win-win negotiation and shows the salesperson's interest in working with the customer.
- Agree to a solution only after it is certain to work for both parties.

### Negotiation Outcomes

Any sales negotiation has four possible outcomes: win-win, win-lose, lose-win, and lose-lose. Only the *win-win* outcome will further the business relationship and set the stage for future sales agreements, as shown in Figure 6.4.

| | | BUYER | |
|---|---|---|---|
| | | **Win** | **Lose** |
| **SALESPERSON** | **Win** | Both the buyer and the salesperson are satisfied with the agreement, and the business relationship is in good shape. A problem-solving partnership is developing. | The salesperson is satisfied with the agreement, but the buyer is dissatisfied, and may even feel manipulated or taken advantage of, so the business relationship is in trouble. |
| | **Lose** | The buyer is satisfied with the agreement, but the salesperson feels manipulated, and may reciprocate in future negotiations or reduce customer service. The business relationship is in trouble. | Both parties are dissatisfied with the agreement. Thus, the bond of trust between them may be so damaged that they are unlikely to enter into any future business agreements. |

**FIGURE 6.4**

SALES NEGOTIATION OUTCOMES

**Win-Win Negotiations**
The kind of negotiations in which both parties feel satisfied with the outcome; the only kind of negotiations that professional salespeople seek!

*Salespeople and customers can express their win-win frame of mind through their communication styles.*
Corbis

**Seller Win-Buyer Win Agreements.** When both parties feel satisfied with the outcome, you have the basis for a continuing mutually beneficial relationship. **Win-win negotiations** are the *only* kind that lead to long-run success for salespeople and the only kind that professional salespeople seek. One study found that when both buyers and sellers engage in cooperative tactics (that is, seek to negotiate with open and accurate information, offer mutually advantageous concessions to each other, and respect each other's goals), deadlocks are less likely to arise and negotiation satisfaction is higher than when both parties engage in competitive (win-lose) tactics.[2]

**Seller Win-Buyer Lose Agreements.** When the salesperson feels good about the agreement but the buyer is dissatisfied, the business relationship is in trouble. A buyer who feels taken advantage of may refuse to have anything more to do with the salesperson or the company he or she represents. Some disaffected buyers may also feel vindictive and seek to destroy the salesperson's relationships with other prospects and customers, perhaps through negative word-of-mouth.

**Seller Lose-Buyer Win Agreements.** Sometimes salespeople offer buyers an extraordinarily low price on a temporary basis in order to win an order from a new customer. They think that they'll be able to make up the profit loss on future orders from the customer. Unfortunately, an unusually low price or other one-time concession can create buyer expectations for similar "super deals" in the future. And customers may be angry if they aren't continued. Automobile manufacturers and dealers have fallen into this trap by offering cash rebates and low interest or even no interest loans on new cars in order to stimulate sales and compete with foreign competition. When they return to normal pricing strategies, customers look elsewhere for a good deal. Occasionally prospects or customers who know that a salesperson wants their business badly will pressure for a "seller lose-buyer win" agreement, thinking erroneously that it will be to their long-run advantage. For instance, a buyer may assert, "I'll buy from you only if you lower your price by 10 percent;" or "I don't want the free warranty program, so just reduce my price by the cost of that program;" or "I'll buy your product if you throw in some free merchandise along with it." On such deals, the buyer may temporarily win the upper hand by squeezing the seller. Sellers can't stay in business by losing on each agreement, though, so they must find a way to make it back from the buyer, perhaps by cutting corners on quality or service.

**Seller Lose-Buyer Lose.** A "lose-lose" agreement that results in a loss for both parties leads to a deteriorating situation and the eventual end of the relationship. Occasionally, lose-lose agreements can be sustained for a while if both parties somehow believe that they are winning. For example, a short-sighted buyer may force a salesperson eager for new business to accept an unprofitable agreement. In order to make the agreement profitable, however, the salesperson may put the buyer's purchase on a low priority for delivery, neglect to inform him or her about special discounts, and generally ignore service requests. Gradually, both buyer and seller will see this relationship as a lose-lose situation and end it. In negotiating sales agreements, it all boils down to this: Both buyers and sellers are best off in the long run when they conscientiously strive to reach win-win agreements. Try your hand at creating a win-win outcome in the following *It's Up to You.*

## IT'S UP TO YOU

You have finished your presentation to a prospect who seemed interested in and agreeable to your selling proposition. He has been smiling much of the time, and he hasn't even interrupted you or asked any questions during your presentation. Now, however, the prospect's smile turns to a blank stare and he says nothing. What do you do next?

## PLANNING FOR OBJECTIONS

To deal effectively with sales resistance, ideally, you should learn as much as you can about the prospect; then an objection is less likely to take you by surprise.[3] If you know or anticipate prospect objections your confidence in addressing those objections will likely increase. Research shows that a salesperson's confidence can significantly increase customer satisfaction with sales presentations, as well as success in closing sales.[4] Therefore, one of the best ways to minimize objections is to learn what the customer's objections are likely to be *before* you begin the sales presentation, then adapt the sales presentation to cover these points.

By raising the issue during your presentation, you can forestall the objection. That is, you mention it and handle it before the prospect actually raises it. This puts you in a better position to control the negotiations, thereby improving your chances for making the sale. If the salesperson can successfully anticipate prospect objections, he or she can soften or preempt them by including evidence, testimonials, and demonstrations in the sales presentation and subsequent negotiations. This strategy requires several preliminary steps, which we discuss in the following paragraphs.

### Keep a Running File of the Most Typical Objections

Develop a master list of prospect objections that come up in your own experience and that of other salespeople and classify them according to type, such as product, price, delivery, installation, service, or company. Include successful and unsuccessful ways of dealing with each objection. In sales meetings and informal discussions, tap sales colleagues' knowledge about various types of prospect resistance and successful methods for dealing with each. Somewhat like an entertainer who learns to ad lib or have a joke ready for every situation, the salesperson can learn a technique to defuse nearly every objection.

### Determine Whether the Objections Are Valid or Not

As mentioned before, some objections are merely defense mechanisms the prospect uses to stall or slow down the sales process in order to gain some time to think about the purchase.[5] Valid objections, on the other hand, are those concerns that won't go away and will prevent the sale from taking place unless the salesperson can satisfactorily defuse them. It may take considerable interaction with a prospect or customer before you can begin to feel confident about what's a valid or invalid objection from that particular individual. Sometimes, cultivating a friendly conversational relationship with receptionists or other employees in the prospect's company can provide insights about generally invalid objections. For example, a receptionist might casually remark something like, "Bob, our purchasing manager, is so fearful of making a mistake that he buys only from the biggest and best-known companies." If your company is a small one, it now becomes apparent that Bob will probably not reveal this invalid objection but merely throw up other smokescreen objections to rationalize not buying. As a salesperson for a small company, you will need to reassure this purchasing manager on any sales proposal that your company provides a money-back, no-risk guarantee if unsatisfied with any of your products. Or, alternatively, you may invite him to make a small initial purchase as a test run of your firm.

## Sell the Prospects on the Benefits

By emphasizing the bundle of benefits that the prospect will derive from the product, you can resolve many objections or push them into the background. Salespeople must remember to cover intangible benefits as well as the tangible ones. Brand image, expertise and experience in the area, state-of-the-art technology, timely delivery, flexible credit terms, prompt installation, training assistance, and outstanding post-purchase service may be more important to some customers than quality or price differences among competing products. Salespeople should prepare a list of specific objections relating to their products that can be offset by persuasive evidence, proof, and convincing testimony of the product's tangible and intangible value. Stressing the product's *bundle* of benefits can usually overcome most objections. Several general rules can help salespeople successfully negotiate prospect and customer objections, as outlined in Table 6.3.

TABLE 6.3

### GENERAL RULES FOR NEGOTIATING OBJECTIONS

- Don't be defensive about objections. Welcome the objections as a sign of prospect interest.

- Make sure you understand the objection before you answer it.

- Don't disparage the prospect's objection and risk deflating the prospect's ego.

- Lead the prospect to answer his or her own objection by politely asking for elaboration on the objection.

- Never argue with the prospect. You don't win sales by wining arguments.

- Don't over answer or belabor the point in dealing with an objection and risk insulting the prospect's intelligence.

- Don't be drawn into pointless squabbles over some objection. Tell the prospect that's all the information you have at this time and move to another benefit.

- Don't fake an answer. Admit you don't know but promise that you'll find an answer promptly. No salesperson has all the answers. In fact, some salespeople believe that a promise to find information is one way to ensure a return sales call.

- Confirm your answers to objections but don't put the prospect on the defensive by asking, "Have I fully answered your question?" This can come across as condescending and arrogant, which may cause some prospects to bring up more objections merely to try bringing you down a notch or two.

# SPECIFIC TECHNIQUES FOR NEGOTIATING BUYER OBJECTIONS

As we noted earlier, prospects may bring up objections for many different reasons. Unless the salesperson can ease the prospect's anxieties by emphasizing benefits to be derived at minimal risk, the sale may be lost. Various methods have been developed and tested to handle prospect objections, as outlined in Table 6.4. In fact, these methods, used effectively, can sometimes lead to an immediate close or move the salesperson much closer to consummating the deal. Let's discuss and illustrate some of the different strategies for negotiating resistance or dealing with objections under five categories: put-off, switch focus, offset, denial, and provide proof.

### Put-Off Strategies

**Put-Off Strategies**  A set of strategies for handling a prospect's objections that require the salesperson to delay dealing with the objection initially.

One set of strategies for handling a prospect's objections are **put-off strategies** because they require the salesperson to delay dealing with the objection initially.

**I'm Coming to That.**  Although most objections should be answered as they are raised, some objections are best put off until later in the presentation because a premature answer may turn off prospects. "What's the price?" is a typical question that should be answered later in the sales presentation after product benefits have been fully discussed. The salesperson can delay the exact answer to the price question by saying,

> That's a good question. I think you'll be pleased by the value you'll receive for your dollars. But, if you don't mind, I'll return to price in just a few minutes because there are three product-service options I need to lay out for your consideration. You'll want to

|  | TABLE 6.4 |
|---|---|
| **SPECIFIC TECHNIQUES FOR NEGOTIATING BUYER OBJECTIONS** | |

| Put-Off Strategies | Offset Strategies |
|---|---|
| • *I'm Coming to That* | • *Compensation or Counterbalance* |
| • *Pass-Off* | • *Boomerang* |
| **Switch Focus Strategies** | **Denial Strategies** |
| • *Alternative Product* | • *Indirect Denial* |
| • *Feel, Felt, Found* | • *Direct Denial* |
| • *Comparison or Contrast* | **Provide Proof Strategies** |
| • *Answer with a Question* | • *Case History* |
| • *Agree and Neutralize* | • *Demonstration* |
| • *Humor* | • *Propose Trial Use* |

make sure that one of them satisfies your particular needs before
we zero in on price. Let me first briefly outline the benefits offered
by the basic product package, then I'll cover the benefits offered in
the comprehensive and the deluxe product packages.

In fact, this salesperson's presentation may be so convincing that the
prospect may even drop the objection later on.

**Pass-Off.**  Salespeople cannot avoid or counter all objections or criticism of
their products. Sometimes the best response to a prospect's objection is to
smile and say nothing. This approach is especially appropriate if the objection is not serious or really requires no attention. In fact, the salesperson may
simply quietly acknowledge the objection by a head nod and move on in the
presentation. For example, a regional buyer for a grocery store chain mut-
tered about his dislike of the salesperson's company advertisements. Rather
than seek to justify his firm's ads, the salesperson merely smiled, agreed with
the buyer, and went on with his sales presentation.

## Switch Focus Strategies

A second set of strategies for negotiating prospect objections relies on the
salesperson's ability to switch the prospect's focus through various tactics.

**Alternative Product.**  Some sales reps are inclined to help prospects identify
purchase criteria, such as product features, necessary for a purchase to transpire
and the products that do or don't meet those criteria. Such efforts can enhance
salespeople's selling effectiveness.[6] Most times the salesperson will have more
than one product alternative or model to sell. Each product will have its advantages and disadvantages compared to the others. When an objection is raised
about a feature of one product, the salesperson can switch the prospect's focus
to another product variation until one is found that will satisfy the prospect. For
example, one prospect was disappointed that a computer software salesperson's
program could not simultaneously print an invoice and a billing statement. The
salesperson addressed the objection by turning the buyer's attention to a new,
higher-priced program that included the desired printing capability.

**Feel, Felt, Found.**  A versatile technique that enables the salesperson to
agree with the prospect's objection, confirm that it's a normal reaction to the
product, and then disconfirm the objection over the longer run is called
"feel, felt, found." For instance, a prospect may comment, "This computerized lighting system is too complex for me to operate. I'm not a very mechanical person." In response, the salesperson can say:

I know how you *feel* because I'm not very mechanical myself. In fact,
many of my customers *felt* the same way when they first saw all the
gauges and buttons on this model, but they soon *found* that they only
need to use three buttons to do everything most people want. The
other twelve buttons are just for fine-tuning the main three operations. You'll be amazed how comfortable you'll be with all the buttons
in a few weeks, and you'll be happy to have the extra options.

**Comparison or Contrast.**  By comparing the product with another acceptable or unacceptable alternative, salespeople can often dissolve prospect resistance. For instance, a favorable comparison with other alternatives can address a prospect's objection regarding the price of a computerized credit information service: "A report from a traditional credit bureau costs ten dollars or more per name and may take days to receive. But our online service enables you to instantly obtain a complete credit report on any of more than four million people in the Delaware Valley area for less than ten cents per name."

Notice that the salesperson renders the objection neutral or inconsequential without arguing about or minimizing the prospect's concern.

**Answer with a Question.**  This versatile approach technique separates valid objections from invalid ones or allows the salesperson to zero in on the specific reason for buyer resistance. It essentially turns the responsibility for providing an answer to the objection over to the prospect. Moreover, a question can help clarify the objection for both the buyer *and* the seller. By the salesperson asking a question, the prospect is not invited to raise another objection but rather forced to address his or her own objection. For instance, a potential client might say, "I don't think your company has enough expertise or experience in accounting to audit a company the size of ours." The client representative for the accounting firm might reply, "What is it that makes you think that we don't have sufficient expertise or experience?" This response forces the prospect away from the generalized resistance to a more specific objection with which the rep can deal.

**Agree and Neutralize.**  In response to many objections, the salesperson can state some level of agreement and then go on to neutralize the objection. For example, a prospect may say to a salesperson for a contracting firm, "Your firm is estimating that it will take nearly twice as long and cost 25 percent more to complete this office building than any of your competitors." The salesperson can say:

> Yes, you're right. That's because our completion estimates are accurate, and our cost projections include the highest quality materials and the work of skilled professionals. If we build it, you'll never have to tell your commercial tenants about any delays in their move-in date. And you won't hear any complaints from them about the quality of the materials or the work. We do it right the first time. Our way does take a little more time and money initially, but it will save you time and money over the long run.

Essentially, this approach allows the salesperson to concede the objection and then provide more information to support his or her company's position. It offers a means for justifying the existence of the objection.

**Humor.**  Telling a humorous story to ease the tension and defuse an objection can be an effective approach when skillfully done. A funny anecdote may relieve the uneasiness and allow the sales presentation to be continued even if

**ON THE FRONTLINES**

## *SOQ NOP*

The senior regional sales manager from John Deere was wearing an odd tie tack. It was in the shape of a cross. The vertical letters spelled out DEERE, the horizontal SOQ NOP. When asked what the letters stood for, his reply was, "Sell on quality, not on price." He added, "It's my toughest job in down markets to make my own people realize that the objective is to sell the benefits, not just resort to price [as the only selling leverage]. I tell them a story. I was going after a sale [for Deere] some years ago. It came down to two final contenders. The fellow making the buy called me in to give me one last chance. His message in a nutshell was 'You're just too high on the price side. No hard feelings, and we hope we can do business with you again in the future.' I was about to walk out the door, unhappy to say the least. Then I had an inspiration. I turned and said, 'Those are nice-looking boots you've got on.' He was a bit surprised, but said, 'Thanks,' and he went on to talk for a minute or so about those fine boots, what was unique about the leather, why they were practical as well as fine. I said to him at the end of his description, 'How come you bought those boots and not just a pair off the shelf in an Army-Navy store?' It must have taken twenty seconds for the grin to spread all the way across his face. 'The sale is yours,' he said, and he got up and came around his desk and gave me a hearty handshake."

***Source:*** *From* A Passion for Excellence *by Thomas J. Peters and Nancy K. Austin. Copyright © 1985 by Thomas J. Peters and Nancy K. Austin. Used by permission of Random House, Inc.*

the objection has not been fully addressed. Not every salesperson can tell a humorous story well, but for those who can, humor is a valuable tool. For example, if the prospect says the price is too high, the salesperson might tell a story similar to the one mentioned in *On the Frontlines* above.

### Offset Strategies

A third category of strategies dealing with objections uses the technique of **offset strategies**—offsetting the objection with a benefit.

**Compensation or Counterbalance.** Countering an objection that cannot be denied by citing an even more important buying benefit is an effective means of addressing an objection. By using this approach, the salesperson is telling the prospect that the seller's offering isn't perfect, but that its advantages far outweigh the disadvantage that the prospect has raised. For instance, a retailer may complain to a manufacturer's rep, "I don't think I'll have much success selling your *Dustlifter* hand vacuum cleaner in my store. It runs for only fifteen minutes before it has to be recharged, while the competitive *Quick Pickups* runs for thirty minutes before recharging." In replying, the salesperson might point out the following:

**Offset Strategies**
A set of strategies for dealing with objections that uses the technique of offsetting the objection with a benefit.

*Using humor effectively can be a valuable way for a salesperson to defuse a tense situation with a buyer.*
Corbis

That's correct, but their hand vacuum weighs twice as much as ours, so the householder's hand is under considerable strain and discomfort while using theirs. Our studies show that the typical person uses a hand vacuum for more than ten minutes at once only about 8 percent of the time. We decided to make it as light-weight and comfortable to use as possible while covering more than 90 percent of the usage times. I think we made the right trade off, don't you?

**Boomerang.** Turning the objection into a reason for buying, but avoiding making the prospect look simple-minded for raising the objection, is called the "boomerang" method. If you are selling anything that has a safety concern associated with it, the boomerang method is a good technique for responding to objections such as price, design, weight, or size. For instance, a Fortune 500 company CEO who wants to buy two corporate airplanes for top executive use might say, "Your airplanes are fifty thousand dollars more than your competitors." In response, the salesperson can say, "Yes, and there's an important reason for that—construction quality and safety features. Do you and your top executives really want to fly in an airplane built by the lowest bidder?"

Notice that with this response, the objection becomes the reason for making the purchase. The boomerang technique is especially useful for objections not strongly backed by facts; the objection can be defused before the facts can be marshaled to support it. Read *From the Command Post* on p. 191 about how some small high-tech companies offset their size disadvantages in competing against giant competitors.

## FROM THE COMMAND POST: CHARGE OF THE LILLIPUTIANS

High-tech companies were the business juggernauts in the 1990s. Not so, any longer! A sea change has taken place. Many dot-coms have fallen by the wayside; hardware and software firms are merging, struggling, or going bust; and venture capitalists and Wall Street pundits are no longer enamored with e-commerce. Despite these phenomena, however, some companies have been able to rise above the fray and succeed despite tenuous circumstances. Surprisingly, some of these companies are Lilliputians. And not only have they held their own despite their David-like stature in the market, but some of them have captured very large accounts.

What has led to the success of many small high-tech players? First, because they lack deep pockets, the high-tech dwarfs must "outthink" the Goliaths. Instead of relying on conventional selling approaches, their sales forces must develop close partnerships with customers by helping them improve their own profitability. Doing so typically requires a more steadfast commitment than that of their competitors to providing the highest level of customer service and understanding of their customers' businesses. Devotion to such service means that these small vendors are ever ready to serve clients at any hour of the day or night. This commitment is backed up by ensuring that all salespeople and managers include their work, home, and cell phone numbers on their business cards and invite customers to contact them anytime or anywhere.

Because they are small players on an uneven playing field with giant players, these little companies often make use of "guerilla" marketing tactics. For instance, to demonstrate their technological strength and product superiority to prospects and customers, they often use promotions that confront their large competitors with a challenge (e.g., daring a larger competitor to face off with them in a competing-product contest). So, when small size is the objection, the Lilliputians stress small size as a reason to buy because the customer gets more personalized service and higher-quality products.

## Denial Strategies

A fourth category of techniques for dealing with prospect objections calls for denying the objection, either indirectly or directly. These strategies are often effective in responding to negative rumors about your company, products, or services.

**Indirect Denial.** Using this approach, the salesperson agrees with the prospect's objection but then inoffensively follows with a disclaimer. It recognizes that prospects and customers do not like to be contradicted; that is, they prefer to deal with salespeople who will bend a bit (just like a boxer who rolls with punches to soften the blow from the other boxer). For example, a prospect for a truck manufacturer might say, "I can't take a chance on buying from you because your truck tires have a reputation for poor quality." Using the indirect denial method, the salesperson can answer as follows:

> You're absolutely right. We did have a quality control problem in some of our older plants about seven years ago. But now we have

state-of-the-art manufacturing equipment and modern quality control procedures in all our plants. For the past three years, our truck tire quality has consistently been among the best in the business as rated by several independent research laboratories. We've regained nearly all our old customers, and we're anxious to win back your business, too. Let me show you what we have to offer.

**Direct Denial.** Occasionally, prospects or customers will relate some incorrect information to a salesperson as a reason for not buying. In these instances, the salesperson needs to refute what the prospect has said and then explain the true situation. The ideal means of using this technique is to be earnest, but not offensive. Ruffling the prospect or customer's feathers may allow you to win the battle (addressing the objection) but lose the war (not closing the sale).

Many rumors, both true and false, tend to circulate about companies or industries from time to time, and some can hurt sales badly. For example, false rumors have been floated about McDonald's using worms in their hamburgers and about Procter & Gamble's corporate trademark symbolizing a satanic cult. Negative publicity about a salesperson's company or products can make sales calls particularly challenging. Today, a common rumor about a company is that of impending bankruptcy. When a salesperson is confronted with such a rumor, it's usually best to confront the rumor or accusation head-on, "Yes, I've heard that rumor myself, and I can assure you that there's absolutely no truth to it. Our company is in strong financial condition. In fact, to put that rumor to rest, I've taken to carrying our annual report, which shows our latest accounting audit. Here's a copy. You'll see that a well-known accounting firm gives us a complete bill of health. In fact, the next few years should be among our best ever."

### Provide Proof Strategies

The fifth category of responses to objections involves providing proof of the qualities of the product by citing a case history, giving a demonstration, or letting the prospect use the product on a trial basis.

**Case History.** Relating the experience of another prospect who purchased the product and is now extremely satisfied with it can effectively turn objections around. Although you might present the story in various lengths or dramatizations, the bottom line will be to show how satisfied other customers are with your company's product. For example, a sales rep for an agricultural feed producer could say, "Mack Turkey Farms has seen their average bird's weight increase by nearly a pound since they started using our K240 turkey feed last year."

**Demonstration.** All good salespeople know their product's advantages and disadvantages versus those of competitors. A demonstration that dramatizes these major advantages is one of the best ways to overcome the prospect's various objections. A demonstration can reveal that the prospect's objection is

## *What a Dinghy!*

A boat manufacturers' rep sells pleasure boats made by several manufacturers to retailers throughout the Midwest. Like many top salespeople, he is creative in dealing with buyer objections. One time he tried to sell a yacht dealer a pontoon boat, but the dealer wasn't interested. The dealer told him, "We sell expensive yachts! No one has ever come in here and asked for a mere pontoon boat." The sales rep promptly quipped, "I bet that no one has ever come in here and asked for a haircut, either. But if a barber pole was put up, someone would!" Following this insightful comment, the sales rep convinced the dealer to display four pontoon boats . . . and the pontoon boats all sold within two weeks. Now this upscale yacht dealer is one of his biggest customers for pontoon boats.

not applicable. Salespeople using demonstrations, however, should carefully avoid unfair or deceptive product demonstrations that are mere "surrogate or false indicators" of a product's benefits. In addition to their being unethical, prospects eventually see through misleading demonstrations and lose trust in the salesperson. The professional salesperson only uses demonstrations that substantiate legitimate advantages.

**Propose Trial Use.**  A good way to deal with many potential objections simultaneously is to propose that the buyer use the product on a trial basis for a short period. Free trial use often resolves objections, including those related to people's fears of new technology. Apple computer dealers have urged people, "Take an Apple out for a test drive. See for yourself how user-friendly a computer can be." This no-risk trial helps salespeople by enabling prospects to try out products that they might not risk buying for reasons unrelated to quality, such as the product's small market share, as in Apple's case. This technique is most appropriate for wary customers. As they use the product for a few weeks they can discern whether the product is appropriate for them. Essentially, the trial allows the prospect to identify clearly the benefits of the product, which in some cases can show prospects a good alternative to the products they're currently purchasing or considering.[7] This method is also called the "puppy dog" close, because after trying the product, they are more likely to appreciate and feel that they should make the purchase (like the puppy, "How can I pass up buying him after he wagged his tail so eagerly and licked my face so many times? Well, I can't!"). *On the Frontlines* above describes one creative use of this method.

One sure way to become a better salesperson is to learn, practice, and master the different techniques for handling buyer objections and to know in what negotiating situations to use them. Salespeople with these skills in their repertoires will win many sales that less-prepared salespeople will lose.

## A MAJOR NEMESIS: PRICE RESISTANCE

Prospect resistance to price is probably the most common and sometimes most difficult one for salespeople. Of course, if people only bought on the basis of price, eventually only one seller would remain in each product category, the one with the lowest price. Most buyers, in fact, are more concerned about relative value for their money than absolute price. Usually, a price objection means that the salesperson has not convinced the buyer of the product's value in terms of its price. Professional salespeople seldom sell on the basis of price—they sell on value. One creative firm confronts price objections head-on in its sales presentations when salespeople make the following statement, "The bitterness of an inappropriate product lasts far longer than the sweetness of a giveaway price."[8]

**Perceived Value** A product's value from the prospect's perspective.

*Value,* or more accurately **perceived value,** is determined by the prospect mentally dividing what he or she perceives as the bundle of benefits offered by the perceived price, as in this equation:

$$\text{Perceived Value} = \frac{\text{Perceived Benefits}}{\text{Perceived Price}}$$

The essential job of the salesperson, therefore, is to convince the prospect that the perceived benefits to be derived by the prospect *significantly* exceed the product's perceived price (which can include many intangibles such as the inconvenience in switching to another supplier). Although every salesperson frequently hears the objection that the price is too high, prospects can have various meanings. It's the salesperson's job to sort out the real meaning of the price objection and deal with it appropriately. To find out the real reason for the price objection, the straightforward reply to a question about high price is to ask, "Why do you think the price is too high?" If the objection is not merely a stalling tactic by the prospect, salespeople can address price resistance in several ways, as detailed in Table 6.5.

### Value Analysis and Industrial Buyers

**Value Analysis** Usually a written financial analysis that shows how a product is the best value for the money.

In order to deal specifically with price resistance, the industrial sales representative is always prepared to provide the industrial buyer with a **value analysis.** Sometime called value engineering or value assurance, value analysis shows how the salesperson's product is the best value for the buyer's (organization's) money.[9] It is usually a printed document that assesses a product's cost as compared to its value and is often presented as part of the sales proposal. Most industrial salespeople spend much of their time trying to provide alternative—better, cheaper, more efficient—products for their customers, and this often involves replacing a competing product. A value analysis is absolutely essential for such competitive situations. Three basic approaches to the preparation and presentation of a value analysis are (1) unit cost, (2) product cost versus value, and (3) return on investment. Let's examine each of these approaches.

| TABLE 6.5 |
| --- |
| **ADDRESSING PRICE RESISTANCE** |

- Break the price down into *smaller installments over time.* "It costs your company only about eighty cents a day more than the competitive product, less than the price of a cup of coffee."

- Make *price-value comparisons* with competitive products. "This superb Acer mainframe computer provides all the features of the IBM for twenty-five hundred dollars less."

- Emphasize the product's *one-of-a-kind uniqueness.* "Our ZX-330 fax machine is the only fax available that gives you all these high-tech, high-performance features at this low price."

- Work down from higher priced *product alternatives* to a level that the prospect finds acceptable. "You can buy the premier model at sixty-three hundred dollars, the champion at fifty-four hundred, or the challenger model for forty-two hundred dollars. Which one do you think will best fit your needs?"

**Unit Cost.** A value analysis using the unit cost approach simply breaks the cost of the product down into smaller units. If you can show that your product's price per unit is lower than the competing product's price per unit, and that you offer the same or better quality, you will probably make the sale. For example, a large baking company might need a particular kind of detachable bolt that workers use to secure its large bread-cooling trays to stationary racks. These bolts are frequently replaced for safety. Currently, the buyer purchases packages of ten bolts from your competitor for $120, or $12 per unit. You know that you can beat the competitor's price by selling in larger packages, so you provide a simple value analysis showing how the buyer can obtain packages of fifty high-quality bolts for $500 or $10 per unit, seventy-five bolts for $630 or $8.40 per unit, or one hundred bolts for $700 or $7 per unit.

**Product Cost Versus Value.** For a broader portrait of a product's value, you could prepare a value analysis that reveals the product's costs *over time.* Returning to the example above, your competitor is also selling the large bakery special switches for dough mixers in its central baking facility for fifty-five dollars per unit. You offer the customer a similar switch for one hundred dollars. You know that the customer must replace your competitor's switch every three months, and you can prove that your switch will last three times as long. Furthermore, you know that the customer uses twelve of these switches in the baking facility at one time. Your value analysis of this situation for an eighteen-month period might look like the chart on p. 196.

*Competitor Switches:*   12 × $55 = $660
*Your Company Switches:*   12 × $100 = $1,200

| Elapsed Time | Competitor Company | Your Company |
|---|---|---|
| 0 months | $  660 | $1,200 |
| 3 months | $  660 | ———— |
| 6 months | $  660 | ———— |
| 9 months | $  660 | $1,200 |
| 12 months | $  660 | ———— |
| 15 months | $  660 | ———— |
| 18 months | $  660 | $1,200 |
| Total cost/18 months | $4,620 | $3,600 |
| Total customer savings with your switches | | $1,020 |

**Return on Investment.** Finally, industrial buyers are interested in what percentage return on investment they can expect from the purchase of a particular product. *Return on investment* (ROI) refers to the amount of money expected from an investment over and above the original investment. Because it produces measurable results expressed as a percentage return, many companies view an industrial purchase as an investment. For example, you are now trying to sell the baking company from the examples above a computer inventory and ordering system. After discussions with the buyer and plant supervisor, you and the baking company agree that computerization would save the company at least five thousand dollars per month in hourly wages paid to employees in the inventory and ordering systems. The monthly cost of your equipment is four thousand dollars, including full customer technical assistance and repair and replacement service. Now you can prepare a simple table to reveal the customer's potential ROI for this arrangement:

| Value of Hourly Wages Saved | $5,000 per month |
|---|---|
| Cost of Equipment | −$4,000 per month |
| Customer's Cost Savings | $1,000 per month |

Return on Investment ($1,000/$4,000) = 25 percent per month

Whether or not they are engaged in industrial selling specifically, all consultative salespeople should carry out their own value analysis programs on their own products versus those of competitors and actively participate with their prospects and customer organizations to ensure the calculations are correct. You should be aware that many organizations regularly perform value analysis studies on the products they buy and sell to discover ways to provide their own customers with the same basic product at a lower price, or a better product at the same price. Take time to hone your value analysis skills and make sure your customers know that purchasing your product gives them real value for their money.

## Price Resistance and "Reality"

Admittedly, your product's price can often be a selling obstacle for the buyer. And as buyers more and more view products as being commodity-like, price is likely to remain a major factor in their purchase decision. Nonetheless, professional salespeople recognize that prospects and customers often raise price objections merely to try for a better deal (even when they already know that they are being offered one) or to slow down the selling process. In fact, prospects' price resistance may well be a ploy to conceal their real reason for not buying. Therefore, through careful unveiling of the prospect's sales resistance, professional salespeople can discern how critical price is to the buyer and which selling strategy to employ to successfully deal with it.

## SUMMARY

Without sales resistance, there would be little need for salespeople. Prospect objections are usually positive signs of interest and involvement in the sales presentation. Uncovering and negotiating the prospect's key objection is one of the salesperson's most important and challenging tasks. Several objectives and strategies help salespeople negotiate prospect resistance. Every sales negotiation has four possible outcomes, but only the win-win outcome will further the buyer-seller relationship and encourage future negotiations.

Anticipating objections and preempting them in the sales presentation is one of the best ways to minimize objections. The most common objection is to price, which means that the salesperson has not convinced the prospect of the value of the product. Perceived value can be determined by the ratio of the prospect's perceived benefits to the product's perceived price from the prospect's viewpoint. Techniques for negotiating prospect's objections can be divided into five basic categories: put-off, switch focus, offset, denial, and provide proof strategies. Value analysis can show prospects that your product offers the best value for their money.

## KEY TERMS

| | | | |
|---|---|---|---|
| Objection | Keystone objection | Put-off strategies | Perceived value |
| Invalid objections | Win-win negotiations | Offset strategies | Value analysis |
| Valid objections | | | |

## CHAPTER REVIEW QUESTIONS

1. What do we mean by "buyer objections and resistance"?

2. How can a salesperson distinguish between valid and invalid objections?

3. Outline some basic negotiating strategies.

4. Describe the four possible outcomes in any business negotiation.

5. What steps are involved in planning for prospect objections?

6. What do we mean by "perceived value"? How do prospects determine perceived value?

7. What are the three basic approaches to preparing and presenting a value analysis and how does each approach work?

8. Give some basic techniques for handling objections in each of the five categories discussed in the chapter.

## TOPICS FOR THOUGHT AND CLASS DISCUSSION

1. Why are objections sometimes called the salesperson's best friends? Wouldn't it be better for salespeople if prospects had no objections to buying their products?

2. Explain the concept of the buyer's "arch of resistance" and the "keystone" objection.

3. Why is the term "negotiation" appropriate for describing how the salesperson should handle prospect resistance and objections?

4. Describe some ways in which a salesperson could change the prospect's perceived value for a product.

## PROJECTS FOR PERSONAL GROWTH

1. Go to the Business Periodicals Index online or at your school library or do a computer search to find five articles on *business negotiation*. Read at least three of them, then prepare a list of guidelines that a salesperson might use. In class, compare the list you developed with those developed by classmates also given the same assignment.

2. Ask four professional salespeople about their philosophies and strategies in negotiating prospect objections and resistance. Judge from your discussions whether they believe in win-win or win-lose outcomes in negotiating with prospects. Explain your reasons for making this judgment about each salesperson.

3. Ask three professional salespeople who each sell to different customer categories what their favorite techniques are for handling buyer resistance and objections. Do the negotiating techniques differ with the customer type? Why or why not?

## CASE 6.1 NEGOTIATING PRICE WITH A TASKMASTER

Chuck Johnson and his sales manager, Tom Barnhart, have been trying to sell DuraFlor residential sheet vinyl to Bargain City Stores for many years. Johnson and Barnhart work for McGranahan Distributing Company of Toledo. McGranahan's handles the DuraFlor line of resilient flooring products, which includes both flooring tile and sheet vinyl. In the resilient flooring market, the six competing major manufacturers all use "traditional" marketing channels of independent distributors, who sell to retailers, who, in turn, sell to the general public or contractors.

Bargain City operates a chain of sixty-five discount stores throughout Ohio, Michigan, and Indiana, with headquarters in Toledo, Ohio. The firm concentrates on secondary markets, and although they stock all the major product lines that other mass merchandisers offer, they have an excellent do-it-yourself building materials department. Don Schramm is the chief buyer for this department, and his strategy is to buy good value at the low end of the market to sell in Bargain City outlets. It is commonly known throughout the industry that Bargain City buyers always want good product quality at the lowest possible prices, with low price being their top priority.

The product that Johnson and Barnhart are attempting to sell to Mr. Schramm is a low-end line of twelve-foot sheet vinyl flooring called Imperial Accent. This line has twelve different patterns and fifty-six stock-keeping units. McGranahan's sold the Imperial Accent line to Schramm seven years ago, and the sales volume was $250,000. Now, with Bargain City's expansion, Johnson estimates the first-year order volume should be more than $500,000. Johnson lost the business when another distributor offered Schramm a 15 percent discount on a similar product made by Congolese Manufacturing. At the time, DuraFlor was unwilling to meet the competitor's lower price, asserting that its superior brand awareness increased retailer inventory turnover and justified a higher price.

DuraFlor controls more than 60 percent of the entire resilient flooring market, but only 30 per-

cent of the low-end twelve-foot sheet flooring market. DuraFlor has tended to neglect this market because the low-end market is a fiercely competitive one. The manufacturing process, called rotogravure, is so common that no manufacturer has a competitive cost advantage. The process allows virtually any picture to be made into a pattern. Thus, competitors can copy top sellers, making it difficult to maintain styling advantages.

Recently, Chuck heard that Bargain City's current distributor for twelve-foot sheet vinyl is having financial problems and can't keep its customers' stores stocked. On the chance that Bargain City might be looking for a new supplier, Tom called Mr. Schramm and was delighted to hear him confirm a sales call appointment with him and Chuck.

Chuck and Tom have decided to ask the DuraFlor district manager, Ron Harris, to participate in the sales presentation to Bargain City because to win the Bargain City business his firm must ultimately lower the price to McGranahan Distributing. McGranahan's current profit margin is 24 percent on the DuraFlor product.

In the pre-call strategy meeting, Johnson, Barnhart, and Harris decide to stress Imperial Accent's improved styling and other product features. They will point out the inventory turnover benefits it offers Bargain City because of its high brand awareness with the store's customers. The three of them agree that they will have to do some "paper-and-pencil" selling by demonstrating in specific numbers how profitable the DuraFlor line would be for Bargain City. They also agree that Johnson and Barnhart will finish the sales call with a review of the inventory monitoring, prompt delivery, and sales support that McGranahan's can provide.

After waiting in the lobby of Bargain City's large headquarters building for thirty-five minutes, a receptionist leads the three men to Mr. Schramm's office. Schramm's assistant buyer, Sixto Torres, is also there and, seeing the three of them march in, comments,

(continued)

## NEGOTIATING PRICE WITH A TASKMASTER

(CONTINUED)

"Oh boy, they're bringing in the big guns today. We're in for a real dog-and-pony show, Boss." Everybody laughs, and greetings are exchanged all around.

Then Tom Barnhart says, "We appreciate the opportunity to review the merits of the Imperial Accent line with you today, Don. I'm sure by the conclusion of our meeting that you'll agree that it offers an attractive profit opportunity for Bargain City."

"I'll be the judge of that," snaps Schramm, peering menacingly over his bifocals while leaning forward in his chair.

"Here are the twelve patterns in the Imperial Accent line," says Chuck Johnson, as he lays the patterns before Schramm and Torres. "As you can see, DuraFlor has restyled the line with five new patterns, including geometric designs, floral, and the always-popular brick patterns. We've also brightened the color palette in the line because market research has shown us that low-end buyers prefer brighter colors."

"What do you think of this pattern, Sixto?" asks Harris, holding up a bright red, rather garish thirty-six-by-thirty-six-inch sample.

"It's really ugly," replies Torres. "I wouldn't have it in my house. But who cares what I think about the pattern—how does it sell?"

"It's brand new, and we don't have any data on it yet," answers Harris.

Barnhart jumps in. "Don, Sixto, here's a list of the top twenty-five sellers nationwide, by color and by pattern. We suggest you begin by stocking all the patterns to see how they sell in your different markets. We'll ship new inventory promptly to any of your stores as needed."

Schramm leans forward, "Mm, so we won't have to stock anything in our warehouse?"

"That's right, Don, we'll handle all the inventory concerns and my salespeople will regularly call on all of your stores to make sure the twelve-inch roll racks are fully stocked," says Barnhart.

Harris chimes in, "The Imperial Accent line is really coming on strong lately, Don." Holding up a sample of the new embossing, he continues, "Our improved rotogravure process allows us to emboss the product now, enabling it to hide subfloor irregularities better than any product on the market. We're also using new 'hi-fidelity' inks that give these brighter colors."

Schramm puts his glasses on and folds his arms as his assistant picks up one of the samples and compares it to a sample of the Congolese product they are now carrying. "This doesn't look any different from the Congolese product," says Torres. "How many mils is the wear layer on your product?"

"Eight," says Harris.

"Congolese has a ten-mil wear layer," replies Torres.

"That's because they pump it up with air. We don't do that. Our research shows this product is the most durable in its product class." Harris is tired of competitors making claims that imply greater durability, while what they're doing is literally blowing hot air into the product. DuraFlor has always been conservative in its product claims, perhaps too conservative.

Harris continues talking, interrupting Barnhart, who is urging the discussion back to what McGranahan's can do for Bargain City. "Don, look at this profit opportunity," says Harris, handing a sheet of paper to Schramm. "If you buy Accent from McGranahan's at two dollars and five cents per square yard and sell it for three ninety-nine, you'll make almost 49 percent gross margin. Now with sixty-some stores, eight rolls per store, and seven turns a year, with the average roll being, say, one hundred square yards, that's a profit of $369,000. I know it will take a while to get the Congolese off your racks, but you could be generating these kinds of profit dollars in a year or two." Harris smiles and looks at Schramm.

Schramm crosses his arms again and stares at the sheet Harris has put on his desk. He rubs his eyes and grimaces slightly. "Well, for one thing, Ron, if I were to pay two dollars and five cents per square yard for this product, Sixto would have my job the next day. It's nice of you to try and help

(continued)

## CASE 6.1

# NEGOTIATING PRICE WITH A TASKMASTER

[CONTINUED]

me run my department, but if I made a 49 percent margin on this product, it wouldn't exactly be a bargain for the customer, now would it?"

"I think Ron was just trying to point out the profit potential, Don. Obviously, you'll be changing the numbers to fit Bargain City's marketing strategy," offers Johnson. "And remember that 2 percent of all your purchases will accumulate in a fifty-fifty co-op advertising fund."

"We're only paying a dollar eighty-two per square yard for the Congolese product. Can you meet that price?" asks Schramm.

"We'll sure try," quickly responds Barnhart. "What about it, Ron, can we get there?"

"I don't know for sure," says Harris to Schramm. "Let me talk to the product manager and get a price to Tom, and he'll give a price to you. If we can meet Congolese's price, will you give us the business, Don?"

"Maybe," Schramm replies. "Come back with your best price and we'll see. The products look similar to me, your styling has improved, and the co-op program is good. But I'll look at what your competitors are offering before I make up my mind."

"Remember, Don, we'll carry all the inventory, service your stores so the managers won't have to remember to order, and deliver the products right off our own truck so you won't take any risk of damage during delivery. And those costs are all in the price of the goods. You'll never get a bill for delivery charges. What have you got to lose? How about giving us a shot at the sheet goods business?" pleads Johnson.

"We'll see," says Schramm.

Later that week Harris calls Barnhart with a wholesale cost that would yield McGranahan's a price of $1.90 per square yard with a normal margin. Barnhart calls Johnson into his office and asks if he will be willing to take a 2 percent commission instead of 3 percent in order to help bridge the 8 percent gap. Thinking that it is critical to meet the competitor's price of $1.82 in order to win the business, Johnson agrees to take the cut in his commissions. Barnhart

calls Schramm with the price of $1.82 per square yard, reviews all the benefits of the Imperial Accent line and the services provided by McGranahan's, and asks for the order. Schramm says he will let him know in a few days, after he hears from other suppliers.

When Schramm calls back three days later, he says McGranahan's can have the business if they will take another nickel off their price. Apparently, the Congolese distributor has lowered the price to keep from losing the business. Barnhart really doesn't have a nickel to give. He has already cut the price to the bone, and another nickel off will reduce McGranahan's gross margin to 17 percent, not too attractive considering all the services they will be providing. Barnhart thinks for a few minutes, then calls Johnson in to discuss the new terms that Bargain City is requesting.

*Reprinted with permisson of James T. Strong, University of Akron.*

## Questions

1. Should McGranahan's lower the price to Bargain City by another five cents? Should Johnson agree to take an even lower commission to win the order?

2. How successful do you think Johnson, Barnhart, and Harris were in negotiating price resistance during the sales call? What types of techniques did Johnson, Barnhart, and Harris use to negotiate resistance? Do you think more persistence could have won the three-member sales team the Bargain City order?

3. Do you think it was a good idea to bring Ron Harris, the district manager of DuraFlor, along to help make the sales presentation to Bargain City? Why or why not?

4. How well overall did the sales team (Johnson, Barnhart, and Harris) do in negotiating concessions? What, if anything, should they have done differently?

5. What would you advise Chuck Johnson and Tom Barnhart to say in responding to Mr. Schramm's request for another nickel cut in price to win the Bargain City business?

# LEARNING TO HANDLE PROSPECT OBJECTIONS

Rachel Glassman sips her morning coffee as she waits for the last trainee to return from the morning break. Rachel, regional sales training manager for a multinational machine tool company, is in the middle of a long and intense day of sales training for recently hired salespeople. Today's training concentrates on negotiating prospect resistance and objections. From past experience, she knows that this part of the company's five-week training program is one of the most difficult for new representatives to master. Over the years, Rachel has tried many approaches to help trainees learn negotiation strategies and tactics. One of the best approaches, she believes for two reasons, is to combine video simulations with role-playing. First, former trainees who used the videos claim that the simulations hit close to what they later experienced in real sales situations. This testimonial makes current trainees more responsive. They understand that what they are viewing will be of value to them once they are assigned to a sales territory. Second, when sales trainees role-play immediately after they view the videotapes, they practice and reinforce negotiation strategies and techniques they just learned.

Today Rachel is presenting some simulated selling situations in which a sales representative deals with customer resistance or objections. In the first three segments, which three trainees viewed along with Rachel before the morning break, the videos followed a representative through a sales presentation and showed how salespeople handle various types of customer objections. The last two segments, which Rachel will present to the three trainees after the break, are again vignettes of sales presentations where the salesperson encounters various types of customer resistance and objections. In these videotapes, however, at the point when the objection is raised, the tape stops and each trainee is asked to recommend a strategy or technique to deal with the situation. When all sales trainees have made a recom-

mendation, the simulation is restarted and the viewer observes how the representative actually handled the customer's objection.

The essence of these two videotaped situations, along with brief summaries of how the three sales trainees responded, follows.

## Situation #1

A salesperson is just completing a sales presentation of a Power Spraywater broom to Cecil Jergens, a purchasing agent for National Industrial Equipment. The salesperson's concluding statement is "As you have seen, Mr. Jergens, the water broom enables workers to simultaneously wash away and sweep up tough dirt and grime from factory or plant floors in minutes. At the price of $34.95 per unit, it's a tremendous bargain, and I'm sure that each one of your plant managers will want several."

"Yes, the water broom looks like a useful product," responds Mr. Jergens, "but your price is nearly three times the price of our heavy-duty industrial brooms, which do a good clean-up job. I don't see the value in paying three times as much for a product that does the same job."

**Trainee Bob:** "Mr. Jergens seems to have some hidden agenda. I think he's probably buying the industrial brooms from a friend of his whom he has dealt with for years. I don't think there's much of a chance for a sale here."

**Trainee Pete:** "Mr. Jergens still isn't convinced of the benefits of the water broom relative to its price. I think the sales rep has to restate the benefits of the water broom in terms of worker time saved, cleanliness of the plant floors in ridding them of ground-in oil and grease as well as dirt, and improved worker morale. The salesperson ought to point out that the water broom's benefits relative to its price are actually much greater than the traditional industrial broom's benefits compared to its price. Doing so will indicate to Mr.

(continued)

# LEARNING TO HANDLE PROSPECT OBJECTIONS (CONTINUED)

Jergens that he will receive more value for his dollars by buying the water broom.

**Trainee Allison:** "At three times the price of the industrial brooms, perhaps the price of the water broom is too high. I'm sure the sales rep has some room to negotiate on price, so I'd recommend offering the water broom at a lower price—say $29.95 to see how Mr. Jergens responds."

## Situation #2

After making the sales representation and demonstration, a sales representative for Tool Storage Cabinet, Inc., asks the purchasing agent for Tebbets Machining Company this question: "May I go ahead and order five of these welded steel tool chests for your plant, Mr. O'Connor, so your machinists can soon have the peace of mind that comes from knowing that their valuable tools are secure?"

"Well, I know the machinists want more secure tool chests," replies Mr. O'Connor, "but I don't think they're going to like the combination locks on the doors. They're used to using keys, and it's going to slow them down a lot to have to remember and work the combinations each time they want to open the doors of their tool chests."

**Trainee Bob:** "The engineers who designed those tool chests weren't very customer oriented. They should have known that the machinists would want access by keys instead of a combination lock. I'd go back to headquarters and tell them that we need to redesign the locking device on our tool storage chests."

**Trainee Pete:** "I'd turn this apparent disadvantage into an advantage. I think the sales rep could correctly say that the locks were purposely designed with combination locks for some well-thought-out reasons. First, keys get mislaid, lost, or stolen, and anyone with the key can open the tool chest. Combinations are not likely to be lost or stolen. Second, if a key is left at home, the machinist must return home for the key, but a

combination is carried around in one's head. Third, when there is turnover in the plant, a new machinist can securely use the former employee's tool chest by merely changing the combination, rather than having to rework the entire locking device for a new key. Fourth, talented thieves can pick open key locks, but few thieves can open combination locks. By pointing out these advantages of the combination lock, I think the sales rep can overcome the prospect's objection."

**Trainee Allison:** "I'd tell Mr. O'Connor that I bet some of the machinists will prefer the combination lock to the key lock tool chests, and that I'd appreciate him taking a little poll to find out. Then I'd tell him that we can provide both types of locking devices, depending on what the machinists want. If I found out later that our company didn't offer anything but the combination lock, I'd call Mr. O'Connor back and tell him that I'm sorry but I was mistaken about our selling the key-lock type. Then I'd ask for an order for the combination-lock tool chests, assuming that some of the machinists will prefer them."

## Questions

1. Look at the two situations one at a time. In your opinion, which of the three sales trainees seems to be on the best track toward handling the objection in each situation? How do you think the prospect will respond to the other two sales reps' approaches in each case?
2. Which one of these sales reps would you prefer to be assigned to a territory where you were the sales manager? Why?
3. What overall advice would you give the sales reps to help them in negotiating prospect objections or resistance?
4. What do you think of the process of setting up a situation via videotape, stopping the tape to let sales trainees explain how they would deal with the situation, and then showing how the sales rep actually dealt with the situation?

## CHAPTER 7

# Confirming and Closing the Sale: Start of the Long-Term Relationship

*"The secret of success is constancy to purpose."*
Benjamin Disraeli

## After Reading This Chapter, You Should Understand:

- Why some salespeople fail to close.
- When to attempt a trial close.
- What trial closing cues are and how to make use of them.
- Key principles of persuasion in closing.
- Effective closing techniques.
- How to deal with rejection.
- What immediate post-sale activities must be performed.

INSIDE PERSONAL SELLING:
## Meet Marc Gedansky of OceanLake

**M**arc Gedansky closes a sale by focusing on his customer's problem, not his company's technology. Gedansky is Vice President of Sales and Business Development for OceanLake, which sells wireless connectivity technology to translate Internet content for web-enabled cell phones and other mobile devices. If a company wants to make Internet content available through mobile devices, it can use OceanLake's technology to reformat the information to fit the smaller screen on a PDA or cell phone.

Gedansky works toward closing sales by helping prospects recognize and make decisions about solving a troublesome problem. "Don't focus on what your product does," he advises. "Focus on the problem that's causing the customer pain." Only when it is clear to both Gedansky and

the prospect that there is a problem—and that OceanLake can solve it—does he explain features and benefits. "It helps your customers; it helps your employees; it helps your prospects gain access to information. Is that of value to you?" he asks. If the prospect agrees, he is nearing a close.

"Assuming I have gotten the prospect's agreement on the problem and solution, I then try to create a sense of urgency," says Gedansky of his typical approach to closing. He believes that salespeople often lose sales, not to competition, but to buyer inertia: "The prospect did not buy anything at all. Why? Because you could not convince them there was a compelling reason to make a decision to buy."

To overcome inertia, Gedansky tries to quantify the pain whenever possible by putting a dollar figure on what indecision is costing the prospect. For example, he might point out that a prospect could save ten thousand dollars a day by using OceanLake's technology. "When you get prospects to think in those terms, you instill a sense of urgency," he says. "You also get them to understand the consequences of delaying a decision—and you may get a decision without going through a lengthy evaluation process."

When prospects don't buy, Gedansky is driven to find out why, because of advice he received from an early mentor. "You will not be an effective salesperson until you take full responsibility for somebody not buying from you, regardless of the situation," he stresses. Sometimes he finds that the company has no problem that OceanLake can solve; sometimes company management sees the problem as such a low priority that it is not worth the investment to solve. When a prospect doesn't buy at all, Gedansky checks periodically to see if the company's priorities have changed. When a prospect buys from a competitor, he looks at the reasons, which may be price or a particular feature. "I try to be as objective as possible so I can analyze and learn from a lost sale," he summarizes.

**Close** the stage in the selling process where the salesperson tries to obtain the prospect's agreement to purchase the product.

ow comes every salesperson's moment of truth. You've gone through the preceding five steps of the PSP brilliantly. Your qualified prospect has witnessed a solid sales presentation and demonstration, you've addressed all of his questions, you've dealt adeptly with his objections, and he seems extremely convinced of the merits of your product. Now, you must only ask for the order—close the sale—and you can count the prospect as one of your customers. But are you ready to seize the challenge of inducing the prospect to approve the purchase? By the end of this chapter you will be armed with the knowledge to do just that!

The **close** is defined as those activities involved in eliciting a positive buying decision from the prospect. It should be a natural step in the sales process and not forced. If you have done your job effectively in the preceding five steps of the PSP, the close should evolve almost automatically. That is, the prospect's desire and conviction for the product should be keen and his or her questions or objections should have been addressed, so the time should be ripe to ask the prospect to make the purchase.

Although a sale is typically closed after completion of the previous five steps in the PSP, professional sales personnel *constantly* evaluate when they

**FIGURE 7.1**

THE PERSONAL SELLING PROCESS

should close the sale. This assessment indicates whether to close the sale now or continue with the selling process. You may be able to close earlier with some prospects than with others and close earlier in some situations than in others. Don't be surprised if you haven't completely finished those five PSP stages and the prospect is ready to sign the order form—take the order now. After all, your primary purpose is to make sales—not sales presentations.

A common saying on the stage is "It's easier to get on than it is to get off." This is also true in sales. The close is the final curtain. Closing is the make-or-break time of selling, the moment of truth, when having some small morsel of extra knowledge or skill often makes the difference between earning or losing a commission. Only one question really matters: "Can I close this buyer?"[1]

## CLOSING AND CONFIRMING THE SALE

The close is that stage in the selling process where the salesperson tries to obtain agreement from the prospect to purchase the product. Some scholars and practitioners prefer to use the term "confirming sales" instead of "closing sales." In their view, *closing* incorrectly implies the end of the selling process, when in fact much hard work must follow the sale in terms of service to satisfy the customer and win repeat business. Professional salespeople realize that their job has just begun after the prospect has agreed to buy. Why? Because only attentive efforts will retain the current sale, maintain the prospect's satisfaction with the purchase, and enhance the relationship with this account (for example, secure additional business and referrals).

### Closing is Part of the Ongoing Selling Process

Instead of viewing the close as the end or the pinnacle of the PSP, professional salespeople regard the close as simply a vital part of the *ongoing* selling process and buyer-seller relationship. No matter how clever the closing strategies used, the salesperson is unlikely to make the sale unless he or she has done a good job in each stage of the PSP leading up to this point. Conversely, no matter how brilliantly the salesperson has performed in the preceding stages of the PSP, the sale can still be lost unless the salesperson uses the right closing strategy and tactics.

### What the Close Represents

A successful close confirms the *win-win* agreement reached with a buyer and the continuance of the buyer-seller relationship. It indicates that the salesperson has done a thorough selling job (so far) and that the buyer is pleased with his or her purchase decision (at least so far). Because of its widespread acceptance, and for convenience, we will frequently use the term "closing the sale," but keep in mind that the close is *not* the end but merely a *continuation* of the selling process. Read the following *From the Command Post* to see how web auction sites have been successfully closing sales again and again and again.

# FROM THE COMMAND POST: WEB AUCTION SITES JUST KEEP ON SELLING MORE AND MORE

Web auction sites (such as eBay, UBid, Amazon Auctions, Sotheby's, QXL, and TripBid) have become one of cyberspace's favorite and most successful web venues. Started chiefly to help consumers buy and sell such prosaic items as candy dispensers, automobiles, and second-hand products, collectively they represent a behemoth channel of distribution. Web auction users buy collectibles of all kinds, in addition to clothing, sports equipment, and almost anything else that's legal. And their success has been colossal. Millions of goods exchange hands daily through these sites, generating billions of dollars in annual sales revenues.

Why are these sites so effective? First, they provide a convenient commerce platform on the Internet. Second, most continue to seek out additional customers, increase the offerings sold on their sites, expand into global markets, and offer users an enjoyable and exciting experience.

In efforts to thrive in cyberspace, some auction sites have moved into the business-to-business (B2B) and business-to-consumer (B2C) channels, rather than being merely a consumer-to-consumer (C2C) alternative. Businesses, whether producers, wholesalers, or retailers, can buy or sell myriad kinds of items (for example, copiers, computers, and cars) on the web sites. Even giant companies, like IBM and Sun Microsystems, are marketing their products on auction web sites. In addition, numerous businesses are using these web sites to sell directly to consumers. To complement and promote all of these activities, some auction companies are advertising their business services aggressively—not only online but via television, direct mail, and print ads to attract larger user bases.

For many dot-coms and cyberspace firms, the road to glory has been paved with potholes and insurmountable obstacles. For web auction companies, though, sticking close to their strengths and goals, plus adept execution, has led to amazing growth, success, and increasing aspirations.

## AVOIDING THE CLOSE

Despite the significance of closing the sale and its natural sequence in the PSP, some salespeople unfortunately avoid the close. This happens with both experienced and inexperienced sales personnel. Whatever the reason, a failure to close abruptly ends the buyer-seller relationship that had just begun. Let's look at some reasons why sales reps may fail to close.[2]

### Experienced Salespeople

Some experienced salespeople become so involved in the selling process that they don't even try to close until they've finished their sales presentation and product demonstration. Such behavior can either delay the sale or result in the prospect's raising more and more objections or the salesperson's talking past the point of making a sale (so the prospect becomes "cold"). Still other veteran salespeople become so complacent about selling techniques that have worked well in the past that they avoid trying new closing methods in new selling situations. Consequently, their closings become stale and ineffective.

The best salespeople are sensitive to every opportunity to close and are always shaping their closes to fit the individual prospect and selling situation. This often means trying new closes, or at least old closes with new twists—both of which not only improve closing effectiveness but also help keep the selling job interesting and exciting.

## New Salespeople

Some new salespeople find it extremely difficult to close sales for three basic reasons: a lack of confidence in themselves, the product, or the company; guilt about asking people to part with their money; or a general fear of failure that causes them to postpone the close as long as possible.

1. Lack of confidence is common in new salespeople who are thrust into new selling situations without adequate training. One way to help overcome this lack of confidence is to talk with other salespeople, those who are also new and dealing with the same confidence problem themselves and with sympathetic veterans who can tell stories about their own shaky confidence during their first few months in sales. Sales managers understand this common problem and can usually help by providing support, information on confidence-building books and exercises, and perhaps additional training. In addition, having the sales manager accompany the new rep on sales calls can provide a source of comfort and confidence for the novice salesperson. In fact, the manager may be able to assist the salesperson with the close without stealing the individual's "thunder." One computer salesperson asked his sales manager to accompany him on what would turn out to be his first sale. Both the sales manager and the salesperson attempted trial closes that eventually led to an order. After the sale, the manager and sales rep evaluated the sales call as a means of enhancing the salesperson's knowledge and confidence regarding his ability to close a sale.

2. As children, we are taught not to ask people for money—it simply is impolite. If you harbor guilt feelings about asking people to make a purchase commitment, those beliefs also might spring from your negative perceptions about the role of selling. Professional salespeople, however, realize that they are helping people solve problems and are performing a vital and important societal function. People only spend money when they believe the purchase will answer their needs. A sale is thus confirmation of your useful and important role in the buyer's life and livelihood.

3. Fear of feeling rejected is common in selling. Therefore, some salespeople consider the close so terribly important and dramatic that ironically they can never find just the right moment to make the close. Procrastination provides comfort to salespeople who fear that all their previous work in the selling process may come to naught. Fear of failure can be overcome by recognizing that few products are sold on the first sales call. Failure on

## ON THE FRONTLINES

# *Perseverance Pays Off*

A salesperson was assigned to a territory that included a large federal government installation in a major city. This installation used about five thousand personal computers (PCs), and a major computer manufacturer seemed to have a lock on the business because the head purchasing agent preferred that brand.

On the salesperson's initial call, the head purchasing agent told him that the installation bought only the large competitor's PCs and that the salesperson would be wasting his time trying to sell any other brand. Refusing to give up, the salesperson cultivated a relationship with the head purchasing agent's assistant. The salesperson made it a point to call on the installation at least once a month, when he would teach the assistant all about PCs. After about ten months, the assistant called the salesperson and asked him to stop by the following morning. Arriving early, the sales rep met the assistant who said that his boss had taken early retirement so that he was now the head purchasing manager. Before the sales rep could even congratulate him on his promotion, the newly appointed head purchasing manager asked the salesperson whether his firm's PCs met all government specifications. After

checking to make sure that they did, the sales rep was delighted to hear the new head purchasing manger say, "Okay, what's the fifty-PC price?"

The PC salesperson personally installed each one of those fifty PCs and instructed the buyer's employees how to use them. He also arranged for his company's service manager to meet with his counterpart at the installation to set up a two-day course for the repair technicians and a spare parts inventory system. Everything ran smoothly for three months, upon which another order came in, this time for 150 PCs! Those 200 PCs enabled the salesperson to make 225 percent of his annual sales quota and were largely responsible for a key promotion in his career.

Later, the new head purchasing manager told the PC sales rep that his refusal to give up and his willingness to share information without any apparent return convinced him to put in the first order for fifty PCs. The sales rep's thorough follow-up on those PCs and the support provided by his company's service department earned the second order for 150 PCs. Success usually yields to salespeople who never quit trying and make the most of opportunities when they appear.

a particular closing attempt certainly does not mean that the sale is irretrievably lost. There will be other opportunities. The best salespeople, however, share one winning attitude: They never give up.

*On the Frontlines* contains an inspiring story about a salesperson who was so patient and persevering that when the close came, it actually took him by surprise.

## THE TRIAL CLOSE

There is no single, best time to attempt a close. Some situations, though, almost cry out for an attempted close, as we discuss on the next page.

## When to Close

Closing attempts, are especially appropriate in three situations:

1. When you have completed a presentation without the prospect raising any objections, try to close. Doing so may elicit objections from the prospect which you can then deal with.

2. When the sales presentation is completed and all questions and objections have been addressed, closing is logical.

3. If the buyer indicates an interest in buying the product by giving a "closing signal," the time is appropriate to close.

Professional salespeople who are prepared to close anywhere, anytime know their *ABCs—Always Be Closing.*[3] In fact, they learn to use subtle trial closes early and often throughout each stage of the selling process. Some salespeople refer to the **trial close** as a "miniclose," but when handled properly, a small trial close can quickly become the *big close*. A trial close is simply a way to see whether the prospect is ready to buy and thus ready for the close.

**Trial Close** any well-placed attempt to close the sale; can be used early and often throughout the selling process.

Let's say that a salesperson has thoroughly discussed the product features, advantages, and benefits with a prospect who seems interested in the product. The salesperson might then ask, "Should I tell our warehouse personnel to reserve a hundred units for you?" or "Would next week be a convenient time for you to take shipment?" If the prospect says yes to either question, the sale is confirmed and the trial close has been successful. But if the buyer isn't ready to place the order, the salesperson can simply resume the sales presentation and patiently wait until the buyer again seems ready to place the order—either during the same presentation or during a later sales call. Salespeople should continue with their sales presentation when they encounter such caution signs as the following:

- A trial close fails to elicit a positive response from the prospect.
- An interruption disrupts the prospect's frame of mind.
- Another objection or request for more information arises.

## Trial Closing Signals

Salespeople must not only learn *how* to close but *when* to close, given the various verbal *and* nonverbal "trial closing signals." A *trial closing signal* is a verbal or nonverbal indication that the customer may be ready to make the purchase. Positive *verbal* signals occur when the prospect asks specific questions about the product or says something positive about it, or when the salesperson does a good job answering a particular objection. *Nonverbal* signals occur when the prospect begins showing substantial interest in the product and in what the salesperson is saying, and conveys this through positive body language. When salespeople notice a trial closing signal, they can immediately follow it up by using one of the closing techniques that we discuss later in the chapter. Doing so often leads to an early sale. If not, just continue where you left off in the sales presentation. The verbal and nonverbal closing signals summarized in Table 7.1 should help you recognize trial closing opportunities and time your trial closes effectively. *It's Up to You*, on p. 213, puts you in charge of a sales presentation. How would you handle the close?

| TABLE 7.1 |
| --- |

## TRIAL CLOSING SIGNALS

### Verbal Signals

When the prospect asks

- about product price, delivery, installation, or service.
- about any special discounts, deals, or special incentives to buy.
- a hypothetical question about buying: "If I do decide to buy . . ."
- who else has bought the product.
- what other customers think about the product.
- if a special feature is included or available.
- if the product can accomplish a particular task.
- the salesperson for his or her opinion about one product version versus another.
- what method of payment is acceptable.

When the prospect says

- something positive about the product.
- that he or she has always wanted some special product feature.

When the salesperson

- successfully answers one of the prospect's objections.
- asks if the prospect has any more questions and the prospect says no or is silent.

### Nonverbal Signals

When the prospect

- begins closely studying and handling the product.
- tests or tries out the product.
- seems pleased by the product's performance or by some product feature.
- looks more relaxed.
- becomes more friendly.
- increases eye contact with the salesperson.
- looks over the order form or picks up the pen the salesperson has handed him or her.
- nods his or her head in agreement or leans toward the salesperson.
- begins to listen more intensely to the salesperson.
- loans the salesperson a pen.
- picks up, fondles, smells, tastes, or closely studies the product.
- unconsciously reaches for his or her checkbook or wallet.

When the salesperson

- finishes the sales presentation.
- completes a successful product demonstration.
- hands the order form and a pen to the prospect.

## IT'S UP TO YOU

You are a salesperson for a large industrial chemicals company. You arrive at a potential customer's plant just in time for an appointment with a purchasing agent, scheduled three weeks ago. You have prepared and practiced a brilliant one-hour sales presentation focusing on specific benefits that you think will overwhelm the agent and stimulate her to immediately buy one hundred thousand dollars in chemicals from you. As soon as you walk into her office, the purchasing agent says, "I'm sorry, but I only have fifteen minutes to spend with you today. I've looked over your product brochures and I'm impressed. I've decided to place a twenty-five thousand dollar order with you." What do you do now?

## PRINCIPLES OF PERSUASION IN CLOSING

In developing closing strategies for various buyer negotiating styles and buying situations, salespeople can benefit from at least a rudimentary understanding of the basic principles of persuasion, as outlined in Table 7.2. Any one or various combinations of these seven principles can be effective when used within the overall framework of a closing strategy.[4] As you read each principle, think about how you might make use of it now and when you become a salesperson.

**TABLE 7.2**

### PRINCIPLES OF PERSUASION IN CLOSING

**Consistency Principle.** Prospects and customers want to be perceived as logical and consistent in thought and behavior; thus past thoughts and behaviors have a strong effect on future thoughts and behavior.

*Application.* When a group life insurance salesperson asks the prospect to agree on *each* of various reasons to buy group life insurance for the firm, such as the importance of financial planning for retirement, the need for a forced savings plan, or to provide family security in case of loss of income, the salesperson is building to the close using the consistency principle of persuasion. By gaining individual agreement to *each* of the advantages, the salesperson makes it harder for the prospect to turn down a group policy, as such a refusal would be inconsistent with earlier agreements.

**Commitment Principle.** Prospects' prepurchase efforts to learn about a product tend to increase their commitment to buying the product

*Application.* A dealer who makes a special trip to a manufacturer's warehouse sale has taken action that is consistent with buying. The more effort the dealer takes to reach the sale, the greater the consistency effect and the higher the likelihood of buying.

(continued)

> ### TABLE 7.2
>
> ## PRINCIPLES OF PERSUASION IN CLOSING (CONTINUED)
>
> **Reciprocity Principle.** Most cultures have a convention that if one person does something for a second person, the second person is obligated to reciprocate the favor. Often, the reciprocated favor is even greater than the original favor.
>
> *Application.* When a salesperson provides special services to a prospective account beyond "favors" extended by competitors, the salesperson is often rewarded with a large order that exceeds the value of the original service provided.
>
> **Social Validation Principle.** Prospects are more likely to purchase a product when people (and companies) similar to themselves or their desired reference groups have also purchased it.
>
> *Application.* Salespeople can increase the likelihood of the prospect's buying a product by providing product testimonials and stories from other satisfied customers similar to the prospect and his or her reference groups.
>
> **Authority Principle.** Prospects are more likely to buy from salespeople who are perceived as expert in their field.
>
> *Application.* Salespeople with relevant expertise or even symbolic expertise can be effective in persuading prospects. Prospects often attribute expertise to salespeople who look and act the part.
>
> **Scarcity Principle.** As products become more scarce, they are perceived as more valuable and desirable. Thus, the likelihood of persuading a prospect to buy increases if the product, price, or the opportunity to buy are perceived as fleeting.
>
> *Application.* Salespeople frequently use an "impending event" close, which consists of telling a prospect to buy now before something occurs that decreases or eliminates the availability of the product or the current price. "This low price is only good through this week, then the price goes up ten percent," or "These PCs are so popular that this is the last one in stock."
>
> **Friendship Principle.** Prospects are more easily persuaded by salespeople they like. Perhaps this is an offshoot of the consistency effect, because not to buy from a friend would be inconsistent behavior.
>
> *Application.* Salespeople use this principle by ingratiating themselves with prospects. Four effective ways to promote liking are *similarity, praise, cooperation,* and *physical attraction.* Salespeople encourage prospects to like them by reflecting similar attitudes, backgrounds, hobbies, and lifestyles. Subtle praise or compliments are also effective. In team selling, a good-cop, bad-cop approach can be used where one of the salespeople positions him or herself as fighting for (cooperating with) the customer with a tough sales manager. Finally, salespeople try to maximize their attractiveness through grooming, dress, and personality.

## CLOSING TECHNIQUES

A wide range of basic closing strategies have been developed over the years, and the salesperson can tailor each to fit a particular prospect and his or her own personal selling style. Table 7.3 provides a reference tool for several effective closing strategies. This is not a comprehensive list, but it does introduce you to a reasonably extensive repertoire of useful ideas for closing sales, some of which will be appropriate for your selling style and for the selling situations

| | TABLE 7.3 |
|---|---|
| **CLOSING TECHNIQUES** | |

| Closing Technique | Explanation |
|---|---|
| **Clarification Closes** | |
| Assumptive Close | Assume that the purchase decision has already been made so that the prospect feels compelled to buy. |
| Choice Close | Offer the prospect alternative products from which to choose. |
| Success Story Close | Tell a story about a customer with a similar problem who solved it by buying the product. Alternatively, provide satisfied customers' written or verbal testimonies supporting the product. Especially effective are endorsements from people well known and respected by the prospect. |
| Contingent Close | Elicit prospect's agreement to buy if the salesperson can demonstrate the benefits promised. |
| Counterbalance Close | Offset an undeniable objection by balancing it with an important buying benefit. |
| Boomerang Close | Turn an objection around so that it becomes a reason for buying. |
| **Psychologically Oriented Closes** | |
| Stimulus-Response Close | Use a sequence of leading questions to make it easier for the prospect to say yes when finally asked for the order. |
| Minor Points Close | Secure favorable decisions on several minor points leading to eventual purchase of the product. |
| Standing Room Only (SRO) Close | Suggest that the opportunity to buy is brief because demand is high and the product is in short supply. |
| Impending Event Close | Warn the prospect about some upcoming event that makes it more advantageous to buy now. |
| Puppy Dog Close | Let the prospect use the product for awhile and, as with a puppy, an emotional attachment may develop, leading to a purchase. |

(continued)

| | TABLE 7.3 |
|---|---|
| **CLOSING TECHNIQUES** (CONTINUED) | |

| Closing Technique | Explanation |
|---|---|
| **Straightforward Closes** | |
| Ask for the Order Close | Ask for the order directly or indirectly. |
| Order Form Close | While asking the prospect a series of questions, start filling out basic information on the contract or order form. |
| Summary Close | Summarize the advantages and disadvantages of buying the product before asking for the order. |
| **Concession Closes** | |
| Special Deal Close | Offer a special incentive to encourage the prospect to buy now. |
| No Risk Close | Agree to take the product back and refund the customer's money if the product doesn't prove satisfactory. |
| **Lost-Sale Closes** | |
| Turnover Close | Turn the prospect over to another salesperson with a fresh approach or better chance to make the sale. |
| Pretend-to-Leave Close | Start to walk away, then "remember" another benefit or special offer after the prospect has relaxed his or her defenses. |
| Ask For Help Close | When the sale seems lost, apologize for not being able to satisfy the prospect and ask what it would have taken to secure the sale, then offer that. |

in which you typically find yourself. However, take care not to limit yourself to just one or two different strategies. The more strategies you know and experiment with, the greater your chances for closing sales with a vast array of different buyers. When using any of these techniques, however, keep in mind that the response you receive from the prospect will determine whether you have closed the sale or whether you must continue the selling process and attempt another close later on.

The closing techniques can be categorized into five groups: clarification closes, psychologically oriented closes, straightforward closes, concession closes, and lost-sale closes.[5] Let's briefly discuss these strategies.

## Clarification Closes

Clarification closes improve prospects' knowledge and understanding of the seller's offering or overcome their lack of clarity about it.

**Assumptive Close.** If the prospect shows a strong interest in your product, you may close the sale by expressing the assumption that he or she will purchase the product. This can be done verbally or nonverbally. These kinds of statements show a verbal assumption: "Should I alert our credit department to activate an account for you?" or "Will you verify your shipping address to make sure that the product is delivered precisely where you want it?" Taking out the order form, handing the prospect a pen and a completed order blank, or handing the product to the prospect indicate nonverbal assumptions of the purchase. This technique can appear throughout the sales presentation in statements that make the purchase sound routine. For instance, a salesperson might say early on, "After you take delivery, you'll find that this product more than suits your needs." Repeating this kind of statement is likely to be reinforcing and quite persuasive, and can seem encouraging and comforting to the prospect, thus leading to his or her favorable purchase decision. It makes the purchase seem so natural that not making it would seem almost illogical to the prospect.

**Choice Close.** Asking prospects which of two or more alternative products they prefer limits opportunities to say no. Questions that can help set up the choice close include "Which of these two chairs do you think would be most appropriate for your office staff—the Commodore model or the Executive?" "Will you want the five-year or ten-year service plan?" This method removes the potential confusion of considering several products at once by narrowing the choice for the prospect. Furthermore, it omits products the prospect does not need and focuses on those most suitable. In essence, the approach narrows the prospect's choice of alternatives, thus making the buying situation less frightening and clearer for the prospect.

**Success Story Close.** Relating a story about how another one of your customers solved a similar problem with the product can reassure a prospect about buying now. A salesperson might say something like this:

> You know Al Rakowski, the purchasing agent for Superior Plumbing Supplies in Pebbleville? Well, Al was having a heck of a time getting packaging materials that would hold up in shipping some of Superior's heavier plumbing parts to customers. He tried every conceivable type of box offered by every packaging materials and container company you can name. When I heard about his problem, I told Al that I'd give him ten of our new reinforced "Tough Guy" brand containers to test by shipping Superior's most troublesome products to California and back. If our "Tough Guys" didn't hold up, I promised to pay the shipping charges. But, if they did hold up, I wanted an order for five thousand. Well, when our "Tough Guys" came back looking almost brand new and the plumbing parts didn't have a mark on them, Al called me all excited and

insisted on an order for ten thousand more. If you want to listen to a true believer in our "Tough Guy" containers, just give Al a call.

**Contingent Close.** Convincing the prospect to agree to buy if you can show that the product will do what you have said it will do is called a contingent close (or trap close). To set up this contingency, the salesperson might say, "If I can show you how your company can cut production costs by 20 percent without losing quality, will you buy?" By setting up this contingency, the salesperson has effectively closed the sale if the product claims can be substantiated.

**Counterbalance Close.** Prospects who raise a legitimate objection to buying the product can often be closed on that point of resistance if it can be counterbalanced with a benefit. The prospect may object:

> Your company's automatic conveyor belt system is just too expensive for our warehouse operations. We'll just stay with our manual system.

As a counterbalance, the salesperson might reply

> Mr. Greenhaus, you said you were planning to add another person to your warehouse crew. How much will you pay that new employee in wages and benefits—$20,000 to $25,000? Well, our equipment costs only $14,500 fully installed, plus you'll increase warehouse productivity enough that you won't need to hire another person. You'll save over five thousand dollars the first year and more thereafter because our equipment won't demand a pay raise. I don't see how you can go wrong with it, do you?

**Boomerang Close**
turning a prospect's objection or point of resistance around so that it becomes a reason for buying.

**Boomerang Close.** In the **boomerang close,** the salesperson turns the prospect's objection or point of resistance into a reason for buying (recall Chapter 6). For instance, a prospect might remark

> I like the looks and modern style of this automatic warehouse garage door, but it's so slow that it takes twice as long to open and close as our other warehouse garage doors. I'm afraid that our mechanics and customers will lose patience with its slowness.

The salesperson might truthfully counter

> Yes, this new model opens and closes at about half the speed of the older models. I'm sure you know how dangerous these heavy garage doors are and, like most managers, you can probably tell some tragic stories about people being hit by them. Based on our study of these accidents over the past five years, we found that cutting the garage door speed in half would probably reduce the number of accidents by 75 percent. Warehouse managers who are using this new door say that it takes only a few days to adjust to its pace, and there hasn't

been an accident reported yet. I think you'll find that the added safety more than compensates for a little slower operation.

## Psychologically Oriented Closes

These kinds of closes focus on the prospect's emotions, thus inducing a response from the prospect that is psychologically based.

**Stimulus-Response Close.** By steering prospects through a series of leading questions to which they almost have to answer yes, the salesperson builds a pattern of positive responses that helps the prospect make the purchase commitment. For instance, the salesperson might ask the following questions: "You would like to increase the quality of your promotional brochures, wouldn't you?" or "You would like an energy-efficient air conditioning system in your office building, wouldn't you?" This approach to closing is common among inexperienced salespeople because it can be readily learned and has proven effective in various situations. However, because the stimulus-response closing approach is rather mechanical and requires little prospect participation except to provide positive responses, it can come off as condescending and insulting to more sophisticated buyers.

**Minor Points Close.** Starting with minor decisions, prospects are asked to make incrementally larger decisions until the sale is closed. Salespeople might start by asking, "Which size do you prefer most?" "Do you like the stationary or the portable model?" "Are you interested in our service plan?" In answering these sequential questions, prospects develop an increasing commitment toward buying the product. Focusing the prospect on minor issues/decisions is less difficult for both the salesperson and the prospect than focusing too soon on more major issues.

**Standing Room Only (SRO) Close.** By implying or showing that many others are interested in buying the product, a salesperson can put psychological pressure on (that is, instill a sense of urgency) the prospect to buy now. Although this may be an honest description of the competition for a high-demand product, the SRO close has sometimes been associated with questionable ethics. For example, some real estate salespeople have been known to deliberately schedule their appointments with potential buyers to overlap so that it appears that a lot of people are interested in the property. Seeing other buyers waiting to see the property can pressure prospects to make a quick decision to buy. In another situation, a salesperson may tell a buyer, "Companies have been snatching up these new cell phones the minute they lay their eyes on them. If you think your field supervisors will want them, I'd suggest you place your order now for the twenty, so I can put them on hold until Tuesday. That should give your people enough time to make up their minds, shouldn't it?" The SRO close is probably inappropriate or even unethical for most organizational selling situations, unless you can *honestly* state—and show—that the product really is in great demand. Remember: the level of trust a buyer has in a salesperson determines whether or not there will be an ongoing relationship.[6]

**Impending Event Close.** An early warning about a price increase, product shortage, or other event can show the prospect the advantage of buying now. Salespeople who give their customers timely information that helps them buy wisely and efficiently will gain the trust and gratitude of customers. On the other hand, nothing will irritate customers more than not hearing of upcoming price increases or product shortages or later finding out that they bought a product just before it went on sale. Never use the impending event close in a dishonest, manipulative way. Salespeople who do so jeopardize all future sales to customers whom they have duped. Providing evidence of an impending event can enhance your credibility and increase the likelihood that you'll close the sale. For instance, one copier sales rep received a fax from her firm's headquarters noting that copier prices would increase at the end of the week. Seizing the opportunity, the salesperson took the fax to her prospects to alert them to the imminent price increases. As a result, several of her prospects took advantage of the lower prices by making their copier purchases prior to the week's end. By looking out for her customers, this salesperson improved her customers' trust and satisfaction with her and her company.

**Puppy Dog Close.** Who can resist a friendly puppy dog? People who take a puppy into their home for a few days usually become so attached that they want to keep it. Similarly, when salespeople let prospects try a product in the office for a few days or weeks, they usually form an attachment that makes it difficult to return the product—thus, the **puppy dog close**. For example, an aircraft manufacturer's sales rep who has arranged for two or three trial uses of a corporate helicopter might visit the prospect's buying team afterward and say, "Well, your colleagues seem pretty pleased with our 'copter's performance. May I take that as a sign that you'd like to own the aircraft?"

**Puppy Dog Close** letting the prospect try the product for a few days or weeks before buying. Akin to a cuddly puppy, most people grow attached to something they have for awhile.

### Straightforward Closes

Straightforward closes entail salepeople asking directly for the order.

**Ask for the Order Close.** An effective, but sometimes overlooked, close is to simply ask for the order in a graciously assertive way: "Let me use my laptop computer to order the product for you now so we can start solving your company's production line problems as early as next week." If you have done everything "right" in the PSP, this may be the best way to consummate the deal. One salesperson learned the importance of this close the hard way, as described in *On the Frontlines*.

*The quickest way to express your nonverbal assumption of a close is to hand the prospect a pen and your purchase agreement.*
Larry Williams/Corbis

**Order Form Close.** Salespeople use verbal and nonverbal signals to gently pressure the prospect into buying. By asking the prospect a series of basic questions, such as an address and telephone number or the correct spelling of a name, and writing the information on the contract, the salesperson leads the prospect toward the close. After the basic information is filled in, the salesperson hands the order form and a pen to the prospect and, in a friendly way, says something like "Okay, just sign on the dotted line there, please."

**Summary Close.** Also called the T-Account or "Ben Franklin Close"

## ON THE FRONTLINES

# *Ask and Ye Shall Receive*

Tom, a loan sales rep for a mortgage banking firm, was transferred into a new territory that had outstanding potential. He called primarily on real estate agents, asking them to recommend his firm to their clients rather than competitive lenders. To facilitate his efforts, Tom decided to call on the top real estate producers in his territory. One particular real estate company became his target account.

In addition to providing requisite information for the real estate agents in that targeted firm, he called on them every Monday, Wednesday, and Friday (as the firm was large and presented a golden opportunity for Tom). This led to his being invited to all of the real estate company's social gatherings and meetings. Over time, he became intimately familiar with many of their agents.

Tom's belief was that such efforts would lead to lending success. Well, that almost didn't happen!

One day during a sales meeting that Tom attended, the real estate firm's best agent declared that she needed a loan quote and started to call one of Tom's competitors. There Tom sat, as the agent started to call the competition. All of a sudden, she looked up, saw Tom, and said, "Oh, I'm sorry. Aren't you in the lending business?"

Tom closed his almost-lost deal, but more importantly, he learned a critical lesson: No matter how often you call on an account, or how well you know your customer, always ask for the order!

**Source:** *Thomas Kranig, "Learning Lessons from the Field," SellingPower.com, Most Memorable Sale (September 28, 2001). Reprinted with permission.*

because of his rational approach to decision making, a summary close uses a simple analysis in the form of a T-graph to show the advantages and disadvantages in buying the product. It's usually best for the salesperson to assist but to let the prospect actually prepare the T-account so that it becomes the prospect's analysis, not the salesperson's. Seeing that the product's benefits far outweigh its costs usually leads the prospect to make the purchase decision. This method is particularly apt if negotiations have taken up several sales calls and many points have been addressed. Furthermore, this type of close helps offset the prospect's forgetting certain points and reinforces points that the prospect may have objected to earlier. Below is a summary close example for considering the purchase of several laptop computers from a well-known manufacturer.

### Laptop Computer

| Advantages | Disadvantages |
|---|---|
| large active-matrix LCD screen | relatively heavy |
| professional looking | no carrying case |
| includes three-year warranty | latest software not included |
| large RAM and hard drive | |

## Concession Closes

When salespeople employ a concession close, they give something free to the prospect to entice him or her to make the purchase.

**Special Deal Close.**  When the prospect remains hesitant to make the purchase commitment despite the salesperson's best efforts to close, a special deal may provide the incentive to buy now. The salesperson might declare, "If you'll agree to sign the contract, I'll call my boss to see if she'll approve delaying your first payment until January." Or "If you buy today, I'll include the one-year service contract for free." Avoid using the same concession with the same customer often; otherwise, the customer may only buy the product again if you repeat the concession offer. Also, this close requires caution. For instance, a young computer system salesperson tried to close a particular prospect by stating, "If you purchase the system today, I'll include additional memory with no extra charge." The buying committee shot back, "We don't need more memory. Instead, just reduce the price of your system by the cost of the extra memory!"

**Price Discount** any reduction off the standard list price of a product.

Offering a **price discount** is a common way to close sales. Salespeople often are authorized to offer prospects and customers reductions off the standard list price for various reasons, including paying within a certain time, buying a large quantity, buying out of season, cooperating with promotional campaigns, and serving a designated function or role in the channel of distribution. Reminding prospects and customers of a price discount can often tip the balance toward closing the sale. *Price Discounts* discusses how price discounts work.

**No Risk Close.**  Prospects differ widely in the degree of risk they perceive in various purchase decisions. Some professional buyers are especially fearful about making a mistake that costs their companies a lot of money. One common way to alleviate the fear of making a purchase mistake is to offer prospects a money-back guarantee if they are not fully satisfied with the product. A variation on this close is to let the prospect try the product with a free time-limited trial or small sample. Small trial-sized units and money-back guarantees are all methods to close sales by taking some of the risk out of buying.

### Lost-Sale Closes

When salespeople think they will lose the sale, they can still try a lost-sale-close as a last-ditch effort to win the sale.

**Turnover Close.**  In team selling situations, when the prospect fails to respond to one salesperson's sales closing techniques, the prospect can be turned over to another salesperson with a different style and closing approach. Usually this method employs some plausible—and truthful—excuse, such as a meeting or telephone call, so that the prospect doesn't think that the first salesperson is upset with him or her. This turnover close may position the first salesperson as the all-business, unyielding negotiator, while the second salesperson is friendly and flexible. To make this switch in salespeople, the first salesperson might say

I've sorry but I've got to run to a meeting now, but Neil Stacey—who's as knowledgeable as I am about desktop publishing systems—will give you more information and answer any questions you might have.

## PRICE DISCOUNTS

- **Cash discounts** reward buyers for paying the invoice within a specified time period. A typical offer to most organizational buyers is *2/10, net 30.* If the customer pays within ten days, 2 percent is taken off the total bill. No discount is given if the customer pays after the tenth day, and the entire amount is due within thirty days.

- **Quantity discounts** allow the buyer a lower price for purchasing in multiple units or above a certain dollar amount.

- **Noncumulative discounts** (one-time): "I can let you have one for $530 or two for $950."

- **Cumulative discounts** (summary of annual purchases): "We offer a 4 percent discount on total sales over $5,000; for sales over $10,000, we offer a 5 percent discount."

- **Trade discounts** are given to middlemen (retailers, wholesalers, and distributors) for performing various functions for the manufacturer, such as breaking bulk, storage, financing, or transportation. "Wholesalers receive 40 percent off the list price, and retailers receive 30 percent off."

- **Seasonal discounts** are price reductions given to buyers who buy products out of season. "We're offering a 15 percent discount on all bathing suits ordered before March 15th."

- **Promotional allowances** are concessions in price given to customers who participate in a promotional campaign or sales support program. "We'll give you $2,000 on each order of one hundred to help offset your local newspaper's advertising on behalf of our new line of cameras."

**Pretend-to-Leave Close.** When a prospect fails to respond after several trial closes, the salesperson can excuse himself or herself to do another task. Seeing the salesperson start to walk away, most prospects will let down their guard and may even feel disappointed to see the salesperson leave them. At that moment, the salesperson can suddenly turn around and come back to tell the prospect about one final benefit or incentive to buy that he or she failed to mention. Catching the prospect off guard often leads to a successful close.

**Ask For Help Close.** Even after the salesperson appears to have lost the sale, another chance to close remains. At this point, salespeople can apologize to prospects for being unable to satisfy them, and then ask them what it would have taken to make the sale—the **ask for help close.** Thinking the salesperson has admitted defeat and merely wants to improve his or her selling skills by humbly asking for help, many prospects readily reveal their real objection at this point or what it would *really* have taken for them to buy. With this information, the salesperson can now deal with the real objection and offer whatever the customer says he or she wanted to close the deal.

**Ask For Help Close**
even after the sale seems lost, the salesperson asks the prospect what could have been done to make the sale. Oftentimes, the prospect will give a previously undisclosed reason or objection, which the salesperson can then answer and secure another chance to close the sale.

## LETTING CUSTOMERS CLOSE THE SALE

Professional salespeople who strongly advocate win-win selling sometimes advise turning the tables on tradition by *letting the customer close* the sale. Most sales can't close until the prospect is ready to buy, and by that time, he or she is as anxious to move ahead as the salesperson. It is in customers' best interests to close win-win problem-solving agreements quickly so they can start receiving the desired product benefits as soon as possible. As one salesperson puts it: "My hit ratio, in fact, is a lot better on major sales when I let the customer close than it used to be when I tried to trial-close him every sentence or two." When the proposed sales agreement is obviously a win-win situation, *customers* will often try to trial close the salesperson by asking questions like, "How soon can I get the product?" or "What credit terms do you offer?"

To motivate customers to help close the sale, clearly show the product's added value in solving customer problems and increasing customer success. Successful closes depend on all the phases of the PSP from prospecting through sales presentation and resolving prospect objections. If each stage of the selling process goes well and blends smoothly with the preceding and following stage, the prospect inevitably will help the salesperson close the sale.

## SILENCE CAN BE GOLDEN IN CLOSING

According to some sales trainers, "Whenever you ask a closing question, shut up. The first person to speak loses." Why is it so important not to speak after asking a closing question? Because you have just hit the ball into the prospect's court and the pressure is on the prospect to hit it back by answering your closing question and committing to the purchase. If you speak first after the closing question, the ball automatically bounces back into your court. One study found that more high-performing than low-performing salespeople use silence in closing.[7]

Now, it may sound easy to just remain silent for a few seconds, right? But this seems to be one of the hardest tasks for salespeople or anyone else. Let us say you ask this closing question: "Well, Mr. Thurstone, which model do you like best—the Mohawk or the Eagle?" If you remain silent, Mr. Thurstone is pressured to commit himself to one of the models and probably make the purchase. If you speak first, Mr. Thurstone can avoid answering. If you break the silence by saying, "Oh well, we can return to that decision later," Mr. Thurstone slips off the hook and you must set up another closing opportunity. Of course, professional salespeople avoid antagonizing the prospect by being pigheaded about using this close. If the prospect remains silent for a long time and shows no inclination to answer, then you must move on to another benefit that may lead to a different trial close.

# CLOSING MISTAKES

Many sales are lost because the salesperson makes simple mistakes in the closing stage of the PSP. Every salesperson has made most types of mistakes at least once, but top professionals learn the fundamentals and make fewer mistakes than less successful salespeople. Some of the most common mistakes that hamper sale closings are outlined in Table 7.4. Read these over several times so that when your turn comes to close a sale, you'll avoid them.

**TABLE 7.4**

### CLOSING MISTAKES

- **Talking past closing signals:** Salespeople can become so enamored with their sales presentation and demonstration that they don't stop until they've finished; they talk past several prospect closing signals, despite being aware of them. They then must spend more time reselling prospects.

- **Failing to recognize prospect buying signals:** Salespeople sometimes fail to hear and see closing signals while they are making their sales presentations and demonstrations. If you miss a closing signal, the opportunity to close the sale must wait until another closing signal opportunity.

- **Projecting a lack of confidence:** Salespeople who don't believe in themselves, their products, or their companies will manifest a lack of confidence that prospects will pick up and mirror back with reluctance to buy.

- **Being reluctant to try trial closes on early calls:** Every sales call is an opportunity to close the sale. Salespeople who make no attempt to close until the third or fourth call will often miss closing opportunities and may lose many sales to more assertive salespeople.

- **Inflexibility in using closing techniques:** For every selling situation, the salesperson should plan alternative closing strategies in case the preferred ones don't work. Some salespeople, though, succeed with one closing technique, then fall into the habit of relying on it almost exclusively. No one closing technique is appropriate for all customers or for all times with any one customer. Professional salespeople learn to use an array of closing techniques, as the selling situation requires.

- **Giving up too soon:** Persistence is an essential quality for the successful salesperson. Sales are rarely closed on the first sales call.

- **Lingering too long after the close:** Generally, after a sale has been closed (the order form signed), the salesperson should make a polite but speedy exit. Lingering too long afterward can endanger a sale because the prospect may think of more objections that the salesperson cannot successfully negotiate.

- **Failing to practice closing skills:** As with any professional, whether doctor, lawyer, entertainer, public speaker, or baseball player, sales skills can become rusty or sloppy habits can form unless you devote considerable time to regular practice and improvement. Salespeople who rehearse the likely closing skills needed for each individual sales call develop a significant advantage over salespeople who don't practice.

- **Failing to understand the need to close:** Only the most naïve salesperson fails to understand that the close is an essential stage in the selling process. An outstanding sales presentation will not ensure that the buyer will buy. Unless the salesperson asks for the order through skillful use of trial closes, many sales will never be consummated.

# HOW DO YOU HANDLE SALES REJECTION?

If you simply cannot close the sale, admittedly, you may well experience negative emotions. After all, you have expended effort to attain a highly desired goal but were unable to achieve it.[8] Nonetheless, you should not feel discouraged or personally rejected. Not even the best salesperson makes a sale every time. In fact, some sales success (or "hit") ratios can be markedly low depending on the product, competition, and prospects.

## No One Wins All the Time

Let's use a baseball analogy. In challenging activities like closing sales, you can have a moderate batting average and still achieve great success. Ty Cobb stole 94 bases in 144 attempts during his best year, for a success rate of two out of every three. But it wasn't Cobb's success rate that made him a legendary figure. Another ballplayer, Max Carey, had 94 percent success one year when he stole 51 bases out of 54 tries. If Carey had kept up that ratio, he would have stolen 135 bases and far surpassed Cobb's long-time record. But Carey didn't try often enough. The difference in the level of fame between Cobb and Carey points out that it's not how many times you *fail*, it's how many times you *try* that usually determines outstanding success.[9]

---

**TABLE 7.5**

### CONSTRUCTIVE WAYS TO DEAL WITH REJECTION

- Never equate your worth as a human being with your success or failure as a salesperson. Base your long-run opinion of yourself not on whether you win or lose, but on how honestly and fairly you play the game.

- Separate your ego from the sale. Prospects are not attacking you personally. If a prospect doesn't buy, he or she simply believes that at this time the product fails to fit his or her needs or offer the best value for the money.

- Don't automatically assume that you or your selling skills are the problem. The prospect may be a difficult person or may be having a bad day. These are not your fault.

- Move on to other prospects. When one prospect rejects your product, simply look in your prospect file for other promising prospects on whom you can call. The more prospects you have, the more confident you'll feel.

- Positively anticipate rejection, and it will not overwhelm you. Expect it, but don't create it. Think in advance how you will respond to rejection.

- Remember that nearly all types of selling produce many more rejections than successes. Considering the law of averages, each rejection increases the chances of a success on the next sales call.

- Recognize the possibility that the prospect may at this time have to refuse for various reasons, such as timing, shared decision making, or budget constraints. And realize that many prospects will feel uncomfortable revealing to you reasons that reflect on their power.

*Source:* Adapted from Tom Reilly, "Salespeople: Develop the Means to Handle Rejection," *Personal Selling Power* (July–August 1987),15. Reprinted with permission.

## Learning from Sales Rejection

In his book *How to Master the Art of Selling*, Tom Hopkins argues that salespeople must develop positive attitudes toward sales rejection. Instead of failure, view rejection as

- A learning experience that will enable you to do better next time.
- Negative but helpful feedback that will spur you to more creative approaches.
- An opportunity to develop a sense of humor and begin to lose your fear of future rejection.
- The motivation you need to spend more time practicing selling skills and improving performance.
- Just part of the selling game you must accept in order to continue to play and win.[10]

Depicted in Table 7.5 are some effective means for dealing with sales rejection. Think about how you can use these right now in your everyday life and how you will employ them as a sales rep in the future. Table 7.6 shows ways to interact with a prospect who chooses not to buy from you.

*When you lose a sale, view the situation as a learning experience, not as a personal failure.*
Photo Disc

---

| TABLE 7.6 |
| --- |
| **WHAT TO DO WHEN THE PROSPECT DOESN'T BUY** |

- **Don't burn any bridges.** Never show disappointment, frustration, impatience, anger, or any other sour grapes reaction to the prospect. If you are a good sport, future opportunities to sell the prospect are more likely to come your way.

- **Analyze lost sales.** Review the selling process from start to finish to see what might have gone wrong or been improved upon. Be as objective as you can so that you benefit from this postmortem.

- **Help the prospect shop the competition.** If the prospect wants to continue to look at competitive products before buying, you can help him or her by outlining the specific criteria on which to judge the quality and overall performance of products in the category. You should, of course, have already identified your product's performance on these specific criteria for the prospect.

- **Call back with new information or appeals.** Continue to keep the relationship alive by providing the prospect with relevant information, such as interesting articles on the industry, new product introductions, special deals, or upcoming price changes.

- **Schedule another sales appointment.** Arrange for another sales appointment whenever you have a new sales proposal or product in which you think the prospect might be interested.

- **Never give up.** As long as a prospect needs your product category, don't give up on making the sale. Organizational and operational changes can quickly change buying criteria. Many long-term relationships and profitable sales arrangements have emerged after years of prospect refusals to buy.

# IMMEDIATE POST-SALE ACTIVITIES

As mentioned at the beginning of this chapter, a sale's close is not really an ending but the *continuation* of a buyer-seller relationship. Therefore, sales personnel must engage in special post-sale efforts.

### Serving and Satisfying the Customer

During the immediate post-sale period, the professional salesperson has some critical activities to perform. As noted below, these tasks include providing requisite service to the customer and ensuring that the customer remains satisfied with his or her purchase decision.

- Call or write within a few days to *thank* customers for their orders, reassure them about their purchases to relieve any dissonance or anxiety, and let them know that you are there to help them with any problems. Solving little problems for customers can substantially increase customer satisfaction and help further the long-run buyer-seller relationship. After a sale, some salespeople make it a practice to send customers a little "thank you" gift—including items, such as candy, wine, flowers, fruit baskets, clever toys, and tickets to the theater or a sports event.
- Check on your customers' orders to ensure prompt delivery. If delivery will be delayed, call the customers to warn them. Although such news is rarely welcome, customers will appreciate receiving advance warning that allows them to make appropriate adjustments in their operations.
- Contact the credit and billing department to confirm that they have the correct information on your customers' orders before sending out invoices. Few things irritate customers more than receiving and having to straighten out erroneous bills.
- Try to be present when the product is delivered to the customer. Assisting with installation and start up will do wonders for furthering that long-run relationship. The customer will see that you are committed to providing a high level of service.
- Promptly update your customer sales records. Do so before you forget; then you'll be prepared for the next call. Include the latest sale, personnel or organizational changes, new problems and needs, purchase plans, or any other relevant developments.

### Keeping the Customer Sold

After closing the sale, professional salespeople celebrate their success only a short time because they understand that keeping the customer sold can be as challenging and time consuming as winning the order in the first place. Some salespeople have made the analogy that keeping a customer is like trying to keep a lover who is continually pursued and romanced by others from straying. You can't take either the lover or your customers for granted. You must work at pleasing customers, making sure that they are satisfied with the current relationship, and doing everything you can to improve upon it so that

## KEEPING UP ONLINE: HOTMAIL

**N**early all companies today utilize email. However, not everyone in a firm may have his or her own private email account. How could a salesperson send confidential messages to a person at a company who must share an email account? Although no email guarantees complete confidentiality, you can ensure some degree of privacy with separate email accounts. Check out the following web sites offering email services to see how you might organize your work email to send and receive confidential messages to prospects and customers

http://www.hotmail.com/
http://www.eudora.com/

they are not tempted to leave you for competition. Ignoring your customers only serves to make them susceptible to competitors' efforts.[11] Even when the buyer-seller relationship matures into a partnership or marriage, the professional salesperson keeps up the tender loving care and continues to treat the customer like a new lover instead of an old spouse. Remember: Keeping your old customers is much easier and more profitable than winning new ones.

## SUMMARY

The sales close is an integral part of the ongoing personal selling process. A successful close confirms the sale and furthers the buyer-seller relationship. Salespeople should be prepared to use a trial close at any propitious time during the selling process. Numerous verbal and nonverbal cues can alert salespeople to an opportunity for a trial close. Some salespeople fail to close because of insufficient confidence, feelings of guilt, or fear of failure. Successful closure usually takes several sales calls, so persistence pays off. Several basic principles of persuasion can be effectively applied within the framework of different closing strategies. The five basic categories of closing techniques are clarification, psychologically oriented, straightforward, concession, and lost-sale closes. No one succeeds in closing sales all of the time, so salespeople must learn to deal both with rejection and with the prospect after a sale falls through. Professional salespeople have several immediate post-sale tasks to carry out if they are to satisfy customers and develop a positive long-run buyer-seller relationship.

## KEY TERMS

| | | |
|---|---|---|
| Close | Boomerang close | Price discount |
| Trial close | Puppy dog close | Ask for help close |

## CHAPTER REVIEW QUESTIONS

1. What do we mean by a "trial close"?

2. What verbal and nonverbal cues from the prospect indicate that it's time for a trial close?

3. When should salespeople try to close?

4. What are some reasons that some salespeople don't even attempt to close?

5. What are some principles of persuasion?

6. Describe as many as you can of the closing strategies discussed in the chapter.

7. Outline several closing mistakes.

8. Discuss some ways for a salesperson to deal with rejection.

9. What should a salesperson do when the prospect doesn't buy?

10. List some immediate post-sale activities of a successful salesperson.

## TOPICS FOR THOUGHT AND CLASS DISCUSSION

1. Which do you think is a more appropriate term for stage 6 in the personal selling process: (a) closing the sale or (b) confirming the sale? Why?

2. What would you say to a salesperson friend who must overcome low self-confidence, guilt, and fear-of-failure problems before attempting to close sales?

3. Which of the closing strategies provided in Table 7.3 do you think you would prefer to use in your professional personal selling career? Why?

4. Why can salesperson *silence* oftentimes be effective after attempting a trial close?

5. What would you do if a prospect didn't buy from you following the fifth sales call when you thought for sure you'd achieve a successful close?

6. Assume you have just made a substantial sale. What steps would you take to further the buyer-seller relationship?

7. What do we mean by "rejection"? Why are most of us so afraid of it? How do you personally cope with various types of rejection in your life?

## PROJECTS FOR PERSONAL GROWTH

1. Ask three business-to-business salespeople to explain their favorite closing strategies. Give each strategy a name. How many of them are discussed in this chapter? Do you consider any of the closes used by the three salespeople manipulative or questionable? Why?

2. Share stories with other members of your class about how you have recently used one or more of the seven basic principles of persuasion to negotiate something. Do any of your classmates have a favorite persuasion technique that they rely on most often?

3. Survey five people in different occupations about how they deal with rejection. Would these methods also apply to personal selling? Explain how.

## TALK, TALK, TALK!

After working at Choi Company for four years as a supervisor in the shipping department, Fred Liska was recently asked if he would like to be considered for a position on the sales force. Although he's been taking college courses at night for two years, Fred won't earn his degree for several years, so he jumped at the chance to become a sales representative for the company.

Mr. Choi, who started the company after emigrating from South Korea fifteen years ago, has always taken a special interest in Fred. He personally recommended him for sales because he thinks his personality and conscientiousness make him an ideal salesman. Although Choi Company has no formal training program for new salespeople, Fred had the opportunity to learn how to sell firsthand by spending three weeks traveling on sales calls with Pete Hayes, one of Choi Company's senior sales reps. Pete told Fred, "Just follow me around, and watch and listen. If you have any questions, save them until after each sales call."

Pete seemed to know all the people on his sales calls by their first names, and he spent as much time socializing as selling. Not once during the three weeks did he complete a full sales presentation, and he often failed to discuss some product features and benefits. Although it looked as if Pete mainly took orders instead of doing creative selling, Fred had to admit that Pete secured quite a few orders. In fact, during the three weeks, Pete received nearly every order he asked for—oftentimes even before he was halfway through a sales presentation. "Well," Fred thought to himself, "Choi does make the best instrument carts in the industry, so maybe they sell themselves."

Fred mentally rehearsed what he knew about Choi carts. They are made of sturdy welded steel with rubber-padded, nonconductive, nonslip surfaces and a heavy bottom shelf that helps protect against tipping or failing. Each cart has two swivel and two rigid rubber wheels for easy mobility while carrying up to thirteen hundred pounds of equipment or instruments. Attractively finished in gray enamel, the carts contain a utility drawer that can hold tools, supplies, and other small items. The price is $395.90 per cart, or $3,459 for ten.

On the first Monday after completing his three weeks of field training, Fred nervously approaches his first sales call. The prospect is Deborah Connors, purchasing agent for Scientific Laboratories, a Chicago-based firm specializing in conducting laboratory analyses for medical doctors. After introducing himself and handing Ms. Connors his business card, Fred begins his sales presentation. Because nothing is more impressive than seeing the instrument cart as it is being described, Fred has wheeled one right into Ms. Connor's office. As he is explaining some of the features, advantages, and benefits of the Choi instrument cart, Fred notices Ms. Connors moving the cart back and forth and feeling its surface. She pulls out the cart's drawer and smiles when she sees the neat little compartment trays inside. At this point, she interrupts Fred's presentation to say, "If we do decide to buy, how long will it take for delivery?"

Fred answers, "Two weeks," and continues with his sales presentation, showing several pictures of the cart being used at various types of companies.

Studying the pictures, Ms. Connors asks, "Will the Choi cart really carry thirteen hundred pounds? It doesn't look that strong."

Fred replies, "One of our largest customers, Metropolitan Hospital, regularly carries equipment weighing over fifteen hundred pounds on the carts without any problems." Fred thinks to himself, "If she doesn't quit interrupting, I'll never get through my sales presentation," but he doesn't let any irritation show and smoothly continues with the presentation and demonstration. At this point, Fred pulls out the special drawer with compartment trays and mentions that Choi is the only cart available with this feature.

(continued)

## CASE 7.1

# TALK, TALK, TALK! (CONTINUED)

Ms. Connors smiles and remarks, "Yes, I think putting those compartment trays inside the drawer is a really clever idea. I don't know how many times I've needed a test tube, some tape, or a pair of scissors when I'm carting laboratory samples and instruments from one room to another. We could keep basic supplies in those little drawers and save a lot of time and extra steps." Fred nods his head and continues to point out other features of the cart. He smiles to himself, thinking, "I'm almost done with my sales presentation. Nothing much left to talk about except the price."

Just then, Ms. Connors's secretary interrupts to say that Henry Bauman, the vice president of operations, needs to see her right away in his office. Ms. Connors excuses herself and says, "Ask my secretary to schedule another appointment with me, Fred. I know what this meeting with Mr. Bauman is about, and it's going to take the rest of my time today. Thanks for coming in."

Fred feels deflated. "Boy," he thinks, "what lousy timing. In two more minutes, I would have finished my sales presentation and started my close. I'm sure she would have placed an order when I asked for it." Dejectedly, he picks up his sales presentation materials, places them on the cart, and pushes it out to Ms. Connors's secretary's desk to schedule another appointment.

## Questions

1. Do you believe Ms. Connors would have placed an order when Fred completed his sales close? Why?
2. What do you think of Fred's sales presentation? What improvements would you suggest?
3. Could Fred have tried a trial close before Ms. Connors left for the other meeting? If so, what should he have said?
4. What advice would you give Fred for future sales calls?

## SHE'S GOT PERSONALITY . . . AND A LOT MORE!

Peggy Markley is a sales rep for Versatile Office Equipment (VOE), selling the Assurance brand of portable photocopiers, facsimiles, word processors, and dictation machines. Peggy is a genuinely friendly person whom everybody seems to like because she makes it so obvious that she likes people. She has a smile and a friendly word for nearly everybody she encounters on a sales call. Her beautiful personality makes people take special notice of her. Once she has made a sales call, she seldom has to reintroduce herself to anyone. In each of her five years as a sales rep for VOE, Peggy has surpassed her annual quota, earning her membership in the company's High Flyers Club. Her record for keeping customers is unmatched by any other VOE sales rep.

Training seminars for new salespeople often feature stories about her attention to customers. One of the favorites is about the time she was making a sales presentation in a prospect's office when they were interrupted by a phone call from the hospital saying that the man's pregnant wife had just gone into labor and would soon be delivering a baby. Because the prospect had taken public transportation to work, Peggy insisted on driving him to the hospital so he didn't lose any time. They arrived just in time for the man to see his first baby being born. Well, his wife was so grateful that Peggy became a family friend who was frequently invited to dinner. Peggy also won a profitable account. Surprisingly, none of the other customers whose appointments she had to cancel that day were upset with her when they heard the story. In fact, all of them readily rescheduled their appointments.

Peggy seems to routinely do thoughtful things for her prospects and customers—whether it's bringing in hot cider and doughnuts on a wintry day in January, dropping off mail for them at the post office on her way to another appointment, or lending them her copy of a great book that she has just finished reading. Many of her customers say,

"Peggy's more like a friend than just a salesperson." But Peggy Markley is not just a nice person. She's a top-notch sales professional, and her sales presentations and demonstrations are considered as good as anybody's. She stresses product quality, delivery, and customer service instead of price, pointing out that paying a little higher price for the best gives the greatest value in the long run. One of her typical strategies in dealing with price objections is to compliment a customer on her or his clothes or accessories. For example, she might say, "Your briefcase is so handsome and professional looking; I'm sure you didn't buy it because it was the lowest-priced one. You bought it because it was the best value for your money, right? Well, the same principle applies here—you'll get more value for your dollars by buying Assurance products. No other company comes close to matching our product quality, prompt delivery, return privileges, money-back guarantees, or customer service at this competitive price." To reinforce her statements, Peggy always carries around a notebook of testimonial letters from satisfied customers and a list of prominent companies currently using Assurance products. Frequently, she brings a technical expert from Versatile's engineering, operations, or design departments along with her on a sales call to help analyze a customer's unique problems and suggest a solution. Extremely conscientious about warning her customers about upcoming price changes or product shortages, she frequently offers to set aside inventory for them at the current price for delivery later.

Recently, Peggy has been asked to spend two weeks in Versatile's Training and Development (T&D) department to help prepare a comprehensive sales training program for newly hired salespeople. The new director of T&D, Frank Sherry, hired from the local university, quickly heard about Peggy's unique sales abilities and decided to ask her to help develop the new sales training pro-

(continued)

### CASE 7.2

# SHE'S GOT PERSONALITY . . . AND A LOT MORE! (CONTINUED)

gram. After talking to Peggy, he was surprised to learn that she had never gone through any formal sales training herself. She had shifted into sales from the customer relations department when the company issued a general call for new salespeople from in-house staff. About five years ago, after spending two weeks learning about the company's products and a week traveling with a senior sales rep, her sales manager gave her her own territory and told her to just "go sell 'em." As Peggy told Mr. Sherry, "I don't think I could teach anybody to sell the way I do. The things I do are just natural extensions of my personality. I care about people, and I try to make them feel important. I've never tried to analyze what I do."

Frank Sherry knows that Peggy is well liked and respected in the company and that her association with his new training program will give it credibility. He also believes that she has some unique selling concepts and approaches that he and his staff can draw on and convert into meaningful formats to teach others. He tells Peggy he doesn't expect her to try to design a training program herself. He wants her to just sit down with him and other members of the T&D staff and describe what she does during a typical working day, concentrating especially on her interactions with prospects and customers. Peggy agrees to do this.

### Questions

1. Do you think Peggy uses any particular persuasion principles or selling strategies that others might learn, or is her success largely attributable to her unique personality?

2. Assume that you are Frank Sherry and you must develop a teachable model or system to train others how to do what Peggy seems to do almost instinctively. Based on the limited information provided, identify and give examples of the specific principles of persuasion and closing strategies that Peggy applies in her personal selling activities.

3. Should new salespeople be taught to sell like Peggy Markley, or should each sales trainee be allowed to develop his or her own personal style, closing strategies, and persuasive techniques? Why?

4. Outline a sales training module for new sales trainees that integrates the basic persuasion principles with different closing strategies.

## CHAPTER 8

# Following Up: Keeping Customers Satisfied and Loyal

*"Providing quality service to customers is an investment in future sales."*

*Anonymous*

## After Reading This Chapter, You Should Understand:

- Why it's so important to keep customers.
- The concept of customer service.
- Customer service expectations, perceptions, and satisfaction.
- Several important post-sale follow-up activities.
- How to assess satisfaction with customer service.
- Why customer loyalty is critical for long-run profitability.
- The 8Cs of customer loyalty.

## Meet Barbara Bleiweis of Oracle Corporation

**B**arbara Bleiweis knows that an attentive, responsive salesperson can make a real difference for customers. As Business Development Manager at Oracle Corporation, she is part of a sales team that sells sophisticated software for database management, online services, and other applications to government agencies and businesses. From first contact to final contract, an Oracle sale may take as long as 18 months. Throughout this period—and beyond—Bleiweis looks for every opportunity to personalize her service and add value "so customers and prospects know that I am committed to their success."

One way she builds strong relationships is by ensuring that all of the appropriate Oracle resources are available to answer questions and support the customer's needs,

from the contract stage through project planning, implementation, and completion. Another way is by managing the tiniest details to smooth the way for each project's success. "Customers and prospects get my full attention," Bleiweis explains. "They appreciate that I handle even simple services such as finding a large conference room for a meeting on short notice and confirming the schedule with attendees." Her constant attentiveness reinforces the message that "I want to make sure you are satisfied with how things are going."

Because Oracle wants to create a long-term bond with its customers, the company not only trains its salespeople in customer satisfaction, it regularly conducts satisfaction surveys to obtain customer feedback and identify possible areas for improvement. Bleiweis welcomes this feedback, seeing any customer comments as opportunities to provide more service. "When customers have nothing to say, it means they believe you can't do anything more for them," she explains. When customers do have concerns, however, she tells them, "'This is what I am definitely going to do, this is what I think I can do, and this is what I definitely can't do.' I encourage customers to focus on me as someone who can help address their concerns and make a difference."

Recently, Bleiweis was part of an Oracle sales team competing for a contract to handle part of a U.S. government agency's $2 billion technology modernization program. Instead of making a highly structured, formal sales presentation, she initially focused on establishing a good rapport with agency management. "We wanted to make it a comfortable and collegial atmosphere," she remembers. Bleiweis arranged for Oracle consultants with special expertise to attend the meetings along with the Oracle sales team. As the discussions progressed from the agency's general needs to specific technical challenges that had to be overcome, the Oracle experts were able to suggest practical solutions. "Our involvement came across as constructive," she says, an involvement that solidified the relationship with Oracle.

**Y**ou've closed the sale! Way to go . . . Congratulations . . . Great job! But your selling job is NOT over. Admittedly, some salespeople believe that once they've closed the sale, their work is essentially done. Why? Because they love the challenge—making the sale—but they place little importance on post-sale follow-up efforts. Today's professional salespeople, however, know that after consummating a sale, their work is far from over. In fact, some salespeople believe that the *real* selling job begins only after the sale is closed. Now the sales professional shifts focus onto retaining the current sale, generating customer satisfaction, and keeping the customer's business. The post-sale follow-up activities are designed to ensure customer satisfaction, build customer loyalty, and maximize long-run sales volume and profit.

Many textbooks on personal selling devote their final chapter on the PSP to "follow-up" or "service after the sale." This is potentially misleading for those trying to learn about how sales are made today. The fact is that customer service must be provided not just in the **follow-up** after the sale is closed, but *throughout* the PSP. Numerous customer complaints are about service. Excellent customer (or prospect) service should be a significant part of your mission for success in selling. The most successful salespeople know that if they serve a valuable prospect (for example, provide the needed information), the prospect will appreciate the special attention and may sooner or later become a valuable customer. Let's discuss follow-up and customer service as you should practice them during the selling process as a whole, and then turn our attention to specific post-sale activities.

**Follow-up** Customer service provided, not only after the sale is closed, but throughout the selling process.

## WHAT IS CUSTOMER SERVICE?

**Customer Service** A concept that has five basic dimensions: reliability, tangibility, responsiveness, assurance, and empathy.

**Customer service** is a somewhat elusive concept; different customer groups have their unique definitions. However, based on studies on service quality, five basic dimensions of service have been identified:[1]

- *Reliability*—the ability to perform the desired service dependably, accurately, and consistently.
- *Tangibility*—the physical facilities, equipment, and appearance of sales and service people.
- *Responsiveness*—the willingness to provide prompt service and help customers.
- *Assurance*—employees' knowledge, courtesy, and ability to convey trust and confidence.
- *Empathy*—the provision of caring, individualized attention to customers.

**Reliability** Ability to perform the desired service dependably, accurately, and consistently; the single most important component of customer service.

Salesperson **reliability** is the single most important factor for about half of all customers surveyed.[2] Customers must have confidence that the expected service will be delivered accurately, consistently, and dependably.

### Service Creates Sales

Professional salespeople realize that many customers buy on the *promise* of a great product and service, but it's the actual *performance* of great service that

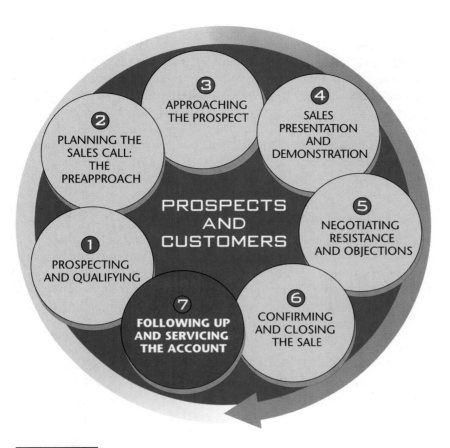

**FIGURE 8.1**

THE PERSONAL SELLING PROCESS

persuades them to become repeat customers. Therefore, you shouldn't promise more than you can actually deliver, as customers have long memories—especially when promises aren't kept. The Strategic Planning Institute in Cambridge, Massachusetts, through its *PIMS (Profit Impact of Market Strategy)* program, analyzed the performance of twenty-six hundred companies over fifteen years. Its studies show that the companies that customers perceive as having the highest quality also tend to garner the highest results by almost any financial measure—sales, market share, asset turnover, or return on investment.[3]

Satisfied customers tend to be loyal and provide the stable sales base that is essential to long-term profitability. The *PIMS* database reveals that those companies rated high on customer service charge 9 percent more on average for their products and grow twice as fast as companies rated poorly.[4] A pattern of one-time buyers is a warning signal that customer expectations are going unmet.

Many industrial firms specialize in providing superb customer service. For example, superior service enables Weyerhaeuser Company's wood products division to charge a healthy premium for its commodity two-by-four lumber. Weyerhaeuser developed a computer system for retail home centers and lumberyards that allows homeowners to custom design their own decks and other home building projects. Premier Industrial Corporation, a distributor of industrial parts in Los Angeles, charges up to 50 percent more than competitors for every one of the 250,000 items it sells. Premier commands such premium prices through superb customer service. When a Caterpillar tractor plant in Decatur, Illinois, called Premier to replace a ten-dollar electrical relay that had stopped an entire production line, a Premier sales representative found the part and rushed it to the airport for a flight to St. Louis where another Premier sales rep took it to Decatur. By 10:30 P.M. that night, the Caterpillar production was running again. The message is clear: *Customers are willing to pay for superior service.*

### Training Salespeople in Customer Service

The best companies train, retrain, and motivate their salespeople to provide superior customer service. For instance, a large seller of computerized services to health-care organizations requires that all of its salespeople take three weeks of sales and customer service training each year. And service quality is often an integral part of the reward system for sales and service people, as illustrated in *From the Command Post.*

### Building Customer Relationships Through Service

Providing a high level of service to customers increases the value products provide and can strengthen the buyer-seller relationship. After all, adept customer service sends a strong signal to customers that they committed precious company resources to the right purchase decision. Sales personnel increase the value their products provide through a variety of activities.

**Value-Added Activities.**  First, service-oriented salespeople can urge their companies to simplify ordering procedures for customers by online computer entry or fax-order entry, or by personally taking orders from customers.

## FROM THE COMMAND POST: CUSTOMER SERVICE PAYS

Many of seven thousand U.S. hospitals are adding guest relations programs to train and motivate physicians, nurses, and other employees in patient hospitality. One community hospital, for example, provides special incentives for quality service performance. The organization sets up a fund of ten thousand dollars for its Guaranteed Services Program, from which it pays patients who have a justified complaint, ranging from cold food to long waits in the emergency room. Any money not spent out of the fund at the end of the year is divided among the hospital's employees. If, for example, no patients have collected for a complaint by the end of the year, each of the hundred employees receives a hundred-dollar bonus. In the first six months after implementing the Guaranteed Services program, the hospital had to pay out only three hundred dollars to patients.

Second, a salesperson can find ways to help the customer become operational quickly and efficiently. This includes arranging for special packaging or coding on boxes; just-in-time (JIT) delivery; helping the customer receive, handle, store, or transfer products; and training the customer's staff to use the new products. For instance, Fastenal Company, the nation's largest distributor of nuts, bolts, and other similar kinds of products, operates 980 stores for factories and commercial builders. As part of its customer service, it will manage the hardware-parts inventory for its customers.[5]

Salespeople can also assist customers in producing, marketing, and distributing products to their own customers. Other services include minimizing downtime by securing replacement parts quickly and obtaining swift resolution of customer complaints. Even periodically sending customers thoughtful little reminder gifts, such as pens, calendars, notepads, and other advertising specialties with the company logo on them, or cards for special occasions, such as birthdays, wedding anniversaries, and holiday greetings, can give the salesperson a perceived service edge on competitors. Customers like to think they're appreciated, and thoughtful little efforts can make a tremendous difference in their perceptions of service.

**Service Differentiation.** *Customer service strategy* calls for segmenting customers based on their desired level of service, then identifying those service segments that can be served at a profit. While market segmentation focuses on what people and organizations *need*, **customer service segmentation** focuses on what they *expect*. To effectively segment customers, it is necessary to find out how much they value different levels of service, and then estimate the costs and benefits of providing the desired service. Service level expectations normally correlate closely with the dollar amount of the sale. Rolls Royce and Mercedes automobile manufacturers provide whatever service their customers want, including twenty-four-hour roadside assistance. Premium-priced shipping firms such as United Parcel Service and Federal Express provide similar kinds of high-level service.

Customer service expectations can be greatly influenced by seemingly minor visible cues such as the personal grooming of the service providers and the quality of their uniforms; the appearance of brochures describing the service; age and condition of service trucks and equipment; the friendliness, professionalism, and courtesy of service personnel; and the product's temporary packaging or wrapping after it has been purchased or serviced. Customers tend to have a higher opinion of a product's quality and its supporting service when special attention is paid to the service *presentation*, such as the well-groomed IBM repair people dressed in business suits or the expensively decorated office of a law firm. For example, after promoting a guaranteed private room and home-like environment for giving birth, obstetrics admissions at St. Joseph's Hospital in St. Paul, Minnesota, jumped 10 percent.

Extra service cannot be stored in inventory, so some idle capacity is always required to accommodate sudden increases in demand. But service quality drops off sharply when demand considerably exceeds the theoretical capacity. Whenever customer service demands exceed capacity, salespeople should give their best customers first priority and cut back on service to less

**Customer Service Segmentation** A strategy for grouping customers with similar service expectations into service segments and then developing a service plan for each segment.

valued customers. Service organizations ranging from popular restaurants to fuel oil companies often do this by seating preferred customers first during prime dining hours or supplying loyal customers first when unexpectedly cold weather increases demand for fuel oil.

## Product and Service Quality

**Product Quality** Perceived performance of the tangible product in satisfying customer expectations.

Quality consists of two components: product and service. **Product quality** is the *degree* to which the product or service offered performs as promised. It is concerned with the perceived performance of the tangible product or service in satisfying customer expectations. **Service quality** includes all the activities that *support* the sale, from the initial contact through the post-sale servicing, and denotes the *degree* to which these activities meet or exceed customer expectations and enhance a product or service's value. It can include product information, technical assistance, financing, order processing, delivery, installation, maintenance and repair, parts availability, and attitudes of service personnel as perceived by prospects and customers.

**Service Quality** All activities supporting the sale, from the initial contact through the post-sale servicing, that meet or exceed customer expectations and enhance the value of a product.

## Perceived Service Quality and Customer Satisfaction

**Perceived Service Quality** The quality of service individual customers believe they deserve and expect to receive.

In most competitive industries, producers eventually match product quality, so the *real* competition boils down to service quality and, beyond this, to **perceived service quality.** FedEx defines service as "all actions and reactions that customers perceive they have purchased."[6] Most companies have general customer service policies, but *perceived* service quality refers to the quality of service that individual customers *believe* they deserve and expect to receive relative to what they actually receive. Salespeople, as the single most important part of the company's prospect and customer service program, must be sensitive to each individual prospect's and customer's service demands and expectations.

When it comes to perceived service quality, salespeople essentially must deal with four basic kinds of prospects and customers, each pulling them in a different direction. For simplicity, we can categorize customers as either good (profitable, cooperative), or bad (neither very profitable nor cooperative) and demanding either lots of service or little service. How do you serve these four different types of customers? Here is some advice:

- *Good customer/Lots of service:* Working extra hard to please this customer should be a joy for you. If not, start to change your attitude immediately.
- *Bad customer/Lots of service:* You may eventually have to speak with your sales manager about this customer, but look to yourself first. Are you providing the wrong kinds of service to the wrong people in the organization? If the customer was once "good" and then turned "bad," (stopped buying or paying bills), find out why. You may be able to save the situation.
- *Good customer/Little service:* Nothing wrong with this situation, right? Wrong! Are you constantly monitoring the service situation with this

customer, making sure that the appropriate people in the organization receive the products and services they need? Beware of your complacency; after all, competition is waiting in the wings.

• *Bad customer/Little service:* Once again, you should look to yourself first. Is the customer "bad" because you have not been providing appropriate services to the appropriate people? Speak with your sales manager about the potentially salvageable situation, too.

Rising customer service expectations and a decreasing tolerance for poor service are expected to have the greatest impact on salespeople's effectiveness in the years ahead. Service quality depends on *customer perceptions*, not on what the seller thinks. Technical Assistance Research Programs Institute (TARP) found that, on average, one out of every four customers is dissatisfied enough with customer service to switch suppliers. More than 90 percent of these unhappy customers will never again buy from that company and will tell at least nine other people about their negative experience.[7] These results suggest why many executives consider "service quality" to be one of their chief business concerns.

Customers have certain overall expectations for service quality, influenced by their past experience, personal needs, advertising, and word-of-mouth information. *Customer satisfaction is generally assured when the seller meets or exceeds the customer's expectations for perceived service quality.* If a gap exists between what they expect and what they perceive they receive, (i.e., getting less than what is expected), customers are usually disappointed in the quality of the service.[8]

Perceived service quality, rather than price or product quality, is the *deciding factor* in customer satisfaction. Poor service is typically the number one reason for switching to competitors. Salespeople can never afford to be complacent about customer service because any service quality standard less than 100 percent may not be good enough. To appreciate quality from the dissatisfied customer's perspective, read the words of an IBM executive: "We make 300,000 components. Don't say to me, '97 percent are okay.' Say instead, '9,000 were defective.' You don't really want 9,000 angry customers, do you?"[9] Read *From the Command Post* on p. 244 to see how to use the Internet to enhance customer service.

## IMPORTANCE OF CUSTOMER SATISFACTION

Many organizations proclaim the importance of customer satisfaction to their employees. Whether espoused in speeches by top-level executives, in organizational policy manuals or credos, on office or store signage, or in company newsletters, such efforts are designed to instill in employees the belief that customers are the driving force behind their success. That is, satisfied customers lead to favorable firm and employee results. Let's take a look at how satisfied customers can affect an organization.

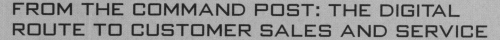

# FROM THE COMMAND POST: THE DIGITAL ROUTE TO CUSTOMER SALES AND SERVICE

Despite the financial malaise that enveloped many organizations at the start of the 21st century, several companies are still successfully marketing their wares. Maybe it's not "like the good old days," but these companies have not succumbed to an economic and business malaise. Instead, these companies are obtaining digital help to continue an unremitting commitment to building customer relationships and providing a high level of customer service to maintain those relationships.

Beyond serving as an additional selling tool, web sites are a convenient and easy-to-use means of servicing customers. For example, web sites enable customers to track the status of their orders, retrieve billing information, and obtain answers to their questions about technical problems. By giving customers direct access to such information, these web sites free up salespeople to spend more time in face-to-face selling and developing closer relationships with prospects and customers.

Web sites offer substantial benefits for sellers. Receiving web site hits and inquiries can enhance prospecting efforts, reduce selling costs, and translate into substantial sales revenue. And, not least, employing a web site as a supplemental service provider can reduce a firm's need for service personnel and technical support engineers. Digital sales and service are a "win-win" for both buyers and sellers.

## The Economics of Customer Satisfaction

Keeping satisfied customers is a lot cheaper than finding new ones. Studies have shown that it is five to six times more costly to attract new customers than to keep current ones. This ratio has been found to be virtually the same for online or offline businesses. According to research conducted by the Boston Consulting Group, selling to a current customer via the web costs about seven dollars versus thirty-four dollars to win a new customer.[10] Many experts contend that the major reason for a company's existence is to satisfy customers. Without such satisfaction, the rest of a company's goals and efforts will be compromised, at least in the long run. Therefore, professional salespeople are constantly vigilant about keeping their customers satisfied, and they seek to satisfy their prospects as well by providing them pre-sale service to induce them to buy later on. Several compelling reasons exist for keeping profitable customers satisfied. These explanations revolve around (a) company profits, (b) impact on the selling organization, and (c) the morale of sales and other company employees, as noted below.

Company profits will increase through retention of profitable customers. This desired situation develops because

- Reducing customer defections by 5 percent can increase profitability anywhere from 25 percent to 95 percent.[11] Obtaining a new account after losing a customer is costly (remember, the cost of retaining an existing customer is about one-fifth or less that of obtaining a new customer).

- The longer a customer stays with the seller, the further costs to service that customer tend to decrease (the learning curve of dealing with the customer becomes less steep over time).
- The seller can charge higher prices (even premium prices) for its products if the customer has confidence in and loyalty to the company.
- The customer provides free word-of-mouth advertising for the company (thus providing the salesperson with referrals).
- The customer will increase his or her purchases over time.
- The customer will pay less attention to competing brands and be less persuaded by competing offerings.
- The customer purchases other products as the seller adds them to its product mix.

Conversely, dissatisfied customers can have an extremely negative impact on companies and their salespeople because

- Dissatisfied customers are likely to switch suppliers and stop buying from the salesperson's company.
- Dissatisfied customers are likely to tell other people about their bad experience. This decreases prospective customers' interest in purchasing from the salesperson's firm.
- Research shows that dissatisfied customers tell eleven other people about their negative experience.[12]
- Customers are less likely to buy again if a problem is not resolved satisfactorily.
- Customer dissatisfaction can lead to low employee morale.

Research indicates that customer dissatisfaction directly affects employee turnover. That is, the more dissatisfied customers a firm has, the less likely employees are to stay. Companies with many dissatisfied customers usually see sales force turnover higher than the typical industry annual average of about 20 percent. Replacing salespeople who leave increases recruitment, selection, and training costs. In addition, opportunity costs arise from lost sales during the departing salesperson's absence from his or her territory.

## Types of Customers vis-à-vis Satisfaction Levels

As is now obvious, how salespeople attend to their customers strongly affects customer satisfaction and customer responses toward the salespeople and their selling organization. Six different kinds of customers have been identified based on their level of satisfaction.[13]

Customers who are completely satisfied and keep returning to the company are referred to as *loyalists*. These customers' needs and the performance of salespeople match up well. Thus, such customers are often the easiest to serve. In this loyalist camp are individuals who are extremely satisfied, whose experiences with your company far exceed their expectations; therefore, they share their strong feelings with others—and become *apostles*.

On the downside, *defectors* are those who are neutral, quite dissatisfied, or more than dissatisfied. These individuals may have been satisfied previously but have encountered failures left uncorrected by the firm. *Vigilantes* are those defectors who have had a bad experience and are eager to tell others about their anger and frustration.

Another customer who can make life miserable for salespeople and their companies is the *mercenary*. These customers seem to defy the satisfaction/loyalty rule. They appear to be and often say that they are totally satisfied but still have almost no loyalty. This type of customer seeks low prices, buys on impulse, looks for fashion trends, or chases something new for the sake of change. Such customers do not stay long enough in the relationship to return a profit, so they are sometimes called "butterflies" because of their tendency to flit and flutter from one supplier to another.

*Hostages* are trapped. These buyers experience the worst the seller has to offer but must just grin and bear it. Companies with a monopolistic advantage see little reason to respond to hostages. If these customers can go nowhere else, why bother to correct their problems? For at least two reasons: First, if the competitive environment suddenly shifts, nonresponsive companies will pay the price as their hostage customers quickly defect. Second, hostages are difficult and expensive to serve. They may be trapped, but they still take the opportunity to complain and ask for special service. Hostages can destroy company morale, and their negative impact on per unit costs can be dramatic.

Overall, the sales rep's goal is to develop and maintain loyalists and apostles and prevent the other four kinds of customers from emerging. After all, a satisfied customer represents a bright future for the salesperson; a rankled customer represents a nightmare.

## CUSTOMER FOLLOW-UP STRATEGIES

In order to maximize customer satisfaction following a sale, salespeople should consider several basic service strategies. Essentially, such activities focus on (a) performing customer service, (b) enhancing customer satisfaction, and (c) obtaining customer referrals,[14] as enumerated below:

- *Express appreciation for the customer's business.* Salespeople should be conscientious about showing genuine appreciation for their customer's business. Appreciation can be shown in many ways, from merely saying "thank you" in a sincere, enthusiastic way (in person, telephone call, email, or handwritten note) to sending the customer a useful gift, such as an address book or small calculator with the seller's logo.
- *Make sure products are delivered and installed on time.* Whenever possible, the salesperson ought to be on hand when the customer's order is delivered. By being there, the salesperson reassures the customer that he or she cares about pleasing the customer and that any potential problems will be promptly resolved. In addition, the salesperson learns to see this important aspect of service from the customer's viewpoint.

• *Assist customers with credit arrangements.* Dealing with company credit personnel can often be frustrating for customers. A salesperson who has already made it a point to establish and maintain good relationships with the credit department can serve as an effective go-between during the credit-granting process and insulate the customer from potential problems.

• *Help customers with warranty or service contracts.* When customers need repair service or need to return a defective product, it's best for the salesperson to serve as the liaison person with company service people. Not only will customers appreciate your saving them time and effort, but you can become acquainted with the company's customer service people.

• *Represent customers in solving their problems with your company.* Customers don't know your company's organization, policies, procedures, or personnel, so the best salespeople serve as their customers' advocates within the company, whether handling product repairs, exchanges, returns, or complaints. Having one contact person on whom they can count to take care of problems can be a tremendous relief to customers. Let your customers know that you *want* them to call you whenever they have a problem, and that you will strongly represent their interests in any dispute with your company. Learning who's who in providing customer service within your company and developing a positive personal relationship with them ahead of time should help you avoid many bureaucratic problems in promptly obtaining service for you customers

*Whenever possible, the salesperson should be on hand when the customer's order is delivered.*
Mug Shots/Corbis

• *Keep customers informed.* Customers want to know about possible product shortages, price changes, upcoming sales, introduction of new products, and any other information that may affect them or their business operations. Customers will quickly lose trust in salespeople who allow surprises that adversely affect them or their businesses.

• *Ask customers about their level of satisfaction.* As we have learned, an absence of customer complaints does not indicate that they are satisfied. It is part of the professional salesperson's job to solicit customers' opinions regarding their level of satisfaction and what services they believe should improve. Even if their company also surveys overall customer satisfaction periodically, salespeople can obtain product-specific and detailed feedback information while showing genuine concern for customers by asking about their level of satisfaction with their products and supporting services. Sometimes the salesperson will discover that a competitor's product and service are unsatisfactory—and that creates an opportunity to replace that competitor's product.

• *Think of prospects and customers as individuals.* The best salespeople meet as many employees as possible in their customer's organizations, not just the purchasing agents and managers. Whenever possible, see how and by whom your products and services are used. *Selling by walking around the customer's site* is a service-oriented strategy many top salespeople use. It allows them to meet the buying organization's employees, understand their jobs, and develop personal relationships at all working levels. Dean Witter, the brokerage firm, probably expresses the customer service concept best: *"We measure success one investor [customer] at a time."*

- *Ask customers how else you might help them.* Salespeople should regularly ask customers what other services they would like or what problems they'd like solved. For many years, DuPont Company sold only adhesives to the shoe industry. Only after a DuPont salesperson asked Reebok International how DuPont could assist it further did DuPont come up with the idea of inserting flexible plastic tubes into the soles of Reebok's new ERS lines. The tubes gave the sneakers a more lively, bouncy feel, and the success of the ERS lines jumped Reebok's net earnings sharply—making Reebok an even more loyal customer of DuPont.

- *Empathize with and be sensitive toward the customer.* Promptly return customer phone calls, letters, emails, or faxes. Also, proactively seek ways to provide extra services to the customer. Treating customers fairly, honestly, and with respect at all times will demonstrate that the customer is truly important to you. Making product and service recommendations when appropriate shows the customer that you are serving him or her like a consultant. Also, use precise language that is most meaningful to customers to enhance communication and understanding between you. Working with customers to plan a mutually profitable future together shows customers that you focus on win-win solutions.

As you can see, today's professional salespeople have much to do after closing a sale if they hope to keep their customers satisfied and loyal. With this in mind, read *It's Up to You* and determine what needs to be done to rectify the situation.

## IT'S UP TO YOU

In reviewing your territory's annual sales report provided by your sales manager, you notice that one of your steady customers, a large paint and wallpaper wholesaler, bought no painting or wallpaper supplies from your company during the past six months. Normally, this wholesaler makes two big orders a year, one in each half of the year. You called on this customer twice during the past six months to check in and to leave some new product information brochures. Each time, your meeting was cordial, and the buyer didn't mention any problems. You made no sales presentation either time because this customer has a direct computer hookup with your company's order-processing department, and the usual practice has been to merely replenish basic stock. The only change in the customer's organization has been the promotion of one of the senior buyers, whom you know casually, to director of purchasing.

What has probably led to the current situation with this customer? What steps should you take to rectify it?

## *Salesperson . . . and Serviceperson*

Richard Angarita, a sales rep for Rainin Instrument Company, a supplier of laboratory instruments in Woburn, Massachusetts, sold more than one hundred systems in eighteen months, at prices up to thirty thousand dollars, in a territory where the previous sales rep sold only two instruments in two years. Considered a sales consultant by customers, Mr. Angarita is thoroughly familiar with the products he sells because he is both the territory's salesperson and a highly trained service technician. He sells, installs, repairs, and trains customers how to use his company's products. An expert at explaining product features and benefits, he quickly gains the trust of his customers by providing quality service promptly. He makes sure that the equipment will meet the customer's expectations or he won't sell it to them. After all, he's the service technician who must resolve any later problems or complaints.

## Handling Customer Complaints

Successfully handling complaints is a critical activity, and doing so can be even more important online than offline. As Jeff Bezos, CEO of Amazon.com, puts it, "In the physical world, if I make a customer unhappy, they'll tell five friends . . . on the Internet, they'll tell 5,000."[15] Professional salespeople recognize complaints as opportunities to improve relationships with customers. Customers who complain are likely to be more satisfied in the long run than those who do not complain.[16] A TARP study showed that up to 70 percent of customers who complain will buy from the seller again if their complaint is resolved satisfactorily. More than 95 percent will buy again if their complaints are resolved promptly.[17] Salespeople should be hesitant to engage in subsequent sales efforts when an existing customer problem with a prior sale has yet to be resolved. Such endeavors could lead the aggrieved customer to view the salesperson as a mere "huckster" having little concern for the buyer. In dealing with customer complaints, sales and service people should follow the guidelines noted in Table 8.1 on p. 250.

## Customers Who Don't Complain

As you may have guessed from our earlier discussion about the two customer types who receive little service, you cannot afford to assume that no complaints means customers are satisfied. Because few dissatisfied customers actually file a complaint, sellers do not know the true extent of customer dissatisfaction. Many unhappy customers simply forego a complaint, especially

| TABLE 8.1 |
| --- |

## BASIC RULES FOR HANDLING CUSTOMER COMPLAINTS

- Anticipate customer complaints and try to resolve them before the customer expresses them.

- Listen closely and patiently to customers' complaints without interrupting.

- Never belittle a customer's complaint. Few customers actually complain, and those who do are a valuable source of feedback and information that can help improve the quality of your product and service.

- Encourage customers to talk and fully express their feelings so that they vent their emotions.

- Don't argue with customers or take their complaints personally. You gain nothing by making a customer angry, and there is no surer way to do so than to argue over the customer's version of the complaint.

- Record the facts as the customer sees them. If you take the complaint over the telephone, let him or her know that you are carefully recording the facts without passing judgment.

- Reassure customers that you hear and understand their complaints accurately by verbally repeating the information as you record it. This repetition reassures customers about your accuracy and interest. Asking nonthreatening or nonjudgmental questions to clarify their various points can also help them to know that they are communicating successfully.

- Empathize with customers and try to see the situation from their point of view.

- Don't make excuses for service problems or criticize your firm's service personnel.

- Ask customers how they would like to have their complaint resolved instead of volunteering what you're going to do. Customers may have quite different expectations about how to solve their problem, and you may offer the wrong solution or much more than they expect. By asking customers what they want, you'll meet their expectations and not overdo in making amends.

- Resolve problems promptly and fairly, even if that means the sale will become unprofitable.

- Thank customers for voicing the complaint. Welcome them as people who care enough to try to help you improve your products and services.

- Follow up to ensure that a customer's complaint has been resolved to his or her satisfaction.

- Keep records on all customer complaints and their outcomes so that, through analysis, you can spot patterns of problems.

when a purchase is not expensive, and buy elsewhere next time. Measuring customer satisfaction with service performance is essential. Even if their companies regularly measure overall customer satisfaction, salespeople should verify their own customers' level of satisfaction with their products and services. Just as competitors' poor service will create additional sales opportunities for you, your poor service creates an opportunity for competitors and must be promptly addressed. Read *On the Frontlines* on p. 249 to see how one salesperson minimizes complaints by making sure that he meets customer expectations.

## CLOSING WITH THE CUSTOMER SERVICE TEAM

Although you are usually the one to ask for the prospect's business, you rarely close alone. It is important for salespeople engaged in organizational selling to work smoothly and effectively with marketing and other in-house teams in order to gain their support in cultivating the best possible relationships with customers. If you have done your job properly, by the time you ask for the prospect's business, you will already know all the post-sale details—product availability and delivery schedules, whether or not the customer will receive credit approval, and so on. No salesperson alone can adequately provide all the services that his or her customers expect. It is necessary for salespeople to work closely with their company's customer support or service team. Customer service policies and procedures are extremely important because so many aspects of customer service cross departmental lines. Immediately before you close the sale, however, you should once again check with colleagues and friends in the (1) customer credit, (2) order-processing, and (3) product delivery teams to iron out any potential difficulties. Let's quickly describe the role these three teams play.

### Credit Team

Two natural sources of conflict arise between salespeople and credit managers. The first essentially is geographical. Credit is still a centralized function in most companies, whereas salespeople usually operate from decentralized regional offices. Beyond physical distance, some natural conflict emerges between the roles of salespeople and credit managers. Salespeople are expected to be their customers' advocates for credit approvals, while the credit department's job is to protect the company from entering into sales agreements with customers who are unlikely to pay.

The best salespeople actively search for ways to minimize the effects of these sources of conflicts. Some companies are encouraging their credit managers to spend a week or two each year in sales territories to further their understanding of the needs of customers and salespeople. Another good approach to improving the working relationships between salespeople and customer service departments is to schedule joint training meetings. Such meetings can foster better understanding by conducting role-playing exercises where salespeople play the role of credit managers and credit managers play the role of salespeople in negotiations. In companies that require their salespeople to collect overdue accounts, salespeople quickly understand the problems of the credit department. Some common complaints that salespeople and credit managers express about each other are shown in Table 8.2 below.

### Order-Processing and Product Delivery Teams

The goal in designing a physical distribution system is to develop minimum cost systems for a range of customer service levels, then provide the service

TABLE 8.2

## POTENTIAL CONFLICTS BETWEEN CREDIT AND SALES

### Credit Department Complaints About Salespeople

- Salespeople often over commit the company.

- Salespeople approve payment delays for customers without even notifying the credit department.

- Salespeople will do almost anything to avoid refusing credit to a customer, including going around the credit department to appeal to upper management for support.

- Salespeople often argue for the profit "potential" of marginal prospects and thereby compromise the credit manager and jeopardize the company's profits.

- Salespeople sometimes write large orders for normally low-to-moderate-volume customers without obtaining a financial update or even considering that one might be needed.

- Salespeople promise special credit services that simply cannot be performed.

- Salespeople won't address even the possibility that a customer might not pay. To them, every customer is "as good as gold."

### Salespeople's Complaints About the Credit Department

- The credit department doesn't explain what it needs to evaluate prospects and customers. The sales department is excluded from the policy and the process.

- Excessive demands on prospective customers weaken sales potential.

- The sales department has to "patch up" customer relationships after negative credit department contacts with customers.

- The credit department exists in a corporate ivory tower and doesn't understand the difficulty in the field.

- The credit department is too quick to condemn a customer who's past due and won't negotiate to save the account. It is too short-run oriented.

- The credit department doesn't notify salespeople in time when a customer is past due or when the account has been referred for third-party collection.

- The sales department isn't notified when a customer's credit is being reevaluated.

*Source:* Excerpt from Nathaniel Gilbert, "The Missing Link in Sales and Marketing: Credit Management," *Management Review* (June 1989): 24–30.

level that generates the highest profits or sales minus distribution costs. Salespeople and company transportation managers must learn to appreciate the full range of policies, procedures, and activities that affect customer perceptions of service, such as complaint procedures, minimum order sizes, order cycles, inventory returns, stockouts, and promised deliveries. Salespeople should cultivate good relationships with people in order processing and transportation by carefully checking customer order forms to minimize any potential misunderstandings and by keeping customer service people informed about any unique customer requirements. When salespeople show that they care about their customers by providing such extra services, the feeling usually becomes contagious and is picked up by the order-processing and transportation staff. When both salespeople and transportation managers start seeing their functions through the eyes of the customer, they begin to think differently. Frito-Lay is one company that doesn't worry excessively about costs when it comes to making sure customers receive the products they need when they need them, as noted in *From the Command Post.*

It is unfortunate that the people responsible for order processing and product delivery often miss out on the excitement of cultivating a new customer and increasing business with an old one. If you want an excellent relationship with these important teams, you will take the time to tell managers and workers the story of a successful sale and thank them for their hard work in supporting that sale. This will give them not only a sense of excitement surrounding your closed sale, but also some specific ideas about that particular customer's order-processing and delivery expectations. Also, it will have the added benefit of making your customers especially memorable to people whom you may occasionally have to call upon for rush delivery, special delivery terms, and the like.

As with credit managers, transportation managers can develop a customer orientation by participating with salespeople in training meetings that include interactive role-playing. Good relationships between salespeople and personnel who handle traffic and transportation, inventory control, warehousing and packaging, and sales and order service will help avoid customer complaints like those depicted in Table 8.3.

## FROM THE COMMAND POST: SERVICE TO SALES

Frito-Lay is dominant in the snack food industry and famous for its customer service. Its ten thousand route drivers visit most stores, large and small, up to three times a week to make sure that their snacks are fresh and appropriately displayed. In its dedication to customer service, Frito-Lay will spend several hundred dollars to send a truck to restock a single store with a couple of thirty-dollar cartons of potato chips. And plant managers do not hesitate to run overtime to make sure salespeople have all the product they need. Each of Frito-Lay's twenty-five thousand employees is taught to live by one motto: "Service to Sales."

TABLE 8.3

## SOME COMMON CUSTOMER SERVICE COMPLAINTS

### Order Processing and Billing

- Invoice had errors
- Discount not taken off price
- Name and address incorrect
- Not notified about late shipment
- Special instructions not followed
- Missing paperwork

### Inventory Control, Warehousing, and Packaging

- Product out of stock
- Wrong product sent
- Unordered product sent
- Product package not sealed properly
- Damaged product sent
- Poor quality product shipped
- Wrong product quantity shipped
- Incorrect papers packaged with product
- Packaging inadequate to protect product

### Traffic and Transportation

- Product delivered prior to date wanted
- Product delivered too late
- Product lost in transit
- No tracking of delayed product
- Requested customer routing not followed
- Specific handling instructions ignored
- Errors on the bill of lading
- Delivery people left product outside in rain or snow
- Delivery people refused to carry product inside
- Delivery people didn't deliver invoice

## KEEPING UP WITH RISING CUSTOMER SERVICE EXPECTATIONS

In order to provide improving quality service, salespeople and their backup customer service teams must stay close to customers and their evolving expectations. Staying close to customers means keeping in mind several basic concepts.

### Only Customers Can Define Customer Satisfaction

Continually soliciting customer feedback is the best way to determine what customer service is and should be. Carlson Systems, a distributor of fasteners and packaging products, asks its customers to fill out regular "report cards," rating the company from poor to excellent on such services as handling back orders or invoice errors.[18]

*Nothing is ever gained by making a customer angry, and there is no surer way to do so than to dispute the customer's version of a complaint.*
Ed Bock/Corbis

Usually, the seller's policies, systems, and procedures, not employee motivation, stand in the way of better customer service. When salespeople and other front-line people are asked for suggestions on how to better serve customers, they respond with numerous practical ideas. An example of a firm that understands the importance of the customer service relationship is presented in *From the Command Post.*

## FROM THE COMMAND POST: SERVICE-ORIENTED WHOLESALER

Bergen Brunswig Drug Company is a drug wholesaler selling to 9,500 hospitals, regional drug chains, and independent drug stores nationwide. Its salespeople are called "consultants" to emphasize the service focus of their jobs. Bergen Brunswig's 235 salespeople offer customers various computer programs to speed ordering and delivery. A comprehensive training program, with hands-on experience in all departments of the company as well as pharmacies, ensures that Bergen Brunswig Drug Company salespeople can implement any service program the firm offers. *Space Management*, a merchandising program

based on product sales data, helps retailers keep the right products in the right place at the right time. For a monthly fee, Bergen Brunswig advises customers on product and shelf arrangement. *Compu-Phase* is a computer system for processing prescriptions, storing patient information, and updating prices. The "Good Neighbor Pharmacy" advertising program gives retailers the advertising benefits enjoyed by chains without sacrificing their local identity. Beyond order entry, shelf management, and inventory control systems, Bergen Brunswig offers financial management programs.

### Everyone Serves a Customer

Salespeople have customers, receptionists have customers, traffic managers have customers, custodians have customers—everybody in the organization has internal customers (other employees) to serve and all directly or indirectly serve the external customers (prospects and customers). Serving internal customers well leads to the kind of teamwork that creates synergistic results and success for the entire organization in satisfying external customers.

### Customer Service Is a Partnership with the Customer

Salespeople and their companies who most consistently provide the highest quality customer service usually have developed a partnering relationship with customers, as described in *From the Command Post*.

## EVALUATING CUSTOMER SERVICE

Regular checkups for your customer service performance are critical to sales health. An easy way to assess how satisfied your customers are is to have them complete a brief questionnaire, like the one depicted on p. 257.

Such questionnaires also can ask customers about *how important* each of the service-related statements is. Those items that customers consider unimportant would require less service attention from the salesperson than those service-related activities that customers consider important.

### Moving Beyond Customer Satisfaction to Customer Loyalty

Customer satisfaction is essential to the success of a company or salesperson. Increasingly, however, companies are seeing *customer loyalty* as the critical

## FROM THE COMMAND POST: BETTER SERVICE THROUGH PARTNERSHIP

As the demand for quality service grows, many manufacturers form partnerships with just a few of their resellers—wholesalers, distributors, and retailers. Partnerships between manufacturers and middlemen bring cost savings through larger purchase volumes, reduced competition, and predictable markets. In addition, the usual adversarial role among channel members is replaced with one built more on trust and cooperation.

To facilitate service delivery, many buyers and sellers have interconnected their computer systems. Designs Inc., a retail chain, has linked its computers directly to Levi Strauss Company. Now, Levi Strauss knows which of its products is selling fastest because sales data are transmitted directly from the point of sale to the manufacturer's computers. Sharing data enables Levi Strauss to anticipate and make timely delivery of needed products to Designs.

# CUSTOMER SERVICE QUESTIONNAIRE

*Indicate the extent to which you agree with each of the following statements using the following scale:*

**5-Strongly Agree;   4-Agree;   3-Neither Agree nor Disagree;   2-Disagree;   1-Strongly Disagree**

XYZ Company insists on error-free records. ____

XYZ Company employees tell you exactly when services will be performed. ____

Employees of XYZ Company give you prompt service. ____

XYZ Company employees are always willing to help you. ____

Employees in XYZ Company are never too busy to respond to your request. ____

The behavior of employees of XYZ Company instills confidence in you. ____

You feel safe in your transactions with XYZ Company. ____

Employees of XYZ Company are consistently courteous with you. ____

Employees of XYZ Company have the knowledge to answer your questions. ____

XYZ Company's operating hours are convenient for you. ____

XYZ Company employees give you personal attention. ____

XYZ Company has your best interest at heart. ____

Employees of XYZ Company understand your specific needs. ____

The more strongly a customer agrees with each of the above statements, the greater the satisfaction with the level of service the salesperson and firm provide.

***Source:*** *Adapted from C. David Shepherd, "Service Quality and the Sales Force: A Tool for Competitive Advantage,"* Journal of Personal Selling and Sales Management 19 (Summer 1999): 73–82. *Copyright © 1999 by Pi Sigma Epsilon, Inc. Reprinted with permission.*

metric that will determine whether their business thrives, merely survives, or dies in the fierce competition ahead. One study found that increasing customer retention by 5 percent could double a small firm's profitability in about ten years and could double the average *Fortune* 500 company's revenue growth rate almost immediately.[19] A majority of offline companies are focusing on customer loyalty as the key indicator of how well they're doing.

By focusing on customer satisfaction, some companies have improved their customer retention rates, at least initially. But much of this early success has proven elusive over the longer run as competitive promises lure customers away. Most customers who later switched to a competitor reported that they were "satisfied" or even "highly satisfied" shortly before leaving. Yet, they weren't loyal. Why isn't customer satisfaction enough? A major part of the problem may be in the measurement of customer satisfaction.

## Corrupted Customer Satisfaction Measurement

General Motors' executives were early advocates of customer satisfaction surveys as they tried to stop the steady erosion of their market share to foreign car companies. Management and employee evaluations, recognition, and bonuses were based partly on statistically rigorous calculation of scores from customer satisfaction surveys. Customer satisfaction ratings improved dramatically to 90 percent or higher, but market share and profits continued to decline and customer retention rates remained largely unchanged below 50 percent.[20] What went wrong? Several factors corrupted customer satisfaction measurement. Let's look at some of these.

**Playing the Customer Satisfaction Game.** Rewards based on customer satisfaction scores encouraged various unproductive, questionable behaviors. Some automobile dealerships, for example, played the ratings game by offering special discounts and incentives to customers who agreed to complete a survey checking "highly satisfied" in all categories. A few dealers brazenly displayed a copy of the survey form showing exactly how to mark it "properly" at the highest level. Some just threw away poor ratings from customers.

**Early Surveys Can Mislead.** Dealers also discovered that they could obtain the highest scores by surveying customers shortly after they bought a new car when it was too early for any problems to have shown up. Even dealers who didn't try to "game" the customer satisfaction studies found that customers were reluctant to participate in long surveys. Some customers were surveyed by automobile dealerships as many as a ten times in a single year, so they started giving perfunctory, although usually positive, answers to the tedious surveys.

**Full Satisfaction Required.** Companies and their salespeople sometimes boast about customer satisfaction ratings of four or higher on a five-point scale, where one equals very dissatisfied and five equals very satisfied. But recent studies show that this level of satisfaction isn't good enough to keep customers loyal.[21] To achieve loyalty, customers need to consistently rate you 5 on a 5–point scale. In other words, customers must be fully satisfied.

**Cumulative Satisfaction Is Key.** Some salespeople think of customer satisfaction in terms of a specific transaction, but this is too limited. The customer's cumulative satisfaction, based on his or her total purchase, consumption, and service experiences over time with you and your company, must be continuously measured and monitored. Cumulative satisfaction is much more predictive of future customer purchase behavior than satisfaction on any single transaction.[22] So salespeople must work to provide full satisfaction with each and every customer purchase, then follow up to make sure that the customer's actual product use and service experiences are fully satisfactory.

**Changing Customer Expectations.** Surveys of customer satisfaction are usually taken over a few days or weeks. However, consistent, long-run satisfaction is unlikely to endure from survey to survey. Consumers are satisfied for short periods of time while their expectations for products and services continue to rise in response to personal desires, advertising promises by competitors, word-of-mouth hyperbole, and such. Consumer expectations seem to have become infinitely elastic; that is, they are continually rising for every product and service. What customers were satisfied with yesterday isn't good enough to win their satisfaction and loyalty tomorrow. If customer satisfaction isn't enough, then we must move to the next level and find ways to create customer loyalty.

## What Drives Customer Loyalty?

**The 8Cs of Loyalty.** Recent research by Srinivasan, Anderson, and Ponnavolu has identified eight factors, or the **8Cs,** that appear to drive customer loyalty both online and offline.[23] Companies can benchmark and compare their performance on these 8Cs versus their past performance, managerial goals, or competitors. Salespeople, too, can evaluate their interactions with prospects and customers according to the 8Cs, as described below:

- *Customization*—the degree to which products, services, and the transactional environment are tailored to the individual characteristics and requirements of each customer. Each customer has his or her own unique personality and communication style (as we'll discuss in chapter 11). Savvy salespeople often try to arrange sales calls in settings where their customers are most comfortable (whether the golf course, a good restaurant, or the ballpark), and they present products and services that best match their customers' interests (for example, high quality, durability, low price, creative design, fast delivery, or some combination). The more you can customize your products, services, and the negotiating environment to individual customers, the more likely you'll close the sale and further the relationship.

- *Contact Interactivity*—the extent of high quality, mutually desired communication and interaction with customers. In personal selling, listening is more important than talking, but providing an easy flow of communication exchanges between you and your customers is essential for positive, long-run rapport. The best customer-salesperson relationships are those in which you genuinely like each other and feel comfortable speaking openly and honestly together. You might not become close friends with all your customers, but you can develop open communications and a high level of contact interactivity with each. For example, you might send regular newsletters by postal mail or email to keep customers informed about upcoming price changes, inventory shortages, new products, or any other items of interest. In each newsletter, you can ask customers for feedback about their product/service needs, concerns, complaints, and opinions with respect to your performance on various criteria important to them. Take a tip from some politicians who regularly ask their constituents, "How am I doing?" Salespeople who don't solicit opinions from customers are unlikely to keep their repeat purchase business.

- *Cultivation*—the degree to which salespeople provide customers with desired information and helpful cross-selling offers. Salespeople should proactively help customers find products and services they need. Nordstrom, the department store chain, is well known for its salespeople writing letters and making phone calls to customers. After purchasing a suit from Nordstrom, one of the authors of this text received five handwritten letters and two phone calls over a period of two years from the salesperson regarding upcoming sales and the recent arrival of new shirts, ties, or shoes that might go well with the suit. Organizational sellers engage in similar activities. They use the phone, email, fax, or regular

**8Cs** Eight factors (customization, contact interactivity, cultivation, care, community, choice, convenience, and character) found to drive customer loyalty. These 8Cs are moderated by customer trust and satisfaction.

mail, as well as face-to-face contact, to inform their accounts about new product releases or imminent events (for example, price increases, product deletion decisions) that are likely to affect the buyers. Customers appreciate cross selling and information that they think is meant to be helpful.

- *Care*—the extent to which a salesperson demonstrates special concern for the customer's welfare in all pre- and post-purchase interactions. Genuinely caring for customers can develop loyalty far beyond mere customer satisfaction. USAA, the giant insurance company headquartered in San Antonio, regularly shows that it cares about customers. During the U.S. military's 1991 call-up for Operation Desert Storm, USAA notified its customers (mainly active duty, reserve, and retired military people) that they could add to their life insurance before going overseas and that they should ask about reduced premiums for their car insurance if their car was not going to be driven as much while they were in the Persian Gulf. In contrast, most other insurance companies refuse to sell life insurance without special clauses in the contracts that exempt the company from paying if a policyholder is killed in war. Salespeople who act as advisers and consultants to their customers can encourage them to remain loyal by showing genuine caring in ways that go beyond the immediate bottom line.

- *Community*—the degree to which customers can share opinions among themselves about a company's products and services. Harley-Davidson customers, who affectionately call themselves "HOGS," have bonds among their community members that act as strong deterrents to buying any other motorcycle or accessory brand. For its hundredth anniversary, Harley-Davidson sponsored a yearlong celebration for their customers, beginning with a five-continent road tour and ending with a huge party in Milwaukee for about two hundred thousand loyal customers. Salespeople who willingly give their customers the names of other customers (who have granted permission) to ask about the performance of their products and services can develop communities that will help past customers sell future customers. Communities of customers strengthen a common bond among salespeople and their customers even when complaints arise.

- *Choice*—the range of desired products and services from which customers can choose. Most customers don't want to buy products from several different salespeople if they can conveniently buy everything they need from one salesperson (one-stop shopping). Even if his or her company offers only some of the products needed, a resourceful salesperson will offer to find and deliver those other products to the customer, too. This value-added service gives customers the feeling that they can go to you for fulfillment of all their product needs, and many will gladly pay a premium price for such service.

- *Convenience*—the ease with which a customer can conduct negotiations and transactions with a seller. Customers want products and services provided when and where needed with minimal effort on their part, and without hassles. Installation and maintenance of products or return of flawed products must be convenient for customers to become loyal repeat buyers. Here is another aspect of convenience: customers want to avoid hardball negotiations with salespeople. Salespeople who see interactions with customers as contests with a clear-cut winner may win a few sales, but they will never win the long-term loyalty of customers.

• *Character*—the image and reputation that a seller projects to customers. Some companies are fortunate enough to have a highly visible person within their companies, usually the founder, to represent them in positive ways. These people often are so likable or so well respected that they give the company a positive character, personality, or reputation. Thousands of investors around the world proudly call themselves "bogleheads" in honor of John Bogle, founder of Vanguard Group (a giant mutual fund investment firm). They credit him personally for ensuring that Vanguard's mutual fund management costs remain the lowest in the industry. Bogle's well-known frugal ways, straight-talking personality, and reputation for integrity have helped make Vanguard the most trusted of all financial firms. Only a few people can inspire such loyalty from customers, but all salespeople can learn from Bogle's example that a favorable reputation is invaluable to sales success and long-run customer relationships.

**Moderators of the 8Cs of Loyalty.** Each of the foregoing eight characteristics is so interconnected that it cannot be considered adequately in isolation from the others. Moreover, although the 8Cs directly affect customer loyalty, two critical moderating variables, cumulative customer satisfaction and trust, influence their overall effectiveness. Unless businesses and their salespeople can maintain a bond of trust with customers and continuously provide full satisfaction in each purchase experience, customer loyalty will suffer even when the 8Cs are highly positive. It's a big task, but companies and salespeople who can do all this will likely produce a substantial payoff in long-run profitability.

## SUMMARY

Winning a new account is five to six times as expensive as increasing sales from an existing account. Therefore, salespeople should engage in several post-sale activities to ensure that profitable customers stay satisfied and do not defect to competitors. Customer satisfaction and the perceptions of the quality of a company and its products are largely determined by the service they receive. Customer service has five dimensions, the most important of which is *reliability*. Service quality is determined by customer perceptions, not what the seller thinks. The absence of customer complaints does not necessarily mean that customers are satisfied, because few dissatisfied customers will actually complain. The rest start buying from another supplier. Customer complaints should be recognized as opportunities to improve the customer relationship.

Customer service strategy calls for segmenting the customers to be served, then identifying those segments whose service expectations can be profitably met. Salespeople need the help of the company's customer service team and internal staff to satisfy their customers' service expectations. Salespeople and their companies who provide the highest quality service usually form partner-like relationships with customers. Customer service expectations and standards will continue to rise, and it will be up to professional salespeople to sell and coordinate this customer service.

Sales organizations should regularly assess how satisfied their customers are with the service they receive. After difficulties measuring customer satis-faction, many companies are moving on to the holy grail of selling (that is, customer loyalty). Eight factors (8Cs) have been identified as driving cus-tomer loyalty. The presence of these 8Cs, along with customer satisfaction and trust, should help companies and their salespeople create the loyal customers needed to maximize profits over the long run.

## KEY TERMS

Follow-up

Customer service

Reliability

Customer service segmentation

Product quality

Service quality

Perceived service quality

8Cs

## CHAPTER REVIEW QUESTIONS

1. What most influences customer perceptions of a company's overall quality?

2. Name and define the five dimensions of cus-tomer service. Which one of these dimensions do customers perceive as the most important?

3. What proportion of dissatisfied customers will actually complain? Why?

4. How do you define customer dissatisfaction?

5. What is the major reason customers switch to competitors?

6. Name some basic customer follow-up strategies.

7. List some positive and negative actions that can affect post-purchase relationships with cus-tomers.

8. Why should customer service markets be seg-mented?

9. About what percentage of customers who com-plain will buy again from the seller if their complaints are resolved promptly?

10. Name three complaints salespeople have about credit managers and three that credit managers have about salespeople.

## TOPICS FOR THOUGHT AND CLASS DISCUSSION

1. What is your personal definition of customer service and what do you consider the most important dimensions of customer service?

2. How do you think customer service expecta-tions are changing?

3. Why do only a low percentage of dissatisfied customers ever complain?

4. Have you ever made a formal complaint about a product? Why? Was your complaint answered? How?

5. As a new salesperson, how would you go about gaining the cooperation of your company's cus-tomer service team in solving your customers' problems?

6. Explain this statement: "Everyone serves a customer, either an internal one or an external one."

7. How does forming a buyer-seller partnership affect customer service?

8. How do you account for the disparity in customer service among retail store chains?

## PROJECTS FOR PERSONAL GROWTH

1. (a) Ask four of your classmates to brainstorm with you about which commercial and non-profit organizations consistently provide the best customer service. Come up with three examples of each category, then take turns explaining the reasons for each selection. (b) Ask each of your four classmates to select two organizations that usually provide the worst customer service. Take turns explaining why. As each of your classmates gives his or her explanations, write down the key points. After everyone has finished, identify the key criteria your classmates mentioned that cause them to perceive organizations as providing the *best* and the *worst* customer service.

2. In your college library, find two articles about how companies measure business customer satisfaction and two articles on measuring consumer satisfaction. From the perspective of the customer (business and consumer), critique the methods described for handling customer complaints. As part of your critique, consider the channels of communication both kinds of customers have for providing feedback to sellers. How effective and efficient are these channels? Finally, outline an ideal system for obtaining regular feedback on customer satisfaction and promptly resolving customer complaints.

3. Select two area companies and contact the customer service manager for each by telephone, email, or letter. Be sure to tell the manager that you're doing a school project, because that should help you obtain responses. Ask the following questions: (a) How does your company define customer service? (b) Who is responsible for customer service? (c) How do you measure your customers' level of satisfaction with your products and services? (d) What is your general process for handling customer complaints? After obtaining this information, write your own critique of the way the two companies are dealing with these critical concerns for retention of customers.

## ADDRESSING CUSTOMER PROBLEMS: SERVICE OR DISSERVICE?

Rob Azar is excited. Actually, he is thrilled. He has just closed a big order with an account that had stopped buying from his company. Most of the other sales reps said it couldn't be done, but Rob knew he could do it. After all, they didn't call him the "Slammer" for nothing. At the first of the year, Rob was promoted to account representative at Master Mailers, Inc., a mailing equipment manufacturer. Although he has been with Master Mailers only about three years, he has quickly moved up through the ranks. In fact, in his three years with the company, he has been promoted at the end of each year. Interestingly, Rob always experiences high sales at the beginning of a year, but his sales taper off toward the end of the year. This has never really concerned him because his final numbers are all that matter, and he always surpasses his sales quotas. Besides, after he "blows" through a territory, he is always promoted out of it, so the year-end drop off isn't a problem for him.

Rob has been in his new assignment for only three months, and, as usual, he is going like gangbusters. He has a city-center hospital assignment that contains both users and nonusers of his company's mailing equipment. While his old territory consisted of many smaller accounts, his new territory has larger accounts that have much more potential. As a result, he must spend more time becoming acquainted with these accounts and understanding their needs.

On this particular day, Rob is pleased with himself. He has just closed a substantial order with one of his higher potential accounts, Union Hospital, which has been buying only 20 percent of their mailing equipment from Master Mailers. Rob really went after this account, knowing there was a lot more business to be had there. The head of purchasing, Marilyn Krane, has been with the hospital for years. During the sales call, she told Rob about her reluctance to buy from him because the hospital experienced several customer service problems with Master Mailers in the past. Rob, who is known for his exceptional ability to negotiate prospect resistance and objections, convinced Ms. Krane to give his company another chance by assuring her that he will be personally responsible for the account and that Union Hospital could count on him to promptly resolve any problems they might have with his company or its products. In reality, Rob has a team of people behind him to service the account, and if anything does go wrong, he plans to direct Ms. Krane to one of them. When Rob brings all the paperwork back to the office and receives hearty congratulations from his district sales manager, Roger Stone, he gives the order to Joan Newman, the district office administrative assistant, to process.

The following Friday, Rob learns that the mailing machine that Union Hospital ordered is in short supply. Although the usual product delivery time is five to ten working days, delivery time for this particular model has been pushed back to three to four weeks. When Rob finds out about the delay, he runs to his manager, telling him that he needs his help in securing a unit in five days for the hospital order. Mr. Stone is upset with Rob because it's standard practice for all salespeople to check on product availability before guaranteeing a delivery date. Nevertheless, he immediately calls the company's vice president of manufacturing. The vice president tells Mr. Stone that faster delivery on that particular model is impossible because of higher production priorities. Mr. Stone in turn tells Rob he has no option but to call the account promptly and explain the delay in delivery. Rob is not eager to call Ms. Krane because he knows she will be upset, and he's afraid that she may cancel the order. Besides, it is already Friday afternoon. He decides to wait until Monday to call the account, hoping that in the meantime he'll think of something.

On Monday, Rob has several sales calls to make and, before he knows it, the day is over and

(continued)

# ADDRESSING CUSTOMER PROBLEMS: SERVICE OR DISSERVICE? [CONTINUED]

he still hasn't called Ms. Krane. On Tuesday morning, he receives a phone message from Ms. Krane asking for confirmation of the scheduled delivery date. Rob waits until he knows she will be out to lunch before returning her call and leaves a brief message on her voice mail saying that he will call back. For the next two days, he deliberately plays telephone tag with Ms. Krane. Finally, on Thursday, Rob knows he must let her know that the new mailing machine is not going to be delivered that Friday. Ms. Krane is angry when Rob tells her the bad news, but he calms her down by assuring her it will be only one more week before delivery, and that he will bring her a "loaner" machine on Friday morning, which he does. The next week passes and still the new equipment has not been delivered to Union Hospital. A deeply upset Ms. Krane leaves another message for Rob asking about the promised delivery, but Rob doesn't bother to return her call. He rationalizes that the hospital has the "free" use of a loaner machine, so there isn't any big problem. When the equipment is finally delivered the following week, Rob calls to make sure that it's working to the hospital's satisfaction. Ms. Krane seems calmer, but not all that happy. Rob figures he'll wait a couple of weeks for matters to settle down, and then take her out to a four-star restaurant for lunch to smooth her ruffled feelings.

About two weeks later, before Rob has had a chance to invite Ms. Krane for lunch, she calls to ask his help in straightening out a billing problem. Rob suggests they discuss it over lunch the following day. At lunch, he takes notes on the problem. It seems that Master Mailer has billed the hospital for a feature that the new mailing machine does not have. Rob explains that this is a minor problem and promises to take care of it. He takes the erroneous invoice and says he will call Ms. Krane within two days to let her know the problem has been resolved. But Rob is so busy over the next two days that he has no time to take care of the

billing problem. In fact, it slips his mind until he receives another phone message from Ms. Krane asking whether the hospital's bill has been corrected. When he calls Ms. Krane back, he assures her that he is working on the problem and that it will be resolved shortly. Back in his office that day, Rob makes a point of giving the problem invoice to Joan Newman to handle. After all, he reasons, he's a sales rep, not a credit rep.

About a month later, Rob receives an urgent phone call from Ms. Krane. It seems that Master Mailers' credit department has notified Union Hospital that all its future purchases will be on a C.O.D. basis because the hospital has failed to pay its last invoice. Ms. Krane is furious, saying Union Hospital does not do business this way. After Rob apologizes, he promises that he will resolve the matter that day. Rob immediately returns to the office, and in about four hours he has the situation settled. Mr. Stone, who has heard about the problem from his secretary, asks Rob why the credit department has so mismanaged the Union Hospital account. Reluctant to explain the whole embarrassing set of circumstances, Rob puts Mr. Stone off by saying, "You know Credit's philosophy: 'The customer is always wrong.' But I got it straightened out, Boss. Got to run now to another sales appointment. Talk to you later." Rob calls Ms. Krane the following morning to let her know that everything is fine and that the hospital's account is completely straightened out.

Over the next two months, Rob is extremely busy chasing down new sales. Since he hasn't heard from Ms. Krane, he assumes all is well with the Union Hospital account. Actually, he doesn't feel that comfortable calling Ms. Krane with the delivery and billing problems so fresh in her mind. By the middle of the third month, Rob calls Ms. Krane to set up another sales call, figuring that by this time, all the past problems have been put to rest and he can safely approach her for additional

(continued)

# ADDRESSING CUSTOMER PROBLEMS: SERVICE OR DISSERVICE? [CONTINUED]

orders. When Rob arrives at the hospital, he is surprised to see one of his biggest competitor's mailing machines in an office. He pokes his head into the office and comments to the woman using it, "Is that a new machine?" The woman replies, "Yes, it is. We just got this machine this week and four others just like it. It's a great little machine. I really love it." Rob feels his stomach sink as he thinks about losing out on a sale of five brand new units. Boy, could he have used those commissions! He approaches Ms. Krane's office with a growing sense of discouragement about winning a larger share of Union Hospital's business.

## Questions

1. Do you consider Rob is a good salesperson? Is he customer service oriented? Why or why not?
2. What customer service mistakes did Rob make in handling the Union Hospital account? What should he have done differently?
3. What should Rob have done after making his initial sale to Union Hospital?
4. What advice would you give Rob now in his efforts to win a higher share of business from Union Hospital?

## CASE 8.2 A SLAM-DUNK THAT REALLY HURTS

After graduating from the City College of New York, where he majored in political science and was a third-team All-American basketball player (and almost made it to the NBA), Darren Jones took a sales position in his home state of New York with Olympia Sports Company. Olympia is one of the country's largest manufacturers of sporting equipment, and sells to wholesalers, retail stores, and large high schools and colleges. Although it faces considerable competition from better-known companies like Wilson and Spaulding, Olympia enjoys a good reputation for the quality of its products.

Darren, nicknamed "Dr. D" by his teammates and college basketball fans, loves sports and believes that selling athletic equipment is the ideal job for him. He is especially happy with his territory because it covers New York, New Jersey, and Pennsylvania, and states where he is well known for his basketball success. Darren's customers like him because of his outgoing personality and his incredible knowledge of college and pro sports. Most customers flash a big smile and say something like, "Always good to see Dr. D!" when they see Darren coming.

Darren seems to be on target for meeting his sales quota in his second year of selling. His regional fame and easygoing personality were his biggest help in meeting his quota in his first year. His normal sales presentation goes something like this: After introducing himself (and usually gaining immediate recognition as Dr. D) and his company, Darren hands the prospect several product brochures. Then he talks about sports until the prospect turns to business with a question like, "So, Darren, what's Olympia offering these days?" Because he is always careful to find out beforehand exactly what the prospect is interested in, Darren almost always has a specific piece of product information or even a sample product to show the prospect right away. Surprisingly, most customers seem to need little more than that before Darren closes another sale.

Recently, Darren was upset to learn that two of his retail customers have made major equipment purchases from another, smaller supplier. Darren knows the competing salesperson that "stole" these accounts. Reggie McArthur is a short, slight man of about the same age as Darren. Darren recalls that once last year he arrived at a customer's office just as Reggie was coming out of it. When he entered the customer's office, Darren was confronted with the sight of several competing product brochures and sample products placed in a careful arrangement on the customer's desk. After making two or three mildly disparaging remarks about the brochures and sample products, which the customer laughed off, saying, "Be nice now, Dr. D, that guy's got to make a living, too," Darren talked sports for a little while and left the office with a small order for some knee pads.

Darren chuckles as he thinks about Reggie, whom he has come to regard as a wimp. "The guy is always trying to make up for his inadequacies," thinks Darren. "He acts like a flunky ball-boy for his customers, writing cute thank-you notes after every sale, actually delivering equipment for customers (he looked like he was breaking his poor little back last month when I saw him delivering that backboard), and always doing errand work like hand-delivering credit paperwork and asking customers to fill out surveys." Darren can't understand how anybody can act in such a self-demeaning way with customers. Doesn't Reggie's company have personnel to do that minor stuff? "You sure won't see Dr. D doing flunky stuff like that," he thought to himself.

In addition to the loss of these two accounts, Darren's sales manager recently warned him that Olympia has received several complaints about faulty bolts in weight-lifting benches and basketball backboard mounts. Apparently, bolts on several of Olympia's midrange models are literally snapping into two pieces after only a couple of months' use. So far, nobody in Darren's territory

(continued)

## A SLAM-DUNK THAT REALLY HURTS (CONTINUED)

has made a complaint, except for the high-school basketball coach who told him a couple of months ago that the top two bolts of a new backboard had popped when one of his players made a slam dunk. The coach was somewhat concerned because many of his better players have always "abused" the equipment this way without breaking any bolts. Darren arranged to have two new bolts installed. Then, to test out the new bolts, he made a half-dozen picture-perfect slam dunks himself . . . as the coach and his team watched admiringly and yelled, "You da' man, Dr. D!"

Now, about a week after the sales manager's warning, Olympia's CEO has circulated an urgent memorandum to the sales staff about the faulty bolts problem. The CEO is requesting all salespeople to quietly inform customers who purchased certain models of benches and backboards that they should refrain from using the equipment until replacement bolts are sent to them. The salespeople are also being asked to check each customer's equipment within one week of shipment of the new bolts. Darren is irritated by this memo because it seems to him that management is making a big deal out of a small problem. "Well, I'll let my customers know they're getting new bolts," he thinks to himself, "but I don't have time to check up on every customer afterwards. I'm a sales rep bringing in big bucks for the company. I can't be wasting my time and the company's with service problems."

Two weeks later, while Darren is watching a pro basketball game on television, he receives a telephone call from his sales manager. At first not recognizing his manager's voice because it sounds so "down-in-the-mouth," Darren learns that a female senior at one of his high-school accounts broke her arm yesterday when an Olympia weight-lifting bench collapsed under her and a fifty-pound free weight glanced off her arm. After relaying this message, Darren's manager asks, "Did you make sure they changed the bolts in that bench?" Darren admits that he didn't check, to which his boss snarls in reply, "This could have been a lot worse, but as it is, we're probably facing a lawsuit. You'd better come into the office tomorrow morning at around eight-thirty to discuss the situation with the regional sales manager. I'll see if we can get one of our lawyers over here, too. We've got a real problem on our hands."

After gulping out an "Okay," Darren hangs up the phone and slumps in his chair to think, the sounds and images from the television becoming a confusing blur.

### Questions

1. When faulty equipment is sold to customers, is it the salesperson's problem or that of the company's manufacturing and quality control departments?

2. What do you think of Darren's response to his CEO's memo? How would you have responded? Do you think the memo was adequate? Did Darren have any evidence that the faulty bolts could be any more than a "small problem"? Should service problems cause a salesperson to disrupt his daily sales calls? How might a salesperson plan for service problems?

3. What can Darren and his district and regional sales managers do at this point? What would you do if you were Darren? Do you believe that notification of the problem should absolve Olympia and Darren from blame? Why or why not?

4. From the information provided in this case about Darren's sales presentation and customer service methods and his relationships with his competitors and with personnel in his own company, what do you infer about Darren's overall attitude toward his selling activities? Outline a plan for him to improve himself in these areas.

# PART THREE

# Understanding and Communicating with Customers

## CHAPTER 9

# Understanding Organizational Markets

*Salespeople must understand not only the needs of their
customers but also those of their customers' customers.*

Anonymous

## After Reading This Chapter, You Should Understand:

- Four kinds of organizational buyers.
- Roles of the members of the buying center.
- Major steps in the buying process and the three types of buying situations.
- Why, what, and how organizational markets buy products and services.
- Six negotiation styles of organizational buyers.
- Buyers' preferred relationships with salespeople.
- Decision-making styles of buyers.
- How to do business in international markets.

**INSIDE PERSONAL SELLING:**

## *Meet Jeanne Connor-Osborn of Sikorsky Aircraft*

**W**ho needs a helicopter—and why? That's what Jeanne Connor-Osborn, a Sikorsky Aircraft sales manager, must determine when selling medical helicopters to hospitals, aircraft operators, ministries of health, and governments. Some customers are transporting victims from traffic accidents; others are flying patients to hospitals two states away. "I need to know what customers must do, down to the weight of the patients they will lift and the types of patients they will handle," says Connor-Osborn. "We recently won a contract because our competitor didn't fully understand the customer's business. We pointed out that the other aircraft didn't have the range to reach the customer's top five referral hospitals—the customer's customers—a majority of the time. Understanding the need behind the need gives you the advantage every time."

Connor-Osborn also must understand how different organizations buy. For example, the buying process of hospitals supported by state or federal funds may be regulated. Some organizations hire consultants to help develop product specifications. "Recently, we worked with a consultant who had a medical transport background but no specific aviation background," says Connor-Osborn. "Although he was well-versed regarding specific aircraft features, we had to carefully explain the effect that the combination of features would have on the helicopter's performance."

Selling to buyers in different countries is another challenge. In Japan, for example, helicopters cannot land on roads to pick up traffic victims. As another example, the Canadian government centralizes medical care for certain specialties and buys helicopters to move patients from smaller hospitals to specialty centers.

Connor-Osborn forges long-term relationships by being prepared to respond to customers' needs and concerns. Recently, she submitted a proposal to a hospital that wanted to buy two helicopters, each capable of carrying two patients and a four-person medical crew. The hospital asked Sikorsky and a competitor to make presentations. Two vice presidents, two directors, a medical specialist, and a salesperson from the competing firm arrived in a deluxe helicopter. They brought pictures of their helicopters signed by company employees and answered questions for two hours.

Connor-Osborn knew the competing helicopter was performing a similar mission at another hospital, but under less demanding requirements. Representing Sikorsky, she came alone to the meeting toting just one cardboard box packed with presentation material. "I focused on the customer's mission," she says. "I knew which hospitals and trauma centers it served. I anticipated the board's questions and the criteria it would use to evaluate the proposals. I could even explain what would happen if they had to land at an alternate airport." Because she was thoroughly prepared, having talked in detail to the hospital's management, pilots, nurses, and mechanics about their specific concerns, she made the multi-million dollar sale.

271

As a consumer, you've undoubtedly interacted with a variety of salespeople at retail stores, including clothing, computer, music, cell phone, health club, and shoe sales personnel. Some of these salespeople were probably little more than order takers who gave you almost no help, while others may have worked patiently with you to find just the right product or service to satisfy your needs. Perhaps you have formulated some strong views—positive or negative—of salespeople based on these experiences. However, before you make up your mind about all salespeople, remember that all of these exchanges were between a salesperson and you—a consumer. Less visible to consumers but vitally important to the business world is personal selling that occurs predominately between a salesperson or sales team and an organizational buyer or buying team. The end results of interchanges between a salesperson and a consumer or a salesperson and an organizational buyer follow the same basic personal selling process (PSP), but distinct differences emerge in the sales rep's level of preparation, the nature of the interaction and negotiations, and the extent of customer service. Why? Because organizational buyers make purchases for their companies in ways different from consumers making purchases for themselves. While professional buyers often do want to satisfy some *personal* objectives in making a business purchase, they must be concerned primarily with achieving their company's objectives.

As a college graduate pursuing a profession in selling or sales management, you will probably spend most of your career selling to organizations. The highest-earning salespeople sell to various types of organizations, including manufacturers, resellers, governments, and not-for-profit organizations. All of these organizational types purchase a vast assortment of goods and services, and each has its own perspectives and procedures. In this chapter, we will discuss the buying practices and viewpoints that salespeople must understand in order to sell successfully in organizational markets.

Salespeople identify four types of organizational markets:

1. *Industrial Markets*: Also called *manufacturer* or *producer* or *business markets*, these organizations buy goods and services for the production of other products and services that are sold, rented, or supplied to other organizations and final consumers.

2. *Reseller Markets*: These individuals and organizations (retailers, wholesalers, and industrial distributors) buy goods *to resell or rent* to other organizations and ultimate consumers.

3. *Government Markets*: These markets include federal, state, and local governmental units that buy goods and services for conducting the functions of government.

4. *Nonprofit Markets*: These markets include organizations, such as universities, colleges, hospitals, museums, libraries, and charitable institutions that are not profit oriented and that buy goods and services for carrying out their functions.

# WHAT ORGANIZATIONAL BUYERS WANT FROM SALESPEOPLE

Organizational buyers want to buy from salespeople they can trust to deliver on their promises, provide reliable service, and supply them with precise, accurate, and complete information. They expect salespeople to forewarn them about upcoming price changes, product shortages, employee strikes, delivery delays, or anything else that might affect them and their organizations. Buyers want to do business with salespeople who are truly looking out for their organization's best interests and who help them look good personally—in other words, they want a trusted, reliable consultant, business partner, and friend if possible. Indeed, research suggests that when a "commercial friendship" develops between buyers and sellers, buyers are more loyal, have greater satisfaction, and are more inclined to provide favorable word-of-mouth promotion about the seller's firm.[1]

## Creating and Maintaining Long-Term Relationships

Relationships in organizational markets are critical. Instead of taking a short-run view by making as much profit as possible on each transaction, salespeople who successfully sell to organizations understand that it is a much more profitable strategy for their companies and themselves to create and nurture long-term relationships with customers. Negotiations with buyers must always be *win-win* (*both parties satisfy their needs*), never *win-lose* (*only the seller's needs are satisfied*). Professional salespeople do not try to win a contest or competition. In fact, you will not succeed over the long run by beating customers in negotiations. Even if you do have the power to take unfair advantage of a customer, never yield to the temptation. The lifetime value of a loyal customer is much greater than any profit from a one-time sale—no matter how large—and the buyer-seller relationship may be ended by an unbalanced outcome. Thus, salespeople should focus on creating and building long-run relationships, not merely making short-run sales transactions. In other words, salespeople are really selling relationships, not just products and services.

## Selling the Relationship

Essentially, when sales personnel sell the relationship, they are engaging in relationship selling. **Relationship selling** includes all activities aimed at creating, developing, and maintaining successful exchange relationships with prospects and customers. Salespeople calling on organizational prospects and customers should make managing these relationships their main focus. It is folly for a salesperson who wishes to develop a trusting, long-lasting buyer-seller relationship to mislead or withhold information or manipulate the buyer in any way. Instead, strive to make sure that all parties are satisfied in all transactions or agreements. Relationships between buyers and sellers are more effective and long-lasting when both parties cooperate with one another, have mutual trust in one another, and realize that each of them needs the other.[2] In dealing with organizational customers, keep in mind the slogan Vidal Sassoon used to sell hair treatment products: "If you don't look good, we don't look good."

**Relationship Selling**
Focuses on all activities aimed at creating, developing, and maintaining successful exchange relationships with prospects and customers.

## INDUSTRIAL MARKETS

Largest and most diverse of all the organizational markets, industrial markets offer outstanding opportunities for anyone considering a professional selling career. There are more careers in industrial selling than in other kinds of selling because many more transactions occur at the business level between members of the channels of distribution. In addition, almost all industries buy from and sell to one another in creating products for the final consumer. Thus, the dollar volume of industrial marketing transactions far exceeds that in consumer markets.

### North American Industry Classification System (NAICS)

**North American Industry Classification System (NAICS)** Covers more than nineteen thousand industry descriptions, used to identify new business prospects and their general product and service requirements by up to six digits of specificity.

One of the best basic sources for identifying new business prospects and their general requirements is the **North American Industry Classification System (NAICS)** published by the U.S. Office of Management and Budget (OMB). NAICS, pronounced "nakes," replaces the old Standard Industrial Classification (SIC) System and provides for standardization in reporting economic data between Mexico, Canada, and the United States. NAICS is more detailed than SIC and provides better coverage of services such as health care, entertainment, and financial institutions. As illustrated in Figure 9.1, the

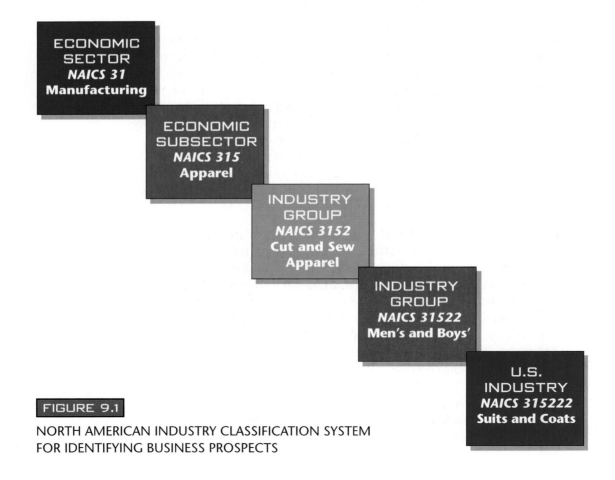

ECONOMIC SECTOR
*NAICS 31*
**Manufacturing**

ECONOMIC SUBSECTOR
*NAICS 315*
**Apparel**

INDUSTRY GROUP
*NAICS 3152*
**Cut and Sew Apparel**

INDUSTRY GROUP
*NAICS 31522*
**Men's and Boys'**

U.S. INDUSTRY
*NAICS 315222*
**Suits and Coats**

**FIGURE 9.1**

NORTH AMERICAN INDUSTRY CLASSIFICATION SYSTEM FOR IDENTIFYING BUSINESS PROSPECTS

NAICS code starts with the broad industry category identified by two digits then focuses more specifically on products and services with each additional digit. For more information, check out www.naics.com.

### Industrial Market Characteristics

Industrial markets differ significantly from consumer markets in the areas of (a) demand, (b) buyers, (c) purchasing process, and (d) marketing mix, as outlined in Table 9.1. Let's briefly discuss these differences.

**Demand.** Industrial demand tends to be **derived demand:** demand for the industrial good comes from demand for a consumer good. For example, Ford Motor's demand for sheet steel from a steel manufacturer as an input in manufacturing automobiles is derived from consumer demand for Ford automobiles.

**Derived Demand**
Demand created as a result of consumer demand; typical of industrial markets.

**TABLE 9.1**

### INDUSTRIAL VERSUS CONSUMER MARKET CHARACTERISTICS

| Characteristics | Industrial Market | Consumer Market |
|---|---|---|
| **Demand** | Derived | Direct |
| | Price inelasticity | Price elasticity |
| | More volatile | Less volatile |
| | Relatively few buying centers | Many individuals or households |
| **Buyer** | Buying centers | Individual or household buyers |
| | Professional | Amateur |
| **Purchasing Process** | Long negotiations | Short negotiations |
| | Infrequent purchases | Frequent purchases |
| | Large order size ($s or units) | Small order size ($s or units) |
| | Servicing expected | Servicing not expected |
| | Reciprocity often demanded | No reciprocity demanded |
| | Often lease | Seldom lease |
| **Marketing Mix:** | Customized, more technical | Standardized, less technical |
| *Products/Services* | Formal bids | List prices |
| *Price* | Emphasis on personal selling | Emphasis on advertising |
| *Promotion* | Shorter channels | Longer channels |
| *Distribution* | Buy direct from producers | Buy through middlemen (for example, retailers) |

If the demand for automobiles weakens, so will the demand for sheet steel to produce automobiles. Price *elasticity* of demand (the degree to which demand is sensitive to changes in price) is another characteristic of industrial demand, especially in the short run, when industrial producers find it difficult to make changes in production methods. In *consumer* markets, sometimes even a small upward change in price will have a large negative impact on consumer demand, meaning that demand is *elastic* with respect to price. In industrial markets, however, a comparatively small change in price usually will have little or no impact on overall demand, meaning that demand is *inelastic* with respect to price. Finally, industrial demand is characterized by *volatility*. Because industrial goods are so affected by final consumer demand, a small change in consumer demand creates a much larger change in the demand for industrial goods and services.

**Buyers.** Industrial buyers tend to be geographically concentrated. About half of the nation's producers are in seven states: New York, California, Pennsylvania, Illinois, Ohio, New Jersey, and Michigan. Industrial buyers are also usually grouped into buying centers or committees, which typically include technical experts and top management. Salespeople need to be well trained and well prepared to make presentations before such groups of experts.

**Purchasing Process.** Industrial purchases are less frequent and normally require a longer negotiation period than do consumer purchases. This is because the industrial product is generally made to order, which requires agreement on exact specifications, and because industrial buyers often require formal bids, which requires time for the seller to prepare precise cost estimates. If the product is complex and expensive, industrial organizations often buy directly from producers instead of going through industrial distributors or other middlemen. Major airlines, for example, buy their aircraft directly from manufacturers such as Boeing or Lockheed Martin.

**Reciprocity** In industrial buyer-seller relationships, an informal agreement between two or more organizations to exchange goods and services on a systematic and more or less exclusive basis. In other words, "you buy from me, and I'll buy from you."

**Reciprocity** often figures in industrial buying. Taking our cue from the old saying, "If you scratch my back, I'll scratch yours," we can define reciprocity, in the context of industrial organizations, as a *mutual exchange of benefits.* In other words, "I'll buy from you if you'll buy from me." A company that procures hardwood veneers and laminates, for example, might buy its office desks and bookcases from its biggest customer, an office furniture maker. Most such reciprocal arrangements are not backed by a formal contract, though some companies have a "trade relations" departments to keep track of their reciprocal buying arrangements with various customers and suppliers. Companies that develop long-term relationships based on reciprocity have found it to be a beneficial competitive tool.[3] Smaller companies tend to make most use of reciprocal agreements. However, systemic practice of reciprocity can also damage morale in a company's sales force and its purchasing department. Surveys show that most purchasing agents and salespeople dislike reciprocity because it restricts their ability to negotiate for the best terms with reciprocating partners.[4]

Finally, even though reciprocity may sound like a reasonable business practice, the Federal Trade Commission and the Justice Department's antitrust division prohibit it if it becomes anticompetitive. Contracts requiring an exclusive supplier arrangement, exclusive dealing, or tying agreement generally have been found illegal in court. Buyers must be able to show that they are obtaining competitive prices, quality, and service from suppliers with whom they are reciprocating.

*Leasing* in lieu of purchasing is a rapidly growing option in industrial organizations. Each year, U.S. companies lease billions of dollars worth of equipment, ranging from power plants and offshore drilling rigs to office copiers and forklift trucks. Company cars, computers, and machine tools that have high obsolescence are frequently leased to save capital investment funds and ensure the latest technology.

**Marketing Mix.** The many differences between industrial and consumer markets in terms of demand, buyers, and purchasing process require that companies selling to industrial organizations develop marketing mixes tailored to specific customer groups and their unique needs. Because sellers must anticipate and satisfy the changing needs of industrial customers who, in turn, are trying to satisfy the needs of their own customers, it is easy to understand why personal selling is the most important factor in their marketing mixes. Every successful company knows that the only way to sell to industrial organizations is to have salespeople who make it their job to understand their customers' organizations inside and out. For this reason, companies make major investments in training their industrial salespeople. As the role of purchasing becomes more strategic to the success of most organizations, salespeople must develop unique *value propositions* for their prospects and customers. Motorola, for example, seeks to establish relationships only with parts suppliers that can provide cutting-edge technology to increase the perceived value of Motorola's products for customers and thereby strengthen its competitive position in diverse markets. Cisco Systems enhances its value proposition by selling directly to organizational customers from its web site. At anytime, buyers can log on to www.cisco.com and start through the stages in the buying process. In the early stages, customers can search first for specific products, specifications, prices, and lead times. Then, before making their final selections, they can try different configurations online to see how proposed changes affect prices. After ordering, buyers can go online whenever they wish to check the delivery status of their purchases and order follow-on services, parts, or product upgrades.

## The Role of the Industrial Buyer

**Industrial buyers** (frequently called *purchasing agents*) are buying experts for their organizations. Large companies have purchasing departments with many purchasing agents, each specializing in buying a particular product or service from various salespeople who call on them. Over the past few decades, the industrial buyer's role and responsibilities have expanded from being little more than a clerk to those of an executive. With increasing competition world wide, the industrial buyer has had to become a highly sophisticated career professional. Skillful purchasing, especially during times of resource shortages, is a major determinant of an organization's profitability. Thus, an organization's success largely depends on industrial buyers' ability to do the following well:[5]

**Industrial Buyer** The buying expert for an organization. Also, sometimes called the purchasing agent.

*Foundation goods, such as industrial robots, are used in the production process but do not become part of the finished product.*
Charles O'Rear/Corbis

- Negotiate favorable prices and purchase terms.
- Develop alternative solutions to buying problems while keeping organizational departments informed about negotiations.
- Protect the organization's cost structure (its cost of doing business).
- Ensure reliable, long-run sources of supply.
- Maintain good relationships with suppliers.
- Manage the procurement process (reorder procedures, order expediting, order receipt, and record control).

To successfully develop and maintain long-run relationships with customers, you must keep in mind all of the foregoing goals of industrial buyers. Unless you help them succeed, you won't succeed. "Win-Win" relationships are the only ones that last.

### What Do Industrial Markets Buy?

We can develop our perspective on the industrial buying process, with its diffused buying influences and diverse products and services, by classifying goods on the basis of their relationship to the organization's production process and cost structure. Industrial buyers are interested in three basic categories of goods and services. The categories are described below and Table 9.2 illustrates product examples.

**Foundation Goods**
Goods used in the production process that do not become part of the finished product, such as fixed major equipment and office equipment.

1. **Foundation goods** are used in the production process but do not become a part of the finished product (for example, installations, accessory equipment, office equipment).

**Entering Goods**
Ingredients or components that become part of the finished product, such as raw materials and semimanufactured goods.

2. **Entering goods** are components that become part of the finished product (for example, raw materials, semimanufactured goods, parts, manufacturing services).

**Facilitating Goods**
Goods consumed while assisting in the ongoing production process, such as maintenance and repair items.

3. **Facilitating goods** are goods and services consumed in the production process (for example, maintenance and repair items, operating supplies, business services).

### How Do Industrial Markets Buy?

**Buying Centers.** In larger organizations, it's realistic to refer to industrial purchasing operations as **buying centers,** because several people participate in purchasing decisions. A buying center consists of all people in the organization who participate in or influence the purchase decision process. This includes anyone playing any of the following six roles in the buying process:

**Buying Center**  In a buying organization, a group of organization members who participate in the purchase decision.

1. *Initiators:* People who first recognize or anticipate a problem that may be solved by buying a good or service.

| TABLE 9.2 |
|---|
| CLASSIFICATION OF INDUSTRIAL GOODS |

**Foundation Goods**

**Installations:** Items considered part of the fixed plant of the purchaser.

*Examples:* Large machine tools, printing presses, electric generators, elevators.

**Equipment:** Capital investment items not regarded as part of the fixed plant.

*Examples:* Motor trucks, portable tools, typewriters, desks.

**Entering Goods**

**Raw Materials:** Unprocessed primary materials from agriculture and other extractive industries.

*Examples:* Wheat, livestock, cotton, crude petroleum, iron ore, lumber.

**Semimanufactured Goods:** Finished output of one manufacturer or processor that undergoes additional changes in its form by another.

*Examples:* Sheet steel, basic chemicals, cement, textiles sold to garment manufacturers, flour sold to bakeries.

**Parts:** Manufactured products that can be installed as a component of larger products.

*Examples:* Electric motors, automobile batteries and tires (original equipment), thermostats for refrigerators.

**Contract Manufacturing Services:** Part of the manufacturing process contracted to an outside organization.

*Examples:* Dyeing, casting, cutting, or shaping services performed by a company on materials supplied by the customer.

**Facilitating Goods**

**Maintenance and Repair Items:** Quickly consumed and highly expendable items that help ensure the continued satisfactory functioning of plant and equipment.

*Examples:* Repair parts, lubricants, nails, cleaning materials, paint.

**Operating Supplies:** Items required for day-to-day operations.

*Examples:* Copier paper, cash-register tape, pencils.

**Business Services:** Services provided by others, often involving the use of supplies.

*Examples:* Printing services, janitorial or cleaning services, business repair services, consulting or advertising services.

2. *Gatekeepers:* People who control information or access to decision makers are **gatekeepers.** Purchasing agents, technical advisers, secretaries, and even telephone switchboard operators can assume this role by preventing salespeople from seeing users or deciders. In situations where sales reps

**Gatekeeper** Person who controls information or access to decision makers. Examples include technical advisers, secretaries, security guards, and even telephone switchboard operators.

**Influencers** People who can influence the purchase decision by helping set product specifications, negotiating purchasing procedures and prices, or providing information about evaluating alternatives.

cannot win over gatekeepers, they will have to find ways to subtly go around them to make sales.

3. *Influencers:* **Influencers** affect the purchase decision by helping set product and service specifications, negotiating purchasing procedures and prices, or by providing information about evaluating alternatives. Technical specialists usually are important influencers.

4. *Deciders:* In many cases these are higher-level managers who have power to select or approve suppliers and final purchase decisions. For routine purchases, the purchasing agents are the deciders.

5. *Buyers:* People with formal authority to order supplies and negotiate purchase terms within organizational constraints.

6. *Users:* People who will actually use the product or service purchased. Users are generally people in production, including machine operators, shop foremen, and supervisors. Users often initiate the buying proposal and help decide product specifications.

Successful salespeople must know all members of the buying center and the roles they play, because each one can influence the purchasing decision. What's more, salespeople must provide each member the precise information needed to facilitate the eventual sale. Because several individuals take part in the buying process, the ultimate sale is likely to be time consuming. So patience and diligence are required when selling to buying centers.

Some salespeople virtually move in with their large customers; that is, they work with them on a daily basis and may set up an office near by or even in the buyer's headquarters or factory.[6] Doing so helps them keep attuned to the multiple buying influences in order to do some multilevel, in-depth, consultative selling. Ask the salespeople in any company: "Are you, with most customers, dealing with the same purchasing agents today as you were five years ago?" Usually, the answer is no. People in the customer organization are continually changing—they may leave the company, receive a promotion to a different job, take a long vacation, retire, or become ill. Farsighted salespeople acquaint themselves with *all* possible members of the buying center to keep their relationship with the customer from depending on just one person. In other words, they don't put all their eggs in one basket, i.e., one relationship.

**Types of Buying Situations.** Industrial buyers face a series of decisions that depend on each buying situation. Figure 9.2 illustrates three basic types of buying situations: (1) straight rebuy, (2) modified rebuy, and (3) new task. Purchasing agents are most influential in straight rebuys and modified rebuys, which involve, respectively, routine and limited problem-solving skills. But engineers are most influential in new task buying, which requires extensive problem-solving skills.

***Straight Rebuy.*** A routine, programmable decision is a *straight rebuy,* where the buyer reorders something from a supplier on the "approved list." Examples of straight rebuys include purchases of bulk chemicals, utilities, or office supplies. Suppliers on the approved list strive to maintain product and service quality and encourage automatic-reordering systems to save the purchasing agent's time and keep out other suppliers. Suppliers not on the

INCREASING COMPLEXITY

| Extensive Problem Solving | Limited Problem Solving | Routine Response |
| --- | --- | --- |

NEW TASK BUY | MODIFIED REBUY | STRAIGHT REBUY

### FIGURE 9.2

THREE TYPES OF INDUSTRIAL BUYING SITUATIONS

approved list must try to get their foot in the door by offering something new or by providing an incentive such as price discounts or greater service to obtain a small order. Once on the list, and after performing well on a small order, the salesperson can seek larger orders.

***Modified Rebuy.*** A more complex decision process requiring more information and involving more decision participants is a *modified rebuy*. Such purchases come about when the buyer seeks a change in product specifications, prices, supplier performance, or the like. In this situation, "in" suppliers run scared trying to protect their relationship with the buyer, while "out" suppliers offer customers various inducements to switch to them. Examples of modified rebuys are consulting services and new company cars or trucks.

***New Task.*** A supplier's greatest opportunity comes when the buyer considers purchasing a product or service for the first time. Examples of a new task might be the purchase of a huge installation such as a heating plant or the construction of a new building. The first-time purchase of a complex new product or service calls for the largest amount of information and the most decision participants. Buyers must determine product specifications, price limits, delivery terms and times, service requirements, payment terms, order quantities, acceptable suppliers, and the selected supplier. As we mentioned in chapter 5 (the sales presentation), such a process often begins with specialized sales teams of salespeople and technical specialists who make comprehensive presentations "selling the company" to the potential customer. The new task buying situation comes up rather infrequently, but it is vital that salespeople be well prepared to make their presentations for these purchase situations because winning the contract can lead to many spin-off rebuys later on. Try resolving an organizational purchase problem in *It's Up to You* on p. 282.

**Stages in the Buying Process.** Today's industrial buyers often know much more about industrial selling behavior than the industrial salesperson knows about industrial buying behavior. So salespeople who fail to understand how their potential customers make their buying decisions will be severely disadvantaged. Thoroughly researching and understanding the

## IT'S UP TO YOU

Y ou recently sold an air conditioning and heating system to Beecher Company, a small manufacturer. You were even present when the system was installed. After about a month, you receive a call from Beecher. The buyer is arguing that the new system is not effective—their building is either too hot or too cold, and employ-ees are constantly complaining about the room temperature. The buyer is demanding that the new system be removed and a better one installed at no additional cost. What is your first step? If you need further information, where will you look or whom will you ask? How will you resolve this problem?

customers' buying process is one of the selling secrets of super salespeople. There are eight major stages in the industrial buying process: (1) recognizing the problem, (2) describing the basic need, (3) developing product specifica-tions, (4) searching for suppliers, (5) soliciting proposals, (6) evaluating pro-posals and selecting suppliers, (7) setting up the order procedure, and (8) reviewing performance. Let's discuss each of these steps briefly.

***Recognizing the Problem.***  The window of opportunity opens for alert sales-people when a business customer complains about your competitor's equip-ment or products, or when machines break down, supplies and inventories become low, materials are in short supply, current products or services are unsatisfactory, new equipment is being installed, or new products are under consideration. Of course, if yours are the products and services not performing well, you're challenged to do something fast to keep the customer's business. You must remain continually sensitive to means of improving the customer's profitability by anticipating problems and alerting customers to opportunities (recall discussions about post-sale follow up in chapter 8).

***Describing the Basic Need.***  After recognizing the problem, the industrial buyer tries to better define the needed item's general characteristics through discussions with company engineers, research and development scientists, or line managers. At this stage, the buyer organization usually conducts a feasi-bility study to determine whether it would be better to make the item them-selves or to buy it.

***Developing Product Specifications.***  The buying organization develops detailed technical specifications to ensure that no error is made by the indus-trial buyer or the suppliers in providing the exact item needed. Any confusion about the exact specifications (dimensions, quality, or quantity) can result in costly manufacturing delays for the customer and lost business (rejected items) for the supplier. Many times, especially with government customers, suppliers will try to work with buyers to write tight specs designed to enable their own companies to secure the business. Most buyers, though, oppose any product specifications so rigid as to limit consideration of supplier alternatives. This is because no buyer wants to be dependent on a sole supplier unless the buyer has extreme leverage over the supplier (for example, a large company whose purchases represent a major share of a small company's sales).

**Searching for Suppliers.** Using product specifications as the guide, the buyer tries to identify qualified potential suppliers (sometimes called *vendors*). Trade directories and recommendations from other industrial buyers are useful in this search phase. Aggressive sales organizations will probably have already solicited business with most potential customers, but unsolicited "call-ins" are still a valuable source of sales. And inside salespeople who handle these call-ins must be as well trained as outside salespeople. Beyond this, salespeople should ensure that their company and its offerings are listed in all appropriate trade directories and that the company's reputation as a supplier remains favorable. Repeat business and referrals from satisfied customers are the fastest, most secure ways to a profitable sales operation.

**Soliciting Proposals.** Industrial buyers will usually invite qualified suppliers to submit proposals for producing and selling the specified items. After reviewing these proposals, the buyer will often invite formal presentations by the more promising potential suppliers. Thus, professional salespeople require training in researching, preparing, and presenting proposals so that they can "sell" the company as well as the technical product. In preparing and presenting sales proposals, professional salespeople keep in mind five basic decision criteria used by nearly all organizational buyers:

1. *Performance criteria:* How well will the product or service do the required job?
2. *Economic criteria:* What is the total cost associated with buying and using the product or service?
3. *Integrative criteria:* Will the supplier be flexible and responsive in working closely with us to meet our changing requirements and expectations?
4. *Adaptive criteria:* How likely is the seller to produce and deliver according to specifications and terms?
5. *Legalistic criteria*: What legal or policy parameters must be considered in buying the product or service?[7]

**Evaluating Proposals and Selecting Suppliers.** In reviewing the proposals prior to awarding a contract, industrial buying organizations evaluate the potential supplier on various criteria. These criteria vary depending upon the size and nature of the buying organization as well as the type of product. Delivery capability, product quality, service, technical ability, and price are usually most important in buying technically complex products. In this stage, it is especially important for salespeople to keep in mind that the engineering department is usually the most influential in new-task buying, while the purchasing department has the most influence in straight rebuys and modified rebuys.

**Setting Up the Ordering Procedure.** Instead of preparing a new contract for each periodic purchase order, most industrial buyers prefer *blanket contracts* that establish an open purchase arrangement over a stated period at a certain price so that reorders are routine. Computerized ordering procedures are

## KEEPING UP ONLINE:
## GENERAL ELECTRIC CORPORATION

eneral Electric (GE) Corporation produces a wide array of different products and offers a variety of services to various markets. Visit their web site at http://www.ge.com/ and describe the different markets their salespeople must serve. Does GE have a different sales force for each of these markets? How might GE use its web site to obtain customer feedback on its performance?

common for staple supplies. An order is automatically printed out or emailed to the designated supplier whenever inventory reaches a specified level. Salespeople often suggest setting up blanket purchase agreements when they win an order because such an arrangement encourages single-source buying through automatic reordering.

***Reviewing Performance.***  Many industrial buyers proactively and regularly contact the end-user departments in their company to obtain feedback on suppliers' performance. These performance reviews, which can be relatively casual conversations or detailed, formal ratings, shape relationships with suppliers by continuing, modifying, or terminating purchase orders. Salespeople should constantly review their own performances so that problems are "nipped in the bud." Read *Keeping Up Online* to discover how one web site may help prevent you from making key mistakes during the buying process.

## RESELLERS

Resellers include all those intermediary organizations that buy goods for reselling or leasing to others at a profit or for conducting their own operations. Resellers serve as purchasing agents for their customers, so they buy products and brands that they think will appeal to their customers.

### Kinds of Resellers

The following are three categories of resellers:

1. *Industrial distributors*, which sell to manufacturers and producers
2. *Wholesalers*, which sell to retailers
3. *Retailers*, which sell to consumers

**Industrial Distributors.**  Industrial distributors in the United States number about twelve thousand, with each generating an average yearly sales volume of about four million dollars. E-commerce between businesses represents more than 90 percent of the estimated four trillion dollars in e-commerce sales in 2003.[8] They handle a variety of products: maintenance, repair, and operating (MRO) supplies; original equipment (OEM) that becomes part of the manufacturer's finished products; and tools, equipment, and machinery used in the operation of the business. There are three kinds of industrial distributors. *General-line distributors* (mill supply houses) are the "supermarkets" of industry because of the broad range of products they carry. *Specialist firms* stock a narrow line of related products, such as bearings, abrasives, and cutting tools. General-line houses have been developing specialist departments, so the difference between these two types has blurred. A third type, the *combination house*, operates like a wholesaler as well by selling to retailers and institutions in addition to manufacturers and construction firms. Industrial distributors are increasing in importance as their sales volume continues to exceed the growth of our gross national product. Generally, salespeople who work for industrial distributors sell to manufacturers and constructions firms.

**Wholesalers.** Wholesaling organizations serve the buying requirements of resellers who, in turn, sell to consumers. The three basic types of wholesalers are (1) merchant wholesalers; (2) agents, brokers, and commission merchants; and (3) manufacturers' sales branches. Merchant wholesalers, often called distributors, account for more than 80 percent of all wholesalers in the United States.[9] Salespeople who sell to retailers work for various types of *full-service* and *limited-service* merchant wholesalers (for example, brokers, agents, or manufacturer's sales branches).

**Retailers.** More than 1.6 million retailers in the United States employ more than twenty million people. This number has stayed relatively constant over the past twenty-five years, while sales volume has quadrupled to nearly three trillion dollars annually.[10]

*Chain stores*—centrally owned and managed groups of retail stores—account for more than one-third of all retail sales even though they comprise less than one percent of all retail establishments. Despite the growing importance of chains, *single-unit, independently owned stores* remain prevalent in retailing. This ownership category accounts for more than 90 percent of all retail stores. Most retail salesclerks are little more than order takers and have traditionally been paid poor hourly wages. Only recently have a few large chains begun offering commissions on sales to all of their retail salespeople, thereby providing the incentive for them to do creative selling.

## Reseller Buying Situations

Salespeople dealing with *reseller* buyers should know that resellers generally find themselves involved in three types of buying situations. Let's discuss each briefly.

**New-Product Situation.** The *new-product situation* arises when suppliers seek distribution for a newly developed product. Because storage and display space are always at a premium, the buyer often must determine what item to drop if the new product is to be ordered for stock. Many buyers estimate potential profit per cubic foot before making a decision. Buyers typically consider such factors as profit margins, product uniqueness, seller's intended positioning and marketing plan, test market results, promotional support, and seller's reputation when determining whether to take on a new product. Also, many supermarket chains demand "slotting allowances"—payments up front before they will make room for a new product on their shelves. Some supermarkets even demand "pay to stay" payments to keep the manufacturer's product on the shelves.

**Selection of the Best Supplier.** Resellers must *select the best supplier* from several, when space limitations permit only one or two brands in a product category, or when they require a private-label supplier for their own house brand. For example, Sears chose Whirlpool Corporation to make its private-label Kenmore clothes washers, so Whirlpool has the inside track in selling its other brands of home appliances, including KitchenAid and Roper, to Sears stores.

**Better Set of Terms from Current Suppliers.** The third buying situation comes about when the reseller wants to obtain *a better set of terms from current suppliers*. McDonald's, the world's most successful food franchiser, decided a few years ago to buy all its food and nonfood products from one supplier. Golden State Foods Corporation, which was supplying McDonald's burgers, buns, and potatoes, was forced to take on a line of paper products to keep McDonald's business, which accounted for 80 percent of Golden State's sales at the time.

### Reseller Information Systems

In recent years we have seen the rapid rise of the *professional reseller manager*, who is more scientific and information oriented than his or her predecessor. Although electronic point-of-sale (POS) systems and in-store computers began appearing in retail outlets in the early 1970s, computer software packages to efficiently managing inventory, purchases, cash flow, and accounts payable information were slow in arriving. Installation of checkout scanners has generated an abundance of timely and specific data about consumer response. Instead of receiving monthly or bimonthly reports about how a brand is doing, retailers now receive weekly or even daily data for every item and size. They are learning precisely how a price cut, promotional coupon, store display, or quantity discount actually affects sales and profits. For example, Nestlé Foods Corporation discovered that a combination of store displays and newspaper ads resulted in large volume increases for its chocolate drink, *Quik*. Warner-Lambert found that store displays were far more effective than newspaper ads or price promotions, and its sales force now focuses on providing incentives to supermarket managers to set up in-store displays.

### Computer-Assisted Buying

Today's customers place increasing value upon having timely information and will often award their business to the seller who provides the best information. For instance, after outfitting its salespeople with laptop computers, Evan-Picone Hosiery sharply reduced the turnaround time between receiving, manufacturing, and delivering sales orders. In addition, the company can spot

---

### TABLE 9.3

## SPECIAL INDUCEMENTS IN SELLING TO RESELLERS

**Automatic Reordering Systems:** Seller sets up the system and provides forms for reseller to automatically reorder products.

**Preticketing:** Seller places a tag on each product, listing its price, color, size, manufacturer, and identification number so the reseller can track products sold.

**Stockless Purchasing:** Seller carries the inventory and delivers goods to the reseller on short notice.

**Cooperative Advertising:** Seller shares costs when reseller advertises seller's products.

**Advertising Aids:** Seller provides in-store displays, glossy photos, broadcast scripts, television videotapes, and print ads.

**Special Prices:** Seller reduces prices for store promotions to attract customers.

**Sponsorship of In-Store Demonstrations:** Seller sets up in-store demonstrations to show shoppers how products work and to persuade them to buy.

**Generous Allowances:** Seller gives attractive allowances for reseller returns, exchanges, and markdowns of seller products.

**Source:** *From Philip Kotler,* Marketing Management: Analysis, Planning, Implementation, and Control *(Englewood Cliffs, N.J.: Prentice-Hall, 2000). Copyright © 2000 by Philip Kotler. Reprinted by permission of Pearson Education, Inc. Upper Saddle River, NJ.*

---

fashion trends earlier now that they know the status of every order for every product. This information has helped Evan-Picone serve its customers better and thereby win more sales.

As reseller information systems based on computerized purchasing operations increase in sophistication, the professional salesperson's job will rapidly shift toward providing buyers with detailed and comprehensive data. Some large manufacturers' sales forces have already edged ahead of the competition by providing retailer customers with individualized merchandising service. For example, salespeople for R. J. Reynolds Tobacco show retail customers various ways to increase profits by better use of display space, new merchandising techniques, and improved inventory control. See Table 9.3 for several other sales tools that can help salespeople make their offerings more attractive to resellers.

## GOVERNMENT MARKETS

The U.S. government, fifty state governments, more than three thousand county governments, and nearly eighty-seven thousand local governments purchase well more than a trillion dollars worth of goods and services annually. Federal, state, and local governmental unit spending has increased rapidly over the years with increasing services provided for citizens. Total purchases in the trillions of dollars makes the United States federal government the largest customer in the world.[11]

## Sales Opportunities in Government Markets

Government markets offer opportunities for both producers and middlemen to sell everything from spacecraft to toothpaste—everything needed to provide citizens with necessary services such as national defense, fire and police protection, education, health care, water, postal service, waste disposal, and public transportation. Government purchasing patterns sometimes change abruptly in response to budget constraints and the service demands of citizens, which can present a problem—or an opportunity—for sellers. The **FedBizOpps.gov** web site lists federal government procurement opportunities over twenty-five thousand dollars. Through this single portal, commercial vendors seeking federal markets for their products and services can search, monitor, and retrieve opportunities being solicited by the entire federal contracting community.

**FedBizOpps.gov** Web site that contains all federal contracting community solicitations for purchases exceeding twenty-five thousand dollars.

## How Do Governments Buy?

Governments spend public funds derived largely from taxes. So, by law, their purchases must be made on the basis of bids or written proposals from vendors. Although purchasing procedures are rigorous in order to ensure quality products and honest, efficient expenditures, selling to governments can be profitable for sellers willing to cope with some bureaucratic red tape. Government purchasing agents have the basic goal of obtaining goods and services from the lowest-cost, qualified supplier. Sometimes, however, this goal comes second to such objectives as favoring small businesses, minority-owned companies, or suppliers from depressed areas.

Federal buying serves two sectors, civilian and military. For the federal government's civilian sector, the General Services Administration (GSA), through its Office of Federal Supply and Services, buys all general goods and services (such as office furniture, equipment, supplies, vehicles, and fuels) for use by other government agencies. Defense Department purchases are made by the Defense Logistics Agency (DLA) and the three military services, the army, navy, and air force. DLA operates specialized supply centers that function as "single managers" for purchasing and distributing construction materials, electronics, fuel, personnel support, and industrial and general supplies used in common by the army, navy, and air force. In addition, each branch of the military buys its specialized needs through its own supply system.

Both the GSA and DLA function as wholesalers and resellers for other government units. Together they account for most federal contracts for goods and services, although nearly five hundred other offices in Washington have their own buying functions and procurement policies. Most states have procurement offices to help carry out these massive federal government purchasing activities. Booklets explaining the procedures to follow in selling to governments are available at state purchasing offices and the U.S. Government Printing office. For more information, see the following web sites: http://www.access.gpo.gov/su_docs/ and http://www.access.gpo.gov/#business.

# FROM THE COMMAND POST: THE PRIME MINISTER AS HIGH-TECH SALESPERSON

**P**art of successful personal selling involves persuading buyers to try new ways of thinking and doing. Politicians, too, often must convince their constituencies to adopt a certain philosophy, belief, or idea. And, like salespeople, some politicians are more adept at this than others. In fact, even the prime minister of a country must sometimes sell staff members—including some technophobes—on communicating in new ways! At the same time, the staff is working to sell the prime minister on other issues. Thus, efficient and effective communication is essential to "selling" ideas back and forth.

Janez Drnovsek, prime minister of Slovenia, faces just such a situation. Drnovsek discovered cyberspace in 1992, and since then nothing has been the same for his cabinet ministers. They all have desktop and laptop computers and virtually paperless offices. They spend hours each day receiving, processing, and sending email mails from other government officials. And when Drnovsek sends an email their way, they know that they must quickly prepare a reply.

Most cabinet meetings are conducted online. Each of the country's fifteen cabinet ministers receives cabinet business over a secure system that informs them of the meeting's issues (for example, taxes); then, ministers vote on the topic by clicking a button. They can even attach a note and send it to other cabinet members or just to Drnovsek.

The system also keeps track of what government email files each minister received and whether it was opened. Thus, cabinet members efficiency has been enhanced, as they no longer can claim (as in the past) that they have not received a certain written report. Meeting topics not resolved online sometimes require a face-to-face conference, but cabinet ministers only take their laptops—no paper or pens—to these meetings and, even then, some ministers "attend" via videophone!

Although ministers complain about some facets of the system—such as receiving emails at all hours of the day and night, and even during weekends and holidays—the system clearly has facilitated communication among government officials. In fact, rather than rely strictly on his staff to gather and filter information for him, Drnovsek often emails his ministers directly for the facts. Drnovsek thus represents a government official, who after his fancy was captured by the juggernaut of technology, "sold" the idea to his staff and is now reaping the rewards.

***Source:*** *"Brave New World,"* The Economist *(October 20, 2001): 53. Copyright © 2001 The Economist Newspaper Ltd. All rights reserved. Reprinted with permission. Further reproduction prohibited. www.economist.com.*

Oftentimes, government agencies must "sell" their ideas and viewpoints on various issues to people within their own organizations and to other government agencies. Consider the anecdote in *From the Command Post* about a prime minister who sells high-tech communication to his staff.

## NOT-FOR-PROFIT MARKETS

Nonprofit organizations, also called *noncommercial, nonbusiness,* or *not-for-profit* organizations, include colleges, hospitals, libraries, charities, churches, museums, or organizations such as the National Organization for Women (NOW), the American Association of Retired People (AARP), and the Red Cross. Too often, salespeople and their companies overlook many nonprofit organizations as prospects, perhaps thinking the opportunities for profitable sales are limited. This is a big mistake. Although nonprofit organizations themselves may not strive for profits, they can offer highly profitable opportunities for salespeople who are energetic and persistent enough to learn about the operations, goals, and problems these diverse organizations face while keeping in mind their unique characteristics. Many nonprofit organizations use buying processes similar to those of commercial businesses and buy everything from janitorial services to automobiles. However, nonbusiness organizations do have several distinct characteristics that salespeople must keep in mind throughout the selling-buying process and the ongoing relationship. The most important of these characteristics include

- *Multiple Objectives:* Nonprofits' "bottom line" consists of multiple nonfinancial and financial goals, such as the social impact of their efforts, the number of people served, and the amount of donations or gifts received.
- *Services and Social Change:* Rather than selling a tangible product, most nonprofits distribute ideas and services to change people's attitudes and behaviors.
- *Public Scrutiny:* Their dependence on public support, their tax-exempt status, and their operation in the public interest often place nonprofit organizations under close public scrutiny.
- *Dual Management:* Management in nonprofits usually includes both professional managers and artistic specialists; this **dual management** sometimes leads to conflicts about organizational goals, activities, and expenditure of funds.

**Dual Management** A management system in which both professional managers and specialists without managerial training run an organization, sometimes resulting in conflict. Typical of many nonprofit organizations.

## NEGOTIATING STYLES OF ORGANIZATIONAL BUYERS

Salespeople must be prepared to interact with a variety of behavioral styles in dealing with organizational buyers. Six different kinds of buyers have been identified.[12] Let's take a quick look at each.

Some organizational buyers are *hard bargainers* who keep several suppliers competing aggressively against one another to win the business. These buyers negotiate strenuously to win every possible concession from the salesperson. They tend to see the negotiations as a contest with every weapon pulled out to win. In dealing with hard bargainers, salespeople must guard against being pressured into an unprofitable agreement, because hard bargainers will readily switch to a new supplier who offers better terms next time.

*Facilitators* try to work efficiently and cooperatively with salespeople to reach mutually acceptable agreement. They understand that win-win arrangements are to each party's advantage and are a joy to work with. *Straight-shoot-*

*ers* exhibit honesty and integrity throughout negotiations and refrain from pressur-
ing the salesperson into concessions.
Salespeople must avoid the temptation to
take advantage of straight-shooters
because these buyers will be good long-
run customers as long as they are treated
fairly. *Socializers* enjoy the camaraderie in
interpersonal relationships and don't
want to be rushed through the sales presentation and close. Salespeople who stay
relaxed and informal in their sales presentations and spend some time in friendly
chit-chat will usually close sales with
these buyers. One study found that highly
sociable buyers are particularly focused on
the salesperson's ability to solve their
problem relative to less socializing buyers.[13]

*Does the prospect in this
situation look like a hard
bargainer, facilitator,
straight-shooter, social-
izer, persuader, or considerate buyer?*
Walter Hodges/Corbis

*Persuaders* try to make their own sales presentations about the reputation
and quality of their companies. Sometimes persuaders simply want to tell a
salesperson (who may be representing a better known organization) that their
organization deserves respect, too. Other times they are interested in convincing the salesperson that their organizations are successful and that treating
them well in purchasing agreements can lead to a long-term profitable relationship. Be patient and let persuaders tell their story. Show respect to them
and their organizations and express appreciation for their business.

*Considerate buyers* empathize with salespeople and try to work with them
to reach mutually acceptable agreements. These buyers are so considerate that
they will frequently accept product substitutes or even compromises in the
purchase agreement. Again, salespeople must never shortchange considerate
buyers just because they are more flexible than, say, hard bargainers.
Considerate buyers understand that a successful partnership always requires
give-and-take, so take a reasonable approach to negotiations. When you have
customers such as these, you are fortunate; treat them well.

Obviously, some buyers' negotiating styles will be harder to work with
than others. The challenge to the professional salesperson is to work out *win-
win* agreements with diverse buyer personalities.

## BUSINESS ORIENTATION OF ORGANIZATIONAL BUYERS

Organizational buyers differ with respect to the preferred kind of relationship
they have with salespeople. We can categorize three types of customers with
respect to their preferred relationship.[14] *Commercial friends* interact with salespeople like personal friends, as they share intimacy and casual conversation

and engage in joint leisure activities beyond the usual sales call (for example, attending sporting events). Such relationships tend to be long term. *Customer coworkers* treat salespeople almost like a fellow employee and meld both personal and business aspects of the relationship. They tend to form less intimate, but still long-term, buyer-seller relationships. *Business acquaintances* maintain a formal relationship with salespeople and are reliant on them for economic gain. Although the association is cordial—and may even incorporate discussions of personal life—it lacks intimacy and does not entail interaction beyond the business context.

Before even the first sales call, professional salespeople determine the kind of relationship their prospects and customers desire and adapt their behavior accordingly. This avoids a first impression of behavior that the customer considers inappropriate (for example, too chummy, too formal). Once you have done some background research, you will be better able to determine the best likely balance between product/service discussion and personal exchange. For instance, salespeople who spend more time discussing how their product or service can satisfy the prospect's needs and revealing more intimate personal information about themselves have better interaction with prospects on an initial sales call than those who do not conduct themselves in this fashion. Furthermore, salespeople who spend more time responding to customer-provided information and questions are more likely to interact again with the buyer than sales reps who do not engage in such behavior.[15] Read *On the Frontlines* to further consider which selling strategy to use with different decision-making styles of buyers.

## ON THE FRONTLINES

# *Buyers and Decision-Making Styles*

Buyers' firms tend to have one of three kinds of *decision-making styles*—planning oriented, entrepreneurially oriented, and bureaucratically oriented. A buyer's style influences his or her preferences for the seller's selling strategy. Therefore, the selling strategy a salesperson uses with a given customer should reflect that customer's decision-making style.

A *planning-oriented* style entails making decisions based on long-run considerations, as the needs of the firm are carefully evaluated and planned. It requires detailed information and consultations with multiple departments. The *entrepreneurially-oriented* style usually involves no formal policies and has one or two decision makers whose preferences and actions lead to the decision. Other company members provide little input, and decision making employs minimal technical information. A *bureaucratically-oriented* style is characterized by utilization of formal rules and policies that determine information flows, activities, and interactions among company members. The information matrix in Table 9.4 suggests how salespeople should attend to each type of buyer.

| | | | TABLE 9.4 |
|---|---|---|---|

## TYPE OF DECISION-MAKING STYLE

| Decision-Making Style Characteristics | Planning-Oriented Style | Entrepreneurially-Oriented Style | Bureaucratically-Oriented Style |
|---|---|---|---|
| Nature of buyer | Large company | Smaller company | Government or nonprofit agency |
| Number/type of decision maker | Group | One or two | Formal hierarchy |
| Number/type of sellers involved | Experts in selling firm matched with experts in buying firm | One person | Salesperson makes initial contact and fulfillment of order and follow-up done by support department |
| Decision-making time for buyer | Medium | Low | High |
| Decision-making procedure | Problem-solving oriented | Simple | Complex |
| Emphasis in sales presentation | Solution-oriented nature of the product or service | Innovative nature of the product or service | Product or service specifications and price advantages |

*Source:* Adapted from Arun Sharma and Rajnandini Pillai, "Customers' Decision-Making Styles and their Preference for Sales Strategies: Conceptual Examination and an Empirical Study," Journal of Personal Selling and Sales Management 16 (Winter 1996): 21–33.

## INTERNATIONAL NEGOTIATIONS

As domestic markets become saturated, nearly every company is interested in increasing international sales. This is little more than wishful thinking until the company's sales representatives find global customers, build trustful relationships, and bring the global sales concept to reality. With intensifying global competition, salespeople play major roles in helping the U.S. remain economically strong. Perspectives on negotiation strategies, time, desire to be liked, and the willingness to make concessions vary greatly from country to country. Therefore, U.S. salespeople who sell in overseas markets cannot be ethnocentric and assume that the U.S. way of conducting business is the only way. Rather, they must be extremely sensitive to individuals in international markets and cognizant of accepted business practices in those locales. To do otherwise is pure folly. So professional sales personnel must be especially aware of cultural differences that they will encounter when doing business with international organizational buyers and how those differences will influence the buyer-seller relationship.

### International Views of Negotiation

Buyers from other countries often see U.S salespeople as negotiating with a "winner-take-all" attitude. This attitude assumes that negotiation is a contest where the objective is to outwit the other side. It emphasizes bluffing, confrontation, areas of disagreement, and legalistic aspects of contracts. Europeans, by contrast, prefer to develop buyer-seller relationships up front that encourage win-win negotiations based on trust. Europeans want the agreement to be good not only for themselves but also for the other party. They are no more principled or generous, but they understand what's in their own long-run best interests. If an agreement is good for both parties, they acknowledge the added incentive for both parties to fully implement the agreement. Forcing the other party to accept an unfavorable agreement increases the likelihood that he or she will try to find ways to squirm out of the arrangement or to cut corners in implementing it.

International negotiators generally believe that trust and shared interests characterize a healthy relationship, not some complex legal contract. They place more importance on thoroughly understanding the other negotiators and their perspectives, so they like to spend time socializing before transacting business. This knowledge provides insights that facilitate the negotiations and improve the relationship. One successful Rockwell International salesperson made seven trips to Venezuela trying to close a sale for three jet transports. He shared several four-hour lunches with the prospect, discussing everything from politics to women, without any mention of his products or terms of sale. The prospective customer wanted to size up the U.S. sales representative before discussing business. Long, drawn-out negotiations that require socializing first are common even when U.S. companies deal with global suppliers.

### Concessions

Russians and Eastern Europeans are tough negotiators because they are slow to make concessions. They realize that any concession that they could make now can also be made next week. In contrast, Americans tend to make concessions quickly when negotiations don't move along quickly. Cultures also differ in the importance that negotiators attach to feelings of friendship toward the other party and their desire to create goodwill with their opponent. Russian and Eastern European negotiators, for instance, do not seem to care about their popularity with Westerners, so it is much easier for them to be rigid, inscrutable, and unwilling to reciprocate when the other side makes a concession.

U.S. salespeople negotiating in Japan frequently have found the pace of negotiations so frustrating that they've made expensive concessions long before the Japanese are even ready to negotiate. Japanese, Middle Eastern, and Latin American negotiators generally build in a great deal of maneuvering room between their opening stance and their planned final position. Extreme negotiation stances initially are part of their strategy so that they have plenty of maneuvering room to make concessions that will not hurt. Other cultures, such as the Latin Americans, assume that their opponents are also overreaching, and that every opening offer or asking price is highly negotiable.

## Know Your Negotiating Partner

When you engage in international negotiations, make yourself aware of local customers, traditions, customs, habits, and sensitivities. More than courtesy, this is a matter of practicality to avoid misunderstandings, enhance mutual respect, and increase the chances for success in the negotiations. In some countries, personal selling must be unobtrusive. For example, European industrial buyers dislike being seen with salespeople in public. Private areas are usually set aside at trade shows where negotiations between buyers and sellers can be conducted out of sight. France goes so far as to prohibit door-to-door selling. Before you approach customers in other countries, learn and be ready to adapt to unfamiliar behavioral rules. Read *On the Frontlines* for some insights on selling in Japan.

## Guidelines for Doing Business in International Markets

When you sell to global buyers, you may find that your typical way of selling in the domestic market is totally inappropriate for international buyers. Some caveats and guidelines for doing business with organizational buyers in international settings appear in Table 9.5.

## ON THE FRONTLINES

### *Selling in Japan*

Sales calls are not taken lightly in Japan. Professional salespeople never make a cold call on a Japanese prospect without a formal introduction. If a salesperson doesn't know anyone to make the introduction, he or she can contact the U.S. office of the Japanese company, call a U.S. federal or state government representative in Tokyo, or hire a consultant.

Relationships in Japan are based largely on trust. Insisting on a written contract will leave a negative impression with most Japanese businesspeople. Be content to seal the initial deal with a handshake and leave signing a written contract to another meeting. Do not try to ingratiate yourself *during* a business meeting by telling a joke or using humor. Even though Japanese businesspeople may laugh heartily before or after a business meeting, and later in a social setting, their business meetings are always strictly business.

Always accept after-hours social invitations, but never bring your spouse because the Japanese business executives will not bring theirs. At dinner, let the Japanese host pick the subjects of conversation. Wait for your host's toast before you sip your drink, and always keep your neighbor's glass full. Do not brag about yourself or members of your family during conversation because Japanese etiquette is to be humble, even about your children. An old Japanese saying is, "The nail that sticks up gets hammered down." To sell successfully in Japan, you must adapt your behavior to gain your prospect's respect and trust.

| | TABLE 9.5 |
|---|---|

## CONSIDERATIONS IN DOING INTERNATIONAL BUSINESS

**Don't Be in a Hurry:** U.S. salespeople usually want to get down to business, believing that "time is money." Rushing any negotiation generally puts salespeople at a great disadvantage and leads them to push forward without sufficient information. In other countries, U.S. salespeople must fight the temptation to try closing the sale quickly. Asian and South American cultures find our standard American directness offensive.

**Understand Time:** Salespeople who hope to negotiate business deals in developing nations may need to adjust their attitude toward time. Business appointments are flexible to people in most developing countries. If something comes up that's more important than business, like a festival or a wedding, then business is postponed. In Latin countries, it is called the "mañana" (tomorrow) syndrome. In Spain, people also move at a leisurely pace. Most offices and shops close for siesta (1:30 to 4:30 P.M.), and restaurants rarely reopen until after 9 P.M. and get into full swing about 11. However, attitudes toward time may vary widely within a given country. In São Paulo, Brazil, the pace is much like that of a large city in the United States. But in Rio de Janeiro, business discussions begin only after considerable socializing and when a feeling of simpatico (warm empathy and deep understanding) are established. People in developing countries also have a habit of "looping" their conversations. They may begin a conversation by talking about the last time they saw you or some other chitchat, then move into substantive issues concerning the business at hand—only to switch abruptly back to some social topic. This looping process is seldom a part of conversations with someone from their own country.

**Continue Gathering Information:** Even when well prepared, no salesperson has all the facts before negotiations begin. Some information is always missing, and some is soft information based on assumptions, opinions, or rumors. Therefore, it is important to use small talk during socializing and the negotiations themselves to obtain valuable information about your international counterparts and what issues they perceive as most important. Inexperienced salespeople tend to think that small talk at the beginning of negotiations is merely a perfunctory routine, not something truly useful.

**Be Comfortable with Silence:** Salespeople who try to fill any negotiating vacuum with talk can make serious mistakes. Japanese, Chinese, and Koreans use silence as a bargaining weapon when negotiating with U.S. salespeople. Because most Americans are uncomfortable with long periods of silence, they will often jump in and lower the price, just to start the conversation going again.

**Never Be Confrontational or Argumentative:** Seldom is anything gained in negotiations by losing your cool or attacking the other party. Such behavior makes it clear to the other side that you consider the negotiations a contest, not a shared partnership. Even belligerence contrived to gain a concession will be offensive to most negotiators and will seldom contribute to furthering the relationship. Always negotiate with a *buyer win-seller win* attitude and convey that feeling to international buyers.

**Thoroughly Prepare Before Any Negotiations:** Learn about the other parties' culture, religion, ethical standards, and social customs. Most U.S. salespeople are already at a language disadvantage in dealing with global prospects and may have to work through an interpreter. They cannot afford to neglect their homework in learning about their international prospects. Knowledge is power in any negotiation but especially in international negotiations.

(continued)

| TABLE 9.5 |
| --- |

## CONSIDERATIONS IN DOING INTERNATIONAL BUSINESS (CONTINUED)

**Stay Open to Different Negotiating Styles:** In Western countries, specific issues are tediously negotiated. Only after agreement has been reached on each of these separate issues is an overall agreement achieved. In Japan and Russia, however, packages are negotiated first. Individual issues will be discussed in increasing detail but will not be finally decided until after reaching agreement on the entire package.

**Try Negotiating by the Other Side's Rule Book:** Quoting a local proverb as the reason for doing something is far more likely to encourage agreement and obtain desired results. For example, when a U.S. business executive in Beijing wanted to exclude an item from a contract and met Chinese resistance because they wanted to operate on the basis of trust, the executive cited an old Chinese adage: "Man is mortal. What if one of us were to have an accident or pass away? How would our successors know what to do, in case of our absence, if we didn't leave a written record of our agreements?"

## Business Etiquette in Other Cultures

U.S. salespeople must learn as much as they can about local business etiquette when negotiating in different countries. Avoiding a mistake in business etiquette can often make the difference between successful and unsuccessful negotiations. Some major issues to be aware of and sensitive to are the following:

- *Use of business cards*—Always carefully read the prospect's title aloud and treat the business card with respect. Never just thrust it into your pocket without glancing at it.
- *Use of first names*—Avoid the temptation to use first names when meeting prospects from another country, which can appear disrespectful. Even in the United Kingdom, people may work with one another for decades but still use last names when addressing each another.
- *Eye contact*—Excessive eye contact can come across as too aggressive in many countries. In fact, in many Arab countries, men tend to avoid looking at women, as a sign of respect, when conversing with them.
- *Understanding what "yes" means*—In some cultures, such as Japan's, a positive response often is no more than a sign of politeness indicating that you are heard. It does not imply a positive response to your question.
- *Acceptance of gifts*—Always be careful about giving gifts to a man's wife. Always, too, make sure that any gift conveys no negative cultural meaning. For example, in Russia, giving cutlery says that "you are cutting the relationship." And in Japan, white (flowers or any item) connotes death.
- *Interpretation of smiling handshakes*—Even the common U.S. practice of smiling while shaking hands can suggest insincerity in some countries, for example, Germany.

- *Use of one's voice*—U.S. salespeople too often speak in loud, overly enthusiastic voices that prospects from other countries can interpret as overbearing and aggressive. Even in the United States, it's a wise practice to adapt one's voice to the tone and level of the prospect.
- *Posture and body language*—One's posture or body language can unintentionally convey offensive messages. For instance, in Arab countries, crossing your legs and showing the sole of your foot sends a negative message. In South American countries, the U.S. customary "okay" sign made by forming a circle of one's thumb and forefinger is tantamount to someone thrusting his middle finger upward in the United States.
- *Distance between buyer and seller*—While conversing with each other, people in many countries tend to stand much closer together than do people in the United States. For example, a U.S. salesperson who moves away from a Latin American prospect to regain his or her comfort zone of space may risk offending the prospect.
- *Awareness of host country holidays*—Some U.S. salespeople have made the incredibly naïve mistake of ignoring host country holidays and thinking that the host country also celebrates U.S. holidays.
- *Use of the term "foreigners"*—Never use the term "foreigners" when selling abroad. You are the foreigner there, not they.
- *Importance of face-to-face contact*—In many countries, such as Italy, face-to-face contact and negotiations are nearly always necessary to reach successful agreements, so the telephone, emails, and faxes won't do the job.
- *Importance of humility and modesty*—In many countries, humility and modesty—whether sincere or not—are characteristics always displayed in public. Exhibiting arrogance or over-confidence can be counterproductive to personal selling success. Even in the United States, salespeople should not overlook the value of humility and modesty, especially when first meeting prospects.

## SUMMARY

In this chapter we discussed organizational markets and how and why they buy. We examined the three types of purchasing situations, as well as the organizational buying process. In addition, we reviewed the four major kinds of organizational buyers—industrial, reseller, government, and nonprofit organizational markets. Then, we described the submarkets within each of these larger categories. Resellers include industrial distributors, wholesalers, and retailers who buy goods for reselling or leasing to others at a profit or for conducting their own operations. Government markets include the federal government and all state and local governments, which purchase goods and services in order to provide citizens with necessary services such as fire and police protection, education, and health care. Nonprofit markets, which include institutions and organizations such as colleges, hospitals, libraries, and charities, purchase goods and services in order to provide people with services, attract donations, or change public attitudes about social concerns and problems. Various roles of individual industrial buyers and industrial salespeople were also examined. Six kinds of organizational buyers were analyzed vis-à-vis their negotiation styles, three kinds of purchasers were described with respect to the kind of relationships they prefer to have with sellers, and three kinds of decision-making styles of buyers were presented. Finally, we explored doing business in international markets and what salespeople need to know and do to sell successfully in different cultures.

## KEY TERMS

Relationship selling

North American Industry Classification System (NAICS)

Derived demand

Reciprocity

Industrial buyer

Foundation goods

Entering goods

Facilitating goods

Buying center

Gatekeeper

Influencers

FedBizOpps.gov

Dual management

## CHAPTER REVIEW QUESTIONS

1. Compare and contrast industrial markets and consumer markets.

2. Explain why industrial demand is *derived* demand. Why are industrial markets more price inelastic and volatile than consumer markets?

3. Name the different criteria by which a company will measure the success of its purchasing agent.

4. What six roles can different members of a buying center play in the industrial buying process?

5. List, discuss, and give examples of the three types of industrial buying situations.

6. Name and describe the sequential stages in the industrial buying process.

7. Compare and contrast the three different types of decision-making styles used by professional buyers: (1) planning oriented, (2) entrepreneurially oriented, and (3) bureaucratically oriented. How would you negotiate with buyers who exhibit each of the three styles?

8. Briefly discuss government markets. What are two sectors the federal government buys for? How are most government purchases made? What sources of help in dealing with the government are available?

9. What five major characteristics distinguish nonprofit markets from the three other organizational markets?

10. Provide some basic guidelines and rules of business etiquette for salespeople selling in international markets.

## TOPICS FOR THOUGHT AND CLASS DISCUSSION

1. How would you go about becoming acquainted with members of an organization's "buying center"? How would you determine which specific role each person played?

2. What do you think about the practice of reciprocity in business?

3. If you were a small business owner who wanted to obtain some federal government contracts,

how would you find out how to sell to the government? Outline the steps that you would take.

4. What do you think are some of the reasons that U.S. salespeople sometimes fail when trying to negotiate contracts with prospects from other countries? What might they do to increase their success?

5. Of the four different types of organizations (manufacturers, resellers, governments, and nonprofits), which do you think you would most like to call upon as a salesperson? Which would you least like to call on? Why?

## PROJECTS FOR PERSONAL GROWTH

1. Your company's R&D department has developed a chemical compound made from corn by-products that provides airtight sealing properties when coated over various substances. R&D scientists believe that this product, tentatively named Sealatron, will have many uses in the heavy construction industry. They say it may be appropriate for a final coating on top of the outer insulation wrappings for large oil and gas pipes, power lines, and perhaps sewer and water mains. It might also be used for waterproofing the exteriors of commercial buildings. Go to your school library and use the North American Industry Classification System (NAICS) to research the potential markets for this new chemical sealant. How specifically can you define the potential markets by NAICS digits? Once you've found the level of specificity that you want, how will you use the NAICS information?

2. Assume that you sell for a small clothing manufacturer that wants to supply your company's undershirts, undershorts, and trousers to one or more of the military branches. Go to *FedBizOpps.gov* and see what information you can find about federal government solicitations for clothing contracts. What other web sites did you visit to find more information? Keep at it until you find at least two solicitations that you believe your company could bid on. Find out how, when, and where to submit your bid.

3. Select a country (other than the United States) in which you would like to sell products and services for a U.S.-based company. What are some basic considerations and rules of etiquette that you need to know and follow in order to sell successfully in this country?

## NOW WHAT AM I GOING TO DO?

Eaton Electronic Company, a manufacturer of electronic motors and controls with annual sales of about $150 million, was a steady customer of Mectronic Supplies Company for nearly four years. Eaton regularly bought all of its rheostats and resistors from Mectronic, and the relationship between the two companies had become almost like a partnership based on mutual trust and respect. Keith Shepherd, a senior sales rep for Mectronic who has serviced the Eaton account for the past four years, developed a particularly close relationship with two Eaton buyers, Debbie Roseman and Roger Dommermuth. The three of them even used to meet for an informal lunch every other Thursday.

Then, three months ago, a leveraged buyout of Eaton Electronic Company by National Electric Corporation brought about several changes in Eaton's management, from the senior level down through middle management. Eaton's fifty-five-year-old director of purchasing took early retirement and was quickly replaced by Herb Cuthbert, a purchasing manager from National Electric. Within the past two weeks three senior Eaton buyers, including Debbie Roseman and Roger Dommermuth, resigned to take jobs with other companies. Keith Shepherd was surprised by the sudden turnover of so many people. He only learned about Debbie and Roger leaving late last week, and neither has gone to a company that would be interested in buying anything Mectronic sold.

Early this morning, when calling on the new director of purchasing, Keith was told that all current purchasing arrangements would be reviewed for total performance and that, based on that review, some "changed relationships" with current suppliers might occur. From his preliminary review, Mr. Cuthbert said, "It looks like we're going to be dropping some suppliers. In fact, I'm not impressed by the performance of your company, Keith. You were up to a week late on three out of twelve shipments last year. Late shipments can cost us several thousand dollars in production downtime, and such poor performance will no longer be tolerated. I haven't looked at the number of defective parts or the quality of service that we've gotten from each supplier, but those will be other factors in our deci-

sions to drop or retain current suppliers. Finally, I should alert you that we will be requesting new sales proposals from the present and potential suppliers before signing any purchasing agreements for the coming year. In the future, we will expect our suppliers to be price competitive in addition to supplying quality products and total service."

Ever since his interview with Mr. Cuthbert, Keith has been thinking of what he might do to keep the Eaton business. He doesn't really know how well his company has performed over the past year; in fact, he was surprised to learn of the late deliveries because nobody at Eaton ever complained to him about the shipments. Perhaps, he thinks to himself, he has taken the Eaton account for granted because of the good relationships he enjoyed with Debbie Roseman and Roger Dommermuth. Herb Cuthbert, on the other hand, seems to be all business. Keith doubts that Cuthbert ever does anything in an informal way! The people who are replacing Debbie and Roger won't be starting until next Monday, so Keith doesn't know what to expect.

Keith can't afford to lose the Eaton account. It represents almost 15 percent of his annual commissions, and losing that amount would be a severe blow to his family's standard of living. Also, such a large account loss might jeopardize a promotion to sales supervisor that Keith's sales manager has hinted might be forthcoming.

Keith decides to drive to a local cafe for a cup of coffee to calm his nerves and to think. While slowly drinking his coffee, Keith considers the changed situation at Eaton and tries to devise a strategy to keep this important account.

### Questions

1. Do you think Keith has been doing a good job serving the Eaton account? Why or why not?
2. In what stage of the buying process is Eaton's new purchasing organization? What is the buying situation from their perspective?
3. What specific actions would you advise Keith to take now?
4. If Keith manages to retain the Eaton account, what advice would you give him for long-run maintenance of the account?

# DO I REALLY HAVE TO WORRY ABOUT ALL THESE PEOPLE?

Linda Stephens is a sales engineer for McDonnell-Cummins Company, which sells specialty chemicals, plastics, and polymer products to large consumer goods companies. After graduating from Michigan State University with a degree in chemical engineering, Linda interviewed with several companies and received three job offers. She decided to take the job as sales engineer with McDonnell-Cummins because it offered the best overall compensation package (including perks like a new car and an expense account) as well as a career path that could lead to top management. After three months of intensive training that included classroom lectures and discussions, laboratory demonstrations of products, videotapes, lots of reading material, and several examinations, Linda feels confident of her knowledge of the company's products and believes that she is prepared to make effective sales presentations to customers.

Still, on her first sales call at the headquarters of Gamble & Simpson, a large consumer products manufacturer, she is a little apprehensive as she walks into the huge lobby and sees many other people—apparently salespeople—waiting. After she introduces herself to the receptionist and says she is here for a 9 A.M. meeting with Bill Constantin in the purchasing department, she takes her Gamble & Simpson visitor's pass and sits down in a comfortable chair to wait for Mr. Constantin. (She learned his name from the call reports that the previous sales engineer handling this account had submitted.) Within a few minutes, Mr. Constantin's secretary, Marie Doyle, comes down to the lobby to greet Linda and escort her back to Mr. Constantin's office. Marie says that Mr. Constantin can spend only about fifteen minutes with Linda because he has to prepare for an emergency meeting scheduled for 9:30 A.M. with the vice president of purchasing.

Arriving at Mr. Constantin's office, Linda introduces herself and gives Mr. Constantin her business card. Bill Constantin seems somewhat harried and preoccupied, so Linda thinks she had better forget the small talk and get down to business. Handing a packet of product brochures to Mr. Constantin, she tells him that her company will be introducing several new products over the next few months and that she wants to give him some preliminary information about them. Linda makes a short presentation on each of five new products, while Mr. Constantin listens and leafs through the brochures. Upon finishing her presentations, Linda asks if he has any questions. Mr. Constantin replies, "Not at the moment, but I'll probably have some later when I get a chance to read the brochures and talk to some of the R&D people. Right now, I've got to get ready for my 9:30 meeting."

At that moment, Mr. Constantin's manager, Esther Hughes, pokes her head in the door and says that she'd like to talk with Mr. Constantin after his meeting with the VP. Mr. Constantin quickly introduces Linda to Esther and leaves for his meeting. Esther was hired as purchasing manager only a month earlier, so she is still progressing up the learning curve at Gamble & Simpson. She asks Linda a few questions and requests copies of the product brochures to bring her up to date on what McDonnell-Cummins is offering. She remarks that at her previous company she bought from a competitor of Linda's company. Ms. Hughes soon excuses herself and asks Marie if she would mind taking Linda out to the laboratory to introduce her to some of the research and development people who use the products that Mr. Constantin buys for them.

In the laboratory, Linda meets Dr. Stuart Forbes and Dr. Li Chu, two scientists who provide detailed specifications to Mr. Constantin for products they need in their work. Li Chu says that he is working on a new idea for a laundry detergent for which he needs a polymer with particular properties. He asks

(continued)

## DO I REALLY HAVE TO WORRY ABOUT ALL THESE PEOPLE? (CONTINUED)

Linda if her company can provide such a product. Linda admits that she isn't sure, but says that she will talk to her company's R&D people and let him know as soon as possible. While in the laboratory, Linda also meets Fred Burnett, a laboratory technician who carries out most of the experiments designed by Drs. Forbes and Chu. Mr. Burnett is an uninhibited young man about Linda's age who cracks a couple of lighthearted jokes along the line of "What's a nice person like you doing in a place like this?" Finally, on the way out of the laboratory, Marie introduces Linda to the director of R&D, Dr. Leland Birsner, whose approval is required for any product requests submitted to purchasing. Dr. Birsner seems rather dour, but he is polite enough and says that he hopes Linda will keep him informed about any new products her company is developing. Taking this as her cue, Linda hands him another packet of brochures from her briefcase.

Later, while walking back to the lobby with Marie, Linda asks who will make the purchasing decision on her products. Marie responds, "Oh, lots of people have input. It's usually more of a group decision than any one person's, although the R&D director and the purchasing manager have the final say."

Leaving Gamble & Simpson, Linda is a bit overwhelmed by the possibility that each of the people she's met have input in deciding whether or not to purchase her company's products. Her first job, she decides, is to prepare an organizational chart of the Gamble & Simpson buying center to help her understand the multiple roles played by the different people. Then she will develop some strategy tactics for developing and keeping good relationships with all of these people.

### Questions

1. In terms of buying-center roles (initiators, gatekeepers, influencers, deciders, buyers, and users), how should Linda classify each of the seven people (Marie Doyle, Bill Constantin, Esther Hughes, Dr. Stuart Forbes, Dr. Li Chu, Fred Burnett, and Dr. Leland Birsner) she met at Gamble & Simpson?

2. Which of these people do you think has the greatest input on purchase decisions? Why?

3. What advice would you give Linda in her efforts to think up a strategy and tactics to develop and maintain good relationships with all of these buying center members?

4. Now that her first sales call is over, what should Linda do to follow up with some or all of the Gamble & Simpson people?

## CHAPTER 10

# Strategic Understanding of Your Company, Products, Competition, and Markets

*Customers don't care how much you know about your products until they know how much you care about them and their needs.*

*Anonymous*

## After Reading This Chapter, You Should Understand:

- Why in-depth knowledge about your company, products, competition, and markets helps you become a more successful salesperson.

- How to evaluate your firm's competition.

- Various sources of information and their potential uses.

- The growing professionalism in purchasing and its impact on personal selling.

- How to keep current on product developments, competitors, and markets.

## INSIDE PERSONAL SELLING:
### Meet Christi Rose of Pitney Bowes

To stay abreast of her company's products, competition, markets, and industry, Christi Rose does everything from attend training to dial in for a weekly phone message from the chief executive officer. As a major account executive for Pitney Bowes, she sells mailing equipment—postage meters, folding and inserting machines, addressing equipment, and shipping systems. Rose joined Pitney Bowes because she heard about its extensive training program for young sales professionals. Once hired, she spent an intense month studying the company's products and honing her selling skills. Then she and other new reps "went into the field with seasoned sales reps who helped us learn the business and how to sell," she remembers.

Her company's mission statement is to "deliver shareholder and customer value by providing leading edge global inte-

grated mail and document management solutions for organizations of all sizes." To apply this mission, Rose learns everything she can about a customer's business, future direction, and problems.

Recently, for example, she heard from a customer that its mail center was unable to track the hundreds of incoming packages received every day. She immediately thought about a Pitney Bowes system that records the addressee's name via a bar code and captures a signature through a handheld device. This allows the user to check a database and find out whether a missing package was actually delivered and who signed for it. Next, says Rose, "I read up on the competitor and the deficiencies of its product. Then I called the customer's operations manager and vice-president of technology to ask if I could come in to discuss the technological advantages of our solution. They agreed, and within days, the system was sold."

One day every month is set aside for an internal marketing meeting. "If new products are being introduced, we role-play sales situations and learn to operate the new products to certify that we can sell them," she says. Every Sunday evening, CEO Michael Critelli records a voice-mail telling the entire organization about company growth, market share, revenue, and other key topics. And once a year, corporate executives meet with each sales district to discuss the previous year's performance as well as the coming year's goals for the company, division, and district.

When she visits with customers, Rose listens carefully for clues about emerging market trends. "I have to keep on top of everything from postal rates to the shipping industry and changes within carriers like FedEx and UPS," she says. "I subscribe to industry journals, and I go to meetings of the Mailing Systems Managers Association and the Postal Customer Council. All these sources help me guide customers in the right direction if things are about to change."

305

ow, we've certainly discussed a lot about how to sell in the past several chapters. You may feel more than ready to head out into your sales territory and become the successful salesperson you know you can be. Well, it's great that you have such confidence and eagerness. You *have* learned a lot! You now know how to efficiently find and qualify new prospects, collect valuable preapproach information, smoothly contact a customer for the first time, make a sound sales presentation, adroitly handle sales resistance, skillfully close the sale, and attend to critical post-sale activities. But, as a professional salesperson, you also must be intimately familiar with the selling environment in which you'll operate; otherwise, you'll waste a lot of energy. Now we'll add knowledge of your company, its products, your competitors, and target markets to make you fully prepared to start making sales calls.

Several studies have shown that more effective salespeople have richer and more interrelated knowledge about their customers and selling strategies than do less effective salespeople.[1] How do salespeople acquire this knowledge? At one time, salespeople were given a price book and told, "Go make some sales calls to see if you can get some orders." With no training and little product knowledge, most of these salespeople failed miserably and soon left the company. Today, many products are complex and customer needs are diverse, so new salespeople require thorough training about their company, its products, competitors, and markets before calling on customers. Many companies provide much of this essential knowledge in formal training programs that make use of videotapes, lectures, demonstrations, role-playing sessions, computer exercises, and trainee interaction with each other and seasoned salespeople.[2]

One *Fortune 500* company, for example, uses a three tiered sales training program that extends over three or four *years*. The first tier includes two weeks of classroom and demonstration lab work in the company's modern training center. Most of the second tier training occurs in the district sales offices, where the manager's monthly staff meetings are followed by two hours of sales training. Each district office includes a library of training modules on VCR cassettes for sales trainees' use. The third training tier takes place in the homes of the sales reps. Each rep receives a PC or workstation on which he or she completes computer-assisted homework exercises in preparation for classes at the district office. The in-home PCs are networked so that messages, such as assignments, can be broadcast simultaneously to the reps.

High-performing salespeople must have detailed knowledge about their (1) company, (2) products, (3) competitors, and (4) markets. Being deficient in any of these categories will lead to inefficient and ineffective selling efforts. This chapter focuses on these four areas, their importance, and how salespeople learn this requisite information.

## STRATEGIC UNDERSTANDING OF YOUR COMPANY

Company history, organization, mission statement, culture, philosophies, goals, objectives, strategies, tactics, policies, and procedures are among the first subjects sales trainees study. Companies take different approaches to teaching these basics. Some companies present this information in formal training programs, and others provide it in manuals and handouts. Whatever the approach, every salesperson needs to thoroughly understand his or her company in order to knowledgeably develop selling strategies and respond to customer questions. Let's see why.

## Company History

Studying the company's history may not seem particularly interesting at first, but this knowledge provides perspectives and insights that will serve the salesperson well throughout a career. It may be intriguing to see how humbly the company began. What new sales trainee would not be inspired by the story of young Steve Jobs and Steve Wozniak? Jobs and Wozniak raised thirteen hundred dollars by selling Jobs' Volkswagen bus and Wozniak's Hewlett-Packard handheld calculator, then built the first personal computer "for the rest of us" in a tiny garage.[3] Today, Apple Computer is known all over the world. Most companies were started by one determined individual with a marvelous vision. Because a company's present business philosophies and slogans often trace back to its founder, a study of company history generally begins with the founder's life and philosophies. Usually the company's librarian or personnel manager can recommend a good book on the company and its founder. Many customers will enjoy hearing the story of a company's origins, and it may help win respect for the salesperson's professional knowledge.

## Growth and Development

Another aspect of a company's history is its record of growth in sales, market share, profits, and new products. Reading annual and quarterly reports or independent financial analysts' evaluations of the firm (for example, *Value Line, Standard and Poor, Dun & Bradstreet, Morningstar*) can keep you current about company growth and development and give you an advantage in closing sales. If a potential customer asks, "How's this new product been selling so far?", a knowledgeable salesperson could truthfully answer, "It's the fastest growing new product in the industry; we're barely able to keep up with orders. Your two major competitors have already placed large orders." Sharing this information not only reassures, but also helps persuade the customer to make the purchase in order to keep up with competition. Without such timely knowledge, a salesperson would have to answer, "Gee, I don't know. Let me check with the home office." Most likely, the customer would delay buying until the salesperson reports back—or buy from someone else in the interim.

## Company Organization

Many companies carefully maintain one or more organization charts. An organization chart provides an overview of a company's chain of command, communication flows, and overall structure. The organization chart might be anything from a single sheet of paper giving the names of company officers and executives, to an elaborate wall chart kept in the company's main boardroom or on the company's web site.

New salespeople can learn a lot about the positions and unique roles of key individuals by studying the organization chart. Most companies maintain a separate, detailed organization chart for the sales department showing the hierarchy of sales managers, sales support people, and the most important people the sales organization: the salespeople. The way a company structures its organization chart suggests what's really important to top management. If a sales force is structured by geographic location, for example, this could suggest that management considers specific geographic markets large enough to justify special attention. A sales force structured by customer type, however, may reflect management's concern with identifying and solving problems and issues for specific customers or customer types.

## Mission Statement

**Mission Statement** Sets forth in writing the organization's orientation, goals, basic values, and sense of purpose.

The **mission statement** provides an understanding and feel for the organization's orientation, goals, basic values, and sense of purpose. In describing the essence of the company's business and what it seeks to accomplish, the mission statement lays out the company's vision and direction for the next ten to twenty years. It also can help motivate salespeople to extraordinary performance. For example, it is much more satisfying and challenging for salespeople to think of their jobs as helping to create cleaner, healthier, more attractive home environments for families rather than as merely selling home air and water filters. Newport News Shipbuilding's classic mission statement remains unchanged since their founding in 1886: *"We shall build good ships here—at a profit if we can—at a loss if we must—but always good ships."* What an inspirational message that provides for Newport News Shipbuilding salespeople to relay to customers who ask about the quality of a ship they're planning to buy.

## Culture

Every organization has its unique *culture* or operating climate. This culture may be defined as a set of formal or informal values that establish rules for dress, communicating, and behavior on everything from problem solving to ethics. A highly centralized organization run by authoritarian management will create a sales climate sharply different from that of an organization where authority is decentralized and management employs a more consultative or democratic style. The organization may have no one pervasive climate, but various climates that depend on the department or unit.

Not only does an organization have its own culture, but the sales force within the firm has its own culture. Although the two are related—because the company's culture usually sets the overall tone for the sales organization's culture—points of difference may arise between the two. For instance, a firm's corporate culture may be formal, but the culture within a given sales manager's selling team still might be somewhat informal owing to the sales manager's leadership style. Company culture is important to your success as a salesperson. It will affect your job satisfaction, performance, commitment to the firm, and motivation.[4] Thus, it's a good idea for a new salesperson to size up both the organizational and sales force culture quickly and learn what is acceptable and expected behavior. A few coffee breaks or lunches with more experienced salespeople and staff can prove invaluable in understanding the corporate culture and managerial climate.

## Goals and Objectives

*Goals* and *objectives* are terms often used interchangeably, and we see no value in trying to distinguish between them here. Companies generally apply one of the terms to long-run, less quantifiable targets, such as becoming the most innovative company in the industry, and the other term to short-run, quantifiable targets such as earning a 15-percent return on investment in the next year. Good salespeople know the goals and objectives of their company, the marketing department, and each successive organizational unit (sales region, division, branch) in which they work. They use this knowledge to formulate more compatible and realistic personal goals and objectives. For instance, it would probably be unrealistic for a salesperson to forecast an increase of 30 percent in territorial sales if the company and the region's overall forecast is for a 5 percent sales decline. Awareness of the company and sales department forecasts can help keep a salesperson from making serious personal sales forecasting errors.

## Strategies and Tactics

A **strategy** is a total program of action for using resources to achieve a goal or objective. A **tactic** is a short-run, specific action comprising part of the larger strategic plan. A small company might develop a sales strategy, for example, to compete against IBM by concentrating its field sales force calls on small businesses, because IBM focuses its resources more on large companies. Sales tactics might include use of Spanish-language videotapes and brochures for sales presentations to Hispanic customers. Salespeople who understand their companies' strategies and tactics will have useful guidelines for making their own personal selling decisions in the field. In order for any organization to succeed, every member of the team needs to know the overall plan (strategy) as well as the individual tasks (tactics) to employ.[5] Company strategic success has been directly linked to salesperson effectiveness.[6]

**Strategy** A long-run total program of action for using resources to achieve an overall goal.

**Tactic** A short-run, specific action comprising part of the larger strategic plan.

## Policies

To ensure consistency, continuity, and expeditious organizational decisions on routine matters requires setting general rules of action called "policies." Policies are predetermined decisions for handling recurring situations efficiently and effectively. Knowledge of company policies helps salespeople make better field decisions and better serve customers. For example, a salesperson who is familiar with the company's policy of not shipping goods until payment has been received for the previous shipment can prevent customer embarrassment or annoyance. In order to negotiate price and terms with the buyer, the salesperson must thoroughly know the company's credit policies and credit terms. Some companies offer discounts for quantity purchases or to buyers who pay

## IT'S UP TO YOU

One of your better customers has just called you to complain about the latest batch of packaging that your company delivered. It seems that the company's telephone number and address are incorrect on all the packaging. You check the order to see how such a mistake could have been made, and you notice that the customer made the mistake in filling out the order. Your company's policy is to take back any packaging misprinted by its fault. But customers are responsible for any errors that they make in ordering, and this is clearly printed on the order form. This customer has been increasing its purchases from you by about 10 percent a year, and last year bought $17,500 worth from you. The invoice price of the misprinted packaging is $1,250. What is your next move? What strategy can you develop for dealing with such problems?

the invoice within a specified number of days. Even the salesperson's own financial planning requires knowing whether the company's policy is to pay commissions to salespeople when the order is accepted, when the goods are shipped, or when the customer pays the invoice. Most companies pay commissions when the goods are shipped. Consider how to address the problem in *It's Up to You* above, which pertains to an issue concerning company policy.

*Studying their company's history will provide perspectives and insights that enable salespeople to better understand their company, its products, and organizational culture.*

Jan Butchofsky/Corbis

# STRATEGIC UNDERSTANDING OF YOUR PRODUCTS

Studies consistently show that more effective salespeople have greater knowledge about their company's products.[7] Few customers will respect or buy from a salesperson who is poorly informed about the product's technical details and its application to their problems. Therefore, professional salespeople must be technically qualified and knowledgeable about their products. They must understand what their products can and cannot do for customers and how they can best be used. When salespeople feel technically deficient, they should seek intracompany experts who can assist them with the needed knowledge or jointly meet with prospects or customers. Salespeople who really understand their products develop a pride and confidence that shines through to prospects and helps gain their confidence and trust—and most likely, the sale.

As product cycles shorten and technology advances at an ever-accelerating pace, salespeople must work harder to keep informed about company products. What do salespeople need to know about their products? The answer is simple—EVERYTHING. And believe it or not, this is not an exaggeration. Essentially, salespeople selling to producers need to know how the products they sell are made, packaged, shipped, and received by the customer; unpackaged; sent to the buyer's production line; picked up; placed into the final product or adjoined to other parts; then packaged and shipped to their customer's customers; and how they perform. Listed in Table 10.1 are a few of the many questions that salespeople must be able to answer about their product line.

---

**TABLE 10.1**

### REQUISITE PRODUCT KNOWLEDGE OF PROFESSIONAL SALESPEOPLE

- Where does the product come from? Where is it mined, grown, assembled, or manufactured? How is it shipped to the present location? Does shipping significantly affect its quality or price?

- Who designed the product? How is the product made? What kind of machines produced it?

- How should the product be used? What are the manufacturer's recommendations regarding care and maintenance? What can be learned from other customers who have used the product? Do any special features or advantages distinguish this product from competitive products on the market?

- What kind of guaranty or warranty does the company offer on the product? What kind of repair and maintenance service does the company provide? Does the company have a service department or service centers? Where are they located?

- What happens if a product is broken in delivery? Is the customer protected? What is the procedure for returning the product if it proves unsatisfactory?

## Products from the Customer's Perspective

Most products and services offer a range of functional, psychological, and sensory (sight, hearing, smell, touch, and taste) attributes. A bar of soap may become much more appealing and satisfy a wider array of the customer's functional and psychological needs when it is conveniently and attractively shaped, contains a special moisturizing agent, gives off a pleasant scent, feels good to the touch, and has a pleasing, eye-catching wrapper. In a related fashion, earth-moving equipment becomes much more appealing to industrial buyers when it is well designed for operator use and the seller guarantees that it will be replaced or repaired within twenty-four hours of any breakdown.

It is not enough simply to explain to a customer the basic functions or general uses of a product. A customer is really looking for *personal benefits or solutions to his or her problems* before anything else (recall FAB). Salespeople must use their product knowledge to present products in ways that match the needs and desires of customers. Various customers may view the identical product quite differently, depending on their individual needs. Consider the following conversation between a computer salesperson and a prospective customer:

> *Customer:* "What different types of personal computers do you sell?"
>
> *Salesperson:* "Well, I have sold some firms personal computers (PCs) that help them manage their clients' stock and bond investments. I sold desktop publisher PCs that would streamline their efforts and get the work done in a timely fashion. Mary Jones, Inc., a public relations firm, bought several PCs to keep records on its customers and to develop creative presentations for clients. The physics department over at the university purchased our PCs in order to assist its faculty to analyze the statistical results of their experiments.
>
> *Customer:* Wow, sounds like you sell a wide range of computers!
>
> *Salesperson:* No. Actually, we sell just one basic PC, but people buy it for a lot of different reasons.

## Selling Multiple Products

Product knowledge problems are compounded when salespeople must handle several lines of products. A salesperson who carries five product lines has nearly five times as much work to know all the products and keep them straight. When you need a systematic way to stay informed about your products, consider developing, maintaining, and carrying for ready reference a simple *product knowledge worksheet*, as shown in abbreviated format in Table 10.2. You can update this worksheet and add relevant questions as you receive new questions from prospects and customers. Either a file on a laptop computer or a handwritten hardcopy will do. In addition to the product knowledge worksheet for your own products, it's important to have a *competitive analysis worksheet* (as illustrated in Table 10.3 on page 316). If the comparison will be favorable, consider using a side-by-side comparison of your products versus those of leading competitors.

TABLE 10.2

## PRODUCT KNOWLEDGE WORKSHEET

| Characteristics | Product A | Product B | Product C | Product D |
|---|---|---|---|---|
| **Customer Benefits** | | | | |
| 1. | | | | |
| 2. | | | | |
| 3. | | | | |
| **Features** | | | | |
| 1. | | | | |
| 2. | | | | |
| 3. | | | | |
| **Advantages** | | | | |
| 1. | | | | |
| 2. | | | | |
| 3. | | | | |
| **Initial Price** | | | | |
| **Estimated Life** | | | | |
| **Estimated Lifecycle Cost** | | | | |
| **Size** | | | | |
| **a. Weight** | | | | |
| **b. Dimensions** | | | | |
| **Installation Ease** | | | | |
| **Required Service** | | | | |
| **Return Policy** | | | | |
| **Warranty** | | | | |
| **Trade-in Allowance** | | | | |
| **Other Characteristics** | | | | |

## Interaction with Other Products

Not only must salespeople know their products thoroughly, they must also know how these products work with *other* products. For example, a customer may ask, "What color printers are compatible with this PC?" or "Does this PC come with a built-in CD burner?" Without understanding how his or her products interact with other equipment and stack up against competitive products, the salesperson cannot reassure the customer and may risk losing the sale. It is especially important for salespeople to know everything about the product and compatible ancillary equipment when selling a product without a well-known brand name. For example, although Research In Motion, a small, relatively unknown company, introduced the *BlackBerry*—an interactive emailer and pager—its salespeople were able to make it a quick success by effectively showing its advantages versus compatible products.

### Knowledge About Product Service

Most products, whether tangibles such as mainframe computers and oil derricks, or intangibles such as group life and health insurance, require service. All products eventually need servicing, repairs, changes, or replacements. For instance, companies purchasing life and health insurance for their employees need and expect advice as demographic factors and lifestyles change. Professional sales reps know what services their companies provide for each product, the costs of those services, which are most appropriate for different customers, and how they can be included in the buyer's purchase order.

## STRATEGIC UNDERSTANDING OF YOUR COMPETITION

Because salespeople nearly always sell in a competitive environment, they must understand competitors' products and services almost as well as their own company's. Customers will have confidence in a salesperson who can knowledgeably compare his or her own product's features and advantages with those of a competitor. This confidence, however, can be undermined if the salesperson gives in to the temptation to disparage the competition in front of customers. Negative comments such as, "Our competitor's machine is pathetically slow and has one of the worst repair records on the market" often work against the salesperson who is trying to win the trust and respect of customers. It's always better to make product comparisons in positive terms, such as, "Our tabletop copiers average about five thousand copies before you need to change the toner cartridge— nearly twice as many as any other comparable machines—and our repair record is one of the best. In fact, using an objective study by *Consumer Reports*, allow me to compare our record with those of others." Read *From the Command Post* to see how fierce competitors are trying to "one-up" each other.

### The *Thomas Register*

**Thomas Register** The primary source of locating suppliers for most *Fortune* 500 companies. Published annually, it provides information about 170,000 manufacturers of product categories, specific products, names of the companies, branches, top executives and their job titles, affiliation data, and credit rating.

One of the most comprehensive and widely used sources of information about who makes what products and where they can be purchased is the *Thomas Register of National Manufacturers*. The **Thomas Register** is the primary source of locating suppliers for most Fortune 500 companies. Published annually, it provides information about 170,000 manufacturers of product categories, specific products, names of the companies, branches, top executives and their job titles, affiliation data, and credit rating. Available in several hardcopy volumes at most large libraries, the *Thomas Register* also is online at www.thomasregister.com, with

# FROM THE COMMAND POST: BATTLING OVER BREAKFAST

Several companies (Kellogg, General Mills, Quaker Oats, Nestlé/Nabisco, and Post) have been fighting for market share in the ready-to-eat breakfast cereal business for decades. Each percentage point of market share means millions of sales dollars. For seventy-five years, Kellogg has dominated the breakfast cereal business. But the total consumer market for breakfast cereals continues to lose share to fast-food restaurants, microwaveable food, breakfast drinks, and energy bars. Even the venerable Wheaties brand, long promoted as the "breakfast of champions," was extended to a new *Wheaties Energy Crunch* bar in efforts to capture some of the rapidly growing "energy bar" market.

As the total breakfast cereal market declines, Kellogg's dominance has been undercut by the innovative sales and marketing programs of competitors. In San Antonio, for instance, General Mills targeted Hispanics by advertising in ethnic media, employing Spanish speaking salespeople, sponsoring Hispanic seasonal celebrations (for example, Cinco de Mayo), and offering resellers price discounts on large volume purchases. Subsequently, Kellogg reluctantly removed its salespeople and retreated from the San Antonio market.

In the mid-1990s, while some cereal marketers cut back sharply on promotional expenditures, others maintained their sales promotion and other marketing efforts. For example, after the U.S. government endorsed oat bran as a cholesterol fighter, Quaker Oats and General Mills began promoting new health benefits for their respective Quaker Oats and Cheerios brand cereals. Other breakfast cereal makers reformulated and revitalized some of their old brands, then promoted their augmented nutritional value (calcium, folic acid, iron, or vitamins B6 and B12). Some companies are also employing web grocery delivery service to sell regional brands of breakfast cereals.

Kellogg has not been standing still in the face of all this intense competition. They are creating consumer excitement by adding fruit to old cereal brands like Special K, and trying innovative new strategies such as introducing new cereal brands, then withdrawing them quickly from the market. With the purchase of Keebler snack products, Kellogg increased the efficiency of its salespeople, who can now sell Keebler and Kellogg products together.

Even in the mature market of breakfast cereals, there is ongoing excitement as the battle over breakfast continues, giving salespeople more benefits to present to their wholesaler and retailer customers.

---

thousands of online catalogs and links to company web sites, plus millions of downloadable CAD drawings. Salespeople who know that their products' customers are manufacturers of certain types of products can search by product, company, or brand name. For example, a salesperson who sells equipment to companies that manufacture machine lathes can type in *machine lathes* at the *Thomas Register* web site and go to a web page that lists the different types of lathes. From this web page, the salesperson can, in a few more keyboard clicks, find the address of prospect companies, catalogs, web sites, order and request for quotation (RFQs) forms, computer assisted design (CAD) drawings, and email addresses to contact. Although used mainly by purchasing agents, savvy salespeople can effectively and efficiently use the online or offline *Thomas Register* to locate manufacturer prospects for their products and services.

TABLE 10.3

## COMPETITIVE ANALYSIS WORKSHEET

For each dimension below, rank our company versus competitors on a scale of 1–5, with 1 being the highest.

| Product Dimension | Our Firm | Competitor A | Competitor B | Competitor C | Competitor D |
|---|---|---|---|---|---|
| Sales growth | | | | | |
| Market share | | | | | |
| Sales force | | | | | |
| Financial strength | | | | | |
| Marketing strategy | | | | | |
| Marketing mix | | | | | |
| Image/Reputation | | | | | |
| New products | | | | | |
| Product quality | | | | | |
| Pricing (value) | | | | | |
| Promotion | | | | | |
| Installation | | | | | |
| Delivery | | | | | |
| Billing/Invoicing | | | | | |
| Repair | | | | | |
| Customer service | | | | | |

### Competitive Analysis Worksheet

Many professional salespeople maintain well-organized files on competitors and their offerings. They keep running files on each of their competitors—products they sell, competitive advantages and disadvantages, major customers, products that each customer buys and for what use, names of competitive salespeople, and their estimated sales volume. A salesperson can prepare a competitive analysis worksheet, like the one shown in Table 10.3, with input from customers and systematize information about competitors' product and service offerings versus his or her own company's.[8]

## STRATEGIC UNDERSTANDING OF YOUR MARKETS

Where are your company's present and future markets? Who are and will be its customers? Economic, technological, political-legal, cultural-social, ethical, and competitive environments are continuously changing. Companies that have prospered most over the years are those that have successfully antici-pated and responded to the many dynamic changes in the macromarketing environment.

Timely customer feedback is critical to the company's response to a dynamic environment. Salespeople are supposed to be the "eyes and ears" of the company in the marketplace, but sales and marketing managers often ignore this information-gathering function of salespeople. Thus, the company loses a valuable early-warning system about changing customer needs and the evolving marketing environment. Most salespeople and their companies' managers believe they know the market thoroughly. Yet, overwhelming evi-dence indicates that they do not. Important innovations rarely come from firms currently dominant in a given industry. Numerous industry leaders have been slow to recognize technological developments that changed their mar-kets forever, as shown in Table 10.4.

Beyond anticipating and adjusting to changes in the environment, an organization must apply marketing and sales planning to its relationships with all its influencing publics, not just customers. All of these publics (for example, the financial community, suppliers, governments, employees, stock-holders, and the general public) should be considered *stakeholders* in the com-pany. Each of these publics influences the operation of sales and marketing organizations for better or worse, thus the potential reaction of each must be considered in developing strategies and tactics.

| TABLE 10.4 | |
|---|---|
| **COMPANIES SLOW TO RECOGNIZE OPPORTUNITIES IN MARKETS THEY DOMINATED** | |
| **Company or Industry** | **Innovative Product or Service** |
| Parker Brothers, Mattel | Video games |
| Kendall (cloth diaper cleaners) | Disposable diapers |
| Levi Strauss | Designer jeans |
| Goodyear, Firestone, Goodrich | Radial tires |
| Swiss watchmakers | Digital watches |
| Anheuser Busch, Miller | Light beer |
| Coke, Pepsi | Diet soda |
| Wine producers | Wine coolers |
| Eversharp, Eberhard Faber | Ballpoint pens |
| IBM | Microcomputers |
| Converse, Keds | Running shoes |
| Keuffel & Esser (leading manufacturers of slide rules) | Calculators |

## Keeping Informed

Successful salespeople work at staying well informed about the industry they serve and about business in general. They regularly do their own personal market research at local university or college libraries or via the web. They keep alert to trends in their customers' industries and regularly read publications about their customers' industries. They join trade associations that publish current developments in the industry and can supply membership lists that lead to new customers. And they attend trade shows and seminars where they can interact with customers and learn more about their customers' businesses.

An abundance of information about prospects and companies is available in most college and large city libraries and over the Internet from company web sites and in online databases. At a library, check with the business reference librarian to learn about the many sources of company information available in hardback volumes, microfilm, or online. Sales professionals read the annual reports of their customers, their competitors, and their own companies, and study analyses on these companies prepared by financial companies such as Dun & Bradstreet, Standard and Poor's, and Value Line. They periodically review data from *Dun & Bradstreet's Million Dollar Directory, Ward's Directory of Major U.S. Private Companies*, and *Thomas' Register of National Manufacturers*. They go to the **Business Periodicals Index** at a library or on the web to find specific business articles about a company, product, issue, or problem. They regularly read general business publications such as *Business Week, Wall Street Journal, Forbes*, and *Fortune* in order to keep up with the latest happenings in the business world and to project a more informed image to prospects and customers. They don't rely on just one source for information, but rather try to corroborate data with various sources.

**Business Periodicals Index** A cumulative subject index listing business articles from more than 160 periodicals.

For salespeople and their managers, particularly valuable information can be found in the *Source Book of Demographics and Buying Power for Every Zip Code in the U.S.A.* (http://einsys.einpgh.org/MARION/ABJ-4716). It provides population, socioeconomic characteristics, buying power, and other demographics for zip code areas throughout the United States. Each zip code area is assigned a *purchasing potential index* number based on its consumption potential across a variety of product categories. For instance, if the purchasing potential index for a certain zip code is 115 for purchase of office desks, then that zip code has a 15 percent greater potential to buy office desks than the U.S. average. Conversely, if a zip code has an index of 85 for the purchase of punch press machines, then its purchasing potential for that product is 15 percent below the national average. Purchasing potential information can be extremely helpful to salespeople in identifying which zip codes in their sales territories offer the most buying opportunity for their particular products and services.

A second source of useful data on an area's effective buying income is the *Survey of Buying Power* published annually in *Sales and Marketing Management* magazine (www.salesandmarketing.com/salesandmarketing/index.jsp). An overall indicator of an area's buying power is the *buying power index (BPI)*, expressed as a percent of total U.S. sales. The higher an area's BPI, the greater the ability of that market to buy general merchandise. For example, a city with a BPI of .3242 has a higher potential ability to buy than a city with a BPI of only .2783. A serious limitation of the BPI is that it only calculates potential for buying general merchandise. Specific product categories require a customized BPI.[9]

After you've identified some high potential buying areas, you might next go online to *SalesLeadsUSA* (http://lookupUSA.com) and use the free database service to search the addresses and phone numbers of more than eleven million businesses in the United States and Canada by name, type of business, NAIC code, names of key executives, and more. Sales leads can also be found at *Harris InfoSource* (www.HarrisInfo.com), which provides information on more than 350,000 companies and 600,000 key decision makers.

Online, you will find countless other valuable sources of information for salespeople. Companies that produce similar products and services often belong to industry trade associations, which means you can start at the Federal Consumer Information Center web site (www.pueblo.gsa.gov/crh/trade.htm), where you will find lists of hundreds of associations, both commercial and not-for-profit, by type of activity (for example, automobile, banking, insurance, utilities, and military) and alphabetically. At this web site, you will find a brief statement about whom the association represents and what they do, and the association's address, telephone and fax numbers, email address, and web site address.

When you contact an association or go to its web site, you can obtain valuable prospecting information and perhaps the membership directory. Some good places to find company web sites are Internet search engines such as *Yahoo's Business and Economy* (http://www.yahoo.com/Business and Economy/Companies/), which provides links to companies in more than one hundred industry categories. Overall, the Internet is home to hundreds of searchable online databases, some free and some for a fee. Table 10.5 shows some of the various information sources available to resourceful salespeople. Most of the trade directories, business guides, indexes, and government publications usually can be found in hardcopy at larger libraries, and in many cases on the Internet, as well. Colleges and universities generally allow their students free access to the many Internet sources of information. Log on to the U.S. Census Bureau's web site, in *Keeping Up Online*, to discover how much government information is readily available at the click of a mouse.

## KEEPING UP ONLINE: U.S. CENSUS BUREAU

The U.S. Census Bureau has an abundance of data for the entire nation. Check out the offerings at http://www.census.gov. How could a salesperson make use of these data? Do you see any problems in using these data?

TABLE 10.5

## SOURCES OF INFORMATION

### Trade Association Directories

- **Encyclopedia of Associations** (Gale Research Company, Detroit; http://library.dialog.com/bluesheets/html/bl0114.html) Provides detailed information on thousands of nonprofit membership organizations worldwide.

- **National Trade and Professional Associations of the United States and Labor Unions** (Columbia Books, Washington, D.C.; http://dir.yahoo.com/Business_and_Economy/Organizations/Trade_Associations) Contains data on about five thousand organizations, trade and professional associations, and national labor unions.

- **Directory of Corporate Affiliations** (National Register Publishing Company, Skokie, IL. www.corporateaffiliations.com/Content/index.html) Cross-references more than three thousand parent companies with their sixteen thousand divisions, subsidiaries, and affiliates.

### Business Guides

- **Thomas Register of National Manufacturers** (www.ThomasRegister.com) Leading and most comprehensive purchasing guide to the manufacturing industry. Database includes more than 189,000 companies and 72,000 product categories. Provides comprehensive company information on 550,000 industrial distributors, manufacturers, and service companies classified in 6,000 product and service categories. Buyers and engineers can access supplier information through e-commerce enabled catalogs, brochures, fax forms, line cards, and hotlinks to supplier web sites. Users can negotiate and complete the entire buying/selling process online.

- **Reference Book of Corporate Managements** (Dun & Bradstreet, New York; http://www.loc.gov/rr/business/duns/dunsindx.html) Identifies more than thirty thousand executives who are officers and directors of twenty-four hundred large corporations. Also, at this Library of Congress web site are numerous additional Dun & Bradstreet business publications.

- **Standard & Poor's Corporation Services** (Standard & Poor's Corporation, New York; http://www.standardandpoors.com) Provides various services, including: *Industry Surveys* (trends and projections); *Outlook* (weekly stock market letter); *Stock Guide* (monthly summary of data on five thousand common and preferred stocks); *Trade and Securities* (monthly listing of statistics on business, finance, stocks and bonds, foreign trade, productivity, and employment).

- **Dun & Bradstreet Information Services** (http://www.dnb.com) Provides the latest business news and trends plus corporate profiles and financial information for privately held companies.

- **Standard & Poor's Register of Corporations,** (Standard & Poor's Corporation, New York; www.netadvantage.standardandpoors.com) Contains a cross-section of U.S. companies plus some international companies. Information includes company name and address, parent company name, NAIC codes, year started, sales, number of employees, market territory, and executives.

(continued)

> ### TABLE 10.5
> ## Sources of Information (CONTINUED)

- *Standard Directory of Advertisers* (National Register Publishing Company, Skokie, Illinois; http://www.bowker-saur.co.uk/Products/Business/redbooksadvertisers.htm) Profiles detailed information on more than twenty-four thousand U.S. and international advertisers who each spend more than two hundred thousand dollars annually on advertising. Each listing includes advertising expenditures by media, agency, annual sales, and key contact personnel.

### Indexes

- *Business Periodicals Index* (H. W. Wilson, New York; www.silverplatter.com/catalog/wbpi.htm) Cumulative subject index listing international English-language business articles from about six hundred magazines, journals, and other periodicals.

- *Wall Street Journal Executive Library* (Dow Jones, Princeton, New Jersey; http://www.executivelibrary.com/) Indexes of business articles published in the *Wall Street Journal* and many international newspapers, magazines, journals, and web sites. Also includes many business reference sources and tool kits. Articles arranged into corporate news and general news.

- *CommerceNet* (http://www.dnb.com) An index of web sites for major companies, where you can find annual reports, earnings data, and product information.

### Government Publications
### (www.access.gpo.gov/su_docs/locators/cgp)

- *Survey of Current Business* (U.S. Department of Commerce, Bureau of Economic Analysis, Washington, D.C.) Updates twenty-six hundred different statistical series in each monthly issue. Includes data on gross national product, national income, international balance of payments, general business indicators, employment, construction, real estate, and domestic and foreign trade.

- *Monthly Catalog of United States Government Publications* (Superintendent of Documents, U.S. Government Printing Office, Washington, D.C.) Lists federal publications issued each month, by agency.

- *Monthly Checklist of State Publications* (Superintendent of Documents, U.S. Government Printing Office, Washington, D.C.) Lists state publications received by Library of Congress.

- *Census Data:* Provides an extensive source of information on the United States.

- *Bureau of the Census Catalog of Publications:* Is an index of all Census Bureau data, publications, and unpublished materials.

  - *Census of Retail Trade:* Provides data on the number of retail operations, sales, payroll, and personnel by primary metropolitan statistical areas (PMSAs), counties, and cities with populations of twenty-five hundred or more by kind of business.
  - *Census of Wholesale Trade:* Same as above but for wholesalers.
  - *Census of Selected Services:* Provides data on hotels, motels, beauty parlors, and other retail service organizations.

(continued)

**TABLE 10.5**

## SOURCES OF INFORMATION (CONTINUED)

- *Census of Housing:* Provides detailed data on various housing characteristics, including occupancy, financing, equipment, and facilities by state, metropolitan areas, and city block.
- *Census of Manufacturers:* Provides various data on manufacturers, including value added, employment, payrolls, new capital expenditures, cost of materials, and value of shipments for 450 manufacturing industries classified by geographic region and state, employment size, and type of establishment.
- *Census of Population:* Provides social and economic description of U.S. population with cross-classification of inhabitants for metropolitan statistical areas, urban areas, and all locales of one thousand people or more.
- *Census of Agriculture:* Provides data for all farms and for farms with sales of twenty-five hundred dollars or more by county and state.

### Internet Information Sources

- ***Fortune 500 and Fortune Global 500*** (http://fortune.com/fortune500 or http://fortune.com/global500) Lists the top 500 U.S. companies and the top 500 global companies as compiled by *Fortune;* the lists can be downloaded in spreadsheet form or ordered on disk.

- ***Hoover's Online*** (http://www.hoovers.com/) This database provides brief company profiles; links from the company profile to financial statements, news, and quotes for the selected company are provided.

- ***Encyclopedia of Associations*** (Thomson Company http://library.dialog.com/bluesheets/html/b10114.html) Provides a database of eighty-one thousand professional societies, trade associations, labor unions, cultural and religious groups, fan clubs, and other nonprofit organizations of all types.

- ***Federal Consumer Information Center*** (www.pueblo.gsa.gov/crh/trade.htm) Lists the name, address, telephone number, email and web sites for hundreds of commercial and nonprofit associations by major activity and alphabetically.

- ***Yahoo's Business and Economy*** (http://www.yahoo.com/Business_and_Economy/Companies/) Yahoo, an Internet search engine, provides links to companies in more than one hundred industry categories from its Companies page.

- ***PR Newswire*** (http://www.prnewswire.com/) Offers the latest press releases on companies, industries, and executives; releases are from participating PR Newswire members.

- ***Companies Online*** (http://companiesonline.com/) Partnership between Dun & Bradstreet and Lycos provides a search engine for information on more than one hundred thousand public and private companies.

- ***Dun & Bradstreet Information Services*** (http://www.dbisna.com/) Includes industry data and business reference solutions, such as the *Dun & Bradstreet Million Dollar Directory,* which includes in-depth information on more than a million leading U.S. public and private businesses.

(continued)

TABLE 10.5

## SOURCES OF INFORMATION (CONTINUED)

- **Wall Street Journal Online** (http://www.wsj.com) Includes the *Dow Jones Interactive Publications Library*, a searchable database of articles published in more than five thousand newspapers, newswires, magazines, trade and business journals, transcripts, and newsletters.

- **Lexis/Nexis** (http://www.lexis-nexis.com/) *Lexis-Nexis* is an online, full-text database that contains comprehensive information in the areas of business, news, government, finance, patents, company information, law, legislation, and other items of value to salespeople implementing the selling process. Sources include newspapers, journals, wire services, research reports, press releases, transcripts, codes, and regulations. One of the strongest features of Lexis-Nexis is that it is updated continuously throughout the day, which makes it a fantastic resource for current information. Another advantage of Lexis-Nexis is that you can access the full text of articles you are viewing and print or download that information at your computer workstation, without having to track down your information piece by piece. However, Lexis-Nexis is a complicated online service, and often requires assistance on use. Also, you must pay for the service unless your school has purchased it for free use by students.

- **STAT-USA** (http://www.stat-usa.gov/stat-usa.html) A service of the United States Department of Commerce, this web site provides vital economic, business, and international trade information from hundreds of government offices and divisions.

- **BigYellow** (http://www1.bigyellow.com) Find more than sixteen million U.S. business telephone listings, one hundred million U.S. residential telephone listings, or more than fifteen million email addresses from all over the world; also includes global directories.

- **Internet 800 Directory** (http://www.inter800.com) Find any toll-free 800 or 888 number; this is a free service for users.

## Understanding Professional Buyers

Once salespeople could rely chiefly on personal creative selling skills, but now they usually deal with professional buyers or purchasing agents who mostly want the salesperson's assurance of on-time delivery, product quality, and reliable service. They want to feel sure a product will positively affect their company's profits, and they are demanding greater service and more concessions in price while reducing the number of approved vendors for their local operating units. Professional buyers expect a salesperson to not only know their needs well, but also have keen knowledge about *their* customers' needs.[10]

Salespeople also need to know how their product is compatible with the buying organization's strategy. That is, how does the product fit in with the customer's strategy and achievement of objectives? Such knowledge can be helpful in crafting the sales presentation and in demonstrating to buyers that the salesperson's offering does more than solve a problem: it actually helps them achieve their firm's goal.

*Professional salespeople need an extensive knowledge base to work effectively with their increasingly demanding customers.*

William Taufic/Corbis

One overriding goal of most customers is higher profitability. To assist in achieving this goal, salespeople should help customers *sell through* to their own customers. This can be done in many ways, such as sharing marketing research findings, recommending promotional strategies, or helping train the employees of customers.

**Professional Knowledge Is Essential.** Salespeople who can demonstrate that they have studied the customer's business and understand the customer's problems in serving its own customers will have a firm foundation upon which to build a sales relationship. Such a well-grounded, long-term relationship will be based on mutual trust, cooperation, interdependence, social relationships, adaptation, and commitment.[11] Although friendliness and an outgoing personality help, professional knowledge is essential for success in sales. The major attributes that buyers want from sales personnel are directly related to salesperson knowledge:[12]

- Thoroughness and follow through
- Knowledge of product line
- Willingness to go to bat for buyer within the supplier's firm
- Market knowledge and willingness to keep the buyer informed
- Imagination in applying products to the buyers' needs
- Knowledge of the buyer's product line
- Diplomacy in dealing with operating departments
- Preparation for well-planned sales calls
- Regularity of sales calls
- Technical education

**Buyers Are Human, Too.** Although novice salespeople sometimes think that organizations buy for purely rational reasons, remember that professional buyers are human beings with needs and motivations that cannot help but influence their purchase decisions. For instance, a corporation will seldom buy a multimillion-dollar executive airplane unless the CEO becomes personally excited about it and conveys this enthusiasm and support for the acquisition to the company's purchasing agent. In working with buyers, a perceptive salesperson can soon determine whether emotional as well as rational factors might influence a purchase decision. Emotional factors can include the reward/punishment system for purchase mistakes, perceived purchase risk, buyer self-confidence, perceived image of the supplier, or the personal relationship between the salesperson and the buyer. Perceptive salespeople will make all necessary efforts to satisfy the emotional as well as the rational needs of a buyer.

# Will the Real Prospects Please Stand Up?

Finding potential buyers who have the *need*, *authority*, *money*, and *eligibility* to buy is a never-ending struggle in sales. Salespeople spend more time in prospecting and qualifying leads than on any sales activity, but developing truly qualified prospects still is a major conundrum for many salespeople. Like the long-running television show, *To Tell The Truth*, it would be great if salespeople could just ask the real prospects to please stand up. But most salespeople must rely on prospect lists generated from customer referrals or purchased from commercial companies. Such lists, however, are fraught with difficulties. Names and addresses may contain many errors, contain entities that may lie outside the target market, or the list may be badly outdated, especially with regard to contact people. To attend to these problems, some software companies have developed programs that assist sales organizations in verifying their prospect lists. With the aid of these increasingly sophisticated software programs, less time is being wasted in trial-and-error phone calls and travel to determine whether or not a name and address on a prospect list is accurate—and a potential customer. Recently developed software enables sales organizations to examine their prospects' target markets and develop their own target market list through sequential analyses. With such high-tech assistance and more sure to come, salespeople are increasing their effectiveness and efficiency by spending less time with unqualified prospects and more time closing sales.

## Sales Management Information Systems

The increasing sophistication of professional buyers and their access to information will continue to challenge salespeople to find new sources and faster methods of obtaining information for customers. One particularly fast and valuable source is the company's management information system (MIS). In some progressive companies, a subset of the management information system (MIS) is the **sales management information system (SMIS)**—an ongoing process of collecting, sorting, classifying, storing, analyzing, interpreting, retrieving, and reporting information for the development of sales strategies and tactics. More companies are insisting that salespeople assume responsibility for gathering marketing intelligence on a continuous basis for the company MIS and SMIS. For instance, one large industrial and consumer chemical manufacturer tells its salespeople, "Don't just sell—get information. What do our customers need? What's the competition doing? What sort of financial package do we need to win the order?" Salespeople can play an integral role in collecting such information if given the charge to do so—and incentives as well.

**Sales Management Information System (SMIS)** An ongoing process of collecting, sorting, classifying, storing, analyzing, interpreting, retrieving, and reporting information for the development of sales strategies and tactics.

Developments such as the information explosion, ever more complex products, the shift from local to global competition, the growing professionalism of buyers, and customers' continued development of sophisticated management information systems to determine order quantities and potential suppliers, make it increasingly important that salespeople have ready access to essential information from the SMIS. Read *On the Frontlines*, on p. 325, to find out how firms use database marketing to overcome one of their major problems.

In this age of exponential growth of information, salespeople who want to excel must understand that they cannot rest or rely for long on what they already know. They must tirelessly search online and offline for information that can help in the personal selling process and in building long-term, professional, and trustful relationships with customers. Salespeople who have the most timely and best information to share with customers will achieve major advantages over competitors.

## SUMMARY

To be effective and efficient revenue generators, salespeople today need to keenly understand their company and their company's products, competition, and markets. Whether selling low-tech or high-tech products, salespeople must present product features, advantages, and benefits that match their customers' needs and wants. After completing the company's training program, the most successful salespeople keep up to date by reading professional and general business magazines, and by making use of trade association directories, business guides, indexes, the web, and government publications in searching for specific information. The roles of professional buyers for organizations are expanding dramatically, as top management more clearly understands their impact on profitability. To keep pace with professional buyers and computerized purchasing systems, salespeople must be continuously seeking information from offline and online sources to better serve their customers.

## KEY TERMS

| | | |
|---|---|---|
| Mission statement | Tactic | *Business Periodicals Index* |
| Strategy | *Thomas Register* | Sales Management Information System (SMIS) |

## CHAPTER REVIEW QUESTIONS

1. Why is it critical that salespeople understand their company and their company's products, competition, and markets? How might salespeople acquire this understanding?

2. Why is it important for salespeople to understand their company's culture and that of the sales department? How would you suggest that a salesperson quickly learn about the culture of his or her company and department?

3. Name the ten attributes that industrial buyers say they like in salespeople.

4. What are some of the offline and online sources through which salespeople can find information to help them better serve customers?

5. What is the *Thomas Register*? How might salespeople use it?

6. For what specific purposes can an SMIS be used? How are salespeople expected to contribute to development of a SMIS?

## TOPICS FOR THOUGHT AND CLASS DISCUSSION

1. In what ways might the company's stakeholders, other than customers, affect personal selling?

2. If you were a new sales trainee about to start a two-week training program, what instructional methods would you prefer? Why?

3. Why do you think that the role of company purchasing agents is expanding?

4. Do you think it's necessary for salespeople to know nearly as much about competitive products as they do about their own company's products? Or is it sufficient to just know the major strengths and weaknesses of competitive products? Why?

5. Why do you think so many product innovations come from smaller companies instead of the most dominant company in the industry?

6. Name some offline and online sources of information you have used to find information. What information were you looking for? Were you successful in finding what you needed?

## PROJECTS FOR PERSONAL GROWTH

1. Contact two business-to-business salespeople and ask what their firms' policies and procedures are for
   (a) processing special rush orders.
   (b) approving customer credit.
   (c) delivering and installing products.
   (d) opening new customer accounts.
   (e) handling returned or damaged goods.

2. Ask each of the two salespeople you contacted above to describe their company's culture. Is their sales department culture different from their company's overall culture? If so, why?

3. Choose a company of interest to you, then use a (a) trade association directory, (b) business guide, (c) index, and (d) government publication to learn as much as you can about the company's history, mission, organization of the sales force, products sold, markets served, and major competitors. Which source(s) proved most helpful? Write a three-page report summarizing what you discovered about the company that would be important in selling to them.

4. Choose a favorite product or service that you have recently purchased, then prepare a product knowledge worksheet comparing the product you bought versus three competitive products you might have purchased.

## GEE, WHAT COULD HAVE GONE WRONG?

"You can find him in the warehouse," said the store clerk in response to Marty's question. Marty Simpson began his walk toward the back of the store, but he stopped and inspected some of his chief competitor's products displayed prominently at the end of the aisle. They sell some good products, he thought, but ours are better. He smiled and felt confident that next time he was in this store, he would be looking at his own company's aisle display. Marty was here in Houston, Texas, where Consolidated Cabinet Company had just begun selling its products, to see Arnold Burke, owner of Burke's Kitchen and Bath Store.

Marty had just returned from Consolidated's twenty-fifth annual sales meeting in Dallas. At the meeting, Consolidated, a relatively small furniture manufacturing company, had unveiled its new line of kitchen cabinets to its salespeople. The high-quality cabinets—premium priced, all-wood construction—were a step up for Consolidated, which in the past had marketed low- to mid-priced cabinets made of particleboard and wood veneer. The low-end cabinets were mainly segmented toward the do-it-yourselfer and were primarily sold in retail home center stores under the store's private label. However, the company believed the best market for this new line was the kitchen contractor. Kitchen contractors shop at specialty stores for their cabinets, where quality products sell at prices much higher than at home center retailers. For Consolidated this represented a new channel of distribution where they planned to sell at a premium price under their own "Consolidated" brand.

This would be Marty's first meeting with Arnold. Marty saw Arnold in the warehouse talking with two men, and waited until Arnold finished his conversation to approach him.

**SIMPSON:** Mr. Burke, my name is Marty Simpson, and I represent Consolidated Cabinet Company. I was wondering if you might have a few minutes to hear about our exciting new line of high-quality kitchen cabinets.

**BURKE:** Well, actually I'm a little busy at the moment. What was the name of your company again?

**SIMPSON:** Consolidated Cabinet Company. I promise this will only take a few minutes, and I also promise it will be well worth your time.

**BURKE:** Well, okay.

**SIMPSON:** Great!

[Marty proceeded to pull out his selling aids and began explaining the new cabinet line.]

**SIMPSON:** We call this line the Classic America, and you can see from the picture in the brochure that it is a beautiful piece. Let me tell you a few things about it. It's completely made of wood and comes in the finest hardwoods. As you know, the benefit of all wood is that it will retain its quality look forever. Each piece is handcrafted so that you can be assured of the highest quality with few defects. The designs are classic raised panel so they won't go out of style. The hardware is all metal, and the hinges are the highest grade so it will always close, and you will never have to replace them. And they're available in thirty-two different cabinet designs. Well, what do you think?

**BURKE:** Frankly, I'm happy with my current supplier and its line I'm carrying now. I've done business with them for a long time, and they provide excellent service. I don't see that you're offering any better deal, and their product seems to have the same things as yours, so I can't see changing now.

**SIMPSON:** Well, Mr. Burke, think it over and in a few weeks I'll check to see if you've changed your mind.

(continued)

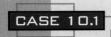

## GEE, WHAT COULD HAVE GONE WRONG?
(CONTINIUED)

Marty left wondering if he had given a good presentation, and if he could have done anything during the presentation that would have improved his chances.

**Questions**

1. What do you think Marty did wrong in his sales presentation?

2. Would Marty have benefited from using any sales aids? Explain.

3. What should Marty say to Mr. Burke when Marty calls back?

## I'LL COOK HIS GOOSE

**B**eth Morelli was in her first year of selling business forms for Forms International. She was walking down the hall to the office of Chuck Stoner, purchasing agent for Forest Building Supply (FBS). Beth knew little about FBS, except that it was a division of a large multinational enterprise and that FBS had just opened this office two months ago. Even before Beth entered the office, she was apprehensive because she always had difficulty approaching new accounts, especially ones she didn't know much about. But the sight of Bill Reilly made her even more concerned. Reilly, a sales representative for Troy Corporation, a major competitor of her company, had been a nemesis of hers from day one. Seeing him leave Stoner's office made Beth realize that she had a major selling job ahead of her. Beth's boss, who had covered the territory before her, warned her about Bill Reilly. Not only had Reilly covered the same territory for six years, he was well liked and respected by customers. And sure enough, even though Beth felt confident that her products were superior to those of any competitor's, including Troy Corporation's, in her first three months Reilly managed to beat her out at four different accounts.

As they passed each other in the hallway, Bill Reilly greeted Beth cordially and asked, "How are things going?" Beth was always a little surprised by Reilly's friendly greeting each time they met because they were in head-to-head competition on many accounts. After a light-hearted chat, Beth excused herself so she wouldn't be late for her appointment with Stoner. Reilly called to her, "Good luck." As she walked towards Stoner's office, Beth thought, "If he wasn't such a tough competitor, I might really like Bill Reilly."

As she entered Stoner's office, Beth was pleased to see him stand up, smile, and extend his hand. Beth returned the handshake cordially.

**MORELLI:**   Good morning, Mr. Stoner. You seem to be in a good mood.

**STONER:**   Yes, I am. Bill Reilly just gave me two tickets to tonight's baseball game. My son's going to be thrilled.

**MORELLI:**   Well, that's nice, but I heard there's a 50-50 chance of rain tonight.

**STONER:**   [Looking a little annoyed] I sure hope not. What do you have to show me today?

[Beth makes her sales presentation, explaining her company's services and showing examples of her company's business forms.]

**MORELLI:**   So, Mr. Stoner, what do you think?

**STONER:**   Well, your products do look good, but, I'm not sure they're any better than Troy's.

[Beth thinks for a moment. She wants desperately to win this account.]

**MORELLI:**   Well, Mr. Stoner, from what I've seen, I'm not sure why anyone would be interested in Troy's products. They have slow service, old-fashioned looking products, and high prices. Our company's a lot more progressive. Troy's been having some union problems lately that have affected their customer service. Did you know that they sent one hundred cases of business forms to Metropolitan Hospital last month, and all had the wrong address on them? Every one of them had to be returned, and for two weeks the hospital had to ration forms to keep from running out. Customers can't afford many mistakes like that, can they?

[Beth thinks to herself, "That ought to make Stoner nervous about choosing Reilly's company over mine."]

(continued)

## CASE 10.2

## I'LL COOK HIS GOOSE (CONTINUED)

**MORELLI:** Mr. Stoner, if I can take an order this week, I'm authorized to give you a 10 percent discount on the entire order. How many cases of forms can I order for you?

**STONER:** Well, I've got to run to a ten o'clock meeting now, but I'll get back to you when I decide. Thanks for coming in.

Before Beth could say another word, Stoner was standing up and heading out the door to his meeting. As Beth was gathering up her presentation materials, she wondered what her chances were of landing a big order.

### Questions

1. How do you think Mr. Stoner perceived Beth Morelli's sales presentation?

2. What do you think Beth should have done differently? Why?

3. How would you compete with a competitive salesperson like Bill Reilly?

4. What advice would you give Beth if Mr. Stoner calls her later? What should Beth do if Mr. Stoner doesn't call her?

## CHAPTER 11

# Communicating Effectively with Diverse Customers

*"Half the world is composed of people who have something to say and can't and the other half who have nothing to say and keep on saying it."*

*Robert Frost*

## After Reading This Chapter, You Should Understand:

- The five modes of communication.
- The three dimensions and four levels of listening.
- The formats and types of questions.
- How to use space in the buyer-seller interaction.
- The use of body language.
- The four communication styles, sources of conflicts between them, and how to flex with different communication styles of buyers.
- How to build trust with prospects and customers.

## INSIDE PERSONAL SELLING:
## *Meet Ewell Hopkins of Sapient Corporation*

Effective communication is the key to selling services—especially the business strategy consulting, systems design, software implementation, and research services that Ewell Hopkins sells on behalf of Sapient Corporation. As Director of Client Relations, Hopkins needs top-notch communication skills to uncover a prospect's problems before he can begin to sell anything: "We interpret a business need, reach consensus with the client through workshops and other interviewing processes, agree on the ultimate goal, and then design a solution to meet that goal."

Hopkins considers listening more important than talking in a sales situation. "You can't learn anything when you're talking," he notes. "More importantly, prospects look for someone who understands their unique needs. If you start off talking, prospects will

be concerned that you are not prepared to listen or understand their needs."

To probe for needs, goals, and information, Hopkins asks open-ended questions beginning with "Why . . . ?" or "How . . . ?" and explains his rationale for asking so prospects understand where the discussion is leading. "You don't want people wondering why you're asking the question," he stresses.

Not long ago, Hopkins met with a Canadian financial firm seeking a creative way of using technology to strengthen relations with existing customers and attract new customers for its retirement products. He had to prove that he understood the prospect's challenge and could help the prospect reach its goals. This required listening actively and empathetically to the prospect's management and its customers. "We established why customers want retirement accounts and what they liked about working with an investment provider," Hopkins says. Based on this research, the client and the Sapient team collectively came up with the idea of an interactive game to make retirement planning more appealing to the prospect's customers.

When Hopkins meets in a prospect's office, he looks around for conversation-sparking ideas. "People put things in their personal space for a reason," he observes. "You can discuss virtually anything if it's in plain view." In a group meeting, he lets the prospect's representatives sit first and notes how they position themselves versus one another: "If I bring two or three colleagues, I spread them out so my people are not all seated on one side with the prospect's people on the other side. I will intentionally sit on 'their' side."

After the sale, Hopkins closely monitors progress toward meeting deadlines and ensures that the Sapient team is fully informed about the client's needs and situation. This requires good internal and external communication. He stays in touch with the client and advises his colleagues of any special pressures or requests that affect the project. "People don't like to work in isolation," Hopkins explains. "If you explain the context and show how they fit into the big picture, people are much more motivated to do a quality job."

**D**o you think that you're an effective communicator? If you are, that's great! But most people require training to become effective communicators. As a college student, you've probably had a lot of practice and become a pretty good speaker. But how much practice and how good have you become at the other half of communication, that is, listening? Of course, you listen carefully in class for anything that might be on an upcoming exam. But what about outside of class? Before responding, candidly answer the following questions: Do you always carefully listen and try to fully comprehend what another person is saying? Do you "cool your jets" long enough to let the other person finish before you start speaking? Do you seldom interrupt other people while they're talking . . . and rarely complete their sentences for them even when they seem to be hesitating? Do you avoid anticipating or prejudging what the other person is going to say? Do you stay away from thinking about your own reply until the other person has finished talking? Are you good at putting yourself in the other person's shoes and empathizing with his or her viewpoint even when it disagrees with yours? Are you perceptive in picking up subtle, underlying points and body language beyond an individual's spoken words?

If you have honestly answered yes to all the foregoing questions, you are probably an excellent listener. If you answered no to one or more, you, like most of us, could improve your overall communication skills. As indicated by the questions you answered, communicating isn't *just* about speaking clearly, audibly, articulately, or even persuasively. It involves much more. By the end of this chapter, you will not only learn what communication is and how to do it effectively, but you should also be well on your way toward becoming a better communicator—an invaluable asset for a salesperson or, for that matter, anyone in any career or walk of life.

Successful salespeople, like successful people in most any profession, are excellent communicators. So central is communication to successful selling and marketing that the words of Marion Harper, Jr., from many years ago are still true today:

> More and more it is becoming apparent that marketing is almost entirely communications. The product communicates; the price communicates; the package communicates; salespeople communicate to the prospect, to the trade, to management and to each other; also, prospects, dealers, management and competitors communicate.[1]

## WHAT IS COMMUNICATION?

**Communication** A process in which information and understanding are conveyed in two-way exchanges between two or more people.

**Promotion** Typically, a one-way flow of persuasive information from a seller to a buyer.

**Communication** is a process whereby information and understanding are conveyed between two or more people. Communication should not be confused with the related concept of promotion. **Promotion** is typically a one-way flow of information and persuasion from seller to buyer, whereas communication is a *two-way exchange*.

We use five distinct modes of communication: (1) listening, (2) writing, (3) talking, (4) reading, and (5) an often overlooked means—*nonverbal* communication. Of the first four modes, the average person, unlike many salespeople,

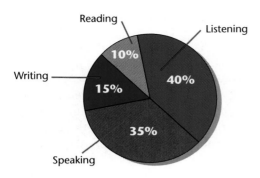

**FIGURE 11.1**

TIME SPENT IN COMMUNICATION

normally spends more time *listening*, as shown in Figure 11.1. Nonverbal communication, sometimes called "body language," is expressed through our bodies (face, arms, hands, legs, and posture) or our voices (rate of speech, volume, pitch, tone, accent, rhythm, emphasis, and pauses). And it has significant meaning in buyer-seller exchanges, as you will see later in the chapter.

Keen listening is especially important for salespeople. You can't learn anything about prospects and customers while you're talking. In fact, to succeed at personal selling, you must learn to be an expert listener, one who shows empathy and respect for prospects and continually strives to enhance rapport with them. Keep in mind that you, the salesperson, are not the only one with a message to communicate. Customers want you to understand them and comprehend *their* message *first*. Unfortunately, a chronic complaint of buyers is that salespeople simply do not listen to their customers. Without listening attentively to customers, solving their problems and satisfying their needs will be virtually impossible. Read *It's Up to You* and give your communication skills a try.

## IT'S UP TO YOU

You are in the middle of your sales presentation to a buying committee at a large company. As the presentation has unfolded, you seem to be doing fairly well: one of the prospect's representatives seems particularly interested. She is responding favorably to your questions, and, in turn, is asking you a lot of questions. What is troubling you, however, is that the prospect keeps interrupting your presentation, and you make little progress. Some of her comments pertain to questions or issues relevant to the presentation; others, however, are totally unrelated ones or ones that you will answer later in the presentation. You don't want to offend the prospect by telling her to stop interrupting, but you also want to complete a solid, informative, convincing presentation before you run out of time and some of the members of the buying committee have to leave. What is your next move? How will you conduct the rest of this call?

# DEVELOPING COMMUNICATION SKILLS

Today's top professional salespeople continually increase their communication effectiveness and efficiency by improving their skills in (1) listening, (2) asking questions, (3) using space, (4) interpreting nonverbal communication, and (5) dealing with alternate communication styles of buyers. Let's discuss these skills and ways that you can develop and use them in your sales career.

**Sensing** Most basic aspect of listening, it includes hearing words, inflection, and paralanguage (for example, speed of speech, use of colloquialisms), as well as observation of nonverbal language (for example, body language, facial expressions).

**Processing** Refers to operations within the salesperson's mind that give meaning to the prospect's message through understanding, interpreting, evaluating, and remembering the communication.

**Responding** Assures the prospect that the salesperson has been listening accurately and is encouraging the communication to continue.

**Marginal Listening** Occurs when salespeople hear the prospect's words but are easily distracted and may allow their minds to wander.

**Evaluative Listening** Seller concentrates on what the buyer is saying but fails to sense what is being said through nonverbal or subtle verbal cues.

**Active Listening** Occurs when the salesperson receives a message, processes it, and then responds to it to encourage further communication.

## Listening

Becoming an effective listener does not mean that you must give equal attention to everything you hear. On any given day, you may hear or have the opportunity to hear an incredible quantity and variety of messages from family, friends, colleagues, subordinates, superiors, radio and television broadcasts, prospects, and customers, and from interactions with service people of all kinds—from taxi cab drivers to restaurant waiters to health care professionals. Although you may have plenty to hear, relatively little of it will merit your full attention, and you require only certain ways to listen to them to be an effective communicator. Your mind processes messages of importance to you, filters those that seem irrelevant, and perhaps dismisses some summarily.

**Three Dimensions of Listening.** We refer to three dimensions of listening.[2] The first dimension is **sensing.** The most basic aspect of listening, it entails hearing words, inflection, and paralanguage (for example, speed of speech, use of colloquialisms), as well as observing nonverbal language (for example, body language, facial expressions). **Processing,** the second dimension, refers to operations in the salesperson's mind that give meaning to the message through understanding, interpreting, evaluating, and remembering the communication. After sensing and processing the message, salespeople engage in the third dimension, **responding** to the message. Listeners send information back to speakers indicating that the speakers' message has been received correctly. Responding assures the prospect that the salesperson has listened accurately and is encouraging the communication to continue.

**Levels of Listening.** In addition to the foregoing three dimensions of listening, a *hierarchy* of listening involves four kinds of listening, from least effective to most effective.[3] When **marginal listening** occurs, salespeople hear words but are easily distracted and may allow their minds to wander. This flawed kind of listening can cause the salesperson to miss a key point or important material provided by the buyer.

**Evaluative listening** entails concentrating on what the buyer is saying but not sensing what is being said through nonverbal or subtle verbal cues. As a result, the salesperson is likely to process the buyer's message inaccurately and not understand the true meaning of the communication.

**Active listening** occurs when the salesperson receives a verbal and nonverbal message, processes it, and then responds to it to encourage further communication. Moreover, active listeners provide verbal and nonverbal feedback to the buyer. Salespeople who actively listen tend to use all of their senses to clearly understand the message—and communicate that to prospects.

The highest level of listening is **active empathetic listening (AEL)**. With AEL, the salesperson

> . . . receives verbal and nonverbal messages, processes them cognitively, responds to them verbally and nonverbally, and attempts to assess their underlying meaning intuitively by putting [himself or herself] in the customer's place throughout.[4]

By putting yourself in the customer's shoes, you show genuine concern for your prospect. And when you show sincere concern for prospects, they are likely to respond favorably to you and your offering. Top-performing salespeople are effective active empathetic listeners. An illustration of the four different levels of listening is provided in Table 11.1.

**Guidelines for Effective Listening.** Effective listening is an active process. As noted above, even when salespeople hear a prospect's words, they must observe body language and listen carefully for voice inflection and tone to fully understand what the words mean. The guidelines described in Table 11.2 are those that effective listeners employ.

**Active Empathetic Listening (AEL)** Highest level of listening when the salesperson receives verbal and nonverbal messages, processes them cognitively, responds to them verbally and nonverbally, and attempts to assess their underlying meaning intuitively by putting self in the customer's place throughout.

---

**TABLE 11.1**

## EXAMPLES OF FOUR LEVELS OF LISTENING

Car Buyer: I'm not sure I like this car's color.

Salesperson responds with *marginal listening:* Let's take a test drive. [The salesperson has not really heard what the prospect was saying.]

Salesperson responds with *evaluative listening:* There's a classic blue one over there. Let's take a test drive. [The salesperson failed to sense what the prospect was saying owing to a failure to sense the prospect's verbal and nonverbal cues.]

Salesperson responds with *active listening:* What is it that you dislike about the color of the car? Is there anything else you don't like about the car? [The salesperson accurately sensed verbal and nonverbal messages, but failed to put himself or herself in the prospect's shoes.]

Salesperson responds with *active empathetic listening:* You seem to be saying that this car is not right for your company. What are the really key features that you want your car to have? We'll consider only cars that have those particular features. [The salesperson has identified with the prospect's perspective to better empathize and understand what the prospect was attempting to communicate.]

***Source:*** *Copyright © 1999 by Pi Sigma Epsilon, Inc. From* Journal of Personal Selling and Sales Management *19, No. 1, (Winter 1999): 16–17. Reprinted with permission.*

## TABLE 11.2

## GUIDELINES FOR EFFECTIVE LISTENING

- **Ask Probing Questions:** As a salesperson, your most important tool is the probing question. Probing allows you to uncover a sales opportunity. Further, questions can stimulate a need for your product and ultimately convert the prospect into a customer.

- **Paraphrase the Information You Hear:** In paraphrasing, you restate the prospect's key words for emphasis and understanding. Be careful when using this technique, however, to avoid annoying customers by echoing everything the prospect says. A *confirmatory paraphrase* simply restates a prospect's comment to confirm an attitude or fact. This technique can help build rapport and a climate of empathy and mutual understanding. For example, you can say, "Then, it's my understanding that you think your plant manager would like us to implement our 'just-in-time inventory response' program right away." Paraphrasing indicates to the prospect that you are attentively listening, understanding his or her concerns, and showing genuine concern for what is being said.

- **Use a Leading Phrase When Appropriate:** With a leading phrase you subtly encourage prospects to reexamine and modify their views by interpreting their words to make your point. For instance, when the prospect comments, "Your product may be the best, but it is just too expensive," a leading paraphrase would be, "If I understand you correctly, you think that price is a more critical consideration than product quality." You have to be careful in using leading paraphrases because your interpretation of their words can irritate prospects. A prospect might testily retort, "I didn't say that quality is less important than a reasonable price. I said that we need both." Hearing this response, you would be wise to back off a little and reply, "I'm sorry I misunderstood. I know that you just want the best value for your company. And, I assure you, Mr. Peters, that our product will be your best buy over the long run because our quality is much higher and our price is only a little higher than our competitors'."

- **Clarify the Information:** Sometimes in communicating with prospects, conversations become a little vague. It's better to seek clarification before the sale is made than after the sale is closed and corrective action is impossible. Make sure that you understand exactly why, where, when, and how the product or service is desired by asking follow-up questions to clarify your understanding. For example: "Now, let me make sure I understand exactly *when* you need the stronger steel and *where* it should be delivered. If one of our big trailer rigs dumped a load of steel in the wrong place, you'd probably come looking for me. You said to deliver one trailer load to Twelfth and Market Streets on the morning of August 31st at 7:30 A.M.—right?"

- **Use Affirmative Responses:** Salespeople can convey to prospects and customers that they are actively empathetically listening by nodding their heads, maintaining good eye contact, and by an occasional comment like, "I see," "Okay," "Yes," or "Uh-huh." Doing so informs the prospect of your listening and allows you to acknowledge that what the prospect is saying is important to you.

(continued)

| TABLE 11.2 |
| --- |
| GUIDELINES FOR EFFECTIVE LISTENING (CONTINUED) |

- **Welcome Pauses and Silences:** Don't be fearful of long pauses or silences in communicating with prospects. Remember the old saw: "Silence is golden." A common mistake of rookie salespeople is to try to fill any gap in communication with words. Short pauses or longer silences give both you and the prospect some time to think and to make sure that you haven't overlooked anything. Silences by the salesperson also encourage the prospect to continue talking and providing more information about the purchase decision and reasons for buying. Most prospects and customers like to talk—so let them! You will likely only gain from your silence (now's the time to use your listening skills!).

- **Summarize the Conversation:** At the conclusion of the sales call, it's a good idea to summarize the sales interview so that the prospect has a final chance to correct any errors or misunderstandings. Summaries demonstrate to the prospect that you have been an attentive listener throughout the selling process. This summary can also reassure the prospect that you are a thorough, conscientious, and empathetic professional.

## Asking Questions

Studies have shown that the more questions salespeople ask, the more successful they are in closing sales.[5] Top salespeople know that superior selling is *less telling, more asking.* They are nearly always excellent questioners. They know exactly what information they need, so each of their questions has a specific purpose. They develop questioning skills and approaches that enable them to quickly discover the following:

- The best prospects
- The prospect's real needs
- What, when, and how they buy
- Who influences the purchase decision
- What product or service benefits they want
- Why prospects seem to prefer one brand over another
- How quickly the prospect wants the product
- How the prospect will pay for the order
- What kind of post-purchase service the prospect will require
- The competition and what they offer

**Question Formats.** Here are three basic question *formats* that experienced salespeople use: (1) open-ended, (2) closed, and (3) semi-open questions. *Open-ended questions* usually begin with words such as *who, what, why, where, when,* and *how.* They allow prospects to answer in their own words and are best for eliciting general background or prospect feelings, confirming understanding of a comment, and probing for subconscious feelings. Open-ended questions look like these: "What kind of benefits are you seeking from this

## KEEPING UP ONLINE: BIZJOURNALS.COM

**B***izjournals.com* is a daily online newspaper that provides exclusive local business intelligence in fifty-eight U.S. major markets, such as New York, Chicago, and Minneapolis-St. Paul. Its access to news and information can provide salespeople the competitive edge for the market or markets they choose. Visit Bizjournals.com at http://www.bizjournals.bcentral.com. How might bizjournals.com assist you in your sales career? How might it help you improve your communication skills with prospects and customers?

---

product?" "How do you think you'll use the product?" "Why do you believe that Brand A is better than Brand B?"

*Closed questions* usually can be answered directly with simple yes or no responses. They are best for ensuring that you are on the right track, confirming information, and narrowing the focus of discussion. Closed questions often begin with some form of the verbs *be, do,* or *have.* Some examples of closed questions are the following: "Are your office computers networked?" "Do you think Mr. Johnson would be interested in buying laptop computers for the sales force?" "Will he be back from vacation next Monday?"

*Semi-open questions* seek precise information and thus tend to have only one or a few possible answers. They help you obtain specific facts. Semi-open questions include the following: "When can we set up an appointment?" "What day do you want us to deliver the equipment?" "What's your preference—the mahogany executive desk or the walnut one?" "Do you want to pay by cash or credit?" Read *Keeping Up Online* above and determine how its web site can assist you in formulating questions for prospects.

**Types of Questions.**  Professional salespeople use six basic *types* of questions: **probing questions, evaluative questions,** strategic questions, tactical questions, **dichotomous questions,** and multiple questions. Each of the six has a different purpose and appropriate time in which to be used. Table 11.3 offers detailed information about the six major types of questions.

Asking the right types of questions in the right format, in the right tenor, and in the right context is both an art and a science. Undoubtedly it requires practice to produce effective results over time. But just as verbal questions are critical in the sales job, so are written questions sent to prospects and customers in the form of a questionnaire. Read *From the Command Post* on p. 344 to see how some companies are making increased use of cyberspace to ask important questions whose answers can ultimately affect marketing and sales force efforts.

**Probing Question**  Used to search for information when prospects and customers have difficulty articulating their precise needs.

**Evaluative Question**  Used within the open-ended question format to stimulate prospects and customers to talk about their general or specific goals, problems, and needs.

**Dichotomous Question**  Used to set up a clear-cut "either-or" answer for prospects and customers.

**TABLE 11.3**

## QUESTION TYPES, PURPOSES, APPROPRIATE USE, AND EXAMPLES

| Question Type | Purpose | When To Use | Example |
|---|---|---|---|
| **1. Probing** | Allows you to dig for information when prospects can't seem to articulate their needs or wants. | Any time after rapport has been established with prospect. | "Bob, what do you think the plant manager means by his comment?" |
| SILENCE | Encourages the prospect to keep talking. | Whenever you want the prospect to elaborate on his or her thoughts and feelings. | |
| CONSEQUENCE | Points out the disadvantages of continuing to use the prospect's present product. | During the early part of the sales presentation. | "Ms. Byrd, if you continue to use a dot matrix printer while other departments are using laser printers, aren't you afraid that top management will think your reports are less professional?" |
| ENCOURAGEMENT | Encourages prospect to continue talking by nodding agreement, making supporting sounds, looking interested, leaning forward, etc. | Anytime you want the prospect to keep talking and expanding on something. | While nodding the head, make supporting responses such as, "Yes, I see," "Go on," "Uh huh," "I didn't know that," or "Is that right?" |
| ELABORATION | Obtains more information from prospect along the same line. | Best to mix with other probes. Overuse may limit range of information obtained. | "Will you tell me a little more about the problems you're having with your current product?" |

(continued)

TABLE 11.3

## QUESTION TYPES, PURPOSES, APPROPRIATE USE, AND EXAMPLES (CONTINUED)

| Question Type | Purpose | When To Use | Example |
|---|---|---|---|
| CLARIFICATION | Requests prospect to supply additional information on specific subject. | When you need clarification about some topic or to obtain more detailed information. | "Can you explain what you mean by that?" |
| TOPIC CHANGE | To switch topics. Must be done subtly to keep from irking prospect. | When you believe you have obtained all the information you need about a given subject. | "May I ask you a question on a somewhat different topic?" |
| DIRECTIVE | Aimed at obtaining facts about a focused topic. | Within your sales presentation. | "Who will be using the facsimile machine?" |
| VERIFYING | Designed to obtain prospect confirmation of information. | To verify presales call information and set stage for further questioning. | "Are you still the purchasing agent responsible for buying truck axles?" "Do you think you'll need to buy about five thousand axles this year?" |
| LEADING | To check for understanding, obtain feedback, or answer an unspoken question. | Use later in the sales call to determine options desired and to obtain agreement on purchase decision. | "Do I understand correctly that you prefer the upgraded model?" |
| LOADED | Emotionally charged words designed to bring out strong prospect feelings. | After rapport has been established with prospect. This can be most effective in the later stages of the sales presentation or during the close. | "Don't you think that anybody who drives a foreign car is unpatriotic?" "Doesn't it make you sick to see people wearing animal fur coats?" |

(continued)

TABLE 11.3

## QUESTION TYPES, PURPOSES, APPROPRIATE USE, AND EXAMPLES (CONTINUED)

| Question Type | Purpose | When To Use | Example |
|---|---|---|---|
| **2. Evaluative** | Open-ended questions designed to stimulate prospects to talk about their goals, problems, and needs. | To learn about the prospect's goals and what he or she thinks, feels, wants, and hopes. | "What do you think about the design for your new office?" "What are the problems with your current inventory system?" |
| DIRECT | Ask direct questions to obtain the views and opinions of prospects. | To learn about the prospect's beliefs and attitudes about selling firm, the seller's products, the product type, and such. | "What is your opinion of this kind of product?" "How do you know about our firm?" |
| INDIRECT | Learn indirectly what the prospect thinks or feels without producing a negative reaction. | When the prospect may not want to directly express his or her thoughts and feelings. | "What do you think most people in your department will say about this new photocopier?" |
| **3. Strategic** | Allows you to continue productive questioning even when the prospect is negative. | Anytime during sales call with negative prospect to uncover underlying needs and attitudes. | "Why do you think our mainframe computer isn't in the same league with the IBM computer?" |
| **4. Tactical** | To "hit the ball" back into the prospect's court when dealing with a tough question. | When the prospect asks a sensitive or irritating question to put you on the defensive. | "Don't you think that small businesses are as capable as large firms in providing quality service?" "Didn't virtually every business start out small?" |

(continued)

**TABLE 11.3**

## QUESTION TYPES, PURPOSES, APPROPRIATE USE, AND EXAMPLES (CONTINUED)

| Question Type | Purpose | When To Use | Example |
|---|---|---|---|
| **5. Dichotomous** | "Either-or" questions that set up alternatives for prospects. | During the sales close to force an indecisive prospect to make a choice. | "Would you prefer the table model or the floor model lamp for the office?" "Do you want the regular strength or industrial strength?" |
| **6. Multiple Choice** | Offer the prospect a range of choices in pushing for a purchase decision. | During the close to force a prospect to come to a decision. Offer only two or three choices to avoid confusing the prospect and delaying a decision. | "Which of the three do you want to order—the regular, large or extra large quantity?" |

## FROM THE COMMAND POST: SURVEYING CUSTOMERS VIA EMAIL

**M**ost marketing organizations are keenly aware of the difficulties associated with designing and administering surveys of customers. Phone and mail questionnaires can be very costly and time-consuming to create, distribute, and analyze. An increasing number of sales organizations have turned to developing and sending surveys to prospects and customers via email. Why? Because email offers several significant benefits: quick turnaround, increased response rates, lower costs, and faster analysis of responses.

Without requiring technical training or expensive new equipment, questionnaire design software enables salespeople to develop their own questionnaires and obtain desired feedback from prospective and current customers. Salespeople can create the survey instrument on their own computers, then distribute it instantly via email to hundreds or even thousands of recipients with a mouse click or two.

Typically, respondents are instructed to go to a web site containing the survey. Depending on the software, respondents may be able to respond to the questionnaire directly from the initial email. As a result, completed survey responses often come back within hours instead of the days or weeks needed with traditional postal mail surveys. What's more, survey responses usually can be downloaded directly into statistical packages for speedy data analysis. Finally, with tight budget constraints, another major advantage of email surveys is that there are no postage costs!

## Using Space or Proxemics

The manner in which a salesperson utilizes space with prospects and customers can dramatically influence the success of his or her buyer-seller interactions. Let's see how.

**Proxemics.** **Proxemics** refers to the way people use space. Salespeople need to be aware of the proxemics of every sales situation, especially with new prospective customers, because their spatial relationship to prospects has a proven impact on the outcome of the sales presentation. You must be careful about moving too close toward a prospect who wants a little more space, or too far away from a prospect who prefers a little more intimacy. The first prospect may think that you're trying to be dominating, intimidating, or even sexy. The second prospect may perceive you as standoffish or formal. Believe it or not, where you stand in the prospect's office may well be the determining factor in your winning or losing the sale.

**Zones of Buyer-Seller Interaction.** People in the United States appear to recognize four zones of human interaction: (1) *intimate*—for loved ones or close friends, (2) *personal*—for business acquaintances, (3) *social*—for opening most sales presentations, and (4) *public*—for selling to a group. In each situation, people are most comfortable with an appropriate distance between themselves and the persons with whom they are communicating. Prospects tend to stake out a zone or surround themselves with a "private sphere" in which they feel most comfortable.

*Intimate zones* are about an arm's length (roughly two feet) and are reserved for loved ones or close friends. In general, avoid entering a prospect's intimate space, because many prospects resent this space invasion as a pushy attempt to dominate. If you're alert, you'll notice prospects recoiling when you move into their intimate space. Quickly move back when the prospect seems uncomfortable or tries to pull back.

*Personal zones* (two to four feet) are areas that strangers or business acquaintances are normally allowed to enter. Some prospects are even uncomfortable with new salespeople in this area. Desks or tables are often used as barriers to keep salespeople and others from coming closer than this personal zone.

*Social zones* (four to twelve feet) are best for most sales presentations. You should begin the sales presentation in the middle of the social distance zone, six to eight feet, in order to avoid putting the prospect on the defensive. This is especially true if you are not well known to the prospect. Later, as rapport grows, prospects may invite you into their personal space by pulling their chair closer or moving out from behind their desk. Highly successful salespeople gradually move closer to prospects as they prepare to close the sale.[6]

*How a salesperson uses interpersonal physical space will have a dramatic impact on the success of the buyer-seller interaction.*
Jose Luis Palaez/Corbis

**Proxemics** Refers to the spatial relationships of people and objects.

*Public zones* (more than twelve feet) are typical when a salesperson makes a presentation to a group of people. This distance is about the same as that between a teacher and students in a classroom. It is nonthreatening and allows people to feel comfortable and secure in their own territorial zones.

### Interpreting Nonverbal Communication: Kinesics or Body Language

**Kinesics** Describes bodily gestures and movements with regard to what these gestures and movements communicate to other people.

Much of human communication is nonverbal, even though most of us are unaware when we communicate this way. **Kinesics** is a term describing any movement in our bodies, including shifts in posture (body angle); facial expressions; eye movements; or arm, hand, and leg movements. Every movement or gesture from a shrug of our shoulders, to crossing our legs, to the subtle wink of an eye is a part of kinesics or body language. Unconscious movements or changes such as a throbbing neck muscle, heavy breathing, or a blushing face can reveal many emotions, including tenseness, frustration, anger, or embarrassment.

**Reading Body Language.** Everybody reads and uses body language to some degree or another. Many professional athletes are expert readers and users of body language—and this ability gives them a real competitive edge. For example, clever opponents might observe that a football quarterback slaps the center with the back of his right hand a split second before the snap. On pass plays, some linesmen will lean back with their shoulders up and hand barely touching the ground to enable them to step back and block more effectively. Centers will sometimes tighten their grip on the ball just before the snap. In baseball, players converse by body language. Catchers call pitches with their fingers, and coaches use various body language signs to tell batters to bunt or base runners to steal. Some players tip off when they are going to try to steal by the way they crouch just before taking off, and some pitchers make an unconscious facial expression when they are about to throw a curve ball.

Some salespeople become expert at reading body language and use this ability to determine prospects' mental states during a sales call. Prospects are always sending signals via body language. Some of the messages are obvious. For instance, when prospects start clearing off their desk or reading their mail, they are signaling that they want to end the interview. When this happens, you should acknowledge the value of the prospect's time and try to quickly close the sale. If it appears that your close won't be successful this time, ask for another appointment, thank the prospect, then exit. Most body language is more subtle. One highly successful salesperson claims he knows of two unmistakable clues of intent to buy: (1) when prospects put their fingers on their chins, they are ready to buy; and (2) when they put their hands over their mouths or on or near their noses, they are not yet ready to buy.

**Sending Body Language Messages.** Learning to read and use nonverbal language can also be important to sales success. In a pioneering study of nonverbal communication, Edward T. Hall predicted 74 percent of the time whether or not a sale would take place by observing nonverbal language only.[7] You will make better sales presentations when your nonverbal language is harmonious with your verbal expression. We have all seen speakers whose body language wasn't in harmony with their words and voice inflections. It's almost like watching a movie where the sound and the action are not synchronized.

Nonverbal messages have several channels or vehicles: (1) distance and proximity, (2) general appearance and personal hygiene, (3) body postures and movements, (4) face, (5) arms, (6) hands, (7) legs, and (8) voice characteristics. Distance and proximity we discussed above; the others are described below.

1. *General Appearance and Hygiene:* Good grooming and personal hygiene are essential to salespeople who wish to send positive messages to prospects and customers. Shined shoes, neatly pressed shirt or blouse and suit, clean and trimmed fingernails, and neatly combed hair will enhance your communication effectiveness. Clothing style, quality, and fit can say a lot about a salesperson. What you wear should be stylish or in vogue, it should appear to be of sufficient grade, and it should complement your height and size very well. Also, most salespeople should refresh their mouths by brushing their teeth, gargling with mouthwash, or using a breath mint or spray before calling on the next customer.

2. *Body Movements:* Prospects who make side-to-side movements with their bodies are usually expressing negative feelings, perhaps anxiety and uncertainty, and prospects who move their bodies back and forth are expressing positive feelings. When prospects lean toward you, they usually are interested in what you're saying and showing a positive reaction. Prospects who lean away from you, however, are communicating negative emotions, perhaps disinterest, boredom, hesitation, wariness, or distrust.

3. *Posture:* A rigid erect posture conveys defensiveness, while a sloppy posture suggests disinterest or boredom. People who share the same opinion in a group tend to unconsciously assume the same body postures. When prospects agree with you, they may imitate your body posture. This is a signal to attempt a trial close.

4. *Eyes and Facial Expressions:* Some people have rubber faces that openly show approval, disapproval, concern, relaxation, frustration, impatience, and the range of human emotions. Other people have stone faces that reveal little about what's going on inside their heads. Eyes are the most important features on our faces. When we are interested or excited, our pupils tend to enlarge. Magicians have long known this and use their eye reading skills to identify which card we picked out of a deck. Jewelry salespeople are often so expert at reading people's eyes that jewelry buyers sometimes wear dark glasses so that salespeople cannot see their level of interest in different pieces!

5. *Eye Contact:* Eye contact in our culture conveys sincerity and interest, while eye avoidance suggests insincerity and dishonesty. Long contact usually indicates rapt attention, but eye contact that lasts too long may invade the prospect's privacy and be considered threatening. People can smile with their mouths and with their eyes. In fact, unless the eyes are smiling, the person's mouth smile may be insincere. John Molloy, author of several books on dressing for success, gives a different and somewhat

# DO EYE CONTACT AND SMILES KILL SALES FOR SALESWOMEN?

According to best-selling author, John T. Molloy, sales training for women often doesn't work because it's based on the assumption that women sell the same way men do. Interviews with saleswomen revealed that male sales trainers usually tell saleswomen to always maintain good eye contact or they will turn their buyers off. But many of the women interviewed ignored this advice because they had learned that too much eye contact can also turn their buyers on. Moreover, several of them pointed out that their training in nonverbal communication instructed them to handle a sales call in a way that came off as too sexy. According to the women interviewees, the silliest advice they received was to keep smiling all the time. Two women, one who sold computers and one who was an attorney turned salesperson, said that if they continuously smiled, prospects tended to not take them seriously. They predicted the results of Molloy's research before it started by declaring, "Smiles can kill sales." If a woman is too smiley, prospects often ask, "What's a nice girl like you doing in a job like this?" Molloy's research indicated that in some technical sales fields the main problem women have is not being taken seriously. Accordingly, he found that women who avoid smiling for at least the first ten minutes of the first meeting with a prospect tend to be more successful. More so than men, according to Molloy, saleswomen must establish the fact early on that they are serious professionals.

***Source:*** *Excerpt from John T. Molloy,* Molloy's Live For Success *(New York: Bantam Books, 1983), 91.*

controversial perspective on eye contact and smiling for women (see above).

6. *Arm, Hand, and Leg Movements:* Like the maestro leading the orchestra, our arm movements express our intensity of feeling. If we wave our arms frantically, we are in distress or trying to catch someone's attention. Similarly, when we make stiff, jerky movements with our arms, we express determination or aggression. If we move our arms gracefully and slowly, we express warmth and gentleness. People from some cultures have been teased about being unable to talk without using their hands. Hand language is challenging to decipher because hand movements must be interpreted within a given situation. People often show impatience by tapping their fingers on a desk. Clenched fists are a strongly defensive or offensive gesture. Touching the fingertips of one hand to the fingertips of our other hand to form a kind of steeple indicates dominance or weighing of alternatives. Prospects may cup their mouths with their hands to whisper a secret, or cover their eyes to show embarrassment. When prospects handle a product roughly, they are suggesting that they find it of little worth. Handling a product gingerly generally indicates that they feel the product is valuable. To suggest high quality, clever salespeople often remove their products, whether knives or perfume, from fancy packages in front of prospects. Prospects who cross their legs in an open position toward the

salesperson are sending a message of confidence, interest, and cooperation. But prospects who cross their legs away from a salesperson are sending a negative message.

7. *Voice Characteristics:* Voice qualities such as pitch, sound articulation, resonance, tempo, and nonlanguage sounds or vocalizations such as laughing, yawning, grunting, and expressions like *uh-uh* for "no," *uh-huh* for "yes," and *ah* or *er* for hesitation are called *paralanguage*. One study found that using a speaking rate somewhat faster than that of normal conversation leads to increased selling effectiveness.[8] Also, a salesperson's accent can influence selling effectiveness; that is, those who speak the local dialect are likely to be more successful and perceived as more credible than those who do not (that is, those who have an accent).[9]

It's a good idea for you to audiotape your sales presentation practice sessions so that you can critique your own voice characteristics (see Table 11.4) and nonverbal communication. Varying your speech pattern by increasing its volume or pace can help emphasize key points during your sales presentation. Speaking in a quiet voice can sometimes draw attention to your points as well. Determine the pace or speed of delivery of your presentation by the prospect's preferences and the complexity of the presentation. You can cover easy to grasp material at a faster rate of speech, but slowing down at times will give emphasis to important points.

## Putting It All Together

So now you see what it takes to be an excellent communicator—and thus a successful salesperson as well. Listening, speaking, giving verbal and nonverbal signals, and receiving verbal and nonverbal cues require practice, practice, and more practice. Rome wasn't built in a day, and professional sales rep communication skills aren't either. But steadfast dedication to the concepts that we have thus far discussed in this chapter will assist you in becoming a successful salesperson. Read *On the Frontlines* to see how one canny salesperson

| TABLE 11.4 |
| :-- |

## SALESPERSON VOCAL QUALITIES

| Voice Quality | Potential Problems |
| --- | --- |
| Volume | Do you speak too loudly or too softly? |
| Pitch | Is your voice too high or too low? |
| Clarity | Do you slur your words, or do you enunciate clearly? |
| Resonance | Is the timbre or tone of your voice unpleasant? |
| Inflection | Do you speak in a monotone, or do you use changes in inflection to emphasize points? |
| Speed | Do you speak too fast or too slowly? |

## ON THE FRONTLINES

# *Whose Show Is This Anyway?*

After earning his college degree in marketing, Marvin Gibson took a job with Universal Building Supplies, headquartered in Delaware. After a six-week training course, Marv was assigned a territory in southeast Pennsylvania notorious for one tough purchasing agent, Mike Bitters of Henderson Modular Homes (HMH). A warning from the previous salesperson in the territory unnerved Marv about calling on Mr. Bitters even though the account had a high volume potential. The previous salesperson had been insulted and thrown out of Mr. Bitters' office on the first sales call for "wasting his valuable time," so he never called on HMH again. He told Marv, "Mike Bitters is a domineering jerk. Nobody can sell him anything. He hasn't changed suppliers in twenty years, so there's no use even calling on him."

Marv avoided the HMH account during his first three months on the job. But one day when he was in a particularly upbeat mood, Marv decided to give the notorious Mike Bitters a try. Arriving at Henderson Modular Homes headquarters, Marv felt a lump in his throat as he asked the receptionist if he could see Mr. Bitters. The receptionist smirked and called Mr. Bitters' secretary. To his and the receptionist's surprise, Mr. Bitters would grant him exactly five minutes but not a minute more. So off Marv trotted to Mr. Bitters' office where, through a half-opened door, he saw a large, rough-featured man in his early sixties staring down at some papers. Knocking on the door, Marv said, "Mr. Bitters, I'm Marv Gibson from Universal Building Supplies. May I come in?"

"Yeah, but get straight to the point. I'm busy and don't have time to waste bullshooting with a salesman."

Glancing quickly around the office, Marv noticed a plaque on the wall to the right of Mr. Bitters' desk and blurted out without thinking, "That's an impressive plaque; what's that for?" Well, those turned out to be the magic words. Mr. Bitters launched into a story about how he had been chosen Pennsylvania's top purchasing agent five years ago and exactly what led to his selection. Marv didn't say a word for thirty minutes. He just listened intensely with a few appropriate nods of his head and "mmm . . . huhs." At the end of the half hour, Mr. Bitters said curtly: "I've got to go to a meeting. Leave your product brochures with my secretary." Then, he got up and left without so much as a goodbye or a handshake.

Thinking he had failed like everyone else, Marv felt a little depressed as he drove home after his last sales call that night. But the next morning to his delight, he learned that Mr. Bitters had called and placed a large order and given Marv credit for being a persuasive salesperson. After that, Marv called on Mr. Bitters regularly and within two years, HMH had become Marv's biggest customer. According to Marv, what really won over Mr. Bitters was that: "I unwittingly encouraged him to tell his own story. No other sales rep had ever shown any interest in Mr. Bitters personally. They were all too intimidated by his gruff reputation."

***Source:*** *Story related to one of the authors by a former student who became a successful salesperson. Names of people and companies have been changed.*

used his communication skills—especially listening—to cultivate a relationship with an erstwhile gadfly of a prospect.

At the outset of this chapter we asked you a series of questions regarding how effective a communicator you thought you were. Well, now let's see how REALLY effective you are. Take the following communication "test" in Table 11.5. Be objective in your response to each statement. After completing the test, you will be able to determine whether you are truly an effective communicator. Additionally, you will be able to see how to improve in areas where you might be less than effective. Good luck!

---

**TABLE 11.5**

## ARE YOU AN EFFECTIVE COMMUNICATOR?

Use the scale below to respond to the statements that follow. (When responding to the statements, assume that you are involved in face-to-face interaction with another individual.)

5 = Strongly Agree   4 = Agree   3 = Neither Agree nor Disagree
2 = Disagree   1 = Strongly Disagree

**When I have face-to-face communication:**

1. I focus only on the other person. ___

2. I try to maintain regular eye contact when the individual is talking. ___

3. My nonverbal gestures communicate that I am listening carefully. ___

4. I remain genuinely interested throughout the interaction. ___

5. I ask for more details when I do not completely understand what the individual is saying. ___

6. I paraphrase questions to make sure I understand before answering. ___

7. I do not interrupt another who is speaking. ___

8. I do not change the subject frequently when communicating. ___

9. I never try to finish another speaker's sentences. ___

10. I try hard to understand fully what the individual is saying. ___

11. I respond with useful statements rather than merely replying "yes" or "no." ___

12. I offer relevant information regarding questions another asks me. ___

13. I show eagerness and enthusiasm in my responses. ___

14. I answer all questions at the appropriate time. ___

The higher your score on each of the statements, the better your communication skills are likely to be.

***Source:*** *Adapted from Rosemary P. Ramsey and Ravipreet S. Sohi, "Listening to Your Customers: The Impact of Perceived Salesperson Listening Behavior on Relationship Outcomes,"* Journal of the Academy of Marketing Science *25 (Spring 1997): 127–137.*

## COMMUNICATION STYLES

Our prospects and customers are continuously sending us verbal and nonverbal signals about their personalities and how to most effectively communicate with them. Your capacity to correctly detect and understand the messages that buyers send you—whether verbal or nonverbal—will affect your success.[10] Your ability to respond to these specific messages rather than relying on your own predispositions or flawed beliefs about customers will influence how effective you are with buyers.[11] In addition, the stage of your relationship with the buyer (that is, early, middle, late), as well as the buyer's **communication style,** influence your communication style.[12]

Because we are all mixtures of diverse personality characteristics, it may seem overly simplistic to classify everybody in a simple typology. But before we can begin to understand the complex personalities of our prospects and customers, we need ways to classify them.

### Classifying Communication Styles

David Merrill, Roger Reid, Paul Mok, and Anthony Alessandra, among several other researchers, have developed taxonomies for classifying people's preponderant behavior and communication styles.[13] Most of these behavior models classify people into one of four distinct categories based on two dimensions: (1) assertiveness and (2) responsiveness. **Assertiveness** is the degree to which a person attempts to control or dominate situations and direct the thoughts and actions of other people. **Responsiveness** is the level of emotions, feelings, or sociability that a person openly displays.

Using Figure 11.2, we can plot an individual's degree of assertiveness and responsiveness and classify him or her into one of four communication styles:[14] (1) Amiable, (2) Expressive, (3) Analytical, or (4) Driver. Let's discuss the people who use these four communication styles and how you can sell to them.

**Communication Style**
The way a person sends and receives messages in communicating with other people.

**Assertiveness** The degree to which a person attempts to control or dominate situations and direct the thoughts of other people.

**Responsiveness** The level of emotions, feelings, or sociability that a person openly displays.

*Watch out! How can you recognize that these salespeople may be pushing this buyer too much?*
Eyewire, Getty Images

**Amiables.** Open, relatively unassertive, warm, supportive, and sociable people who "wear well" with others, *Amiables* are the most people oriented of all of the four styles. As shown in the upper left-hand corner of Figure 11.2, they are high in responsiveness and low in assertive behavior. In communicating, their voices are enthusiastic and congenial, and their body language warmly animated. Coworkers and salespeople may perceive them as compliant and easygoing because they emphasize building a trustful relationship and work at a relatively

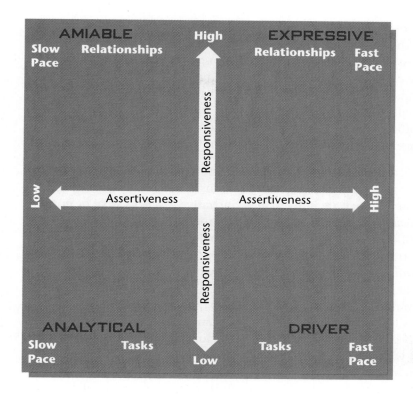

**FIGURE 11.2**

COMMUNICATION SYLES

slow pace. They readily share their personal feelings and are often charming storytellers. Generally, they are deliberate in making decisions or taking action because they want to know how others feel first. Amiables prefer friendly, personal, first-name relationships with others. They dislike interpersonal conflicts so much that they will often say what others want to hear rather than what they really think. Amiables are understanding listeners and easily make and keep friends. They don't like pushy, aggressive behavior. Cooperative team players, their theme song might be *Getting to Know You*. Amiables' offices will probably be decorated in a comfortable, open, friendly style with informal seating arrangements conducive to close contact. On their desks, you'll probably find family pictures and various personal items. Family or group pictures and personal mementos are likely hanging on their office walls.

**Expressives.** In the upper right-hand corner of Figure 11.2 are the *Expressives* who rate high in both responsiveness and assertiveness. Enthusiastic, spontaneous, talkative, and extroverted, they work at a fast pace. They operate largely on intuition and express their views dramatically. They dislike being alone. If no one's around, they'll spend a lot of time on the telephone. Full of ideas, Expressives may daydream and chase a lot of rainbows. Their usually excellent persuasive skills enable them to excite others about their ideas. They seek approval and recognition for their accomplishments and achievements. They are usually creative and can think quickly on their feet. Uninhibited in giving verbal or nonverbal feedback, they readily share their personal feelings. They believe that success depends more on "whom you know than what you know." Expressives tend to become involved in too many activities and may not be strong on follow-through due to their impatience and relatively short attention spans. Their desks are often cluttered and disorganized. Hanging on their office walls will be awards, provocative posters, and motivational slogans. Their offices are usually decorated in an open, friendly style, and the seating arrangement invites interaction and contact.

**Analyticals.** *Analytical buyers*, in the lower left-hand corner of Figure 11.2, tend to be low in both assertiveness and responsiveness. Logical, controlled, and self-contained, they are not very demonstrative in their verbal or nonverbal communication. They like organization, structure, and self-discipline and work at a deliberate pace. Being systematic problem solvers who ask many detailed questions, they like sales presentations to be based on facts. Analyticals will probably be most persuaded by objective product tests conducted by independent research organizations, expert testimonials, and comprehensive warranties. Security conscious, they prefer predictability. They want to know how a product or service works and what proof you have of its quality. Analyticals like organization and structure and dislike too much involvement with other people. They work slowly and precisely by themselves and prefer an intellectual work environment that allows them to self-actualize. They rarely share their personal feelings and are slow in giving nonverbal feedback. Precise, detail-oriented, and time-conscious, they are likely to be critical of their own and other people's performance. They exhibit a skeptical "show me" attitude and like to see details in writing. They like salespeople to be organized and professional, with all the facts at their fingertips. In their desire for information, Analyticals may keep collecting information even beyond the time a decision is needed. Clues that help you to identify Analyticals are offices that appear functionally organized with everything in its place. Office walls often have charts, graphs, and pictures relating to their job. Pictures of people are unlikely. Furniture and seating arrangements are formal and impersonal.

**Drivers.** *Drivers*, in the lower right-hand corner of Figure 11.2, tend to be assertive and unresponsive. Controlled and decisive, they operate at a fast pace and are goal-oriented in their relationships with others. Strong-willed, impatient, tough, "take-charge" personalities, Drivers show a low tolerance for the feelings, attitudes, and advice of others. Believing that success depends on themselves, they need to control situations and people and actively seek leadership roles. They thrive on decision making and producing results. Inflexible, impatient, and poor listeners, they tend to ignore facts and figures and rely more on their "gut feel." A theme song for Drivers might be *My Way.* Clues identifying the Driver personality are desks piled high with work projects. Their offices are decorated to indicate power and control, and the walls may contain honors and achievement awards or a large planning sheet/calendar. Seating arrangements are likely to be closed, formal, and positioned for power. Some Drivers even raise their chair heights or choose extra large desks to project their dominance over others.

Although most people show characteristics of all four communication styles at least occasionally, most prospects or customers will exhibit a preponderate communication style. It is the salesperson's job to identify that style early on and adapt the presentation accordingly. Table 11.6 provides a quick reference tool for the four communication styles, with their respective characteristics listed by their key variables.

**TABLE 11.6**

## SUMMARY OF COMMUNICATION STYLES

| Key Variables | Amiable | Expressive | Analytical | Driver |
|---|---|---|---|---|
| Communication Style | Responsive nonassertive | Responsive assertive | Nonresponsive nonassertive | Nonresponsive assertive |
| Pace of Communication | Slow and easy | Fast and spontaneous | Slow and systematic | Fast and decisive |
| Personal Focus | Human relationships | Influencing others | Analytical process | Results |
| Wants To Be | Liked | Admired | Correct | In charge |
| Wants You To Be | Pleasant | Stimulating | Precise | To the point |
| Decision Making Is | Participatory | Spontaneous | Deliberate | Decisive |
| Risk Orientation | Avoids risks | Takes risks | Calculates risks | Controls risks |
| Seeks | Close relationships | Recognition | Accuracy | Productivity |
| Office or Work Space | Personal Relaxed Friendly Informal | Stimulating Personal Cluttered Friendly | Structured Organized Functional Formal | Busy Formal Efficient Structured |
| Personal Appearance | Casual Conforming | Fashionable Stylish | Formal Conservative | Businesslike Functional |
| Achieves Acceptance By | Conformity Loyalty | Playfulness Stimulating environment | Correctness Thoroughness | Leadership Competition |
| Gains Security By | Close relationships | Flexibility | Preparation | Control |
| Wants to Maintain | Relationships | Status | Credibility | Success |
| You Should Support Their | Feelings | Ideas | Reasoning | Goals |
| Personal Fears | Confrontation | Loss of prestige | Embarrassment | Loss of control |
| Under Tension Will | Concede Compromise | Argue Use sarcasm | Withdraw Reconsider | Confront Verbally attack |
| Irritated By | Insensitivity Impatience | Boredom Routine | Surprises Unpredictability | Inefficiency Indecision |

(continued)

| | TABLE 11.6 |
| --- | --- |

### SUMMARY OF COMMUNICATION STYLES (CONTINUED)

| Key Variables | Amiable | Expressive | Analytical | Driver |
| --- | --- | --- | --- | --- |
| **Measures Personal Worth By** | Compatibility with others Depth of relationships | Acknowledgment Recognition Applause Compliments | Precision Accuracy Systematic process | Results Track record Measurable progress |
| **Needs to Know (Benefits)** | How it will affect their personal relationships | How it enhances their status Who else uses it | How to justify the purchase logically | What it does What it costs When it can be delivered |
| **Salesperson Should Appreciate the Prospect's** | Feelings | Creativity | Knowledge | Goals and achievements |

### Developing Communication Style Flexibility

Pairing a salesperson and prospect with different communication styles can be tricky. Let's see how the professionals manage.

**Dimensions of Communication Style.** Besides differences in levels of responsiveness and assertiveness, styles may clash in terms of pace and priority. *Pace* is the speed at which a person moves. People who are high in assertiveness (Expressives and Drivers) prefer a fast pace in talking, thinking, and making decisions. Whereas, those who are low in assertiveness (Amiables and Analyticals) prefer a slow pace. *Priorities* identify what a person considers important. Goals, objectives, and task achievement are highest in priority for those who are low in responsiveness (Analyticals and Drivers), while relationships with other people are the top priority for those who are high in responsiveness (Amiables and Expressives). Table 11.7 illustrates the types of conflicts that occur when people with different styles try to communicate.

As you can see in Table 11.7, Amiable/Driver pairings or Expressive/Analytical pairings encounter both pace and priority problems when they try to communicate with each other. All other communication style pairings, except for identical styles, must deal with either a pace or a priority problem.

**Style Flexing.** The many possible conflicts between salesperson and prospect communication styles illustrate the need for every salesperson to cultivate the ability to *flex* with prospect communication styles. *Style flexing* will enable you to sell to your prospects *in the way they want to be sold*. If prospects talk and move fast, you should adjust your rate of speech and movements to match theirs. If they like to take their time and engage in light conversation, relax and allow more time for the appointment. If prospects are task oriented,

**TABLE 11.7**

## SOURCES OF CONFLICTS BETWEEN COMMUNICATION STYLES

| Style Match-Up | Shared Dimension | Area of Agreement | Area of Conflict |
|---|---|---|---|
| Amiable with Expressive | High responsiveness | Priorities | Pace |
| Analytical with Driver | Low responsiveness | Priorities | Pace |
| Amiable with Analytical | Low assertiveness | Pace | Priorities |
| Expressive with Driver | High assertiveness | Pace | Priorities |
| Amiable with Driver | None | None | Both |
| Expressive with Analytical | None | None | Both |

shift your focus to tasks. If they are relationship oriented, you should stress relationships, too. When you meet another person's behavioral style needs, a climate of mutual trust begins to form. As a bond of trust develops, the other person will begin to tell you what he or she really needs. Instead of a contest, you will foster a compatible, productive relationship that will likely result in a sale and long-term customer. Table 11.8 shows flexing approaches to employ with prospects or customers exhibiting one of the four foregoing communication styles.

**TABLE 11.8**

## FLEXING WITH PROSPECT COMMUNICATION STYLES

### Selling to Amiables

- Approach Amiables in a friendly, neighborly way with a sincere greeting and a warm handshake. Use a relaxed, informal pace to build trust, friendship, and credibility.
- Plan to get to know them personally. Be agreeable, professional but friendly.
- Try to get to know the prospect personally. Ask nonthreatening questions about their interests and activities. Be agreeable and supportive, professional, but friendly. Show them that you genuinely like them.
- Present the product or service in a close interactive way so that you develop a good relationship. Make the demonstration meaningful and congenial.
- Deal with resistance and objections by using testimonials from other people, personal assurances, and guarantees.

(continued)

TABLE 11.8

## FLEXING WITH PROSPECT COMMUNICATION STYLES (CONTINUED)

- Close in a warm, reassuring way. Do not be pushy or aggressive.
- Follow up with friendly personal letters, notes, and phone calls to make sure that they are satisfied with the product or service.

### Selling to Expressives

- Approach Expressives boldly by introducing yourself first and extending your hand. Tell them that you are delighted to meet them. Enthusiastically ask questions to learn about their needs, goals, and dreams.
- Ask questions that will allow them to brag a little. You can obtain clues from the pictures, trophies, awards, and interesting art objects that you are likely to see in their office.
- Show appreciation for their abilities and achievements. Compliment them on their accomplishments if you can do so sincerely.
- Present your solution with stimulating stories and illustrations that relate to them and their goals. Be confident and animated throughout your presentation and demonstration. Spice up your sales presentation with interesting stories and illustrations.
- Deal with resistance and objectives candidly and confidently.
- Close with lively appeals that provide positive support for achievement of their dreams and goals.
- Follow up by confirming the purchase in writing. Your letter should be friendly, clear, and cordial.

### Selling to Analyticals

- Approach Analyticals in a gracious, genial way but quickly move on to the task at hand.
- Be prepared to answer a series of detailed questions about the product, its use, and performance.
- Make your sales presentation logical, objective, and deliberate, citing many facts and figures.
- Deal with resistance and objections by providing detailed analysis and research findings.
- Close by summarizing the benefits and deficits for purchasing the product.
- Follow up with reassuring information from survey or research findings that support their purchase decisions.

(continued)

**TABLE 11.8**

**FLEXING WITH PROSPECT COMMUNICATION STYLES** (CONTINUED)

### Selling to Drivers

- Approach Drivers directly with a firm handshake and in a confident, businesslike manner.

- Plan to be well prepared, organized, fast paced, and to the point.

- Present your selling points clearly and directly by showing how the products and services will help them achieve their goals. Involve the prospect in a hands-on product/service demonstration.

- Deal with resistance and objections directly. Do not try to double-talk or pass over prospect concerns, because drivers go after the answers they want like tenacious pit bulls.

- Close in a straightforward, professional way by emphasizing the bottom line results or benefits.

- Follow up by asking how well the product/service is helping them achieve their goals. Suggest additional products that may help them improve results.

## COMMUNICATION AND TRUST BUILDING

We have discussed throughout this book the importance of salespeople being trustworthy. After all, the foundation of a solid and mutually valuable buyer-seller relationship is trust. Your words and actions communicate to prospects and customers how trustworthy you are or are likely to be. Saying one thing (for example, "We always deliver on time") and then doing another (delivering the product two weeks late) violates the trust a buyer may have placed in a salesperson. Alternatively, consistent words and actions maintain or enhance a buyer's trust in the sales rep. Five "trust builders" have been identified that professional salespeople use to communicate to buyers that they are deserving of trust.[15]

### Candor (Words)
- Sales presentations are balanced and fair (product strengths and limitations are mentioned).
- What the salesperson says agrees with what the buyer knows to be true.
- The proof the salesperson uses to support statements is credible.
- Subsequent events prove the statements to be true.

### Dependability (Actions)
- The salesperson's actions fulfill his or her prior (verbal) promises.
- The actions fit a pattern of prior dependable action the salesperson has established.
- The salesperson refuses to promise what cannot be delivered.

### Competence (Ability)
- The salesperson displays technical command of products and their applications.
- The salesperson has the skill, knowledge, time, and resources to follow through on promises and do what the buyer wants.
- The salesperson's words and actions are consistent with a professional image.

### Customer Orientation (Intent)
- The salesperson understands the buyer's needs and places them on par with own and organization's needs.
- The salesperson gives fair and balanced presentations and offers clear statements of benefits.
- The salesperson advises rather than sells (that is, doesn't push an unneeded product on a buyer).

### Likableness (Personality)
- The salesperson makes efficient use of the buyer's time.
- The salesperson is courteous and polite.
- The salesperson and buyer share and talk about areas of commonality; this extends to non-business topics.

If you can put the above five trust builders into practice while flexing your communication style with that of your prospect or customer, you are well on your way toward gaining rapport and developing a long-term sales relationship.

## SUMMARY

In this chapter we examined principles and theories of communication and communication skills for the professional salesperson. After stating that listening is the most important communication skill for the salesperson to learn and practice, we described requisite communication skills for the salesperson. We discussed four levels of listening (marginal, evaluative, active, and active empathetic), three question formats (open-ended, closed, and semi-open), and six distinct types of questions (probing, evaluative, strategic, tactical, dichotomous, and multiple choice). Proxemics (the use of space) and kinesics (nonverbal communication) were also shown to be important to selling success.

We learned that the best salespeople are constantly sharpening their ability to (1) listen, (2) ask questions, (3) use space, and (4) communicate nonverbally. We also discussed how an individual's levels of assertiveness and responsiveness could be plotted in four directions, yielding four basic communication styles: (1) Amiable, (2) Expressive, (3) Analytical, and (4) Driver. Quickly comprehending each new prospect's communication style and flexing to that style will help salespeople sell to prospects and customers in the way in which they want to be sold. Finally, we described five trust builders that salespeople can use to establish enduring buyer-seller relationships.

## KEY TERMS

Communication

Promotion

Sensing

Processing

Responding

Marginal Listening

Evaluative Listening

Active Listening

Active Empathetic Listening (AEL)

Probing Question

Evaluative Question

Dichotomous Question

Proxemics

Kinesics

Communication Style

Assertiveness

Responsiveness

## CHAPTER REVIEW QUESTIONS

1. Differentiate between communication and promotion.

2. Outline the four levels of listening and give an example of each.

3. Name the three basic question formats. What kind of response would you expect from a customer for each format?

4. What are some guidelines to facilitate good listening?

5. How would you describe the difference between proxemics and kinesics?

6. Briefly describe how you would sell to each of the four communication styles: Amiable, Expressive, Driver, and Analytical.

7. What do we mean by "style flexing" and why is it important to salespeople? Give an example of style flexing in a selling situation.

8. Describe the different dimensions of vocal quality. What might a salesperson do to improve his or her vocal qualities?

9. Give examples of five trust builders when negotiating with prospects.

## TOPICS FOR THOUGHT AND CLASS DISCUSSION

1. Can you think of any people—in your own or public life—who appear to be effective communicators? What do you think makes them so effective? How might you incorporate some of their communication techniques into your own repertoire of techniques?

2. Do you think that women tend to be better at some communication skills while men are better at others? Or do you believe that gender is largely irrelevant to communication skills? If you think gender differences arise in communication skills, how do you account for these differences?

3. Which do you think conveys the most accurate information—people's words or their body lan-

guage? Why? Do you think you can tell more readily whether or not people are being honest with you by hearing their words or reading their body language? Why?

4. Rank each of the communication modes (talking, listening, reading, writing, and body language) in terms of your own personal effectiveness using each. What has helped make you good in the highest ranked mode and relatively weak in the lowest ranked one? What advice do you have for a person who wants to improve in each area?

5. Are you consciously aware of your use of body language when communicating? Do you have certain mannerisms that other people have commented on? What are they? What do you think they convey in communication?

6. In your opinion, which communication style do you most often use? Do you flex this style when communicating with different people? Give some examples of your own style flexing with different people (for example, family members, friends, clergy, teachers, coaches, police officers, new acquaintances).

7. Try to think of an example of each of the four communication styles among your own family and friends. How well do they fit the different qualities under their primary style in Table 11.6 on pages 355–356? Do you ever notice yourself adjusting to any of these people's style when you communicate with them? Do you get along better with some of these people than with others? Consult Table 11.7 on page 357 to see if your two styles match up well or poorly. Do you think your communication style match-ups help explain your relationships?

8. Which of the trust builders do you think is most important for people in learning to trust someone? Why is that one most important? How well do you generally do at trust building?

## PROJECTS FOR PERSONAL GROWTH

1. Make a simple two-column chart on a separate piece of paper (or on your computer)—a "T" design will do. In the left-hand column list the six types of questions salespeople use, leaving plenty of space between each entry. Then, in the right-hand column put down in your own words as much information as you can about each question type—how and when to use it, the expected or desired response, and examples.

2. If your class is small enough and students are willing, ask everyone in class to classify each other student into one of the four communication styles: amiable, expressive, analytical, driver. [Only students who are willing to have their communication styles categorized need to participate.] Which style appears to be most prevalent in your class? Now discuss how a salesperson using one of the communication styles would negotiate with the students exhibiting each of the four communication styles.

3. As an experiential exercise, ask for student volunteers who believe that they know their own communication style to try to sell something, perhaps a textbook, to students with different communication styles. After observing the role play, other students should offer their perceptions of the interaction and negotiations.

4. If you're confident enough, ask one of your classmates to give you an honest appraisal of your vocal qualities. Were you surprised by the evaluation? Why? What might you consider doing to improve your voice quality?

5. Prepare a fifteen-minute sales presentation on a product with which you are familiar. Rehearse it several times, then, ask a friend to watch you while you give your presentation and ask him or her to note positive and negative verbal and nonverbal communication. In a critique afterward, compare the effect you thought you were having to the effect your friend thought you had during the presentation. Any surprises? (If you have the resources, try doing this exercise with a video camera then an audiotape recorder.) *With a video camera:* After taping your presentation, play it back while observing and listening to all modes of communication, then play it back with the sound off so you can analyze body language. *With an audio recorder:* Record your presentation, then analyze your voice characteristics. Whether you make your presentation to a friend, videotape it, or merely

record it, ask yourself the following questions: Do I look and sound sincere? Would I buy from myself? With respect to verbal and nonverbal communication, what do I like about my presentation? What don't I like? How might I improve my communication?

6. Over the next two days, find two people who are giving a speech or an address, whether in person or on television, and take the time to hear and watch the whole presentation. Evaluate their verbal and nonverbal communication. What advice would you give these people to improve their communication effectiveness? Do you think they made their points? What did you find convincing and/or inspiring about what they said and did? Did they look or sound at all insincere? What was basically good about their "performances," and what was basically bad about them?

# MIRROR, MIRROR ON THE WALL

Sally Blakemore is beginning her first field day on her job as missionary salesperson or "detail person" for Bevan-Warner Pharmaceutical Company. Having completed a three-month training program, she is now ready to call on hospitals and medical offices in the Philadelphia area to introduce and explain her company's pharmaceutical products to health care professionals. Ms. Blakemore will not directly sell or take orders for her company's product. She is called a detail person because her job is to give doctor "deciders" all the details needed to convince them to prescribe the Bevan-Warner pharmaceuticals for their patients.

As she learned in her training program, few doctors can keep up with the latest pharmaceutical products because of their hectic schedules. Most tend to rely heavily on detail people to keep them up-to-date. Sally Blakemore's job is to provide in-depth information on the chemical make-up of the product, how it interacts with other medicines a patient may be taking, and its potential side effects. To gain the trust of the medical professionals, detail people must know their products thoroughly and answer questions in a straightforward, professional way. In addition, the detail person must communicate effectively with diverse physician personalities.

On the first day of fieldwork, Sally is calling on three doctors: (1) Dr. Peter Hartman, an orthopedic surgeon, (2) Dr. Elizabeth Butterfield, a general practitioner; and (3) Dr. Janice Winer, a gynecologist. Her predecessor, who was promoted to district sales manager after three years in the field, tried to help Sally understand the personalities of the three physicians. Here's the way he described each one:

"*Dr. Peter Hartman* is a tall, thin man about fifty-five years old who tends to be somewhat irritable and generally preoccupied. He's definitely not Mr. Warmth. I always get the feeling in talking to him that he doesn't quite believe me. I can never keep him listening to me for more than ten minutes, and he always sits on the edge of his chair like he's ready to jump up at any time. He's got a reputation as a loner in that he doesn't socialize with any of the other doctors or nurses. His wife divorced him three years ago after they raised three children—two of whom are doctors. I think the other one is a struggling artist. With Hartman, you'll need to get straight to the point because his favorite line is, 'Give me the short version and nothing but the facts, please.' He won't ask many questions, but he'll expect to see the research that backs up product claims; so leave him all the technical product literature you can and send him more between visits. I've found that he actually reads those reports, so it will help you on your next call to have him high up on the learning curve."

"*Dr. Elizabeth Butterfield* is one of the nicest, least pretentious people you'll ever meet. She's everybody's mother. Although she has a heavy load of patients every day, her spirits never seem dampened. She's always laughing and telling playful little one-liners, often about her size—she is over six feet tall and 'full figured,' as they say. Her husband's a high school principal, and they have five children, ranging in age from four to twenty. Her patients love her, and so does nearly everyone else. Dr. Liz will always find fifteen or twenty minutes to see you no matter how backed up her schedule is. I hear that she often stays in her office until ten o'clock at night seeing patients. And her nurses say she is just as upbeat at the end of the day as she is at the beginning. The thing that always amazed me is that she'll remember your name after meeting you once, and she'll remember the names of any family members you've talked about, too. She always asked how my mother was doing. It's a joy to call on her because she makes you feel that she likes, trusts, and respects you."

"*Dr. Janice Winer* is a super-intelligent woman, about thirty-seven years old, who I heard was

(continued)

## MIRROR, MIRROR ON THE WALL (CONTINUED)

number one in her medical school class. She's perpetual motion and all business. She moves fast, thinks fast, and makes decisions fast. I don't think I have ever met anyone who is more organized and efficient. Her whole office staff is the same way. You know how most doctors seem to have a lot of patients in the waiting room? Well, I've never seen more than two or three in her waiting room at any on time. At first, I thought it was because she didn't have many patients. Then her receptionist showed me her appointment book—she's booked up solid for months ahead of time, but she's simply one of those rare doctors who's nearly always ready to see you at approximately the time of your scheduled appointment. You don't waste time with her on chitchat. She'll greet you politely, then say, 'Okay, what have you got?' You can be halfway through a product presentation and she'll stop you and say, 'Okay I'm sold on it. What else do you have?' I never really got to know her personally, but I understand she got married last year to a corporate executive who is twenty years her senior."

Ever since listening to her colleague describe the people she will meet on her first three calls, Sally has felt anxious about whether her own personality will mesh or clash with the personalities of the three physicians. In college, her classmates

used to jokingly call her "grind" because of her unwillingness to break her habit of studying at the university library every weeknight from seven to eleven. True, she graduated with a 3.8 average on a 4.0 scale, but she certainly doesn't think of herself as a grind, because she was an officer in the student marketing club and a sorority member. She saved her partying for the weekends. Thinking about how others might describe her, Sally imagines they might mention traits like quiet, reserved, intelligent, hard-working, cooperative, organized, goal oriented, determined, and likable. "Hmmm," she thinks to herself, "I'm not sure what personality type I am. I seem to be a mixture of several types, like most people. Oh well, no use worrying any more—best to just get going."

### Questions

1. How would you categorize the personalities of each of the three physicians on whom Sally will be calling?
2. What personality type is Sally?
3. Which of the physicians do you think Sally will best communicate with? Why? With which one will she have the most difficulty communicating? Why?
4. What advice would you give Sally before she calls on each physician?

# HE KEEPS GOING AND GOING AND GOING

Clare Suzuki is an account representative for Burton, Dirksen, & Lipton, a New York advertising agency. She and Earl Webb, a vice president of the agency, are in the midst of making a sales presentation designed to win the advertising account for the *Lovable Tramp* line of dry dog food manufactured by National Foods Corporation. The account could be worth more than five million dollars to BD&L. Sitting at a big, round table in a comfortable conference room are seven National Foods representatives: the vice president of marketing, the director of brand management, the brand manager, two assistant brand managers, a product development manager, and a marketing research manager. All seven project serious demeanors and are dressed virtually alike in dark gray suits with blue shirts and neckties in different shades and patterns of red. All have laptop computers before them on the table.

Mr. Webb and Clare carefully rehearsed their presentation for two days before flying to National Foods headquarters in Milwaukee. Mr. Webb's part of the presentation was timed to last about an hour, and Clare's was to be about twenty-five minutes. Mr. Webb starts his presentation by telling a couple of old jokes, which seem to fall flat. No one laughs, although a few smile slightly with clenched teeth. Then, throughout his overly wordy PowerPoint presentation, Mr. Webb tells several mildly interesting stories about his experiences in the advertising business but presents little analytical data or client benefits for hiring his advertising firm. Mr. Webb tends to think of himself as a raconteur with down-home charm. Although not denying his extroverted personality, Clare has often thought that he is a little too full of himself and that he tends to be a bit corny at times.

Only once during his presentation does anyone interrupt Mr. Webb to ask a question. And Mr. Webb doesn't ask any questions of the National Food executives. As Mr. Webb is about to finish his part of the presentation—nearly seventy minutes long—Clare glances around the room to see how the National Food executives are reacting at this point. Two people are doodling on the handouts that she and Mr. Webb passed out, National's vice president of marketing is quietly tapping his fingers on the table, another person is leaning back in his chair with his hands clasped behind his head, the product management director is pouring a cup of coffee, and two assistant brand managers are whispering to each other and smirking.

Clare has fifteen PowerPoint slides to show in her concise presentation, which is designed to win the sale by stressing the benefits that Burton, Dirksen, & Lipton can provide clients . . . and she'll have to keep the lights dimmed. The original plan was not to take a break between Mr. Webb's presentation and her own because the two are so interconnected. But now Clare fears that Mr. Webb is so engrossed in his long-winded presentation that he doesn't notice how bored and weary the audience has become. Still, Clare doesn't think she can risk suggesting a break and upsetting Mr. Webb's game plan. She's hoping that Mr. Webb will suggest taking a short break, but he gives no indication. He is smiling that self-satisfied smile that she has seen so many times near the end of his presentations. But over the years, Clare has adjusted to his personality and genuinely likes him.

Soon Mr. Webb finishes, briefly introduces Clare with a mildly humorous comment, then sits down. Standing up and glancing over at Mr. Webb for an indication of whether there should be any change in the presentation strategy, Clare sees him pick up the presentation booklet and turn to her part without looking up. Clare's presentation will be succinct, but it's filled with financial data that she would like her audience to hear with refreshed minds.

(continued)

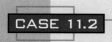

CASE 11.2

# HE KEEPS GOING AND GOING AND GOING

[CONTINUED]

## Questions

1. How do you think the audience received Mr. Webb's presentation? Why? What nonverbal communication do you think that Mr. Webb should have picked up on?

2. What communication style do you think the business executives from National Foods are most used to hearing? What do you think Mr. Webb's communication style might be? Do you think Mr. Webb is a good communicator? Why? Is a lack of questions a good sign for how well the presentation is going over with an audience? Should Mr. Webb have tried to involve the audience in the presentation? How?

3. What do you think Clare should do now? Should she suggest a five-minute break? . . . Continue with her part of the presentation as planned? . . . Forget about using the fifteen slides, turn up the lights in the room, and ask for any questions? . . . Or should she turn on the lights to wake everybody up and then show the fifteen slides even though they won't be as effective in full light?

4. Can you suggest anything else that Clare might do to help ensure that her part of the presentation goes over well?

5. Depending on what you suggest, what should Clare say to Mr. Webb when the two of them discuss the presentation later? Should Clare offer Mr. Webb any suggestions on improving his sales presentations in future sales calls? If so, how should she broach this delicate matter? What would be appropriate for her to say to her boss?

## CHAPTER 12

# Managing Your Time and Your Territory

*"What may be done at any time will be done at no time."*

Scottish proverb

## After Reading This Chapter, You Should Understand:

- Why salespeople must be concerned about efficiency as well as effectiveness in allocating their time.
- How salespeople function as field marketing managers.
- How to use ROTI to manage the territory.
- Methods for using time wisely.
- Efficient routing strategies for sales calls.
- Ways to prioritize accounts.
- How to avoid falling into time traps.

## INSIDE PERSONAL SELLING:

## Meet Lance Perkins of GE Medical Systems

Lance Perkins is a fair-sized company all by himself. As executive account manager for General Electric's Medical Systems unit, he helps hospitals achieve goals such as cutting costs, boosting productivity, and improving quality through annual purchases of more than $25 million worth of goods (CAT scanners, x-ray equipment, and more) and services (such as repair contracts, consulting, and financing). Perkins is the main company contact for hospitals in his territory and coordinates the sales efforts of other GE specialists. If a hospital executive mentions building plans, for instance, Perkins will suggest GE Industrial Systems, "because we sell roofing, tile, even power systems for emergency generators."

In addition to meeting monthly sales goals, Perkins must progress through a

series of activity milestones leading to each sale, because nine to eighteen months may pass between an initial meeting and a signed contract. GE also evaluates the leadership skills of its sales professionals. "In this sales position, you manage a lot of other people," says Perkins. "You may have ten or twelve other salespeople who are in touch with each hospital. I establish the relationship and bring in other specialty sales reps to supplement my discussions with customers."

Working on commission, Perkins learned to identify his best sales opportunities—the 20 percent of customers who account for 80 percent of his sales volume. "Fresh in the territory, it takes at least a year before you get the pulse of the market and figure out how to work smarter instead of harder," he observes. Although he initially reacted to every lead, he gradually began focusing on larger accounts, narrowing his contact list from sixty hospitals to fewer than twelve.

Perkins spends about three days a week visiting customers. The rest of the time he sets appointments, updates customer files and sales forecasts, obtains quotes, and coordinates the work of other GE specialists through email, teleconferences, and meetings. Despite his busy schedule, Perkins makes cold calls every week. "Many salespeople have call reluctance," he says. "If they don't set a time to do it, they just won't do it." Without the cold calls, the milestones, and information about past sales—such as when a service contract expires—Perkins might miss potential sales.

Instead of writing call reports about customer contacts, Perkins creates "trackers," spreadsheets listing how much money each deal will generate, what milestone each deal is at, and the probability that a deal will close—and when. He constantly reviews and revises his trackers to see which sales may close in a given month and where he needs more support from other GE personnel. Managing his time and his territory, says Perkins, "is really like running a business and trying to figure out what the cash flow will be."

As a student, you have almost total control over how you spend your time. Although professors put demands on you, you still can prioritize your preparation time. After all, no one is really forcing you to do everything at once. And although you may not have as much free time as you'd like, nonetheless, you have tremendous discretion over how to spend that time, too. Generally, you choose what activities and pursuits you want to do and when you want to do them. Well, believe it or not, so do many salespeople!

## SELF-MANAGEMENT

Unlike people in most jobs where performance is usually judged subjectively by a boss, a professional salesperson's performance is fairly easily measured and depends mainly on personal abilities and how well he or she manages a sales territory. Few jobs demand more self-management than professional selling. Self-management, where boss and worker are the same person, is probably more difficult than management where feedback from various sources can keep you on track and motivated. As your own manager, you must decide what to do, and how and when to do it. You set the daily performance standards—whether high or low—for yourself. You decide whether to be hard driving or complacent, to be customer-service oriented or indifferent, to use modern technology or not, and in the long run, to succeed or fail.

Some salespeople have even worked out a system of rewards and punishments to motivate their own behavior. For example, if they successfully sell a new account, they may buy themselves a nice gift or take the afternoon off to play golf. On the other hand, if they fail to accomplish some task on time, they may punish themselves by working overtime that night on paperwork.[1] Whatever method you use to motivate yourself, your success as a professional salesperson will be greatly affected by how effectively and efficiently you manage your time and your sales territory.

## EFFECTIVENESS AND EFFICIENCY

**Effectiveness** Results-oriented focus on achieving selling goals.

**Efficiency** Cost-oriented focus on making the best possible use of the salesperson's time and efforts.

Successful salespeople understand that their success depends not only on their effectiveness but their efficiency, too. **Effectiveness** is *results oriented* and focuses on achieving goals (for example, sales revenue, profitability). **Efficiency** is *cost oriented* and focuses on expending minimum time, effort, and resources on tasks (for example, number of miles driven, expenses incurred). The combination of effectiveness and efficiency produces sales success, as depicted by the following formula:

*Effectiveness + Efficiency = Sales Success*

Time is a precious, nonexpandable resource. Consequently, salespeople must work to optimize their use of this precious commodity. One national study of nearly ten thousand sales representatives showed that they spend 33 percent of their time in face-to-face selling, 20 percent in travel, 16 percent in

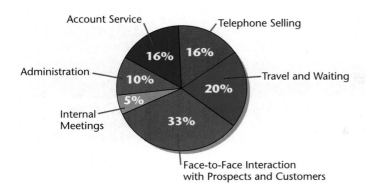

**FIGURE 12.1**

HOW SALESPEOPLE SPEND THEIR TIME

phone selling, 16 percent in account service and coordination, 10 percent in administration, and 5 percent at internal company meetings (see Figure 12.1).[2]

Although spending one-third of their time in face-to-face selling may not seem impressive, this is a higher percentage than many other studies have found. Perhaps growing professionalism among salespeople and increased use of the latest telecommunication tools have contributed to greater face-to-face selling time.

The extent of face-to-face selling time can have a tremendous impact on a salesperson's effectiveness and efficiency. Assuming the typical salesperson works forty hours per week and takes a two-week vacation, salespeople who spend 25 percent of their time in face-to-face selling have just five hundred hours a year (40 hr./week $\times$ .25 $\times$ 50 weeks/yr. = 500) in which to sell. Those salespeople whose efficiency allows them 33 percent face-to-face selling time have 660 hours a year (40 $\times$ .33 $\times$ 50 = 660) or 160 hours more to achieve selling goals. Table 12.1 on p. 372 shows, given each of these assumptions, the worth of an hour of the salesperson's time at different earning levels. For a salesperson earning one hundred thousand dollars a year, each hour of selling time costs more than two hundred dollars if only 25 percent of the time is spent in face-to-face selling. That cost drops to $152 an hour if selling time is increased to 33 percent. Thus, it's obvious that increased efficiency yields a substantial pay-off for a salesperson.

The most successful salespeople are the best prepared to make maximum use of their limited face-to-face selling time with prospects. Effective salespeople tend to possess the following characteristics:

- Their product knowledge, competitive knowledge, and face-to-face selling skills are excellent.
- They serve as clearinghouses of information, advisers, relationship builders, problem solvers, customer advocates, and deal makers.
- They use their influence to work with both internal staff and customers. Because salespeople generally have no subordinates, they must work through others over whom they have little or no direct control.

| TABLE 12.1 |
|---|
| WHAT IS ONE HOUR OF SELLING TIME WORTH? |

| Earnings | Approximate Worth of One Hour | |
|---|---|---|
| | 25% of Time Face-to-Face (500 Hours/Yr.) | 33% of Time Face-to-Face (660 Hours/Yr.) |
| $ 40,000 | $ 80 | $ 61 |
| 50,000 | 100 | 76 |
| 60,000 | 120 | 91 |
| 70,000 | 140 | 106 |
| 80,000 | 160 | 121 |
| 90,000 | 180 | 136 |
| 100,000 | 200 | 152 |
| 150,000 | 300 | 227 |
| 200,000 | 400 | 303 |
| 300,000 | 600 | 455 |
| 400,000 | 800 | 606 |
| 500,000 | 1,000 | 758 |

Influencing others to change their priorities and interrupt their schedules is a major part of the sales job.

• They understand that providing customer service is as important as making the sale. Therefore, they do not abdicate responsibility for installation, implementation, and service to technical support staff. They continue to maintain a close post-sale relationship that their customers find valuable.

Put your time- and relationship-management skills to work when you read the following *It's Up to You*.

## IT'S UP TO YOU

Your district manager calls you Wednesday evening and says he wants to work with you over the next two days as you make each of your sales calls. Last week, you scheduled four two-hour sales calls on both Thursday and Friday of this week, so your appointment book is filled. However, two of these accounts, one on each day, are notorious for canceling out at the last minute. You are fearful of this happening while your boss is working with you, and you are trying to decide how to avoid two hours of idle time each day in case of last-minute cancellations. What, if anything, should you say to your boss? What is your next move?

## SALES ACTIVITIES

Based on a study of nearly fourteen hundred salespeople from fifteen manufacturing industries, salespeople spend their time carrying out ten basic activities, as seen in Table 12.2. Depending on the industry, the prospects or customers, the products, and the situation, though, these activities will vary in importance. Therefore, you will want to determine the relative weight to assign to each of these activities in your given market environment and set your time priorities accordingly.

### What's Your Job Description?

Beyond understanding the general activities of salespeople, you need to know the exact performance expectations for your specific job assignment. One of the first tasks for a new salesperson should be to obtain a copy of his or her job description and make sure that it is current and accurate by verifying the

**TABLE 12.2**

**BASIC ACTIVITIES OF SALESPEOPLE**

| Basic Activities | Examples of Tasks Involved |
|---|---|
| Selling Process | Search out leads; prepare sales presentations; make sales calls; negotiate resistance. |
| Working with Orders | Process orders; expedite orders; handle shipping problems. |
| Servicing the Product | Test equipment; provide training; supervise installation. |
| Managing Information | Disseminate and gather information from customers; provide feedback to superiors. |
| Servicing the Account | Take inventory; set up point-of-purchase displays; stock shelves. |
| Attending Conferences or Meetings | Attend sales meetings; set up and staff exhibits at trade shows. |
| Training/Recruiting | Recruit new sales reps; train new sales reps. |
| Entertaining Customers | Take clients to dinner, golfing, stage plays. |
| Traveling Out of Town | Travel overnight to sales appointments. |
| Working with Distributors | Establish and maintain relationships with distributors; extend credit; collect past-due accounts. |

**Source:** Adapted from William C. Moncrief, "Selling Activity and Sales Position Taxonomies for Industrial Salesforces," Journal of Marketing Research (August 1986): 261–270.

SALES
REPRESENTATIVE

| | |
|---|---|
| **Position:** | District Sales Representative |
| **Reports to:** | Regional Sales Manager |
| **Division:** | Food Processing Machinery |
| **Purpose of Position:** | To sell and/or lease all manufactured and agency equipment and parts in the assigned territory and/or to assigned customers, and assist on national account promotions and sales. |

POSITION
RESPONSIBILITIES

1. Manage territory to create and maintain an environment for customers or potential customers to buy, use, and recommend products from our company.

2. Call regularly on major, unpenetrated accounts to build future business.

3. Complete studies and quotations, make technical and sales presentations, close sales and leases, draw sales contracts and other sales documents on machinery, and obtain parts orders.

4. Maintain representation and liaison between customers and all departments within our company to gain and maintain a high level of acceptance in our customers' organizations.

5. Work with Customer Service and other departments to ensure prompt and adequate service to customers to include using sound business judgment in handling pricing problems, pressures for concessions, and difficult negotiations.

6. Monitor competitive market posture to advise on necessary redesign of equipment, modification of pricing policy, or similar changes as may be indicated.

7. Assist the Credit Department in establishing customer's financial condition.

8. Maintain expenses at a prudent level and evaluate entertainment and conference expenditures to ascertain their potential to generate sales.

9. Implement aggressively all divisional product line promotional programs.

10. Manage time and utilize available resources to provide adequate coverage to customers.

11. Assist management in preparing accurate sales forecasts, quotas, and financial reports.

POSITION
REQUIREMENTS

1. B.S. degree (Engineering, Technical, or Business)
2. One or more years experience in the food industry
3. Willing to relocate

**FIGURE 12.2** POSITION DESCRIPTION

description with the sales manager. If you don't know what is expected, you will find it impossible to set meaningful time priorities. Figure 12.2 shows a typical job description for a salesperson.

In addition to a current job description, salespeople need to know what they are expected to achieve during a given time period. Salespeople and their sales manager should mutually agree on what is to be accomplished, then establish explicit time-based objectives such as quotas for sales calls, unit sales, and new customers during the quarter. Knowing what must be accomplished by a certain date will help you better manage your territorial activities and will help reduce the stress of uncertainty about your role and performance. After all, how will you know where you are going and whether you've arrived if you never establish goals?

## Salespeople as Field Marketing Managers

For many companies, the modern professional selling job has evolved into that of *field marketing manager* for a sales territory. Today's salespeople have more responsibilities than ever before, and they must fill many roles. They are largely their own bosses in their sales territories, working with groups of people over whom they have little control and who often impose conflicting demands and expectations on them. For example, customers may expect salespeople to help them obtain extended credit on purchases while the company accounting department is putting pressure on them to collect overdue accounts. Salespeople today perform many functions similar to those of marketing or sales managers, as illustrated in Table 12.3 on p. 376. They are involved in analyzing customer problems, setting sales objectives, doing financial analyses, coordinating members of a selling and customer service team, educating or training customers in the proper use of products, and controlling their activities and time to maximize productivity.

As field marketing managers, salespeople research the needs of their prospects and customers, analyze evolving markets to spot opportunities for new products and new customers, forecast sales for their territories, continually study buyer behavior to keep in touch with changing markets segments, devise marketing strategies to help customers improve their profitability, and use central information systems to keep themselves and customers informed. In contrast to sales or marketing managers, however, salespeople are responsible for managing only their own activities, not those of other people in a sales force or marketing department.

## Return on Time Invested

**Return on time invested (ROTI)** is a financial concept that can help salespeople spend their time more profitably with prospects and customers. To calculate ROTI, salespeople divide the result achieved by the amount of time incurred to accomplish that result (that is, result achieved/time). The *result* can be measured in various ways, such as dollar sales to a customer, profits on a certain product category, or new customers won. For example, if a salesperson spends sixty hours in preparing a sales call, making a sales presentation, and providing service to a customer who orders $90,000 worth of products, the ROTI is $90,000 (the result achieved) divided by sixty hours (the time

**Return on Time Invested (ROTI)** The designated return achieved calculated by dividing the result achieved by the amount of time incurred to accomplish that result.

TABLE 12.3

# THE SALESPERSON'S MANAGEMENT AND MARKETING ACTIVITIES

## Management Activities

| | |
|---|---|
| Problem Analysis | Analyzing customer problems that can be solved by the salesperson's products or services. |
| Objectives Setting | Establishing sales volume and market share levels needed in a territory to ensure a strong competitive position. |
| Financial Analysis | Evaluating the impact a customer's purchase will have on that customer's personal or business financial health. |
| Supervision and Coordination | Working with others in the salesperson's own firm to answer questions, supply information to prospects, provide customer service. Coordinating efforts of a company selling team. |
| Training | Educating buyers in the proper and productive use of products sold by the salesperson. |
| Controlling | Reviewing personal time allocations to various prospects, customers, and other tasks to determine how to become more productive. |

## Marketing Activities

| | |
|---|---|
| Research | Investigating prospect and customer needs and recommending product changes or new product ideas. |
| Market Analysis | Determining the size and needs of various market segments. Continually searching for new market opportunities. |
| Sales Forecasting | Predicting sales volume for different customer groups and individual accounts to help allocate selling time. |
| Buyer Behavior | Studying the buying process to become more effective in adjusting to different motivational and behavioral needs of prospects and buyers. |
| Marketing Strategy | Understanding the overall marketing strategy of customers in order to assess the impact of purchases on their inventory, distribution, product development, pricing, sales, and profits. |
| Information Systems | Using computers and other telecommunications technology to supply and access data needed in salesperson's competitive efforts and those of the buyer's or seller's company. |

*Source:* Adapted from Thomas R. Wotruba and Edwin K. Simpson, Sales Management: Text and Cases *(Boston: PWS-Kent, 1992).*

# KEEPING UP ONLINE: FIRST VIRTUAL CORPORATION

First Virtual Corporation specializes in video networking products such as videoconferencing. Visit their web site at www.fvc.com to examine their offerings. How could a company's salespeople use these services to improve their time and territory management?

incurred), or $1,500. Another salesperson who invests thirty hours of time to make a sale of $25,000 has an ROTI of $833. The higher the ROTI is, the better the salesperson's performance. Salespeople must keep accurate hourly records to know their ROTI for different activities, customers, and products. Although this may sound like tedious record keeping, it only takes a few minutes a day to record this information, and ROTI calculations can help salespeople manage their time more effectively and efficiently. Simple *sales call planning and results* sheets can be completed each week, then filed in folders or put on a computer for later analysis. Read *Keeping Up Online* to discover excellent tools for saving time.

## SETTING PRIORITIES

Setting priorities is essential. Salespeople who don't set priorities will often work on relatively minor tasks first because they are the easiest to complete and provide the feeling of accomplishment. Priorities should relate to specific objectives to be accomplished over a certain time period, such as a year, quarter, month, or week. Once you've determined your selling objectives, order them according to their importance and assign a date for their completion.

*Salespeople who don't set priorities will often work on relatively minor tasks first because they are the easiest to complete and provide an immediate sense of accomplishment.*
Photo Disc

### Three Axioms in Personal Selling

Top-performing salespeople always set priorities in their work; they recognize the truth of three axioms: Parkinson's Law, Concentration Principle, and Iceberg Principle. Let's briefly discuss each of these.

**Parkinson's Law.** The axiom that work tends to expand to fill the time allotted for its

**Parkinson's Law** Work expands to fill the time allowed for it.

completion is **Parkinson's Law.** For example, if you have eight hours to write a sales proposal, you will probably take that much time to complete the task. But, if you had only four hours to write the proposal, you would somehow manage to complete it within that time.

**Concentration Principle** Most sales, costs, and profits come from a relatively small proportion of customers and products; also known as the "80-20" rule.

**Concentration Principle.** Often called the "80-20" rule, the **concentration principle** says that most of your sales, costs, and profits come from a relatively small proportion of your customers and products. For example, a large cosmetics producer markets its products in more than fifty countries, but only eight countries account for 86 percent of the company's sales and 90 percent of profits. Also, about 20 percent of its sales reps account for more than half of its sales.[3] A pharmaceutical company increased its sales 250 percent over four years by eliminating sales calls on 330,000 small accounts in order to concentrate on 70,000 major ones.[4] Later in this chapter you'll see how you can determine which of your accounts are more important than others and thus deserve more of your attention and effort.

**Iceberg Principle**
Analogous to an iceberg, most sales problems are hidden beneath the surface of overall positive sales totals.

**Iceberg Principle.** Analogous to an iceberg that shows only 10 percent of its mass above the water, many sales problems can remain hidden beneath the surface of overall positive sales totals—the **iceberg principle.** That is, *total* company or sales office sales do not reveal a complete picture of the effectiveness and efficiency of sales operations. For instance, *total* sales could be increasing dramatically, yet *certain* territories, products, or classes of customers may be "bleeding red ink" and proving to be marked profit drains to the company. As a result, many companies send their sales managers sales, cost, and profitability reports analyzed by territory, product, customer, and salesperson. Salespeople should not hesitate to ask their sales managers for detailed analyses relevant to their territories. If this information is unavailable to you, you can develop your own analyses on products and customers within your territories.

### Performance Measures

All salespeople want to know how well they're doing. Having this information helps you determine how far you are from your goals and what you need to do to reach them. For example, you may need to reset some priorities. A balance of several *quantitative* and *qualitative* standards is better than relying on one performance measure, such as sales volume, because you will obtain a more complete picture of your performance. For instance, if you emphasize keeping sales and service expenses low, you may find sales revenue and profits adversely affected.

*Quantitative measures*, like dollar or unit sales volume or net profit by product or customer, affect sales or expenses directly and usually can be measured objectively. *Qualitative measures*, such as the salesperson's product knowledge, customer relationships, or ethical behavior, have a more indirect and longer-run impact on sales and expenses and thus must be evaluated on a more subjective basis.

Most prospects and customers place more importance on qualitative measures of salesperson performance than quantitative ones. For instance, prospects and customers prefer to interact with salespeople who are effective listeners, can address questions and issues well, don't waste time, and have strong communication skills.

Another way to look at sales activities is as efforts and results. *Sales efforts* include selling activities, such as the number of sales calls made on potential new accounts, or nonselling activities, such as the number of service calls, displays set up, collections made, or customer complaints handled. *Sales results* include measurable outcomes, such as the number of orders obtained, average dollar amount of orders, percent of quota achieved, and gross margin by product or customer type. Table 12.4 shows quantitative measures of a salesperson's selling efforts and selling results. Let's discuss two important kinds of salesperson performance measures: sales quotas and customer reviews of performance.

**TABLE 12.4**

## QUANTITATIVE MEASURES OF SALESPERSON PERFORMANCE

| Personal Selling Efforts | Personal Selling Results |
|---|---|
| **Sales Calls:**<br>• Number of calls on current customers<br>• Number of calls on new prospects<br>• Number of sales presentations<br>• Number of sales demonstrations<br>• Selling time versus nonselling time<br>• Call frequency ratio per customer type | **Orders:**<br>• Number of orders obtained<br>• Number of orders canceled by customers<br>• Average order size (dollars or units)<br>• Batting average (orders ÷ sales calls) |
| **Selling Expenses:**<br>• As percent of sales volume<br>• As percent of sales quota<br>• Average per sales call<br>• By customer type<br>• By product category<br>• Direct selling expense ratios<br>• Indirect selling expense ratios | **Sales Volume:**<br>• Dollar sales<br>• Unit sales<br>• Percent of sales quota obtained<br>• Sales by customer category<br>• Sales by product type<br>• Market share |
| **Customer Service:**<br>• Number of service calls<br>• Number of customer complaints<br>• Percent of sales (units/dollars) returned<br>• Delivery cost per unit sold<br>• Displays set up<br>• Delivery cost per unit sold<br>• Average time spent per call | **Margins:**<br>• Gross margin for territory<br>• Net profit for territory<br>• Gross margin by customer and product<br>• Net profit by customer and product |
| | **Customer Accounts:**<br>• Number of new accounts<br>• Number of lost accounts<br>• Number of overdue accounts<br>• Dollar amount of accounts receivable<br>• Collections from accounts receivable<br>• Percent of accounts sold |

**Sales Quotas.** Derived from sales forecasts, sales quotas provide performance objectives and motivational incentives for salespeople. Usually stated in terms of dollar or unit volume, sales managers rely heavily on them as standards for appraising the performance of individual salespeople.[5] To spur themselves on to greater performance, some top-performing salespeople establish even higher quotas—inspirational—for themselves than those assigned by their sales manager. If your company does not assign you specific quotas, you should establish your own goals or quotas for various performance measures in your territory. Here are four types of quotas that salespeople ought to consider: (1) *sales volume quotas*, such as dollar or unit sales; (2) *financial quotas*, such as gross margin, net profit, or expenses; (3) *activity quotas*, such as the number of sales calls made or the number of dealer training sessions given; and (4) *combination quotas*, which include both financial and activity goals. It is important to have activity quotas as well as financial quotas because meeting activity quotas can continue to motivate salespeople who fail to meet financial quotas.[6]

One problem in using quotas in business-to-business selling is that sales may rely on the efforts of several people, including telemarketers, inside salespeople, or even a selling team. When several people influence sales, many companies use team or group quotas and split commissions on some predetermined basis among group members. It is important for salespeople to understand clearly how and when commissions will be distributed in order to avoid disputes later.[7] Most companies pay commissions after orders are *shipped*, but some pay when orders are *received* and others not until orders are *paid*.

**Customer Reviews of Performance.** Customers are increasingly conducting annual reviews of supplier performance. Salespeople should ask for an annual evaluation of their performance by customers and participate in this review process at a special meeting. Obtaining feedback from customers is one of the most effective ways to keep from losing touch with customers. Staying on top of your customers' needs and your performance in satisfying them demonstrates your commitment to the firm. The more committed you are to an account, the more satisfied the account is likely to be and the less likely it will switch suppliers.[8]

## ACCOUNT AND TERRITORY MANAGEMENT

**Sales Territory** A control unit that contains customer accounts.

A **sales territory** is a control unit that contains customer accounts. Most salespeople are assigned a geographical control unit such as a state, county, zip-code area, city, or township because these are the bases for a great deal of government census data and other market information. Other market factors such as buying habits and patterns of trade flow can also define territories.[9] Companies establish sales territories to facilitate sales planning and control by enhancing market coverage, to increase sales, to keep selling costs low, to reduce travel time, to improve salesperson rewards and morale, to strengthen customer relations, and to coordinate selling with other marketing func-

## KEEPING UP ONLINE: INSTANT YELLOW PAGES

Assume that you are a sales representative for a candy manufacturer in Connecticut who calls on candy retailers throughout that state. How might you improve your effectiveness and efficiency by using yellowpages.com to identify prospects?

tions.[10] With escalating selling costs, territory management is becoming increasingly important.[11]

Once the geographical control unit has been established, the next step is to analyze the customers and prospects in the territory on the basis of their sales potential. Accounts must first be identified by name. Many sources provide this information. Computerized directories represent one of the most effective sources for identifying customers quickly. The *Yellow Pages Online* (www. yellowpages.com) contains a huge database of U.S. and international businesses by name, mailing address, and phone numbers. Read *Keeping Up Online* and think about how the Yellow Pages Online web site can help your selling.

Salespeople can also use company records of past sales, trade directories, professional association membership lists, directories of corporations, publishers of mailing lists, trade books and periodicals, chambers of commerce, federal, state, and local governments, and personal observation by the salesperson. Once you've identified potential accounts, the next step is to estimate the total sales potential for all accounts in each geographical control unit. After you make those sales estimates, classify the accounts according to their annual buying potential. Those with the highest sales potential you can assign to category A and give the largest share of your time. Next, classify the average potential accounts as category B. Finally, those accounts with very little sales potential are in category C. Now you can decide which accounts to make sales calls on and which ones to contact by telephone or by direct mail. As illustrated in Figure 12.3 on p. 382, the concentration principle is usually evident after ranking customers by sales potential. Here, customers in category A (20 percent) account for about 70 percent of the sales volume, category B (25 percent) for 23 percent of sales, and customers in category C (55 percent) account for only 7 percent of sales. Many companies use computer programs to assist their salespeople in account analysis, planning, and control.

### Portfolio Analysis Approach

Many organizations still refrain from helping their salespeople with computerized mathematical models because they are so complex. Also, not every sales call can be accurately programmed because of the diverse variables that affect success and failure. A *portfolio analysis approach* provides an alternative to the

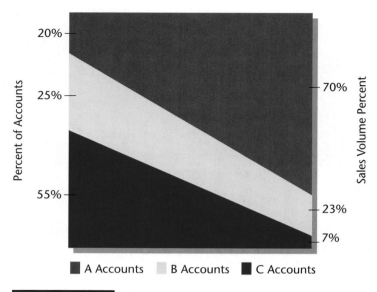

**A Accounts**     **B Accounts**     **C Accounts**

**FIGURE 12.3**

RANKING CUSTOMERS ACCORDING TO THE CONCENTRATION PRINCIPLE

analytical rigor of the mathematical models. In this approach, the sales call strategy is based on the account's attractiveness. Account attractiveness depends on two dimensions: account opportunity and strength of position. *Account opportunity* refers to the prospect's need and ability to purchase the product; *strength of position* refers to the strength of the selling firm's position with the prospect.[12] Presented in Figure 12.4 is a portfolio analysis approach. Segment 1 represents what most companies call a key account. Segment 2 would be considered a potential customer or prospect. Segment 3 is a stable account, and Segment 4 represents a weak account. This kind of matrix allows salespeople to set calling priorities among their accounts and establish sales call strategies for them.

Note that the above approach involves the salesperson's assigning a *generalized* assessment concerning the attractiveness of an account. An alternate approach to determining how valuable an account is uses *quantitative* information by considering (1) the present profit contribution of a customer and (2) the customer's potential profit contribution. Once this determination is made for all accounts, each account can be positioned into one of four quadrants:

- High present profit contribution and high potential profit contribution (desirable accounts)
- High present profit contribution and low potential profit contribution (developed accounts)
- Low present profit contribution and high potential profit contribution (developing accounts)
- Low present profit contribution and low potential profit contribution (undesirable accounts)

## STRENGTH OF POSITION

|  | **Strong** | **Weak** |
|---|---|---|
| **High** | **SEGMENT 1**<br>**Attractiveness**<br>Accounts are very attractive, since they offer high opportunity and since sales organization has a strong position.<br><br>**Sales Call Strategy**<br>Accounts should receive a high level of sales calls, since they are the sales organization's most attractive accounts. | **SEGMENT 2**<br>**Attractiveness**<br>Accounts are potentially attractive, since they offer high opportunity, but sales organization currently has weak position with accounts.<br><br>**Sales Call Strategy**<br>Accounts should receive a high level of sales calls to strengthen the sales organization's position. |
| **Low** | **SEGMENT 3**<br>**Attractiveness**<br>Accounts are somewhat attractive, since sales organization has strong position, but future opportunity is limited.<br><br>**Sales Call Strategy**<br>Accounts should receive a moderate level of sales calls to maintain the current strength of the sales organization's position. | **SEGMENT 4**<br>**Attractiveness**<br>Accounts are very unattractive since they offer low opportunity and since sales organization has weak position.<br><br>**Sales Call Strategy**<br>Accounts should receive minimal level of sales calls and efforts should be made to selectively eliminate or replace personal sales calls with phone sales calls, direct mail, etc. |

ACCOUNT OPPORTUNITY (vertical axis label)

### FIGURE 12.4

ACCOUNT ANALYSIS

The analysis will suggest to the salesperson the value of each account and which ones merit attention and which do not.[13] Following the portfolio analysis, salespeople are now prepared to undertake the next phase of account management—territorial routing.

**Territorial routing** is devising a plan or pattern to use when making sales calls. The primary goal is to minimize nonselling time (for example, traveling and waiting) and maximize selling time for salespeople.[14] A well-designed routing system also helps salespeople reduce their selling costs, improve their territory coverage, and improve their communication with sales managers, customers, or others who, by knowing their routing pattern, can more easily locate them on short notice. In many companies, individual salespeople still route themselves because they know their territories and customers best.

**Territorial Routing**
Devising a travel plan or pattern to use when making sales calls.

Depending on the geographical distribution and number of prospects and customers, routing systems can be quite complex. A basic pattern can be made simply by locating all the accounts on a map and determining the optimal order for visiting each and the fastest route to take. Before developing a routing plan, you must decide the number of calls to make each day, the call frequency on each class of customer, the distance to each account, and the method of transportation. With this information, you can locate present and potential customers on a map of the territory. In the past, accounts were often identified on a map by marking their location with felt-tip pens, or using different colors of pushpins for each account category. Today, salespeople can use various computer programs to obtain a complete routing plan in minutes. The overall objective in developing a routing path is to minimize backtracking and crisscrossing, thereby enabling the salesperson to use time in the most efficient manner.

### Routing Patterns

Depending on the sales territory's size and shape, routing patterns are commonly straight or circular. With a *straight-line* route the salesperson starts at the office and makes calls in one direction until he or she reaches the end of the territory. *Circular patterns* start at the office and move in a circle of stops until the salesperson ends up back at the office. Two less common and more

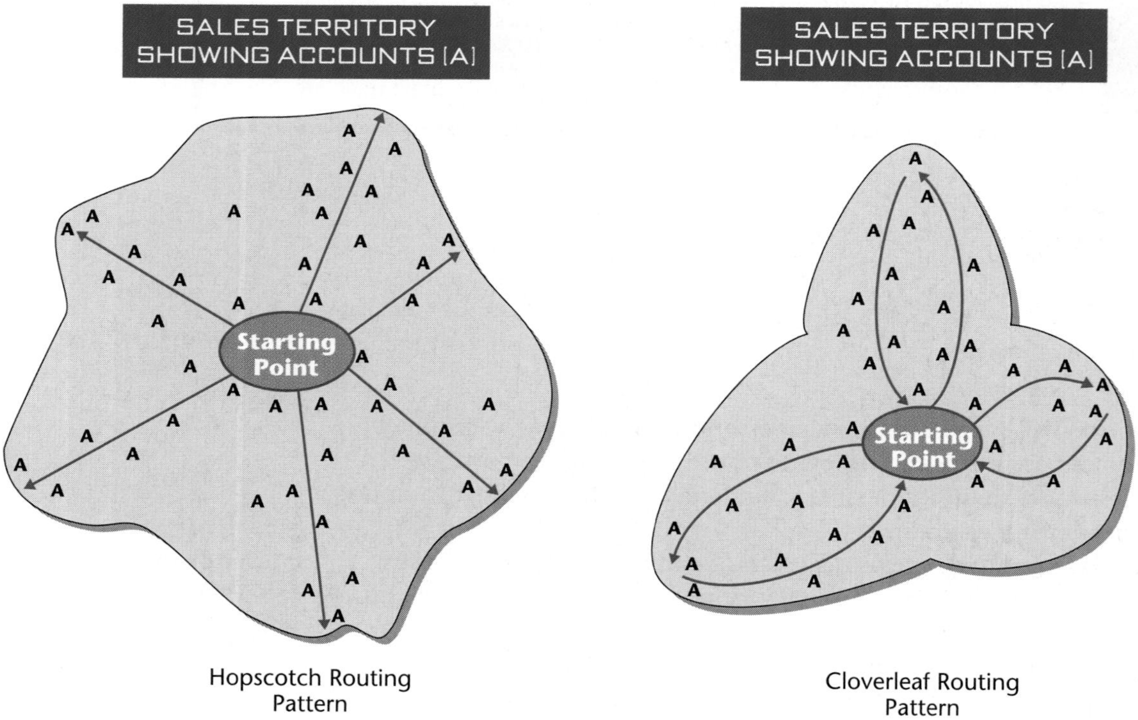

Hopscotch Routing
Pattern

Cloverleaf Routing
Pattern

**FIGURE 1 2.5**

HOPSCOTCH AND CLOVERLEAF ROUTING PATTERNS

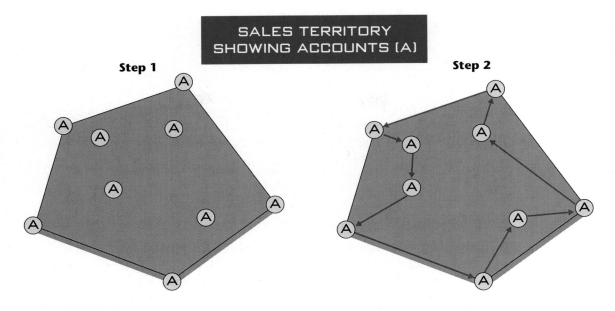

SALES TERRITORY
SHOWING ACCOUNTS [A]

**FIGURE 12.6**

"OUTER RING" ROUTING PATTERN

complex route patterns are the cloverleaf and the hopscotch. Used when accounts are concentrated in specific parts of the territory, a *cloverleaf* route is similar to a circular pattern, but rather than covering an entire territory, the route circles only part of a territory. The next trip is an adjacent circle and the pattern continues until the entire territory is covered. With *hopscotch* patterns the salesperson starts at the farthest point from the office and hops back and forth calling on accounts on either side of a straight line back to the office. For speed, the salesperson may fly to the outer limits of his or her territory then drive back calling on customers. On the next trip the salesperson would go in another direction in the territory. Hopscotch and cloverleaf patterns are depicted in Figure 12.5.

In the "outer ring" approach to routing, shown in Figure 12.6, the salesperson first draws an outer ring around the customers to be called upon. Then, those customers inside the ring are connected to the outer ring route using angles that are as obtuse as possible. General principles underlying this "outer ring" approach of routing include the following:

- Customers in close proximity to each other should be visited in direct succession.
- Sales calls should be made along the way to eliminate sharp angles in the route.
- Avoid using the same route to and from a customer because retracing your steps is the most acute angle of all.
- Routes already traveled should not be crossed.
- Daily travel routes should be as circular as possible.[15]

## KEEPING UP ONLINE: EMPOWER GEOGRAPHICS

*mpower Geographics* is a web site at which salespeople can locate prospects and customers on maps using criteria such as sales, driving distance, markets served, lead distribution, or work load. Investigate www.empowergeo.com/pages/about_territory.htm and consider how a salesperson might use such maps to improve efficiency and effectiveness in territory management.

### Using Computer Programs in Routing

Numerous computer-based interactive models have been successfully applied to sales force routing and territory management.[16] One computer model, called *nearest-city*, can start from any given geographic point and select the shortest, least cost distance between accounts. Nearly all computer routing models require input from salespeople on each customer's sales potential, call length, profit contribution, and estimated share penetration. Based on this information, the computer models realign sales territories into more manageable account groupings and route sales reps in terms of call frequencies, travel time, and length of call.

With the help of sophisticated software programs, you can quickly and conveniently develop your own optimal routing and scheduling strategies on your computer. In recent years, more elaborate sales force automation models have become available from companies such as Siebel Systems, which sells *enterprise relationship management* (ERM) software to direct and monitor sales, customer service, and call center relationships with prospects and customers. In the years ahead, comprehensive mathematical models and software programs that allow more effective and efficient scheduling and routing of salespeople will become available. You can see some current mathematical models and formulas used in salesperson routing at www.nada.kth.se/~viggo/wwwcompendium/node104.html. To test your ability to develop an efficient territorial routing plan, try out some of the problems at www.courses.psu.edu/mktg/mktg220rso3/qwrap.htm. The above *Keeping Up Online* suggests another web site of interest for providing time management assistance.

## WORKING SMARTER

Effort alone will not produce favorable sales results. To increase efficiency, salespeople also need to learn to work smarter.[17] Two means of doing this are by using the latest telecommunications technology and managing time better.

### Using the Latest Technology

As discussed in chapter 2, salespeople have at their disposal a wealth of technological advances to assist them to perform their job more efficiently and effectively. Electronic beepers, cellular phones, email, facsimile machines, laptop computers, word-processing and spreadsheet software, time management software, and other devices are valuable tools in the salesperson's selling arsenal.

The experiences of diverse companies attest to the value of laptop computers to their salespeople and customers. To help in managing territories, completing paperwork, and gaining more face-to-face selling time, one pharmaceutical firm equipped their salespeople and sales managers with laptop computers. Now the company's salespeople can obtain information on and for their thousands of physician customers in a few seconds. Administrative tasks are taking about 20 percent less time and reports are more accurate. The firm estimates that every 1 percent boost in a rep's effectiveness increases revenue by $6.7 million per year.

At a life insurance company, salespeople use their laptop computers to compute instantly how different options can change the cost of a prospect's insurance policy. Prior to laptops, such calculations took days or even weeks. At one large oil company, computers are freeing field sales representatives from administrative functions, yielding sales productivity gains of 15 to 20 percent. Salespeople from a marketing services group of a large data-processing firm are saving an average of 4.4 hours per week on various sales-related tasks and serving customers information needs faster. A steel manufacturer estimates a 20 to 25 percent reduction in clerical errors for laptop users. And salespeople with laptops at an electronics manufacturer have gained two to three hours a week in selling and servicing time. Other organizations have seen improvements in budgeting and controlling expenses. Read how some firms have expedited their sales reps' capabilities in *From the Command Post*.

## FROM THE COMMAND POST: IT'S ALL IN THE PALM OF MY HAND

PalmPilots (and other handheld devices) have become the sine qua non as well as de rigueur in the selling arena. Few sales personnel today would be caught without one. Their potential for increased sales productivity is almost limitless. In fact, without one, a salesperson may well be bereft of crucial information and the means with which to close a sale, provide customer service, or execute customer reorders. Depending on its configuration, sales reps can scan their products' UPC bar codes, align the device with their PCs, and email purchase orders to company headquarters. And all this can be done instantly by salespeople whenever and wherever they want. No longer do salespeople need to incur long delays while playing "phone tag" with their sales managers and other support people to obtain or send critical information.

Handheld high-tech devices have significantly decreased the time required to place orders, transfer them to company headquarters, and enter them into the supplier's accounting software. Some companies have cut the amount of time formerly needed to perform these activities by almost 99 percent! Not only is ordering time expedited, but salespeople now have more time to spend on building customer relationships. And because handheld devices are becomingly increasingly user-friendly, salespeople can quickly become attuned to their features and advantages, thus minimizing the former "learning curve" disadvantages of adopting new technology.

## Managing Time Better

Many organizations provide time-management training for their sales reps. Nonetheless, some salespeople find multiple reasons for using time inefficiently.

**Excuses about Time.**  Some salespeople are chronically late, disorganized, and generally inefficient in using time. Part of the problem is often the person's attitude toward time and the acceptance of excuses for its inefficient use. Some of the most common excuses are offered in Table 12.5.

---

**TABLE 12.5**

### EXCUSES FOR POOR TIME MANAGEMENT

- **Insufficient time:** There is always enough time to accomplish essential tasks. A salesperson who believes that he or she has insufficient time can usually overcome the problem by reassessing priorities for daily activities. Some tasks can be postponed or delayed indefinitely.

- **Too many demands on my time:** Learning to say no is probably the most important timesaving technique you can learn. Letting other people preempt your priorities with their own allows them to control your time. Whenever someone places an unexpected demand on your time, ask yourself: Is this unplanned activity more important than what I had planned to do with this time? If it isn't, give a courteous but brief explanation of why you cannot comply with the request.

- **I can do it better myself:** Some salespeople have such a need for control and perfection that they waste time doing unimportant tasks that could be delegated to others. Ask yourself whether such tasks are the best use of your time. If someone else can do minor tasks well enough for you, you gain more time to spend on important projects.

- **If I only had more time each day:** Everyone has the same twenty-four hours each day, but some people learn how to use those hours more efficiently. Working more hours every day produces mental and physical fatigue that can be counterproductive to overall performance.

- **I don't have time to plan:** The old saying, "Ask a busy person if you want something done," illustrates the importance of planning the use of one's time. People who achieve a lot have learned how to manage their time by skillful planning.

- **I can't find time to work on big projects:** Because many complex projects cannot be finished quickly, people tend to let them go until they can find large blocks of time. Schedule at least an hour every day to work on major projects so that you do not procrastinate and create a panic situation later when the deadline draws near.

- **Unexpected problems disrupt my plans:** Whenever the unexpected occurs, ask yourself the key question: Is this more important than what I had planned to do at this time? If it isn't, don't do it.

- **If only I could work faster:** Most people make mistakes when they hurry. When you lack the time to do everything on your list, setting priorities is the key: Do high-priority tasks and ignore low priorities.

- **It's better to do small tasks first:** This is the exact opposite of what the best time managers do. Create the habit of doing your most important tasks early in the day before minor tasks crowd them out.

*Paperwork can be a dreaded and time-consuming chore for salespeople who aren't good time managers.* Photo Disc

**Paperwork.**   One of the most dreaded and time-consuming tasks of salespeople is handling their *paperwork*. Like other sales-related activities, paperwork ought to be scheduled on the salesperson's daily or weekly planning calendar. Some companies put the two hundred to seven hundred pages of memos, newsletters, brochures, reports, announcements, and other sales-related materials sent to salespeople each week onto audiotapes. The tapes are recorded according to topics, so salespeople can choose exactly what they want to hear.

**Customer Service.**   Another time-consuming but important activity is providing *customer service*. Although it is hard to predict *which* customers will want *what* services *when*, salespeople must recognize that customer service is a regular part of their jobs and must be scheduled like any other activity. The suggestions below may assist you in focusing your customer service activities:

- Segment your customers according to costs and the potential profits in providing them with superior service.
- Remember that all customer contacts, whether through telephone operators, receptionists, secretaries, delivery and repair personnel, or customer service people shape the perceptions of your company's service. Try to encourage all these customer-contact people to treat prospects and customers well.
- Continually stress the importance of customer service to people in your company and reinforce this attitude by your own actions.
- Design and use measures of service effectiveness, such as the percentage of on-time deliveries, the length of time it takes to repair a product, and the level of customer satisfaction.

The professional salesperson must learn to work smarter instead of harder. *On the Frontlines* below suggests how salespeople can do exactly that!

**Time Traps.**  Many salespeople hurt their efficiency by falling into daily traps that waste their time. The most successful salespeople learn how to avoid time traps so that they make the most of each hour and each day. Some of the most common time traps are given in *The Box of Time Traps* on p. 391.

**A Plan for Each Day.**  Every salesperson can benefit from preparing a daily to-do list of projects and tasks ranked into A, B, and C categories of importance. Work first on all the A priorities until no more work on them can be done; then, move on to the B categories, and finally work on the C category tasks. Although the A items are likely to be complex or long-term projects, use the *Swiss cheese* approach to punch little holes in such tasks at every opportunity because they are your top priority. For example, if one of your A priorities

## ON THE FRONTLINES

# *A Prosaic High-Tech Selling Tool*

Most salespeople want to stand out from the pack, excel, and be recognized as among the best in their field. In this high-tech age, there are manifold ways of achieving this goal. One sometimes overlooked means, perhaps because it is so commonplace today, is email.

Email can be an efficient and effective means of selling. It requires, though, careful attention in execution. Otherwise, it can become just another selling tool—and not a particularly useful one at that. Prospects and customers are flooded with myriad email missives day in and day out, many of which they do not read or even open. Therefore, fine-tuned email messages can be an extremely valuable weapon in the selling battle. Several means of doing this are available.

The accuracy of the database must be checked. Names and addresses, as well as any other pertinent information purchased from the database provider (for example, company size, nature of industry, contact people) must be correct. Otherwise, precious promotional dollars and efforts will be wasted on emails that never reach a legitimate prospect or customer.

Additionally, lists need to be segmented to enhance financial return. Email prospects who have shown an earlier interest in a company's offerings should receive specially tailored information or discounts that the more general customer email list does not receive. Just as segmentation works for marketing products and services to target markets, it is also beneficial for providing customer service with technical support updates and advance notice of new product introductions.

Once an email distribution list has been completed, the campaign should be thoroughly evaluated and tested. Evaluation can help determine the effectiveness and efficiency of email efforts. For instance, the tests can provide salespeople with information on the number of email messages sent, delivered, opened, examined, and forwarded successfully, as well as the addresses from which the message was bounced back and the reason for this. With such feedback, the salespeople can refine their email lists until they largely contain only qualified prospects and customers.

For those sales force members who work for companies who have a legitimate business (offering a substantive product or service) and emphasize customer service, email sales activities may be just the extra medicine required to achieve renewed sales health.

## THE BOX OF TIME TRAPS

- Calling on unqualified or unprofitable prospects.
- Insufficient planning for each day's activities.
- Poor territorial routing and travel plans.
- Making too many cold calls.
- Taking long lunch hours and too many coffee breaks.
- Making poor use of waiting time between appointments.
- Spending too much time entertaining prospects and customers.
- Not using modern telecommunications equipment such as a car phone, beeper, facsimile, and laptop computer.
- Doing tasks that could be delegated to a staff person or to automated equipment.
- Failing to prioritize work.
- Doing work that isn't a part of the job description.
- Procrastinating on major projects or on contacting high potential prospects, resulting in redundant preparation and paperwork.
- Inefficient handling of paperwork and disorganized record keeping.
- Putting too many documents into a pending file, so that you wind up handling each sheet of paper several times as you look through the pending file periodically.
- Failing to break up huge, long-range goals into small, currently manageable tasks.
- Ending workdays early, especially on Friday afternoons.
- Failing to insulate self from interruptions on sales calls or while doing paperwork.
- Letting sales meetings and discussions veer too far off course.
- Conducting unnecessary meetings, visits, and phone calls.
- Socializing excessively during or between sales calls.
- Allowing other people to preempt your priorities with their own.

is preparing a sales proposal for a large client, take every opportunity to work on that report during your day, perhaps by looking up a reference in the library or doing a few calculations. By doing a small piece of this major project every day, you will complete it before you know it. Follow these tips in your daily planning:

- Outline your daily tasks and activities.
- Arrange them in A-B-C priority order.
- Work on the A priorities until you can do no more, then work on the B priorities, and finally the C priorities.
- Delegate as many tasks as you can.
- Control interruptions.
- Don't let other people preempt your priorities.

**Steps to Manage Your Time More Effectively.** Although numerous guidelines have been suggested by time management experts, most seem to agree on the following steps:

| DAILY SCHEDULE | DATE _____ |
|---|---|
| **Hours** | **Appointments/Activities** |
| 8:00 | |
| 9:00 | |
| 10:00 | |
| 11:00 | |
| 12:00 | |
| 1:00 | |
| 2:00 | |
| 3:00 | |
| 4:00 | |
| 5:00 | |
| Evening Hours | |

**FIGURE 12.7**

DAILY SCHEDULE SHEET

- *Accomplish one major objective each day:* Pick one important task and concentrate on completing it. If you develop this habit, it will prevent you from filling up your day with low-priority activities.
- *Each weekday afternoon, write down your schedule for the next day:* Committing your schedule to writing will force you to think carefully about your plan. It will help you set realistic deadlines and motivate you to accomplish the plan, as well as achieve any call quotas and sales goals that have been set for you. Use a daily schedule sheet like the one pictured in Figure 12.7.
- *On Friday afternoon, plan your schedule for the following week:* By the middle of Friday afternoon, you have a good idea of what you've accomplished—or failed to accomplish—that week. The pressure has eased, so you can think clearly. It's the ideal time to decide what you need to accomplish the following week. This tactic allows you to mentally rehearse your schedule over the weekend so that you'll have a psychological headstart Monday morning. When you arrive at the office, you'll hit the ground running.
- *Reduce one time-waster each week:* You can never quit wasting time altogether, but you can waste less of it. For example, by closing your door to concentrate on writing or reading reports, you can reduce time lost to drop-in visitors.
- *Concentrate on keeping meetings shorter and more productive:* As Peter Drucker says in *The Effective Executive:* "Meetings are by definition a

concession to deficient organization. For one either meets or one works. One cannot do both at the same time." You can, however, take steps to keep meetings manageable. Mail out an agenda to meeting participants; put a suggested time limit beside each item on the agenda and stick to it; start and end the meeting on time; and take five minutes at the end of a meeting to summarize decisions and who will be responsible for what.

- *Concentrate on high priorities:* Salespeople must learn to work on high priority projects first, even when only a little can be accomplished on the project that day, before switching to lower priority tasks.
- *Spend your time as if you had to buy it:* If you look at your time as a precious asset like gold that costs you money to use up, you'll learn to use it more productively.
- *Stop procrastinating:* Change your "do-it-later" habit into a "do-it-now" habit. Some salespeople delay work on large projects until they can find large blocks of time. But this approach can cause them to leave their most important projects until the last minute when they are forced to finish them quickly and poorly.
- *Schedule some personal time every day:* The best way to obtain personal time is to schedule it in your daily appointment book, so that it's protected from intrusions. Listen to music, read a book, talk with friends and family, or go for a long walk. Personal time is not a luxury or something to postpone until you can fit it into your schedule. It's a requirement for maintaining a healthy balance and control in your life.
- *Good intentions are not enough:* As the old saying goes: "The road to hell is paved with good intentions," so stop talking about how you're going to manage your time better and start doing it now.[18]

Few, if any, human beings have ever reached or maintained for long optimal effectiveness and efficiency. Nevertheless, salespeople should keep careful track of how they use their time each day, so that they can find ways, even small ones, to increase their number of productive hours. Such continuous efforts can soon pay off in higher sales and greater income.

## SUMMARY

Top-performing salespeople are usually efficient and effective managers of their territories. Operating much like field marketing managers, they try to maximize their return on time invested (ROTI). They understand the various qualitative and qualitative measures of performance and conduct annual reviews of their own performance with their individual customers. They use the most efficient account analysis and routing plans, sometimes developed by computers. They are excellent time managers who learn ways to work smarter by utilizing the latest technology and by avoiding the classic time traps that plague lesser salespeople.

## KEY TERMS

Effectiveness

Efficiency

Return on Time Invested (ROTI)

Parkinson's Law

Concentration Principle

Iceberg Principle

Sales Territory

Territorial Routing

## CHAPTER REVIEW QUESTIONS

1. Define and distinguish between the terms *effectiveness* and *efficiency*.

2. How do salespeople actually spend their time?

3. What are the basic activities of salespeople?

4. Why is a job description important to a salesperson?

5. Identify the major *management* and *marketing* activities of salespeople.

6. Describe the concept of return on time invested (ROTI).

7. Name at least five *quantitative* and five *qualitative* measures of salesperson performance.

8. Give some guidelines for better time management.

9. What are the classic time traps into which salespeople can fall?

10. What are some steps salespeople can take to manage their time better?

## TOPICS FOR THOUGHT AND CLASS DISCUSSION

1. Why are salespeople described as operating like field marketing managers? Do you believe that this is an accurate representation of the typical field salesperson? Explain.

2. Do you think that most job descriptions for salespeople accurately reflect their current duties and responsibilities? Why?

3. Pick a routine task in your life and map out a plan for improving your efficiency and effectiveness in accomplishing it.

4. How do time traps disrupt your time management? How can you avoid these traps?

5. What techniques do you use to plan, organize, and set priorities in your daily activities? Do you use the "Swiss cheese" approach for large or complex projects? Give an example of how you do or how you might.

6. Do you allow other people to frequently preempt your priorities in use of your time by substituting one of theirs? Give an example. How might you deal with future situations where someone wants you to accept his or her priority for time use instead of yours?

## PROJECTS FOR PERSONAL GROWTH

1. Contact three salespeople and ask them how they plan, organize, and prioritize their daily activities. Mention that you are a student working on a class project. Evaluate their approaches in terms of ROTI.

2. Classify four of your student friends on the basis of your perceptions of their effectiveness and efficiency. Then ask these student friends these two questions: (a) "What techniques do you use to plan, organize, and set priorities in your daily activities?" and (b) "What *time traps* are most responsible for wasting your time each day?" Compare your friends' answers with your prior classification of them. Any surprises?

3. For the coming week, write down how you spend each hour of the seven days. At the end of the week, compute approximately how much of your time you used productively and how much you wasted. Draw up a plan for better managing your time and use it throughout a second week. At the end of this second week, evaluate whether or not you obtained more productive time. What made the difference?

4. Go to the library and search out three current articles on managing a sales territory. Summarize them and report what you learned to your classmates.

## CASE 12.1

# TIME IS NO OBJECT

Steve Burbank and his fiancée, Diane Boutilier, had shared a gloriously long weekend of sun-bathing, swimming, boating, and gambling in Atlantic City, New Jersey. While driving back to New York City late that evening, Steve thought about how fortunate he was, at age twenty-six, to have a pretty, fun-loving fiancée and a great job that gave him a lot of independence. Steve had accepted the job with Pearson Machine Tools after graduating from the State University of New York with a degree in marketing. His first year with Pearson had been spent in training—learning about the machine tools and different customer needs. With a guaranteed salary of $48,500 for the first year and no sales pressure, Steve had enjoyed the training even though he didn't take some of it too seriously. After all, training programs always give the theoretical approach, while the real work is different, or so he thought.

Only a month ago Steve had been assigned to his own territory and on Monday would begin his first long field trip. Arriving home that evening, Steve felt mellow but tired, and he had fallen asleep without setting his alarm clock for 7:00 A.M. as he had planned in order to catch an 8:30 A.M. flight to Boston. Steve had learned about the "hop-scotch" routing pattern in training, and he was going to use it this week to fly to the farthest point of his territory, then rent a car and make sales calls on the way back home.

Although he missed his 8:30 A.M. flight to Boston, Steve caught another flight about an hour later. Arriving in Boston around 10:30 A.M., he rented a car at the airport, checked into a convenient motel, and started telephoning the four accounts he planned to call on that day. Following a busy signal on each of his first three calls, Steve decided to just drive over to the first customer's office, which was only twenty minutes away. On the drive over he realized that he probably should have set up precise appointments for each of his customers before leaving on this trip, but he had sent out postcards last week informing

them that he would be calling on them sometime this week.

11:00 A.M. Upon announcing his business purpose to the receptionist at his first account's office, Steve was shocked to learn that the purchasing agent, Burt Haywood, had suffered a mild heart attack two days ago and was in the hospital. As of yet, no one had been assigned to handle Mr. Haywood's work. After expressing his sympathy and good wishes for Mr. Haywood's quick recovery, Steve decided to go to lunch because it would be nearly noon before he could make it across midday traffic to his second account.

11:30 A.M. Because he was on an expense account, Steve picked out one of the better restaurants nearby but had a fifteen-minute wait for a table. After being seated, he ordered a cocktail and the restaurant's special broiled lobster lunch. Although expensive, it was delicious, and Steve was in a better mood now, especially after a second cocktail.

1:15 P.M. Arriving at Simpson's Electronics Company, Steve found three other salespeople waiting in the reception area for Robin Wolfe, the purchasing manager. Taking a seat, Steve chatted pleasantly with Mr. Wolfe's secretary, then began reading the latest copy of *Sports Illustrated* he had in his briefcase. Steve always took magazines with him on sales calls to help make the waiting time go faster.

1:45 P.M. Mr. Wolfe's secretary ushered Steve into Mr. Wolfe's office where the two engaged in light conversation. "Well, I didn't expect to see you today, Steve. How have you been?"

"Fine, Mr. Wolfe, how about yourself? Guess you saw the Lakers and 76ers basketball game on television last night. It was quite a contest. I love to see L.A. and Philadelphia play." After discussing the game for another 10 minutes, Steve asked whether Mr. Wolfe was ready yet to replace that old punch press they had talked about over the phone three weeks ago. To his dismay, Steve

(continued)

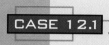

## TIME IS NO OBJECT (CONTINUED)

learned that Mr. Wolfe had bought a new machine from one of Pearson's biggest competitors who was offering a 15 percent discount special this month. Greatly disappointed, Steve blurted out: "We've got a 20 percent discount special on our best model punch press all this month. It's the one we talked about."

"I'm sorry, Steve," replied Mr. Wolfe, "but I didn't get any promotional literature from you, so I didn't know about it. The guys in the foundry would have preferred your machine. With all the business we give you Steve, I'd think you'd want to keep me better informed about upcoming deals."

"I was going to mail the promotional pieces out last week, but since I was coming down to see you this Monday, I didn't think it would be necessary," responded Steve.

2:30 P.M. Really upset on missing out on a $65,000 dollar order, Steve consoled himself with a candy bar and a soft drink before calling on his last two accounts for the day. On the first call, he learned that Louise St. Germain—the head buyer at Crown Laboratories—had started her vacation today and wouldn't be back for two weeks. Someone was filling in for her, but that person didn't have authority to buy equipment—only supplies and maintenance items.

2:45 P.M. Telephoning his last account for the day, Steve was relieved to hear that Ken Endicott was in and would see him as soon as Steve arrived. It was only a five-minute drive, so Steve took a short coffee break.

3:15 P.M. Upon arrival, Steve and Mr. Endicott exchanged friendly greetings and light banter for a few minutes, then Mr. Endicott's secretary buzzed him. Mr. D'Arcy, the vice president of purchasing, wanted to see him immediately. Apologizing for the interruption, Mr. Endicott left but told Steve to relax as he would probably be back within a half hour. Again Steve took out his magazine to read.

4:00 P.M. Mr. Endicott returned and told Steve that he had an emergency project to do for his boss but that he would be glad to see Steve early tomorrow morning. Although Steve had another customer scheduled for tomorrow morning, he said that would be fine and waved goodbye.

4:10 P.M. Leaving Mr. Endicott's office, Steve was feeling down because it hadn't been a good day. It was already past four o'clock, so he decided against trying to reach any more customers for the day. Instead, he drove back to his motel for a quick nap before dinner. Tomorrow had to be a better day!

### Questions

1. How would you evaluate Steve Burbank's management of his time and territory?
2. What would you recommend to help him improve his effectiveness and efficiency?
3. How might Pearson's training program have better prepared Steve for managing his territory?

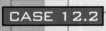

## WORKING SMARTER . . . OR JUST HARDER?

It was another typical morning for Jim Rosenthal. His two young children, three-year old Bobby and five-year old Kim, were yelling and screaming at each other and resisting their mother's attempts to bathe them. It was always a hassle in the morning because both Jim and his wife, Mary, worked outside the home. Jim was a sales representative for Cranson Industrial Scales, and Mary was a loan officer with First Regional Bank. Jim took the kids to nursery school each morning at 7:30 A.M., and Mary picked them up before 6:00 P.M. each night. Jim loved his family dearly, but oftentimes he was relieved to drop the kids off at nursery school and head out on sales calls. In his car, he could find a little peace and quiet, if traffic conditions weren't too bad, and focus his attention on his sales calls for the day.

This morning, Jim was sitting at the kitchen table gulping down a cup of black coffee and trying to complete some paperwork that the district sales manager had been bugging him about for more than a week. Work hadn't been going too well lately. He hadn't made a sale in a week, and his annual sales quota seemed increasingly unreachable. Jim called on more than two hundred accounts in his middle Atlantic territory selling various types of Cranson industrial scales and measuring devices for automatically weighing products and packages on assembly lines. Around 6 to 7 percent of his accounts purchased more than twenty-five thousand dollars a year from him and accounted for nearly 75 percent of his total sales. More than half of his accounts bought less than five hundred dollars, making up around 5 percent of his sales; and the rest of his accounts tended to fall into the two thousand to five thousand dollar purchase range, accounting for about 20 percent of his sales. Jim had never actually tried to classify his accounts by dollar volume or profitability, but he believed he knew within a few hundred dollars what most accounts bought annually. Of course, his figures weren't exact because accounts would sometimes phone in orders

directly to headquarters, but Jim received credit for those sales, too.

Jim made it his practice to call on each of his accounts at least three times a year, and he called on many eight to ten times because they were conveniently located on his way to or from other sales calls that ended early or were cancelled. Jim believed that you couldn't afford to neglect accounts because they were small because they might quickly grow into large accounts. Surprisingly, some of his biggest accounts didn't seem to require as many sales calls or as much service as some of his smaller accounts. Some of the big accounts ordered almost routinely at certain times of the year, and Jim always made a point of calling on them around that time. Several small accounts, however, demanded a lot of customer service, and some called Jim two or three times a month about various problems that Jim spent time correcting, either in person or by phone through the Cranson headquarters field support staff. Although he never said so, Jim sometimes thought that certain of these small accounts were probably more trouble than they were worth. But his commitment to customer service kept him responding to their requests.

Jim couldn't figure it out. Five years ago, when he had half as many accounts, he had little trouble making his annual sales quota. But in the last few years, as his customer list doubled, it seemed that Jim had less and less time and was finding it harder and harder to make quota. It just didn't make any sense. He was working harder and accomplishing less. Jim also believed that he was working "smarter" than ever. He had even devised his own routing pattern, shown in Figure 12.8, by printing a capital *G* on a map of his territory at the location of his thirteen giant accounts (those buying more than twenty-five thousand dollars of Cranson products yearly), a capital *C* at the location of about fifty of his medium-sized customers (those buying more than two thousand dollars'

(continued)

# WORKING SMARTER . . . OR JUST HARDER?

### (CONTINUED)

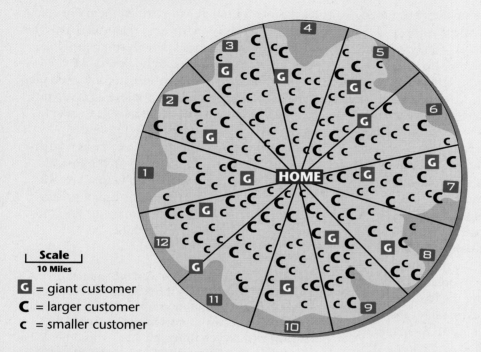

Scale
10 Miles

**G** = giant customer

**C** = larger customer

**c** = smaller customer

**FIGURE 12.8**

JIM'S TERRITORIAL ROUTING ZONES

worth of Cranson products yearly), and a small *c* for more than 120 small customers who bought less than two thousand dollars each year. Next, he traced a circle around his territory and drew twelve radius lines (each about twenty-five miles long) from his home in different directions to the outer edge of his territory to create twelve zones. On Friday, he always scheduled appointments by phone with customers in a particular zone for the following week. Then, starting each Monday, he would work his way out and back home each day of the week making sales calls within that zone. He would schedule appointments with the largest accounts in the zone first then schedule the smaller accounts in between sales calls on the large accounts. Because some zones had many accounts and a lot of customer service needs, Jim frequently

found it necessary to work the same zone two straight weeks or more to cover them all.

Jim had heard about maximizing a salesperson's return on time invested (ROTI) in sales training courses, but it sounded like too much work maintaining records on sales analyzed by the time invested. He wasn't convinced that ROTI was even a good indicator of proper time use. Some of his current accounts had purchased little from him for years; then one day, they made a big purchase mainly because he had kept the relationship going and therefore was one of the first sales reps they thought of when they decided to switch suppliers. Jim's normal practice was to spend at least an hour on a sales call with the giant accounts, about thirty to forty-five minutes with the large accounts, and

(continued)

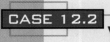

## WORKING SMARTER . . . OR JUST HARDER?

(CONTINUED)

twenty minutes or so with the smallest customers. Of course, the actual time Jim spent with each prospect or customer varied substantially depending on how busy the customer was, his or her frame of mind, type of problems, and need for information.

Lately, traffic jams and scarce parking spots in his highly congested territory were becoming frustrating. He had been thirty to forty-five minutes late for three appointments this past week, and two of his customers had said they'd have to reschedule appointments because they didn't have any additional time to see him.

Jim had often thought about using a mobile phone so he could at least let customers know when he was going to be late and perhaps reschedule the appointment over the phone. But he had been so pressed for time during the last few months—what with making extra sales calls, trying to meet his sales quota, doing all the paperwork that headquarters required, and coping with the kids at night while he and his wife tried to keep up with the numerous household chores.

Jim felt tired a lot of the time and seldom had time for lunch or even a coffee break. Usually, he bought a can of soda and a hotdog at a conven-ience store for lunch and gobbled them down in his car on the way to the next sales call. Lately, he noticed himself becoming increasingly irritable with his wife and kids at night, and it bothered him that he was obviously bringing some job pressures home with him. Unless sales picked up fast, Jim wasn't sure that he would be able to take his annual two-week vacation with his family. Perhaps, he thought, he might work every other day during his vacation to wrap up his annual sales quota. Right now, it would help if he could just have a good night's sleep instead of tossing and turning for several hours worrying about his quota and the next day's schedule.

### Questions

1. Do you think that Jim is working smarter or just harder? What do you think about Jim's sales call allocation and routing plan for his accounts? Can you suggest any improvements?
2. How well do you think Jim invests his time? What might he do differently?
3. What advice would you give Jim about achieving his annual sales quota?
4. What would you suggest to Jim to help him deal with the stress in his life?

# PART FOUR

# Achieving Success in Personal Selling

**CHAPTER 13**

Ethical and Legal Considerations in Personal Selling

**CHAPTER 14**

Starting Your Personal Selling Career

**401**

# Ethical and Legal Considerations in Personal Selling

*"A Society with no other scale but the legal one is not quite worthy of man."*

*Aleksandr Solzhenitsyn*

## After Reading This Chapter, You Should Understand:

- What ethics are and the ethical image of salespeople.
- Ethical concerns of salespeople in dealing with customers, competitors, employers, and coworkers.
- Behavior salespeople have a right to expect from their employers.
- Legal and ethical issues in foreign markets.
- How to approach ethical decisions.

## INSIDE PERSONAL SELLING:
# Meet Renata Bitoy of Houghton Mifflin

Ethical questions can arise in any personal selling situation, even when the product is a college textbook. Just ask Renata Bitoy, a sales representative for the College Division of Boston-based Houghton Mifflin Company. Bitoy travels to campuses in the Midwest, visiting with professors to discuss their needs and presenting her company's textbooks and educational materials.

During the comprehensive training all new sales reps receive, Bitoy and her colleagues were introduced to Houghton Mifflin's standards of ethical behavior and its Code of Employee Conduct. The code lays out company policies and procedures related to payments and gift-giving, discrimination, sexual harassment, conflict of interest, privacy and confidentiality, fraudulent behavior, and other workplace issues.

"In our training course, we discussed relationship building with the professors and

the administrative support staff," remembers Bitoy. "We are in this business for the long term, and if you want to build strong relationships, you must earn the customer's respect and show you are genuinely interested in improving how students learn."

Misrepresentation, for example, is inappropriate and unprofessional: "You have to be honest with the professors to gain their trust and keep their business year after year," she says. For this reason, she is careful never to disparage another publisher's books or mislead professors about the availability of a textbook.

When professors are trying to decide which textbook to assign, they frequently request a free review copy of each text under consideration. But what happens to review copies after the decision has been made? Most unadopted textbooks are placed in the department library as a resource for students and faculty. Bitoy prefers this because the text is in use and visible, which means the department may consider it later should needs change.

"Some departments don't have the space and ask that I pick up the texts," she says. "Then I can place them at another school for consideration. On occasion, however, a text will be sold to a used book vendor. This is problematic because books sold to used book vendors will ultimately increase the price that students pay for textbooks in the future. In my tenure at Houghton Mifflin I have come across only one instructor who abused the system." Her solution to this ethical question, therefore, is to discover as much as possible about her customers, their teaching needs, and their patterns.

"The more you learn about your customers, the better you can determine how to proceed in a particular situation," says Bitoy. "Some situations have the potential for higher value over time. You have to determine how much service to provide in each case." This is a delicate balancing act, because the actions Bitoy takes today will influence the future course of her relationship with her customers.

**403**

Throughout your life, you've undoubtedly faced difficult issues that forced you to make decisions concerning what's right and what's wrong. In a few instances, you may have experienced tremendous conflict about the issue; in others, you made your decision without hesitation. Some situations probably provided no guidelines for decision making; in others, some general policies or philosophies assisted you in formulating your decision. Ethical issues confront all of us every day—and dealing with them can be fraught with great uncertainty and uneasiness. As you move into your professional selling career, ethical issues will abound in great variety and complexity. Your successful attention to ethical concerns will affect your ultimate effectiveness as a salesperson . . . as well as your satisfaction with your career choice.

Some people seem to have developed almost an immunity or insensitivity to high ethical standards. Individuals cheat in school and on their income taxes, their resumes, their insurance claims, and almost anywhere the chances of detection are low. Don't despair, though, there is some good news. People seem to be getting fed up with such ethical decay, and many are calling for adherence to higher standards of conduct by politicians, businesspeople—and perhaps even us.

## WHAT ARE ETHICS?

**Ethics** Moral code that governs individuals and societies in determining what's right or wrong.

**Ethics** may be defined as the study of what is good and bad or right and wrong. Ethics constitute a moral code of conduct governing individuals and societies. They deal with matters as they *should* be, not necessarily as they are. According to the great humanitarian Dr. Albert Schweitzer, ethics is " . . . an obligation to consider not only our own personal well-being, but also that of other human beings." People may differ sharply about what is ethical or unethical behavior, especially in complex, competitive areas such as business. Thus, a need exists for thorough analysis and evaluation before developing ethical standards for business decision making.

### Business Ethics

In business, a decision that is "right" or "wrong" has usually been made on the basis of *economic* criteria. Some salespeople have the idea that if it's legal, it's ethical. But people are not ethical simply because they stay within the law. Ethical behavior and legal behavior are not the same. A salesperson can be dishonest, unprincipled, untrustworthy, unfair, and uncaring without breaking the law.[1] In fact, some businesspeople have two sets of ethical standards—one that they use in their personal life and one that they employ in the office. And the set that guides their personal conduct is likely to be on a higher moral plane than their office set. Many U.S. companies recognize this problem, as more than 38 percent offer ethics training,[2] and about 20 percent of large corporations have appointed ethics officers.[3]

Most of us would probably agree that doing what we personally believe is wrong is unethical. Thus, a salesperson who believes that it's wrong to pressure

## KEEPING UP ONLINE: E-CENTER FOR BUSINESS ETHICS

At the *E-Center for Business Ethics*, you can find insightful information and perspectives about business ethics and corporate codes of conduct. You can also enroll in a ten-week online program leading to an "Ethics Certificate." Visit their web site at www.e-businessethics.com. How might salespeople benefit from earning an ethics certificate?

prospects to buy a product that they don't really need, yet does so anyway, is acting unethically. Salespeople must work assiduously at being ethical at all times. Why? Because it's the right thing to do, and because a salesperson's reputation for ethical behavior and integrity is one of the most valuable assets he or she can bring to negotiations with prospects and customers. Shakespeare described the importance of guarding one's reputation in act 3, scene 3 of *Othello*:

> Who steals my purse steals trash; 'tis something, nothing;
> 'Twas mine, 'tis his, and has been slave to thousands;
> But he that filches from me my good name
> Robs me of that which not enriches him
> And makes me poor indeed.

Once a salesperson's reputation is damaged, it is extremely hard to repair and, at the very least, takes a long, long time. So don't ever allow yourself to be tempted to do anything unethical because nothing else will destroy your career faster. Read *Keeping Up Online* to see how you can add to your knowledge of ethical issues.

### Ethical Image of Salespeople

By far, the vast majority of sales reps are strongly ethical. However, largely because of its persuasive nature, high visibility, direct contact with customers—and a few people who call themselves salespeople but are really more like con artists—personal selling unfortunately continues to attract criticism about low ethical standards. Door-to-door salespeople and car salespeople have borne much of this criticism. But, apparently, not just these salespeople have a tainted image. Even business-to-business sales personnel, through questionable conduct, have served to tarnish the image of professional salespeople. In a survey of two hundred sales managers—ranging from major corporations to privately held companies—nearly half admitted that their salespeople had lied on a sales call.[4] To counter this negative image, today's salespeople must hold themselves and their companies to a high standard of ethics and avoid even the appearance of questionable ethics. They must be paragons of trustworthiness; that is, their conduct must demonstrate to their

## ON THE FRONTLINES

# *Honesty Is Not for Sale*

Salespeople constantly face ethical dilemmas. These dilemmas may occur between sales managers and salespeople, between salespeople, and most likely between salespeople and their customers. Because money is involved in selling to customers, this interaction is especially ripe for ethical conflicts. How salespeople choose to react to each ethical situation will have a long-term effect on their company and their personal success.

Some buyers may try to "bait" salespeople to determine how they will react to a questionable request. Their intent is to separate ethical salespeople from unethical ones, remaining a customer of the former and rejecting the latter from further consideration.

To illustrate, a salesperson may be calling on a prospect company that could become a major account. As the initial sales interview approaches its conclusion, the buyer, in what appears to be an earnest question, asks the salesperson: "How much of a kickback (i.e., bribe) will I receive, given the unusu-

ally large size of my order?" How the salesperson responds to this question will probably affect subsequent business with the individual. Assuming, of course, that the buyer is ethical, which is generally the case, the buyer is seeking a response that demonstrates high ethical conduct on the part of the salesperson. A reply such as: "If this is what it takes to do business here, I don't want anything to do with it," is the kind of response that the honest purchaser is looking for. Any response that indicates that the salesperson is not honest will likely result in the loss of this sale and any future purchases from the buyer. As a guiding principle, salespeople must never compromise their integrity nor let anyone intimidate them by asking for "special favors." In the rare case where the buyer is dishonest, it's better to lose that business than to compete unethically for it. As an old adage states: "Even crooks like to do business with people they can trust."

customers that their word is "golden." Trustworthiness in sales personnel has a strong positive impact on the ways in which salespeople and their customers interact.[5] Read *On the Frontlines* for a sense of how salespeople must sometimes make ethical decisions under extreme pressure.

## ETHICAL CONCERNS OF SALESPEOPLE

Salespeople work in a business environment "ideal" for ethical conflict:

> The sales organization is unique. . . its members work apart from each other, experiencing little daily contact with supervisors, subordinates, or peers. . . . The resulting impact on ethical decision making can be negative, since individuals interacting in a group produce decisions at higher levels of moral reasoning than when acting alone . . . instances of role stress which [provide] many unique opportunities for ethical issues and dilemmas [can] arise.

The central nature of selling—a negotiation between buyer and seller—is inherently a laboratory of ethical scenarios.[6]

Therefore, professional salespeople must be ethically sensitive in their interactions with a variety of people and organizations, including their customers, coworkers, competitors, and their own companies. In fact, how right or wrong sales managers perceive salespeople's behavior toward others to be can influence the rewards or discipline managers recommend.[7] Moreover, companies have ethical obligations toward their employees.

## Customer Relationships

It is never smart to engage in unethical practices with customers, even when the customer is the instigator. Even dishonest and unethical customers don't trust and will eventually stop dealing with unethical salespeople. Losing such customers in the short run may simply be the price an ethical salesperson must pay for long-run success in selling. Professional salespeople build long-run relationships of mutual trust, respect, and confidence with customers. Any loss of personal or company integrity in the eyes of customers jeopardizes these relationships. Read *It's Up to You* to try your hand at dealing with an ethical issue in selling. Next, we discuss some areas in which ethical problems can arise with customers.

**Special Gifts.** Bribes, payoffs, and kickbacks are clearly illegal and can bring about serious legal problems for violators. Nevertheless, some salespeople insist on "showing their appreciation" to customers by giving them *expensive* gifts. Sometimes, especially around the holiday seasons, some customers will drop subtle hints that they expect a nice gift for all the business they've been giving you. One survey of sales managers revealed that almost nine out of ten believed that not paying bribes would put their companies at a competitive disadvantage.[8] Such ambivalence on the part of sales managers places salespeople in an awkward situation unless companies have established clear policies that address the issue of gift giving—something most salespeople want.[9] Numerous companies

## IT'S UP TO YOU

You are a salesperson for Atlas Sporting Goods, Inc., a manufacturer of sports equipment and apparel. While trying to negotiate a $125,000 sale with a buyer for one of the largest retailers in your territory, the buyer says to you, "You know what, young man? Our deal would be a lot sweeter if you could see your way to getting me a complete set of your company's titanium golf clubs with a pro bag and pull cart. What do you think, partner?" If you negotiate this sale, your commission will be five thousand dollars, and you will surpass your annual quota by fifteen thousand dollars and receive a twenty-five-hundred-dollar bonus. The golf clubs, bag, and cart would cost you about nine hundred dollars because you, as an employee of Atlas, can buy them at cost. At retail, they would sell for about two thousand dollars. What factors will influence your decision? If you choose to say no, how will you attempt to salvage the sale?

*Professional salespeople do not engage in unethical and illegal activities like bribes, payoffs, or kickbacks.*
David Pollack/Corbis

have solved this problem for salespeople by refusing to allow their employees to accept any gifts from suppliers. What's more, many supplier companies have stopped the practice of giving Christmas gifts to customers, offering instead to contribute to the customer's favorite charity.[10]

**Entertainment.** Taking a customer or prospect to dinner, to play golf, or to a ball game or special event is generally an acceptable and often expected part of doing business. Moreover, it can provide additional time for the buyer and seller to discuss business and impart much important information in a relaxed setting. But lavishly entertaining a prospect or customer may well be a disguised bribe to influence a purchase. For example, pharmaceutical company salespeople have been roundly criticized for treating doctors to fine meals at expensive restaurants, offering free tickets to Broadway shows and sporting events, offering cash to listen to sales presentations, and even providing free trips to expensive resorts to influence the most intimate and important of medical decisions, viz., selection of drugs to prescribe for patients.[11]

**Overpromising.** In order to win the sale, some salespeople will promise much more than they can deliver. Later, they think that the customer will accept some reasonable excuse. Promising an unrealistic delivery date in order to make a sale is not only an ethical violation, it's poor business practice. Customers prefer to buy from salespeople whose word and promises can be relied upon. A maxim to follow as a salesperson is: "Promise only what you can deliver."

**Misrepresenting or Covering up the Facts.** A few salespeople try to cover up the facts or distort the truth to make a quick sale. For example, pharmaceutical sales reps for Purdue Pharma touted the advantages of a powerful painkilling medication that cost three hundred to four hundred dollars for a bottle of one hundred. Simultaneously, law enforcement personnel had been warning pharmacists about the hazards of this morphine-like drug, as it had the capacity to induce addiction. Yet, Purdue Pharma's sales reps were remiss by not admitting this catastrophic weakness in their sales presentations to pharmacists. In fact, 120 users of the drug died over a four-year period, and several other users became severely addicted to it. The salespeople's allegedly unethical conduct resulted in pharmacists' decision not to stock the drug. Once salespeople have gone down the slippery slope of misrepresentation (or lying), "reconstituting integrity is next to impossible."[12]

**Manipulating Order Forms.** During sales contests or approaching sales quota deadlines, some salespeople are tempted to finagle their actual sales records by shifting orders from one period to another or overselling some products. Customers are not always aware of how much inventory they need, so the unethical salesperson may try to persuade them to overbuy. Overselling and order manipulation not only cheat customers but are also unfair to other colleagues competing in the sales contest or striving to make quotas. In one *Fortune* 500 data-processing firm, sales reps who had already exceeded their annual quota by December would hold orders and submit them at the start of the new year. Doing so would allow them to jumpstart their quota drive for the new year.

**Disclosing Confidential Information.**  In an effort to ingratiate themselves with important customers, some salespeople reveal confidential and potentially harmful information about their customers' competitors. Customers who receive such information have to wonder whether these salespeople are also telling competitors confidential information about their companies. Thus, a seed of mistrust is planted that will likely inhibit future communication with customers. Ethical salespeople play it straight with all their customers and earn a reputation for being honest and trustworthy.

With more sophisticated computer technology and software and Internet-based buying, large amounts of data—for example, product preferences, purchase patterns, customer demographics and psychographics—can be subtly collected and analyzed for use by salespeople or for sale to other companies. A Federal Trade Commission (FTC) study found that more than 90 percent of commercial web sites collect at least one type of personally identifying information from visitors, and 57 percent gather some type of demographic information.[13] Yet, the FTC found that only 14 percent of the sites surveyed reveal what they do with the personal information they collect.[14] "Cookies"—small files placed on computer hard drives when a prospect or customer visits certain web sites—are the most common means of obtaining this information. Because they can track one's movement on the web, they pose a threat to privacy. With few regulations on business use of this information, companies can buy and sell information about customers to gain competitive advantage. Companies who want to be both ethical and socially responsible should clearly post their privacy policies on their web sites for browsers to read. TRUSTe is a nonprofit organization, supported by a network of corporate, industry, and nonprofit sponsors, working to advance global trust in the Internet through its seal and certification program. It grants TRUSTe awards to web sites that adhere to its established privacy principles and agrees to comply with its oversight and resolution process. Web sites that display the trustmark must disclose their information collection and privacy policies in a straightforward privacy statement. Anyone who believes that his or her privacy has been compromised can file a compliant at the TRUSTe web site (www.TRUSTe.org). Take a closer look at the TRUSTe web site in *Keeping Up Online.*

## KEEPING UP ONLINE: TRUSTE

Do you believe that organizations like TRUSTe help or hinder salespeople in doing their jobs? Why? Take a look at the TRUSTe web site at www.TRUSTe.org to see how it might be useful to a salesperson, prospect, customer, or competitor.

**Showing Favoritism.**  Salespeople will almost always like some customers more than others, but the ethical salesperson cannot afford to show favoritism by, say, moving a favored customer's deliveries ahead of others' orders or making sure preferred customers receive scarce products while others do not. One study found that more than 50 percent of salespeople surveyed believed that showing favoritism toward a customer poses an ethical conflict.[15] In addition, customers who are discriminated against will deeply resent such unequal treatment and may refuse to buy from salespeople even suspected of such behavior.

### Treatment of Coworkers

A few excessively aggressive salespeople will behave unethically even in competing with their own company sales colleagues. Unethical behavior among coworkers can destroy employee morale, work against company goals and objectives, and ruin the reputation of the company. In fact, the kind of feedback salespeople give their sales peers influences peer job satisfaction and even performance.[16] Let's look at some examples of what would generally be considered unethical behavior in dealing with one's colleagues.

**Sexual Harassment.**  Salespeople, whether males or females, may become perpetrators or victims of sexual harassment that violates both ethical and legal codes of conduct. In 1980, the Equal Employment Opportunity Commission wrote its guidelines defining sexual harassment as a form of sex discrimination, and therefore, illegal under Title VII of the Civil Rights Act of 1964. The EEOC definition follows:

> Unwelcome sexual advances, requests for sexual favors, and other verbal or physical conduct of a sexual nature constitutes sexual harassment when (1) submission to such conduct is either explicitly or implicitly a term or condition of an individual's employment, (2) submission to or a rejection of such conduct by an individual is used as a basis for employment decisions affecting such individual, or (3) such conduct has the purpose or effect of unreasonably interfering with an individual's work performance or creating an intimidating, hostile, or offensive working environment.[17]

**Quid Pro Quo Harassment**  Where a person in authority demands sexual favors from an employee in exchange for a job advantage, such as being hired or promoted.

**Hostile Environment**  A pattern of sexual behavior that makes the job so unpleasant that the victim's work is adversely affected.

As indicated in the EEOC definition, the law recognizes two types of employment-related sexual harassment: (1) **quid pro quo harassment,** where a person in authority demands sexual favors from an employee in exchange for a job advantage, such as being hired or promoted, and (2) **hostile environment,** where a pattern of sexual behavior makes the job so unpleasant that the victim's work is adversely affected. An open demand for job-related sexual favors is clearly recognized as illegal. But with respect to *hostile environment harassment*—for example, hazing, joking, and sexually suggestive talk—interpretation of the law becomes fuzzy. Where does good-humored kidding cease and harassment begin?

Experiencing sexual harassment is much more common for women than for men.[18] Some women fear filing a sexual harassment case because it may lead to public humiliation, possible job loss, and threats to their family happiness. Many, therefore, opt to leave the job or suffer in silence. Nevertheless, many women have filed legal suits, and some have received substantial awards from juries. In a recent study of salespeople, half reported having been involved in office romances.[19] This statistic may portend increased sexual harassment in sales offices.[20]

**Stealing Customers from Colleagues.**  Encroaching on another salesperson's territory or trying to convince a customer doing business in two different territories to make all purchases from your territory are unethical practices. Salespeople found guilty of poaching on other salespeople's territories may face reprimands from management and possible loss of their jobs. One *Fortune* 500 company took a unique approach when one of its saleswomen crossed over into a colleague's sales territory to make a sale. Rather than censuring the errant salesperson, management decided to give both salespeople credit for the sale and one-half of the commission, as well as requiring both sales personnel to install and service the computer at the new account.

**Undermining Coworkers.**  Occasionally, salespeople become so obsessed with their own lust for success that they deliberately undercut their coworkers. Failing to relay a customer's telephone message to a sales colleague or telling the boss's secretary some disparaging remark made by another salesperson about the boss are examples of unethical activities. Such viciously self-serving salespeople usually underestimate other people, who will quickly size them up and begin to shun them. Few salespeople succeed for long by disparaging colleagues. Remember the moral of the old saying: "To hold someone else down, a part of you has to stay down, too."

## Treatment of Competitors

Perhaps it can be argued that "all is fair in love and war," but this is certainly not the case for ethical salespeople in dealing with competitors. Initiating unethical practices against competitors can stimulate unethical retaliatory action from them and lead to accelerating aggressive activity that soon crosses the line into legal violations. Let's consider potential problems that could arise.

**Disparaging Competitors.**  Making negative, exaggerated statements about competing products and companies is an unethical practice that may create retaliation from competitors. Even the best companies are sometimes guilty of disparaging competitors. One *Fortune* 500 company was accused of using sales demonstrations that "unfairly" denigrated the competition by purposely misusing materials and devices to assess the effectiveness of the competitor's product. Describing the weaknesses of a competitor's offerings relative to yours is acceptable, but going to excessive lengths to impugn the integrity of the offerings is simply unfair and unethical.

**Tampering with Competitors' Products.**  It is unethical and illegal for salespeople to damage competitors' products, tamper with their displays and point-of-sale materials, or reduce their product shelf space in retail stores or elsewhere. Salespeople who stoop to such activities may also anger retailers and wholesalers who naturally resent any unauthorized tampering with their displays. A small producer of cereal was set upon by its behemoth competitors in efforts to get its product off grocery shelves. Its competitors slashed open the small producer's cereal boxes on the shelves; the small manufacturer, angered by the attack, responded in kind! This open warfare hurt all parties involved, including the retailers, until such futile activities ceased.

**Competitive Snooping.** Salespeople use many ruses to obtain valuable information about competitors. To obtain competitive pricing information, for instance, some salespeople ask customers to solicit bids from competitors. Some pretend to be customers at professional conferences, trade shows, and exhibits, or on plant tours of the competition. Such practices are neither uncommon nor illegal, and some would argue that such behavior is okay because "nearly everybody does these things." But salespeople who are trying to maintain the highest ethical standards will see such practices, at best, as questionable.

## Salespeople's Ethics and Their Company

Salespeople and other employees sometimes believe that standards of ethics don't fully apply when dealing with an organization, whether it's the Internal Revenue Service, an insurance firm, or their own company. After all, they reason, it's not human, it's just a big bureaucratic organization with lots of money. But when large numbers of people start taking home a few ballpoint pens or paper tablets, padding expense accounts, or doing personal business on company time, the costs of doing business can go up dramatically. Eventually, these abuses translate into higher prices to customers, fewer company employees, lower profits, and lower wages and salaries, as the company loses sales to lower-cost competitors. Let's discuss some of the more obvious and problematic tactics.

**Expense Account Padding.** Salespeople can easily pad their expense accounts by taking friends out to dinner and claiming they were entertaining customers or by submitting excess claims for meal expenses, mileage, taxi fares, tips, and the like. Padding one's expense account, however, may be viewed as stealing by sales managers and can lead to dismissal if discovered. An expense account should *not* be considered a supplement to or extension of your salary. It is provided by the company to assist you in the performance of your job (so don't bite the hand that feeds you!).

**Unauthorized Use of Company Resources.** Making personal telephone calls on company phones, using company copying machines for personal purposes, keeping company promotional premiums intended for customers, taking home supplies from the office for personal use, and driving a company car on unauthorized personal trips are unethical activities that can significantly add to company costs. Beyond ethics, U.S. businesses lose billions of dollars yearly to thefts committed by employees. One study found that approximately one-third of job applicants claim to have stolen merchandise, ranging in value from twenty-five dollars to fifteen hundred dollars, from an employer.[21] Some employees rationalize stealing from their own companies by claiming that the company owes it to them for underpaying them, or that they're just borrowing something that they will pay back later, or that "everybody else does it," so it must be all right.

**Personal Use of Company Time.** U.S. workers steal more than $120 billion in time each year from their companies. Some employees go beyond long lunch hours, personal telephone calls, and excessive socializing to actually "moonlighting" on part-time jobs during the same hours that they are supposed to be working for their primary employer. Because of their independence and freedom, salespeople have many opportunities to convert company time to personal use, but ethical sales reps will give their companies a full day's work even if they have made all of their scheduled sales calls for the day. There is always some customer servicing or paperwork to be done. In the Midwest sales branch office of a major manufacturer, many salespeople took off Friday afternoons for socializing. Branch management, after getting wind of this behavior, started scheduling mandatory in-branch sales training for Friday afternoons!

**Fabrication of Sales Records.** Because many companies base their performance evaluations of salespeople at least partially on their sales *activities* as well as sales *results*, some salespeople are tempted to falsify their number of sales calls, service calls, or promotional mailings to customers. Smart salespeople realize that activity quotas are guides designed to help them learn what it takes to achieve top performance. Falsifying sales activity records may become a habit that causes salespeople to become lazy with consequent adverse effect on their sales performance. One *Fortune* 500 company required sales reps to submit their daily call reports from the previous week to their manager every Monday morning. One of their less productive salespeople completed the call reports each Monday morning by obtaining company names and addresses from a phone book. What he recorded on the call report appeared to be a legitimate prospect but was in reality a falsehood. Eventually, the salesperson was terminated for sub-par performance.

**Manipulation of Customer Orders.** To win sales contests or meet their annual quotas, salespeople may persuade customers to over-order products with the promise that they can return them after the contest or end of the year. Not only does this unethical practice harm sales colleagues who are competing fairly in the contest, but it also creates unnecessary costs for the company and hurts the image of the company and its salespeople with customers.

## Employer Ethics with Their Salespeople

Ethical salespeople have a right to expect ethical treatment from their companies, especially with regard to compensation, sales territories, sales quotas, hiring, promoting, and firing policies.

**Compensation.** Prompt, accurate payment of salary, commissions, and bonuses as well as timely reimbursement of selling expenses are basic requirements for any ethical company in dealing with its salespeople. Any company that tries to delay payments or cheat salespeople out of their fair commissions or reimbursement for selling expenses will see its sales force turnover skyrocket.

## KEEPING UP ONLINE: U.S. EQUAL EMPLOYMENT OPPORTUNITY COMMISSION

The EEOC works to ensure that companies provide equal employment opportunities for all applicants. Visit the EEOC online at www.eeoc.gov. Have the actions of the EEOC helped or hurt sales forces in the United States? Justify your answer.

**Sales Territories.** Sales managers must ensure that salespeople are involved in the fair assignment of sales territories. Ideally, each salesperson should receive a territory that has an equal sales potential. Whenever territories must be reassigned, split up, or moved to national accounts, the salespeople should receive early warning of the impending change and be given an opportunity to negotiate a new territorial assignment. This is especially important because salespeople's satisfaction with their sales territory affects their performance.[22]

**Sales Quotas.** Setting unrealistically high sales quotas for salespeople, then applying constant pressure to produce sales, is unfair and unethical. Moreover, it destroys motivation. Salespeople should be involved in setting their own quotas, so that they will view the quotas as fair. An important aspect of sales force motivation and loyalty to the company is the salespeople's perception that they are being treated fairly and ethically. This may not always be the case, though, as some sales managers tend to play favorites. Research has found that salespeople who are viewed as desirable work partners, as well as desirable social partners and friends, by their sales managers are evaluated more favorably than those who are not perceived so favorably.[23]

**Hiring, Promoting, and Firing.** Although all forms of discrimination have been legally prohibited since the 1964 Civil Rights Act (which was made even more powerful by the Equal Employment Opportunity Act of 1972), continuing evidence suggests that *sexism, racism,* and *ageism* still influence managerial decisions in hiring, promoting, and firing salespeople. Over the long run, the most successful companies are those that provide equal opportunities for all employees and base decisions on job performance.[24] Read *Keeping Up Online* above to find out more about the EEOC.

## THE COMPANY'S ETHICAL EYES AND EARS IN THE FIELD

Misguided managers will sometimes employ unethical means to achieve short-run sales and profit levels. Read *From the Command Post* to see how management in some large firms have pushed their salespeople too far. To counter

## FROM THE COMMAND POST: BETRAYAL FROM THE TOP

Financial statements aren't what they used to be! Although financial statements presumably represent an objective appraisal of an organization's financial condition at a given point in time, an increasing number of companies have been hauled into court for alleged accounting malfeasance. High ranking executives from Enron, Global Crossing, Adelphia, Tyco, ImClone Systems, WorldCom, and several other companies have been accused by the federal government of illegal activities, such as "cooking the company books" to report inflated earnings. Millions of company employees and shareholders feel betrayed and angry by such apparent dishonesty in the executive suites of several U.S. corporations. What's more, many employees trusted the integrity of top management at their companies and kept their 401(k) retirement money invested in their employer's stock. Now, some of these companies have declared bankruptcy and virtually wiped out employee retirement funds.

What caused these egregious lapses in ethical and legal standards by formerly honored and trusted executives? Many set increasingly ambitious and eventually impossible sales and earnings objectives for their companies. Struggling to increase or maintain sales and earnings projections in a declining economy caused some senior executives to resort to financial manipulation in efforts to maintain the stock price of their companies. By engaging in highly questionable, if not outright illegal, accounting practices (for example, recording product shipments to channel members as actual sales, or recording routine operating expenses as capital assets to be written off over several years), these executives have badly damaged faith in business leadership. Without ethical leadership from the top on down, no organization can expect to develop healthy, profitable relationships with prospects and customers which are essential to company success. No short-run payoff is ever worth the devastation that such behavior inflicts on individual companies and industry in general. Despite any glib comments to the contrary, "honesty is always the best policy" whether you're a salesperson or a CEO.

unethical behavior, some companies (for example, Texas Instruments) have an ethics officer who answers anonymous employee questions in the monthly company magazine or in weekly online news columns on ethics. Professional salespeople should accept the role of customer representative or spokesperson whenever they spot questionable marketing activities, such as those discussed below.[25]

## Product Quality and Service

Poor product quality, unsafe products, unreasonable return policies, and poor servicing of products after the sale are examples of unethical practices that salespeople should not have to tolerate from their companies. If the company persists in shady activities, a salesperson would probably be better off seeking a job with a more ethical company. Over the long run, unethical companies are unlikely to prosper competing against ethical companies.

### Pricing

Some companies or salespeople routinely inflate list prices so they can appear to offer customers a discount. And salespeople are often accused of taking advantage of uninformed customers or those less aggressive in negotiating. Ethical salespeople, however, will not resort to price gouging or taking advantage of a naïve customer. Though you may make the sale now, customers will eventually find out that they paid too much and refuse to buy from you again.

Salespeople can legitimately offer price and quantity discounts if they make them available on an equal basis to all customers. One aggrieved customer called a salesperson from a large computer manufacturer complaining that he had been charged a higher price for the exact same computer system than paid by a colleague at another firm. The customer demanded a refund for the difference between what he paid and what his colleague paid, or he would remove the system from his office and cancel the sale. The salesperson's management quickly agreed with the customer's demands.

### Distribution

Some unethical salespeople will sell lower quality products and inferior services to young people, the elderly, non-English-speaking Americans, and poorly informed people, often at prices as high or higher than those for better quality products and services.[26] Unscrupulous firms and salespeople tend to prey on people who are undereducated, dependent on credit, unaware of their legal rights, and unable to read or speak English.

### Promotion

Deceptive advertising, misleading product warranties, phony promotional contests, and dishonest fund-raising activities are unethical and perhaps illegal. Unfair or stereotypical representation of gender, racial and ethnic minorities, sexual orientation, the disabled, or senior citizens may be viewed as merely insensitive instead of unethical, but such promotions can upset major customer groups. Whenever salespeople hear customers commenting negatively about the company's promotional efforts, they should relay this information to sales and marketing management. No salesperson should be expected to work under the cloud of unethical advertising.

## BEHAVING ETHICALLY, EVERY DAY

When you interact with prospects and customers, you represent yourself and your firm. Your conduct will send them strong signals regarding what kind of person you are and for what kind of company you work. Furthermore, how you behave on the job will affect how your management, colleagues, and peers perceive you. Behaving morally and ethically will cause people to speak well of you and enhance your success as a salesperson. And, if you have any doubt about that, let us put that to rest! Research has found that more ethically sensitive salespeople perform better and have greater success than do

| TABLE 13.1 |
|---|

## ETHICAL IDEAS FOR SALES PERSONNEL

1. Ethical conflicts and choices are inherent in personal selling.

2. The law is the lowest common denominator of ethical behavior.

3. No single satisfactory standard of ethical action agreeable to everyone exists to assist you in making on-the-job decisions.

4. Ethical action has diverse and sometimes conflicting determinants (for example, the customer, management, your peers, industry standards, competition).

5. Your value system will have a dramatic influence on your ethical conduct.

6. The lower you are in the corporate hierarchy, the greater the likelihood that you will feel pressure to engage in unethical conduct.

7. Your company's top management will set the tone for its ethical conduct.

*Source:* Adapted from Clarke L. Caywood and Gene R. Laczniak, "Ethics and Personal Selling: Death of a Salesman as an Ethical Primer," Journal of Personal Selling and Sales Management 5 (August 1986): 81–88.

their less ethically sensitive counterparts.[27] When performing your sales job, it may be helpful to reflect on the ideas presented in Table 13.1.

In efforts to assist employees, some firms have established codes of ethics or codes of conduct that describe behavior considered acceptable and unacceptable in the execution of their jobs. Some codes are detailed and strict, and others are more general in nature. Their purpose, irrespective of their content, is to provide guidelines for employees about appropriate job deportment. Studies have found that salespeople want their firms to provide ethical policies to assist them in their jobs.[28] Some professional associations also have created codes of conduct, and following them is a requirement for membership. The American Marketing Association (AMA) has developed a code that even includes behavior on the Internet, as shown below.

## AMA CODE OF ETHICS

Members of the American Marketing Association are committed to ethical professional conduct. They have joined together in subscribing to this Code of Ethics embracing the following topics:

### Responsibilities of the Marketer

Marketers must accept responsibility for the consequences of their activities and make every effort to ensure that their decisions, recommendations and actions function to identify, serve and satisfy all relevant publics: customers, organizations and society.

Marketers' Professional Conduct must be guided by:

1. The basic rule of professional ethics: not knowingly to do harm;

(continued)

# AMA CODE OF ETHICS (CONTINUED)

2. The adherence to all applicable laws and regulations;
3. The accurate representation of their education, training and experience; and
4. The active support, practice and promotion of this Code of Ethics.

### Honesty and Fairness

Marketers shall uphold and advance the integrity, honor and dignity of the marketing profession by:

1. Being honest in serving consumers, clients, employees, suppliers, distributors, and the public;
2. Not knowingly participating in conflict of interest without prior notice to all parties involved; and
3. Establishing equitable fee schedules including the payment or receipt of usual, customary and/or legal compensation for marketing exchanges.

### Rights and Duties of Parties in the Marketing Exchange Process

Participants in the marketing exchange process should be able to expect that

1. Products and services offered are safe and fit for their intended uses;
2. Communications about offered products and services are not deceptive;
3. All parties intend to discharge their obligations, financial and otherwise, in good faith; and
4. Appropriate internal methods exist for equitable adjustment and/or redress of grievances concerning purchases.

It is understood that the above would include, but is not limited to, the following responsibilities of the marketer:

### In the area of product development and management:

- disclosure of all substantial risks associated with product or service usage;
- identification of any product component substitution that might materially change the product or impact on the buyer's purchase decision;
- identification of extra cost-added features.

### In the area of promotions:

- avoidance of false and misleading advertising;
- rejection of high-pressure manipulations, or misleading sales tactics;
- avoidance of sales promotions that use deception or manipulation.

### In the area of distribution:

- not manipulating the availability of a product for the purpose of exploitation;
- not using coercion in the marketing channel;
- not exerting undue influence over the reseller's choice to handle a product.

### In the area of pricing:

- not engaging in price fixing;
- not practicing predatory pricing;
- disclosing the full price associated with any purchase.

### In the area of marketing research:

- prohibiting selling or fundraising under the guise of conducting research;
- maintaining research integrity by avoiding misrepresentation and omission of pertinent research data;
- treating outside clients and suppliers fairly.

### Organizational Relationships

Marketers should be aware of how their behavior may influence or impact the behavior of others in organizational relationships. They should not demand, encourage or apply coercion to obtain unethical behavior in their relationships with others, such as employees, suppliers, or customers.

(continued)

## AMA CODE OF ETHICS (CONTINUED)

1. Apply confidentiality and anonymity in professional relationships with regard to privileged information;
2. Meet their obligations and responsibilities in contracts and mutual agreements in a timely manner;
3. Avoid taking the work of others, in whole, or in part, and representing this work as their own or directly benefiting from it without compensation or consent of the originator or owner; and
4. Avoid manipulation to take advantage of situations to maximize personal welfare in a way that unfairly deprives or damages the organization of others.

**Any AMA member found to be in violation of any provision of this Code of Ethics may have his or her Association membership suspended or revoked.**

### American Marketing Association Code of Ethics for Marketing on the Internet Preamble

The Internet, including online computer communications, has become increasingly important to marketers' activities, as they provide exchanges and access to markets worldwide. The ability to interact with stakeholders has created new marketing opportunities and risks that are not currently specifically addressed in the American Marketing Association Code of Ethics. The American Marketing Association Code of Ethics for Internet marketing provides additional guidance and direction for ethical responsibility in this dynamic area of marketing. The American Marketing Association is committed to ethical professional conduct and has adopted these principles for using the Internet, including online marketing activities utilizing network computers.

### General Responsibilities

Internet marketers must assess the risks and take responsibility for the consequences of their activities. Internet marketers' professional conduct must be guided by

1. Support of professional ethics to avoid harm by protecting the rights of privacy, ownership and access.
2. Adherence to all applicable laws and regulations with no use of Internet marketing that would be illegal, if conducted by mail, telephone, fax or other media.
3. Awareness of changes in regulations related to Internet marketing.
4. Effective communication to organizational members on risks and policies related to Internet marketing, when appropriate.
5. Organizational commitment to ethical Internet practices communicated to employees, customers and relevant stakeholders.

### Privacy

Information collected from customers should be confidential and used only for expressed purposes. All data, especially confidential customer data, should be safeguarded against unauthorized access. The expressed wishes of others should be respected with regard to the receipt of unsolicited e-mail messages.

### Ownership

Information obtained from the Internet sources should be properly authorized and documented. Information ownership should be safeguarded and respected. Marketers should respect the integrity and ownership of computer and network systems.

### Access

Marketers should treat access to accounts, passwords, and other information as confidential, and only examine or disclose content when authorized by a responsible party. The integrity of others' information systems should be respected with regard to placement of information, advertising or messages.

*Reprinted by permission of the American Marketing Association.*

## GOING BEYOND ETHICS: LAWS AFFECTING BUSINESS-TO-BUSINESS PERSONAL SELLING

Among the most important federal laws for business-to-business salespeople to understand are the Robinson-Patman Act, Sherman Act, and Clayton Act. These acts cover price discrimination, collusion, price fixing, restraint of trade, exclusive dealing, reciprocity, tie-in sales, business and product descriptions, orders and terms of sale, unordered goods, secret rebates, customer coercion, and business defamation.

### Price Discrimination

The Clayton Act prohibits a seller (salesperson) from discriminating on price or terms of sale among different customers when the discrimination would injure competition. It also makes it illegal for a buyer to knowingly induce or accept a discriminatory price.

Under the Robinson-Patman Act, a seller (salesperson) cannot sell at different prices in different markets, or charge different prices to different purchasers for the same quality and quantity of goods. Differences in price or terms of sale can be successfully defended only if (1) the price differential was given in good faith to match, not beat, a price offered by a competitor; or (2) the price differential represents a cost saving resulting from different manufacturing techniques or quantities in which the products are sold or delivered. Price reductions are permissible when based on quantity ordered, closeout sales, lower shipping and selling costs, good faith meeting of competition, and lower commissions paid to salespeople. For their own legal protection, sellers should establish accounting procedures that can certify cost differences in selling to certain customers.

*Several federal, state, and local laws affect how salespeople do their jobs.*
Jose Luis Palaez/Corbis

## Price Fixing

If two or more competing sellers conspire to set or maintain uniform prices and profit margins, they are involved in **price fixing.** Even an informal exchange of price information between competitors or discussion of pricing policies at trade shows has been found to be illegal by the courts.

**Price Fixing** Two or more competing sellers conspiring to set or maintain uniform prices and profit margins.

## Collusion

Competing sellers who agree to set prices, divide up markets or territories, or act to the detriment of a third competitor are involved in an illegal arrangement called **collusion.**

**Collusion** An illegal arrangement in which competing sellers agree to set prices, divide up markets or territories, or act to the detriment of a third competitor.

## Exclusive Dealing

**Exclusive dealings** are agreements in which a manufacturer or wholesaler grants one dealer exclusive rights to sell a product in a certain trading area and insists that the dealer not carry competing lines. These actions are illegal under the Clayton Act.

**Exclusive Dealing** Agreements in which a manufacturer or wholesaler grants one dealer exclusive rights to sell a product in a certain trading area or insists that the dealer not carry competing lines. Illegal under the Clayton Act.

## Restraint of Trade

Dealers cannot be prohibited from selling competitors' products as a condition of receiving the right to sell the manufacturer's product. Under both the Sherman Act and the Clayton Act, agreements made between competitors to divide a market into noncompetitive territories or to restrict competition are restraints of trade.

## Reciprocity

Reciprocity, or purchasing from suppliers who buy from your company, is a controversial but not uncommon practice. Reciprocity agreements that eliminate competition are illegal, and the Department of Justice and the Federal Trade Commission (FTC) will intervene to stop systematic reciprocal buying practices deemed to be anticompetitive.

## Tie-In Sales

A **tie-in** occurs when a seller (salesperson) requires a customer to buy an unwanted product along with the desired product. Such requirements are prohibited.

**Tie-In** Refers to an often-illegal situation in which a seller requires a customer to purchase an unwanted product along with the desired product.

## Unordered Goods

Section 5 of the FTC Act prohibits companies from shipping unordered goods or shipping larger quantities than customers ordered.

## Orders and Terms of Sale

It is illegal for sellers to substitute goods different from those ordered, to misrepresent delivery dates, or to fail to fill an order within a reasonable time. Key terms of sale, such as warranties or guarantees, the ability of the buyer to cancel a contract or obtain a refund, and important facts in a credit or financing transaction cannot be concealed or misrepresented.

## Business Descriptions

Salespeople must never misrepresent their company's financial strength, length of time in business, reputation, or particulars about its plant, equipment, and facilities.

## Product Descriptions

It is illegal to lie about how a product is made. A salesperson may not state that a product is "custom-made" or "tailor-made" when it is actually ready-made. In addition, no statements can be made about "proven" claims unless scientific or empirical evidence is available to substantiate the truth of the claims.

## Secret Rebates

Salespeople cannot secretly reward a dealer's salespeople for pushing sales of their company's products. Even if the dealer's management approves such an incentive plan for their employees, this practice may violate the Sherman Act if it results in unfair discrimination among competing dealers.

## Customer Coercion

Salespeople cannot make fictitious inquiries that harass a competitor or pressure anyone into buying a product through scare tactics, coercion, or intimidation.

## Business Defamation

Many companies and their salespeople have been sued by competitors for making slanderous statements about them that caused financial damage, lost customers, unemployment, or lost sales. The Federal Trade Commission can impose cease and desist orders or obtain an injunction against companies that engage in unfair or deceptive practices through their salespeople. What's more, private lawsuits may be brought against the offenders. **Business defamation** can include the following offenses:

- **Business slander** occurs when unfair and untrue *oral* statements are made about competitors that damage the reputation of the competitor or the personal reputation of an individual in that business.
- **Business libel** occurs when unfair and untrue statements are made about a competitor in *writing* (usually a letter, sales literature, advertisement, or company brochure) that damage the competitor's reputation or the personal reputation of an individual in that business.
- **Product disparagement** occurs when false or deceptive comparisons or distorted claims are *made during or after a sales presentation* about a competitor's products, services, or properties. These statements are considered defamatory *per se;* that is, a defamed company or individual needs not prove actual damages to win a favorable verdict, only that the

**Business Defamation** Any action or utterance that slanders, libels, or disparages a competitor, causing the competitor financial damage, lost customers, unemployment, or lost sales.

**Business Slander** Unfair and untrue *oral* statements made about competitors that damage the reputation of the competitor or the personal reputation of an individual in that business.

**Business Libel** Unfair and untrue statements made about a competitor in *writing* (usually a letter, sales literature, advertisement, or company brochure) that damage the competitor's reputation or the personal reputation of an individual in that business.

**Product Disparagement** False or deceptive comparisons or distorted claims *made during or after a sales presentation* about a competitor's products, services, or properties. These statements are considered defamatory *per se.*

## KEEPING UP ONLINE: FEDERAL TRADE COMMISSION

The Federal Trade Commission (FTC) is the agency most involved in regulating U.S. business practices. Sometimes, however, the FTC encourages firms within an industry to establish their own set of trade practices. If businesses could agree on their own set of trade practices, do you think it still would be necessary to have a Federal Trade Commission? Why? Go to the FTC web site at www.ftc.gov/ to see the wide range of business practices, both online and off-line, that come under its regulatory authority.

statement is untrue. Below are the kinds of statements that may be judged defamatory:

- Untrue comments that a competitor is engaging in illegal or unfair business practices
- Untrue remarks that a competitor fails to live up to its contractual obligations and responsibilities
- Untrue statements regarding a competitor's financial condition
- Untrue statements that a principal in the competitor's business is incompetent, of poor moral character, unreliable, or dishonest

When the FTC receives a complaint or believes that a company is violating a law, it issues a complaint to the company stating that it is in violation. If the company persists in the questionable practice, the FTC can issue a cease-and-desist order demanding that the business stop the practice or risk civil penalties in court of ten thousand dollars per day for each infraction. Read *Keeping Up Online* above to find out more about the FTC.

A reputation for integrity and high ethical standards in dealing with all people at all times is one of the most valuable possessions of the professional salesperson. Ethics will pay off in the long run because nearly all customers—even those who are not ethical themselves—prefer to do business with a salesperson who is ethical.

## ETHICS AND REGULATION IN INTERNATIONAL SALES

Salespeople in international selling face shifting ethical standards and accepted modes of behavior as they go from one country to another. Selling practices that are illegal or unethical in one country may be accepted ways of doing business in another. Yet, salespeople who engage in acceptable practices abroad may be criticized or even prosecuted for violation of U.S. law. International salespeople are restrained by three laws.

1. U.S. law prohibits American companies from trading with some foreign countries—which vary depending on our political relationships.

2. Salespeople must obey the *laws of the host country* where they operate even though they may differ sharply from U.S. laws. Some foreign countries actually have more restrictive business laws than in the United States. For example, Greece sued Colgate for giving away razor blades with its shaving cream. France and Sweden regulate across-border flows of mailing lists and data about citizens. Japan restricts compilation of computerized mailing lists. More often, U.S. companies and their salespeople face particularly difficult moral and ethical issues in foreign countries with less-restrictive business laws. For instance, in some countries, payment of bribes to high-level military officials in order to sell weapons to their government is the expected way of doing business.

3. The multinational firm is subject to *international laws* that are enforced across national boundaries. Gifts, bribes, and payoffs have consistently been identified in studies as the major abuses in international personal selling. One case, for example, involved payments of nearly thirty-eight million dollars made by Lockheed Aircraft Corp. to government officials in Japan, Italy, and the Netherlands to win sales for its L1011 Tri Star and F-104 Starfighter jet airplanes. The Foreign Corrupt Practices Act prohibits U.S. firms from giving such bribes to host country personnel. Both the United Nations and the European Economic Community are standardizing commercial codes that deal with such issues as product safety and environmental standards, and making them binding on all companies whose nations endorse the codes. Eventually, perhaps, ethical standards can be established among trading partners.

Sales representatives planning to sell products or services in a foreign country should check with the U.S. Department of Commerce for information about each country's legal restrictions on imports and U.S. restrictions on exports. For example, sales of some categories of technological equipment and processes are restricted by U.S. law or by edict of the State Department or Defense Department, and such items are not allowed to leave the country. Then, before beginning any transaction within the foreign country, sales representatives should contact the commercial attaché at the U.S. embassy for information on the specific legal requirements in conducting business there.

In international negotiations, salespeople must not confuse ethical standards and the law. Ethical practices vary greatly from one country to another. "Lubrication bribery," or small amounts of money to grease the wheels of bureaucracy, is deeply entrenched in some parts of the world. A lubrication bribe, or *baksheesh*, is often the accepted and expected way of doing business in the Middle and Far East. In Italy, a *bustarella* (an envelope stuffed with lire notes) persuades a particular license clerk to do his job. By contrast, *mordida* ("the bite") ensures that a Mexican government inspector will not do his job. *Whitemail bribery* buys influence at high levels.

Even though payoffs and bribes sometimes seem necessary to do business in some countries, a study of sixty-five major American corporations (forty of

---

### TABLE 13.2

## DOING BUSINESS IN FOREIGN COUNTRIES

1. When operating in foreign markets, no single standard of ethical behavior applies to all business decisions. A wide range of standards and modes of ethical conduct will confront salespeople selling in international markets.

2. In developing countries, not the laws of the country, but the degree of enforcement of those laws will most likely determine the lower limit of acceptable business behavior of sales personnel.

3. The upper level of ethical conduct pertaining to doing business in foreign markets is not clearly defined.

4. Flagrant unethical behavior by sales personnel may attract substantial attention in foreign countries and might lead to regulatory action aimed at the offending company.

5. Salespeople must be intimately familiar with the foreign country in which they are operating to avoid an ethnocentric posture and ethical misjudgments.

**Source:** Adapted from Gene R. Laczniak and Jacob Naor, "Global Ethics: Wrestling with the Corporate Conscience," Business (July-September 1985): 3–10.

---

which admitted to making questionable payments abroad) found that these payments usually just shift orders from one American company to another. If both companies follow the same ethical standards, no payment is needed. Interestingly, though, a study of eight hundred senior executives in fifteen developing countries determined that, out of twenty-one major trading nations, firms in the United States (as well as in Russia and Asia) are *most likely* to pay bribes when seeking business in emerging nations. This is occurring despite the U.S. government's ratification of the *1999 Anti-Bribery Convention of the Organization for Economic Development and Cooperation*, which is aimed at prosecuting U.S. companies that foster corruption in international markets.[29] Table 13.2 provides useful propositions concerning doing business in foreign countries.

## MAKING ETHICAL DECISIONS

Whether selling domestically or internationally, ethical standards must be a part of the salesperson's individual value system and incorporated into his or her decision-making process. Table 13.3 on p. 426 suggests a five-step process for ethical decision making.

A salesperson's reputation for ethical conduct is an invaluable advantage in developing and maintaining long-run relationships with customers. Even if the value system one developed from youth does not naturally lead toward consistent ethical decision making, it makes economic sense over the long run

| TABLE 13.3 |
|---|

## ETHICAL DECISION-MAKING CHECKLIST

**1. General Questions**
- Who is responsible to act?
- What are the consequences of the action? (Benefits-Harm Analysis)
- What rights, and whose rights, are affected? (Rights-Principles Analysis)
- What is fair treatment in this case? (Social Justice Analysis)

**2. Solution Development**
- What solutions are available to me?
- Have I considered all of the creative solutions that might permit me to reduce harm, maximize benefits, respect more rights, or be fair to more parties?

**3. Selection of the Optimum Solution**
- What are the potential consequences of my solutions?
- Which of the options I have considered does the most to maximize benefits, reduce harm, respect rights, and increase fairness?
- Are all parties treated fairly in my proposed decision?

**4. Implementation**
- Who should be consulted and informed?
- What actions will ensure that my decision achieves the intended outcome?
- Implement the decision.

**5. Follow-Up**
- Was the decision implemented correctly?
- Did the decision maximize benefits, reduce harm, respect rights, and treat all parties fairly?

*Source:* Adapted from Patrick E. Murphy, "Implementing Business Ethics," *Journal of Business Ethics* (December 1988): 913.

to always be seen as a salesperson who can be trusted to do the right thing in all situations. So, whether you're just naturally an ethical person or someone who only wants to be as successful as possible in your career, remember that people with many years of experience in sales and in all walks of life have found truth in the adage that investing in ethics pays big dividends in the long run.

## SUMMARY

Ethics is the study of what's right and wrong and serves as the basis for a code of conduct for interactions among people. Salespeople need training in ethical conduct for dealing with customers, competitors, coworkers, and their own companies. In addition, companies have a responsibility to act ethically with their salespeople. International selling is affected by U.S. laws, laws of the host country, and international laws enforced across national boundaries, as well as varying ethical expectations in different countries. Salespeople and their companies should bear in mind that what is legal or ethical in the host country may not be in the United States. Yet, the salesperson and his or her company will be held responsible for their conduct in both countries. Cultural differences make it critical that salespeople understand the legal, ethical, and social mores of any countries in which they are attempting to sell their company's products.

## KEY TERMS

Ethics

Quid Pro Quo Harassment

Hostile Environment

Price Fixing

Collusion

Exclusive Dealing

Tie-In

Business Defamation

Business Slander

Business Libel

Product Disparagement

## CHAPTER REVIEW QUESTIONS

1. What are ethics?

2. Discuss some of the more common ethical concerns of salespeople.

3. Can you explain the difference between *quid pro quo* and *hostile environment harassment*?

4. Describe some of the ways that professional salespeople can be the ethical "eyes and ears" of their companies.

5. Name and briefly describe several of the most important federal laws affecting business-to-business selling.

6. What are the three most common kinds of business defamation?

7. Why should salespeople be especially careful about business defamation during or after the sales presentation?

8. What are three different sets of laws international salespeople must abide by?

## TOPICS FOR THOUGHT AND CLASS DISCUSSION

1. How do you think your ethical values were formed? Who had the most influence on you? Why?

2. Why must salespeople concern themselves with ethical issues? Isn't it enough to understand and operate within the law?

3. Do you believe that ethical standards in the United States are relatively stable or changing? Do you think U.S. ethical standards are becoming higher or lower? Why?

4. Why do countries differ so sharply about what is ethical or unethical behavior? Do you think that all countries would ever adopt an international code of ethical behavior in business?

5. How do you think you would handle a situation in which you are trying to make a multimillion dollar sale to a foreign country and that country's trade representative makes it clear that he expects a substantial bride?

6. Have you ever been a victim of sexual harassment? How did you deal with it?

7. What do you think are today's major ethical issues?

8. Do you have any personal guidelines for what is ethical or unethical behavior? Would you like to see everyone use your guidelines?

## PROJECTS FOR PERSONAL GROWTH

1. Locate and interview two salespeople. Ask them how they decide whether a particular behavior is ethical or unethical. Did they receive any training in ethics during their sales training program? Do their companies have codes of ethics? What punishments or penalties accompany ethical violations?

2. Write down two ethical dilemmas that you have personally faced. How did you decide what to do in each case? In retrospect, do you think your decisions were the right ones? Who was affected by your decision? How? Would you be willing to tell your friends the total truth about the dilemma and how you resolved it? How do you think they would react?

3. Go to your college or public library and look through issues from the 1940s or 1950s of popular magazines such as *Life* or *Time* and compare them with recent issues. Do you think the advertisements seem more or less ethical than those of today? Why do you think so, and what might account for the differences?

## CASE 13.1
# IT'S THE SHORT-RUN THAT MATTERS MOST!

After graduating from Eastern Michigan University, Stewart Dickinson accepted a sales position with Spearhead Technologies, Inc., a small, fast-growing measuring instruments firm, in Kalamazoo, Michigan. After completing his first year on the job, Stewart felt a little disappointed because he didn't make his annual sales quota. Although the sales manager, Sylvia Ambers, did not express any disappointment at Stewart's year-end performance review, she did tell him that she thought he could do better. And she suggested that Stewart talk with some top-performing sales-people in the company to see if he could pick up some sales tips. In fact, she said that she had arranged for Stewart to meet next Wednesday with George Fagus, who had been with the company only two years but had exceeded his sales quota each year.

Stewart was a little apprehensive when he met George for lunch at a popular Kalamazoo restaurant. George was a smooth-talking, former varsity football player at the University of Nebraska who exhibited supreme confidence. The two had met only casually and had never really talked. What's more, Stewart knew that Sylvia had probably asked George to give him some selling advice. After exchanging some pleasantries and other small talk about sports, George said, "Stu, let me level with you. Sylvia has asked me to help you out. I understand that you had an okay year, but you're a bright, energetic guy who can do better."

"George," responded Stewart, "I've worked really hard this year but it's been tough selling measuring instruments in this down market, especially when our competitors are offering better deals than we are."

"I hear you, George. But to play in the big leagues, you've got to be aggressive and creative! Let me give you a personal example. At the beginning of last quarter, it didn't look like I was going to make my sales quota this year, either. So, I shifted to a creative strategy. I told a couple of my biggest customers that I'd heard rumors about a big price increase in our line of measuring instruments next quarter, and I advised them to stock up now. Both of these big customers doubled their orders for the month. On another one of my sales calls, the prospect said that he was about to place a big order with a major competitor, Midas Measures, because he needed some measuring devices specially tailored to some new equipment his company had recently purchased. His company's production manager needed the new instruments within two weeks, so he wasn't even considering buying from Spearhead because he had heard that it took us nearly a month to deliver. Well, between you and me, Stu, he was right, but why should I just give up and let some competitor take that business? I told the prospect that if he would sign the order form today, I'd put a rush on his order, fax it in immediately, and have it delivered within nine days. Of course, it ain't goin' to happen, but I got the order instead of the competitor, who probably wouldn't have delivered on time either. When the prospect doesn't get the instruments within nine days, I'll just give him an excuse about a screw-up in production. 'Hey, it's not my fault,' I'll tell him . . . 'I did my best!'"

Stewart thought for a moment and replied, shaking his head, "George, I'm not comfortable misleading or lying to customers about delivery dates."

"I don't like it either, Stu, but I've found if you don't use every weapon in your arsenal to make a sale, you're going to lose it. Remember the trainers told us never to be negative about competitors before, during, or after a sales presentation? Well, that advice's for wimps. If I subtly plant a little negative information about a competitor during the sales presentation or afterward, it helps me win the sale. Besides, our competitors are always badmouthing our products. You gotta fight fire with fire, don't you?"

George winked at Stewart. "Stu, I've found that if I can bring my biggest customers a little

(continued)

## IT'S THE SHORT-RUN THAT MATTERS MOST!

(CONTINUED)

insider information about their competitors, they reward me with a big order. Just the other day, I told the purchasing manager at Giant Gears, Inc., that their major competitor, Pitt Manufacturing, was upgrading their warranties to five years on all their products. That little bit of information got me a 25 percent larger order than usual. What's the harm in telling them something that they're going to find out about soon anyway?"

"But, George," said Stewart, sitting back and crossing his arms, "Aren't you concerned that when you don't deliver an order on time, you'll lose that customer's future business? And, if you reveal confidential information to one customer about another one, won't that lead to mistrust in your long-run relationships with customers?"

George split a roll, buttered it generously, and took a large bite. "The game is making sales, not developing relationships. Furthermore, all this talk about customer relationship management is just that—so much talk. I'm not going to be in sales long enough to see any long-run pay off. After another year in field selling, I expect to be a sales manager. Right now, I'm looking good because my sales volume is great. If customers start complaining later, who cares? That's going to be the problem of whoever has taken over my old territory.

I'll have moved on. Stu, it's all about doing what's best for you right now. No matter what anyone says, it's all about the short-run . . . today's transaction . . . even top management turns over about every three years, so who's ever around for the long run? In the long run, we're all dead!"

### Questions

1. What do you think about George Fagus' approach to personal selling? Why do you think he's viewed as a top performer at Spearhead Technologies?

2. Do you think that Stewart should follow George's advice, at least for the next year or so, so he can make his sales quotas? Why? If you don't agree with George's advice, what advice would you give Stewart? What should Stewart do next year at this time if he hasn't made his sales quota? What should he say to his sales manager, Sylvia Ambers?

3. Do you think Spearhead Technologies has any problems in their performance evaluation system? For example, do you think the company is giving equal weight to qualitative performance and quantitative performance? What can the company do to ensure a better balance in its performance evaluation for salespeople? How might an improved performance evaluation system help Spearhead Technologies?

# AFFABLE . . . OR OVERLY AFFECTIONATE?

Following college graduation with a B.S. degree in marketing, Toni Lauder entered a sales training program at National Micro Systems (NMS) headquartered in Philadelphia, where she has been a successful salesperson with her own territory for three years. Toni, at twenty-six, is still single but quite regularly dates one man, Burt Sanford, a twenty-nine-year-old high school mathematics teacher. One of Toni's favorite forms of after-work relaxation is going to the ballet (she took lessons for seven years before college), and she buys season tickets every year. Her boyfriend would rather go to a sporting event, but he willingly goes to the ballet with Toni whenever she asks. In return, Toni often attends 76er basketball or Phillies baseball games with Burt. They have a great relationship, but marriage doesn't seem to be a pressing consideration for either of them.

For the past two years, Toni has exceeded her sales quota and received outstanding performance evaluations. In fact, last year she made the NMS President's Club and received as a reward a two-week vacation trip traveling throughout Switzerland with other top-performing salespeople and senior NMS executives. On the trip, she got to know Samuel Thomas, CEO of NMS, and she enjoyed hearing his perspectives after more than forty years at NMS. He was an approachable, affable man who planned to retire within the next two years. His likely successor, Rick Fleming, could not make the trip because he was involved in negotiating to buy a small manufacturer of parts that NMS incorporates in their products. Toni was awed by the diverse beauty of Switzerland, and she can't stop talking about the trip even two months later. Toni believes that special incentives like the vacation trip in Switzerland with senior executives help motivate NMS salespeople. After all, being on a first-name basis with the CEO of a multibillion-dollar company was a heady experience for all the salespeople. Toni enjoys her work and is optimistic about her future career at the company.

Despite her overall satisfaction with her work at NMS and with her customers, Toni has become increasingly concerned about her relationship with her new sales manager, Tom Whall, a forty-four-year-old married man with three teenagers at home. Tom was recently promoted to district sales manager after eight years as a top-performing salesperson in NMS's California sales office. Prior to entering the sales field, Tom had owned his own small machine tools business for twelve years. Tom is a tall, husky, extroverted guy who often puts his arm around people, whether men or women, when talking with them. He has done this to Toni on several occasions. At first, Toni was a little taken aback by such touching but, as she has seen Tom do it to the salesmen, she's learned to accept it as just Tom being Tom. However, later, Tom has started commenting on Toni's clothes and figure in front of the other salespeople. For example, at the last sales meeting, he whistled when Toni came into the room and said, "Wow, why can't the rest of you guys look that good in the morning! Toni, your smile makes my day. Come take a seat next to me at the conference table." During the meeting, Tom's leg brushed against Toni's several times . . . even after Toni positioned her legs as far as she could away from Tom's side of the table. Toni wasn't sure whether the leg touches were accidental or not.

After the meeting was over, Tom called Toni aside and told her that he wanted to spend the next week riding with her as she called on customers in her territory. This would give him a chance to develop closer relationships with NMS customers and enable him to help Toni become an even better salesperson. During the week, Toni and Tom would have to stay overnight at motels along the way and eat all their meals in restaurants. Toni was concerned about the week with Tom on the road, but she didn't think he would try to come on to her. After all, he is a married man with three super teenage kids whom Toni

(continued)

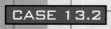

## AFFABLE . . . OR OVERLY AFFECTIONATE?

(CONTINUED)

had met at a party for the salespeople at Tom's house. They seemed like a happy family who got along great. So Toni was quite confident that she had nothing to fear. Nevertheless, she thought about what she would do if Tom did try to make a play for her on the road. What might she say to put him off? She knew that she didn't want to lose her job, yet she certainly wasn't going to have an affair with her boss.

Toni talked to her boyfriend, Burt, about her concerns regarding the upcoming trip with her boss, but he just laughed it off. "Tom is a big, lovable oaf who won't be a problem, Toni. And, as far as leg touching under the table," explained Burt, "That happens all the time when you're sitting at a small conference table. As big as Tom is, I'll bet his legs were bouncing off the legs of people on both sides of him. Even if Tom would try something, I know that you can handle it. I've seen you put people in their place when they've pushed you too far. You have my cell phone number. Just give me a call if you feel you're getting into an awkward situation." Toni felt better after hearing Burt's comments.

Reassured by Burt, Toni confidently picked up Tom at his house on Sunday afternoon to drive to the Hampton Inns motel near the first three sales calls she planned to make with Tom on Monday morning. It was about a two-hour's drive to the motel where Toni and Tom would be in separate rooms across the hall from each other on the third floor. Tom talked a lot as they drove to the motel. At first, he asked her only about her customers, but later he began asking her more personal questions, for example, about her relationship with Burt and her future plans for marriage and children.

When he first shifted his conversation to this more personal area, Toni took a deep breath before saying anything, then gave him short, noncommittal answers, such as, "I don't know. I haven't really thought about it." Toni thought to herself, "Is he just showing personal interest in me as one

of his salespeople, or is he trying to increase the intimacy of our conversation to an unacceptable level?" Toni didn't want to appear defensive or say something that might insult her boss, but she wanted to stop this increasingly intimate conversation. She tried to shift the conversation by asking some questions about how to deal with one of her difficult customers on whom they'd be calling tomorrow. But Tom brushed the question off. "Don't worry about it tonight. We can talk about how to deal with him as we drive over there tomorrow." Tom continued his previous line of questioning but received only brief responses from Toni.

Upon arriving at the motel and checking in, Tom asked if Toni would like to join him for a drink in the motel restaurant/bar. Toni replied, "No thanks, I'm tired and need some rest. We have a full day tomorrow calling on customers. Goodnight." Tom says "Okay," then turns and walks to the bar.

### Questions

1. Do you think Tom's line of questioning while driving to the motel was merely a show of genuine interest and concern for Toni (who's nearly young enough to be his daughter) . . . or not? Did Toni handle the conversation with Tom appropriately? If not, what do you think Toni should have said to Tom when he began asking her rather personal questions? Would your suggested response enable Toni to avoid upsetting Tom?

2. While staying overnight at motels, should Toni go out to dinner each night with Tom or make some excuse each time and eat alone? Why? Should she order or allow Tom to order any alcoholic drinks for her if they do go out to dinner together? What should Toni do if Tom invites her to dance, if they happen to go to a restaurant with live entertainment? Will Tom be insulted if Toni says no to a dance invitation? If so, how might this affect their long-

(continued)

**CASE 13.2**

# AFFABLE . . . OR OVERLY AFFECTIONATE?

(CONTINUED)

run superior-subordinate relationship and Toni's future at NMS?

3. While traveling in her territory with her boss this coming week, what should Toni do if Tom seems to be making advances toward her? Should she just ignore any such attempts, make a joke about them that subtly puts Tom back in his place, or should she take a tough stance up front and tell Tom to back off? Should Toni's first-name relationship with Samuel Thomas, CEO of NMS, be used to keep Tom in his place?

4. What should Toni say and do if Tom has a few drinks and later tries to become affectionate with her at the restaurant or later at the motel? What can Toni do to avoid being alone with Tom?

5. If Toni believes that she has to put Tom in his place verbally, or, worse, fend off his overly friendly touches during the first few days on the trip, what should she do about the remainder of the trip around her territory? Should she tell him to fly back to the office, as she cannot work in this awkward situation? If he refuses to leave, should she cancel the remainder of the trip and go back home, possibly risking her job? Should she call her boyfriend for advice? Should she call Samuel Thomas, CEO of NMS, to tell him about her awkward experience with Tom? What other options might be better?

6. Do you think that Toni's sales manager is creating a hostile working environment for her? Should Toni consider leaving the company? Why or why not?

## CHAPTER 14

# Starting Your Personal Selling Career

*"If it is to be, it is up to me."*
William H. Johnson

## After Reading This Chapter, You Should Understand:

- Some of the many benefits in a personal selling career.

- Various online and offline sources of sales jobs.

- What companies are looking for in new salespeople.

- How you may be screened for a personal selling job.

- Reasons why some candidates for sales jobs are rejected.

- Questions often asked in an interview.

- How to use the PSP to find a good job in personal selling.

- Various suggestions for preparing your résumé and cover letter.

## INSIDE PERSONAL SELLING:
### Meet Tere Blanca de Ulloa of Codina Realty Services

College graduates starting a career in personal sales need perseverance, discipline, and good communication skills, says Tere Blanca de Ulloa, a senior vice president at Codina Realty Services Inc., ONCOR International. As her company's most productive salesperson, de Ulloa sells and leases commercial real estate and land in Miami-Dade County, Florida. She represents owners of office buildings and land as well as tenants looking for office space. Over the years, she has found that prospective salespeople can learn effective sales techniques but often "need to polish their verbal and written communication skills," she says.

De Ulloa took a job in banking after graduating from the University of Miami with a concentration in international finance and marketing. Eighteen months

later, she returned to school for a graduate degree. "The M.B.A. program gave me an overview of all the business disciplines and developed my writing and presentation skills," she says.

Then de Ulloa moved to San Diego and, at the suggestion of friends, pursued jobs in sales. Visiting the University of San Diego campus, she spotted a note on a bulletin board: "Seeking people for positions with Burroughs Corporation." De Ulloa applied, was hired, and began selling computer products to distributors after a week of sales training. Selling for Burroughs "was a terrific experience, and I developed my sales skills," she remembers. Seeking more diversity in sales contacts and wanting to apply disciplines learned in graduate school, she looked into commercial real estate, where "each deal and client is different and finance skills are important, especially when handling investment properties."

Returning to Miami, de Ulloa was hired by Coldwell Banker Commercial Real Estate, completed its training program, and remained with the firm for about two years.

The president of Codina Realty Services recruited de Ulloa when he began expanding the company fourteen years ago. Codina typically recruits through referrals, seeking candidates who have some sales experience—even in a different field. People who want to work in sales must be "absolutely hungry for the job," observes de Ulloa. "Selling is tough because you get negative reinforcement at first. When you are cold calling, the way most salespeople start, you hear 'no' from a lot of people. If you don't have discipline and perseverance, the job will not work out."

Her advice to students considering a sales career? Gain some experience in your chosen field before you graduate. "Get an internship in a company and industry that interests you," she suggests, "and try to work with the sales teams by helping with research, presentations, or marketing materials." Although an internship may not be easy to find, de Ulloa points out that successfully getting such a position demonstrates the kind of discipline and perseverance every sales professional needs.

**435**

ongratulations, you've done it! You have persevered through thirteen chapters of learning about a career in personal selling, and now you're ready to start looking for that entry-level sales position. The good news is that the very tools and skills that you've just learned can help you effectively and efficiently look for a job and sell yourself to an employer. Wow, is the personal selling process flexible or what?

## YOUR CAREER IN SALES

Your career choice will play a major role in determining your income, lifestyle, success, and personal happiness. For highly motivated men and women, a career beginning in professional personal selling offers exceptional benefits and advancement opportunities, because job performance in sales is measured more objectively than in most fields. Some of the many benefits we've discussed that accompany a sales career include

- high earnings potential
- job freedom and independence
- special perquisites such as a company car, company credit card, club memberships, and incentives for superior performance
- opportunities to travel and entertain customers on an expense account
- continuous job challenge and excitement
- tax deductions for home offices and other expenses not covered by the company
- opportunities to meet and interact with new and diverse people
- recognition within the company because top salespeople are the highly visible superstars who directly generate revenues that keep the company financially healthy. In fact, some people have said that everyone's job depends on how well salespeople do their jobs.
- fast track opportunities for promotion all the way to the top of an organization
- jobs for diverse types of individuals with varied backgrounds and personalities to match up with diverse prospects and customers
- high mobility, because good salespeople are always in demand
- chance to contribute to a healthy, growing economy by solving problems and making a real difference in your customers' and your own company's "bottom line"
- multiple career paths in professional selling, sales management, or marketing management

### Career Path Options

Remember from chapter 1 the three major career paths branching out from personal selling? You usually begin your sales career as a sales trainee for a few weeks or months. Then you become a sales representative with a territory of your own to manage. After a few years in the field, you may have an opportunity to make a career designation, either (a) professional selling, (b) sales management, or (c) marketing management. If you choose the *professional selling* path, your first promotion after *salesperson* will be to *senior sales representative*. After several years in this job, you may be promoted to *master sales representative*. Then, top-performing master sales reps are promoted to *national account executive* or *key account executive* with responsibility for selling to a few major customers such as DuPont, Procter & Gamble, or Wal-Mart.[1]

If you choose the *sales management* route, you'll probably advance from *salesperson* to *sales supervisor,* then *sales manager* at the branch, district, zone, division, or regional levels.[2] From this point, you may be promoted to *national sales manager* or *vice president of sales*. The foregoing are all line sales management jobs. Another way to move into management is through the sales staff side. Staff people are at every sales organizational level and may hold positions in sales planning, sales promotion, sales recruiting, sales analysis, or sales training. For example, you might serve as a *sales analyst, sales training manager*, or as *assistant to the sales manager*. Although people in sales management staff positions have no line authority over the sales force, they may hold impressive titles such as *assistant national sales manager* and often switch over to top positions in line management.

Following success in field selling, another alternative open to a salesperson is the *marketing management* career path. This path often starts with promotion to *product or brand manager* for a product category such as Pillsbury's Hungry Jack biscuits or Procter and Gamble's Colgate toothpaste. As a product or brand manager, you're like a president of a company within a larger company. Whatever happens to Colgate toothpaste, whether good or bad, will be largely credited to the product manager since he or she is responsible for marketing it successfully. Success in product management may lead to promotion to *director of product management*, then *vice president of marketing*, and maybe even *president and CEO*.

## Sources of Sales Jobs

Companies recruit salespeople through various *internal* and *external* sources.[3] Among the most widely used *internal sources* are employee newsletters, bulletin board announcements, and *employee referral programs,* which may offer employees a "finder's fee" to recommend potential salespeople. Current salespeople and purchasing agents are especially good sources because they know what sales jobs demand, and they hear about salespeople who are discontent and about to leave. Sometimes the company will make an announcement to all employees that they are looking for people interested in transferring into sales. If too few qualified or interested people emerge from among present employees, the company will use *external sources* such as newspaper advertisements, employment agencies, colleges and universities, career conferences or job fairs, and professional organizations. People interested in sales careers should make a habit of reading the daily *newspapers* covering the areas in which they would like to work. The *Wall Street Journal* is a good source of quality sales jobs across the world.

*Trade journals* offer information on specific types of sales jobs and often have an employment section. If you have an interest in working in a particular industry, you can use a general search engine like www.google.com to find the name of the key trade journal for that industry, then ask your college's business reference librarian to locate the most current copy for you. *Private employment agencies* can sometimes help find sales jobs, but some charge a fee of up to 20 percent of your first year earnings. Employers, not job seekers, will pay the fee for higher caliber sales jobs. Sales Consultants (www.mriscs.com) is one of many international employment agencies that specialize in finding quality sales and marketing people.

On the Internet, you can find all kinds of general job web sites covering diverse job openings in the United States and around the world, as well as web sites that specialize in sales jobs. Don't neglect the general web sites, because nearly all of them have separate listings for many sales jobs. At most of these sites, you can review job openings in the exact city or area of country in which you'd like to work. Moreover, you can prepare and post your résumé, then send it to specific companies or even broadcast it to many companies. Some web sites will send you an email when a job opening appears that matches your job specifications. Some sites provide helpful *personal assessment tools*. After you complete an online self-assessment questionnaire and submit it online, you'll shortly receive a personal analysis and advice by email on how to further develop your sales skills or attitude. You can even compare salaries for different jobs in various markets online. Serving as the bridge between company recruiters and individual job seekers, web sites are continuously upgrading their services. It's worth your time to check out several. *General Job Web Sites* on p. 439 and *Sites That Specialize in Sales Jobs* on p. 440 provide some sites for you to visit.

College and university campuses are most likely to be used by large companies with sales trainee programs. Campus recruiters usually do not expect you to have sales experience, and many companies even prefer college students who have not learned the bad selling habits that many experienced salespeople pick up. Campus placement centers can help you in setting up interviews, preparing your résumé, and providing facilities for meeting with company representatives.

**Cooperative education programs,** offered at universities such as Drexel, Northeastern, and Cincinnati, obtain jobs for students in their chosen career field with one of several thousand participating companies. Students combine their course work with work in their career field of interest during two six-month co-op cycles. By working a year during the educational process, students learn what it's really like in their chosen career field, earn substantial money to help pay for tuition when they return to school, and build impressive résumés. Students who perform well usually receive job offers upon graduation from the company they worked with on co-op.

**Sales internship programs**, offered by such companies as Procter & Gamble and Automatic Data Processing, are also gaining popularity. Although you can learn much in an intern program, you usually earn no money. *Job fairs* bring hundreds of employers and job seekers together in one location for mini-interviews and for students to circulate their résumés. One organizer of job fairs, *Career Concepts*, conducts job fairs in eleven cities and charges the

**Cooperative Education Programs** Students combine their college studies with paid work in their career field of interest during two six-month co-op cycles with one or more of several thousand participating companies. Students often pay for their own college education with money earned in these co-op jobs. Three universities—Drexel, Northeastern, and Cincinnati—are best known for their cooperative education programs.

**Sales Internship Programs** Unpaid study-work programs offered to college students by several companies, for example, Procter & Gamble and Automatic Data Processing, where students learn about career opportunities.

## GENERAL JOB WEB SITES

www.monster.com—contains hundreds of thousands of job listings in all fields and links to related job sites globally, including home pages of companies.

www.marketingjobs.com—lists sales, marketing, and advertising/public relations jobs, provides direct links to companies with openings, and offers ideas and helpful books on finding employment.

www.careercity.com—allows you to search four million job openings and provides links to twenty-seven thousand U.S. companies. Also has free résumé posting and comprehensive salary surveys for all fields.

www.usajobs.opm.gov—includes a résumé builder and email notification of jobs that match your criteria.

www.ajb.dni.us—(America's Job Bank)—provides information on more than a million jobs in all fields at all levels. Allows you to create and post your résumé online.

www.diversitylink.com—lists job opportunities from employers seeking minority candidates.

www.eop.com—home page of Equal Opportunity Publications. Specializes in identifying job opportunities and career fairs for minority or physically challenged candidates.

www.minoritiesjobbank.com—hosted by *Black Collegian* magazine, it offers a job and résumé bank for companies interested in a diversified workforce. Provides valuable career and specific job information to African Americans, Hispanic American, Asian Americans, Native Americans, and women.

www.philanthropy-journal.org—presents a job bank for people looking for employment with nonprofit organizations.

www.espan.com—has about ten thousand job listings that you can search by job title, company, and state. You can post your résumé in less than two minutes.

www.americanjobs.com—allows you to post and send résumés free to potential employers.

www.careerpath.com—contains classified employment ads from more than twenty large city newspapers and many smaller ones.

www.resweb.com—is a job data bank of more than two hundred thousand listings and free posting of your résumé.

www.careerweb.com—provides alerts via email to job openings that match your qualifications; also includes a salary calculator and career fair information.

www.careertips.com—for those who want to pursue employment or education outside the United States.

www.nytimes.com/pages/jobs/index.html—contains jobs listed in the *New York Times* newspaper.

www.hoovers.com—offers various search tools such as sales development assessment questionnaires. This subscription service charges a monthly fee, although many parts of the site are free.

http://jobs.internet.com—specializes in high-tech jobs.

http://jobs.guardian.co.uk—has job openings in the United Kingdom.

www.overseasjobs.com—contains international jobs.

www.bilingual-jobs.com—is for those who speak English plus another language and are interested in working with other cultures within the United States or internationally.

## WEB SITES SPECIALIZING IN SALES JOBS

| | |
|---|---|
| www.salesjobs.com | www.bizwiz.com/salesjobs |
| www.acccessalesjobs.com | www.jobs4sales.com |
| www.marketingjobs.com | www.nasp.com |
| http://sales.monster.com | www.sellingjobs.com |
| www.topsalespositions.com | www.salesengineer.com |

participating companies a fee. Professional associations, such as local chapters of the *American Marketing Association* (www.ama.org) and *Sales and Marketing Executives International* (www.smei.com), encourage students to join and interact with salesperson members. Contacts made at the meetings of such associations oftentimes lead to sales jobs. The *Marketing News,* a biweekly newspaper for AMA members, reports on the marketing profession and describes job openings in a regular section called "The Marketplace." You can learn about sales jobs from a variety of other sources, including employers, professors, friends, acquaintances, and relatives, so keep your résumé up-to-date and stay alert to all opportunities.

## WHAT COMPANIES LOOK FOR IN NEW SALESPEOPLE

Individual companies in different industries, large and small, look for diverse qualities in their sales recruits. At one large company, the personnel director noted, "We search for individuals who are intelligent, quick learners, problem solvers. We don't look for specific academic backgrounds. We've hired some music majors, because they have very logical minds."

Some companies like to hire college athletes because of their competitive drive and ability to work as a team member. It seems that every company has its own idea about what makes a successful salesperson; so learn as much as you can about the type of person a particular company likes to hire before taking an interview or even sending your résumé and **cover letter.** Clues about the type of sales candidates a company seeks can often be found in annual reports and magazine articles about the company. In general, successful sales candidates tend to have the following characteristics:

**Self-Motivation:**
- able to explain why they selected sales as a career path
- exhibit and communicate high energy levels, indicating
  - ability to work long and hard without discouragement

**Cover Letter** Letter that accompanies a résumé and is designed to induce employers to read the enclosed résumé. Oftentimes used by college students and others to identify the position they're applying for if they prefer to not put a job objective on their résumé.

- track record of setting and achieving meaningful goals
- capacity to initiate action and influence events rather than being merely passive observers
- express thoughts and ideas clearly and directly
- organize thoughts logically
- ask insightful questions about the company
- listen attentively

### Interpersonal Skills:

- interact comfortably in a friendly fashion with diverse types of people in different situations
- have persuasive ability to win the confidence of others
- are flexible and adaptable to new situations
- can handle rejection and disappointments without losing confidence or effectiveness

### Planning/Organizing Skills

- can establish realistic short-run and long-run objectives
- can set priorities among tasks
- can develop clear strategies to achieve objectives
- can make sound judgments and decisions based on facts[4]

## HOW COMPANIES SCREEN YOU FOR A SALES JOB

Companies use a great variety of selection tools, techniques, and procedures to select candidates for their sales forces. Most companies use initial screening interviews, application forms, in-depth interviews, reference checks, physical examinations, and tests. Most firms rely most heavily on application forms and job interviews, and they base most final hiring decisions on successful personal interviews—first a screening interview, then a final, in-depth interview with the sales manager to whom you will report.

### Screening Interviews

The initial screening interview is the first hurdle that you must clear to be seriously considered for a sales job. You can prepare for this initial screening by anticipating questions you might be asked and mentally preparing your response to each. Among countless questions that interviewers may ask, see how you would answer some typical ones listed in Table 14.1 on p. 442.

In terms of employment laws, **protected groups** are people who are distinguished by special characteristics such as their race, color, ethnicity, national origin, religion, gender, age (over forty), disability, or veteran status. These particular groups are protected under federal antidiscrimination law, which mandates that people in one of these protected groups cannot be discriminated against in any aspect of employment, whether hiring, promotion, training, discipline, pay, or termination. State laws may protect other groups,

**Protected Groups** In terms of employment laws, protected groups are people distinguished by special characteristics, such as race, color, ethnicity, national origin, religion, gender, age (over forty), disability, or veteran status. These particular groups are protected under federal antidiscrimination law, which mandates that people in one of these protected groups cannot be discriminated against in any facet of employment—including hiring, promotion, training, discipline, pay, or termination.

| | TABLE 14.1 |
|---|---|

## QUESTIONS OFTEN ASKED IN A SCREENING INTERVIEW

- Why do you want to work for our company?
- What do you know about our company?
- Give me some reasons why we should hire you.
- What are your major strengths?
- What are your major weaknesses?
- What were your extracurricular activities in college?
- Were you an officer or leader of any organizations in college?
- Where do you see yourself in five years? Ten years?
- How would your friends describe you? Are they right?
- What is your greatest accomplishment to date? Why?
- What is your greatest failure to date? Why?
- Why do you think you would be a good salesperson?
- Try selling me something you see on my desk.
- What was your best subject in college? Why?
- What was your worst subject in college? Why?
- How much do you expect to earn your first year in sales with us?
- What would you like to tell me about yourself that isn't on your résumé?

such as individuals in certain age groups, people who smoke, and individuals with a particular sexual orientation.

Any questions asked of these protected categories of people must not have the effect of limiting job opportunities for them.[5] As shown in Table 14.2, many questions are illegal to ask a candidate in a job interview.[6]

Employers' concerns about women becoming pregnant and taking maternity leave or having to be absent from work to take care of a sick child make female applicants for sales jobs especially subject to illegal questions by interviewers. Some potential employers have been known to use sneaky means to obtain answers to illegal questions. For example, one sales manager admits that he usually takes female sales applicants out to a fine restaurant for dinner, then casually begins discussing his own family and how his responsibilities to them sometimes impinge on his work. In a relaxed atmosphere, this indirect approach usually causes people to open up and reveal protected information. Many women have lost job opportunities because they've talked too freely about the problems of raising children and having a career. Finally, some company interviewers will simply ask illegal questions that put women in a no-win situation. While you need not answer any question unrelated to job performance, refusing to answer the illegal inquiries may risk alienating the interviewer and cause you to lose the job for some contrived reason.

TABLE 14.2

## QUESTIONS INTERVIEWERS CANNOT LEGALLY ASK

| Subject | Illegal Questions |
|---|---|
| Age | How old are you? What is your birth date? When did you graduate from high school? |
| Appearance | How much do you weigh? How tall are you? What is your race or ethnic background? What is your gender? |
| Marital, Family, and Lifestyle | What is your marital status? Have you ever been divorced? Are you living with anyone? Do you plan to get married? What does your spouse do? Do you have any children? Do you plan to have children (or any more children)? Who will take care of your children while you work? What is your sexual orientation? What is your religion? |
| Medical | What is your medical history? Do you smoke? Do you have, or have you ever had, a drug problem? Do you have AIDS? Have you ever been treated by a psychologist or psychiatrist? Do you have a physical disability? How many days of work each year did you miss on your last job? |
| Military | What type of military discharge do you have? What branch of the military did you serve in? Did you receive an honorable discharge? |
| Home | Do you rent or own a home? Do you live in an apartment or a house? Do you have a mortgage? |
| National Origin | What is your native language? What is your place of birth? How did you acquire the ability to read, write, or speak a foreign language? |

Rationalizing that interviewers who ask unlawful questions don't deserve to be answered truthfully, some women simply lie. A divorced mother of two children, one of whom is severely handicapped, says, "Even though I'm a very reliable worker, I knew if I told the truth, I wouldn't get the job, and I needed this job badly. So I said I wasn't married—which was true—and I had no intention of having children—which is sort of true because certainly I don't plan to have any more children. I got the job. I figured that my kids were none of their business, so it didn't matter what I told them. Once I was hired, what could they do?"[7]

## Screening Tools and Tests

Selection tools and techniques frequently help spot poor candidates and identify highly qualified candidates. Most candidates, however, will fall between these extremes so the screening tools serve largely as supplements to managerial judgment in the selection process. Consultants, such as Boston-based McBer & Co. and Charles River Consulting, who study salespeople can usually predict who will fail at selling but cannot reliably predict which salesperson will do best. Nevertheless, you will probably be thoroughly analyzed, tested, and evaluated as a candidate for a sales job, especially by larger companies.

**Testing.** Various tests help companies increase the probability of selecting good salespeople, reduce sales force turnover, and increase sales productivity. Testing employees and job applicants had its heyday in the 1950s. Companies gathered information on prospective workers through psychological profiles, employment histories, criminal records and personal data, and tests. Use of tests in the selection of salespeople was widespread until the late 1960s. Shifting values in the 1960s and 1970s brought about the Federal Equal Employment Opportunity guidelines that restricted employers on testing unless it could be shown to be a scientifically valid selection tool and that it didn't discriminate against specific racial or social groups. After passage of the Civil Rights Act in 1964, preemployment testing of applicants dropped from about 80 percent of companies to only about 25 percent because of complaints that tests had been used to discriminate against minority groups.

Testing is not illegal if the questions and procedures are relevant to job performance. Small and medium-sized companies are less likely to use testing because they lack the specialized experts and employee numbers to substantiate the validity of their tests. Although most sales managers rely more heavily on the personal interview than any other tool in selecting new salespeople, you may be asked to take one or more of several basic types of tests: (1) intelligence, (2) knowledge, (3) vocational interest, (4) sales aptitude, (5) personality, (6) polygraph, (7) attitude and lifestyle, (8) drug use, and (9) presence of the AIDS virus.

***Intelligence Tests.*** Designed to measure the individual's ability to think and to be trained, intelligence tests include vocabulary, math, and logic questions. Scoring high on these tests still may not win you the job. Some companies have found that those who score above a certain level tend to become bored on the job, while those who score below a certain level have difficulty doing the job. Intelligence tests help sort out these people and thereby reduce costly salesperson turnover.

***Knowledge Tests.*** These tests attempt to gauge how much an applicant knows about a certain market, product, service, or sales technique. Results can indicate what type and level of initial training program may be necessary.

**Vocational Interest Test** Designed to measure how closely an applicant's interests match the interests of other people who have successfully performed a particular job.

***Vocational Interest Tests.*** **Vocational interest tests** attempt to measure how closely an applicant's interests match the interests of other people who have successfully performed the job. Interests are believed to be strong indicators of motivation, and a few firms have found positive relationships between interest test scores and selling success.

***Sales Aptitude Tests.*** These tests measure an individual's innate or acquired social skills and sales ability. Numerous sales aptitude tests are available, including *Diagnostic Sales Intelligence Tests, Empathy Test, General Sales Aptitude Section of Aptitude Tests for Occupations*, and *Sales Aptitude Checklist*. Applicants for some high-tech companies are required to take an *Informational Processing Aptitude Test* to determine if they have the ability to learn technical information.

***Personality Tests.*** There are many complex aspects of personality, including values, social adjustment, emotional stability, temperament, and personal behavior patterns. Personality tests try to measure the behavioral attributes believed important to success in selling, such as assertiveness, initiative, extroversion, and sensitivity to others. Several *Fortune* 500 companies use personality assessment programs to evaluate and make promotion decisions on current employees.

Yankee Cos., Inc., an oil and gas firm, claims to have significantly cut its high turnover rate by using a personality-assessment test. Test takers are asked to review a list of phrases and adjectives, such as "life of the party," "sympathetic," and "aggressive," and then answer two questions: "Which of these adjectives describes how you think you are expected to act by others?" and "Which of these adjectives describes who you really are?"[8]

Personality Dynamics, Inc. (PDI), a management consulting and testing firm, believes that personality has more to do with successful selling than other factors such as experience or training. PDI compares potential salespeople's answers on 179 questions like the following:

1. If the following activities paid the same compensation and carried equal status, which would you choose? (a) representing clients in court, (b) performing as a concert pianist, (c) commanding a ship, or (d) advising clients on electronic problems.

2. Among these statements, which best describes you? (a) I don't need to be the focus of attention at parties, (b) I have a better understanding of what politicians are up to than most of my associates, or (c) I don't delay making decisions that are unpleasant.[9]

Personality tests have shown their effectiveness in hiring top salespeople. For instance, the financial services industry found that people who scored in the extremely high ranges of emotional intensity, recognition motivation, and assertiveness scales of the *Comprehensive Personality Profile (CPP)* earned nearly three times as much in commissions as individuals scoring in the lowest ranges on these same scales.[10]

***Polygraph Tests.*** Sometimes called the lie-detector test, the polygraph measures blood pressure, heartbeat, respiration, and skin reaction in response to questions as indicators of personal honesty. Because of concern about its validity,[11] federal law now severely restricts the use of polygraph testing in hiring except for a few jobs that directly affect public safety or national security.

***Attitude and Lifestyle Tests.*** **Attitude and lifestyle tests** became quite popular in the early 1990s because of the emergence of drug abuse as a major problem in the workplace and legislation that restricted the use of polygraph tests. Their primary purpose is to assess honesty and spot drug abusers. Typical test questions may ask how often the applicant drinks alcoholic beverages or daydreams, or the applicant's opinions about drug use.

**Attitude and Lifestyle Tests** Seek to assess honesty and spot drug abusers. These tests first appeared in the late 1980s when drug abuse became a major problem in the workplace but legislation restricted the use of polygraph tests.

***Drug and AIDS Tests.***  The U.S. Chamber of Commerce estimates that drug and alcohol abuse among workers costs employers tens of billions of dollars each year in lost productivity, accidents, higher medical claims, increased absenteeism, and theft of company property to support drug habits. Today, more than 80 percent of major U.S. companies test current and prospective employees for illicit drug use. Employers are likely to require job seekers and present employees to submit samples of urine or blood for analysis. Workers are protected from surprise tests unless evidence indicates a problem or they hold high-risk jobs.

With companies afraid of wrongful discharge suits and liability for faulty products, drug tests and other types of testing are finding increasing use as a personnel management tool. More than one-third of companies surveyed have a targeted enforcement program with surveillance, search, and detection tactics to identify abusers and dealers. Estimates are that from 4 to 10 percent of employees in any company have a substance abuse problem serious enough to merit treatment.[12] Chevron Corporation carried out anonymous drug testing and found that about 30 percent of all job applicants and 20 percent of their employees tested positive for illegal drugs. Many large companies use urine tests to identify drug abusers among applicants or employees. As part of routine physical exams, some also check current employees and job applicants for diseases such as AIDS. Critics of drug testing argue that it violates constitutional protection against unreasonable search and seizure and invades an individual's privacy. Also, they express doubts about the accuracy of the tests because large error rates can cause innocent people to be classified as drug abusers. Drug tests can be administered only after the company makes a job offer contingent upon a negative test results.[13]

### Personal Interviews

Many recruits will successfully pass screening interviews and testing, but the most important and final hurdle in being hired is the in-depth personal interview. Table 14.3 shows some negative factors that frequently cause candidates for sales jobs to be rejected.

*A personal interview is the most popular technique for selecting salespeople.* Photo Disc

| TABLE 14.3 |
| --- |

## POSSIBLE REASONS FOR REJECTING SALES CANDIDATES

| | |
| --- | --- |
| • Poor appearance | • Evasiveness in answering questions |
| • Weak interpersonal skills | • Failure to ask questions |
| • Late for interview with no excuse | • Cynical attitude |
| • Poor application form or résumé | • Weak sense of humor |
| • Lack of goals or career plan | • Low moral standards |
| • Poor academic record | • Radical views |
| • No extracurricular activities | • Intolerance or prejudice |
| • Inability to express self clearly | • Evidence of wasted time |
| • Insufficient enthusiasm | • Poor personal hygiene |
| • Lack of confidence | • Laziness |
| • Unreasonable expectations | • Lack of ethics |
| • Immature | • Inability to accept criticism |
| • Tactlessness | • Dislike for schoolwork |
| • Discourteous | • Arrogant attitude |
| • Criticisms of past employers | • Unhappy marriage |
| • Lack of vitality | • Poor relationship with parents |
| • Limp handshake | • Socially inept |
| • Unhappy social life | • Overemphasis on money |
| • Narrow interests | • Poor body language |
| • Failure to ask questions about the job | • Failure to thank interviewers for their time |

## SELLING YOURSELF TO A PROSPECTIVE EMPLOYER

With your personal services as the product, you must convince prospective employers that they should buy your services over those of other potential candidates for the sales job. All the steps of the personal selling process apply: (1) prospecting for potential employers, (2) planning your approach, (3) approaching with your résumé and cover letter, (4) making your sales presentation and demonstrating your qualifications in a personal interview, (5) negotiating resistance or persuading the employer that you are the best candidate for the job, (6) attempting to close the sale by enthusiastically asking for the job, and (7) following up to thank the prospective employer for the interview and to reinforce a positive impression. In *each* of the stages of the personal selling process, you should be looking for feedback from the interviewer's body language and voice inflections or tone.

## Prospecting for an Employer

After learning all about what you have to sell (your knowledge, skills, abilities, interests, motivations, and goals) and identifying the type of job you think you'd like, you might begin your personal selling process by looking at the American Marketing Association's MarketingPower.com web site. At this site, you'll find recommended articles and books to help you in your career planning. Two recent book selections are *Careers in Marketing* by Linda Bearman, and *Powerful Planning Skills: Envisioning the Future and Making It Happen* by Career Press. Probably the most famous and most read job-hunting book is *What Color Is Your Parachute?*, which provides insightful advice about nearly every aspect of looking for a job and planning your career. It's revised virtually every year by its author, Richard H. Bolles, so it's always up to date. Go to JobHuntersBible.com to learn more about this exceptional book, which is available in most libraries.

Sources of information about prospective employers include their annual reports found in your college library and usually online, the annual *American Marketing Association* membership directory (company listings), telephone directories in cities where you'd like to live and work, and classified sections of the *Wall Street Journal* (http://online.wsj.com) or hundreds of city newspapers which you'll find at www.onlinenewspapers.com. Before contacting a particular company, first look at its annual report, which can be useful but overly sanguine. Then, find a more objective financial evaluation of the company. Two excellent sources of financial information about publicly traded companies are *Value Line* and *Standard and Poor's*. Both of these sources can be found online (www.valueline.com or www.standardandpoors.com), but some of the desired information may NOT be free, as it will be in your library. Don't hesitate to ask the business reference librarian if you need help. If you are researching only a few companies, you can obtain a list of articles on each from the *Business Periodicals Index* (BPI), which all college libraries have in hard copy and most make available to their students for free online. Again, check with your college's business reference librarian to find offline and online sources.

**College Placement Office.** At your college placement office, find out which companies will be interviewing on campus on what dates, then sign up for interviews with those companies that seem to best match your job skills and requirements. Usually, the college placement office has several books, pamphlets, or files that will give you leads on other prospective employers not interviewing on campus that term. Although campus interviews are convenient, competition can be stiff to obtain the interview time slots available with each company. Moreover, students seldom are offered a job without follow-up interviews with more senior managers at company headquarters. These headquarters interviews may take a full day or more and involve long-distance trips, so you will need to schedule your interviewing time carefully.

Job hunting can be expensive. Printing your résumé, typing cover letters, buying envelopes and stamps, making long-distance telephone calls, incurring travel expenses, and purchasing a new suit or two will require a sizable outlay of money. Although most companies eventually reimburse you for all expenses incurred on a company visit, they seldom pay in advance. Reimbursement can take several weeks, so you may encounter some cash-flow problems over the short run.

**Networking.** According to Forrester Research, about 40 percent of all successful job searches come from networking.[14] People you already know or will meet can help you find a good job. You can cultivate all kinds of people as part of your networks, including any or all of the following: family members, friends, relatives, coworkers, past employers, teachers and professors, fellow students, and service providers such as your family doctor, dentist, lawyer, realtor, or insurance agent. Give each of them a copy of your résumé, tell them the kind of job you're looking for, then periodically follow up to let them know you're still looking. Of course, you don't want to become a nuisance to them but most understand what you're going through and will want to help as much as they can.

When you receive referrals from your networking, use your source as an introduction to the potential employer. For example:

> Mr. Peterman, my name is Bruce Hopkins. Our mutual friend, Chuck Addison, suggested I call you about interviewing with your company for a sales job. First, let me convey Chuck's good wishes to you and your family. He said that you and he worked in the same sales office at IBM about ten years ago and that I should tell you that he's now nearly a scratch golfer. And, if you believe that, he's got a piece of swamp land he wants to sell you. But the reason for my call, Mr. Peterman, is that Chuck said you were a great guy and that you might be able to help me obtain an interview.

Just as in a sales call, it's always an advantage to have a referral because it turns a cold call into a warm call. Even if referrals don't have a job opportunity for you, ask if they might help you with another referral. Sometimes, you can keep going from referral to referral until you make the sale—that is, win the job.

You might even try some networking online by using a web site like the *National Association of Sales Professionals* (www.nasp.com) which includes a registry of member sales representatives—many of whom allow direct email access to them. Approaching any of these sales professionals (whom you've never met) via email will require diplomacy and sincerity—not a shotgun approach to looking for a job. Perhaps, you could ask some of them for advice about starting your sales career.

**Employment Agencies.** Although many employment agencies receive fees from employers for providing good job candidates, others charge job seekers (sometimes thousands of dollars or up to 20 percent of the first year's salary) for helping them find jobs. Make sure you fully understand the fee arrangement before signing up with an employment agency. Some employment agencies may not be worth your time or money because they use a programmed approach to helping you write your résumé and cover letter, and to prospect for potential employers. Potential employers have seen these "canned" formats and approaches so many times that your personal advertisement (your résumé and cover letter) will appear almost indistinguishable from others.

**The Hidden Job Market.** Up to 90 percent of available jobs may not be advertised nor reach employment agency files,[15] so creative resourcefulness often pays off in finding the best jobs in the **hidden job market.** Consider every reasonable source for leads. Sometimes your professors, deans, or college administrators can give you names and contact persons at companies looking for new graduates. Do not be reluctant to let other people know that you're looking for work. Classmates, friends, and business associates of your family may oftentimes be of help, if not directly, at least by serving as an extra pair of eyes and ears alert to job opportunities for you.

**Hidden Job Market**
About 90 percent of available jobs are never advertised nor reach employment agency files, so job applicants must use proactive and creative resourcefulness to compete for these jobs.

## Planning Your Approach

After identifying potential employers looking for people with your abilities and interests, you need to prepare a *résumé* (or personal advertisement) for yourself. An excellent source for help in preparing your résumé is MarketingPower.com, where you'll find American Marketing Association recommendations regarding articles (for example, *Components of a Winning Resume*, and *Ten Resume Mistakes*—both written by Peter Newfield) and books (for example, *The Adams Resume Almanac* by Bob Adams Publishers and *Resumes for Higher Paying Positions* by Cory J. Schulman). Of course, you can find scores of other articles on résumé preparation listed in the *Business Periodicals Index* and numerous books on résumés in your college library, your college bookstore, commercial bookstores, and city libraries. Find two or three that communicate in the style you prefer, then let them guide you in writing the first draft of your résumé.

**Preparing Your Résumé.** Your résumé should focus on your achievements to date, your educational background, your work experience, and your special abilities and interests. If you know what job you want (such as sales representative for a consumer products company), you may want to put your *job objective* near the top of your résumé. If you're unsure what job you want or want to send out the same résumé for several different jobs, then you can describe your job objective in your *cover letter.*

No one format is correct for your résumé. Three basic formats are widely used: (1) chronological, (2) functional, and (3) combined. Using the chronological approach, you would present your schooling, employment, achievements, and activities in order, starting with the most recent. The functional approach places primary emphasis on your accomplishments, skills, and strengths instead of your chronological history. Using the combined approach, you would stress your skills first, then follow with your employment history, which may not directly relate to the job for which you're applying.

No matter which résumé format you use, a little tasteful creativity can help differentiate your résumé from countless look-alike résumés (a la product differentiation in marketing). Most résumés of new college graduates are only one page long, but don't avoid going to a second page if you have something important to present. One student so blindly followed the one-page résumé rule that he left off having served as an army officer—a fact that is usually viewed highly positively by prospective employers, especially if one had leadership responsibilities or gained valuable work experience. To find ideas for preparing your résumé and posting it on the Internet, check out www.marketingingjobs.com and www.collegegrad.com.

**Track Record of Achievement.** Some students make the mistake of merely listing their job responsibilities with different employers without indicating what they accomplished on the job. When looking for a job, students must remember that employers are looking for a *track record of achievement,* and you must distinguish yourself from those who may have had the same assigned job responsibilities but performed poorly. If you made a positive contribution on a job, say so on your résumé—in quantitative terms if you can. Examples:

- reorganized office files to reduce staff searching time by nearly 20 percent
- named employee of the month
- received five-hundred-dollar reward for an innovative customer service suggestion
- increased sales in my territory by 10 percent
- received a 15 percent raise after three months on the job
- promoted to assistant store manager after four months

If your work experience is minimal, consider a "functional" résumé where you emphasize your special skills (for example, organizational, interpersonal, or leadership) and personal attributes (for example, resourcefulness, perseverance, and goal orientation). But be sure to give supporting evidence or examples of these skills and attributes whenever you can. An example of a succinct résumé is provided in Table 14.4 on p. 452.

**References.** Note that this résumé does not include the usual "References furnished upon request" at the bottom. All employers know this, and such obvious statements just take up valuable space on your résumé. When potential employers do ask for recommendations, you are probably close to being hired, so assist those who will write your letters of recommendation for you. You can obtain reference letters from current or former employers, professors, clergy, or any other established adult who can attest to your personal qualities, skills, and achievements. Before giving a potential employer the names of any references, make sure you have received their permission to list them as a reference for you. Today, references are often contacted by email or telephone; however, some companies still prefer to have two or three letters of recommendation for you in their files. To help busy people in writing a recommendation or serving as a reference for you, give each a copy of your résumé and cover letter, and provide answers for the basic questions that most employers will ask, such as the following:

- How long and under what circumstances have you known the candidate?
- In what percentile (25th, 50th, 75th, 95th, 99th) would you rank this candidate in terms of the following qualities: interpersonal skills, writing ability, speaking ability, listening ability, goal orientation, maturity,

TABLE 14.4

## SAMPLE RÉSUMÉ

### CATHERINE JAMES

4111 Sandy Drive
Ocean View, MD 21758
(301) 898-0001 Telephone
(301) 898-0000 Fax
semajc@hotmail.com

**Job Objective:** Salesperson for a high-tech company

**Education**

Earned B.A., with honors, in Marketing Management (June 2003). Dean's List last three semesters. Overall GPA = 3.4/4.0

**Activities and Honors**

Vice President, Beta Gamma Sigma (business administration honorary for top 10 percent of class); Treasurer, Phi Omega Chi Sorority; varsity women's basketball team, 2000–2003; advertising manager for student newspaper, *Coyote Howls.* Selected to Who's Who Among American College Students, 2002–2003.

**Work Experience**

*Summer 2002*—Telemarketing Sales Supervisor, Gibson Kitchens, Inc.

Supervised a telemarketing sales team of seven people contacting homeowners about remodeling their kitchens. Increased sales 25 percent over previous summer's record.

*Summer 2001*—Assistant Sales Representative, Reynolds Food Company.

Traveled with sales representative throughout northern Maryland territory. Set up displays, inventoried stocks, and restocked store shelves. Received cash bonus when sales in our territory were highest in the company during June–August.

*Summer 2000*—Field Salesperson, Carver Towels, Inc.

Sold $25,400 in bathroom and kitchen towels door-to-door in Baltimore, Maryland, area. Selected to "Carver Achiever Club" for meeting sales quota three straight months.

**Hobbies and Interests**

Golf, tennis, jogging, and reading biographies

energy level, adaptability, resourcefulness, willingness to cooperate with others, and integrity? *[Rating yourself will help your reference in case he or she doesn't interact enough with you to evaluate some of the qualities. You can explain that you thought that he or she would appreciate your own appraisal of your qualities.]*

- What do you see as the candidate's major strengths and abilities?
- In which areas do you think the candidate could use more development?
- What is your overall assessment of the candidate's likelihood to succeed as a business-to-business salesperson for our company?
- What other comments might you add that could help us in evaluating the qualifications and potential of this candidate?

*[Perhaps you can suggest something unique here that isn't normally asked in standardized recommendation forms. For example, you can provide an example of your dedication and "quick-study" abilities by explaining how you worked with Habitat For Humanity in Mexico one summer and learned conversational Spanish by studying the language in the evening and speaking it during the day.]*

**Electronic Résumés.** Many large companies now use computer software to receive, sort, store, and retrieve **electronic résumés** from job applicants so that they can later scan thousands of résumés in a matter of minutes to find the best candidates for a job opening. For instance, a company may need a woman who is fluent in English and Chinese, with an undergraduate chemical engineering degree, an M.B.A. degree in marketing management, and two or more years experience working in mainland China, to open up a new sales office there. Candidates who match these requirements can be found quickly in the company's database of résumés. Thus, it's important that your résumé include key words associated with your education, work experience, skills, achievements, personal qualities, and interests. Some web sites will ask you to select the key words for your qualifications and for the type of employment you're seeking. You can post your résumé for employers at most of the web sites listed near the beginning of this chapter. Before posting your résumé to any web site, go to MarketingPower.com and use some of the resources offered there, such as a *free* résumé evaluation.

Posting your résumé online can be a great job search advantage because it extends the life of your résumé before potential employers. Instead of being filed away or thrown away, résumés are now placed in large company data banks for two years or more of potential retrieval when a job opening becomes available. If you're interested in a particular company, go to their web site to see whether or not they have an online résumé submission process. Of course, many colleges and universities are now putting their graduating student's résumés online for potential employers to scan.

**Cover Letters.** Every time you send your résumé to a prospective employer, you should accompany it with a *cover letter* to induce employers to read your enclosed résumé. The typical cover letter is scanned by the addressee in only a few seconds, so you need to make your key points powerfully and succinctly—so that they almost jump out at the reader. In preparing your cover letter, keep some basic guidelines in mind, including the following:

- Address your letter to a specific person by name (not job title or position).
- Clearly identify the position you're applying for, where you found out about it (for example, which web site or publication), and why you are interested in that position.

**Electronic Résumés**
Many large companies now use computer software to receive, sort, store, and retrieve résumés from job applicants so that they can later scan thousands of résumés in a matter of minutes to find the best candidates for a job opening.

*Many companies receive, sort, store, and retrieve electronic résumés from job applicants.* Dex Images/Corbis

- Keep your focus on what you can do for the company, not what you want from the company.
- Look for a special tie-in (for example, you're a long time user of their products) that indicates that you are particularly interested in working for this company.
- Do not overuse self-centered words, such as: *I*, *me*, or *my*.
- Avoid starting too many sentences with *the*.
- Keep your language conversational, not overly stiff and formal.
- Include any follow-up action you plan to take—such as a telephone call or email—and when you'll be calling or emailing. *[Some students are uncomfortable about this, but gracious assertiveness is usually respected.]*
- Thank the addressee for considering you for the position and say that you look forward to hearing from him or her.
- Sign the letter with a medium point pen in black or blue ink.
- Fold your letter neatly, leaving about an inch border at the top, so it can easily be unfolded by the addressee.
- Make your letter less than a page long, print it on quality paper, and mail it in a quality business-size envelope.
- To cut down on competition, consider sending your résumé to fast-growing smaller companies (for example, the ones ranked and described at least annually in *Inc.* magazine) instead of the well-known giant companies to which students graduating from schools all over the world send their résumés.

Together, your cover letter and résumé are your direct mail selling piece and personal advertisement to win a job interview. Although you must not be dishonest or even hyperbolic about stating your accomplishments, you cannot afford to be modest either, because, on average, most potential employers scan résumés in twenty seconds or less. Your résumé must stand out in a positive way from the thousands of others that most companies receive each year. Some *Fortune* 500 companies receive thousands of résumés each week from job applicants, and most are discarded readily because they don't make a strong, positive impression. Creative formats, clever envelopes, or innovative enclosures have helped some job applicants' résumés be selected for further consideration. But, on the downside, résumé formats that are too bizarre usually merit only a laugh or two before they're discarded.

In writing your cover letter, keep in mind your goal of convincing the prospective employer to grant you an interview. Therefore, you must talk in terms of the employer's interests, not just your own. You are answering the question "Why should we hire you?" You may need to send a letter with your résumé enclosed to a hundred or more companies to obtain five to ten interviews, so do not be discouraged if you receive encouraging replies from only a few companies. You'll probably need only a few interviews and just one job offer to start your career.

Review some of the publications and sources mentioned under "prospecting" above and ask your business reference librarian to show you other sources where you can learn about the prospective employer so that you can

| TABLE 14.5 |
| --- |

### SAMPLE COVER LETTER

June 3, 2005

Catherine James
4111 Sandy Drive
Ocean View, MD 21758

Ms. Elizabeth Burton
Sales Manager
Sampson Office Furniture Company
Philadelphia, PA 19106

Dear Ms. Burton:

For nearly thirty years, my father has been buying Sampson chairs, desks, and filing cabinets for his law office. So I know firsthand what high quality products you sell. My career interest is in sales, and I would rather work for Sampson than any other company.

This June, I graduate from Northern Maryland State University with a B.A. in marketing management, and I would like to apply for a job as a sales representative with your company. After successfully working in sales during all three of my summer jobs, I have learned that my interests and abilities are well suited for professional selling. My college course electives (*Personal Selling, Sales Management, Public Speaking, Business Writing,* and *Public Relations*) have been carefully selected with my career objective in mind. My extracurricular activities in sports and campus organizations have also helped prepare me for working with a variety of people and competitive challenges.

Will you grant me an interview so that I can show you that I'm someone you should hire for your sales team? I'll call you next Monday afternoon to arrange an appointment at your convenience.

I look forward to meeting you.

Sincerely,

Catherine James

Enclosure: Résumé

tailor your cover letter. Remember, the employer is thinking in terms of his or her company needs, not yours. A sample cover letter is provided in Table 14.5.

## Making Your Approach

You can approach prospective employers by mail, telephone, or in person. A personal contact within the company who can arrange an interview for you will enable you to avoid competing head-on with the many other candidates looking for a job with the company.

Most students start their approach in the traditional way by mailing their résumé and cover letter to the company's recruiting department. Unless your résumé matches a particular need at that time, it will probably be filed away for possible future reference or simply discarded. Some students send their letter by express mail, mailgram, or address it to a key line executive, for example, Mr. Sanford Biers, Vice President of Marketing, with *personal* written on the envelope. They believe that bypassing the company's personnel office will increase the likelihood of their cover letter and résumé being read by someone with authority to hire. A senior executive may forward your résumé without comment to personnel where it might receive special attention because it came down from the top. Who knows, maybe you're the boss' niece? Some executives will like your chutzpah and tell personnel to schedule you for an interview, while others may resent your attempt to beat the system and reject you from consideration.

## Giving Your Sales Presentation and Demonstration

Your personal sales presentation will occur during the interview with the prospective employer's recruiting team. You'll want to make a positive impression on everyone you encounter in the company even while waiting in the lobby for an interview. Sometimes managers ask their receptionists and secretaries for their opinions of you. Your friendliness, courtesy, professional demeanor, personal habits, and even the magazines you choose to read while waiting can be positive or negative. It will not impress your potential employer if you read a popular magazine like *People* or *Sports Illustrated*. Better to be observed reading something more professional such as *Business Week*, *Fortune*, or the *Wall Street Journal*.

Even when a calamity happens, conduct yourself with class and good humor. One graduating student who was interviewing with a company spilled coffee on her light-colored suit during her first interview of the day. But she conducted herself with such aplomb throughout the rest of the day, even though her clothes were visibly stained, that the company hired her. Her ability to handle confidently and pleasantly such an awkward situation impressed all of the company executives with whom she interviewed.

During the interview, go beyond mere responses to the interviewer's questions. Ask some sensible questions of your own to indicate to the interviewer that you are alert, energetic, and sincerely interested in the job. The personal interview is your opportunity to persuade the prospective employer that you should be hired. To use a show business analogy, you will be on stage for only a short time (during the personal interview), so present an honest but positive image of yourself. You will find it easier to be alert and enthusiastic if you imagine that you are being interviewed on television. A little anxiety can be positive, but be careful to not let this television imaging make you too nervous to do your best. It's a good idea to anticipate and prepare general answers to questions frequently asked by interviewers, like those noted in Table 14.6.

Sometimes interviewers will ask you to *demonstrate* your communication abilities by asking you to write a timed essay about your life, or sell something (such as a desk stapler) to them. Others may deliberately ask you off-the-wall or hostile questions to see how you respond. Interviewers at one *Fortune* 500 company routinely ask candidates for sales jobs simple math questions, such as "What's 8 percent of eighty?", to see whether they can think under stress.

| TABLE 14.6 |
| --- |

## QUESTIONS FREQUENTLY ASKED IN POST-SCREENING INTERVIEWS

- Why do you want to work for our company?
- Tell me what you know about our company.
- Tell me about yourself, your strengths, weaknesses, and career goals.
- Is any member of your family a professional salesperson? If so, what do they sell?
- Why do you want to start your career in sales?
- In three minutes, persuade me that we should hire you.
- What extracurricular activities do you participate in at college?
- What leadership positions do you hold or have you held?
- What benefits have you derived from participation in extracurricular activities that will help you in your career?
- Where do you see yourself within our company in five years? In ten years? Twenty years?
- What is your ultimate career goal?
- What do you consider your greatest achievement to date?
- What is your biggest failure to date?
- What is your favorite subject in school? Why?
- Are you willing to travel and possibly relocate?
- How would your friends and associates describe you?
- How would you describe yourself?
- What do you like most about selling?
- What do you like least about selling?
- If we hire you, how soon could you start work?
- What is the minimum pay you would accept to work in our company?

Another favorite technique of some interviewers is to ask thought-provoking questions like, "If you could be any kind of fruit, what would it be and why?"

Microsoft Corporation is known for asking seemingly off-the-wall questions during interviews to observe a candidate's thinking process. For example: "How many piano tuners are there in Chicago? About how many manhole covers do you think there are in Manhattan? If I dropped a ten-pound bowling ball off the side of a ship in the deepest part of the Pacific Ocean, about how long would it take to hit bottom?" Interviewers aren't looking for a precise answer to these questions, and they certainly won't be impressed if you make some wild guess. Instead, they want you to walk through your problem-solving approach because this is what they are really interested in discovering about you, that is, how well do you analyze and solve problems? For example, with regard to how many piano tuners are in Chicago, you should first estimate (if you don't know) how many people live in Chicago, one of the three or four largest cities in the United States. Then, about how many households would this population probably represent? Next, approximately what percent of these households would have a piano that's played regularly . . . and about how often would these pianos be tuned? Now, you'd want to make an assumption as to how many pianos can be tuned by one skilled person in a normal working day. After gathering all the relevant facts, you can use simple math to produce a ballpark estimate of the number of piano tuners in Chicago. As a capstone, you might say, "Finally, I'd go to the phonebook and count how many piano tuners were listed." Just remember to keep calm and confident during any unorthodox interviewing approaches (even if the interviewer becomes hostile), and you will come off well.

On aptitude and psychological tests, many experts say that it isn't difficult to "cheat" if you are able to "play the role" and answer like the type of person that the company is looking to hire. The so-called safe approach in most personality and preference (interest) tests is to avoid extreme positions on anything not clearly associated with the job you're applying for. However, it is probably in your long-run best interests to be honest in your responses so that you create no unrealistic expectations that you cannot fulfill. It is just as important that you create a true impression and avoid beginning your sales career with a company that isn't right for you.

As a checklist for preparing for the interview, make sure you have done all of the below items:

- Find out the time and place of the interview and make sure you know how to get there. If driving, use one of the web sites that provides driving directions from one address to another at http://maps.lycos.com or www.mapquest.com.
- Learn the interviewer's name and how to properly pronounce it.
- Research the company before the interview.
- Have at least three good questions to ask during the interview.
- Make sure that you dress appropriately for the job for which you're interviewing.
- If you're going for a luncheon interview, do not order anything sloppy like spaghetti or soup that could spill on your clothes. If you're unsure about which fork to use first, wait until your host has picked up one of his or her utensils, then copy him or her.

### Dealing with Resistance and Objections

Sometimes interviewers will bluntly ask: "Why should we hire you?" This requires you to think in terms of the employer's needs and to present your major "selling points" or customer benefits. Other interviewers may bring up reasons why you are not the ideal candidate. For example, he or she may mention the following: (a) "We're really looking for someone with a little more experience;"; (b) We'd like someone with a more technical educational background"; or (c) "We need someone to start work within two weeks." These kinds of statements are similar to *objections* or requests for additional information. In other words, the interviewer is saying: "Convince me that I shouldn't rule you out for this reason."

To overcome such objections, you might respond to each along the following lines: (a) "I've had more than a year's experience working with two different companies during my cooperative education jobs, and I've worked part time with a third company all during college. I'm a fast learner and I've adapted well to each of the three companies. I believe that my working experience is equivalent to someone who has three or four years experience with the same company"; (b) "Although I didn't choose to earn a technical undergraduate degree, I've taken several technical courses in college, including basic engineering courses, chemistry, physics, and two years of math; so, I have a blend of technical and managerial education. I'm confident that I can quickly learn whatever is necessary technically to do the job"; (c) "Well, I do have one more term of school, so I couldn't start full-time work in two weeks, but perhaps we could work out an arrangement where I could work part time during the evenings or on weekends until I graduate."

Good salespeople do not allow an objection to block a sale. Providing reasonable solutions or alternative perspectives can often overcome employer resistance and objections or, at least, allow room for further negotiation toward a compromise solution.

## Confirming the Agreement or Receiving the Job Offer

Although it is not likely that a prospective employer will offer you a job right on the spot, you should nevertheless let the interviewer know that you definitely want the job and are confident that you will do excellent work for the employer. You'll need to use your best judgment as to whether or not to use other closing techniques such as the *summary close* or *standing-room-only* close. For example, with the summary close, you can summarize your strong points that match up with the company's needs to reinforce in the interviewer's mind that you are right for the job. The standing-room-only close (where you let the prospective employer know that you have other job offers and will need to make a decision within a limited time) may be appropriate when you sense that the employer is impressed with you and needs a little push to offer you the job now rather than interview more candidates. This puts the ball in the prospective employer's court to come up with a good offer quickly or risk losing you to another company.

## Following Up

Within a few days after any job interview, whether you want the job or not, business courtesy requires you to write thank-you letters to interviewers. In this letter, you can reinforce the positive impression you made in the interview and again express your strong interest in working for the company. If you don't hear back from the company about the job within a few weeks, it may be appropriate to write another letter expressing your continuing interest in the job and asking for a decision so that you can consider other options if necessary. As a possible reason for this follow-up letter, you might mention an additional personal achievement since the interview, more fully answer one of

TABLE 14.7

## CHECKLIST FOR FOLLOW-UP LETTERS

### After an Interview:

- Express your thanks for the interviewer's time and courteous treatment.
- Provide answers to any questions that you couldn't answer during the interview, for example, your exact college graduation date.
- Clarify any misconceptions.

### To Accept the Job:

- Confirm your acceptance of the job . . . even if previously done by telephone or in person.
- Restate your understanding of the employment agreement, for example, the day and time to start the job, the job title, salary, and other important aspects of the agreement.

### To Turn Down a Job Offer:

- Express thanks for the offer and indicate that you were impressed with the company and the people you met, including the interviewers.
- Graciously decline the offer and give an acceptable reason.
- Extend good wishes for the future to the company and its employees.

### When the Company Turns You Down for a Job:

- Never show that you're upset or angry.
- Politely express your regret that no job is currently available for you.
- Ask if you might be considered for future employment with the company.
- Ask for advice on how you can improve your qualifications to better fit the company's criteria for hiring new employers.

the interviewer's questions, or perhaps send a newspaper or magazine article of interest. A well-written, gracious follow-up letter gives you a chance to make a stronger impression on the interviewer while exhibiting several positive personal qualities such as initiative, written communication skills, sensitivity to others' feelings, and awareness of business protocol. A checklist for sending follow-up letters is provided in Table 14.7.

## YOUR EARLY SALES CAREER

Even though you want to choose a company that you will stay with throughout your working life, it is realistic to recognize that you will probably work for more than one company during your career. If you are not fully satisfied with your job or company during the first few years, remember that you are building experience and job knowledge that will increase your abilities and marketability for future job opportunities. Stay on top of the rapidly changing sales field by becoming a member of *Sales and Marketing Executives-International* where you can interact with other professionals across industries. If you don't do this, at least log on regularly to the S&MEI Executive Library at www.sell.org. It offers an almost endless amount of information, statistics, and news. And it includes a listing of schools where you can hone your skills.

Always keep a positive outlook and do the best you can in every job assignment and your chances for new opportunities will come. Do not be too discouraged by perceived mistakes that you may make in your career. Nearly every highly successful person has made and continues to make many mistakes. View these mistakes largely as *learning experiences,* and they will have less impact on your confidence. Believe that you can probably do whatever you make up your mind to do because it's true. Best wishes to you for a successful and satisfying sales career!

## SUMMARY

You can use your knowledge of the personal selling process to make that first big sale, that is, selling your personal services to an employer. With a college degree, you offer much to potential employers; so use your selling strategies and skills to make them aware of the benefits you offer to their company. Preparing an effective cover letter and résumé are major initial steps in selling your services. Use all the help available online and offline from books, articles, and associates to evaluate your cover letter and résumé and fine-tune them.

Either in your cover letter or résumé, identify the position or job you're seeking. Many potential employers receive hundreds, if not thousands, of résumés weekly; so you will lessen your chance of obtaining an interview if you leave it up to the potential employer to figure out what job your qualifications would fit best in their company. Instead, most will simply discard your résumé and go on to those that do indicate a job objective. When your résumé is at the quality level you want, it's a good idea to post it online where potential employers can find it. Because employers use key words for their job opening to match with key words identifying your qualifications, your selec-

tion of key words for your credentials and desired job are critical.

When you have successfully sold yourself via your cover letter and résumé, you will receive some invitations for job interviews. In preparation for these job interviews, make sure you have a basic sales presentation on why you want to work for the company and what benefits you're offering. Prepare and rehearse your general answers to the typical questions that interviewers ask, but also prepare for some of the seemingly off-the-wall questions they may ask to observe how you go about solving difficult problems.

Practice your interviewing strategy and tactics with a friend and ask for honest feedback about how to improve. Before, during, and after the job interview, make sure you are courteous and considerate in all interactions with gatekeepers (for example, guards, secretaries, administrative assistants) or anyone else you meet at the company, especially interviewers. Your behavior is always being closely observed when you are interviewing. For example, what you read and how you behaved while waiting in the reception area will likely be noticed by a secretary or security guard who may be asked later what he or she thought about you. Exhibit a gracious and friendly but professional demeanor even while waiting for your first interview. Although you're on stage throughout the interviewing process, try to stay relaxed and confident.

After the interview, gracious follow-ups in writing or by telephone, or both, will reinforce your desire for the job, allow you to add important information not covered in the interview, and show that you understand business etiquette. Few job applicants receive a job offer after every interview, but you will substantially improve your chances for success if you carefully follow each of the personal selling steps and use your sales skills. Good luck, we're pulling for you!

## KEY TERMS

Cooperative Education Programs

Sales Internship Programs

Cover Letter

Protected Groups

Vocational Interest Test

Attitude and Lifestyle Tests

Hidden Job Market

Electronic Résumés

## CHAPTER REVIEW QUESTIONS

1. List some of the major benefits of a sales career.

2. What are your basic career options after serving as a successful salesperson for a few years?

3. Name some online sources (web sites) of sales jobs.

4. What general qualities do companies usually look for in salespeople?

5. Give examples of ten questions that you might be asked in an interview for a sales job.

6. Give some examples of questions that interviewers cannot ask members of protected groups.

7. Describe several screening tools used by employers.

8. Job applicants are sometimes their own worse enemies. What are some possible reasons for rejecting job applicants?

9. Why are electronic résumés increasingly used to match up job seekers and employers?

10. What is the purpose of a cover letter? Provide some guidelines for preparing and sending a cover letter.

11. List some questions frequently asked by interviewers.

12. What are some typical objections interviewers give for not considering a job applicant for a job? How might you respond to each of those objections?

## TOPICS FOR THOUGHT AND CLASS DISCUSSION

1. If you post your résumé online, the web sites often ask you to provide key words that will help potential employers looking for people with your qualifications. Come up with five key words that best describe your qualifications for a sales job.

2. What key words often are required for the job you're seeking? Develop five key words that might best match your online résumé with a company and job.

3. How might you positively differentiate your cover letter and résumé from the thousands of others posted online or sent through the mail to prospective employers?

4. What activities would make you thoroughly prepared for a job interview at a company for which you'd like to sell?

5. Have you ever been turned down for a job? What reasons do you think explain why you were turned down?

6. Why do you think that most graduating college students from around the world tend to overlook sending their cover letters and résumés to smaller companies? What do you think are the advantages and disadvantages in working for a small company?

7. If you were hiring new college graduates to become salespeople for a company that you owned, what criteria would you use to select candidates?

8. What screening tools do you think would be most effective in selecting candidates for sales jobs?

## PROJECTS FOR PERSONAL GROWTH

1. Prepare three different cover letters to accompany your résumé and ask several of your friends and a professor to pick out the best one. Ask them why they chose that one.

2. Prepare your résumé using each of the three formats: chronological, functional, and combined. Which of the three formats do you think will be most effective in obtaining your desired job? Ask two professors to pick out the résumé format they consider best for you to (1) mail to prospective employers and to (2) post online.

Did they choose the same format for each? If not, ask them why they chose a different format for each channel.

3. Ask one of your friends to help you rehearse interviewing for a sales position. Tell your friend first to ask you challenging and even off-the-wall questions; then ask him or her to put you on the defensive or raise objections to hiring you. Analyze your performance with your friend to determine how you might have done better.

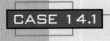

## DEVELOPING STRATEGIES TO OBTAIN A GOOD JOB

Aaron Shipley expects to earn his degree in marketing from the University of Florida about five months from now. Aaron has earned close to a B average during his last two years in college after earning mostly Cs during his freshman and sophomore years. His grades suffered somewhat during the first two years because Aaron tried out for the baseball team, and the sport demanded a lot of his time. Although he made the varsity team as a pitcher, he was hit by a broken bat and suffered a bad bone chip in his arm during the next to last game of his sophomore year. After several months of treatment, the doctor told Aaron that he should stop playing baseball for fear of doing permanent damage to his arm. Aaron was depressed for several months until he met Amata Ventura, a bright, pretty, personable woman who sat beside him in personal selling class during the first term of his junior year. After they dated for a few months, Aaron and Amata both felt that they had met the one they wanted to marry. With Amata supporting him, Aaron really began to focus on earning good grades. They both earned A's in the personal selling class, and Aaron thought it might be a good way to start his business career. Amata wanted to try advertising.

Now, although born and raised in New York City, Aaron wants a job near San Francisco after graduation because he fell in love with the city after visiting it on spring break two years ago. Amata, who lives in Miami, thinks it would be great to live in California, too. Only months away from graduation, Aaron is busy preparing his résumé and cover letter to send to prospective employers. Amata has already prepared her résumé and cover letter and taken two interviews with prospective employers.

Aaron is discussing his résumé with Amata over coffee at the local Starbucks and asks her advice.

**AARON:** Amata, do you think it would make sense for me to put some subtle hints that I'm African-American on my résumé?

**AMATA:** Sure, Aaron, I think it could help. A lot of companies still don't seem to have many African-American managers, and some even advertise that they're looking for minority candidates. Under activities on your résumé, you could include that you were vice president of the Campus African-American Club, and also mention your coordination of last year's Dr. Martin Luther King, Jr. Day activities.

**AARON:** Yeah, guess you're right. I'll make sure I add those items to my résumé. But, what about you? You're a member of a minority, too.

**AMATA:** I think it's pretty obvious that I'm Hispanic American by my last name, don't you. Even my first name, Amata, is Spanish. Of course, I'm a double minority because I'm also a woman, in case you haven't noticed.

**AARON:** Believe me, I've noticed.

**AMATA:** You know that stuff we learned in our personal selling class about our being members of protected groups? Well, in both of my interviews so far, I've been asked illegal questions. Right after shaking hands at my first interview, the interviewer said, "What a pretty name? What nationality is that?" That was okay, because I wanted her to know that I'm from Central America. But later, she asked me if I had a boyfriend and whether we planned to marry soon.

**AARON:** Well, what did you say?

**AMATA:** I told her the truth, Aaron, that I had a boyfriend and that we were planning to marry this summer.

(continued)

## DEVELOPING STRATEGIES TO OBTAIN A GOOD JOB (CONTINUED)

**AARON:** I'm not sure that was wise, Amata.

**AMATA:** Well, I didn't want to lie, especially if I might wind up taking a job at the company.

**AARON:** Have they gotten back to you yet?

**AMATA:** No, they haven't. It's been almost three weeks now, and I really wanted that job.

**AARON:** Amata, I'm afraid you lost that job opportunity when you told the interviewer that you and I were going to be married soon.

**AMATA:** I had no choice. If I told her that she was asking illegal questions, I'm sure that would have just upset her, and I would have lost the job anyway. Some protection I have. Interviewers can ask me anything they want, and I have no options in responding except to lie—and, you know that's not me, Aaron.

**AARON:** I know, Honey. That's one reason I love you so much. There's nothing dishonest or deceitful about you. But, frankly, if they ask me illegal questions in my interviews, I'm going to give them the answers that will help me get the job. Amata, what happens if an interviewer asks if I've ever been arrested? Do you think I'm going to tell them that I was arrested at sixteen for underage drinking and using a false I.D.? No way, that would probably kill my chances for the job. If interviewers are going to play the interviewing game illegally, then I have the right to be dishonest.

**AMATA:** Aaron, who wants a job that you have to lie to interviewers to get?

**AARON:** Well, I do, if it's in California! Once, I'm hired, then I can probably put in a few words to the right person to get you hired, too. Then, we'll be working together. Wouldn't that be great? Imagine driving in to work together each day.

**AMATA:** I don't know, Aaron. It's seems like that would be starting off on the wrong foot for a new job. They're going to find out that you lied later.

**AARON:** Yeah, but it'll be too late then. And they'll soon see that I'm a top performer, so they're going to be happy they hired me . . . and you. They'll be calling us the dynamic duo. Okay, let's not worry about it now, Amata. Let me buy you lunch at your favorite restaurant.

## Questions

1. What do you think about Amata's responses to the illegal questions about future marriage plans asked by the interviewer? Why would an interviewer ask such illegal questions? Do you think that many employers ask illegal questions during interviews? Will Amata's unwillingness to lie help or hurt her in securing a job? Why?

2. What do you think about Aaron's plans to give the interviewers the answers they want in order to win the job? Do you think giving false answers to questions during preemployment interviewers will hurt Aaron later after he's hired? Why?

3. What would you do if an interviewer at a company for which you wanted to work asked you an illegal question? What if the question was "Have you ever been arrested"—and you had an experience similar to Aaron's with the police?

4. What options does an interviewee have when an interviewer asks illegal questions?

5. Is it more difficult for women than men to be honest in an interview when illegal questions are asked? Why?

## CASE 14.2

# A TALE OF THREE "BROTHERS"

Frank Corbett will be graduating from a large state university within five months. Frank is a little apprehensive about leaving college where he has been having the time of his life. He joined a fraternity in his freshman year and has partied nearly every weekend over the past four years. On spring break this year, he and three of his fraternity brothers went to Mexico where he partied most days and nights for a week. In Frank's words, "Man, I'm going to be working for the rest of my life, so I'm going to live it up as much as I can now."

Frank is receiving a degree in marketing, but he isn't sure what career he wants to pursue. His grade point is 2.4 on a 4.0 scale, and he has no activities other than his fraternity where he was named Pledge Master last year. Frank feels little concern about finding his first full-time job, as he is supremely confident: "I have great interpersonal skills. If I get the interview, I'll get the job."

Each of the last three summers, Frank has worked as a lifeguard at a Lake Michigan beach where he's made a lot of friends. Being a lifeguard is a great job from Frank's perspective. "You sit in the sun all day, drink sodas, and watch pretty girls parade by in bathing suits—and, of course, flirt with as many as you can." During his three years as a lifeguard, Frank has received three awards for bravery and has been credited with saving four people from possible drowning.

One of Frank's buddies in the fraternity is R. C. Kline whose I.Q. is rated genius level. R. C. is one of those people for whom everything seems to come easy. He has a 3.8 GPA even though he doesn't study much at all. As R. C. says: "I'm good at playing the education game. You don't have to work hard if you're smart. For instance, I sign up for large classes where the professor can't take role so he doesn't know whether I'm there or not . . . and most times I'm not. I miss a lot of classes, but I always show up for the tests and usually score in the top 10 percent of the class. Nearly all the tests are curved, so an A is almost an automatic for

me." R. C. is also president of his fraternity, although he delegates most of the fraternity work to his vice president, Howard Pevear, who's dedicated and hardworking—and not a party animal like R. C. and Frank. Howard's dad was a member of the same fraternity thirty years ago. So Howard was accepted into the fraternity as a legacy even though some of the brothers thought he was a little nerdy while he was pledging. Howard has turned out to be an unpretentious, likeable guy, although not considered a "face man," that is, someone whom they want to introduce to potential pledges.

It's late on a Friday night, and Frank and R. C. are having a couple of brews at Casey's bar and talking about their future careers. Frank comments, "You know, R. C., I don't have much going for me other than my magnetic personality, good looks, fearlessness, and awesome conversational ability. Even though my grade point is low, I don't see myself having any problem getting a job because I'm going into sales and—as you know—I can talk anybody into doing anything. Getting people to buy will be a piece of cake. And I sure don't have any problem with rejection. Anybody who rejects what I'm selling is just stupid, as I've found in the dating game."

"Yeah, Frank, you and I are a couple of superstars. You in your way and I in my way. I'm a genius, pure and simple, so I can dazzle anybody with my brilliance. I love it when interviewers ask me off-the-wall questions. And I've got a great personality like you—although I'm better looking than you. Nothing can stop us. Any company that wouldn't offer us a job is not a company I'd want to work for. I'm going to take a few campus interviews, and I'll rough out a one-page résumé, but I'm not writing a cover letter, because I don't intend to do anything beyond the campus interviews. Any company that comes to campus to interview is looking for good people to hire . . . and I'm one of the best, so why should I sweat it?

(continued)

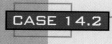

## A TALE OF THREE "BROTHERS" (CONTINUED)

I'll sign up to interview for the jobs and companies I'm most interested in. It's doesn't make sense interviewing with companies that aren't your top choices."

"You're right, R. C. If you've got a lot going for you like we have, why knock yourself out trying to get interviews? I'm with you. I'm going to sign up for campus interviews with *Fortune* 500 companies, then dazzle the interviewers with my personality. We'll have job offers before any of our classmates. Some of those grinds, like our buddy, Howard, are sweating blood worrying about finding a job. Howard is even tailoring his cover letter for each company and plans to send it along with one of three versions of his résumé to more than fifty companies—some of them I've never heard of. He told me that he found a list of fast-growing small companies in a recent issue of *Inc.* magazine. Howard has been researching a bunch of companies in the library and on the Internet, and he told me that he plans to post his résumé online at several employment web sites. Can you believe that Howard's job objective on his résumé is: 'salesperson for a high-tech company'? He's got about half the personality that you and I have, and he has to work his tail off just to pull down B grades. He couldn't make it in sales with his dull personality. We voted him in as vice president of the fraternity only because we knew that he would do most all the administrative work. Overall, I guess he's an okay guy, he just doesn't have any charisma. If you're going to succeed in sales, ya gotta have some charisma! Some guys have it . . . most don't!"

"Let's order another beer, R. C., then go back to the frat house to see what's going on there. Bet, we'll find ol' Howard practicing his interviewing techniques with someone. He's been preparing like there's only one job out there, and he's going to beat out everybody else to get it. Glad we're not so up tight."

### Questions

1. Which of the fraternity brothers—Frank, R. C., or Howard—do you think will be most successful in his job search? Why? Do you think Frank's personality, R. C.'s brilliance, or Howard's diligent work habits will be most impressive to interviewers for sales positions? Why?

2. Do you think Frank and R. C., who both pride themselves on their charisma, will project a positive attitude in their campus interviews with prospective employers? Why or why not?

3. What could upset Frank and R. C.'s plans to just interview on campus for a sales job? Do you think they're clever or naïve in their approach to finding employment? Why?

4. Based on what you've heard, which of the three fraternity brothers do you think will be most successful as a salesperson? Why? Which do you think will be most customer service oriented? Why?

5. Do you think Howard is over-preparing for his job search? Is rehearsing the job interview a good idea when you don't know what questions an interviewer might ask? Why?

6. If you were asked to give Frank, R. C., and Howard some advice in their job search, what would you tell each?

# NOTES

## Chapter 1

1 National Salesmen's Training Association, *The Art and Science of Selling*, vol. 1, *The Salesman* (Chicago: National Salesmen's Training Association, 1918), p. 45.

2 John T. Molloy, *Molloy's Live For Success* (New York: Bantam Books, 1983), 87.

3 Susan Greco, "The Art of Selling," *INC.* (June 1993): 72.

4 Rolph Anderson, "Personal Selling and Sales Management in the New Millennium," *Journal of Personal Selling and Sales Management* 16 (Fall 1996): 17–32.

5 See Gilbert A. Churchill, Neil M. Ford, Steven W. Hartley, and Orville C. Walker, "The Determinants of Salesperson Performance: A Meta-Analysis," *Journal of Marketing Research* 22 (May 1985): 117.

6 "Thriving On Order," *INC.* (December 1989): 49.

7 Thomas N. Ingram, Keun S. Lee, and George H. Lucas, "Commitment and Involvement: Assessing a Salesforce Typology," *Journal of Academy of Marketing Science* 19 (Summer 1991): 187–197.

8 Philip Kotler and Gary Armstrong, *Principles of Marketing* (Englewood Cliffs, N. J.: Prentice Hall, 2000), 14.

9 F. G. "Buck" Rodgers, *The IBM Way: Insights into the World's Most Successful Marketing Organization* (New York: Harper & Row, 1985).

10 Robert Saxe and Barton A. Weitz, "The SOCO Scale: A Measure of the Customer Orientation of Salespeople," *Journal of Marketing Research* 19 (August 1982): 343–351; Michael R. Williams and Jill S. Attaway, "Exploring Salespersons' Customer Orientation as a Mediator of Organizational Culture's Influence on Buyer–Seller Relationships," *Journal of Personal Selling and Sales Management* 16 (Fall 1996): 33–52.

11 Michael A. Humphreys and Michael R. Williams, "Exploring the Relative Effects of Salesperson Interpersonal Process Attributes and Technical Product Attributes on Customer Satisfaction," *Journal of Personal Selling and Sales Management* 16 (Summer 1996): 47–57.

12 Lawrence Crosby, Kenneth Evans, and Deborah Cowles, "Relationship Quality in Services Selling: An Interpersonal Influence Perspective," *Journal of Marketing* 54 (July 1990): 68–81.

13 Kotler, 2000.

14 William C. Moncrief, "Selling Activity and Sales Position Taxonomies for Industrial Salesforces," *Journal of Marketing Research* 23 (August 1986): 261–270.

15 Richard E. Plank and David A. Reid, "The Mediating Role of Sales Behaviors: An Alternative Perspective of Sales Performance and Effectiveness," *Journal of Personal Selling and Sales Management* 14 (Summer 1994): 43–56.

16 Frederick Reichheld and Earl Sasser, Jr., "Why Satisfied Customers Defect," *Harvard Business Review* (November-December 1995): 88; Frederick F. Reichheld, Robert G. Markey, Jr., and Christopher Hopton, "The Loyalty Effect—The Relationship Between Loyalty and Profits," *European Business Journal* (2000): 134–139.

17 James L. Heskett, Thomas O. Jones, Gary W. Loveman, W. Early Sasser, Jr., and Leonard A. Schlesinger, "Putting the Service-Profit Chain to Work," *Harvard Business Review* (March-April 1994):165–166; Rebecca Piirto Healt, "Loyalty for Sale: Everybody's Doing Frequency Marketing—But Only a Few Companies Are Doing It Well," *Marketing Tools* (July 1997): 65; Kenneth Carlton Cooper, "The Relational Enterprise," *Customer Relationship Management* (July 2002): 42–45.

18 Stephanie Bernardo, Elizabeth Meryman, Hanna Rubin, and Judith D. Schwartz, "Superstars of Selling," *Success!* (November 1984): 34–35.

19 Steven P. Brown and Robert A. Peterson, "The Effect of Effort on Sales Performance and Job Satisfaction," *Journal of Marketing* 58 (April 1994): 70–80; Steven P. Brown, William L. Cron, and John W. Slocum, "Effects of Trait Competitiveness and Perceived Intraorganizational Competition on Salesperson Goal Setting and Performance," *Journal of Marketing* 62 (October 1998): 88–98.

20 Sean Dwyer, Orlando Richard, and C. David Shepherd, "An Exploratory Study of Gender and Age Matching in the Salesperson Prospective Customer Dyad: Testing Similarity-Performance Predictions," *Journal of Personal Selling and Sales Management* 18 (Fall 1998): 55–69.

21 Leslie M. Fine and Sarah Fisher Gardial, "The Effects of Self-Monitoring and Similarity on Salesperson Inferential Processes," *Journal of Personal Selling and Sales Management* 10 (Fall 1990): 7–16.

22 F. B. Evans, "Selling as a Dyadic Relationship—A New Approach," *American Behavioral Scientist* 6 (May 1963): 76–79. Other studies supporting Evan's results include: M. S. Gadel, "Concentration by Salesmen on Congenial Prospects," *Journal of Marketing* 28 (April 1964): 64–66; Arch G. Woodside and J. W. Davenport, Jr., "The Effect of Salesman Similarity and Expertise on Consumer Purchasing Behavior," *Journal of Marketing Research* 11 (May 1974): 198–202; Edward A. Riordan et al., "The Unsold Prospect: Dyadic and Attitudinal Determinants," *Journal of Marketing Research* 14 (November 1977): 530–37; Lawrence A. Crosby, Kenneth R. Evans, and Deborah Cowles, "Relationship Quality in Services Selling: An Interpersonal Influence Perspective," *Journal of Marketing* 54 (July 1990): 68–81.

23 J. David Lichtenthal and Thomas Tellefsen, "Toward a Theory of Business Buyer–Seller Similarity," *Journal of Personal Selling and Sales Management* 21 (Winter 2001): 1–14.

24 Herbert M. Greenberg and Jeanne Greenberg, "Job Matching for Better Sales Performance," *Harvard Business Review* (September-October 1980): 128–133; Robert J. Zimmer and Paul S. Hugstad, "A Contingency Approach to Specializing Industrial Sales Force," *Journal of Personal Selling and Sales Management* 1 (Spring/Summer 1981): 27–35.

25 William A. Cron, Alan J. Dubinsky, and Ronald E. Michaels, "The Influence of Career Stages on Components of Salesperson Motivation," *Journal of Marketing* 52 (January 1988): 78–92.

26 Alan J. Dubinsky, Roy D. Howell, Thomas N. Ingram, and Danny N. Bellenger, "Salesforce Socialization," *Journal of Marketing* 50 (October 1986): 192–207.

## Chapter 2

1 Rolph E. Anderson, "Personal Selling and Sales Management in the New Millennium," *Journal of Personal Selling and Sales Management* 16 (Fall 1996): 17–32.

2 A classic examination of market globalization can be found in Theodore Levitt, "Globalization of Markets," *Harvard Business Review* (May-June 1983): 92–102.

3 For a discussion about training sales personnel to assume international sales positions, see Victoria D. Bush and Thomas N. Ingram, "Building and Assessing Cultural Diversity Skills: Implications for Sales Training," *Industrial Marketing Management* 30 (January 2001): 65+; Victoria D. Bush, Greg Rose, Faye Gilbert, and Thomas N. Ingram, "Managing Culturally Diverse Buyer–Seller Relationships: The Role of Intercultural Disposition and Adaptive Selling in Developing Intercultural Communication Competence," *Journal of the Academy of Marketing Science* 29 (Fall 2001): 391–404; Kenneth R.

Evans, Roberta Schultz, and David Good, "Intercultural Interaction Strategies and Relationship Selling in Industrial Markets," *Industrial Marketing Management* 28 (November 1999): 589–599.

4 L. Mark Rivers and Jack Dart, "The Acquisition and Use of Sales Force Automation by Mid-Sized Manufacturers," *Journal of Personal Selling and Sales Management* 19 (Spring 1999): 59–73.

5 Ned C. Hill and Michael J. Swenson, "The Impact of Electronic Data Interchange on the Sales Function," *Journal of Personal Selling and Sales Management* 14 (Summer 1994): 82.

6 *Sales & Marketing Management*, "How Technology is Changing Business Travel," (June 2001): 68.

7 Michael J. Swenson and Adilson Parrella, "Cellular Telephones and the National Sales Force," *Journal of Personal Selling and Sales Management* 12 (Fall 1992): 67–74.

8 SellingPower.com, *Incentives Newsletter,* September 27, 2001.

9 Ginger Trumfio, "For the Love of a Laptop," *Sales & Marketing Management*, Part 2 (March 1995): 32.

10 Data from *Computer World* web site, www.computerworld.com/home/Emmerce.nsf/All/stats/.

11 Peter Svensson, "Business Deals Are Pushing Beanie Baby Auctions Aside," *St. Louis Post-Dispatch*, November 24, 1999, C7.

12 George J. Avlonitis and Despina A. Karayanni, "The Impact of Internet Use on Business-to-Business Marketing," *Journal of Business Research* 29 (September 2000): 441–459.

13 Earl D. Honeycutt, Ashraf M. Attia, and Angela R. D'Auria, "Sales Certification Programs," *Journal of Personal Selling and Sales Management* 16 (Summer 1996): 60–65.

14 "Fools Gold?" *Sales and Marketing Management* (June 1998): 58–62.

15 Don Peppers, "Banking on Strong Customer Relationships," *Inside 1to1* (March 16, 2000): www.1to1.com/publications.

16 Rolph E. Anderson, Joseph F. Hair, and Alan J. Bush, *Professional Sales Management* (Houston: Dame Publications, 1999).

## Chapter 3

1 Bernard M. Bass, "Personal Selling and Transactional/Transformational Leadership," *Journal of Personal Selling and Sales Management* 17 (Summer 1997): 19–28.

2 Marvin A. Jolson and Thomas R. Wotruba, "Prospecting: A New Look at this Old Challenge," *Journal of Personal Selling and Sales Management* 12 (Fall 1992): 59–66.

3 Lee Iacocca with William Novak, *Iacocca: An Autobiography* (New York: Bantam Books, 1984), 39–40.

4 Reprinted with the permission of Simon & Schuster from *The Book of Virtues* by William J. Bennett. Copyright © 1993 by William J. Bennett.

5 For discussions of prospecting methods not included here, see Alan J. Dubinsky, "A Factor Analytic Study of the Personal Selling Process," *Journal of Personal Selling and Sales Management* 1 (Fall/Winter 1980–1981): 26–33; Sean Dwyer, John Hill, and Warren Martin, "An Empirical Investigation of Critical Success Factors in the Personal Selling Process for Homogenous Goods," *Journal of Personal Selling and Sales Management* 20 (Summer 2000): 151–159.

6 Marvin A. Jolson, "Prospecting by Telephone Prenotification: An Application of the Foot-in-the-Door Technique," *Journal of Personal Selling and Sales Management* 6 (August 1986): 39–42.

7 Tricia Campbell, "What's a Referral Worth to You?" *Sales & Marketing Management* (September 1997): 103.

8 Sarah Lorge, "The Best Way to Prospect," *Sales & Marketing Management* (January 1998): 80.

9 "Leads Are a Terrible Thing to Waste," *Sales & Marketing Management* (August 1997): 108.

10 Bradley S. O'Hara, "Evaluating the Effectiveness of Trade Shows: A Personal Selling Perspective," *Journal of Personal Selling and Sales Management* 13 (Summer 1993): 67–77.

11 "Generating Electronic Sales Leads," *Sales and Marketing Management* (August 1996): 93.

12 Sean Dwyer, John Hill, and Warren Martin, "An Empirical Investigation of Critical Success Factors in the Personal Selling Process for Homogenous Goods," *Journal of Personal Selling and Sales Management* 20 (Summer 2000): 151–159.

5 Douglas M. Lambert, Howard Marmorstein, and Arun Sharma, "The Accuracy of Salesperson's Perceptions of Their Customers: Conceptual Examination and Empirical Study," *Journal of Personal Selling and Sales Management* 10 (Winter 1990): 1–9.

6 Willem Verbeke and Richard P. Bagozzi, "Sales Call Anxiety: Exploring What It Means When Fear Rules a Sales Encounter," *Journal of Marketing* 64 (July 2000): 88–101.

7 Tony L. Henthorne, Michael S. LaTour, and Alvin J. Williams, "Initial Impressions in the Organizational Buyer-Seller Dyad: Sales Management Implications," *Journal of Personal Selling and Sales Management* 12 (Summer 1992): 57–66.

8 Alan J. Dubinsky, "A Factor Analytic Study of the Personal Selling Process," *Journal of Personal Selling and Sales Management* 1 (Fall/Winter 1980–1981): 26–33.

9 "If You Get Lemons, . . ." SellingPower.com, *Most Memorable Sale* (October 19, 2001).

10 Carolee Boyles, "3-D Show and Tell," Selling Power.com, *Sales Management Newsletter* (October 16, 2001).

11 Robert B. Cialdini, "Harnessing the Science of Persuasion," *Harvard Business Review* 79 (October 2001): 72–79.

12 Jennifer M. George, "Salesperson Mood at Work: Implications for Helping Customers," *Journal of Personal Selling and Sales Management* 18 (Summer 1998): 23–30.

13 Peter Schulman, "Applying Learned Optimism to Increase Sales Productivity," *Journal of Personal Selling and Sales Management* 19 (Winter 1999): 31–37.

14 Betsy Cummings, "Do Customers Hate Salespeople?" *Sales & Marketing Management* (June 2001): 50.

15 Maxwell Maltz, *Psycho-Cybernetics* (Englewood Cliffs, N.J.: Prentice Hall, 1960), 116.

16 Ibid.

## Chapter 4

1 Arun Sharma, "The Persuasive Effect of Salesperson Credibility: Conceptual and Empirical Examination," *Journal of Personal Selling and Sales Management* 10 (Fall 1990): 71–80.

2 Jon M. Hawes, Kenneth E. Mast, and John E. Swan, "Trust Earning Perceptions of Sellers and Buyers," *Journal of Personal Selling and Sales Management* 9 (Spring 1989): 1–8.

3 Lucette B. Comer and Tanya Drollinger, "Active Empathetic Listening and Selling Success: A Conceptual Framework," *Journal of Personal Selling and Sales Management* 19 (Winter 1999): 16–17.

4 Marvin A. Jolson, "Prospecting by Telephone Prenotification: An Application of the Foot-in-the-Door Technique," *Journal of Personal Selling and Sales Management* 6 (August 1986): 39–42.

## Chapter 5

1 For a discussion about how salespeople adapt their communication style to the buyer's style, see Morgan P. Miles, Danny R. Arnold, and Henry W. Nash, "Adaptive Communication: The Adaptation of the Seller's Interpersonal Style to the Stage of the Dyad's Relationship and the Buyer's Communication Style," *Journal of Personal Selling and Sales Management* 10 (Winter 1990): 21–27.

2 Michael A. Humphreys and Michael R. Williams, "Exploring the Relative Effects of Salesperson Interpersonal Process Attributes and Technical Product Attributes on Customer Satisfaction," *Journal of Personal Selling and Sales Management* 16 (Summer 1996): 47–57.

3 Anthony Alessandra, James Cathcart, and Phillip Wexler, *Selling by Objectives* (Englewood Cliffs, N.J.: Prentice-Hall, 1988), 206.

4 Lucette Comer and Tanya Drollinger, "Active Empathetic Listening and Selling Success: A Conceptual Framework," *Journal of Personal Selling and Sales Management* 19 (Winter 1999): 15–29.

5 For a description of the buying and selling tasks involved in making a sale to a buying team, see Dawn R. Deeter-Schmelz and Rosemary Ramsey, "A Conceptualization of the Functions and Roles of Formalized Selling and Buying Teams," *Journal of Personal Selling and Sales Management* 15 (Spring 1995): 47–60.

6 Betsy Cummings, "Do Customers Hate Salespeople?" *Sales & Marketing Management* (June 2001): 44–51.

7 Mark A. Moon and Gary M. Armstrong, "Selling Teams: A Conceptual Framework and Research Agenda," *Journal of Personal Selling and Sales Management* 14 (Winter 1994): 17–30.

8 Mark Moon and Susan Forquer Gupta, "Examining the Formation of Selling Centers: A Conceptual Framework," *Journal of Personal Selling and Sales Management* 17 (Spring 1997): 40.

9 Moon and Armstrong, 1994.

10 Barton Weitz, Harish Sujan, and Mita Sujan, "Knowledge, Motivation, and Adaptive Behavior: A Framework for Improving Selling Effectiveness," *Journal of Marketing* (October 1986): 174–191.

11 Jerry R. Goolsby, Rosemary L. Lagace, and Michael L. Boorom, "Psychological Adaptiveness and Sales Performance," *Journal of Personal Selling and Sales Management* 12 (Spring 1992): 51–66.

12 Stephen S. Porter and Lawrence W. Inks, "Cognitive Complexity and Salesperson Adaptability: An Exploratory Investigation," *Journal of Personal Selling and Sales Management* 20 (Winter 2000): 15–21.

13 Marvin A. Jolson, "Canned Adaptiveness: A New Direction for Modern Salesmanship," *Business Horizons* 32 (January-February 1989): 7–12.

14 Ed McMahon, *Ed McMahon's Superselling* (Englewood Cliffs, N.J.: Prentice-Hall, 1989), 22–26.

## Chapter 6

1 For an interesting perspective on how to develop creative partnerships, see, for example, two articles by David T. Wilson, "An Integrated Model of Buyer-Seller Relationships," *Journal of the Academy of Marketing Science* 23 (Fall 1995): 335–345; "Deep Relationships: The Case of the Vanishing Salesperson," *Journal of Personal Selling and Sales Management* 20 (Winter 2000): 53–61.

2 Joe F. Alexander, Patrick L. Schul, and Denny E. McCorkle, "An Assessment of Selected Relationships in a Model of the Industrial Marketing Negotiation Process," *Journal of Personal Selling and Sales Management* 14 (Summer 1994): 25–39.

3 Thomas Wood-Young, "Three's a Charm," SellingPower.com, *Sales Management Newsletter* (October 1, 2001).

4 Kenneth R. Evans, Robert E. Kleine, Timothy D. Landry, and Lawrence A. Crosby, "How First Impressions of a Customer Impact Effectiveness in an Initial Sales Encounter," *Journal of the Academy of Marketing Science* 28 (Fall 2000): 512–526.

5 Marvin A. Jolson, "Broadening the Scope of Relationship Selling," *Journal of Personal Selling and Sales Management* 17 (Fall 1997): 75–88.

6 Judy A. Wagner, Noreen M. Klein, and Janet E. Keith, "Selling Strategies: The Effects of Suggesting a Decision Structure to Novice and Expert Buyers," *Journal of the Academy of Marketing Science* 29 (Summer 2001): 289–306.

7 Julie T. Johnson, Hiram C. Barksdale, and James S. Boles, "The Strategic Role of the Salesperson in Reducing Customer Defection in Business Relationships," *Journal of Personal Selling and Sales Management* 21 (Spring 2001): 123–134.

8 Jolson 1997, 84.

9 Robert W. Haas, *Business Marketing*, 6th ed. (Cincinnati, Oh.: South-Western College Publishing), 1995.

## Chapter 7

1 Ed McMahon, *Ed McMahon's Superselling* (New York: Prentice Hall Press, 1989), 113–114.

2 For an interesting discussion about how salespeople view their failures, see Gordon J. Badovick, Farrand H. Hadaway, and Peter F. Kaminski, "Attributions and Emotions: The Effects on Salesperson Motivation after Successful vs. Unsuccessful Quota Performance," *Journal of Personal Selling and Sales Management* 12 (Summer 1992): 1–11.

3 Joseph P. Vaccaro, "Best Salespeople Know Their ABC's (Always Be Closing)," *Marketing News* (March 28, 1988): 10.

4 For an interesting and easy-to-understand discussion about persuasion's use in industry, see Robert B. Cialdini, "Harnessing the Science of Persuasion," *Harvard Business Review* 79 (October 2001): 72–79.

5 Alan J. Dubinsky, "A Factor Analytic Study of the Personal Selling Process," *Journal of Personal Selling and Sales Management* 1 (Fall/Winter 1980–81): 26–33.

6 Annie H. Liu and Mark P. Leach, "Developing Loyal Customers with a Value-Adding Sales Force: Examining Customer Satisfaction and the Perceived Credibility of Consultative Salespeople," *Journal of Personal Selling and Sales Management* 21 (Spring 2001): 147–156.

7 Sean Dwyer, John Hill, and Warren Martin, "An Empirical Investigation of Critical Success Factors in the Personal Selling Process for Homogeneous Goods," *Journal of Personal Selling and Sales Management* 20 (Summer 2000): 151–159.

8 Steven P. Brown, William L. Cron, and John W. Slocum, "Effects of Goal-Directed Emotions on Salesperson Volitions, Behavior, and Performance: A Longitudinal Study," *Journal of Marketing* 61 (January 1997): 39–50.

9 Hopkins, 1982.

10 Based on Tom Hopkins, *How to Master the Art of Selling* (New York: Warner Books, 1982), 87–93.

11 Michael J. Dorsch, Les Carlson, Mary Anne Raymond, and Robert Ranson, "Customer Equity Management and Strategic Choices for Sales Managers," *Journal of Personal Selling and Sales Management* 21 (Spring 2001): 157–166.

## Chapter 8

1 Leonard L. Berry, A. Parasuraman, and Valarie A. Zeithaml, "The Service-Quality Puzzle," *Business Horizons* (September-October 1988): 35–43.

2 Berry et al., 1988.

3 Berry et al., 1988.

4 Eric R. Blume, "Customer Service: Giving Companies the Competitive Edge," *Training & Development Journal* (September 1988): 25.

5 Dan Morse, "Hardware Distributor Sticks to Nuts-and-Bolts Strategy," *Wall Street Journal,* July 3, 2001, B2.

6 Christopher H. Lovelock, *Managing Services: Marketing, Operations, and Human Resources* (Englewood Cliffs, N.J.: Prentice-Hall, 1988), 263–264.

7 *Business Week* (March 12, 1990): 90–91; Joan C. Szabo, "Service + Survival," *Nation's Business* (March 1989): 16–21.

8 Valarie A. Zeithaml, Leonard L. Berry, and A. Parasuraman, "The Nature and Determinants of Customer Expectations of Service," *Journal of the Academy of Marketing Science* (Winter 1993): 1–12; Rolph E. Anderson, "Consumer Dissatisfaction: The Effect of Disconfirmed Expectations on Perceived Product Performance, *Journal of Marketing Research* (February 1973): 36–42.

9 Tom Peters, *Thriving On Chaos* (New York: Alfred A. Knopf, 1987), 103.

10 *Business Week* (July 3, 2000): 72.

11 Frederick Reichheld and Earl Sasser, Jr., "Why Satisfied Customers Defect," *Harvard Business Review* (November-December 1995): 88.

12 Weld F. Royal, "Cashing In On Companies," *Sales & Marketing Management* (May 1995): 88–89.

13 This section is adapted from Thomas O. Jones and W. Earl Sasser, "Why Satisfied Customers Defect," *Harvard Business Review* (November-December 1995): 88–99.

14 Alan J. Dubinsky, "A Factor Analytic Study of the Personal Selling Process," *Journal of Personal Selling and Sales Management* 1 (Fall/Winter 1980–1981): 26–33.

15 Poleretzky, Zoltan (1999), "The Call Center & E-Commerce Convergence," *Call Center Solutions*, 7, 17, (January): 76.

16 Dhruv Grewal and Arun Sharma, "The Effect of Salesforce Behavior on Customer Satisfaction: An Interactive Framework," *Journal of Personal Selling and Sales Management* 11 (Summer 1991): 13–23.

17 *Business Week* (March 12, 1990): 90–91.

18 *Business Week* (January 8, 1990): 33, 86.

19 Geoffrey Brewer, "The Customer Stops Here," *Sales & Marketing Management* (March 1998): 30–36.

20 Richard L. Oliver, "Whence Consumer Loyalty?," *Journal of Marketing* 63 (1999): 33–44.

21 Thomas O. Jones and W. Earl Sasser, Jr., "Why Satisfied Customers Defect," *Harvard Business Review* (November-December 1995): 88–99.

22 Eugene W. Anderson, Claes Fornell, and Donald R. Lehmann, "Customer Satisfaction, Marketing Share, and Profitability: Findings from Sweden," *Journal of Marketing* 58 (July 1994): 54; Michael D. Johnson and Claes Fornell, "A Framework for Comparing Customer Satisfaction Across Individuals and Product Categories," *Journal of Economic Psychology* 12 (1991): 267–286.

23 Srini Srinivasan, Rolph Anderson, and Kishore Ponnavolu, "Customer Loyalty in E-Commerce: An Exploration of Its Antecedents and Consequences," *Journal of Retailing* 78 (2002): 41–50; Rolph Anderson and Srini Srinivasan, "E-Satisfaction and E-Loyalty: A Contingency Framework," *Psychology and Marketing* (forthcoming); Rolph Anderson and Srini Srinivasan, "Customer Loyalty: A Meta-Analysis," Working Paper #101, Marketing Department, Drexel University.

## Chapter 9

1 Linda L. Price and Eric J. Arnould, "Commercial Friendships: Service Provider-Client Relationships in Context," *Journal of Marketing* 63 (October 1999): 38–56.

2 J. Brock Smith and Donald W. Barclay, "Selling Partner Relationships: The Role of Interdependence and Relative Influence," *Journal of Personal Selling and Sales Management* 19 (Fall 1999): 21–40.

3 J. Carlos Jarillo and Howard H. Stevenson, "Cooperative Strategies: The Payoffs and the Pitfalls," *Long Range Planning* (February 1991): 64–70.

4 F. Robert Finney, "Reciprocity: Gone But Not Forgotten," *Journal of Marketing* (January 1978): 54–59.

5 Robert W. Haas, *Business Marketing—A Managerial Approach*, 6th ed. (Cincinnati: South-Western College Publishing, 1995).

6 David T. Wilson, "Deep Relationships: The Case of the Vanishing Salesperson," *Journal of Personal Selling and Sales Management* 20 (Winter 2000): 53–61.

7 Hass, 1995.

8 Charles W. Lamb, Jr., Joseph F. Hair, Jr., and Carl McDaniel, *Marketing*, 6th ed. (Cincinnati, OH: South-Western, 2002), 186.

9 1997 Economic Census (Washington, D.C.: U.S. Census Bureau, January 21, 2000), 7–24.

10 Ibid., 424; Bureau of the Census, *Statistical Abstract of the United States* (Washington, D.C.: Government Printing Office, 2000), 543–544.

11 William O. Bearden, Thomas N. Ingram, and Raymond W. LaForge, *Marketing*, 3rd ed. (Boston: McGraw-Hill Irwin, 2001), 114.

12 Alan J. Dubinsky and Thomas N. Ingram, "A Classification of Industrial Buyers: Implications for Sales Training," *Journal of Personal Selling and Sales Management* 1 (Fall-Winter 1981–1982): 46–51.

13 Gene Brown, Unal O. Boya, Neil Humphreys, and Robert E. Widing, "Attributes and Behaviors of Salespeople Preferred by Buyers: High Socializing vs. Low Socializing Industrial Buyers," *Journal of Personal Selling and Sales Management* 13 (Winter 1993): 25–33.

14 John E. Swan, Cathy Goodwin, Michael A. Mayo, and Lynne D. Richardson, "Customer Identities: Customers as Commercial Friends, Customer Coworkers or Business Acquaintances," *Journal of Personal Selling and Sales Management* 21 (Winter 2001): 29–37.

15 Richard S. Jacobs, Kenneth R. Evans, Robert E. Kleine, and Timothy D. Landry, "Disclosure and Its Reciprocity as Predictors of Key Outcomes in an Initial Sales Encounter," *Journal of Personal Selling and Sales Management* 21(Winter 2001): 51–61.

## Chapter 10

1 Siew Meng Leong, Paul S. Busch, and Deborah Roedder John, "Knowledge Bases and Salesperson Effectiveness: A Script-Theoretic Analysis," *Journal of Marketing Research* 26 (May 1989): 164–178; Harish Sujan, Mita Sujan, and James R. Bettman, "Knowledge Structure Differences Between More Effective and Less Effective Salespeople," *Journal of Marketing Research* (February 1988): 81–86; Steven P. Schnaars, *Megamistakes: Forecasting and the Myth of Rapid Technological Change* (New York: Macmillan, 1989).

2 For a discussion of factors that might influence the effectiveness of a sales training program, see Alan J. Dubinsky, "Some Assumptions About the Effectiveness of Sales Training," *Journal of Personal Selling and Sales Management* 16 (Summer 1996): 67–76.

3 Robert F. Hartley, *Marketing Successes* (New York: Wiley, 1985).

4 Donald W. Jackson, Stephen S. Tax, and John W. Barnes, "Examining the Salesforce Culture: Managerial Applications and Research Propositions," *Journal of Personal Selling and Sales Management* 14 (Fall 1994): 1–14.

5 For an interesting perspective on how the sales force assists the firm in implementing its business strategy, see Madhubalan Viswanathan and Eric Olson, "The Implementation of Business Strategies: Implications for the Sales Function," *Journal of Personal Selling and Sales Management* 12 (Winter 1992): 45–58. Also, for further topics related to the role of the sales force in strategic issues, see an entire issue of *Journal of Personal Selling and Sales Management* 21 (Spring 2001).

6 Artur Baldauf, David Cravens, and Nigel Piercy, "Examining Business Strategy, Sales Management, and Salesperson Antecedents of Sales Organization Effectiveness," *Journal of Personal Selling and Sales Management* 21 (Spring 2001): 109–122.

7 Harish Sujan, Mita Sujan, and James R. Bettman, "Knowledge Structure Differences Between More Effective and Less Effective Salespeople," *Journal of Marketing Research* (February 1988): 81–86.

8 For an alternate approach to evaluating competition, see Alvin C. Burns, "Generating Marketing Strategy Priorities Based on Relative Competitive Positions," *Journal of Consumer Marketing* 3 (Fall 1986): 49–56.

9 "Survey of Buying Power," *Sales and Marketing Management* (Summer 2000).

10 Daniel C. Smith and Jan P. Owens, "Knowledge of Customers' Customers as a Basis of Sales Force Differentiation," *Journal of Personal Selling and Sales Management* 15 (Summer 1995): 1–15.

11 David T. Wilson, "An Integrated Model of Buyer-Seller Relationships," *Journal of the Academy of Marketing Science* 23 (Fall 1995): 335–345.

12 Alvin J. Williams and John Seminerio, "What Buyers Like from Salesmen," *Industrial Marketing Management* 14 (May 1985): 76.

## Chapter 11

1 Marion Harper, Jr., "Communications Is the Core of Marketing," *Printers' Ink* (June 1, 1962): 53.

2 Lucette B. Comer and Tanya Drollinger, "Active Empathetic Listening and Selling Success: A Conceptual Framework," *Journal of Personal Selling and Sales Management* 19 (Winter 1999): 16–17.

3 Comer and Drollinger (1999): 17–19.

4 Comer and Drollinger (1999): 18–19.

5 Camille P. Schuster and Jeffrey E. Davis, "Asking Questions: Some Characteristics of Successful Sales Encounters," *Journal of Personal Selling and Sales Management* (May 1986): 17.

6 John T. Molloy, *Live for Success* (New York: Perigord Press, 1981).

7 Wilbur Schramm, *The Process and Effects of Mass Communications* (Urbana: University of Illinois Press, 1954), 3.

8 Robert A. Peterson, Michael P. Cannito, and Stephen P. Brown, "An Exploratory Investigation of Voice Characteristics and Selling Effectiveness," *Journal of Personal Selling and Sales Management* 15 (Winter 1995): 1–15.

9 John Tsalikis, Oscar DeShields, and Michael LaTour, "The Role of Accent on the Credibility and Effectiveness of the Salesperson," *Journal of Personal Selling and Sales Management* 11 (Winter 1991): 31–41.

10 Patricia Knowles, Stephen Grove, and Kay Keck, "Signal Detection Theory and Sales Effectiveness," *Journal of Personal Selling and Sales Management* 14 (Spring 1994): 1–14.

11 Fred W. Morgan and Jeffrey J. Stoltman, "Adaptive Selling—Insights from Social Cognition," *Journal of Personal Selling and Sales Management* 10 (Fall 1990): 43–54.

12 Morgan P. Miles, Danny R. Arnold, and Henry W. Nash, "Adaptive Communication: The Adaptation of the Seller's Interpersonal Style to the Stage of the Dyad's Relationship and the Buyer's Communication Style," *Journal of Personal Selling and Sales Management* 10 (Winter 1990): 21–27.

13 See David W. Merrill and Roger H. Reid, *Personal Styles and Effective Performance, The Tracom Corporation* (Radnor, Penn.: Chilton, 1981); Paul Mok, *Communicating Styles Technology* (Dallas, Tex.: Training Associates Press, 1982); Larry Wilson, *Social Styles Sales Strategies* (Eden Prairie, Minn.: Wilson Learning Corporation, 1987); Anthony Alessandra, Phil Wexler, and Rick Barrera, *Non-Manipulative Selling* (Englewood Cliffs, N.J.: Prentice-Hall, 1987).

14 For more in-depth explanation of communication styles, see Anthony Alessandra, Phil Wexler, and Rick Barrera, *Non-Manipulative Selling* (Englewood Cliffs, N.J.: Prentice-Hall, 1987); J. Ingrasci, "How To Reach Buyers in Their Psychological Comfort Zones," *Industrial Marketing* (July 1981): 60–64; Anthony J. Alessandra and Phillip S. Wexler with Jerry D. DeenHugh, *Non-Manipulative Selling* (San Diego, CA: Courseware, 1979).

15 Stephen X. Doyle and George Thomas Roth, "The Use of Insight Coaching to Improve Relationship Selling," *Journal of Personal Selling and Sales Management* 12 (Winter 1992): 59–64.

## Chapter 12

1 For a discussion about different tools salespeople can use to manage themselves effectively, see Daniel Sauers, James Hunt, and Ken Bass, "Behavioral Self-Management as a Supplement to External Sales Force Controls," *Journal of Personal Selling and Sales Management* 10 (Summer 1990): 17–28.

2 "How Salespeople Spend Their Time," *Sales & Marketing Management* (January 1990): 39.

3 Paul Markovits, "Direct Selling Is Alive and Well," *Sales & Marketing Management* (August 1988): 76–79.

4 Robert F. Vizza and T. E. Chambers, *Time and Territorial Management for the Salesman* (New York: Sales Executives Club of New York, 1971), 97.

5 For a discussion about how sales executives and sales managers perceive quotas, see David J. Good and Robert W. Stone, "Attitudes and Applications of Quotas by Sales Executives and Sales Managers," *Journal of Personal Selling and Sales Management* 11 (Summer 1991): 57–60.

6 For an in-depth analysis of performance indicators sales managers use to evaluate their salespeople, see Donald W. Jackson, John L. Schlachter, and William G. Wolfe, "Examining the Bases Utilized for Evaluating Salespeople's Performance," *Journal of Personal Selling and Sales Management* 15 (Fall 1995): 57–66.

7 A discussion of salespeople's reactions to their achieving or not achieving their quota can be found in Gordon J. Badovick, Farrand J. Hadaway, and Peter F. Kaminski, "Attributions and Emotions: The Effects of Salesperson Motivation after Successful and Unsuccessful Quota Performance," *Journal of Personal Selling and Sales Management* 12 (Summer 1992): 1–12.

8 For an interesting perspective about rewarding sales personnel for generating a high level of customer satisfaction, see Arun Sharma, "Customer Satisfaction-Based Incentive Systems: Some Managerial and Salesperson Considerations," *Journal of Personal Selling and Sales Management* 17 (Spring 1997): 61–70.

9 For an examination of the impact of territory on salesperson performance, see Bruce Pilling, Naveen Donthu, and Steve Hanson, "Accounting for the Impact of Territory Characteristics on Sales Performance: Relative Efficiency as a Measure of Salesperson Performance," *Journal of Personal Selling and Sales Management* 19 (Spring 1999): 35–45.

10 Emin Babakus, David W. Cravens, Mark Johnston, and William C. Moncrief, "Examining the Role of Organizational Variables in the Salesperson Job Satisfaction Model," *Journal of Personal Selling and Sales Management* 16 (Spring 1996): 33–46.

11 For an interesting discussion about sales territory alignment and realignment, see Andris A. Zoltners and Sally E. Lorimar, "Sales Territory Alignment: An Overlooked Productivity Tool," *Journal of Personal Selling and Sales Management* 20 (Summer 2000): 139–150.

12 Raymond W. LaForge, Clifford E. Young, and B. Curtis Hamm, "Increasing Sales Productivity Through Improved Sales Call Allocation Strategies," *Journal of Personal Selling and Sales Management* 3 (November 1983): 53–59.

13 Alan J. Dubinsky, "Customer Portfolio Analysis," in *Advances in Business Marketing,* ed. Arch G. Woodside (Greenwich, Conn.: JAI Press, 1986), 113–139.

14 Andy Cohen, "Process," *Sales & Marketing Management* (September 1998): 71–78.

15 For a review of various routing models, see Wade Ferguson, "A New Method for Routing Salespersons," *Industrial Marketing Management* (April 1980): 171–178.

16 Ibid.

17 For alternative suggestions about how to work smarter rather than harder, see Harish Sujan, "Smarter Versus

Harder: An Exploratory Attributional Analysis of Salespeople's Motivation," *Journal of Marketing Research* 23 (February 1986): 41–49; Harish Sujan, Barton A. Weitz, and Mita Sujan, "Increasing Sales Productivity by Getting Salespeople to Work Smarter," *Journal of Personal Selling and Sales Management*, 10 (August 1990): 9–19.

18 Thomas J. Quirk, "The Art of Time Management," *Training* (January 1989): 59–61.

## Chapter 13

1 Clarke L. Caywood and Gene R. Laczniak, "Ethics and Personal Selling: *Death of a Salesman* as an Ethical Primer," *Journal of Personal Selling and Sales Management* 5 (August 1986): 81–88.

2 "Firms Making Ethics a Part of Corporate Life," *Mobile Register* (April 16, 1995): 6F.

3 Carl McDaniel and Robert Gates, *Contemporary Marketing Research*, 2nd ed. (Cincinnati, Oh.: South-Western, 1993): 223–226.

4 Michele Marchetti, "Whatever It Takes," *Sales & Marketing Management* (December 1997): 29–38.

5 J. Brock Smith and Donald W. Barclay, "The Effects of Organizational Differences and Trust on the Effectiveness of Selling Partner Relationships," *Journal of Marketing* 61 (January 1997): 3–21.

6 Thomas R. Wotruba, "A Comprehensive Framework for the Analysis of Ethical Behavior, with a Focus on Sales Organizations," *Journal of Personal Selling and Sales Management* 10 (Spring 1990): 30.

7 Joseph A. Bellizzi and Ronald W. Hasty, "The Effects of a Stated Organizational Policy on Inconsistent Disciplinary Action Based on Salesperson Gender and Weight," *Journal of Personal Selling and Sales Management* 21 (Summer 2001): 199–206; Shelby D. Hunt and Arturo Z. Vasquez-Parraga, "Organizational Consequences, Marketing Ethics, and Salesforce Supervision," *Journal of Marketing Research* 30 (February 1993): 78–90.

8 G. A. Churchill, N. M. Ford, and O. C. Walker, *Sales Force Management* (Chicago: Irwin, 1997), 63.

9 Alan Dubinsky, Marvin Jolson, Ronald Michaels, Masaaki Kotabe, and Chae Un Lim, "Ethical Perceptions of Field Sales Personnel: An Empirical Assessment," *Journal of Personal Selling and Sales Management* 12 (Fall 1992): 9–21.

10 For additional perspectives, see Frederick Trawick, John Swan, and David Rink, "Industrial Buyer Evaluation of the Ethics of Salespersons' Gift-Giving, Value of the Gift, and Customer vs. Prospect Status," *Journal of Personal Selling and Sales Management* 9 (Summer 1989): 31–37.

11 Jeff Gammage and Karl Stark, "Under the Influence," *Inquirer Magazine* (March 10, 2002): 10.

12 Betsy Cummings, "Do Customers Hate Salespeople?" *Sales & Marketing Management* (June 2001): 44–51.

13 Edward C. Baig, "Progress in Online Privacy, But Critics Say Not Enough," *Business Week Online*, www.business-week.com (May 13, 1999).

14 Nick Wingfield, "A Marketer's Dream: The Internet Promises to Give Companies a Wealth of Invaluable Data About Their Customers. So Why Hasn't It?" *Wall Street Journal*, interactive.wsj.com (December 7, 1998).

15 Dubinsky et al., 1992.

16 Ajay K. Kohli and Bernard J. Jaworski, "The Influence of Coworker Feedback on Salespeople," *Journal of Marketing* 58 (October 1994): 82–94.

17 "Discrimination Because of Sex Under Title VII of the Civil Rights Act of 1964 as Amended: Adoption of Final Interpretive Guidelines," U.S. Equal Employment Opportunity Commission Part 1604, *Federal Register* (November 10, 1980).

18 Sexual harassment does not occur solely between employees in the same organization; it also occurs between buyers and sellers. See Leslie M. Fine, C. David Shepherd, and Susan L. Josephs, "Insights into Sexual Harassment of Salespeople by Customers: The Role of Gender and Customer Power," *Journal of Personal Selling and Sales Management* 19 (Spring 1999): 19–34.

19 Betsy Cummings, "An Affair," *Sales & Marketing Management* (August 2001): 50–57.

20 For more insights on sexual harassment issues, see Cathy Owens Swift and Russell L. Kent, "Selling and Sales Management in Action—Sexual Harassment: Ramifications for Sales Managers," *Journal of Personal Selling and Sales Management* 14 (Winter 1994): 77–87; Leslie M. Fine, C. David Shepherd, and Susan L. Josephs, "Sexual Harassment in the Sales Force: The Customer is NOT Always Right," *Journal of Personal Selling and Sales Management* 14 (Fall 1994): 15–30.

21 Banning K. Lary, "Why Corporations Can't Lock the Rascals Out," *Management Review* (October 1989): 51–54.

22 Ken Grant, David Cravens, George Low, and William Moncrief, "The Role of Satisfaction with Territory Design on the Motivation, Attitudes, and Work Outcomes of Salespeople," *Journal of the Academy of Marketing Science* 29 (Spring 2001): 165–178.

23 Thomas E. DeCarlo and Thomas W. Leigh, "Impact of Salesperson Attraction on Sales Managers' Attributions and Feedback," *Journal of Marketing* 60 (April 1996): 47–66.

24 Lucette B. Comer, J. A. F. Nicholls, and Leslie J. Vermillion, "Diversity in the Sales Force: Problems and Challenges," *Journal of Personal Selling and Sales Management* 18 (Fall 1998): 1–20.

25 For other perspectives on ethical and moral judgments by salespeople, see Lawrence B. Chonko, John F. Tanner, Jr., and William A. Weeks, "Ethics in Salesperson Decision Making: A Synthesis of Research Approaches and an Extension of the Scenario Method," *Journal of Personal Selling and Sales Management* (Winter 1996):

35–52; and Richard Tansey, Gene Grown, Michael Hyman, and Lyndon Dawson, Jr., "Personal Moral Philosophies and the Moral Judgment of Salespeople," *Journal of Personal Selling and Sales Management* (Winter 1994): 59–76.

26 Alan R. Andreasen, "Revisiting the Disadvantages: Old Lesson and New Problems," *Journal of Public Policy and Marketing* (Fall 1993): 270–275; Judith Bell and Bonnie Maria Burline, "In Urban Areas: Many More Still Pay More for Food," *Journal of Public Policy and Marketing* (Fall 1993): 268–270.

27 *The Economist* (April 22, 2000): 67.

28 Dubinsky et al., 1992.

29 "Executives Are Surveyed on Bribery," *Wall Street Journal,* May 15, 2002, A12.

**Chapter 14**

1 For an examination of hiring practices of key account executives, see Thomas R. Wotruba and Stephen B. Castleberry, "Job Analysis and Hiring Practices for National Account Marketing Positions," *Journal of Personal Selling and Sales Management* 13 (Summer 1993): 49–66.

2 Some reasons for and results of hiring and promoting individuals in selling and sales management can be found in Shankar Ganesan, Barton Weitz, and George John, "Hiring and Promotion Policies in Sales Force Management: Some Antecedents and Consequences," *Journal of Personal Selling and Sales Management* 13 (Spring 1993): 15–26.

3 For an interesting discussion about where firms might obtain their most profitable salespersons, see Rene Y. Darmon, "Where Do the Best Sales Force Profit Producers Come From?" *Journal of Personal Selling and Sales Management* 13 (Summer 1993): 17–30.

4 For more insights, see Timothy J. Trow, "The Secret to a Good Hire: Profiling," *Sales & Marketing Management* (May 1990): 44–55.

5 Theresa Donahue Egler and Jennifer G. Velez, "Your Hiring Practices Could Put You to the Test," *HR Magazine* (March 1997): 126; Laura M. Litvan, "Thorny Issues in Hiring," *Nation's Business* (April 1996): 34; and Julia Lawlor, "Highly Classified," *Sales & Marketing Management* (March 1995): 76–85.

6 For an examination of discrimination in sales force recruitment, see C. David Shepherd and James C. Heartfield, "Discrimination Issues in the Selection of Salespeople: A Review and Managerial Suggestions," *Journal of Personal Selling and Sales Management* 11 (Fall 1991): 67–77; Lucette B. Comer, J. A. F. Nichols, and Leslie J. Vermillion, "Diversity in the Sales Force: Problems and Challenges," *Journal of Personal Selling and Sales Management* 18 (Fall 1998): 1–20; Greg W. Marshall, Miriam B. Stamps, and Jesse N. Moore, "Preinterview Biases: The Impact of Race, Physical Attractiveness, and Sales Job Type on Preinterview Impressions of Sales Job Applicants," *Journal of Personal Selling and Sales Management* 18 (Fall 1998): 21–38; Eli Jones, Jesse Moore, Andrea Stanaland, and Rosiland Wyatt, "Salesperson Race and Gender and the Access and Legitimacy Paradigm: Does Difference Make a Difference?" *Journal of Personal Selling and Sales Management* 18 (Fall 1998): 71–89.

7 Arthur Eliot Berkeley, "Job Interviewers' Dirty Little Secret," *Wall Street Journal,* March 20, 1989, A14.

8 "Can You Pass the Job Test?" *Newsweek* (May 5, 1986): 46–53.

9 Richard Nelson, "Maybe It's Time to Take Another Look at Tests as a Sales Selection Tool?" *Journal of Personal Selling and Sales Management* 7 (August 1987): 33–38; Sara Delano, "Improving the Odds for Hiring Success," *Inc.* (June 1983).

10 Larry L. Craft, "The Career Life Insurance Agent," *Research Brief 96-1,* CraftSystems, Inc. (September 1996).

11 Kenneth A. Kovach, "The Truth About Employers' Use of Lie Detectors," *Business and Society Review* (Spring 1995): 65–69.

12 "Firms Debate Hard Line on Alcoholics," *Wall Street Journal,* April 13, 1989, B1.

13 Michael P. Cronin, "This is a Test," *Inc. Online* (August 1993): 64.

14 Joan Raymond, "The Jaws of Victory," *Newsweek* (March 18, 2002): 38P.

15 Tom Jackson and Davidyne Mayless, *The Hidden Job Market* (New York: Quadrangle Books, New York Times Book Company, 1976), 95–122.

# GLOSSARY

**Active Empathetic Listening (AEL)**—Highest level of listening when the salesperson receives verbal and nonverbal messages, processes them cognitively, responds to them verbally and nonverbally, and attempts to assess their underlying meaning intuitively by putting self in the customer's place throughout. (11)

**Active Listening**—Occurs when the salesperson receives a message, processes it, and then responds to it to encourage further communication. (11)

**Adaptive Selling**—Modifying each sales presentation and demonstration to accommodate each individual prospect. (5)

**Approach**—The first face-to-face contact with the prospect. (4)

**Ask For Help Close**—Even after the sale seems lost, the salesperson asks the prospect what could have been done to make the sale. Oftentimes, the prospect will give a previously undisclosed reason or objection, which the salesperson can then answer and secure another chance to close the sale. (7)

**Assertiveness**—The degree to which a person attempts to control or dominate situations and direct the thoughts of other people. (11)

**Attitude and Lifestyle Tests**—Seek to assess honesty and spot drug abusers. These tests first appeared in the late 1980s when drug abuse became a major problem in the workplace and legislation restricted the use of polygraph tests. (14)

**Augmented Product**—Complete bundle of benefits offered by a product, including its core function, various enhancing characteristics, and supplemental benefits and services. (1)

**Boomerang Close**—Turning a prospect's objection or point of resistance around so that it becomes a reason for buying. (7)

**Business Defamation**—Any action or utterance that slanders, libels, or disparages the product of a competitor, causing the competitor financial damage, lost customers, unemployment, or lost sales. (13)

**Business Libel**—Unfair and untrue statements made about a competitor in *writing* (usually a letter, sales literature, advertisement, or company brochure) that damage the competitor's reputation or the personal reputation of an individual in that business. (13)

**Business Periodicals Index**—A cumulative subject index listing business articles from more than 160 periodicals. (10)

**Business Slander**—Unfair and untrue *oral* statements made about competitors that damage the reputation of the competitor or the personal reputation of an individual in that business. (13)

**Buying Center**—In a buying organization, a group of organization members who participate in the purchase decision. (9)

**Canned (or Programmed) Selling**—Any highly structured or patterned selling approach. (5)

**Centers of Influence**—Individuals or groups of people whose opinions, professional activities, and lifestyles are respected among people in the salesperson's target markets. (3)

**Close**—The stage in the selling process where the salesperson tries to obtain the prospect's agreement to purchase the product. (7)

**Cold Calling**—Approaching or calling a business without an appointment for the purpose of prospecting or selling. (3, 4)

**Collusion**—An illegal arrangement in which competing sellers agree to set prices, divide up markets or territories, or act to the detriment of a third competitor. (13)

**Communication**—A process in which information and understanding are conveyed in exchanges between two or more people. (11)

**Communication Style**—The way a person sends and receives messages in communicating with other people. (11)

**Concentration Principle**—Most sales, costs, and profits come from a relatively small proportion of customers and products; also known as the "80-20" rule. (12)

**Cooperative Education Programs**—Students combine their college studies with paid work in their career field of interest during two six-month co-op cycles with one or more of several thousand participating companies. Students often pay for their own college education with money earned in these co-op jobs. Three universities—Drexel, Northeastern, and Cincinnati—are best known for their cooperative education programs. (14)

**Core Selling Team**—Members of the selling firm assigned to a particular customer to develop and maintain the customer relationship. The team tends to stay together for the duration of the buyer-seller relationship. (5)

**Cover Letter**—Letter that accompanies a résumé and is designed to induce employers to read the enclosed résumé. Oftentimes used by college students and others to identify the position they're applying for if they prefer to not put a job objective on their résumé. (14)

**Customer-Benefit Approach**—An approach whereby the salesperson offers the prospect a specific benefit that can be realized from using the salesperson's product. (4)

**Customer-Oriented Selling**—Salespeople focus on identifying customers' needs and engaging in selling and servicing behaviors that help build and maintain a high level of customer satisfaction in the long run. (1)

**Customer Service**—A concept that has five basic dimensions: reliability, tangibility, responsiveness, assurance, and empathy. (8)

**Customer Service Segmentation**—A strategy for grouping customers with similar service expectations into service segments and then developing a service plan for each segment. (8)

**Data Mining**—Using statistical analyses, such as decision trees, cluster analysis, and regression analysis, to detect relevant patterns between and among variables in a database. (2)

**Data Warehouse**—Corporate-wide database built from information systems already in place in the company. (2)

**Database Marketing**—Use of computers to analyze prospect and customer profiles and purchase patterns to better identify and serve target markets. (2)

**Derived Demand**—Demand created as a result of consumer demand; typical of industrial markets. (9)

**Dichotomous Question**—A question used to set up a clear-cut "either-or" answer for prospects and customers. (11)

**Direct Marketing**—Selling alternatives that bypass or partially substitute for field salespeople, including *direct mail, telemarketing, teleselling, computer salespeople, facsimile,* and *electronic mail.* (2)

**Door-to-Door Canvassing**—Knocking on doors in a commercial area without an appointment to locate prospects. (3)

**Dual Management**—A management system in which both professional managers and specialists without managerial training run an organization, sometimes resulting in conflict. Typical of many nonprofit organizations. (9)

**Effectiveness**—Results-oriented focus on achieving selling goals. (12)

**Efficiency**—Cost-oriented focus on making the best possible use of the salesperson's time and efforts. (12)

**8Cs**—Eight factors (customization, contact interactivity, cultivation, care, community, choice, convenience, and character) found to drive customer loyalty. These 8Cs are moderated by customer trust and satisfaction. (8)

**Electronic Résumés**—Many large companies now use computer software to receive, sort, store, and retrieve résumés from job applicants, so that they can later scan thousands of résumés in a matter of minutes to find the best candidates for a job opening. (14)

**Endless Chain**—A classic method of prospecting in which the salesperson simply asks recently satisfied customers for prospect referrals. (3)

**Entering Goods**—Ingredients or components that become part of the finished product, such as raw materials and semimanufactured goods. (9)

**Ethics**—Moral code that governs individuals and societies in determining what's right or wrong. (13)

**Evaluative Listening**—Seller concentrates on what the buyer is saying but fails to sense what is being said through nonverbal or subtle verbal cues. (11)

**Evaluative Question**—Used within the open-ended question format to stimulate prospects and customers to talk about their general or specific goals, problems, and needs. (11)

**Exclusive Dealings**—Agreements in which a manufacturer or wholesaler grants one dealer exclusive rights to sell a product in a certain trading area and insists that the dealer not carry competing lines. Illegal under the Clayton Act. (13)

**Extranets**—Corporate networks that allow communication between a company and selected customers, suppliers, and business partners. (1)

**FAB**—A memory-aid acronym standing for a product's *f*eatures, *a*dvantages, and *b*enefits that will appeal most to a salesperson's customer. (5)

**Facilitating Goods**—Goods consumed while assisting in the ongoing production process, such as maintenance and repair items. (9)

**FedBizOpps.gov**—Web site that contains all federal contracting community solicitations for purchases exceeding twenty-five thousand dollars. (9)

**Follow-up**—Customer service provided, not only after the sale is closed, but throughout the selling process. (8)

**Foundation Goods**—Goods used in the production process that do not become part of the finished product, such as fixed major equipment and office equipment. (9)

**Gatekeeper**—Person who controls information or access to decision-makers. Examples include technical advisers, secretaries, security guards, and even telephone switchboard operators. (9)

**Hidden Job Market**—About 90 percent of available jobs are never advertised nor reach employment agency files, so job applicants must use proactive and creative resourcefulness to compete for these jobs. (14)

**Hostile Environment**—A pattern of sexual behavior that makes the job so unpleasant that the victim's work is adversely affected. (13)

**Iceberg Principle**—Analogous to an iceberg, most sales problems are hidden beneath the surface of overall positive sales totals. (12)

**Industrial Buyer**—The buying expert for an organization. Also, sometimes called the purchasing agent. (9)

**Influencers**—People who can influence the purchase decision by helping set product specifications, negotiating purchasing procedures and prices, or providing information about evaluating alternatives. (9)

**Intranets**—Internal corporate networks that allow salespeople and other employees within a company to obtain information and communicate with each other. (1)

**Invalid Objections**—Delaying or stalling actions or hidden reasons for not buying. (6)

**Keystone Objection**—The customer's most important objection. (6)

**Kinesics**—Describes bodily gestures and movements with regard to what these gestures and movements communicate to other people. (11)

**Lead**—Anything—a name, address, or telephone number—that points to a potential buyer. (3)

**Marginal Listening**—Occurs when salespeople hear the prospect's words but are easily distracted and may allow their minds to wander. (11)

**Marketing Information System (MIS)**—Any systematized, continuous process of gathering, sorting, analyzing, evaluating, and distributing market information. Can be helpful to salespeople in obtaining leads and prospects. (3)

**Mission Statement**—Sets forth in writing the organization's orientation, goals, basic values, and sense of purpose. (10)

**Missionary Selling**—Educating, building goodwill, and providing services to customers (for example, to doctors and dentists) by giving them samples and information about products and services (such as new pharmaceuticals and medicines, to prescribe or recommend for their patients). (1)

**NAME**—An abbreviation for the process of qualifying a lead in terms of *need* for the product, *authority* to buy, *money* to be able to buy, and overall *eligibility* to buy. (3)

**North American Industry Classification System (NAICS)**—Covers more than nineteen thousand industry descriptions; used to identify new business prospects and their general product and service requirements by up to six digits of specificity. (9)

**Objection**—Anything that the prospect or customer says or does that impedes the sales negotiations. (6)

**Offset Strategies**—A set of strategies for dealing with objections that uses the technique of offsetting the objection with a benefit. (6)

**One-to-One Marketing**—A philosophical change from the traditional approach of looking at customers as mass markets to viewing customers as individuals. One-to-one marketing seeks to sell more products to fewer (selected) customers rather than more products to more customers. (2)

**Order Creating**—The process of identifying prospective buyers, offering them information, motivating them to buy, closing the sale, and following up after the sale has been made to ensure customer satisfaction. Trade, technical, and creative salespeople engage in order getting. (1)

**Order Supporting**—The process of having minimal involvement in sales generation but instead serving as an assistance-provider to customers. (1)

**Order Taking**—Processing routine orders or reorders for products that have been sold previously to the buying firm. (1)

**Parkinson's Law**—Work expands to fill the time allowed for it. (12)

**Perceived Service Quality**—The quality of service individual customers believe they deserve and expect to receive. (8)

**Perceived Value**—A product's value, from the prospect's perspective. (6)

**Personal Selling Process (PSP)**—The seven-stage process of professional personal selling, from prospecting and qualifying prospects to following up and servicing customers. (1, 3)

**Preapproach**—The approach planning stage of the selling process. (4)

**Prenotification**—A technique using an in-person cold call, a mailing, or a telephone call to send a strong signal to the prospect that the salesperson would like to schedule a sales call appointment. (4)

**Price Discount**—Any reduction off the standard list price of a product. (7)

**Price Fixing**—Two or more competing sellers conspiring to set or maintain uniform prices and profit margins. (13)

**Probing Question**—Used to search for information when prospects and customers have difficulty articulating their precise needs. (11)

**Processing**—Refers to operations within the salesperson's mind that give meaning to the prospect's message through understanding, interpreting, evaluating, and remembering the communication. (11)

**Product Disparagement**—False or deceptive comparisons or distorted claims *made during or after a sales presentation* about a competitor's products, services, or properties. These statements are considered defamatory *per se*. (13)

**Product Quality**—Perceived performance of the tangible product in satisfying customer expectations. (8)

**Professional Salesperson**—Salesperson who sees a sales career as a true profession for which he or she must be well educated, well prepared, and thoroughly professional in order to negotiate successfully with professional buyers. (1)

**Promotion**—Typically, a one-way flow of persuasive information from a seller to a buyer. (11)

**Prospect**—A lead that has been qualified as a definite potential buyer. (3)

**Prospecting**—First step in the PSP where salespeople find leads and qualify them on four criteria: name, authority, money, and eligibility to buy. (1)

**Protected Groups**—In terms of employment laws, protected groups are people distinguished by special characteristics such as race, color, ethnicity, national origin, religion, gender, age (over forty), disability, or veteran status. These particular groups are protected under federal antidiscrimination law, which mandates that people in one of these protected groups cannot be discriminated against in any facet of employment—including hiring, promotion, training, discipline, pay, or termination. (14)

**Proxemics**—Refers to the spatial relationships (positions) of people and objects. (11)

**Puppy Dog Close**—Letting the prospect try the product for a few days or weeks before buying. Akin to a cuddly puppy, most people grow attached to something they have for awhile. (7)

**Push Technology**—Combination of data warehousing and email to retrieve and send relevant information and services to prospects and customers. (2)

**Put-Off Strategies**—A set of strategies for handling a prospect's objections that require the salesperson to delay dealing with the objection initially. (6)

**Quid Pro Quo Harassment**—Where a person in authority demands sexual favors from an employee in exchange for a job advantage, such as being hired or promoted. (13)

**Random-Lead Searching**—Generation of leads by randomly calling on organizations. Sometimes called "blind" searching. (3)

**Reciprocity**—In industrial buyer-seller relationships, an informal agreement between two or more organizations to exchange goods and services on a systematic and more or less exclusive basis. In other words, "you buy from me, and I'll buy from you." (9)

**Relationship Selling**—Focuses on all activities aimed at creating, developing, and maintaining successful exchange relationships with prospects and customers. (9)

**Reliability**—Ability to perform the desired service dependably, accurately, and consistently; the single most important component of customer service. (8)

**Responding**—Assures the prospect that the salesperson has listened accurately and is encouraging the communication to continue. (11)

**Responsiveness**—The level of emotions, feelings, or sociability that a person openly displays. (11)

**Return On Time Invested (ROTI)**—The designated return divided by the hours spent achieving it. (12)

**SAD TIE**—A memory-aid acronym standing for *s*tatistics, *a*nalogies, *d*emonstrations, *t*estimonials, *i*ncidents, and *e*xhibits, one or all of which the salesperson may use to spice up a sales presentation. (5)

**Sales Internship Programs**—Unpaid study-work programs offered to college students by several companies, for example, Procter & Gamble and Automatic Data Processing, where students learn about career opportunities. (14)

**Sales Management Information System (SMIS)**—An ongoing process of collecting, sorting, classifying, storing, analyzing, interpreting, retrieving, and reporting information for the development of sales strategies and tactics. (10)

**Sales Megatrends**—Major behavioral, technological, and managerial trends that influence how salespeople and their managers perform their jobs. (2)

**Sales Territory**—A control unit that contains customer accounts. (12)

**Seeding**—Prospect-focused activities, such as mailing pertinent news articles, carried out several weeks or months before a sales call. (4)

**Selective-Lead Searching**—Application of systematic strategies to generate leads from predetermined target markets. (3)

**Selling Center**—Selling organization members assigned to a certain prospect to close a particular sales transaction. After the sale is consummated, the selling center is likely to disband. (5)

**Sensing**—Most basic aspect of listening, it includes hearing words, inflection, and paralanguage (for example, speed of speech, use of colloquialisms), as well as observation of nonverbal language (for example, body language, facial expressions). (11)

**Service Quality**—All activities supporting the sale, from the initial contact through the post-sale servicing, that meet or exceed customer expectations and enhance the value of a product. (8)

**SPIN**—A selling technique that allows the salesperson to identify a prospect's major needs quickly. The acronym refers to *Situation, Problem, Implications,* and *Needs* payoff. (4)

**Spotters**—People who work in jobs where they meet other people and who can help salespeople obtain leads. Also called "bird dogs." (3)

**Strategy**—A long-run total program of action for using resources to achieve an overall goal. (10)

**Survey Approach**—An approach whereby the salesperson asks the prospect to answer a few survey questions, the responses to which establish quickly whether or not the prospect has a need for the salesperson's product. (4)

**Tactic**—A short-run, specific action composing part of the larger strategic plan. (10)

**Telemarketing**—Use of telephone by support staff to help salespeople identify prospects, gather information, and answer inquiries. (2)

**Teleselling**—Conducting the entire personal selling process via telephone. (2)

**Territorial Routing**—Devising a travel plan or pattern to use when making sales calls. (12)

**Territory Blitz**—An intensified version of door-to-door canvassing in which several salespeople join efforts to call on every organization in a given territory or area. (3)

**Thomas Register**—The primary source of locating suppliers for most *Fortune* 500 companies. Published annually, it provides information about 170,000 manufacturers of product categories, specific products, names of the companies, branches, top executives and their job titles, affiliation data, and credit rating. (10)

**Tie-In**—Refers to an often-illegal situation in which a seller requires a customer to purchase an unwanted product along with the desired product. (13)

**Trade Selling**—Field service for distributors and wholesalers that includes expediting orders, taking reorders, restocking shelves, setting up displays, providing in-store demonstrations, and distributing samples to store customers. Trade sellers are usually discouraged from hard selling to customers. (1)

**Trial Close**—Any well-placed attempt to close the sale; can be used early and often throughout the selling process. (7)

**Valid Objections**—Sincere concerns that the prospect needs answered before he or she will be willing to buy. (6)

**Value Added**—Extra benefits, from the prospect's perspective, that one salesperson and his or her products and services have over those of competitors. (5)

**Value Analysis**—Usually a printed document that shows how a product is the best value for the money. (6)

**Vocational Interest Test**—Designed to measure how closely an applicant's interests match the interests of other people who have successfully performed a particular job. (14)

**Wheel of Personal Selling**—Depiction of the seven stages of the PSP as a continuous cycle or wheel carried out by professionals in the field of sales. (1)

**Win-Win Negotiations**—The kind of negotiation in which both parties feel satisfied with the outcome; the only kind of negotiation that professional salespeople seek! (6)

**Written Presentation**—In sales presentations to organizational prospects, the salesperson's explanation of how the prospect can profitably use the product. Also called a sales proposal or business plan. (5)

# NAME INDEX

# ORGANIZATION INDEX

# SUBJECT INDEX

## DATE DUE

Demco, Inc. 38-293

## REAL DEAL UPGRADE CD-ROM

Free with a new textbook, this CD contains tools to help
students succeed: chapter objectives and summaries, a
glossary of key terms, tips on improving study habits, and
a link to the text web site that includes both chapter-
related material and general management resources.

## STUDENT WEB SITE

This site provides additional information,
guidance, and activities that will help
enhance the concepts presented in this
text. The site offers students ACE Self-
Testing, Ready Notes, Flash Cards, Web
Resources, Learning Objectives, Outlines,
and Company Links. In addition, the site
will feature links to important job and
career sites.